T0215696

Lecture Notes in Computer Science   11870

More information about this series at http://www.springer.com/series/7412

Halimah Badioze Zaman · Alan F. Smeaton ·
Timothy K. Shih · Sergio Velastin ·
Tada Terutoshi · Nazlena Mohamad Ali ·
Mohammad Nazir Ahmad (Eds.)

Advances in Visual Informatics

6th International Visual Informatics Conference, IVIC 2019
Bangi, Malaysia, November 19–21, 2019
Proceedings

 Springer

Editors
Halimah Badioze Zaman
Universiti Kebangsaan Malaysia
Bangi, Malaysia

Alan F. Smeaton
Dublin City University
Dublin, Ireland

Timothy K. Shih
National Central University
Taoyuan City, Taiwan

Sergio Velastin
Carlos III University of Madrid
Madrid, Spain

Tada Terutoshi
Toyo University
Tokyo, Japan

Nazlena Mohamad Ali
Universiti Kebangsaan Malaysia
Bangi, Malaysia

Mohammad Nazir Ahmad
Universiti Kebangsaan Malaysia
Bangi, Malaysia

ISSN 0302-9743   ISSN 1611-3349   (electronic)
Lecture Notes in Computer Science
ISBN 978-3-030-34031-5   ISBN 978-3-030-34032-2   (eBook)
https://doi.org/10.1007/978-3-030-34032-2

LNCS Sublibrary: SL6 – Image Processing, Computer Vision, Pattern Recognition, and Graphics

This Springer imprint is published by the registered company Springer Nature Switzerland AG
The registered company address is: Gewerbestrasse 11, 6330 Cham, Switzerland

Preface

The world is going through great economic and technological challenges in this digital economy era. With the advent of the 4th Industrial Revolution (4IR) and Industry 4.0, Visual Informatics has become a significant component in computer science. This multidisciplinary field encompasses that of computer science and information technology and engineering, integrating areas such as computer vision, image processing, pattern recognition, computer graphics, simulation, virtual reality, data visualization and analytics, cyber security, as well as social computing, which can all be applied to various domains of knowledge such as education, medical and health, finance, or security. The Institute of Visual Informatics (IVI) at the Universiti Kebangsaan Malaysia (UKM), also known as The National University of Malaysia, is a center of excellence (CoE) established as an outcome of the first Visual Informatics Conference (IVIC) held in 2009. The institute, which conducts research in the basic areas mentioned earlier, conducts Masters and Doctoral (PhD) Degree programs of research, as well as short Professional Practical Certifications currently in the areas of Data Science and Intelligent Visual Data Analytics. The institute has successfully graduated more than 30 postgraduate students (Masters and PhD) since its inception in 2010. We are indeed indebted to the international fraternity from the last five IVIC conferences (2009, 2011, 2013, 2015, and 2017), who have given us support for the establishment of the institute. Our smart partnerships, through this conference, has helped the institute to grow and enhance research in this area locally and internationally.

The Visual Informatics Research Group and the Institute of Visual Informatics (IVI) at UKM, once again hosted this 6th International Visual Informatics Conference (IVIC 2019), with the objective to bring together experts to discuss and share new knowledge and ideas in this research area so that more concerted efforts can be undertaken nationally and globally. As in the previous IVIC conferences, this conference was organized collaboratively by the Visual Informatics fraternity from various public and private universities and industry from various parts of the world (their names are listed in the proceedings). This sixth edition of IVIC was co-sponsored by Malaysian Digital Economy Corporation (MDEC), National Council of Professors (MPN), and Malaysian Information Technology Society (MITS). The conference was co-chaired by five professors from the UK, Ireland, Taiwan, Japan, and Malaysia.

The theme of the conference, 'Digital Innovation Towards Society 5.0' reflects the importance of digitalization in this fourth industrial revolution digital economy, where disruptive technologies have caused technologies to integrate and result in fusion technologies that bring about interesting emerging technologies such as autonomous and semi-autonomous vehicles, Internet of things (IoT), and Blockchain that will benefit society. The changing landscapes of Industry 4.0 require technologies that are Artificial Intelligence (AI)-driven which will assist future Society 5.0 to make decisions from more precise intelligent predictions that would result in an efficient decision making and smart intelligent applications for the well-being of society and the economy. Thus, the theme of the conference was relevant, apt, and timely.

The conference focused on four tracks:

- Visualization and Digital Innovation for Society 5.0
- Engineering and Digital Innovation for Society 5.0
- Cyber Security and Digital Innovation for Society 5.0
- Social Informatics and Application for Society 5.0

The tracks took place over the course of two days (November 19–20, 2019) and ended with a one-day workshop (November 21, 2019). There were 4 keynote speakers and 65 paper presentations based on topics covered by the 4 main tracks. The reviewing of the papers was conducted by experts who represented the Program Committee from Asia, Europe, Oceania, and the USA. Each paper was reviewed by 3 reviewers and the acceptance rate was 47%. The reviewing process was managed using the EasyChair system.

The conference also included for the first time an exhibition portraying the theme 'Symbiosis of Art, Science, and Technology for Society 5.0' to show how scientific and technological research can be presented in interesting art works that have a great impact on public awareness on the seamlessness of knowledge in art, science, and technology, and its effects on the civilization of societies.

On behalf of the organizing and Program Committee of IVIC 2019, we thank all authors for their submissions and camera-ready copies of papers, and all participants for their thought-provoking ideas and active participation in the conference. We also thank the vice-chancellor of UKM (host university), and vice-chancellors and deans of all IT faculties of the IHLs for their support in organizing this conference. We also acknowledge the sponsors, members of the Organizing Committees, Program Committee members, support committees, and individuals who gave their continuous help and support in making the conference a success. It is our fervent hope that one day IVIC will be held in different host countries such as Asia, Europe, Oceania, the UK or the USA.

November 2019

Halimah Badioze Zaman
Alan F. Smeaton
Timothy K. Shih
Sergio Velastin
Tada Terutoshi
Nazlena Mohamad Ali
Mohammad Nazir Ahmad

Organization

The 6th International Visual Informatics Conference (IVIC 2019) was organized by the Visual Informatics Research Group and Institute of Visual Informatics, Universiti Kebangsaan Malaysia (UKM), in collaboration with local public and private universities in Malaysia, the Multimedia Development Corporation (MDEC), and the ICT Cluster of the National Professors' Council (MPN).

Local Executive Committee

Chair

Halimah Badioze Zaman (UKM)

Deputy Chair

Rosalina Abdul Salam (USIM)

Secretary

Nazlena Mohamad Ali (UKM)

Assistant Secretary

Norshita Mat Nayan (UKM)

Treasurer

Rabiah Abd. Kadir (UKM)

Assistant Treasurer

Ummul Hanan Mohamad (UKM)

Program Committee

Program Co-Chairs

Halimah Badioze Zaman	Universiti Kebangsaan Malaysia, Malaysia
Alan F. Smeaton	Dublin City University, Ireland
Timothy K. Shih	National Central University, Taiwan
Sergio Velastin	Queen Mary Univ. of London, UK
Terutoshi Tada	Toyo University, Japan

Technical Program Committee

Mohammad Nazir Ahmad (UKM) – Head
Halimah Badioze Zaman (UKM)
Nazlena Mohamad Ali (UKM)
Ely Salwana Mat Surin (UKM)
Norshita Mat Nayan (UKM)

Sponsorship

Azlina Ahmad (UKM) – Head
Halimah Badioze Zaman (UKM)
Rosalina Abdul Salam (USIM)
Wan Fatimah Wan Ahmad (UTP)
Bahari Belaton (USM)
Noor Afiza Mat Razali (UPNM)

Publicity (Web Portal)

Noor Afiza Mat Razali (UPNM) – Head
Ang Mei Choo (UKM)
Hanif Baharin (UKM)
Norshahriah Abd. Wahab (UPNM)
Mohamad Taha Ijab (UKM)
Nur Intan Raihana (USM)
Mohd Nadhir Ab Wahab (USM)
Dahlan Abdul Ghani (UNIKL)
Robiatul Adawiah Jamaluddin (IUKL)
Nizam Md Husen (UNIKL)
Noramiza Hashim (MMU)
Anusha Achuthan (USM)
Hajah Norasiken Bakar (UTEM)
Suraya Hamid (UM)
Dayang Rohaya Awang Rambli (UTP)
Prasanna Ramakrishnan (UiTM)
Nurul Amelina Nasharuddin (UPM)
Aslina Baharom (UMS)

Logistics

Riza Sulaiman (UKM) – Head
Mohamad Taha Ijab (UKM)
Syed Nasir Syed Zakaria Alsagoff (UPNM)
Dahlan Abdul Ghani (UNIKL)
Asama Kuder (UKM)
Azreen Azman (UPM)
Hafizhah Suzana Hussien (UKM)
Mohammad Haziq Mohd Johari (UKM)

Zulkepli Mukhtar (UKM)
Mohamad Shahmi Shahril (UKM)

Workshop

Puteri Nor Ellyza Nohuddin (UKM) – Head
Amelia Ritahani Ismail (UIA)
Nur Intan Raihana (USM)
Joshua Thomas (KDU)

Conference Management System

Ely Salwana Mat Surin (UKM) – Head
Mohammad Nazir Ahmad (UKM)
Hafizhah Suzana Hussien (UKM)

Tour

Nurul Amelina Nasharuddin (UPM) – Head
Hajah Norasiken Bakar (UTEM)
Azreen Azman (UPM)

Exhibition

Mohamad Taha Ijab (UKM) – Head
Hanif Baharin (UKM)
Mohammad Haziq Mohd Johari (UKM)
Zulkepli Mukhtar (UKM)

Special Task

Norshita Mat Nayan (UKM) – Head
Siti NorazimahAhmat (UKM)
Nurulhuda Muhamad (UKM)
Anis Najwa Mohd Sharuddin (UKM)

Technical Committee

International

Alan F. Smeaton	Dublin City University, Ireland
Timothy K. Shih	National Central University, Taiwan
Sergio Velastin	Queen Mary University of London, UK
Tada Terutoshi	Toyo University, Japan
Emanuele Trucco	University of Dundee, UK
Hang-Bong Kang	Catholic University of Korea, South Korea
Marta Fairén	Universitat Politècnica de Catalunya, Spain
Erich Neuhold	University of Vienna, Austria
Theng Yin Leng	Nanyang Technological University, Singapore

Tony Pridmore	University of Nottingham, UK
Neil A. Gordon	University of Hull, UK
Hyowon Lee	SUTD, Singapore
Jianguo Zhang	University of Dundee, UK
Jing Hua	Wayne State University, USA
Nick Holliman	Durham University, UK
Qingde Li	University of Hull, UK
Wenyu Liu	Huazhong University of Science and Technology, China
Malcolm Munro	Durham University, UK
Huang Jiung-Yao	National Taipei University, Taiwan
Li Kuan-Ching	Providence University, Taiwan
Khider Nassif Jassim	University of Wasit, Iraq
Kamal Badr Abdalla Badr	Qatar Foundation, Qatar
Yunis Ali	Simad University, Somalia
Furkh Zeshan	University Islamabad, Pakistan
Kamarul Faizal Hashim	University of Dubai, UAE'
Omar Ahmed Ibrahim	University of Mosul, Iraq
Sommai Khantong	Mahasarakham University, Thailand

Malaysia

Azlina Ahmad (UKM)
Aliimran Nordin (UKM)
Amalina Farhi Ahmad Fadziah (UPNM)
Asama Kuder Nseaf (UKM)
Aslina Baharum (UMS)
Azreen Azman (UPM)
Ang Mei Choo (UKM)
Bahari Belaton (USM)
Bavani Ramayah (NOTTINGHAM)
Chiung Ching Ho (MMU)
Dahlan Abdul Ghani (UNIKL)
Dayang Rohaya Awang Rambli (UTP)
Ely Salwana Mat Surin (UKM)
Falah Y. H. Ahmed (MSU)
Fauziah Zainuddin (UMP)
Halimah Badioze Zaman (UKM)
Hanif Baharin (UKM)
Hajah Norasiken Bakar (UTEM)
Hoo Meei Hao (UTAR)
J. Joshua Thomas (KDU Penang)
Jamaiah Yahaya (UKM)
Kasturi Dewi Varathan (UM)
Khairul Shafee Kalid (UTP)

Mahadi Bahari (UTM)
Maizatul H. M. Yatim (UPSI)
Marwan D. Saleh (MSU)
Mohamad Taha Ijab (UKM)
Mohammad Nazir Ahmad (UKM)
Mohammad Adib Khairuddin (UPNM)
Mohd Afizi Mohd Shukran (UPNM)
Mohd Hafiz Faizal Mohamad
  Kamil (UNIKL)
Mohd Nadhir Ab Wahab (USM)
Mohd Nizam Husen (UNIKL)
Mohd Rizal Mohd Isa (UPNM)
Mohd Nazri Ismail (UPNM)
Muhammad Reza Z'aba (UM)
Muslihah Wook (UPNM)
Nor Hidayati Zakaria (UTM)
Nazlena Mohamad Ali (UKM)
Nazmona Mat Ali (UTM)
Noor Afiza Mat Razali (UPNM)
Noor Azah Samsudin (UTHM)
Noor Hafizah Hassan (UTM)
Noor Hayani Abd Rahim (IIUM)
Noorminshah Iahad (UTM)

Nor Asiakin Hasbullah (UPNM)
Nor Zairah Ab. Rahim (UTM)
Norizan Mat Diah (UiTM)
Norshahriah Abdul Wahab (UPNM)
Norziha Megat Mohd. Zainuddin (UTM)
Nur Azaliah Abu Bakar (UTM)
Nur Fazidah Elias (UKM)
Nurulhuda Firdaus Mohd Azmi (UTM)
Noor Afiza Mat Razali (UPNM)
Norshita Mat Nayan (UKM)
Prasanna Ramakrisnan (UiTM)
Puteri Nur Ellyza Nohuddin (UKM)
Rabiah Abdul Kadir (UKM)
Rahayu Ahmad (UUM)
Rahmah Mokhtar (UMP)
Rasimah Che Mohd Yusoff (UTM)
Razatulshima Ghazali (MAMPU)
Ridzuan Hussin (UPSI)
Riza Sulaiman (UKM)

Robiatul A'Dawiah Jamaluddin (IUKL)
Rohayanti Hassan (UTM)
Roslina Ibrahim (UTM)
Rosmayati Mohemad (UMT)
Savita K. Sugathan (UTP)
Siti Nurul Mahfuzah Mohamad (UTEM)
Stephanie Chua (UNIMAS)
Suraya Hamid (UM)
Suzaimah Ramli (UPNM)
Suziah Sulaiman (UTP)
Syed Nasir Alsagoff (UPNM)
Ummul Hanan Mohamad (UKM)
Wan Fatimah Wan Ahmad (UTP)
Zahidah Abd Kadir (UNIKL)
Zarul Fitri Zaaba (USM)
Zeratul Izzah Mohd Yusoh (UTEM)
Zuraini Zainol (UPNM)
Zuriana Abu Bakar (UMT)
Zahidah Zulkifli (IIUM)

Strategic Partners

National Council of Professors (MPN)
Malaysia Digital Economy Corporation (MDEC)
Malaysian Information Technology Society (MITS)
Sistem Perintis Sdn Bhd

Co-organizers

Universiti Kebangsaan Malaysia (UKM)
Universiti Pertahanan Nasional Malaysia (UPNM)
Universiti Sains Islam Malaysia (USIM)
Universiti Teknikal Malaysia Melaka (UTeM)
Universiti Teknologi PETRONAS (UTP)
Universiti Sains Malaysia (USM)
Infrastructure University Kuala Lumpur (IUKL)
Universiti Kuala Lumpur (UniKL)
Universiti Teknologi Malaysia (UTM)
Universiti Malaya (UM)
Universiti Teknologi MARA (UiTM)
Al-Madinah International University (MEDIU)
International Islamic University Malaysia (IIUM)
University of Malaysia, Sarawak (UNIMAS)

Universiti Pendidikan Sultan Idris (UPSI)
Universiti Tenaga Nasional (UNITEN)
Universiti Utara Malaysia (UUM)
University of Nottingham, UK (Malaysia Campus)
KDU Penang University College
Sunway University

Contents

Engineering and Digital Innovation for Society 5.0

Cyber Security and Digital Innovation for Society 5.0

Social Informatics and Application for Society 5.0

Visualization and Digital Innovation for Society 5.0

Content-Aware Video Analysis to Guide Visually Impaired Walking on the Street

Ervin Yohannes[1], Timothy K. Shih[1], and Chih-Yang Lin[2(✉)]

[1] National Central University, Taoyuan, Taiwan
[2] Yuan Ze University, Taoyuan, Taiwan
andrewlin@saturn.yzu.edu.tw

Abstract. Although many researchers have developed systems or tools to assist blind and visually impaired people, they continue to face many obstacles in daily life—especially in outdoor environments. When people with visual impairments walk outdoors, they must be informed of objects in their surroundings. However, it is challenging to develop a system that can handle related tasks. In recent years, deep learning has enabled the development of many architectures with more accurate results than machine learning. One popular model for instance segmentation is Mask-RCNN, which can do segmentation and rapidly recognize objects. We use Mask-RCNN to develop a context-aware video that can help blind and visually impaired people recognize objects in their surroundings. Moreover, we provide the distance between the subject and object, and the object's relative speed and direction using Mask-RCNN outputs. The results of our content-aware video include the name of the object, class object score, the distance between the person and the object, speed of the object, and object direction.

Keywords: Content-aware · Mask-RCNN · Visually impaired · Distance · Speed · Direction · Assistive technology

1 Introduction

The World Health Organization (WHO) reports that around 253 million people have some form of vision impairment and 36 million people are blind. These populations would benefit from navigation assistance to help them in their daily lives. In recent years, Computer Vision (CV) has created opportunities to develop systems that can enable the visually impaired to connect with, recognize, and search their surroundings [1]. However, building such navigation tools is difficult, especially in complex situations. Many methods have already been tried, including inexpensive canes, guide dogs, and electronic travel aids. The difficulties that all of these solutions are trying to solve can be classified into three categories: identifying the position of the person, the person's desired destination, and the best way to get to that destination [2]. Traditionally, the blind and visually impaired have used a cane-like stick to detect object/obstacles in the way. But now, more advanced technology has led to many research papers about smart sticks that can classify object/obstacles via embedded sensors [3]. Researchers have even added GPS into these walking sticks to obtain accurate location information,

© Springer Nature Switzerland AG 2019
H. Badioze Zaman et al. (Eds.): IVIC 2019, LNCS 11870, pp. 3–13, 2019.
https://doi.org/10.1007/978-3-030-34032-2_1

and ultrasound to detect obstacles and potholes when the user is walking indoors or outdoors [4]. Another navigation solution uses a virtual dog [5], which is implemented by combining AlexNet and GoogleNet network for activity recognition. It can help the blind and visually impaired to "see" using audio output from activity recognition.

We propose a new way to help the visually impaired navigate their surroundings through image classification, object detection, and segmentation, which are implemented via deep learning methods. We employ Mask-RCNN, a well-known model that has been widely used to handle such issues. It has already been successfully applied to oral disease detection and segmentation [6]. Moreover, its model can automatically segment nucleic using a microscopic image. A navigation system must be able to perform detection, localization and instance segmentation of a natural image [7]. Mask-RCNN has been applied to hand segmentation using the COCO dataset and combined with Mean Shift to improve the tracking results. Moreover, it can be applied to dynamic hand segmentation for even better accuracy [8].

Using artificial intelligence, computer vision, and pattern recognition for classification, tracking, detection, and recognition can be handled by Mask-RCNN. We want to leverage the advantages of this method to build content-aware video analysis for blind and visually impaired people to classify, track, detect, and recognize object/obstacles around them. We use the COCO dataset, which contains many classes of object/obstacles, for training.

We improve upon the Mask-RCNN results with the distance between the person and object, additionally calculating the object's speed and direction. We obtain the class and score of an object from the Mask-RCNN results and find the distance by using the threshold of the bounding box perimeter between the person and object using two conditions ("medium" and "near") in our system. We then calculate the total distance and frame to get the speed of the object. The direction of the object is found using the origin coordinates, point, and angle, which automatically show the direction. Our contributions are thus threefold. (i) Calculate the distance between the subject and the object; (ii) Calculate the object's speed; (iii) Identify the direction of the object.

The paper is organized as follows. In Sect. 2, we present related literature. In Sect. 3, we describe the Mask-RCNN method and our proposed method. In Sect. 4, we present the experimental results. We draw conclusions and propose future work in Sect. 5.

2   Related Work

The rapid global development of technology has spurred innovative assistive technologies, especially for the blind and visually impaired populations. For instance, recently developed technology can help blind people easily identify clothes using NFC (Near Field Communication) [9]. This system was developed on a Web platform, and clothing characteristics are input manually. Blind people can also recognize products for daily needs using a camera [10] since combining K-means clustering and SIFT method allows for the separation of background and foreground, as well as recognition of product labels.

Today, deep learning has proven to be more powerful than machine learning methods, especially in classification, tracking, detection, and recognition tasks [6, 7]. A deep neural network schema has been used to predict the future short-term speed with a dataset consisting of a vehicle's historic speed and acceleration, steering information, area and driving time [11]. Positive results have shown promise for deep learning methods. New deep learning models for object recognition (Faster-RCNN, R-FCN, Mask-RCNN) and image feature extraction (InceptionResnet and Resnet) rely on simple designs with better results. Mask-RCNN can be applied to synthetic images only with the feature extractor frozen [12].

The latest event-recognition structure using deep local flow in fast region-based convolutional neural network (Fast RCNN) is related to traffic violation recording, monitoring, and control. The definition of the event varies in many aspects, but at its core, an event in video detection is an object that manifests some behavior in the scenes. So, in [13] event-recognition in the video consists of direction and speed of object recognition, detection, and behavior. Content awareness also uses deep object co-segmentation that segments a similar object from various images [14]. The work compares three architectures, including channel-wise attention (CA), fused channel-wise attention (FCA), and channel spatial attention (CSA) for classification between a seen object and unseen object. Content awareness can additionally be implemented on sports data to become a reference in context-aware research, especially sports videos with respect to context-oriented groups, objects, and events [15].

3 Proposed Method

The general framework of our proposed method is shown in Fig. 1. It consists of four main blocks. First, Mask-RCNN outputs name class and object score. Second, the distance between the person and object is found using the bounding box perimeter threshold. Third, the speed of the object is calculated using distance and frame total. Lastly, we determine the direction of the object.

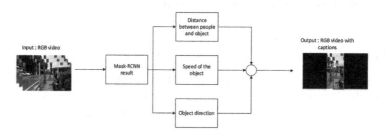

Fig. 1. Framework for the proposed method

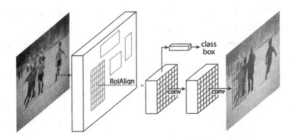

Fig. 2. The Mask-RCNN framework [17]

Fig. 3. Selected portions of a frame. Original image (left); after processing (right)

3.1 Mask-RCNN

Mask-RCNN is a popular deep learning model, especially for instance segmentation [16]. It is derived from Faster RCNN and adds a mask for predicting segmentation on every Region of Interest (RoI). The bounding box regression and existing branch classification run in parallel. The technique applies a similar two-step procedure, with an identical first stage, (which is RPN). The framework of Mask-RCNN is shown in Fig. 2 [17]. For this research, we only take the important parts of an image to be processed by Mask-RCNN. Those parts remain in RGB video, while other parts are converted into the black by setting a value limit for the distance from the left and right sides as shown in Fig. 3.

3.2 Distance Measurement

Distance between the person and object is based on thresholding of the bounding box perimeter. We assume that the bounding box shape is a rectangle. So, we can get the perimeter from the width and height of the bounding box using Eq. (1).

$$perimeter = (2 \ x \ width) + (2 \ x \ height) \tag{1}$$

Here, we have two conditions for the distance: "near" and "medium". "Near" means the perimeter value exceeds 400. "Medium" means the perimeter value is between 300 and 400. This is denoted by Eq. (2).

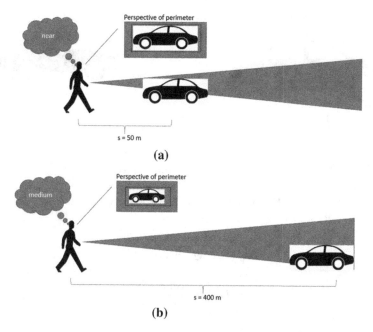

Fig. 4. Perimeter perspective (a) near distance (b) medium distance

$$distance \begin{cases} 300 < perimeter < 400, \; medium \\ perimeter > 400, \; near \end{cases} \qquad (2)$$

We have a perspective on the distance of an object. If an object is far from the person, the size of an object is small (the perimeter is small). In turn, if an object is close to the person, the object's size is large (the perimeter is large) as shown in Fig. 4.

3.3 Speed Perspective

We assume the speed of the object always moves based on the subject's perspective. So, when we refer to speed, we are referring to the speed at which the blind person is moving from the object, and not the actual speed of the object. Many researchers have calculated vehicle speed using static cameras in traffic lights [18, 19]. Besides using simple line applying RoI to obtain the vehicle speed [20], gradient [21], infrared/ ultrasonic sensors [22], and fusion of visual and semantic features [23] have also been used. However, little research about vehicle speed has been done in dynamic cameras. Thus, we need to define the vehicle speed. We use the old coordinates and current coordinates to get the distance by Euclidian distance. Afterward, we divide the distance and frame total by time. Distance and speed are calculated using Eqs. (3) and (4) respectively. The description of vehicle speed can be shown in Fig. 5.

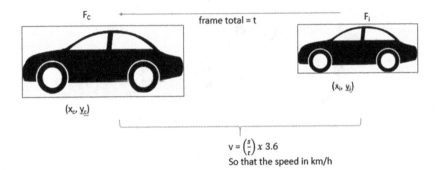

$$v = \left(\tfrac{s}{t}\right) \times 3.6$$
So that the speed in km/h

Fig. 5. Description of vehicle speed

$$s = \sqrt{(x_1 - x_2)^2 + (y_1 - y_2)^2} \tag{3}$$

$$speed\,(v) = \frac{distance\,(s)}{time\,(t)} \tag{4}$$

3.4   Direction

The direction of a moving object is based on the center point, destination point, and angle. The destination point is the same as the center point, and we add speed value inside it so the length of the direction depends on the speed. We can find the angle by calculating two coordinates (x, y) and then incorporating them with the cotangent ($\tan^{-1}$) as shown in Eq. (5).

$$\theta = \tan^{-1}\left(\frac{b}{a}\right) \tag{5}$$

After we get the theta (θ), we insert it into a trigonometric function that rotates a point counterclockwise by an angle around the origin, which must be in radians. The computation of the rotation is shown in Eq. (6), and the description of θ is shown in Fig. 6. R represents rotation, (i, j) represents the destination coordinates, (a, b) refers to the center coordinates, and θ is the angle.

$$R \begin{cases} x = a + cos(\theta) \times (i-a) - sin(\theta) \times (j-b) \\ y = b + sin(\theta) \times (i-a) + cos(\theta) \times (j-b) \end{cases} \tag{6}$$

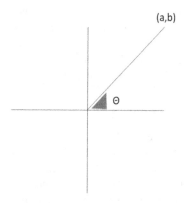

Fig. 6. The description of θ

4 Experimental Results

4.1 Datasets

The dataset uses a common object in context (COCO). COCO is the largest image dataset for object detection and segmentation purposes and can be applied in many platforms, including MATLAB, Python, and Lua APIs. The COCO 2017 dataset contains 123.287 images and 886.284 instances. We use this dataset without any edits.

4.2 Requirements and Results of Mask-RCNN

The computations in this model are complex, so we must use a computer with a lot of memory. Moreover, deep learning implementation uses GPU to get faster results. The

Fig. 7. Mask-RCNN results

software used Python 3, Keras, and TensorFlow. Furthermore, we had to install another library that included numpy, scipy, pillow, cython, matplotlib, scikit-image, opencv-pyhton, h5py, imgaug, and Ipython. Afterward, we could run the Mask-RCNN program to obtain outputs for the name of the label class, score, mask and bounding box. The original results of Mask-RCNN are shown in Fig. 7.

4.3   Distance Analysis

The average distance between the blind person and a detected object can be accurately calculated, but some objects are not detected. This issue comes from the dataset used; not all objects are available in the COCO dataset. One example of an object not available in the COCO dataset in our research is a power pole shown in Fig. 8. It is important for blind people to recognize objects surrounding them. In our work, nearby objects are in red, and those that are a medium distance from the subject are marked in green. The different colors are intended to create system alerts for the blind and visually impaired.

Fig. 8. A missing object in the COCO dataset (Color figure online)

4.4   Speed and Direction Analysis

The speed and direction have the same functions in defining the length of the line. In our research, the speed in each object detection has a different value and no object has a zero value. The description of speed and direction is shown in Fig. 9. The circle represents the center of an object and the circle depends on the width and height of each object. Sometimes, the object's width is greater than the height or vice versa. The arrow represents the direction of each object and it is developed using the center point, destination point, and angle.

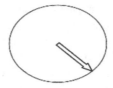

Fig. 9. The description of speed and direction

4.5 Results

The results consist of the name of an object, its score, distance, speed, and direction. The object name and score are obtained from the Mask-RCNN result. Distance is calculated using the thresholding of the bounding box perimeter, for which we assume all bounding boxes are rectangular in shape, and distance can be either "near" or "medium". The speed computation uses distance and frame size over time and is represented by the length of the arrow line. Then, we find direction using a combination of the center point, destination point, and angle. The results are shown in Fig. 10.

Fig. 10. Result of content-aware video analysis

5 Conclusion

In our research, we generate content-aware results that include an object's name, score, direction, and speed. We use Mask-RCNN to achieve image segmentation and object detection and recognition. The results of Mask-RCNN include the object name and score. Then, we use thresholding of the bounding box perimeter to get distance results between the subject (the blind or visually impaired person) and the object.

Next, we calculate distance using Euclidian distance and frame size as a function of time to get speed. Finally, we combine the center point, destination point, and angle to get direction. The results are not fixed, especially for speed and direction, for which the object bounding box continuously updates so that the speed and direction always change. In future work, we will apply another deep learning method and update the dataset or use another dataset since not all objects can be detected (e.g. power pole) using the COCO dataset. Speed also poses a remaining challenge, especially for dynamic cameras, which cannot define speed and direction as easily as static cameras can. For the future work, we will study to the community for looking at the success of our work especially for impaired visually or blind people.

References

1. Yang, K.: Unifying terrain awareness for visually impaired through real-time semantic segmentation. Sensor **18**(5), 1506 (2018)
2. Bai, J.: Virtual-blind-road following-based wearable navigation device for blind people. IEEE Trans. Consum. Electron. **64**(1), 136–143 (2018)
3. Agrawal, M.P., Gupta, A.R.: Smart stick for the blind and visually impaired people. In: 2018 Second International Conference on Inventive Communication and Computational Technologies (ICICCT), pp. 542–545. IEEE (2018)
4. Sen, A., Sen, K.: Ultrasonic blind stick for completely blind people to avoid any kind of obstacles. In: 2018 IEEE SENSORS, pp. 1–4. IEEE (2018)
5. Monteiro, J., Aires, J.P.: Virtual guide dog: an application to support visually-impaired people through deep convolutional neural networks. In 2017 International Joint Conference on Neural Networks (IJCNN), pp. 2267–2274. IEEE (2017)
6. Anantharaman, R., Velazquez, M.: Utilizing mask R-CNN for detection and segmentation of oral diseases. In: 2018 IEEE International Conference on Bioinformatics and Biomedicine (BIBM), pp. 2197–2204. IEEE (2018)
7. Johnson, J.W.: Adapting Mask-RCNN for automatic nucleus segmentation. arXiv preprint arXiv:1805.00500 (2018)
8. Nguyen, D.H., Le, T.H.: Hand segmentation under different viewpoints by combination of Mask R-CNN with tracking. In: 2018 5th Asian Conference on Defense Technology (ACDT), pp. 14–20. IEEE (2018)
9. Rocha, D., Carvalho, V.: MyEyes-automatic combination system of clothing parts to blind people: first insights. In: 2017 IEEE 5th International Conference on Serious Games and Applications for Health (SeGAH), pp. 1–5. IEEE (2017)
10. Mohane, V., Gode, C.: Object recognition for blind people using portable camera. In: 2016 World Conference on Futuristic Trends in Research and Innovation for Social Welfare (Startup Conclave), pp. 1–4. IEEE (2016)
11. Yan, M., Li, M.: Deep learning for vehicle speed prediction. Energy Proc. **152**, 618–623 (2018)
12. Hinterstoisser, S., Lepetit, V.: On pre-trained image features and synthetic images for deep learning. In: Proceedings of the European Conference on Computer Vision (ECCV) (2018)
13. Gu, Q., Yang, J.: Local fast R-CNN flow for object-centric event recognition in complex traffic scenes. In: Satoh, S. (ed.) PSIVT 2017. LNCS, vol. 10799, pp. 439–452. Springer, Cham (2018). https://doi.org/10.1007/978-3-319-92753-4_34
14. Chen, H., Huang, Y.: Semantic aware attention based deep object co-segmentation. arXiv preprint arXiv:1810.06859 (2018)
15. Shih, H.C.: A survey of content-aware video analysis for sports. IEEE Trans. Circ. Syst. Video Technol. **28**(5), 1212–1231 (2017)

16. Yohannes, E.: Building segmentation of satellite image based on area and perimeter using region growing. Indonesian J. Electr. Eng. Comput. Sci. **3**(3), 579–585 (2016)
17. He, K., Gkioxari, G.: Mask R-CNN. In: Proceedings of the IEEE International Conference on computer vision, pp. 2961–2969. IEEE (2017)
18. Dhulavvagol, P.M., Desai, A.: Vehicle tracking and speed estimation of moving vehicles for traffic surveillance applications. In: 2017 International Conference on Current Trends in Computer, Electrical, Electronics and Communication (CTCEEC), Mysore, pp. 373–377. (2017)
19. Kumar, A., Khorramshahi, P.: A semi-automatic 2D solution for vehicle speed estimation from monocular videos. In: Proceedings of the IEEE Conference on Computer Vision and Pattern Recognition Workshops, pp. 137–144. IEEE (2018)
20. Bourja, O., Maach, A.: Speed estimation using simple line. Proc. Comput. Sci. **127**, 209–217 (2018)
21. Czapla, Z.: Vehicle speed estimation with the use of gradient-based image conversion into binary form. In: 2017 Signal Processing: Algorithms, Architectures, Arrangements, and Applications (SPA), pp. 213–216. IEEE (2017)
22. Odat, E., Shamma, J.S.: Vehicle classification and speed estimation using combined passive infrared/ultrasonic sensors. IEEE Trans. Intell. Transp. Syst. **19**(5), 1593–1606 (2017)
23. Tang, Z., Wang, G.: Single-camera and inter-camera vehicle tracking and 3D speed estimation based on fusion of visual and semantic features. In: Proceedings of the IEEE Conference on Computer Vision and Pattern Recognition Workshops, pp. 108–115. IEEE (2018)

Experts' Feedback on DST Elements as Infused in Development Process of Mobile Learning Apps

Hashiroh Hussain[1($\boxtimes$)] and Norshuhada Shiratuddin[2]

[1] IPG Kampus Darulaman, 06000 Jitra, Kedah, Malaysia
hashiroh@gmail.com
[2] School of Multimedia Technology and Communication,
Universiti Utara Malaysia, UUM, 06010 Sintok, Kedah, Malaysia

Abstract. The usage of instructional media (apps) is poorly delivered due to inappropriate content of the presentation. Recent studies showed that perceptions among students and teachers regarding the use of apps are very low. Thus, Digital Storytelling (DST) concept is infused in developing the apps. Nevertheless, students are unable to comprehend DST clearly. The aim of this study is to identify DST elements for the development process of mobile learning apps. Critical analysis is employed based on previous studies to formulate generic DST elements. Eleven DST elements are formed and learning theories are adapted based on correct principles and procedures. This finding is very useful for representing the elements in accordance to the experts' feedback. The elements should contribute a new pedagogical approach for teachers in developing apps with mobile technology.

Keywords: Digital Storytelling · DST elements · Expert feedback

1 Introduction

Digital Storytelling (DST) is a digital narrative with infused multimedia elements, namely narrative-generated videos with images, music or sounds and animations that deliver information effectively [1–3]. DST presents interesting information for specific topics which is introduced by Dana Atchley (pioneer of DST) [4, 5]. Precisely, DST is further classified into three categories according to its content: (i) personal narratives, (ii) stories that examine historical events, and (iii) stories that are primarily used to inform or instruct [6–8].

For educational purposes, this study focuses on the narrative to inform or instruct stories as it involves the creation of multimedia learning materials or teaching products media (apps) [9]. This is because there are still students unable to distinguish DST with non DST [10]. Thus, the application of multimedia technology in learning resources such apps is essential for teachers as it could solve problems of self-learning and different levels of students' knowledge [11]. Besides, it has a positive impact on improving the quality of students' achievement and knowledge with the diversity of the learning resources [12].

© Springer Nature Switzerland AG 2019
H. Badioze Zaman et al. (Eds.): IVIC 2019, LNCS 11870, pp. 14–24, 2019.
https://doi.org/10.1007/978-3-030-34032-2_2

Moreover, teachers are able to better strategize their teaching and learning approaches by including DST concepts in developing learning apps. This would eventually ease teachers in tailoring lessons [13, 14]. This article first explains the DST dimensions, proposed DST elements, learning theories and guidelines. The next section covers the methodology and then the conclusion.

2 DST Concept

The introduction of DST concept has positive impacts in the teaching strategy towards the need for the latest technology [12, 15]. In line with that, high demands for teaching products (apps) have boosted the creation of tablet-based teaching products (apps). However, the usage of apps is poorly delivered due to inappropriate content of the presentation. Recent studies showed that perception among students and teachers regarding the use for apps are very low. Thus, DST concept is infused in developing the apps. Nevertheless, initial study show that students are unable to comprehend DST clearly [16]. The concept of DST is recognized by elements to distinguish DST from other types of media such as film, television, video and blog [17]. Besides, in order to draw audience's attention to listen to stories is based on its elements.

2.1 DST Dimension

As shown in Fig. 1, the Abstract Layer Model by Schafer displays the relation between dimensions of each layer according to the divergent level of complexity [18]. The model categorises the dimensions to determine DST elements [19]. Basically, the model consists of five layers: Origin, Construction, Interaction, Appeal and Presentation [18]. The layers represent the DST dimension, where the clustering of the elements are formed. In performing the proposed dimension, the DST interactive model by Kim, Moon, Han and Chang is designated as a basis based on its suitability that meets with the objective of the study [20]. They discovered four dimensions, namely narrative, tool, interface and output for DST interactive elements. Figure 1 illustrates a brief overview of the mapping process of the proposed dimension performed.

Initially, the Abstract Layer Model by Schafer [18] is mapped to the interactive model by Kim et al. [20] in line with the dimension (layer). As a result, four DST dimensions are formed, namely, narrative, functional, tablet interface and multimedia to comply with the concept of study mainly on DST, tablet based and multimedia technology.

2.2 Proposed DST Elements

Various DST elements are introduced in comprehending DST concepts according to different perspectives of experts. There are 14 key interactive DST elements, namely perspective, intention, personal, dramatic question, engagement, articulation, sound track, tempo, story map, expression, significant content, collaboration, user contribution and minimal suggested by Tenh are validated by seven prominent DST experts, Robin, Porter, Ohler, Lambert, Sapeter, Paul and Fiebich and Schafer [19]. However,

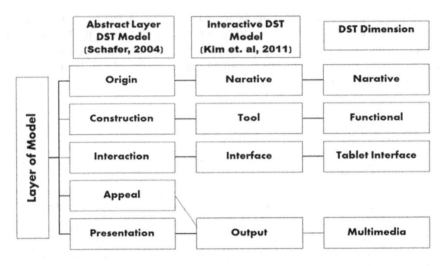

Fig. 1. DST dimensions

the elements are scarce and do not emphasis on touch screen technology. Besides, the elements need to be enhanced based on the latest technology and interactivity. Table 1 lists the initial recommendations of the proposed DST elements in this study. The DST elements are clustered according to DST dimensions: narrative, functionality, tablet interface and multimedia.

Narrative dimensions are situated in the early stage of storytelling process and initiated the preparation of media materials. The elements comprise of story objective, story content and story style. Meanwhile, functional dimension is the interaction between the designer and DST tool during the development process. This dimension involves character, editing media and authenticity in order to produce quality media that gives impact to the story. Tablet interface is another dimension which involves the interaction of the audience on the apps with the story system and consists of elements: interactivity, screen display and collaboration. This is to illustrate the relationship of communication between the story system and the audience. The final dimension is to attract audience with a compelling presentation which involves articulation and story beat using multimedia technology.

Table 1. Proposed DST elements on touch screen tablet.

Dimension	Element	Sources
Narrative	Story objective, story content, story style, character	[5, 21–23]
Functionality	Editing media, authenticity	[6, 24–26]
Tablet interface	Interactivity, screen display, collaboration	[27–30]
Multimedia	Articulation, story beat	[31–33]

2.3 Learning Theories

The proposed DST elements are also integrated with a well-known learning and storytelling theories namely, Cognitive Theory of Multimedia Learning (CTML), Cognitive Load Theory, Connectivism Theory and Neo Aristotelian Theory [34]. In order to justify the selection of the proposed DST elements, correct principles of the theories are adapted as tabulated in Table 2. With theoretical support, DST elements for touch screen tablet are formed to provide a proper guide to ease the development of apps.

Table 2. Adaptation of learning theories in DST elements on touch screen tablet

Element	Principles	Theory	Justification
Story objective	Eliminate the working memory load associated with having to mentally integrate several sources of information	Cognitive Load	Learning objective is focussing on essential learning content
	Signalling	CTML	Learning is effective if designed on essential materials to attract student's attention
Story content	Capacity to know more is more critical than what is currently known	Connectivism	Learning content includes the development of the concept of knowledge to foster students' knowledge
	Limited working memory	Cognitive Load	Learning material content is sufficient and limited
	Dramatical structure	Neo Aristotelian	Storytelling content consists of title and structure and narrative format (story map)
Story style	Personalization	CTML	Message is delivered in conversational style rather than formal style
	Dramatic experience is through audience and character	Neo Aristotelian	Message is delivered in dramatically question for audience's awareness
Character	Object	Neo Aristotelian	Character or image representation provides two-way communication for interactive storytelling
Editing media	Learning may reside in non-human appliances	Connectivism	Various functional tools enable ease of teaching process
Authenticity	Realism	Neo Aristotelian	Digital media are displayed in real situation
Interactivity	Learning is a process of connecting specialized nodes or information sources	Connectivism	Interactivity occurs through the connection between the audience (touch screen interaction) and the story system (apps)

(*continued*)

Table 2. (*continued*)

Element	Principles	Theory	Justification
Screen display	Limited working memory	Cognitive Load	Screen working area is built optimally based on tablet screen size
Collaboration	Learning and knowledge rest in a diversity of opinions	Connectivism	The combination of designer skills and engagement from audience are to create an effective story
Articulation	Modality	CTML	The use of text is presented as narration (spoken words) or using auditory, rather than presented as a written text to accompany the graphics
Story beat	Redundancy	CTML	Combination of animation with voice recording are applied rather than animations, voice recording with text on the screen for effective learning

2.4   Guideline for the Development of Apps with DST Concept on Touch Screen Tablet

Recently, there are many users enable to interact with touch screen devices, even though these interactions are easy to learn [35, 36]. Due to the lack of standards and established guidelines for the interaction of touch screen have triggered an idea of proposing a guideline [37]. With the infusion DST elements in the development process, the understanding of the concept of DST is achieved. A comprehensive analysis is employed to form the seven components of the guidelines, namely, process development, DST element, system requirement, DST dimension, theory and model, DST tool features and DST heuristic, however only five components are displayed based on experts' validation and comments as shown in Fig. 2. In the development process, the creation of apps will undergo four phases of activities: pre-production, production, post production and distribution [38].

The infusion of DST element in the development process is categorized by four dimensions: narrative, functional, interface. The DST element comprises story objective, story content, character, editing media, authenticity, interactivity, screen display, collaboration, articulation and story beat. The guidelines require hardware and software specification for instance, Android as an operating system, touch screen tablet and DST tools (storyboarding, editing and authoring). The features of DST tool are listed as shown in the Fig. 2.

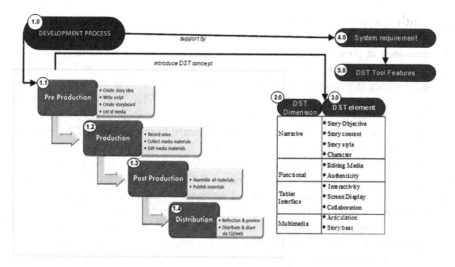

Fig. 2. Guideline for development of apps with DST concept on touch screen tablet [39]

3 Methodology

In this study, a series of activities were carried out as shown illustratively in Fig. 3. The study involves three phases of activities with critical analysis, comparative analysis and expert review, respectively. A critical analysis is carried out using content analysis from previous studies on DST tools. In order to identify suitable DST elements with concrete justification, the adaption of three learning theories and two storytelling theories is employed in order to propose DST elements. Finally, the expert review phase takes place where thirteen appointed experts validate the proposed DST elements with a checklist form. A descriptive analysis is performed to calculate the scores of each element.

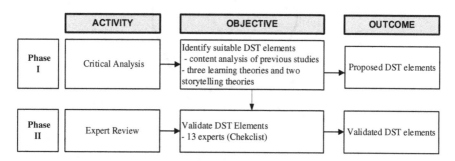

Fig. 3. Summary of activity

4 Findings and Discussion

As mentioned in previous section, the gap on the aspect of mobile technology design with touch screen interaction is identified as a major contribution in the DST elements for touch screen tablet. In order to provide a clear explanation in the design aspect, a detailed characteristic of the DST element is required. Thus, the context of design principles with touch screen interaction is determined according to appropriate narrative elements as a guide in understanding the elements. In proposing the DST elements, a critical analysis was conducted earlier in Table 2 and validated via an expert review.

An expert validation involves thirteen academic lecturers from the Institute of Teacher Education (ITE) and local universities (USM, UM, MMU, UiTM). Their roles are to review and comment the proposed elements based on relevant expertise. An expert's checklist form is to collect data based on the understanding of DST elements. The data is analysed by frequency scores [34]. Figure 4 represents radar chart of experts' feedback on DST elements. Based on the results, it can be seen that the experts strongly agreed on the eleven DST elements proposed in the study as the value of score yielded for each of the elements proposed is more than 8. Only one expert requires a clear explanation on screen display. Table 3 lists eleven DST elements with its summarized design principles based on experts' comments. It is important that justification and comments made by experts are applied in the development process.

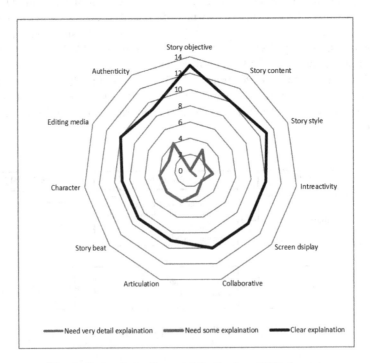

Fig. 4. Radar chart of experts' feedback on DST elements

Table 3. DST elements on touch screen tablet

Dimension	Element	Design principle
Narrative	Story objective	Provide aim and focus of the story based on audience background
	Story content	Provide a headline, type of story and adequate learning materials
	Story style	Show audience's appreciation and awareness with dramatic questions and views
	Character	Provide an image for interaction via two-way communication to draw audience's attention through facial expressions or body language
Functionality	Editing media	Enable media editing (text and images) by changing size and format, move and delete in order to manipulate the media
	Authenticity	Provide a suitable background or image with the correct angle of view
Tablet interface	Interactivity	Enable interaction with audience for navigation via finger input based on the size of media
	Screen Display	Provide suitable and adequate working area on the touch screen
	Collaboration	Enable engagement from audience and designer via interaction with story's system to share stories
Multimedia	Articulation	Provide narration or voice recording and combination of text and voice with effective background music
	Story beat	Enable image display at a certain time at each scene using transition and animation to demonstrate the continuity of the story

5 Discussion

The previous study on the creation of the guideline embarks further study on the DST elements [39]. The DST elements are formed to comprehend DST concept in the development of apps in the guidelines. An experts' validation is carried out after a critical analysis is employed to determine the elements. As a result, eleven DST elements, namely story objective, story content, story style, character, editing media, authenticity, interactivity, screen display, collaboration, articulation, story beat. The elements are clustered based on DST dimensions (narrative, functionality, tablet interface and multimedia).

The experts' validation is to confirm the correct terms and principles of the DST elements. The infusion of DST elements in the development process creates the novelty of the guidelines. Additionally, learning and storytelling theories are pedagogical aspects in adapting the DST elements in the development process. In order to provide a solid justification, the established design principles of DST elements are supported by these theories. This study contributes towards content development of learning material and national agenda as transforming shift towards Education 4.0. In line with that, machine (multimedia technology and tablet) and human development (teachers) will integrate in improving learning and teaching strategy for educational purposes. For future prospect, DST elements can be incorporated with the design of DST tool to create a compelling application for novice designers cum teachers to create their own apps.

References

1. Lambert, J.: Digital Storytelling: Capturing lives, Creating Community, 2nd edn. Digital Diner Press, Berkelay (2006)
2. Porter, B.: Digitales: The Art of Telling Digital Stories. BJP consulting, Sedalia (2004)
3. Signes, C.G.: Integrating the old and new: digital storytelling in the EFL language. Rev. Para Prof. Inglés 16(1&2), 43–49 (2008)
4. Lambert, J.: Digital Storytelling Cookbook, Seven Steps of Digital Storytelling, pp. 9–24. Digital Diner Press, Berkeley (2010)
5. Ohler, J.: Digital Storytelling in the Classroom New Media Pathways to Literacy, Learning, and Creativity, 2nd edn. SAGE Publications, Inc., USA (2008)
6. Abdel-Hack, E.M., Helwa, H.S.A.A.: Using digital storytelling and weblogs instruction to enhance EFL narrative writing and critical thinking skills among EFL majors at faculty of education. Int. Res. J. 5(1), 8–41 (2014)
7. Yuksel, P., Robin, B.R., McNeil, S.: Educational uses of digital storytelling around the world. In: Society for Information Technology & Teacher Education International Conference, vol. 1, no. 1, pp. 1264–1271 (2011)
8. Robin, B.R.: Create: Getting started. University of Houston (2011). http://digitalstorytelling. coe.uh.edu/index.cfm. Accessed 01 Jan 2014
9. Azman, F.N., Zaibon, S.B., Shiratuddin, N.: Pedagogical analysis of comic authoring systems for educational digital storytelling. J. Theor. Appl. Inf. Technol. 89(2), 461–469 (2016)
10. Robin, B.R., McNeil, S.G.: What educators should know about teaching digital storytelling. Digit. Educ. Rev. 22, 37–51 (2012)
11. Adri, M.: Strategi pengembangan multimedia instructional design (suatu kajian teoritis). J. Invotek VIII(1), 2007
12. Yahya, O., Raini, D.P.: Kesan aplikasi perisian cerita interaktif semasa mengajarkan kemahiran bacaan dan kefahaman dalam kalangan murid tahun 4 di Brunei Darussalam. J. Pendidik. Bhs. Melayu 1(1), 27–49 (2011)
13. Siemens, G.: Instructional design in e-learning. Elearnspace (2002). http://www.elearnspace. org/Articles/InstructionalDesign.htm. Accessed 20 Feb 2014
14. Yao, J., Fernando, T., Wang, H.: A multi-touch natural user interface framework. In: 2012 International Conference on Systems and Informatics (ICSAI), pp. 499–504 (2012)
15. Alexander, B.: The New Digital Storytelling: Creating Naratives with New Media. Praeger, USA (2017)
16. Hashiroh, H., Norshuhada, S.: Australian journal of basic and applied sciences usage of digital storytelling for media creation on tablet. In: Proceedings of Social Informtion Technology Teacher Education International Confernce, vol. 9, no. 18, pp. 647–654 (2015)
17. Lowenthal, P.: Digital storytelling : an emerging institutional technology? In: Story circle: Digital Storytelling Around the World, pp. 297–305 (2006). Wiley-Blackwell

18. Schäfer, L.: Models for digital storytelling and interactive narratives. In: 4th International Conference on Computational Semiotics for Games and New Media, pp. 148–155, September 2004
19. Tenh, H.K.: Conceptual model of digital storytelling (DST). Universiti Utara Malaysia (2013)
20. Kim, S., Moon, S., Han, S., Chang, J.: Programming the story: interactive storytelling system. Informatica 35, 221–229 (2011)
21. Robin, B.R.: The educational uses of digital storytelling. In: Proceedings of Society for Information Technology and Teacher Education International Conference, pp. 709–716 (2006)
22. Barrett, H.C.: Researching and evaluating digital storytelling as a deep learning tool. In: Society for Information Technology and Teacher Education International Conference, pp. 647–654 (2006)
23. Zaibon, S.B., Shiratuddin, N.: Adapting learning theories in mobile game-based learning development. In: DIGITEL 2010 - The 3rd IEEE International Conference on Digital Game and Intelligent Toy Enhanced Learning, pp. 124–128, September 2010
24. Rogers, Y., Sharp, H., Preece, J.: Interaction Design: Beyond Human Computer Interaction, 2nd edn. Wiley, Hoboken (2012)
25. Jennings, A., Ryser, S., Drews, F.: Touch screen devices and the effectiveness of user interface methods. In: Proceedings of the Human Factors and Ergonomics Society Annual Meeting, vol. 57, no. 1, pp. 1648–1652 (2013)
26. Miyaji, I.: The effects of digital storytelling through the strategy of evaluation and correction. In: Proceedings of the 9th International Conference on Information Technology Based Higher Education and Training, pp. 129–135 (2010)
27. Yu, K., Wang, H., Liu, C., Niu, J.: Interactive storyboard: animated story creation on touch interfaces. In: 5th International Conference Active Media Technology, pp. 93–103 (2009)
28. Nor'ain, M.Y., Siti Salwah, S.: Investigating cognitive task difficulties and expert skills in e-Learning storyboards using a cognitive task analysis technique. Comput. Educ. 58, 652–665 (2012)
29. Karray, F., Alemzadeh, M., Saleh, J.A., Arab, M.N.: Human computer interaction: overview on state of the art. Int. J. Smart Sens. Intell. Syst. 1(1), 137–159 (2008)
30. Tenh, H.K., Norshuhada, S., Harryizman, H.: Digital storytelling's conceptual model: a proposed guide towards the construction of a digital story. In: International Conference on Teaching and Learning in Higher Education (ICTLHE 2011) (2011)
31. Suwardy, T., Pan, G., Seow, P.-S.: Using digital storytelling to engage student learning. Account. Educ. An Int. J. 22(2), 109–124 (2013)
32. Ohler, J.: Storytelling and new media narrative (2014). http://www.jasonohler.com/storytelling/storytech.cfm. Accessed 01 Jan 2014
33. Mayer, R., Moreno, R.: A cognitive theory of multimedia learning: implications for design principles. Annu. Meet. ACM SIGCHI 91(2), 1–10 (1998)
34. Hashiroh, H.: Garis panduan pembangunan media pengajaran berkonsepkan penceritaan digital untuk tablet skrin sentuh. Univeristi Utara Malaysia (2017)
35. Malizia, A., Bellucci, A.: Viewpoint: the artificiality of natural user interfaces toward user-defined gestural interfaces. Commun. ACM 55(3), 36–38 (2012)
36. Montague, K., Hanson, V., Cobley, A.: Evaluation of adaptive interaction with mobile touch-screen devices. In: Digital Engagement Conference, UK (2011)
37. Norman, D.A., Nielsen, J.: Gestural interfaces: a step backward in usability. Interactions 17(5), 46–49 (2010)

38. Hashiroh, H., Norshuhada, S.: A digital storytelling process guide for designers. J. Telecommun. Electron. Comput. Eng. **8**(8), 13–17 (2016)
39. Hashiroh, H., Norshuhada, S.: Guideline for the development of instructional media with DST concept on touch screen tablet. In: Badioze Zaman, H., et al. (eds.) Advances in Visual Informatics. IVIC 2017. LNCS, vol. 10645, pp. 398–411. Springer, Cham (2017). https:// doi.org/10.1007/978-3-319-70010-6_37

Virtual Environment for VR-Based Stress Therapy System Design Element: User Perspective

Farhah Amaliya Zaharuddin[1,3](✉), Nazrita Ibrahim[1,2],
Azmi Mohd Yusof[1], Mohd Ezanee Rusli[1],
and Eze Manzura Mohd Mahidin[1]

[1] College of Computing and Informatics, Universiti Tenaga Nasional,
Kajang, Selangor, Malaysia
farhahdin@gmail.com
[2] Institute of Informatics and Computing in Energy, Universiti Tenaga Nasional,
Kajang, Selangor, Malaysia
[3] UNITEN R&D Sdn. Bhd., Kajang, Selangor, Malaysia

Abstract. Given that mental stress issue is becoming a big concern in today's society, it is important to highlight available alternatives that may help in reducing stress. One of the options available is virtual reality-based therapy (VR-based therapy). Previous studies conducted show that VR-based therapy has promising results in reducing stress and inducing relaxation. However, most of the studies were only focusing on the effectiveness of the system without taking into consideration the elements that should be included while designing its virtual environment. Therefore, this study aims to identify the possible design elements that should be taken into consideration when designing a virtual environment for a VR-based stress therapy system. An existing system review consisted of system demonstration and interview session was conducted with 12 random participants. During the review, the users were required to use an existing VR-based system and provide their feedback and comments during a short interview session that follows. Based on the review, eight design elements were identified, which were then grouped into five themes; visual attraction, environment setting, user comfort, interaction and navigation.

Keywords: Virtual reality · Stress therapy · Virtual environment · Designing factors

1 Introduction

Lately, virtual reality system has been used as an alternative in reducing one's mental stress. VR-based stress therapy is currently receiving more attention as it provides more advantages compared to conventional techniques such as imagination and Cognitive Behaviour Therapy (CBT). As one of the disadvantages in conventional techniques is low imagination level, therefore, virtual reality is used to enhance the imaginary process by providing the imagination display in graphic form. By using virtual reality, less

H. Badioze Zaman et al. (Eds.): IVIC 2019, LNCS 11870, pp. 25–35, 2019.
https://doi.org/10.1007/978-3-030-34032-2_3

effort is required to build the imagination, thus help the user to focus on therapy session.

Previous studies reported that the application of virtual reality in stress therapy has given promising results which can possibly benefit its users [1]. However, most of the studies only focused on the efficacy of the system to reduce stress. Less attention is given on the virtual environment design and development aspects that may contribute to the effectiveness of the system. As virtual environment is one of the important components in virtual reality system, therefore, there is a need to find out the elements that should be taken into consideration when designing it. Incorporating the right elements in the virtual environment will ensure the effectiveness of the system. Instead of simply designing an environment without any clear guidance, this study aims to help in setting up a basic guideline for future researchers. Once a basic guideline is established, future researchers who wish to study VR-based stress therapy system may use this study as a guide to design their system's virtual environment which in turn will save time by allowing them to focus more on their research problems.

Mishkind et al. [2] in a review of virtual reality treatment in psychiatry highlighted the need for a guidance in developing an effective VR-based system. According to them, since virtual reality is found to be a suitable alternative in psychological therapy, therefore, there is a need for researchers to understand what makes it effective. Additionally, they also highlighted some consideration on what future research could do. It is believed that including information on technical aspects of the system such as field of view and design of the virtual environment, will help researchers in obtaining a better result.

Currently, the elements of a design that should be included in a virtual environment of stress therapy is limited. Prior to commencing this study, a literature survey was done to identify previous works and articles on design elements which should be taken into consideration when designing a virtual environment for a VR-based stress therapy system. Based on the survey, only eight publications [1, 3–9] were found suitable for this study. However, none of these papers discussed on the design elements required when designing a virtual environment for a stress therapy purpose. Thus, this study aims to fulfill the need for identifying and considering the essential design elements in designing a virtual environment for VR-based stress therapy. This study is conducted by asking the users to review an existing system, followed by a short interview to obtain an in-depth description of the review given. Two research questions were built to help in achieving the objective of this study. The research questions are listed below:

- RQ1: What are the design elements that should be taken into consideration when designing a virtual environment for a VR-based stress therapy system.
- RQ2: How the identified elements are recommended to be applied in the virtual environment?

To answer these research questions, the study was not only limited to identifying the elements in the virtual environment design but also applied to any relaxing environment designing process that are not related to virtual reality.

2 Method

The aim of the review is to identify design elements of a virtual environment which help in reducing stress and inducing relaxation. A suitable system was reviewed to collect relevant data from participants. Three methods were used to gather data; observation, talk aloud protocol, and a semi-structured interview.

2.1 Instrument

An existing VR-based relaxation system released in 2016 known as the Guided Meditation VR developed by Cubicle Ninja was the system used in this review. The system was selected based on three reasons. Firstly, the system is a meditation-based system with the purpose of inducing relaxation and reducing stress. Josh Farkas, the Cubicle Ninja founder, in an interview with Stephen Reid explained that Guided Meditation System VR was developed to help users to relax by applying meditation concept embedded with relaxing environment and meditating audio into a virtual reality system to transport the user's mind to a peaceful surrounding [10]. Secondly, the system has a wide range of environment and audio options for its users to choose from. Guided Meditation VR comes with over 30 choices of environments, 15 hours of meditation audio and two modes of navigation. The various options offered in the system helps the researcher to identify more design elements from different aspects. For example, a natural setting for a virtual environment is not only limited to plants and trees, but may also include water elements such as sea and waterfall. Thirdly, the system is still an active system. An active system means the system is still maintained and updated by the developer. Guided Meditation VR is a well-maintained system as its bug and error feedback from the user are taken seriously. Additionally, a continuous update is being done from time to time by adding new environments and audio options. It is important to review an active system in this study in order to ensure that the system reviewed is not obsolete and is still relevant for it to be compared with today's virtual reality technology.

2.2 Participant

Twelve participants (8 males and 4 females) participated in this study. All the participants were randomly recruited from around the researcher's university area. The age of the participants ranges between 18 to 23 years old. Ten participants were students while the other two were research engineers who willingly volunteered to take part in this review. All of the participants were from the field of computer science or information technology.

Based on observations made during the review, participants who were very familiar with virtual reality system gave their feedbacks based on their experience using the system. This group of respondents was most likely to comment on its realistic effects and user experience elements. The rest of the participants gave their opinions based on daily experiences and real-life situations. In addition, it is also noticed that participants who were familiar with computer games and virtual reality system are most likely to require less time to familiarize themselves with the system. They also required less guidance from the researcher in using and navigating themselves through the system.

Data collection and analysis process for this review was done consecutively. Each recorded interview was transcribed and analysed as soon as the review session ended. This procedure helped the researcher to stop the data collection process once the data is saturated. Data collected was assumed to be saturated when similar feedbacks and comments are obtained from the participants.

2.3   Review Procedure

The review began with the explanation on the objectives and procedure of the review to the participant. This step was done to ensure that the participant was made clear of the purpose of the review and what the researcher was trying to achieve and identify at the end of the session.

Once the participant understood the purpose explained, he or she was then asked to use the system on his or her own without consulting the researcher. While using the system, the participant was reminded to evaluate the effectiveness of the system as well as to identify the elements that assisted them to feel relaxed. For the purpose of this review, the system was pre-set by the researcher according to the participant's preference. The participant was asked to choose his or her environment and audio preference based on a list of pre-listed environment and audio set by the researcher. For this review, the system was set as follows:

- Environment: Four options (Beach, waterfall, forest and green garden)
- Audio: Fixed to calming option
- Navigation mode: Fixed to teleport mode

The system was set as above after considering the matters listed below:

- The system was limited to four environment options because there were too many in the system that may result in the review result scope to be too wide. This can indirectly decrease the reliability of the result. The four selected environments which were included in the review were based on the top four preferred relaxing results of a user study done prior to the review.
- The audio option was fixed to calming mode due to the same reason as the environment. Too many options may cause the result to vary too much, hence, making it difficult to analyse. However, the participant was given an option to choose whether they would prefer to listen to additional background audio. If he or she chose to have additional background audio while using the system, the audio was set to calming option.
- The navigation option was fixed to teleport mode because this review aims to get users to give feedback on design elements to be included in a stress therapy virtual environment. In order for the participant to carefully observe the system's environment, he or she requires more freedom to navigate through the virtual environment. Therefore, teleport mode was the best option compared to flight mode as the participant will have more control over his or her exploration.

At the end of the therapy session, the participants were interviewed on their overall perception of the effectiveness of the system to induce relaxation and reduce stress, as well as the virtual environment elements that assisted them to achieve the state. The participants were also encouraged to provide any idea, concern or suggestion that may improve the quality of a VR-based stress therapy system in terms of its virtual environment. Each review session lasted between 30 to 40 min. All feedbacks were audio recorded and transcribed for analysis purposes.

2.4   Data Analysis

Data collected from the review was analysed using thematic analysis. The approach used to perform the thematic analysis is based on a step-by-step outline guide presented by Braun and Clarke [11]. However, the steps were modified to fit the study purpose. Hence, the thematic analysis for this study was done in five stages as depicted in Table 1.

Table 1. Stages of thematic analysis used in this study.

Stage	Description of process
1	Familiarising with the collected data
2	Generating elements
3	Generating theme
4	Reviewing theme
5	Comparing themes and its elements

Stage 1: Familiarising with the Collected Data. Recorded interviews were transcribed word by word. The transcribed scripts were then revised twice while listening to the recorded audio. This was done to ensure that the audio was correctly transcribed. Once the transcription was complete, it was reviewed once again for the third time. The third review only involved reading the script without listening to the recorded audio. The aim of the third review was to help the researcher to become more familiar with the script and to get the overview of the themes to be generated from it.

Stage 2: Generating Elements. Transcribed scripts from the previous stage were loaded into ATLAST.ti, a qualitative data analysis software to help in the coding and theme generating process. During this stage, the scripts were carefully read line by line in order to identify the possible codes to be highlighted. Here, codes refer to any statement in the script that could possibly answer the research questions. Next, the highlighted codes were then assigned to an element. Element refers to a group of codes which have a similar meaning. Each element was given a special name to represent the codes which falls under them.

Stage 3: Generating Theme. The identified elements from the previous stage were listed in a table. At this stage, Microsoft Excel 2016 was used to help in organizing the elements. All the elements listed were screened several times prior to being categorised into several themes. Here, theme refers to a group of elements with similar meanings. During this stage, any element that seemed unrelated was discarded.

Stage 4: Reviewing Theme. The themes generated in the previous stage were reviewed once again. This second review was done to ensure the clarity of the theme. If a theme was found to be too broad, it is then broken into several themes. As for the themes which had similar meaning and were difficult to differentiate from one another, the themes are combined.

Stage 5: Comparing Themes and Their Elements. Themes and elements generated from the current participant were then compared to the themes and elements generated from the script of the previous participant. The two lists were then placed side by side for comparison. The newest list was then updated with any additional themes or elements from the compared list.

3 Result and Discussion

This section discusses the findings from the review which answer the two research questions, RQ1 and RQ2. Findings presented in this section were based on the feedback and comments collected during the system's review session. The results highlighted the design elements that can be considered when designing a virtual environment for VR-based stress therapy. The identified elements may be used as a guide in the decision-making stage of the designing process, specifically to develop an environment for VR-based stress therapy.

Based on the analysis, 69 codes were identified from 12 transcribed scripts which were then grouped into 8 elements and 5 themes. The themes consisted of elements that were grouped together. Table 2 summarises a list of elements and themes identified in this study. Every design element listed is further discussed in the next subsection.

Table 2. List of elements and themes identified.

Identified elements	Generated themes
Presence of animals	Visual attraction
Presence of water feature	
Nature based theme	Environment setting
Realism	
Sense of safety	User Comfort
Free teleportation	Navigation
Selected viewport teleportation	
Active interaction	Interaction

3.1   Design Theme: Visual Attraction

The first design theme identified is visual attraction. Two design elements were recommended to be listed under this theme which were presence of animals and presence of water feature.

Presence of Animals. During the exploration, some participants suggested to include some elements of living matter such as animals in the virtual world. Some of the related comments were; *"...maybe I prefer some kind of living things like small animal like bird...kind of like we can see from far...the mother is feeding its child...so we can feel the family love..."* (Participant 2); *"...ha...but...if possible...it is better if we can have like animal...moving around...for example...butterfly..."* (Participant 4), and; *"...I think you should add another animals if you can create one...yea...maybe one or any animals that move a little...so I can go and touch...it don't have to interact with the animal but I think if you add animals, a nice one...should be a good idea..."* (Participant 7).

Additionally, some participants also commented on how the animals that were presented in the virtual environments helped them to feel calmer *"...because of the fishes...looking at them makes me feel so good..."* (Participant 3,) and; *"... maybe we can add...to enhance the relaxation effect...in my opinion...maybe can add like flying birds...or butterfly...and for example we are here (referring to a river bank point) maybe there are some fishes around...but not every time we are here...we will see the fishes...so...it will more realistic and more peaceful..."* (Participant 5).

Based on the findings, VR-based therapy system developers are encouraged to add animals in the virtual environments that are being built for the purpose of stress treatment.

Presence of Water Feature. Apart from the animal element mentioned above, the inclusion of water feature could also aid in enhancing the relaxing effect of the virtual environment. During the review session, the participants expressed their preference to have water features such as a waterfall as one of the relaxation points. This was captured in the following comments, *"...the water helps me to calm myself...if let say you take out the water...it will reduce the calming effect...or I can say not calming at all..."* (Participant 5); *"...I feel calm because I am at the beach...and the water element at the beach cause me to feel relax..."* (Participant 6), and; *"...Yea...it so perfect...I really like the waterfall...it is fun but the water makes me calm...I just like want to watch the water..."* (Participant 7).

Based on the feedbacks received, it is suggested to include water feature such as river and waterfall in a virtual environment for a VR-based stress therapy as this element help in reducing their stress and make them feel calm.

3.2   Design Theme: Environment Setting

The second theme identified from the review was environment setting. Environment setting refers to how the environment should be designed in term of its visual and audio. Two design elements were recommended to be included under this theme which were nature based theme and realism.

Nature Based Theme. The participants suggested to use nature based environment as the main visual theme. Among the suggested environments received were beach and jungle.

Apart from visual aspect, the participants also suggested to include nature sound-scapes as the main background audio theme in the virtual environment. Such audio could help the users to feel relax in the created world. This was captured in the following comment *"...I want to listen to the water drop sound from the cave..."* (Participant 1) and *"...it is not stressful at all...it is very calm...and listen to the sea... the sea sound..."* (Participant 11).

Therefore, it is highly recommended to include nature based theme in both visual and audio aspects of a virtual environment for a VR-based stress therapy system.

Sense of Realism. The participants expressed their opinion on how the element of realism affects their relaxation. Based on the participants' perspective, they wanted the developed environment to be as real as possible with the real world. Some of the participant's comments on realism in the virtual world were as follows: *"...realism helps...if it not real...it won't give you any effect...if not real...still...it looks like cartoon...it is not relaxing..."* (Participant 10) and *"...realism effect helps me to feel calm...if you decrease the realism effect...it will be too cartoony...and the system would be ineffective...how to say...because you cannot feel that you are not at the side..."* (Participant 11).

On the other hand, visual realism element is also affected by the accompanying audio. While exploring the virtual world, some participants also commented on the accompanying audio that affected their feeling of realism. The feedback received highlighted that the audio should also be realistic for the users to feel their presence in the virtual environment. For example, if the user is sitting near a waterfall, the sound of the waterfall should be loud and the sound should begin to fade out as the user walks away from the waterfall. Few of the recorded comments related to the audio realism were: *"...the waterfall sound is not that clear...too soft...so I can't feel that I am there at the waterfall...the idea is like this...for example...as we go nearer, the sound is louder..."* (participant 5) and *"...I think the sound...it should be a little bit louder... because as of now, I don't feel it real and I am here..."* (Participant 8).

The findings strongly suggest that the virtual environment should be as real as possible while designing a virtual environment to ensure the effectiveness of the system in helping its users to reduce stress. The design should be crafted perfectly to incorporate the visual elements with its audio effects, which hence, increases the sense of realism.

3.3   Design Theme: User Comfort

The third design theme identified was user comfort. One element was recommended to be listed under this theme which was sense of safety.

Sense of Safety. The environment design should be relaxing enough in order to achieve the main aim of the system. Based on the system review, some participants highlighted the importance of having a sense of safety in the environment as they are exploring the world. With the inclusion of safety aspects, it will ease the user's exploration and speed up the relaxation process. This suggestion was raised by two participants: *"...it's quiet and relax...nothing is disturbing and frighten me...no spider or insect frightening me..."* (participant 1) and *"...it feels calm...but at the same time, I am feeling a little bit insecure when been inside the environment...I am scared if suddenly let say something creepy inside there (referring to a bushy area) and suddenly come out..."* (Participant 4).

Therefore, it is suggested to take safety precautions into consideration when designing a stress therapy virtual environment. If there are any animals to be included, it should not make the users feel insecure.

3.4 Design Theme: Navigation

The fourth theme identified was navigation. Two design elements were recommended to be included under this theme which were free teleportation and selected viewpoints teleportation.

Free Teleportation. Some of the participants commented that they want to be given the ability to explore the virtual environment on their own. Some related comments were: *"...we need to have the ability to explore the world...because if not, we can't feel the world...it just like we are watching a video instead of be in the world..."* (Participant 5) and *"...sometimes if we can walk around by ourselves is also good... because we can feel the trees...even though we can't really feel the trees like we touch it, but I think we can help us to feel calmer..."* (Participant 8).

As suggested by the participants, it is convincing to give the user the freedom to explore the virtual environment but, it should however be within some limited boundaries. This is because, based on the researcher's observation, when a user is allowed to navigate their way through without boundaries they tend to 'overly explore the environment' until they're lost and have no idea of their whereabouts.

Therefore, it is recommended to give the users the ability to explore the virtual environment by themselves but with some limitations.

Selected Viewpoints Teleportation. Apart from the free teleportation style suggested, there were also participants who recommended to have selected viewpoints teleportation. Selected viewpoints refer to some viewpoints in the virtual environment which have been pre-set by the developers during the development process. The viewpoints were set at places that were suitable for users to sit back and relax while enjoying the view. In selected viewpoints teleportation, users were only allowed to teleport at and to the selected viewpoints only. Users can choose to sit at one of the viewpoints they preferred.

Some of related participants' comments regarding selected viewpoints teleportation were: *"...if it has the ability to walk around, then it is better...it depends on the situation as well. Just now I am in rush to be at this place...so fast teleportation like what I done is ok...However, if you really want to feel relax and calm, therefore slow explorations is the best..."* (Participant 9) and *"...I prefer to sit wherever I want...for example...I want to be in the water...so I can be here or here (while referring at several places) ..."* (Participant 12).

Therefore, it is also suggested to choose a suitable type of teleportation according to users' preferences. Some users love to have the freedom to feel relaxed, however, some others would love to sit back and relax without the need of struggling and exploring the virtual environment on their own in order to find the best spot for them to sit and relax.

3.5   Design Theme: Interaction

The fifth theme identified was interaction. One design element was recommended to be included under this theme which was active interaction. Active interaction refers to activities that require users to give any instruction to the virtual environment in order to interact. For example, clicking a button to feed fish or pulling a trigger to catch a bird.

Active Interaction. Some of the participants appreciated how a virtual environment could help them feel relaxed. They suggested that it would be more interesting if some user interactions with the virtual world were added. Interactions can help shorten the time taken for the users to achieve tranquillity. One of the comments suggested additional interaction to be included; *"...it will be lovely if there is some interaction... interaction with the environment make me go deeply into the environment...it means I can adapt...I love this thing..."* (Participant 9).

Additionally, the user-virtual environment interaction can also prevent the users from getting bored. Some of the comments quoted: *"...maybe interaction with the animals...for some people who are animal lovers...maybe they love it...because with interaction, they won't be like just moving around only...there are more options that they can do..."* (Participant 11); *"...some activities such as push the trees...interaction with the user la...so...not only teleportation available for the user to interact with the environment..."* (Participant 10), and; *"...that one maybe also helps...because we are not only looking around...we have some interaction...as in inside a game...so it like you having fun inside that environment at the same time...for me...maybe a little bit of interaction will do..."* (Participant 11).

Based on the comments, it was suggested to include some active user-environment interaction in the virtual environment designed for stress therapy.

4   Conclusion

This review is conducted to identify the design elements that should be considered when designing a virtual environment for a VR-based stress therapy system based on the user's perspective. The identification was performed using reviews from an existing system and interview sessions with users.

The users' reviews were categorised into five themes which are visual attraction, environment setting, user comfort, navigation and interaction. Each theme was made up of several design elements. The first identified theme was visual attraction. Two design elements were listed under this theme which included the presence of animals and the presence of water feature. The second theme, environment setting, included two design elements which were nature based theme and realism. As for the third theme, user comfort, one design element was recommended to be included which was sense of safety. The fourth theme was navigation. Two design elements identified were free teleportation and selected viewpoints teleportation. The fifth theme was interaction and the design element identified was active interaction. The future plan for this study is to develop a prototype incorporating all of the identified elements presented in this paper. The developed system will then be used as a tool to reduce stress. Hence, aiming for the users to have a clear mind, feel motivated and remain focus throughout the day.

Acknowledgement. This study was funded by Tenaga Nasional Berhad Seed Fund (U-TE-RD-18-03) in collaboration with TNB Counselling Unit. We would like to thank UNITEN R&D Sdn. Bhd. for fund management.

References

1. Mahalil, I., Rusli, M.E., Yusof, A.M., Yusof, M.Z.M., Zainudin, A.R.R.: Virtual reality-based technique for stress therapy. In: 2014 4th International Conference on Engineering Technology and Technopreneuship (ICE2T), pp. 295–300 (2014)
2. Mishkind, M.C., Norr, A.M., Katz, A.C., Reger, G.M.: Review of virtual reality treatment in psychiatry: evidence versus current diffusion and use. Curr. Psychiatry Rep. **19**(11), 80 (2017)
3. Soyka, F., Leyrer, M., Smallwood, J., Ferguson, C., Riecke, B.E., Mohler, B.J.: Enhancing stress management techniques using virtual reality. In: Proceedings of the ACM Symposium on Applied Perception – (SAP 2016), pp. 85–88 (2016)
4. Taneja, A., Vishal, S.B., Mahesh, V., Geethanjali, B.: Virtual reality based neuro-rehabilitation for mental stress reduction. In: 2017 Fourth International Conference on Signal Processing, Communication and Networking (ICSCN), pp. 1–5 (2017)
5. Andersen, T., et al.: A preliminary study of users' experiences of meditation in virtual reality. In: 2017 IEEE Virtual Reality (VR), pp. 343–344 (2017)
6. Dayang, R., et al.: VReST: an image-based virtual reality stress therapy web application. In: 2011 IEEE International Symposium on IT in Medicine and Education, pp. 733–737 (2011)
7. Shah, L.B.I., Torres, S., Kannusamy, P., Chng, C.M.L., He, H.G., Klainin-Yobas, P.: Efficacy of the virtual reality-based stress management program on stress-related variables in people with mood disorders: the feasibility study. Arch. Psychiatr. Nurs. **29**(1), 6–13 (2015)
8. Das Thoondee, K., Oikonomou, A.: Using virtual reality to reduce stress at work, pp. 492–499, July 2017
9. Waterworth, J., Waterworth, E.: Relaxation island: a virtual tropical paradise. Interact. Exp. (2004)
10. Stephen, R.: Escape reality with guided meditation VR - VIVE blog (2017). https://blog.vive.com/us/2017/03/16/escape-reality-with-guided-meditation-vr/. Accessed 31 May 2018
11. Braun, V., Clarke, V.: Using thematic analysis in psychology. Qual. Res. Psychol. **3**(2), 77–101 (2006)

Factors to Consider When Designing a Virtual Environment to Treat Stress

Farhah Amaliya Zaharuddin[1,3(✉)], Nazrita Ibrahim[1,2],
Mohd Ezanee Rusli[1], Eze Manzura Mohd Mahidin[1],
and Azmi Mohd Yusof[1]

[1] College of Computing and Informatics, Universiti Tenaga Nasional, Kajang,
Selangor, Malaysia
farhahdin@gmail.com
[2] Institute of Informatics and Computing in Energy, Universiti Tenaga Nasional,
Kajang, Selangor, Malaysia
[3] UNITEN R&D Sdn. Bhd., Kajang, Selangor, Malaysia

Abstract. Virtual reality (VR) based stress therapy system refers to a system that applies virtual reality technology in a stress therapy session aiming to reduce mental stress. Previous studies conducted found that the system is effective in reducing stress. However, most of the studies done only aimed to measure the effectiveness of the system in reducing stress without having a guideline on how to design the virtual environment. Therefore, this paper aim to identify potential factors and its elements that must be considered when designing a virtual environment for a VR- based stress therapy application. Systematic literature review technique was employed as a guideline to search for relevant studies. The search was conducted using pre-defined keywords. Potential studies were filtered three times before it was finalised. After the selection process, the chosen studies were reviewed and important data that answers this study's two research questions were extracted for analysis purposes. Ten studies were found to fulfil the inclusion criteria and answer all the research questions. From the review conducted, four factors were identified as aspects that should be considered when designing a virtual environment for a VR-based stress therapy application. In addition, each factor consisted of several elements.

Keywords: Virtual reality · Stress therapy · Virtual environment · Designing factors

1 Introduction

Virtual reality (VR) is defined as a computer-simulated 3D environment that provides an opportunity for its users to experience the virtual world [1]. VR tricks its users into thinking that they are in another world with the help of special sensors, display devices, and sound systems.

The application of VR can be found in various areas such as engineering, tourism, marketing, and education with different usage purpose. Among the purposes are promotion of historical areas as a tourist attraction, marketing strategies to attract

© Springer Nature Switzerland AG 2019
H. Badioze Zaman et al. (Eds.): IVIC 2019, LNCS 11870, pp. 36–47, 2019.
https://doi.org/10.1007/978-3-030-34032-2_4

customers, and training of medical students. As of today, the application of VR is expanded into the field of psychology. In this field, VR is used as an alternative treatment method for mental health-related problems such as phobia [2], anxiety [3], eating disorder [4] and post-traumatic stress disorder (PTSD) [5, 6]. Numerous studies have demonstrated the positive benefits of VR application in the field of psychology which hence, created a good opportunity to conduct rigorous research in this field.

As the use of VR in the field of psychology has shown promising results, an increasing number of recent researches have started to focus on employing VR to reduce stress and induce relaxation [7, 8]. Similar to other VR systems, the development process of VR-based stress therapy requires the consideration of a large number of aspects known as factor.

An article by Mishkind et al. [9] highlighted a gap in determining the potential important factors required to develop a VR-based system. These factors are crucial as it will promote a greater VR application in the field of human psychology. Therefore, there is a need to identify the factors to be considered during the designing process of the virtual environment to ensure the effectiveness of VR-based stress therapy to promote stress reduction and relaxation.

Nonetheless, factors that should be considered when designing a virtual environment for a VR-based stress therapy system are still uncertain. In a study by Dooris [10] on healthy and sustainable settings, it was found that a relationship exists between the surroundings or environment and human health. Like Dooris, Berto [11] also discovered that physical setting plays a role in helping us cope with stress and therefore, this strengthens the connection between environment and the human mental state. Thus, the same concept is used in this study, whereby the idea of a relationship between environment and the human mental state is applied to the VR-based stress therapy system. The design of a virtual environment or environment, as it is known in the original concept, is believed to affect one's mental state.

As such, to determine the factors that should be considered when designing an environment, a preliminary literature survey of past researches on VR-based therapy for stress was done. Results showed that most of the systems only highlighted the main theme employed to develop a virtual environment for a VR-based stress therapy, namely the nature-based elements theme. Moreover, none of the reviewed papers described in detail the design factors that should be considered when developing the chosen environment. Design choices or factors are essentially one of the important aspects in the development of a VR-based stress therapy system. Without a proper and well-thought design, the developed environment may not be effective in reducing stress but instead may become a source of stress to the user.

Even though none of the reviewed papers on VR discussed in detail on matters regarding the choosing and designing of the right environment, this research gap can be addressed by examining researches performed in other domains such as landscape, urban planning, and environmental psychology. Therefore, the main objective of this paper is to review the possible factors and its elements that aid in reducing stress and determine how the identified factors and its elements can be extended into virtual environment design to help in the recovery of stress. Nevertheless, to address the specific details of the design of the virtual environment, specifically for the development of a VR-based stress therapy application, it is imperative to understand relevant context that are to be included. Hence, the aims of this study are as follows:

- RO1: To identify the possible factors to be considered when designing a virtual environment for a VR-based stress therapy application.
- RO2: To list the elements for the identified factors to be considered when designing a virtual environment for a VR-based stress therapy application.

The rest of this paper comprises of Sect. 2, which provides a thorough explanation of the methodology used and Sect. 3 that presents the results and discussion based on data extracted in Sect. 2.

2 Methodology

A systematic literature review was conducted based on the guidelines proposed by Kitchenham [12]. The systematic literature review consists of a step-by-step approach that helps researchers to develop the review protocol. This method was used as it assists in methodically capturing, summarising, synthesising, and critically commenting on the reviewed topic. In this study, the review was done in three phases, i.e. Phase 1 (review planning), Phase 2 (review process), and Phase 3 (review report). Each phase is described in detail in the following subsections.

2.1 Phase 1: Review Planning

The first phase involved identifying the need for the review and defining how the review should be done. All activities conducted in this phase are explained as follows.

Identification of the Need for Review. Based on a preliminary literature survey done, it was found that there is no clear guideline for the factors that should be taken into consideration when designing an environment for a VR-based stress therapy application. Furthermore, there is no systematic review that focuses on the design of the environment. The increasing number of research on the application of VR in stress therapy is a strong evidence as to why a proper guideline for factors that may contribute to the effectiveness of the VR-based stress therapy application is needed.

Apart from that, the guideline will also contribute to the standardisation of the design of the environment. This standardisation is important to build consistency between VR-based stress therapy applications, which will then increase the quality of research in the related field. As such, based on the gaps and potential contributions identified, it is believed that there is a need to conduct a systematic literature review to list potential factors to be taken into consideration when designing an environment for a VR-based stress therapy application.

Defining the Research Question. This systematic literature review aims to identify potential factors that should be considered when designing a virtual environment that aids in the recovery of stress. Besides, the aim is also to obtain descriptions of the elements of the identified factors. Therefore, two research questions were formulated to help achieve the aims as follows:

- RQ1: What are the factors to be considered when designing a virtual environment for a VR-based stress therapy application?
- RQ2: What are the elements of the identified factors to be considered when designing a virtual environment for a VR-based stress therapy application?

The first question helps the researcher to understand the possible factors that should be considered when designing an environment for a VR-based stress therapy application. On the other hand, the second question seeks to assist the researcher to obtain a better description of each factor's elements.

Defining the Search Strategy. This section outlines the search terms and strategy as well as the literature source employed in this review.

Search Terms and Strategy. The search terms used in this review were built based on the following approaches:

i. Direct derivation from terms used in the research objectives and research questions.
ii. Identification of synonyms and alternative words of the terms used in approach (1).
iii. Usage of the Boolean operator OR to incorporate terms used in approaches (1) and (2).
iv. Usage of the Boolean operator AND to combine terms used in approaches (1) and (2).

By combining and interchanging the identified terms, six keywords were formed. Table 1 displays the keywords used to search for related studies.

Table 1. Keywords used for literature search

Keyword 1	"Virtual reality" AND "Stress therapy" ("therapy" was also replaced with "treatment", "healing", and "reduction")
Keyword 2	"Virtual reality" AND, OR "Virtual therapy" OR "Exposure therapy"
Keyword 3	"Virtual reality" AND "Environment" AND "Therapy" ("Therapy" was also replaced with "Treatment")
Keyword 4	"Virtual reality" AND "Relaxation" ("Relaxation" was also replaced with "Meditation")
Keyword 5	"Relaxation" AND "Environment"
Keyword 6	"Relaxation" OR "Environment"

Literature Source. The source for this review was electronic databases, namely, Science Direct, IEEE, Springer, Emerald, ACM, Taylor & Francis, and Scopus. The search was not restricted to the computer science domain but was also expanded to other related domains such as human behaviour research and therapy, landscape and urban planning, as well as environmental psychology. This is because, the results of the preliminary literature survey conducted showed that there are only a few discussions on environment design, especially for VR-based stress therapy application. Therefore, expanding the search to include other domains will help in the identification of more possible factors to be explored in the data gathering process. Factors that were present in other domains may be relevant to be integrated into the VR-based stress therapy application's environment.

2.2 Phase 2: Review Process

The second phase of this review involved the reviewing process of studies found in Phase 1. Activities performed in this phase, i.e. study selection, data extraction, and data synthesis, are explained below.

Study Selection. Selection of studies was done in three stages: (1) initial selection of studies based on the title; (2) selection of studies after reading the abstract; and (3) final selection of studies to be reviewed after reading the full paper.

In the first stage, studies found based on keywords listed in Table 1 were filtered based on its title. At this stage, 297 studies related to the topic reviewed were found. Next, the selected studies were filtered once again based on its abstract, in which 27 studies were shortlisted. In the third stage, the 27 studies shortlisted were thoroughly read through to determine the studies that answers both research questions. By the end of the third stage, 10 studies were found to be relevant for review.

Throughout the selection process, the studies were filtered based on the inclusion and exclusion criteria set for the review. The inclusion criteria includes the fact that the study must: (1) focus on the wellness aspect; (2) discuss on the components or elements that help in the recovery, therapy or treatment process of patients; and (3) offer recommendations or discusses how the components affect a patient's recovery, therapy or treatment process. The exclusion are: (1) does not help in answering the research questions of this review and (2) are not published in English.

During the first stage of the selection, the researcher was more lenient on the inclusion and exclusion criteria. Any titles that contained the words "virtual reality", "VR", "depression", "therapeutic", "relaxing" or any other words potentially related to this study were included to be filtered in the second stage. Nevertheless, if the title of a study is clearly out of scope, it was excluded even though the title contains search words related to this study. In the second stage, the abstract of each selected study was read through while considering the inclusion and exclusion criteria. Any abstracts that fulfilled at least one exclusion criteria were discarded. Lastly, the third stage involved reading the whole paper of the selected studies. In this stage, both the inclusion and exclusion criteria were strictly followed. If a study was found to be relevant and can help answer both of the research questions, important data extraction was done along with the reading process.

Data Extraction. Important data in each study that passed the third stage review was extracted and recorded in a table. The data extracted from the studies were the title, author's details, publication year, and elements of potential factors to be considered when designing a virtual environment for a VR-based stress therapy application.

Data Synthesis. Data synthesis was performed to summarise the evidence gathered from the studies selected after the third stage review, which answered the research questions. The data that answered the first (RQ1) and second (RQ2) research questions were organised in separate tables. Data in each table was analysed by assigning it to a suitable element and an appropriate theme.

3   Results and Discussion

This section is the third phase, i.e. the review report, in which the findings of the systematic review are presented and discussed to answer RQ1 and RQ2.

3.1   Overview of the Studies

Table 2 provides the details of the 10 articles reviewed in this research. The table lists the name of author(s), year of publication, title, and elements of potential factors to be considered when designing a virtual environment for a VR-based stress therapy application.

Each element was analysed and those with similarities were categorised into a group known as a component. By combining the identified components, seven potential elements were generated. The listed elements answer RQ2 of this study. Based on the review done, four factors were generated from the classification of seven elements, thus answering this study's RQ1.

3.2   Factors to Be Considered When Designing a Virtual Environment for a VR-Based Stress Therapy Application

The results of the review show that there are four factors that needs to be taken into consideration when designing a virtual environment for a VR-based stress therapy application as shown in Table 3. The identified factors are visual attraction, environment setting, navigation and interaction.

Factor 1: Visual Attraction. Visual attraction refers to elements that can hold users' attention to continue with the therapy session. This factor helps in distracting users' mind from continuously thinking of the problems that make them stress. Two elements are included in this factor which are water feature and social support. By implementing these elements into a virtual environment, it is believed to help in distracting users' mind by redirecting their attention to a relaxing components. According to Kaplan [13], while an individual's mind is in fascination mode, which can be achieved through visual attraction's elements, he or she tends to forget about their problems or burdens. Hence, the person will achieve a state of tranquillity that indirectly lowers the stress level.

Presence of Water Features. Nordh et al. [14] in their study about parks' components that has restorative potential, found that water elements such as lake and waterfall have a strong influence in creating fascination which is one of the four elements proposed in Attention Restoration Theory. This finding concurs with a study done by Regan and Horn [15], which determined that humans are most likely to look for an environment with greenery and water features when they want to feel relaxed. Another three

Table 2. Details of the reviewed articles

	Name of author(s) and year of publication	Title	Elements of potential components
1	Jiang et al. (2014)	A dose of nature: Tree cover, stress reduction, and gender differences	Nature based theme
2	Wang et al. (2016)	Stress recovery and restorative effects of viewing different urban park scenes in Shanghai, China	Nature based theme Social support
3	Lui et al. (2012)	Development of a mental stress relaxation tool based on guided imagery and Microsoft Kinect	Active interaction
4	Iyendo et al. (2016)	The therapeutic impacts of environmental design interventions on wellness in clinical settings: A narrative review	Water features Nature based theme
5	Nordh et al. (2011)	Assessing restorative components of small urban parks using conjoint methodology	Nature based theme Water features Social support
6	Peschardt and Stigsdotter (2013)	Associations between park characteristics and perceived restrictiveness of small public urban green spaces	Water feature Lighting condition Nature based theme
7	Nordh and Ostby (2013)	Pocket parks for people – A study of park design and use	Nature based theme Water feature
8	Nordh et al. (2009)	Components of small urban parks that predict the possibility for restoration	Water feature Nature based theme
9	Laursen et al. (2014)	Effects of environmental design on patient outcome: A systematic review	Lighting condition Nature based theme
10	Zainudin et al. (2014)	Stress treatment: The effectiveness between guided and non-guided virtual reality setup	Guided and non-guided teleportation

reviewed studies [16–18] also suggested the potential of water features like fountains and waterfalls as a component that helps in the stress recovery process. In short, the reviewed studies proposed that water features have a relaxing effect on the human psychology, thus, strengthening the need to include water features in the virtual environment as one of the visual attraction element.

Social Support. Based on the review done, it was discovered that social support by the presence of people in an environment may influence an individual's emotion. Three of

Table 3. Factors that should be considered when designing a virtual environment for a VR-based stress therapy application.

Factor	Element
Visual attraction	Water feature
	Social support
Environment setting	Nature based theme
	Lighting condition
Navigation	Guided teleportation
	Non-guided teleportation
Interaction	Active interaction

the reviewed studies included presence of people as one of the elements that should be taken into consideration when designing a relaxing environment. Firstly, in a study by Wang et al. [19] on stress recovery and restorative effects of viewing different urban park scenes, it was found that a nature-based environment without people had a higher restorative effect compared to one with people. Nonetheless, their finding contradicted with Nordh et al. [20] who reported that most people prefers to have 'a few other people' in the environment instead of being completely alone or accompanied by too many people. This finding is in line with Peschardt and Stigsdotter's [18] study, which determined that serenity can be achieved at a non-crowded environment where one does not get disturbed by people on bikes.

Based on the result of the reviewed, it is suggested to include people as social support element in a VR-based stress therapy application. However, to prevent the user from feeling suffocated with crowded environment, which in turn may cause anxiety, the number of people to be included in the environment need to be taken into account.

Factor 2: Environment Setting. Environment setting refers to how the environment should be designed in terms of its visual and audio. This factor is important since visual and audio are the main aspects that influence users' perception and comfortability while using the system. Given a situation where an environment is not that relaxing due to elements included are not suitable for relaxing purpose, this situation hence will make the users' feel discomfort, which indirectly, decreases the effectiveness of the system. Therefore, this second factor, which is environment setting will act as a guideline on how to design a relaxing environment in terms of visual and audio in order to ensure that the environment is relaxing enough for the users to reduce their stress. There are two elements included in this factor which are nature-based theme and lighting condition.

Nature-Based Theme. Nature-based environment is typically associated with calmness, happiness, and positive emotions. This theme should be implemented not only in the aspect of visual, but also in terms of its audio.

In terms of visual aspect, nature-based theme can be implemented by creating a nature-based setting such as beach, jungle or flower garden. Based on the review done, four studies highlighted the use of nature-based views and elements in reducing stress. Iyendo et al. [16] conducted a study to investigate the therapeutic impacts of environmental design on wellness in a clinical setting. They reported that an environment incorporated with elements of nature has a positive impact on reducing patients' pain and may also help in blocking negative thoughts and concerns. Results found by Iyendo et al. is in line with another study conducted by Wang et al. [19], which compared the stress recovery levels recorded for nature-based and hardscape environments. The results showed that participants placed at the nature based environ ment had a better stress recovery outcome compared to those placed at the hardscape environment. In addition, two of the reviewed studies [20, 21] found that nature-based elements such as grass, bushes, and natural plants have high potential to be included as one of the components to help in the stress reduction process.

In terms of audio, nature based theme can be implemented through the usage of nature sound as the main background sound.

Lighting Condition. Lighting condition may stimulate emotion. In an environment promoting relaxation, good lighting is essential to achieve tranquillity. In a study examining characteristics of parks and its perceived restrictiveness to a person, it was suggested that both sunny and shady areas are provided to create a relaxing environment [18]. The lighting level in a sunny area should be bright enough to represent the sunlight, whereas in the shady area, mid-key lighting was suggested to represent sunlight that is covered by trees. Besides that, Laursen et al. [21] reviewed the effects of environment design on patients' condition and found that patients placed in a bright environment experienced less stress. Therefore, it is assumed that a bright environment may help in relaxation and stress reduction which then should be implemented in a VR-based stress therapy application.

Factor 3: Navigation. Navigation refers to how users can teleport themselves from one viewpoint to another in the virtual environment. Navigation factor is divided into two which are guided and non-guided. In a guided setup, user movement is fully controlled by the computer, whereby the navigation path and time is pre-set during the development process. On the other hand, in a non-guided setup, the participants are free to navigate themselves to interact with the virtual world. Moreover, navigation path and time in a non-guided setup is determined by the user.

For navigation in a virtual environment for stress therapy, it is suggested that the guided setup is used. Zainuddin et al. [22] conducted a study on the effectiveness of guided and non-guided setups in stress therapy. They reported that the type of interaction used in a virtual environment of a VR-based stress therapy application depends on the type of emotions that needs to be evoked during the treatment of stress. Zainuddin et al. divided emotions into two types, i.e. positive (happy, joyful, confident, and inspired) and negative (nervous, sad, angry, shy, and stressed). Based on their study, if the purpose of stress treatment is to increase the level of positive emotions, a guided setup is recommended to be used. In contrast, if the purpose is to decrease negative emotions, a non-guided setup is recommended.

Nonetheless, in another study by Lui et al. [23], a guided setup was suggested. Guided setup is recommended as it will bring the user through the designated therapy path, which generally applies the same concept that guides the imaginary treatment used by psychiatrists in stress therapy programmes.

Factor 4: Interaction. This factor refers to components related to the communication of users with a virtual environment, i.e. the reaction of elements in a virtual environment to the users' actions and activities done by users of a VR-based stress therapy application. In general, any activities, actions, and reactions between users and the virtual environment are categorised under this factor. Interaction in a virtual environment is divided into two which are passive and active. Passive interaction refers to activities that users naturally do in a real world without thinking. For example, tilt the head to look around which is deemed as a natural habit that we as human naturally do without thinking. Meanwhile, active interaction refers to activities that require users to give any instruction to the virtual environment in order to interact. For example, clicking a button to feed fish or pulling a trigger to play kite.

When designing a virtual environment, it is suggested to use active interaction. Active interaction involves simple motions which helps to prevent the user from feeling bored while undergoing the therapy. Lui et al. [23] in a study on the development of stress relaxation tools, suggested three principles to be followed when designing gestures for user interaction in a virtual environment for a virtual reality based stress therapy. The three principles are: (1) use gentle gestures and avoid aggressiveness; (2) use simple gestures that are easy to be performed; and (3) avoid negative gestures or actions that may touch cultural sensitivity and bring negative emotions. An example of a gesture that can be included in the environment is throwing coins into a fountain, which is associated with wish and hope. The action brings a positive meaning to the users as it indicates that every cloud has its silver lining.

4 Conclusion

The application of VR in stress therapy is not entirely a novel topic. Previous studies on VR-based stress therapy have resulted in the acknowledgement of the effectiveness of VR application in the field of stress therapy. Nevertheless, the lack of a guideline on how to design a proper virtual environment for a VR-based stress therapy application has opened an opportunity to conduct research in a new angle. Therefore, this review aimed to identify the possible factors and its elements that can be used to form a guideline to design a virtual environment for a VR-based stress therapy application. A proper guideline on what to consider during the designing stage will help to increase the success rate of the application.

This review was conducted based on the systematic literature review method, with two research questions as the main guideline. From the review, four factors were identified as aspects that should be taken into consideration when designing a virtual environment for a VR-based stress therapy application. The four identified factors are visual attraction, environment setting, navigation and interaction.

The first factor is visual attraction with two elements, namely, the presence of water feature and social support. Second factor is the environmental setting, which includes two elements which are nature-based theme and lighting condition. Third factor is navigation and this factor is made up of two elements, which are guided and non-guided navigation. Fourth is interaction. There is one element in this factors which is active interaction.

Based on the results of this review, it is recommended that future research expands the review to identify other factors that may be taken into consideration when developing a VR-based stress therapy application.

Acknowledgement. This study was funded by Tenaga Nasional Berhad Seed Fund (U-TE-RD-18-03) in collaboration with TNB Counselling Unit. We would like to thank UNITEN R&D Sdn. Bhd. for fund management.

References

1. Taneja, A., Vishal, S.B., Mahesh, V., Geethanjali, B.: Virtual reality based neuro-rehabilitation for mental stress reduction. In: 2017 Fourth International Conference on Signal Processing, Communication and Networking (ICSCN), pp. 1–5 (2017)
2. Rothbaum, B.O., Rizzo, A.S., McDaniel, D.D., Zanov, M.V.: Virtual reality exposure therapy. In: Encyclopedia of Mental Health, 2nd edn., pp. 370–374 (2016)
3. McCann, R.A., et al.: Virtual reality exposure therapy for the treatment of anxiety disorders: an evaluation of research quality. J. Anxiety Disord. **28**(6), 625–631 (2014)
4. Marco, J.H., Perpiñá, C., Botella, C.: Effectiveness of cognitive behavioral therapy supported by virtual reality in the treatment of body image in eating disorders: one year follow-up. Psychiatry Res. **209**(3), 619–625 (2013)
5. Menelas, B.-A.J., Haidon, C., Ecrepont, A., Girard, B.: Use of virtual reality technologies as an action-cue exposure therapy for truck drivers suffering from post-traumatic stress disorder. Entertain. Comput. **24**(Suppl C), 1–9 (2018)
6. Rizzo, A., Hartholt, A., Grimani, M., Leeds, A., Liewer, M.: Virtual reality exposure therapy for combat-related posttraumatic stress disorder. Comput. (Long. Beach. Calif.) **47**(7), 31–37 (2014)
7. Mahalil, I., Rusli, M.E., Yusof, A.M., Yusof, M.Z.M., Zainudin, A.R.R.: Virtual reality-based technique for stress therapy. In: 2014 4th International Conference on Engineering Technology and Technopreneurship (ICE2T), pp. 295–300 (2014)
8. Soyka, F., Leyrer, M., Smallwood, J., Ferguson, C., Riecke, B.E., Mohler, B.J.: Enhancing stress management techniques using virtual reality. In: Proceedings of the ACM Symposium on Applied Perception – (SAP 2016), pp. 85–88 (2016)
9. Mishkind, M.C., Norr, A.M., Katz, A.C., Reger, G.M.: Review of virtual reality treatment in psychiatry: evidence versus current diffusion and use. Curr. Psychiatry Rep. **19**(11), 80 (2017)
10. Dooris, M.: Expert voices for change: bridging the silos-towards healthy and sustainable settings for the 21st century. Heal. Place **20**, 39–50 (2013)
11. Berto, R.: The role of nature in coping with psycho-physiological stress: a literature review on restorativeness. Behav. Sci. (Basel) **4**(4), 394–409 (2014)
12. Kitchenham, B.: Procedures for performing systematic reviews, vol. 33, no. 2004, pp. 1–26. Keele University, Keele (2004)
13. Kaplan, S.: The restorative benefits of nature: toward an integrative framework. J. Environ. Psychol. **15**(3), 169–182 (1995)
14. Nordh, H., Hartig, T., Hagerhall, C.M., Fry, G.: Components of small urban parks that predict the possibility for restoration. Urban For. Urban Green. **8**(4), 225–235 (2009)
15. Regan, C.L., Horn, S.A.: To nature or not to nature: associations between environmental preferences, mood states and demographic factors. J. Environ. Psychol. **25**(1), 57–66 (2005)

16. Iyendo, T.O., Uwajeh, P.C., Ikenna, E.S.: The therapeutic impacts of environmental design interventions on wellness in clinical settings: a narrative review. Complement. Ther. Clin. Pract. **24**, 174–188 (2016)
17. Nordh, H., Østby, K.: Pocket parks for people - a study of park design and use. Urban For. Urban Green. **12**(1), 12–17 (2013)
18. Peschardt, K.K., Stigsdotter, U.K.: Associations between park characteristics and perceived restorativeness of small public urban green spaces. Landsc. Urban Plan. **112**(1), 26–39 (2013)
19. Wang, X., Rodiek, S., Wu, C., Chen, Y., Li, Y.: Stress recovery and restorative effects of viewing different urban park scenes in Shanghai, China. Urban For. Urban Green. **15**, 112–122 (2016)
20. Nordh, H., Alalouch, C., Hartig, T.: Assessing restorative components of small urban parks using conjoint methodology. Urban For. Urban Green. **10**(2), 95–103 (2011)
21. Laursen, J., Danielsen, A., Rosenberg, J.: Effects of environmental design on patient outcome: a systematic review. HERD Heal. Environ. Res. Des. J. **7**(4), 108–119 (2014)
22. Zainudin, A.R.R., Yusof, A.M., Rusli, M.E., Yusof, M.Z.M., Mahalil, I.: Stress treatment: the effectiveness between guided and non-guided virtual reality setup. In: Proceedings of the 6th International Conference on Information Technology and Multimedia, pp. 374–379 (2014)
23. Lui, A.K.-F., Wong, K.-F., Ng, S.-C., Law,K.-H.: Development of a mental stress relaxation tool based on guided imagery and Microsoft Kinect. In: 2012 Sixth International Conference on Distributed Smart Cameras (ICDSC), pp. 1–6 (2012)

Evaluation of a Virtual Reality (VR) Learning Tool for Fundamental Turbine Engineering Concepts

Hidayah Sulaiman[1]([⊠]), Siti Najiha Apandi[2], Azmi Mohd. Yusof[1],
Rubijesmin Abdul Latif[1], and Nazrita Ibrahim[3]

[1] Informatics Department, College of Computing and Informatics,
Universiti Tenaga Nasional, Kajang, Selangor, Malaysia
hidayah@uniten.edu.my
[2] UNITEN R&D Sdn. Bhd., Kajang, Selangor, Malaysia
[3] Institute of Informatics and Computing in Energy, Universiti Tenaga Nasional,
Kajang, Selangor, Malaysia

Abstract. The education industry have evolved to meet the expectations of current technological trend. The field of mechanical engineering involves the study, design, development, construction, and testing of tools, engines, and machines. One of the critical equipment in the area of power plant engineering is the turbine, which are used to generate power. Students are taught to understand the drawings of these turbines through books or videos and occasionally visit the power plant site. This approach may not be appealing to the digital natives as they prefer to use technology to touch, feel and see the aspects of the turbine at any given time. The lack of engagement, shrinking attention span and obsession with digital devices amongst the younger generation have caused educators to experiment with various means of teaching techniques in ensuring that knowledge is successfully imparted. Hence, this paper provide results of a pilot study on a usability evaluation conducted on a group of undergraduate students to analyze the usability of a virtual reality (VR) application using the System Usability Scale (SUS) instrument. The study also aims to find out if there are any significant differences among gender and computer gamers in using the VR tool. Results indicate that the VR application requires further enhancement in terms of self-learning and interaction familiarity.

Keywords: Virtual learning · Education 4.0 · Engineering education · Usability · Virtual reality

1 Introduction

Blended learning has been recognized as one of the early trends to incorporate technology in classroom lectures. The evolution of classroom teaching from traditional lectures to a more engaging approach in meeting the needs of the younger generations have brought about the use of various technological tools in ensuring that knowledge is disseminated in a more effective manner. This blended approach does not only affect the higher education but also industries worldwide employing these millennials. IBM

© Springer Nature Switzerland AG 2019
H. Badioze Zaman et al. (Eds.): IVIC 2019, LNCS 11870, pp. 48–59, 2019.
https://doi.org/10.1007/978-3-030-34032-2_5

has saved US $200 million in 1999, providing five times the learning at one-third the cost of their traditional methods in providing technical training [1]. Using blended learning through Web-based (80%) and classroom (20%) instruction, Ernst and Young reduced their training costs by 35% while improving consistency and learnability [1]. This is also followed by another success story of Rockwell Collins, where training expenditures were reduced by 40% with only a 25% conversion rate to online training [1]. While there is no doubt that previous research highlights an increasing number of case studies showing success with online learning within the working industries, the higher education also needs to meet these expectations in ensuring that the graduates are fully equipped with the required skillsets and familiarity of using technology. In the case of the engineering graduates working under the power engineering operations, it is quite impossible to realistically recreate in the traditional or 2D simulations of the exact environment of the power plant operations. Hazardous occupations for engineers working with the electrical power line installers and repairers are similarly difficult to simulate, with most current 2D simulators failing to give a feel of the surrounding atmosphere [2]. This limitation presents a major obstacle for educators to explain the required job expectations and highlight technical details of the engineering assets involved within the field. Hence, technology is now offering new solutions in introducing immersive virtual reality application as a complementary approach to classroom teaching [3, 4]. The use of Virtual Reality (VR) has been carried out in various industries namely in the medical field to be used as tool in support of traditional learning [5]. The use of VR allows users to progress at their own pace. The VR-based learning technology will eventually resolve the issue of the 'shrinking attention span' especially amongst younger generations [3]. VR enables complex information to be delivered in a visually attractive and engaging way. Hence, the use of VR is considered to be an effective tool to promote the interest in science and technology namely in the engineering field [6].

The healthcare education industry has also adopted the VR technology to guide medical students and nurses through hands-on procedures such as cardiopulmonary resuscitation and Foley catheter insertion [8]. Medical students and nurses can use VR to practice essential skills without placing lives at risk [5, 7]. By setting aside the manuals and information sheets, students also stand a better chance of retaining information. With students able to rewind training and progress at their own pace, VR systems have been found to suit the learning styles of the digital natives.

The purpose of this paper is to provide a preliminary usability evaluation on an interactive VR tool to improve learning in the engineering education field. The VR application was developed specifically for the mechanical engineering field to allow a close up examination of a power engineering asset. The main expected outcome of the usability testing is to ensure that application meets the expected usability parameters such as ease of use, complexity, support and many more [10]. Usability evaluation of the VR application is important in obtaining feedback to further enhance the development process of the application [9]. It allows the developers to understand problems faced by users and plan the changes to rectify the problems [11]. Hence, it is imperative for every educational learning tool developers to conduct usability evaluation in order to obtain insights on the expectations of the users.

2 Background

2.1 Virtual Reality in Education

In moving towards Education 4.0 or the upcoming Education 5.0, both educators and students need to be exposed to emerging technological trend to meet the expected needs of the industry. Industry players have suggested that graduates of higher education must be industry ready in for them to be exposed to various demands of the working environment [12]. With hundred thousands of engineering graduates each year, the competition of securing a position in an established organization depends on the unique skillset and understanding of the real word working environment. In providing a realistic feel of the working environment, VR can be used to equip these graduates to be immersed in the expected job functions [3, 4]. In the case of the power engineering environment, visualization through VR can accurately illustrate features and processes within the power engineering and energy operations, allowing extreme close-up examination of the components, observation from a great distance, and observation and examination of areas and events unavailable by traditional means. Virtual reality helps to improve engagement through interaction and encourages active participation rather than passivity [13]. Additionally, virtual reality provides the platform for the students to experience a real-time and immersive environment at their own pace. Currently, lectures related to the power engineering and energy operations are taught to students by using traditional presentation materials such as power point slides and videos, as well as practical training on scaled down machines in engineering labs if available [6]. As a result, students often fail to visualize the overall content of the slides, while the practical training or simulations are limited to following the lab manuals or procedure. Students may not be exposed to the worst case scenarios and no mistakes are allowed as a result that it might be hazardous. Hence, the use of VR as part of the power engineering and energy operations hands-on learning allows the student to continuously practice and learn from non-destructive mistakes [6]. VR can also be used to simulate various case scenario and train the students for the right procedure for each case. As opposed to the traditional hands-on simulators or scaled down equipment, the equipment may be jeopardized or damaged which can cause life threatening situations if not operated properly. Hence, the benefits of using the VR assisted learning tool can be seen to have various benefits for the students, educators and universities in terms of: reduce teaching and learning budgets significantly in the long run, reduce learning curve for students, an image of an innovative higher education gaining competitive edge through technologically advanced learning.

2.2 Usability Evaluation for Education Application Using SUS

Usability evaluation allows the system developers to view aspects of the system better. The evaluation would reveal how the users operate the system, would the users find the product or system easy to use, meet the intended goals and most importantly gather ideas on the design issues. There are numerous usability evaluation questionnaires that are designed to measure the system's usability based on the user's perspective and the most widely used evaluation instrument is the System Usability Scale or better known as the SUS [14]. SUS instrument is easy to use and can be appreciated even by non-experts of usability. The generic learning domain has also adopted SUS in evaluating various e-learning tools such as the Learning Management System (LMS), edutainment platforms, and mobile learning applications [15, 22–24]. In the use of virtual reality for education, SUS has been widely used in medical education where the instrument is used to assess the usability aspects of learning effectiveness and satisfaction of the virtual reality application [25, 26]. Results were found to be useful in providing an insight to the usability aspects that require improvement on the VR application according to the SUS questionnaire answered. Although, SUS have been used in various areas of the education industry, nevertheless the adoption of SUS in engineering education is still quite limited. Hence, this study will provide usability evaluation results on a VR application education tool in the mechanical engineering domain. The usability evaluation results would also be used to identify any significant differences among the gender of the undergraduate students or whether or not those who are frequent gamers would find the VR application easier to use.

2.3   V-Turbine Application

The V-Turbine application was developed to provide a platform for digital native students to use an immersive VR learning tool as a supporting tool towards blended learning for engineering subjects taught in the university. Once the students puts on the HMD, the application launches and the welcoming view allows users to be in a workshop environment with the main aeroderivative turbine placed on the table. Figure 1 below illustrates the main view.

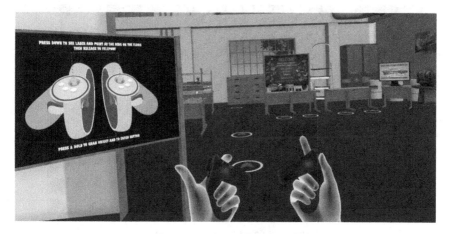

Fig. 1. Main view of the V-Turbine environment

A screen next to the turbine will indicate the names of each part of the turbine. The turbine will then be disassembled where user could pick up each component and learn about the basic functionalities of the turbine components through voice narration. Users will be asked to learn the names and functionalities of the turbine components in order to proceed to the next interactive activity (Fig. 2).

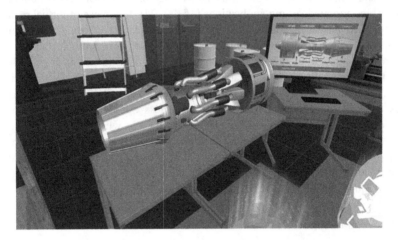

Fig. 2. V-Turbine full view

Figure 3 illustrates the next activity where the user is expected to place the components of the turbine accordingly on the allocated space to assemble the turbine correctly. Error messages will be prompted through voice, if the components are placed wrongly.

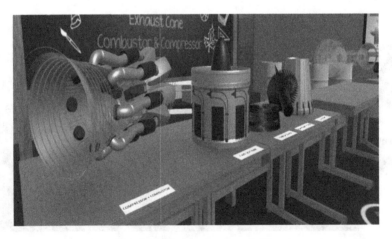

Fig. 3. V-Turbine parts assembly

Words of encouragement are also provided through voice when the components are placed correctly. Figure 4 illustrates the animation on how the turbine works once the turbine is fully assembled.

Fig. 4. V-Turbine animation

3   Methodology

This study conducted a usability evaluation on a VR learning tool that is known as V-Turbine. This tool is created to introduce engineering students to the fundamental concept of aero-derivative turbine for power engineering. Students can have a closer look to the real power engineering asset that may be difficult to demonstrate in a real-life scenario. Upon completion of the development, a preliminary usability evaluation was conducted using System Usability Scale (SUS) questionnaire among a random group of undergraduate students. This preliminary evaluation is important in ensuring that user feel comfortable using the application, find the application interesting ad usable. This phase of the project is important before embarking to the full usability evaluation by the mechanical engineering students.

3.1   Usability Evaluation

SUS was created by John Brooke in 1986 to measure the usability of electronic office systems, but it's now applied to a wide variety of web or technology-based applications to measure how easy or difficult they are to use in order to improve [14, 16]. SUS has also been used in various virtual reality application usability evaluation such as in the medical field [19], automotive [20] and locomotive industry.

SUS consists of 10 questions that can be answered on a five-point Likert scale of "Strongly Disagree" to "Strongly Agree". Table 1 below lists the questions asked using the SUS.

A group of 26 undergraduates were randomly selected from Engineering, Computer Science and Information Technology programme. The respondents' age range is between 20 to 24 years, comprising of undergraduates in the 2nd and 3rd year of studies. Users will have to rank each of the 10 questions above from 1 to 5, based on their level of agreement. The odd numbered questions are positive items, whereas the even numbered items are negative items. The calculation for the SUS score will follow the guideline as per suggested by the authors and creators of the instrument. For each of the

Table 1. Questions derived from SUS instrument.

Question number	SUS questions
Q1	I think that I would like to use this system frequently
Q2	I found the system unnecessarily complex
Q3	I thought the system was easy to use
Q4	I think that I would need the support of a technical person to able to use this system
Q5	I found the various functions in this system were well integrated
Q6	I thought there was too much inconsistency in this system
Q7	I would imagine that most people would learn to use this system very quickly
Q8	I found the system very cumbersome to use
Q9	I felt very confident using the system
Q10	I needed to learn a lot of things before I could get going with this system

odd numbered questions, subtract 1 from the score and for each of the even numbered questions, subtract their value from 5. These new values will be added up for the total score and multiplied by 2.5. The result of calculations is to have a score out of 100. The average acceptable SUS score is 68. If the score is under 68, then there are probably some serious problems with the application's usability that requires critical attention. If the score is above 68, then the developers may look into detail on which components of the SUS requires more attention to make the application better.

4   Results

4.1   Statistics and Descriptive Analyses

A feedback from a set of 26 undergraduate students were collected, ranging between 20 to 24 years old. The aim is to measure usability of using V-Turbine. The students were not allowed to move freely due to the Head Mounted Device's (HMD) sensor, but they are allowed to teleport from one place to another using the HMD console. Each participant completed the task on average about 5 min. Basic demographics were also asked before the students answer the SUS items. The study would also like to see if there are any significance among the gender of students with the usability score and whether or not there are any significant difference if the students were active gamers or non-gamers. Figure 5 below illustrates the distribution of gender among 26 participants with 14 male and 12 female.

As for the number of gamers and non-gamers, this is displayed in Table 2. For this set of undergraduate students, we can see that more than 50% are gamers with the number of hours spent on playing games are more than 6 h per week.

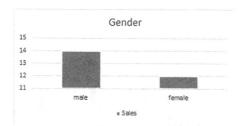

Fig. 5. Gender distribution

Table 2. Frequency of playing computer games

Variable	Frequency	Percent (%)
Games - not playing	11	42.30
Games – playing (1–2 h)	4	15.38
Games – playing (3–5 h)	2	7.69
Games – playing (6–10 h)	4	15.38
Games – playing (>10 h)	5	19.23
Total	**26**	**100**

The SUS scores were calculated to obtain the acceptability range. The range of SUS score for not being acceptable is from 0 to 50, the marginal level is from 50 to 70 and the acceptable level is from 70 to 100. The results as indicated in Fig. 6 displays an acceptable result which is 80 for the SUS score.

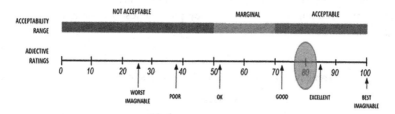

Fig. 6. SUS score

For each individual responses on the SUS questions is displayed in Fig. 7.

An independent-sample t-test was conducted using Statistical Package for the Social Sciences (SPSS) to compare the SUS score between male and female groups. Studies in the area of gaming and virtual reality applications have been conducted in comparing the gender effect in the use of the virtual application. It has been argued that females on average use the computer more than the male, however males have found to be playing video games more than the females [29]. This has also sparked the argument that females can be less comfortable, confident, and capable when using virtual

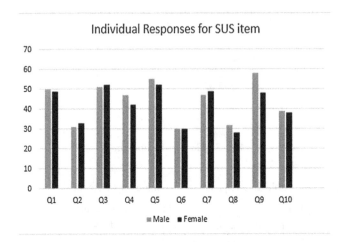

Fig. 7. Individual SUS score

learning environments, especially when it is highly technical and visually complex [28, 29]. In line with previous studies, the usability results of this study would also explore the connotation that men and women do actually differ in the way they use virtual reality applications that have gaming effects.

Results indicate that there was no significant difference in between male (M = 64.64, SD = 18.50) and female groups (M = 66.46, SD = 17.50); t (24) = −.256, p = .800. These results indicate that gender do not have an effect on SUS Score at .05 significance level. To investigate whether males or females would portray any difference if they are gamers or non-gamers, a chi-square statistical analysis was conducted. Table 3 displays the Pearson chi-square results and indicates that males and females are not significantly different whether or not they play games ($\chi2$ = 2.35, df = 1, N = 26, p = .126 > 0.05).

Table 3. Chi-square analysis for gamers or non-gamers

Variable	N	Gender		X^2	p
		Males	Females		
Gamers score				2.35	0.126
Play games	15	10	5		
Not play games	11	4	7		
Totals	26	14	12		

5   Conclusions and Future Works

The blended learning approach of providing a VR application to support the learning process of an engineering subject, has been able to provide the self- learning experience and confidence in users. The tool aims to enhance learnability and interest among the younger generation who are digital natives. The feedback from the students in the usability evaluation of this study indicate that students clearly feel confident and excited when a large asset that is unavailable to be viewed physically can be virtually experienced using the application. However, as a first time user of a VR learning application, students still require technical assistance in using the application. The evaluation also takes into account on whether or not if gender matters when using a VR application. Results indicate that there are no differences in gender when a new application is introduced. Similarly, in evaluating whether or not gamers would have an advantage over non-gamers when using the VR educational application, the statistical analysis have proven that there is no significant relationship on being a gamer or non-gamers. Nevertheless, these digital native portray high level of confidence and excitement whilst using the VR application. Hence, the usability aspects of self-learning and functional familiarity needs to be enhanced further in providing an effective tool for blended learning purpose. Upon completion of the enhanced version taking into account all the necessary usability aspect, larger scale of system testing will be conducted with a bigger cohort of mechanical engineering students to evaluate the learnability and content aspect of the blended learning tool.

Acknowledgments. The authors would like to thank TNB as the grant provider for this project and UNITEN R&D Sdn. Bhd for managing the grant. Thank you for the continuous support and assistance in ensuring that project is carried out smoothly. This work has been supported by the university, and we would like to thank the participating users with their involvement in this project.

References

1. Strother, J.B.: An assessment of the effectiveness of e-learning in corporate training programs. Int. Rev. Res. Open Distrib. Learn. **3**(1) (2002)
2. Khanzode, V.V., Maiti, J., Ray, P.K.: Occupational injury and accident research: a comprehensive review. Saf. Sci. **50**(5), 1355–1367 (2012)
3. Jarmon, L., Traphagan, T., Mayrath, M., Trivedi, A.: Virtual world teaching, experiential learning, and assessment: an interdisciplinary communication course in Second Life. Comput. Educ. **53**(1), 169–182 (2009)
4. Bower, M., Lee, M.J., Dalgarno, B.: Collaborative learning across physical and virtual worlds: factors supporting and constraining learners in a blended reality environment. Br. J. Edu. Technol. **48**(2), 407–430 (2017)
5. Huang, H.M., Liaw, S.S., Lai, C.M.: Exploring learner acceptance of the use of virtual reality in medical education: a case study of desktop and projection-based display systems. Interact. Learn. Environ. **24**(1), 3–19 (2016)
6. Alhalabi, W.: Virtual reality systems enhance students' achievements in engineering education. Behav. Inform. Technol. **35**(11), 919–925 (2016)

7. Moro, C., Stromberga, Z., Stirling, A.: Virtualisation devices for student learning: comparison between desktop-based (Oculus Rift) and mobile-based (Gear VR) virtual reality in medical and health science education. Aust. J. Educ. Technol. **33**(6) (2017)
8. Butt, A.L., Kardong-Edgren, S., Ellertson, A.: Using game-based virtual reality with haptics for skill acquisition. Clin. Simul. Nurs. **16**, 25–32 (2018)
9. Rosson, M.B., Carroll, J.M.: Usability Engineering: Scenario-Based Development of Human Computer Interaction. Morgan Kaufmann Publishers, San Francisco (2002)
10. Qureshi, K., Irfan, M.: Usability evaluation of e-learning applications. In: A case study of It's Learning from a Student's Perspective. School of Computing, Blekinge Institute of Technology (2009)
11. Sulaiman, H., Suid, N., Idris, M.A.B.: Usability evaluation of confirm-a learning tool towards education 4.0. In 2018 IEEE Conference on e-Learning, e-Management and e-Services (IC3e), pp. 73–78. IEEE, November 2018
12. Mohanty, A., Dash, D.: Engineering education in India: preparation of professional engineering educators. J. Hum. Resour. Sustainabil. Stud. **4**(02), 92 (2016)
13. Lindgren, R., Tscholl, M., Wang, S., Johnson, E.: Enhancing learning and engagement through embodied interaction within a mixed reality simulation. Comput. Educ. **95**, 174–187 (2016)
14. Brooke, J.: SUS-A quick and dirty usability scale. Usabil. Eval. Ind. **189**(194), 4–7 (1996)
15. Ayad, K., Rigas, D.: Multi-modal game based learning: satisfaction and users achievement approach. In: WSEAS International Conference on Recent Advances in Software Engineering, pp. 166–171, February 2010
16. Orfanou, K., Tselios, N., Katsanos, C.: Perceived usability evaluation of learning management systems: Empirical evaluation of the system usability scale. Int. Rev. Res. Open Distrib. Learn. **16**(2), 227–246 (2015)
17. Gros, B.: Digital games in education: the design of games-based learning environments. J. Res. Technol. Educ. **40**(1), 23–38 (2007)
18. Bastug, E., Bennis, M., Médard, M., Debbah, M.: Toward interconnected virtual reality: opportunities, challenges, and enablers. IEEE Commun. Mag. **55**(6), 110–117 (2017)
19. Napa, S., Moore, M., Bardyn, T.: Advancing cardiac surgery case planning and case review conferences using virtual reality in medical libraries: evaluation of the usability of two virtual reality apps. JMIR Hum. Factors **6**(1), e12008 (2019)
20. Borsci, S., Lawson, G., Jha, B., Burges, M., Salanitri, D.: Effectiveness of a multidevice 3D virtual environment application to train car service maintenance procedures. Virtual Reality **20**(1), 41–55 (2016)
21. Boletsis, C., Cedergren, J. E.: VR locomotion in the new era of virtual reality: an empirical comparison of prevalent techniques. In: Advances in Human-Computer Interaction (2019)
22. Nakamura, W.T., de Oliveira, E.H.T., Conte, T.: Usability and user experience evaluation of learning management systems. In: Proceedings of the 19th International Conference on Enterprise Information Systems, vol. 3, pp. 97–108 (2017)
23. Belarbi, N., Chafiq, N., Talbi, M., Namir, A.: An experimental case study: comparing perceived usability of two mobile environments of a SPOC. Int. J. Comput. **6**(2), 67–70 (2017)
24. Kaya, A., Ozturk, R., Altin Gumussoy, C.: Usability measurement of mobile applications with system usability scale (SUS). In: Calisir, F., Cevikcan, E., Camgoz Akdag, H. (eds.) Industrial Engineering in the Big Data Era. LNMIE, pp. 389–400. Springer, Cham (2019). https://doi.org/10.1007/978-3-030-03317-0_32
25. Mostafa, A.E., et al.: Designing NeuroSimVR: a stereoscopic virtual reality spine surgery simulator. Science (2017)

26. Gerber, S.M., Müri, R.M., Mosimann, U.P., Nef, T., Urwyler, P.:. Virtual reality for activities of daily living training in neurorehabilitation: a usability and feasibility study in healthy participants. In: 2018 40th Annual International Conference of the IEEE Engineering in Medicine and Biology Society (EMBC), pp. 1–4. IEEE, July 2018

27. Felnhofer, A., Kothgassner, O.D., Beutl, L., Hlavacs, H., Kryspin-Exner, I.: Is virtual reality made for men only? Exploring gender differences in the sense of presence. In: Proceedings of the International Society on Presence Research, pp. 103–112 (2012)

28. Ausburn, L.J., Martens, J., Washington, A., Steele, D., Washburn, E.: A cross-case analysis of gender issues in desktop virtual reality learning environments. J. STEM Teach. Educ. **46**(3), 6 (2009)

29. Annetta, L., Mangrum, J., Holmes, S., Collazo, K., Cheng, M.T.: Bridging realty to virtual reality: investigating gender effect and student engagement on learning through video game play in an elementary school classroom. Int. J. Sci. Educ. **31**(8), 1091–1113 (2009)

Data Visualisation: World Happiness at a Glance!

Angela Siew Hoong Lee[✉], Ammar Kudbuddin, and Phoey Lee Teh

Department of Computing and Information Systems,
School of Science and Technology, Sunway University,
47500 Subang Jaya, Malaysia
{angela1, phoeyleet}@sunway.edu.my

Abstract. The paper aims to visualise the world happiness scores that are reported by the United Nations. Relationship between factors that affect happiness of a country is being identified by performing a clustering analysis on the happiness score. This paper will offer more value and substantial information to practitioners in making vital decisions, by visualizing and identifying the factors exhibited by the data. The results of this study was demonstrated using Tableau tool which is a tool that is able to assist scientist to explore and visualise data using a proposed visualisation-Crisp DM model to obtain insights from the data. This paper fulfils the need for visualisation tools such as Tableau, in assisting researcher to explore and visualize huge and complex dataset in one glance.

Keywords: Data visualisation · Visual analytics · World happiness · Tableau

1 Introduction

Happiness refers to the state of well-being characterized by emotions ranging from immense contentment to intense gladness and joy. It is defined as the sense of pleasure, gratefulness, contentment, joy and many more. Psychologists define happiness as a feeling of positive emotions such as joy, interest, pride, life satisfaction and appreciation of moments [1]. In July 2011, the United Nations General Assembly started a movement, inviting members of different nations to participate in the measurement of their nation's happiness and use this data to help guide their public policy [2]. The 1st World Happiness Report was launched the following year, which eventually drew international attention from all the participating countries [3]. Since then, annual report on nations' happiness has been released every year. Because there is a basic guideline which governments and countries leaders can explore, the study will be useful and the report is use to reflect on the state of happiness in a country which can propel and assist governments to develop and improve the overall state of their country.

Many government leaders have been trying to maximize the potential behind these data by performing data analysis to enhance their country. World Happiness Report has help each country to recognize the factors that play a part in happiness. This study offers more value and substantial information to assist government leaders in making vital decisions by visualizing the factors exhibited by the data for each country and it

© Springer Nature Switzerland AG 2019
H. Badioze Zaman et al. (Eds.): IVIC 2019, LNCS 11870, pp. 60–70, 2019.
https://doi.org/10.1007/978-3-030-34032-2_6

used as a basis to identify which factors that can actually used to identify the score Happiness for each country.

2 Literature Review

United Nations (UN) General Assembly has been releasing yearly reports, which are available to download. Each report outlines the overall Happiness Score based on six metrics, Economy (GDP per Capita), Family, Health (Life Expectancy), Freedom, Trust and Generosity. To ensure high accuracy, top experts from various fields such as economics, psychology, survey analysis and national statistics were called in to describe and ensure every measurement of well-being was effectively used to assess the nation. Every report is organized in order of macro to micro; every chapter is briefly described, which includes the issues such as happiness, mental illness, satisfaction, ethics, etc. [4]. The data used to create each report are obtained via the Gallup World Poll Questionnaire, World Values Survey, etc. [5]. Some of the questions included in the Gallup World Poll Questionnaire were derived from 14 areas of interest such as business & economic, citizen engagement, communications & technology, diversity (social issues), education & families, emotions (well-being), environment and technology, food & shelter, government & politics, law & order, health, religion & ethics, transportation and work [5].

What factors contribute in making a happy society? A person can feel happy while receiving a present. Or, able to cook or provide for friends, such as donation. High involvement in society and activity also can make someone happy. And having good thoughts about friend or relatives can further enhance happiness. This also said that, being contented, possess better social and working connections are happier. Other than making higher wages and living healthier, live longer and contribute more to the country can also create a happy society. Forbes, 2012 [6] has mentions five essential elements that contribute to a happy society. This includes; (1) good physical and mental health; (2) strong internal and external relationships; (3) the ability to view beauty in arts and nature; (4) satisfactory wages and living standard and finally and lastly (5) a good mind that is capable of coping with the storms of life.

On the other hand, environment condition also contributes to the happiness of a society. Season, weather and temperature were among these factors. In the previous study, datasets from the national survey from the International Social Survey Program (ISSP) and the world weather data from the National Oceanic and Atmospheric Administration (NOAA) were studied involving 32 countries. The results showed that average weather variables, include temperature, the speed of the wind, elevation, and GDP, are positively linked with happiness. Psychologist Frederick Herzberg's has gone beyond his study into two-factor theory that shapes the happiness in the working environment [7]. Other than the nature of associating happiness with being recognized for one's value, he intertwined the happiness to the idea of surrounding hygiene and following with company policies, working conditions, wages and advantages [7].

Instead of just putting the weight on what makes a happy society, scientists and researchers have also invested time and effort in learning what makes a happy person. It was said that a person's inner thought about others [8], a person self-acceptance [9], a person lifestyle and experiences also contribute to the fact for a happy person. Overall, it is advisable to go through each day with a positive thinking, and then increased activity, such as helping others to make a person happy, breaths deeply to increase good energy to oneself. Of course, the basics of a happy person are a healthy person, which is to eat healthy meal and have adequate sleep.

Furthermore, researchers have also found that when giving to others most likely causes a person to be happy. It is said that behaving generously can increase happiness but the result is not undeniable [20]. Researches have identified several key factors that contribute towards the effect of good deeds into good feelings. (1) They feel free to choose whether or how to help, (2) They feel connected to the people they are helping, (3) They can see how their help is making a difference [20]. Another study was done on whether the migration of people to other countries would leave an impact to an increase of happiness. The study was done to see if the happiness of a person would increase or what their happiness would be if they had not migrated. There were three types of outcomes that were considered. (1) Positve effect (experiences of enjoyment, happiness, and laughter), (2) Negative effect (experiences of worry, sadness, and anger) [21]. It was said that migration leads a person to be in a happier state for most cases especially when they move to more developed world regions [21].

A research was done by Gallup and GSMA to measure if there was a correlation between the usage of mobile phones/internet usage and a persons happiness. They conducted a survey for adult worldwide to measure if the usage of mobiles phones and the availability of internet access contributed to an increase in happiness in their daily lives [22]. It is said that the economic growth has shown with certainty that the leading driver towards growth and improvement of society is through technological advancement [23]. They then found that there is statiscal significant relationship between the by using multivariate analysis. In another research that was carried out in Spain [23], the correlation between social networks and happiness was done. They observed that people regardless of gender and age tend to have a greater life satisfaction when using social media compared to those who did not. The feeling of being able to communicate with anyone at anytime gives a sense of satisfaction to people [23].

Finally, if countries desire to maintain a happy nation, the discussion above are all equally essential. Happiness can lead to nation development. A person's health and how long he or she can live to be [16] can also form a happy nation. When a nation is poor, the differences in possessions contribute to a big gap in the happiness level [15]. When a nation is relatively rich, wage differences may cause well-being to a lesser degree. In 2009 Nobel-prize-winning economists Joseph Stiglitz and Amartya Sen, put forth a point that promotion of well-being should be the main goal of the government [15]. These aims are vividly portrayed in the mission declaration of the Organization for Economic Co-operation and Development (OECD) [15]. High-income countries with a good technical governance tend to have its people to have a greater level of happiness [24]. Technical quality of governance composes of Government effectiveness, Regulatory Quality, Rule of Law, and Control Corruption [25]. Even if the government of a country is not putting to elevate happiness, it should also not be harming any-one's well-being. Citizens need to understand this and elect politicians who are truly helping them as measuring well-being can make a real difference to a nation's well-being.

There are not many studies that perform visualisation on world happiness, one of the statistician cum blogger has presented world visualisation using D3 [16], and "beeswarm plot", which is essentially a jittered one-dimensional scatterplot to visualise happiness score. Hence, this study intended to extend the zisualization set of data between 2015 to 2017. Besides that, instead of using D3, we have also presented on this paper the potential using Tableau. Other than that, we have also offered an exploration map with the colour scheme scale as the legend as in Fig. 2 (please preview the map in colour visual).

3   Methodology

Happiness Score data was collected from Kaggle.com from year 2015 to 2017. Table 1 describes the collected data. A dashboard development methodology that was based upon a well improved proposed visualisation methodology adapted from CRISP-DM (cross-industry process for data mining). The proposed model is represented in Fig. 1. Happiness is just a case study where this paper focuses on whereas practicioners can use this methodology proposed by us to apply in different types of data when comes to visualisation. For this study, Tableau is used to visualize the data that has been collected.

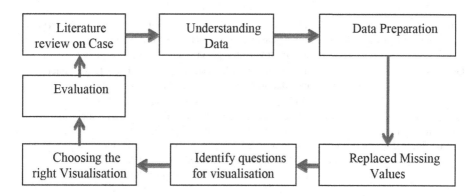

Fig. 1. Proposed model of visualisation - CRISP-DM model

One hundred and six countries with six metrics to measure happiness are collected from a public database (kaggle). The metrics include (1) economy, (2) family, (3) health, (4) freedom, (5) generosity and (6) trust (Government corruption). There has been evident growth in the belief that happiness is the determinant of a positive economic outcome for the top 10 happiest countries [6]. A simple pattern showed that a stable marriage, good health and good income also lead to happiness in a family while unemployment, divorce and income instability leads to depression and terrible outcomes [7].

Table 1. Collected data variables

Variable name	Description	Data type
Country	Name of the country	Nominal
Region	The region the country belongs to	Nominal
Happiness Rank	The rank of the country based on the Happiness Score	Ordinal
Happiness Score	A metric measured based on the happiness scale of 1 to 10	Interval
Economy (GDP per Capita)	The extent to which GDP contributes to the calculation of the Happiness Score (Money) - the quality of life-based on salary	Interval
Family (Social Support)	The extent to which Family contributes to the calculation of the Happiness Score (Social) - the quality of life-based on family	Interval
Health (Life Expectancy)	The extent to which Health contributes to the calculation of the Happiness Score (Physical and Mental state) - the quality of life-based on health and average life expectancy	Interval
Freedom (To Make Life Choices)	The extent to which Freedom contributes to the calculation of the Happiness Score (Physical and Mental state) - the quality of life-based on how they can act in a free-will manner	Interval
Trust (Government Corruption)	The extent to which Perception of Corruption contributes to the calculation of the Happiness Score - trust in the government to avoid corruption	Interval
Generosity	The extent to which Generosity contributes to the calculation of the Happiness Score - how much a country involves in peace-keeping and global aid	Interval
Dystopia Residual *note that variable will be rejected as it does not contribute to happiness score*	The extent to which Dystopia Residual contributes to the calculation of the Happiness Score - Dystopia is an imaginary country which has the world's least-happy people, it is a value equal to the world's lowest national average for each of the six factors	Interval

4   Results

Happiness Score is calculated, with the following six contributing factors, Economy (GDP per Capita), Family, Health, Freedom, Trust and Generosity. Through Table 2, the average Happiness Score among 158 countries is 5.38 out of 10. The lowest Happiness Score recorded is at 2.84, which is a country located at Sub-Saharan Africa. Based on the score recording for significant factor contributing to happiness for the year 2015 is health, on average health is rated at 0.63, and the maximum value recorded is 1.03 by Singapore; translating to Singaporeans valuing health the most and this is a crucial factor to Singaporeans. Family, Freedom and Trust can be categorized as yes or no questions, for example, Family would be whether an individual has anyone such as relatives or friends which they can turn to in times of trouble, while Freedom is whether you are satisfied or dissatisfied with the freedom to choose in life, and lastly, Trust is a perception of whether you think your government or leader is a good leader or not. On average, Family is 0.99 meaning most individuals have someone they can rely on in times of trouble while Freedom recorded an average of 0.43 only, which would suggest that many feel they are not allowed or cannot have the freedom to choose.

Table 2. Summary statistics for the year 2015 World Happiness Report results

Variable	Mean	Std dev	Min	Max	Mode
Happiness Score	5.38	1.15	2.84	7.59	5.19
Economy (GDP per Capital)	0.85	0.40	0.00	1.69	0.27
Family	0.99	0.27	0.00	1.40	0.60
Health (Life Expectancy)	0.63	0.25	0.00	1.03	0.88
Freedom	0.43	0.15	0.00	0.67	0.60
Trust (Government Corruption)	0.14	0.12	0.00	0.55	0.09
Generosity	0.24	0.13	0.00	0.80	0.11

Table 3 represents the 2016 World Happiness Report summary statistics. Similarly, it covers 7 variables and the 5 statistical summaries. Immediately, the average Happiness Score has captured the attention as it shows that 2015 and 2016 has identical values at 5.38. However, the lowest Happiest Score has increased slightly compared to last year at 2.91 which is recorded by another Sub-Saharan Africa country. Trust and Generosity remains as before at an average of 0.14 and 0.24 respectively meaning there are no improvements and it has been stagnant in comparison to 2015.

Table 3. Summary statistics for the year 2016 World Happiness Report results

Variable	Mean	Std dev	Min	Max	Mode
Happiness Score	5.38	1.14	2.91	7.53	3.74
Economy (GDP per Capital)	0.95	0.41	0.00	1.82	0.34
Family	0.79	0.27	0.00	1.18	0.63
Health (Life Expectancy)	0.56	0.23	0.00	0.95	0.65
Freedom	0.37	0.15	0.00	0.61	0.43
Trust (Government Corruption)	0.14	0.11	0.00	0.51	0.08
Generosity	0.24	0.13	0.00	0.82	0.26

Table 4, represents the 2017 World Happiness Report summary statistics. As per mentioned in the descriptions previously, the summary statistics covers 7 variables and 5 statistical fields. Looking at the mean of Happiness Score which is recorded at 5.35, in comparison to the previous 2 years (2015 and 2016), there has been a drop of 0.03 - meaning on average the people are not as happy as before. However, the maximum value for Happiness Score has increased minimally to 7.54 recorded by another Scandinavian country. Norway is ranked as 2017 world happiest country, while Denmark has fallen into 2nd place. More substantially, the minimum value of the Happiness Score has dropped by 0.22 to 2.69 as compared to 2.91 in 2016 - this score was obtained by Central African Republic. The most common value of Happiness Score is 5.07 by 2 countries, Vietnam and Nigeria. As stated previously, Economy, Family, Health, Freedom, Trust and Generosity, all recorded a minimum value of 0.

Table 4. Summary statistics for the year 2017 World Happiness Report results

Variable	Mean	Std dev	Min	Max	Mode
Happiness Score	5.35	1.13	2.69	7.54	5.07
Economy (GDP per Capital)	0.98	0.42	0.00	1.87	0.09
Family	1.19	0.29	0.00	1.61	0.95
Health (Life Expectancy)	0.55	0.24	0.00	0.95	0.64
Freedom	0.41	0.15	0.00	0.66	0.29
Trust (government corruption)	0.12	0.10	0.00	0.46	0.06
Generosity	0.25	0.13	0.00	0.84	0.12

World happiness does not fluctuate much within these three years; the variation are in a smaller amount. From Table 2, 3 and 4, the average Happiness Score among 158 countries is 5.38 out of 10. This is just above the medium overall.

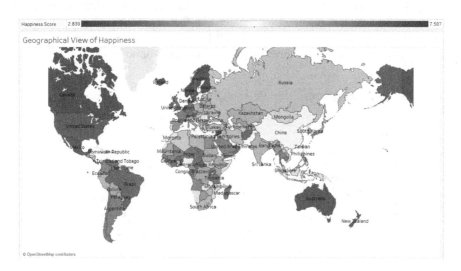

Fig. 2. Geographical view of world happiness using Tableau visualisation tool (Color figure online)

Figure 2 represents the happiness scores around the world on a map. The colour-coordinated red hue represents the lower values; white hue represents the average

Country	Year ID		
	2015	2016	2017
Switzerland	1	2	4
Iceland	2	3	3
Denmark	3	1	2
Norway	4	4	1
Canada	5	6	7
Finland	6	5	5
Netherlands	7	7	6
Sweden	8	10	9
New Zealand	9	8	8
Australia	10	9	10

Fig. 3. Happiness rank based on country (top 10 happiest for 2015, 2016, 2017)

values and blue hue representing the highest values of happiness of the recorded. Countries with happiest people include Switzerland, Norway, Finland, Denmark, Canada, the United States and Iceland.

Figure 3 presents the happiness rank based on top 10 happiest countries. The countries which have been consistently in the top 20 happiest countries are Switzerland, Denmark, Iceland, Norway, Finland, Canada, Netherlands, New Zealand, Australia, Sweden, Israel, Austria, United States, Costa Rica, Belgium, Ireland and Luxembourg. These are all the countries which appeared consistently throughout the three years of 2015, 2016 and 2017. Mexico and the United Arab Emirates in 2015; but not in 2016. Germany and Puerto Rico replaced it. Brazil was top scored in 2015 and 2016, but not in 2017. The United Kingdom and Chile were listed in 2016, but both Puerto Rico and Brazil took over in the top 20 list in 2017. This shows besides the 17 countries which were consistently appearing in the top 20 list; the remaining three countries were constantly shuffling and changing throughout the three years. As mentioned, some of the happier countries include Switzerland, Norway, Finland, Canada, Iceland and others consistently portrayed throughout the three years.

The ranking is arranged as followed: #1 to Switzerland, #2 to Iceland, #3 to Denmark, #4 to Norway, #5 to Canada, #6 to Finland, #7 to the Netherlands, #8 to Sweden and #9 to and New Zealand and #10 to Australia. In the year 2016, Switzerland and Iceland both drop a rank each to second and third respectively, with Denmark climbing two ranks up to first. Norway and Netherlands remained at fourth and seventh rank, while Canada and Finland swapped places to sixth and fifth respectively as compared to the other way in the previous year (2015). New Zealand and Australia went up a rank each as well to eighth and ninth. In 2017, more changes to the rankings were noticed with Switzerland dropping even further down the pecking order to fourth. This is rather surprising as they were 1st two years ago. Iceland remained at 3rd while Denmark dropped a place to second. Norway was the surprise country to jump from 4th for the past two years (2015 and 2016) to first rank in 2017. Canada and Australia, unfortunately, dropped a rank each to seventh and 10th respectively. Finland and New Zealand remained at their ranks at fifth and 8th while Netherlands and Sweden went up a rank to sixth and ninth.

Australia & New Zealand has the most consistent happiness score from 2015 till 2017. Running tightly behind is North America at 7.264, which is only a difference of 0.04 as compared to Australia & New Zealand. The regions of Southeastern Asia, Central & Eastern Europe and the Middle East & Northern Africa do not differ much as well regarding the average happiness score, which translates to people living within these regions are somewhat between average to happy as suggested by their average score. The increases are more prominent in Eastern Asia, Latin America & the Caribbean, and Western Europe, as shown there is a consistent increase in the average happiness score. Through this bar chart, an assumption can be made to assume which are the least happy and happier countries and regions. It can suggest which regions are above average regarding happiness.

Figure 4 shows the average happiness score based on the regions from left to right; Sub-Saharan Africa consists of countries such as Cameroon, Ghana and Kenya, Southern Asia consists of countries, such as India, Nepal and Pakistan, Southeastern Asia consists of countries such as Cambodia, Indonesia and Laos, Central & Eastern Europe consists of countries such as Bulgaria, Croatia, Czech Republic and Estonia., Middle East & Northern Africa consists of countries such as Algeria, Bahrain, Dubai, Egypt, Iran and Iraq, Eastern Asia consists of countries such as China, Hong Kong, Japan and South Korea, Latin America & Caribbean consists of countries such as Argentina, Bolivia, Brazil and Mexico, Western Europe consists of countries such as

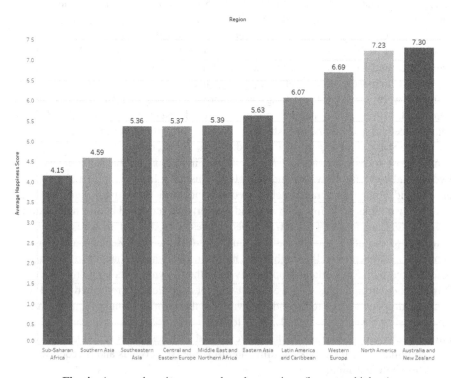

Fig. 4. Average happiness score based on regions (lowest to highest)

Denmark, Finland, Norway and Switzerland. North America consists of only 2 countries the United States of America and Canada and Australia & New Zealand consists of these 2 countries as mentioned by the region. The lowest average happiness score is at 4.17, which is by the Sub-Saharan Africa region while the highest average happiness score is at 7.304, which is by the Australia and New Zealand region. Surprisingly, the happiest countries in the world are not ranked as the 1st in the average happiness score. This is because, in Western Europe, it consists of many different countries with varying happiness scores, thus affecting the position of this region.

5 Conclusion

This study produces the conceptual framework of visualisation techniques to visualize a very complex dataset by exploring the world happiness score from kaggle. On the other hand, using a data visualisation tool in discovering meaningful insights from a huge dataset is useful as you can see the data points in a glance. In this study, it is important for each country government to keep their nation happy and the visualisation of the data allows the country to look at the world happiness at a glance. In future we will use the factors listed here on this paper to do further analysis and predictive modelling and clustering where it can enabled the discovery of new insights to predict the country happiness.

References

1. Khoddam, R.: What is your definition of happiness? Psychology Today, 16 June 2015. https://www.psychologytoday.com/us/blog/the-addiction-connection/201506/whats-your-definition-happiness. Accessed 02 May 2018
2. United Nations General Assembly: Happiness: Towards a holistic approach to development. United Nations, New York City (2011)
3. Sachs, J.D., Helliwell, J.F., Layard, R.: World happiness report 2012. United Nations, New York City (2012)
4. World Happiness Report: Wikipedia, 1 May 2018. https://en.wikipedia.org/wiki/World_Happiness_Report. Accessed 03 May 2018
5. Gallup Poll: World poll questions, vol. 1, no. 1, pp. 1–32. Gallup Poll (2008)
6. Conkle, A.: Serious research on happiness, association for psychological science (2008). https://www.psychologicalscience.org/observer/serious-research-on-happiness. Accessed 05 May 2018
7. Rubin, G.: Forbes Welcome, Forbes.com (2012). https://www.forbes.com/sites/gretchenrubin/2012/02/23/carl-jungs-five-key-elements-to-happiness/#245f129751fb. Accessed 14 June 2019
8. Chanmugham, M.: Forbes Welcome, Forbes.com (2016). https://www.forbes.com/sites/forbescoachescouncil/2016/06/10/money-isnt-everything-five-factors-that-contribute-to-happiness-at-work/2/#3b6c5388295a. Accessed 14 June 2019
9. Parker-Pope, How to Be Happy, Nytimes.com. https://www.nytimes.com/guides/well/how-to-be-happy. Accessed 14 June 2019

10. Holmes, L.: 45 Ways to Be Happier Instantly, HuffPost UK (2017). https://www.huffingtonpost.com/entry/ways-to-be-happier-instantly_us_58cc0e1fe4b0be71dcf46b1a. Accessed 14 June 2019
11. Barter, R. http://www.rebeccabarter.com/blog/2019-01-21_world_happiness/. Accessed 21 Aug 2019
12. Knoema. https://knoema.com/noipuyc/world-s-happiest-nations Accessed 21 Aug 2019
13. Parker-Pope, T.: How to Be Happy, Nytimes.com. https://www.nytimes.com/guides/well/how-to-be-happy. Accessed 14 June 2019
14. Chapman, P. et al.: CRISP-DM 1.0 - Step-by-step data mining guide (2000). http://www.crisp-dm.org/CRISPWP-0800.pdf Accessed 15 June 2019
15. Aknin, L.B., Whillans, A.V., Norton, M.I., Dunn, E.W.: Happiness and prosocial behavior: an evaluation of the evidence (2019)
16. https://www.miqols.org/resources/WHR19.pdf#page=69
17. Hendriks, M., Burger, M.H., Ray, J., Esipova, N.: Do international migrants increase their happiness and that of their families by migrating? (2019)
18. https://s3.amazonaws.com/happiness-report/2018/CH3-WHR-lr.pdf
19. Crabtree, S., Burchell, J.: Do mobile phones make people happier? news.gallup.com (2018)
20. https://news.gallup.com/opinion/gallup/226199/mobile-phones-people-happier.aspx
21. Mochon, F.: Happiness and technology: special consideration of digital technology and internet. Int. J. Interact. Multimed. Artif. Intell. 5(3), 162–168 (2018)
22. https://www.ijimai.org/journal/sites/default/files/files/2018/12/ijimai_5_3_17_pdf_20180.pdf
23. Woo, C.: Good governance and happiness: does technical quality of governance lead to happiness universally in both rich and poor countries? J. Int. Area Stud. 25, 37–56 (2018)
24. Helliwell, J.F., Huang, H.: How's your government? International Evidence Linking Good Government and Well-Being, Cambridge University Press (2008)
25. http://econ.arts.ubc.ca/jhelliwell/papers/Helliwell-Huang-BJPolS2008.pdf

Data Visualization of Supplier Selection Using Business Intelligence Dashboard

Nik Nur Ayuni Nik Alwi[1,2(✉)], Noor Hafizah Hassan[1,2],
Ahmad Fazreen Baharuden[1,2], Nur Azaliah Abu Bakar[1,2],
and Nurazean Maarop[1,2]

[1] Razak Faculty of Technology and Informatics, Universiti Teknologi Malaysia,
Kuala Lumpur, Malaysia
noorhafizah.kl@utm.my
[2] Data Micron Sdn. Bhd., Jalan Pinang, Kuala Lumpur, Malaysia
ayuni@datamicron.com,

Abstract. The emergent of Business Intelligence (BI) tools and techniques could help the transportation company decision maker to make informed decisions regarding their supplier selection. This research aims to help transportation company to identify factors influencing supplier selection in the transportation company also to visualize their data graphically. Other than that, the aim is to highlight the importance of business intelligence dashboard to their business and how it could help them in getting the information from their data thus to aid them to focus straight on the main problem of their company. Data visualization is one of the methods used in this study. BI dashboard of supplier selection is developed throughout this research. Based on the findings, there are three factors that strongly influencing supplier selection which are Price, Quality, and Delivery and data visualization offers a pictorial story platform that makes the decision makers understand the information in a timely manner compared to previous approach which is traditional way that needs the usage of complex queries and involve a time-consuming manipulation. Multiple graphs, charts also other visualizations could be created promptly by using data visualization software or tools. Results from evaluation shows that BI dashboard is very useful to aid transportation company to visualize the information related on supplier selection for decision making process.

Keywords: Business Intelligence · Data visualization · Supplier selection

1 Introduction

Business Intelligence (BI) has become more popular at this time. Gartner states in his report that among many technological tools, BI remains the most favorable on the Chief Information Officer's list (Gartner 2012). BI techniques could be implemented in most of the organizations including the transportation and logistics organization. The main goal of transportation and logistics activities is to meet the customer requirements in a timely and cost-effective manner and this includes the process of planning, executing an efficient transportation and storage of goods from origin point to the point of consumption. In order to achieve the goal, they need a powerful transportation structure

© Springer Nature Switzerland AG 2019
H. Badioze Zaman et al. (Eds.): IVIC 2019, LNCS 11870, pp. 71–81, 2019.
https://doi.org/10.1007/978-3-030-34032-2_7

to bring its advantages into full play. A decent transport system could offer better productivity, diminish operation cost, and improve the service quality (Tseng et al. 2005). By implementing BI techniques in their business, they could better understand their data and identify new pattern that improve business. Selection of the appropriate suppliers is an imperative decision for an operative transportation and logistics company. Proper dealers could lessen the acquiring costs, lessening the manufacture lead time, increase the client gratification and fortify the company competitiveness. According to Weele (2014), selecting the suppliers is one of the most vital phases in the procuring process and it is a foundation of various proceeding activities. Coyle et al. (2010) stated that the supply chain and logistics performance is depends on the transportation provided. Thus, the fleets need to be monitored properly and well-maintained systematically by selecting good suppliers for maintenance. Gitahi and Ogollah (2014) claims that about 20–30% or more cost saving could be obtained if a vehicle is well managed and maintained. To achieve low cost, high value, flexibility and swift response goals, corporations should progressively consider better supplier selection.

Currently, many transportation agencies still using traditional method in delivering their maintenance and service reports and store most of the information stored in Vehicle Management System (VMS). This could lead to a lot of important information losses regarding the suppliers, maintenance and services of their fleets such as low-quality products or services from the suppliers, high cost for maintenance and the spare parts. All these issues could affect their company financially thus cause the ineptitude in their performance. Therefore, Business Intelligence dashboard is important to empowering the decision makers in the transportation agencies to comprehend the information from the analytics presented visually that might go undetected in text-based data analytics.

This paper is divided into seven section. First section describes the overview and needs of the study in supplier selection. In Sect. 2, overview transportation and logistics is described. Section 3 presents the brief information of supplier selection and factors influencing supplier selection based on the previous literature. Section 4 discussed the methodology use in designing the dashboard. Section 5 describes the elements of BI dashboard. Section 6 presented the results of dashboard evaluation with 11 respondents. Finally, in Sect. 7, discussion and conclusion summarize the paper together with the future works.

2   Transportation and Logistics

The history of the transportation and logistics are as long as the history of the mankind. The railroad is discovered in early of nineteenth century while the airplane is discovered in 1903. The invention of sea container in maritime transportation is dated in 1956 and it has impacted the sea transport dramatically. These days, logistics and the broader concept of the supply chain management, is mainly intended as a business function that focus to make goods available anywhere and when needed based on the requirement. Transportation management could be seen as a part of logistics in business processes. Though, it is not only goods, but people also need to be transported. In the past, horse, carriage or ship are the transports they used to travel other than walking.

Currently, there are various types of transportation that made available with different levels in term of cost and comfort (Grazia Speranza 2018). The moving products efficiency is determined by the transportation operation. The progress in the techniques used and the management principles improve moving load, the delivery speed and service quality, costs of the operation and also the facilities usage and energy saving. Transportation is a vital part in logistics manipulation (Tseng et al. 2005). There are three components in this system that are closely linked which are logistics services, information systems and infrastructure/resources. The interactions of those three are interpreted as follows (Tseng et al. 2005). In logistics systems, transport system is the most important economic activity among other business components. The costs spent by logistics companies on transportation are estimated around one third to two thirds of the companies expenses (Tseng et al. 2005). Chang (1998) claimed that based on the National Council of Physical Distribution Management (NCPDM) investigation in 1982, the average of the transportation cost accounted for 6.5% of the market revenue and 44% of logistics costs. Supplier becomes one of the important elements in transportation and logistics industry. To minimize the cost and effective decision making, supplier selection is important element in their business process flow.

3 Supplier Selection

Today competitive and globalized world markets, companies are pressured to find ways to cut the material and production cost. A qualified also reliable supplier is the key element for buyer in reducing their material and production costs (Sonmez 2006). Supplier selection and evaluation is the process of selecting the best supplier that could provide the right quality products and/or services at the right price, at the right quantities and at the right time for the buyer (Sarkis and Talluri 2002). In modern supply chains business, suppliers can be considered as one of the foreseeable sources of external risks. The resilience that stands for adaptive capability to respond to the disruptions and recovering from it needs to be considered in the supplier selection. Selection of the supplier is a challenging task because it involves the evaluation of qualitative and quantitative attributes which is usually imprecise and have limited information. Supplier selection done by prioritize the risk related issues could help in reducing the vulnerability of supply chain to a great extent (Rajesh and Ravi 2015).

3.1 Criteria and Factors of Supplier Selection

According to Stimson (1998), there are six factors that influencing the supplier selection which are price, quality, service, technology, partnership and globalization or localization. Wu et al. (2010) claimed that some other objective functions are minimizing the negative effect of the vendor service rating while Kuo et al. (2010) claimed that minimizing the negative effect of the economic environment and maximizing the service and minimization of risk. Selecting a supplier consists of both quantitative and qualitative process.

Xia and Wu (2007) said that there are two types of supplier selection problems. The first is single sourcing which mean the constraints are not being considered in the supplier selection process. Basically, the buyer only needs to choose which supplier is the best. Second is multiple sourcing which mean that some limitations are being considered in the supplier selection process, for example the quality, the capacity and delivery. In this case, there are more than one supplier to fulfill the buyer's total requirements which mean the buyer need to purchase some part from one supplier and the other parts from other suppliers in order to compensate the shortage of the capacity or the low-quality products from the first supplier. In these circumstances, the buyers need to make two decisions of which suppliers are the best to select, and how much purchase should be made from each of the selected supplier.

There are three basic supplier objectives function evaluation criteria which are price, quality and delivery (Mukherjee 2014; Hosseinei and Barker 2016; Fashoto et al. 2016). Based on the literature review, the most preferable is the price criterion (Chen et al. 2011; Amorim et al. 2016). Price criterion is minimizing the cost, total financial cost, acquiring price, the discounted product, transport and ordering cost, total order cost, and the purchase amount. The quality criterion (Mwikale and Kavale 2012) found that related objective functions are minimizing the rejections, total rejection rate of the product and total amount of the defective units. Delivery criterion related objective functions are minimizing the net late deliveries, the number of delivery lateness, number of the late items and maximizing total amount of on-time deliveries.

Price significance criteria includes the net distributed, expense terms, cash estimates, usage and dispensation costs. The focus is to minimize the total financial cost, acquiring price, the discounted product, transport and ordering cost, total order cost, and the purchase amount. Quality criteria includes the conformance to the settings. The consistency within control limits and the result of quality audits. The focus is to minimize the rejections, the total rejections rate of the product and the total amount of the defective units. Delivery criteria that should be considered are the lead times, on-time delivery the performance, the inventory and the responsiveness. The focus is to minimize the number of delivery delay, number of the late items and take full advantage of total amount of on-time deliveries.

4 Methodology

For designing BI dashboard, one selected company has been chosen to visualize supplier selection. The methodology comprises of three steps which are: Data Preparation, Data Visualization and Evaluation as shown in Fig. 1.

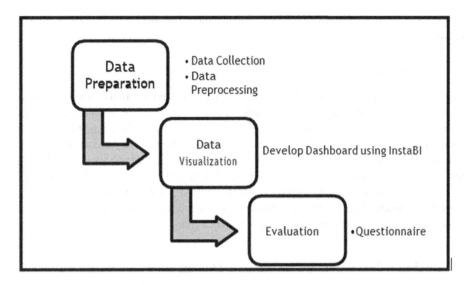

Fig. 1. Research methodology

4.1 Data Preparation

Data preparation is a process of gathering, structuring, cleaning and organizing data so it could be analyzed as part of data visualization. The purpose of data preparation is to ensure that the data is reliable, consistent and accurate so that the information obtained from the analysis is valid. Zheng et al. (2013) stated that data preparation is an essential phase of data analysis comprises the procedures with analysing raw data to harvest quality data and this process includes collecting, integration, transformation, cleaning, reduction, and discretization of the data.

In this study, the data is collected from a local transportation company. The data consists of 24 variables from database of the selected company. Data cleansing or data cleaning is a process of preparing data for analysis by distinguishing and removing unnecessary parts of the data such as incomplete data, duplicated data, or improperly formatted data. All these data could hinder the process, and this will upshot to inaccurate result. Roy et al. (2018) assert that in order to get a good quality information, the data plays a significant role. The data acquired for this research is a structured data. Before the data could be used for data visualization, it needs to be cleaned. There are some redundant data in the variable 'Description' which they are a mixed of Bahasa Melayu and English that referring to the same item.

4.2 Data Visualization

Once the data has been loaded to the database, it could be used for the data visualization. For designing the dashboard, InstaBI is used in this study. There are two stages in designing dashboard using InstaBI. Firstly, the data source needs to be prepared using Business View Designer in InstaBI to extract the data from the database.

Secondly, once the data is published, the dashboard is designed according to the business requirements.

4.3 Dashboard Evaluation

The evaluation is conducted based on the standardized usability questionnaires. Standardized usability questionnaire is designed for evaluating or assessment of software system (Sauro et al. 2016). 12 questions are adopted from the Post-Study System Usability Questionnaire (PSSUQ) for this evaluation. PSSUQ is a research instrument that is developed for the use in scenario-based usability evaluation at the IBM. The system in the question is the changed to BI dashboard to make it suitable for this study. The questionnaire is created in google form and then distributed to 11 expertise in the selected company. The respondents are needed to score the questionnaire between 1–5 which indicates the strongly disagree to strongly agree.

5 Business Intelligence Dashboard Design and Development

The uniqueness of InstaBI tool is that it has the 'Story Board' feature that could be used to create a storyline for presentation. There are 5 dashboards that have been designed in this study which are Landing Page, Summary of dashboard, Supplier overview, Material overview and service overview. The charts in the dashboards is created based on factors of supplier selection discussed in Sect. 3. However, during extracting data from the dataset on the selected company, there is only 1 variable available for this study which is the Price. So, the charts are limited to only Price variable. Quality and Delivery variables are not available in the data.

5.1 Landing Page

The landing page works as the outline of this analysis dashboard. As illustrates in Fig. 2 below, there are 4 icons that indicates the subject areas and number of

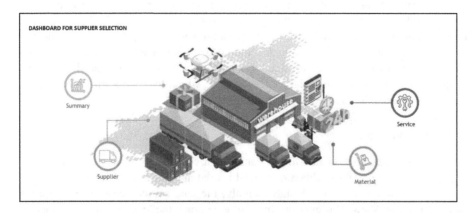

Fig. 2. Business intelligence dashboard landing page

dashboards in this analysis. The element of semiotic is adopted when designing this landing page. Semiotic is basically refer to the sign or symbols to interpret things. Meeks (2018) states that semiotic is the investigation of signs and images, specifically as they convey things spoken and implicit. For instance, icon of truck is used in the landing page to interpret it as the supplier in the landing page and it same as the other icons in the dashboard.

5.2 Summary Dashboard

Summary of dashboard display the element of Total Supplier, Total Spending, Total Materials and Total Services. As for Order Type and Supplier Type, pie chart is used to visualize the data as shown in Fig. 3. Pie chart is used to differentiate the proportion between categories in both attributes. The different between the type could be clearly identify at an instance by using this chart. For decision makers, this kind of information is very important to them, so they could investigate further on the huge gap between those years.

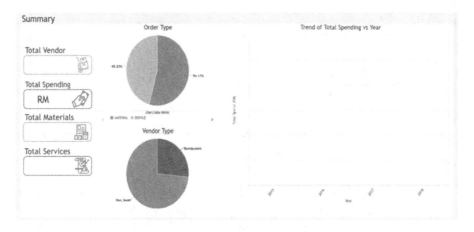

Fig. 3. Summary dashboard

5.3 Supplier Overview

Supplier overview consists of data about the suppliers in the transportation company. At an instance, decision makers of the company could easily determine the total number of suppliers that they have been dealing with which is arranged at the left of the dashboard and also the total number of Depot they have. The list chart is used to show the name of all the suppliers and tree map chart is used to highlight the top 5 suppliers.

5.4 Material and Service Dashboard

Material and service dashboard designed is to provide the decision makers with the information of the suppliers, total material, total spending, vehicle and top order of each group (material and service). By comparing these two dashboards, it could be distinguished that the company has spending the most on the material compared to the service. As for the charts, the bar chart is used to highlight the top material or service and top 10 vehicle for each group. By visualize it this way, the differences of each material or service and vehicle could be distinguished. The line chart is used to show the trends of total spending by year and the label of amount for each year is laid in the chart to reduce the extraneous load of the decision makers. To get the information on the cost and order number whether a high number of order result to a high cost, bar-line combination chart is used. It could be easily distinguished by the decision makers that the high number of material or service order does not result to high cost.

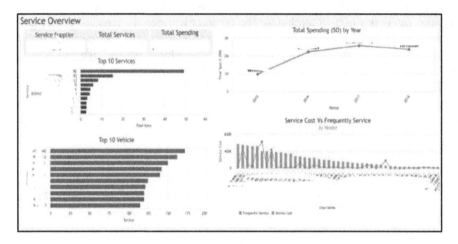

Fig. 4. Service dashboard

The charts in the dashboards shown in Fig. 4 is created based on factors identified in Sect. 3.1 above. However, there is only 1 variable available for this study which is the price. So, the charts are limited to price variable only. Quality and delivery variables are not available in the data. By visualizing the data, the unavailability of quality and delivery variables could be detected. This data alone does not enough and reliable to further the supplier selection analysis in the future.

6 Dashboard Evaluation

This evaluation is conducted which is to evaluate the business intelligence dashboard for supplier selection in transportation industry. The questionnaire is divided into 2 sections. The first section is the personal details of the respondents and the second section is evaluation of the proposed BI Dashboard for the selected company.

6.1 Demographic Information

In this section, the personal details of each respondent are collected. The detail for demographic information as shown in Table 1.

Table 1. Demographics of the respondents

Position	Department	Qualification	Work experience
Consulting director	Business insight and analytics	DBA	20 years
Head of unit	Big data	Not stated	13 years
Executive	Big data	Bachelor's degree	Not stated
Executive	Big data	Masters	Not stated
Executive	Business development	Bachelor's degree	3 years
Executive	Big data	Bachelor's degree	5 years
Executive	Business development	Master	4
Executive	Big data	Master	3 years
Consultant	Sales	Diploma	17
Administrative officer	Administration	Bachelor's degree	8 years
Executive	Big data	Degree	3 years

6.2 Findings from Evaluation

From evaluation conducted with 11 respondents, they are satisfied with the proposed BI dashboard. From the total 11 questions asked, more than 80% of the respondents strongly agree when answering the questions asked on the related items of BI dashboard. In summary, 81.8% of them are strongly agree with the proposed BI dashboard and the other 2 respondents are which are 18.2% agree as shown in Fig. 5. It is clinched that BI dashboard is very useful to selected company to help them to get the insights of their data hence will results to an informed decision making.

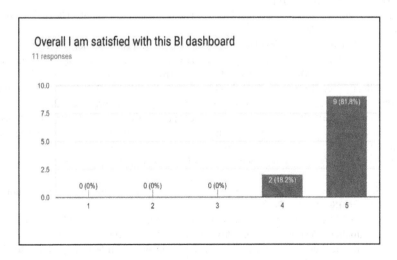

Fig. 5. Summary of BI dashboard evaluation

7 Discussion and Conclusion

The implementation of data visualization in organizations could aid the decision makers in getting information from different departments in a parallel format also make the information more accessible. Price, quality and delivery are the identified factors for supplier selection based on the literature conducted. Business Intelligence dashboard to visualize the supplier in the company has been proposed using InstaBI. Besides, from the evaluation conducted, respondents who involved with the BI dashboard and decision making in the organization confirmed the proposed BI dashboard may help their organization for decision making in supplier selection. To obtain more beneficial and valuable results for supplier selection in future research, some improvements need to be made by the transportation company of this study. Further analysis on the data regarding quality and delivery need to be captured because from both variables there are a lot of information regarding the suppliers that could be obtained. Analysis by using only one variable which is Price might result on unfairness when selecting the suppliers. A thorough analysis for supplier selection need to be conducted in order to get an accurate result of which suppliers are good and otherwise. Data visualization is only a method to help to visualize data into an understandable information.

References

Amorim, P., Curcio, E., Almada-Lobo, B., Barbosa-Póvoa, A.P., Grossmann, I.E.: Supplier selection in the processed food industry under uncertainty. Eur. J. Oper. Res. **252**(3), 801–814 (2016)

Chang, Y.H.: Logistical Management. Hwa-Tai Bookstore Ltd., Taiwan (1998)

Rajesh, R., Ravi, V.: Supplier selection in resilient supply chains: a grey relational analysis approach. J. Clean. Prod. **86**, 343–359 (2015). Business School, Loungborough, 1, 3–34

Chen, Y.J.: Structured methodology for supplier selection and evaluation in a supply chain. Inf. Sci. **181**(9), 1651–1670 (2011)

Coyle, J., Novack, A., Gibson, B., Edawrd, J.: Transportation: A Supply Chain Perspective. Cengage Learning, Manson (2010)

Fashoto, S.G., Akinnuwesi, B., Owolabi, O., Adelekan, D.: Decision support model for supplier selection in healthcare service delivery using analytical hierarchy process and artificial neural network. Afr. J. Bus. Manage. **10**(9), 209–223 (2016)

Gartner: Gartner executive programs worldwide survey of more than 2,300 CIOs shows flat IT budgets in 2012, but IT organizations must deliver on multiples priorities (2012)

Gitahi, P., Ogollah, K.: Influence of fleet management practices on service delivery to refugees in united nations high commissioner for refugees Kenya programme. Eur. J. Bus. Manage. **2**(1), 1–18 (2014)

Grazia Speranza, M.: Trends in transportation and logistics. Eur. J. Oper. Res. **264**(3), 830–836 (2018)

Hosseini, S., Barker, K.: A Bayesian network model for resilience-based supplier selection. Int. J. Prod. Econ. **180**, 68–87 (2016)

Kuo, R.J., Wang, Y.C., Tien, F.C.: Integration of artificial neural network and MADA methods for green supplier selection. J. Clean. Prod. **18**(12), 1161–1170 (2010)

Meeks, E.: Semiotic Lessons & Goals (2018). https://medium.com/@Elijah_Meeks/semiotic-lessons-goals-841afceabb98

Mukherjee, K.: Supplier selection criteria and methods: past, present and future (2014)

Mwikali, R., Kavale, S.: Factors affecting the selection of optimal suppliers in procurement management. Int. J. Hum. Soc. Sci. **2**(14), 189–193 (2012)

Roy, S., Sharma, P., Nath, K., Bhattacharyya, D.K., Kalita, J.K.: Pre-processing: a data preparation step. reference module in life sciences (2018)

Sarkis, J., Talluri, S.: A model for strategic supplier selection. J. Supply Chain Manage. **38**(1), 18 (2002)

Sauro, J., Lewis, J.R.: Standardized usability questionnaires. In: Quantifying the User Experience, pp. 185–248 (2016)

Sonmez, M.: Review and critique of supplier selection process and practices (2006)

Stimson, J.A.: Supplier Selection. PT Publications, Inc., USA (1998)

Tseng, Y., Yue, W., Taylor, M.A.: The role of transportation in logistics chain. In: Proceedings of the Eastern Asia Society for Transportation Studies, vol. 5, pp. 1657–1672 (2005)

Weele, A.J.V.: Purchasing and Supply chain Management: Analysis, Strategy, Planning and Practice, 6th edn. Cengage Learning, Andover (2014)

Wu, M.Y., Weng, Y.C.: A study of supplier selection factors for high-tech industries in the supply chain. Total Qual. Manag. **21**(4), 391–413 (2010)

Xia, W., Wu, Z.: Supplier selection with multiple criteria in volume discount environments. Omega **35**(5), 494–504 (2007)

Zhang, S., Zhang, C., Yang, Q.: Data preparation for data mining. Appl. Artif. Intell. **17**(5–6), 375–381 (2003)

Comparison of User-Centered Design Antibiotic Resistance Awareness App to Existing Antibiotic-Related Mobile Applications

Ummul Hanan Mohamad[(⊠)]

Institute of Visual Informatics, Universiti Kebangsaan Malaysia, UKM,
43600 Bangi, Selangor, Malaysia
ummulhanan@ukm.edu.my

Abstract. Mobile health apps are an effective awareness tool. A user-centred study reported that an ideal awareness app should have the following functional components, (1) information, (2) communication, (3) feedback, and (4) personalized setting. The purpose of this study is to conduct a review of the existing antibiotic-related apps and to compare their functionality. The existing apps were selected from the Google Play Store and Apple App Store, the two major mobile application stores. In total, the search resulted in 1333 apps. After removal of duplicates and discrete viewing, the number of apps was narrowed down to 285 apps. By applying the inclusion and exclusion criteria, only 5 apps were included in the final reviews. Our findings also showed that none of the apps contained all the functionality components that were identified in the user-centred study. As there is still no specific app designed to promote awareness about antibiotic resistance, a user-centred antibiotic resistance awareness app is imperative.

Keywords: Android application · mHealth · Public awareness · Software engineering

1 Introduction

In this Fourth Industrial Revolution (4IR) era, mobile applications (apps) are rapidly growing in the market. Such apps can provide better access to health information [1]. For example, mobile health or also known as mHealth has been developed extensively to fulfil the need of general public and professional healthcare practitioners. In the olden days, health information was commonly distributed through conventional printed materials [2] such as information sheets, pamphlets, brochures, localised event talks, and workshops. Nowadays, with the advancement of the technologies, the mobile application has become a preferred method of health information dissemination due to its versatility. Many of the apps were developed to acquire information and to assist in tracking goals and supporting behavioural changes [3].

According to [4], the usage of smartphones is beneficial in promoting health and social influences. They can influence health behavioural changes among the public, for

© Springer Nature Switzerland AG 2019
H. Badioze Zaman et al. (Eds.): IVIC 2019, LNCS 11870, pp. 82–90, 2019.
https://doi.org/10.1007/978-3-030-34032-2_8

example, through tracking of health information, interaction with the healthcare personnel, accessibility to health info, usage of entertainment. In addition, the mobile application can overcome certain limitations of the conventional approaches in providing health-related information. For example, the mobile application can cover a wider demographic scope and it can be assessed from anywhere at any time [5]. Moreover, some apps encourage two-way communications and they have a built-in function to provide feedback to the users. This extra feature is important to minimise the risk of providing inaccurate information to the users. Besides that, the mobile application also facilitates the possibility of global deployment as some of the mHealth apps can support various functionality such as access to different information, ability to track users, and other features in management [6].

Two types of mobile devices are commonly used for mHealth, namely smartphones and tablets, either from Android or iOS platforms. So far, there has been increasing interest in using the mobile app to promote awareness on many health-related issues [7]. For examples, awareness to exercise, promotion of healthy eating habits, tracking of physical states such as migraine, dissemination of disease prevention awareness such as cancer. In general, these apps are focused on behavioural changes [8]. According to [9], there are several common behavioural modification techniques employed in the awareness app, such as platforms to provide feedback, set goals, self-monitoring, planning of social support, and motivation towards behavioural changes. With multiple functionalities, the mobile app is deemed to be cost-effective to reduce the cost of awareness promotion activities in the long term.

In general, several factors determine the success of a mobile app [10], including the features and functionality of the app [11]. In terms of features, optimal criteria will include attractive visual design, interactive multimedia via audio and video, text sizing comfortable for viewing, online or offline accessibility, optimal screen size, and availability of progress tracking and content sharing through the social media network [12].

Other than that, the proliferation of the internet and social media have also boosted the growth of mHealth apps. In Malaysia, internet usage is as high as 87.4% (28.7 million users) among smartphone users [13]. In addition, other than for communication, the highest online activities recorded are the use of internet included access to social media platform (85.6%) and for information retrieval purpose (85.5%). Indirectly, this opens up a vast potential of using ICT-enabled technology for healthcare purposes. Although the focus has mainly been in the area of disease management, promotion of awareness about other health-related issues via mobile apps has also been blooming. Thus, there is an urgent need to assess the user perceptions of mobile apps in supporting behavioural change and to provide information for researchers and designers to design and develop better health apps based on the insights and perspective of the users [14].

To date, published reviews on existing apps mainly focused on health management or disease prevention. None of the published studies have assessed or compared the functional components of different apps. This information is important for the design and development of an ideal awareness app. Thus, this study aims to compare the mobile app that we designed with the existing mobile apps currently available in the market. Through these findings, the missing gap can be identified and taken into consideration during the development of new apps.

2   Related Works

Many of the apps in the market failed to attract its users because of the design and development lack users input [15]. Thus, it is important that the design and development of awareness app consider User-Centered Design (UCD) to engage users to the app. According to [16], UCD is a process that suited user inputs into the design of application. So far, there have been reviews of existing apps focusing on health management or disease prevention, however, there is yet to be any study that compares and assess the functional components, focusing on developing an ideal awareness app.

Although numerous apps related to antibiotics are available in the app market, it could be seen that the app development pattern focused towards ease of use for professionals or medical personnel [17]. One of the antibiotic-related app category includes antibiotics handbooks (including antibiotic guidelines and dictionaries). This app type is beneficial to assist medical doctors in providing treatment to their patients [18]. However, this information is not suitable to enhance public understanding and awareness on antibiotics and antibiotics resistance issue, simply due to the usage of scientific terms broadly in the apps.

In addition, other types of antibiotic-related apps are dosage calculator. The dosage calculator app is mainly suited for healthcare practitioners but it can also be freely used by the public [19]. However, public is more accustomed to obtaining the needed information from their own doctor with regard to the antibiotic dosage. Considering its function, this type of app did not contribute much to the public awareness on antibiotic and its resistance.

Other antibiotic apps found in the market include medicine reminder [20]. Although this kind of app is more frequently being used by the public, it is generally used as a timely reminder to alert users in following the medication regime. Nonetheless, this app type may help in deterring the occurrence of antibiotic resistance through complete antibiotic consumption by the patients.

Overall, there are many rooms of improvement for the currently available antibiotic-related apps. To do that, the missing functionality can be improved or fulfilled through the newly developed awareness app [21]. Two crucial concern should be addressed; which are to provide the necessary information on antibiotics to the public and to improve the public awareness on antibiotics resistance issue.

3   Methodology

A screening workflow adapted from [11] and [22] was modified accordingly to perform this study (see Fig. 1). Figure 1 shows the four main steps involved in this study, namely identification of functionality components for awareness app, search for the relevant existing apps, selection of final apps, and assessment of the selected apps. The findings from the analysis will help to further improve the user-centred awareness app to fulfil its purpose as an effective awareness tool to combat antibiotic resistance issues.

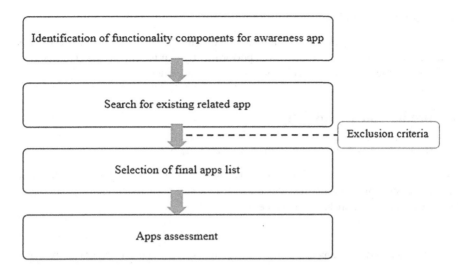

Fig. 1. Screening workflow for comparison of antibiotic-related mobile apps

3.1 Identification of Functionality Components for Awareness App

A mock-up awareness app prototype was made to assess the usability within a pilot study group. A total of 30 participants were selected to evaluate the prototype to provide recommendations or suggestions for the functional specifications and user interface design. Later, all the recommendations are segregated accordingly into several categories of functionality components.

3.2 Search for Existing Related Apps

Initially, three mobile app stores were selected, including Google Play Store, Apple App Store, and Windows Mobile. However, Windows Mobile was excluded as the app store had been discontinued. The search for existing related apps was conducted using keywords which include 'antibiotics', 'antibiotic resistance', 'superbugs', 'pills', and 'antibiotics info'. Next, the search was performed separately in each app store and a list of the search results was compiled.

3.3 Selection of Final Apps List

The search result was reviewed and narrowed down according to the inclusion criteria. The inclusion criteria were relatedness of the app to antibiotics, apps were developed for general purpose, the English language was used, and the ratings of the apps were more than 3. Following that, exclusion criteria were used to eliminate irrelevant apps. The exclusion criteria included apps that were designed as games, apps intended for professional medical practitioners, apps with broad usage such as dosage calculator, dictionary, or medicine reminder, paid apps, and non-human related apps, for example, apps developed for veterinary usage or related to antibiotics for animals.

3.4   App Assessment

The total number of apps was calculated by removing duplicated apps that existed on multiple platforms. The assessment was performed by comparing the selected five apps according to the functionality components identified earlier.

4   Results and Discussion

4.1   Functionality Components for Awareness App

For the comparison of existing antibiotic-related mobile applications to the user-centered design of antibiotic resistance awareness app, four functionality components had been identified and listed in Table 1.

Table 1. Functionality components of user-centered design for antibiotic resistance awareness app.

Functionality	Details
Information	Information on antibiotics and antibiotic resistance, case studies
Feedback	Progress tracking, chat, scores, points
Communication	Information sharing, social media integration, emails, messages
Personalized setting	Profile, password, audio or image support, notification, languages

4.2   Selection of Apps

Based on the initial search in the available app repositories, a total of 1333 apps were found across multiple platforms (Fig. 2). Google Play Store for Android contained more apps (1320) than the Apple App Store (13). However, when redundant apps from multiple search terms in each platform were identified and removed, the number of apps reduced to 293 apps (280 apps from Google Play Store and 13 apps from Apple App Store). Following that, another eight apps were removed from the list due to duplications since they existed on both platforms.

From the list, the 285 were further narrowed down based on the exclusion criteria. A total of 280 apps were excluded. Majority of the apps were excluded because they were created to assist the professional health practitioners. As high as 80% of the apps from the list also functioned mainly as treatment guidelines and antibiotic dictionaries with broad usage such as dosing calculators and medication reminders. Nine of the app were gaming apps (3%). In addition, two paid apps were also excluded. Since this study focused only on the general public, apps with non-human related purposes were also excluded, such as apps created for veterinary antibiotics or animal's antibiotics guides. Hence, the final list included 5 unique apps for comparison.

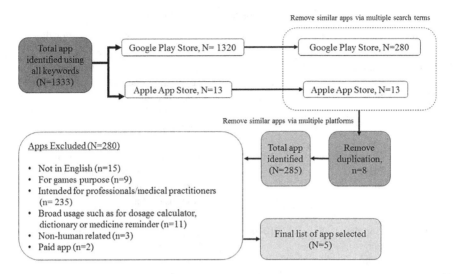

Fig. 2. The screening process for app selection

4.3   App Assessment

Out of the five apps, one of it had been downloaded 500 to 1000 times, another 3 had 1000 to 5000 downloads, and the last one recorded more than 10000 downloads (Table 2). A total of 80% of the apps focused mainly on information about antibiotics but none of the apps stressed on the issue of antibiotics resistance. This was despite one of the apps, Maxxim Waaw 1.0.7, being designed to create awareness.

Since having good usability features contributed to an efficient functionality, these selected apps are sufficient in terms of accessibility and content. All 5 apps can be used online or offline and are filled with information on antibiotics that can be easily understood by the public. However, some features are missing. For example, there is no interactivity through audio or video that can engage users with the app. Two apps, antibiotics, and antibiotics flashcard, lacked eye-comforting text sizing and optimal screen size to display the information.

Moreover, none of the apps had the feedback functionality component. Thus, the user was only getting information through the app but was not informed with their progress or given the opportunity to get more info other than inside the apps. To add, the absent of personalized settings functional component also suggested that user-centered design was also not a priority in these selected apps. Thus, it is essential that the newly developed app takes into account to have all the important functionality of an ideal awareness app encompassing communication, information, feedback and per-sonalized setting.

Table 2. Assessment of selected app

App name	Platform	Rating	Download, N	Short description	Functionality
Maxxim Waaw 1.0.7	Google Play Store	3.8	500+	Create awareness about antibiotic resistance and guides on the appropriate use of antibiotic	Communication
Appibiotic	Google Play Store	4	1000+	Help parents to get information on the correct antibiotics suspension for their kids	Communication information
Antibiotic	Google Play Store	5	1000+	Provide information on antibiotics	Communication information
Classes of antibiotics	Google Play Store	4.1	10000+	Provide information on antibiotics	Information
Antibiotic flashcards	Google Play Store	4.9	1000+	Flashcards that provide a basic classification of antibiotics mode of action and treatment to bacterial infections	Communication information

5   Conclusion

Despite the many mobile apps available in the market, very few are dedicated to antibiotic resistance awareness. Many failed to engage the attention of users. They also lacked positive reviews based on the low number of downloads and low ratings for the apps. Currently, there is no specific app designed to increase the public awareness of issues on antibiotic resistance. The findings from this work validated the fact that there are gaps in the functional components in the existing apps currently available in the market and these gaps can be filled by antibiotic resistance awareness apps with user-centred design. However, there are limitations to this study as the search function within the available mobile application stores were within the capabilities of the system and some unrelated app might have been mistakenly included in this study.

Acknowledgment. This study is supported by Universiti Kebangsaan Malaysia (UKM) under GGPM grant (GGPM-2017-073).

References

1. Abu Hassan Shaari, N.S., Abdul Manaf, Z., Ali, M., Nazlena Shahar, S., Mohamed Ismail, N.A.: Usage of mobile applications in diabetes management. A Rev. Malaysian J. Heal. Sci. **14**(2), 1–10 (2016)
2. Redman, S., Paul, C.L.: A review of the effectiveness of print material in changing health-related knowledge, attitudes and behaviour. Heal. Promot. J. Aust. Off. J. Aust. Assoc. Heal. Promot. Prof. **7**, 91 (1997)
3. Peng, W., Kanthawala, S., Yuan, S., Hussain, S.A.: A qualitative study of user perceptions of mobile health apps. BMC Public Health. **16**, 1158 (2016)
4. Klasnja, P., Pratt, W.: Healthcare in the pocket: mapping the space of mobile-phone health interventions. J. Biomed. Inform. **45**, 184–198 (2012)
5. Dunham, G.: The future at hand: mobile devices and apps in clinical practice. ASHA Lead. **16**, 4 (2011)
6. Dehling, T., Gao, F., Schneider, S., Sunyaev, A.: Exploring the far side of mobile health: information security and privacy of mobile health apps on iOS and Android. JMIR mHealth uHealth **3**, e8 (2015)
7. Edwards, E.A., et al.: Gamification for health promotion: systematic review of behaviour change techniques in smartphone apps. BMJ Open **6**, e012447 (2016)
8. Muhammad, S., Mohamad Taha, I., Norshita, M.N.: The Usability Factors of Cardiovascular Health Monitoring Mobile Application: A Conceptual Model (2018)
9. Coughlin, S., Thind, H., Liu, B., Jacobs, M., Champagne, N., Massey, R.I.: Mobile phone apps for preventing cancer through educational and behavioral interventions: state of the art and remaining challenges. JMIR mHealth uHealth **4**, e69 (2016)
10. Thiruvanackan, K., Mohd. Yusof, M.: Evaluation of mobile health (MHEALTH) application from the pharmacist perspective. J. Inf. Syst. Technol. Manag. **2**(6), 37–54 (2017)
11. Schnall, R., Mosley, J.P., Iribarren, S.J., Bakken, S., Carballo-Diéguez, A., Brown III, W.: Comparison of a user-centered design, self-management app to existing mHealth apps for persons living with HIV. JMIR mHealth uHealth **3**, e91 (2015)
12. Bricker, J.B., Mull, K.E., Kientz, J.A., Vilardaga, R., Mercer, L.D., Akioka, K.J., Heffner, J. L.: Randomized, controlled pilot trial of a smartphone app for smoking cessation using acceptance and commitment therapy. Drug Alcohol Depend. **143**, 87–94 (2014)
13. MCMC: Internet Users Survey 2018 (2019)
14. Dennison, L., Morrison, L., Conway, G., Yardley, L.: Opportunities and challenges for smartphone applications in supporting health behavior change: qualitative study. J. Med. Internet Res. **15**, e86 (2013)
15. Adu, M.D., Malabu, U.H., Callander, E.J., Malau-Aduli, A.E.O., Malau-Aduli, B.S.: Considerations for the development of mobile phone apps to support diabetes self-management: systematic review. JMIR mHealth uHealth. **6**, e10115 (2018)
16. Zain, N.H., Jaafar, A., Razak, F.H.: A user-centered design: methodological tools to design and develop computer games for motor impaired users. In: Proceedings of the 5th International Conference on Computing & Informatics: Computer for Improving the Quality of Life. pp. 223–228 (2015)
17. Fralick, M., Haj, R., Hirpara, D., Wong, K., Muller, M., Matukas, L., Bartlett, J., Leung, E., Taggart, L.: Can a smartphone app improve medical trainees' knowledge of antibiotics? Int. J. Med. Educ. **8**, 416 (2017)
18. Tuon, F.F., Gasparetto, J., Wollmann, L.C., de Moraes, T.P.: Mobile health application to assist doctors in antibiotic prescription–an approach for antibiotic stewardship. Braz. J. Infect. Dis. **21**, 660–664 (2017)

19. Loy, J.S., Ali, E.E., Yap, K.Y.-L.: Quality assessment of medical apps that target medication-related problems. J. Manag. care Spec. Pharm. **22**, 1124–1140 (2016)
20. Chalifoux, P.R.: Medicine reminder and indentification technology (2018)
21. Mohamad, U.H., Nordin, A., Ahmad, A.: Development of SEDAR mobile application for antibiotic resistance awareness (2019)
22. Dute, D.J., Bemelmans, W.J.E., Breda, J.: Using mobile apps to promote a healthy lifestyle among adolescents and students: a review of the theoretical basis and lessons learned. JMIR mHealth uHealth **4**, e39 (2016)

Realization of a 3D Gearbox Model Through Marker-Based Augmented Reality for Edutainment Applications

K. Martin Sagayam[1], Julia Schaupp[2], Alex J. Timothy[3], and Chiung Ching Ho[4(✉)]

[1] Department of Electronics and Communication Engineering, Karunya University, Coimbatore, India
martinsagayam.k@gmail.com
[2] Department of Mechanical Engineering, Technical University of Munich, Munich, Germany
j@schaupps.de
[3] Department of Electronics and Media Technology, Karunya University, Coimbatore, India
alex@karunya.edu
[4] Faculty of Computing and Informatics, Multimedia University, Cyberjaya, Malaysia
ccho@mmu.edu.my

Abstract. Augmented reality (AR) has been proven as a valuable human-computer interface (HCI) for many real-time applications in domains such as education and entertainment. In this paper, we have shown that the modelling of a 3-D gearbox model can be enhanced with marker-based augmented reality (AR). The marker-based augmented reality (AR) visual representation of an automobile's gearbox can improve the understanding of how each moving component interact with each other.

Keywords: Augmented reality · 3D gearbox · Human-Computer Interface · Virtual reality

1 Introduction

The usage of augmented reality (AR) [1] for education and entertainment [2] has become an increasingly important topic in the last years. AR materials is more inter-active for learners, and its usage can promote greater retention and understanding of the subject matter. In this paper, we describe how AR can be used for enhancing the teaching and learning of gearshifts functionality for mechanical engineering. AR is particularly effective in showing the shifting of gears in real-time, a phenomenon that is difficult to observe physically in real-time. In the first phase of this work, 3D models for different gears is generated using Blender 3D. These models are then transferred to Unity 3D. Markers for each gear are created and also transferred to Unity 3D, using Vuforia. Subsequently, the interaction between gears are shown using AR during simulated shifting of gears.

© Springer Nature Switzerland AG 2019
H. Badioze Zaman et al. (Eds.): IVIC 2019, LNCS 11870, pp. 91–99, 2019.
https://doi.org/10.1007/978-3-030-34032-2_9

2 Related Works

AR is the display of the real world, added with virtual objects. It has a wide field of applications; one of which is in the area of teaching. The usage of AR for teaching purposes has been well documented in literature.

AR has been used to enhance teaching in biology classes [3] through an interactive mobile AR application. The AR application was tested on 120 college freshman from the Department of Biology (basic biology is part of the curriculum in the first year). The application contained five different topics: microscope structure, microscope operation, animal and plant cell observation, frog anatomy, and frog bone structure. After four weeks of using the mobile AR application in class, a survey (utilizing Short Feedback Questionnaire and the Likert scale) was performed. Analysis of the survey instrument's results have shown that the usage of AR has enhanced the students' learning efficiency and motivation, and overall academic achievement.

Similarly, AR has been used in the teaching of chemistry [4]. AR was used to enhance the understanding of the space structure of molecules, by implementing 3D control of the molecule. This has been proven to be a more intuitive way of examining the molecule as compared to the 2D manipulation of digital objects using keyboard and mouse. This is realized through a cube with markers on each of its sides, attached to a grip. When the device is held in front of a webcam, the markers are detected and depending on the current position of the cube, a virtual image of the molecule is displayed on the marker. The user can manipulate the virtual object by rotating the grip (cube) and by changing the picture, the camera detects the point-of-view from which the molecule is displayed.

AR has also been used to teach mathematics, through the usage of Unity 3D and Vuforia [5]. The aim was to create an AR implementation, which improves students' spatial imagination by teaching them how to solve the Rubrik's cube as well as other geometry ideas. In the AR application, three scenarios for teaching and learning were developed: Cubic Nets, Three-Dimensional View, and Spatial Cub. In the first scenario, the cubic net is pictured through six markers, and when holding a tablet's camera over it, the different ways to fold the cubic nets into a cubic will be shown. In the second scenario, a tablet was used to view an object made out of stacked cubes, with 3D view of the cubic structure. The final scenario is still in progress. Its aim is to improve visual imagination as well as help to solve the cube through virtually adding the non-visible parts and surfaces of the cubes.

Another AR work in the mathematics field aimed to increase spatial abilities in the mathematics field. The AR application generated for that purpose, displayed mathematical functions in 3D, which contained an additional introduction video as well as the mathematical function itself and several buttons to adjust the displayed 3D function. The application was tested with 30 Engineering students out of a mathematics class, who had subsequently to complete an open survey about their experiences. For the test, students worked in pairs of two, with each pair using a tablet and two acrylic gadgets.

AR was used to instruct engineering students [6] with the aim of improving spatial abilities of engineering students. Using AR-Dehaes (an Augmented Reality book), they realized a five level test in a marker based augmented reality application. A test study with 445 of first year engineering students from different fields has been carried out.

After showing an explanation video and a demo of the used AR book, the students had to complete five difficulty levels of training. Apart from the increase in the spatial abilities of the students through the test, their user feedback was very positive.

3 Creation of a 3D Model of a Manual Gear Using Blender 3D and OTVINTA

3.1 Modelling of the Involute Gear Pairs

To model the involute gear pairs, the OTVINTA Gear Calculator is used. With modul = 1 and a Pressure angle of 20°, for the different teeth number pairs a Python script is generated. The Python script, generated with OTVINTA is then transferred to Blender 3D.

The Python Script, which was used in Blender, generates the shape of the gears (Step 1). The frame is extruded by 10 in positive direction of the z-axis (Step 2). Next, a circle which has the same number of vertices as the gear frame with radius 3 is generated (Step 3) and then connected to the gear frame (Step 4). Afterwards, the circle is extruded by 10 in negative direction of the z- axis (Step 5) and connected to the other end of the gear frame (Step 6). The result is an involute 3D gear (Step 7). The sequence of steps is shown in Fig. 1.

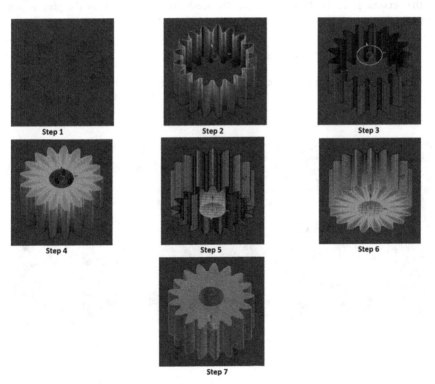

Fig. 1. Modelling of the involute gears pairs is shown in step 1 until step 7

3.2   Modelling of the First Gear

For the first gear, for the countershaft the teeth number 13 and for the pinion shaft the teeth number 27 is used, adding a profile shift of 0.4 (Fig. 2).

Fig. 2. Gears 13/27

3.3   Modelling of the Second Gear

For the second gear, for the countershaft the teeth number 17 and for the pinion shaft the teeth number 23 is used, adding a profile shift of 0.4.

3.4   Modelling of the Third Gear

For the third gear, for the countershaft the teeth number 25 and for the pinion shaft the teeth number 15 is used, adding a profile shift of 0.4. This is shown in Fig. 3.

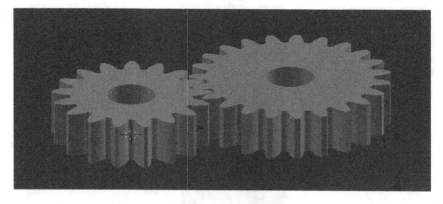

Fig. 3. Gears 25/15.

3.5   Modelling of the Reverse Gear

For the reverse gear, for the countershaft the teeth number 11 is used, for the pinion shaft the teeth number 13 and for the additional gear the teeth number 8 is used, adding a profile shift of 0.2 (Fig. 4).

Fig. 4. Gears 11/8/13.

3.6   Modelling of the Direct Gear

For the direct gear, for both shafts the teeth number 20 is used, adding a profile shift of 0.2 (Fig. 5).

Fig. 5. Gears 20/20.

3.7   Fitting the Gear Pairs Together on the Shafts and Adding Clutch Sleeves

For the shafts, cylinders with a radius of three were generated. For the sleeves, fixed to the gear a radius of 3.5 is used. For the sleeves, fixed to the pinion shaft a radius 3 is used.

At the drive shaft a box, which is representing the motor is added. Another box, connected to the clutch sleeves through bars, representing the manual gear is also added. The colour-coded gears are shown in Fig. 6.

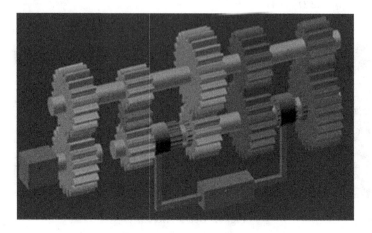

Fig. 6. Composed Blender 3D Model

4 Simulate the Gear Rotation

For the simulation, a duration of 2000 is chosen. The rotation angle for the gears fixed to the countershaft is set at 0° at the point of time 1 and set at −5760° at the point of time 2000. The rotation angle for the drive shaft is set 0° at the point of time 1 and set 5760° at the point of time 2000.

For the gears of the pinion shaft and though the pinion shaft itself (depending on the gear that is currently connected to the pinion shaft) the rotation angle is calculated depending on the teeth numbers of the respective gear pairs. The rotation angle for each gear is shown in Table 1.

Table 1. Rotation angles for different gears

First gear	$\alpha_{13} = -5760°$
	$\alpha_{27} = \alpha_{13}\left(\frac{z_{13}}{z_{27}}\right) = -5760°\left(-\frac{13}{27}\right) = 2773{,}33°$
Second gear	$\alpha_{17} = -5760°$
	$\alpha_{23} = \alpha_{17}\left(\frac{z_{17}}{z_{23}}\right) = -5760°\left(-\frac{17}{23}\right) = 4257{,}4°$
Third gear	$\alpha_{25} = -5760°$
	$\alpha_{15} = \alpha_{25}\left(\frac{z_{25}}{z_{15}}\right) = -5760°\left(-\frac{25}{15}\right) = 9600°$
Reverse	$\alpha_{11} = -5760°$
	$\alpha_{8} = \alpha_{11}\left(\frac{z_{11}}{z_{8}}\right) = -5760°\left(-\frac{11}{8}\right) = 7920°$
	$\alpha_{13} = \alpha_{8}\left(\frac{z_{8}}{z_{13}}\right) = 7920°\left(-\frac{8}{13}\right) = -4873{,}85°$
Idle	None

5   Generating AR Simulation of Gear Rotation Using Unity 3D and Vuforia

5.1   Generating the Markers

For each gear, a marker is generated, using a word processor. To simplify the application for the user, the name of the marker is similar to the name of the gear animation (Fig. 7).

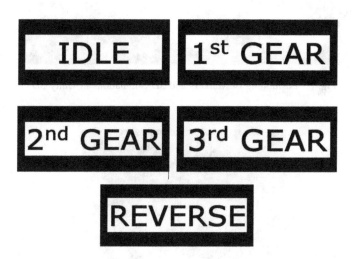

Fig. 7. Augmented reality markers used for each gear

5.2   Loading the Markers to Unity 3D Using Vuforia

The markers are uploaded in a pdf format at the Vuforia Developers Platform to the Target Manager. The markers type is "Single Image" and the width is ten. Subsequently, the markers are imported to Unity 3D.

5.3   Connection the Markers with the 3D Blender Simulation in Unity 3D

First the animation is imported to Unity 3D, which is done by saving the Blender file in a Unity folder. Subsequently, the animation is activated in Unity, so that it is running correctly. Then each of the markers will be connected to the right simulation in Unity 3D. Now, depending on the marker held in front of the camera, the resulting simulation will be performed. Figures 8 and 9 shows the positioning of the markers and the resulting augmented reality images respectively.

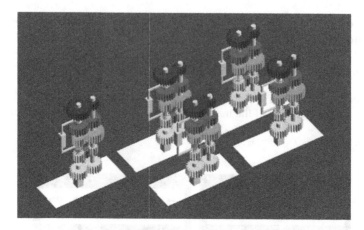

Fig. 8. Positioning of Markers and 3D Simulations in Unity 3D

Fig. 9. 3rd Gear Marker with displayed 3D Simulation of 3rd Gear

6 Results and Discussion

The results obtained with Blender 3D are satisfactory, with three students expressing their satisfaction that the usage of AR has helped their comprehension of the interaction of gears during a gear shift. The possibilities for an extension of this AR application are promising. One example for such an extension could be to model the gear lever and how its movement affects the position of the clutch sleeves. Another example for an enlargement would be to picture the drive (the engine) and the output (the differential/wheels).

At the beginning of each simulation loop, some of the gears are showing a small tug. This should be due to the fact, that blender just accepts one decimal and so is a result of a rounding error. For future works, different values for rotation angle and duration for which only rotation angles for the pinion shaft wheels with at most one decimal are obtained are advisable.

7 Conclusion

In this paper, a 3D gearbox model has been created using unity 3D, blender 3D and OTVINTA. The five sets of markers are created for different gears such as ideal, 1st gear, 2nd gear, 3rd gear and reverse gear. This marker should interact with the system with higher recognition rate. We suggest that the usage of AR for the teaching of gear-shift can be more effective as compared to traditional talk-and-chalk techniques. It can be enhanced in real-time for automobile applications using marker-less AR technique.

References

1. Billinghurst, M., Clark, A., Lee, G.: A survey of augmented reality. HCI **8**, 73–272 (2015). https://doi.org/10.1561/1100000049
2. Selvam, A., Timothy Tzen-Vun, Y., Hu, N., Hau-Lee, T., Chiung Ching, H.: Augmented reality for information retrieval aimed at museum exhibitions using smartphones. J. Eng. Appl. Sci. **11**, 635–639 (2016). https://doi.org/10.3923/jeasci.2016.635.639
3. Chang, R., Yu, Z.: Application of augmented reality technology to promote interactive learning. In: 2017 International Conference on Applied System Innovation (ICASI), pp. 1673–1674 (2017). https://doi.org/10.1109/ICASI.2017.7988257
4. Maier, P., Klinker, G.: Augmented chemical reactions: an augmented reality tool to support chemistry teaching. In: 2013 2nd Experiment@ International Conference (exp.at 2013), pp. 164–165 (2013). https://doi.org/10.1109/ExpAt.2013.6703055
5. Salinas, P., González-Mendívil, E., Quintero, E., Ríos, H., Ramírez, H., Morales, S.: The development of a didactic prototype for the learning of mathematics through augmented reality. Procedia Comput. Sci. **25**, 62–70 (2013). https://doi.org/10.1016/j.procs.2013.11.008
6. Martín-Gutiérrez, J., Luís Saorín, J., Contero, M., Alcañiz, M., Pérez-López, D.C., Ortega, M.: Design and validation of an augmented book for spatial abilities development in engineering students. Comput. Graph. **34**, 77–91 (2010). https://doi.org/10.1016/j.cag.2009.11.003

Users' Perception on Usability Aspects of a Braille Learning Mobile Application 'mBRAILLE'

Lutfun Nahar[✉], Riza Sulaiman, and Azizah Jaafar

Institute of Visual Informatics, Universiti Kebangsaan Malaysia UKM,
43600 Bangi, Selangor, Malaysia
nahar.lutfun3@gmail.com

Abstract. Visually impaired students (VIS) are unable to get visual information that makes their learning process difficult than others. As a developing country, Bangladesh cannot afford for the available costly assistive technologies for VIS. Therefore, mBRAILLE was developed with self-learning capability to assist the blind and VIS in learning Bangla and English Braille easily. The new ISO standard for usability of software suggested that one must evaluate the appropriate usability aspects of any assistive technologies before launching in market. Therefore, this study evaluates four usability aspects (Learnability, Screen/Feature/Interface Evaluation, Accessibility, and Self-Descriptiveness) of mBRAILLE. The evaluation was done by testing the application by the real users. The results show that all the aspects were evaluated by an average score of 6.0 or above, which is in the satisfactory domain. Therefore, it can be said that the application is capable of providing self-learning facility to learn Bangla and English Braille.

Keywords: Usability aspects · Visually impaired students · Braille learning · Assistive technologies · Self-learning

1 Introduction

"mBRAILLE" is a mobile based android application developed for the visually impaired (VI) students of Bangladesh in order to assist their braille learning [1]. The main goal of this application is to help the blind students to learn English and Bangla Braille by themselves without anyone's assistance. Bangladesh is a developing country which contains approximately 750,000 visually impaired people [2, 3]. A recent study reported that the total number of VI people is approximately 87.2 million [4]. Ensuring education for this large number of VI people is not easy. VI students are facing numerous challenges in getting education in Bangladesh [5]. The main challenge is that the blind schools have very limited number of resources [6]. Still now the Braille beginners do not have any technological tool that might assist them in learning Braille as they cannot study by themselves. They only use slate and stylus to write braille [7]. Educational tools and devices that are specially produced for VI are very expensive and beyond the affordability of the blind and VI students in developing countries [8–10]. Therefore, "mBRAILLE" was an attempt of providing these people a suitable software

© Springer Nature Switzerland AG 2019
H. Badioze Zaman et al. (Eds.): IVIC 2019, LNCS 11870, pp. 100–109, 2019.
https://doi.org/10.1007/978-3-030-34032-2_10

on the same hardware that they already have, like mobile phones [1]. Later, Nahar et al. also reported the design of another mobile application for the blind students to learn and practice only Bangla language [7].

In a previous study Nahar et al. proposed the design of mBRAILLE [1]. As "mBRAILLE" is developed for the VI students, usability is a fundamental factor for this application. This article reports the evaluation of different usability aspects of mBRAILLE. In order to achieve this main objective, an intensive evaluation is carried out following the new ISO standard for the usability evaluation [11].

2   Braille Learning Application MBRAILLE

This Application has two main features, English and Bangla. Both features have three sub-features, i.e. Learn Letters, Letter Practice and Tutorial. 'Learn Letters' and 'Letter Practice' sub-features work similarly for both Bangla and English. However, Tutorial contains different sub-features for English and Bangla. Detailed descriptions of all these features are provided in a previous study [1]. The developed interfaces are presented in Fig. 1. The dashed-red arrows show how the English feature will continue one page to another. Additionally, the solid-blue arrows demonstrate how the Bangla feature will continue in the application.

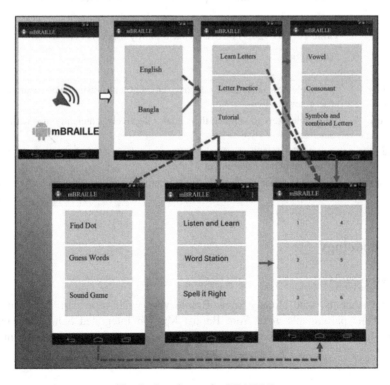

Fig. 1. Interfaces of mBRAILLE.

3 Usability

ISO (the International Organization for Standardization) and IEC (the International Electrotechnical Commission) form the specialized system for worldwide standardization, produced more balanced perspective of Usability than it is typically found in textbooks or individual publications. In 2018, new version of ISO 9241-11, defined the usability as "the extent to which a system, product or service can be used by specified users to achieve specified goals with effectiveness, efficiency and satisfaction in a specified context of use" [11]. There are three main goals of usability that includes Effectiveness, Efficiency and Satisfaction. Together with that, the new version of ISO identifies some usability aspects that are necessary to be evaluated.

3.1 Usability Aspects

The new version of ISO 9241-11 published in 2018 states that usability applies to all aspects of use of any technological products (system or software), including: Learnability, Regular use, Accessibility and Maintainability [as stated in Table 1]. However, it also provides the flexibility of choosing usability aspects appropriate to the developed software/application [12]. For example, Scree/Feature/Interface evaluation, Self-descriptiveness, etc. are important for any touch-based mobile application for the blind people. Therefore, these usability aspects are also considered in this study.

Table 1. ISO 9241-11-2018 stated usability aspects [11].

Usability aspects	Discerption
Learnability	to enable new users to be effective, efficient and satisfied when learning to use a new system
Regular use	to enable users to achieve their goals effectively, efficiently and with satisfaction
Accessibility	so that the system if effective, efficient and satisfying for users with the widest range of capabilities
Maintainability	to enable maintenance tasks to be completed effectively, efficiently and with satisfaction

4 Methodology

4.1 Participants

Five blind students, who already knew Braille very well, were participated in this study. All the participants were from Baptist Mission Integrated School in Dhaka, Bangladesh. Table 2 shows the demographic information of the respondents in this study.

Table 2. Summary of results from questionnaire survey

P*	Sex	Age	Sight	EST*	HS/A*	EBT*
Student 1	M	11	Blind	Yes	Yes	No
Student 2	M	12	Blind	Yes	Yes	No
Student 3	F	8	Blind	No	No	No
Student 4	M	10	Blind	No	No	No
Student 5	F	9	Blind	Yes	No	No

*P = Participants; EST = Experiences in smartphone and touch screen, EBT= Experiences in Braille based assistive technologies, HS/A = Have smart/Android phone.

4.2 Procedure and Setting

mBRAILLE interfaces were used on an Android phone to evaluate its usability aspects. After the detail explanation of how the program works, the respondents were asked to use the application for both English and Bangla features. They used the application (both features) for two weeks before the applications' usability evaluation. Finally, to find out the application usability ratings, the students were asked questions after they used the interface. The questionnaire was designed based on usability goals established during the design and development phase of the interface. Four main usability aspects were considered in this study, namely; Learnability, Scree/Feature/Interface evaluation, Accessibility, and Self-descriptiveness.

Table 3 presents summary of the selected statements of different usability aspects from the questionnaire. During the evaluation once the participants were ready to answer the questions, one person read the statements/questions and asked to rate that statements/questions; and subsequently record the rating for each question. The scoring

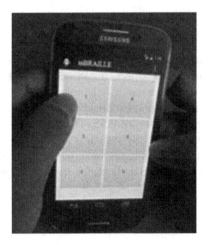

Fig. 2. Testing the application interface.

Table 3. Summary of results from questionnaire survey

Learnability	Screen/feature/interface evaluation
1. Learning to operate the system is easy 2. Time to learn to use the system is adequate/sufficient 3. Facilitates learning for the users with no prior smart phone using experience 4. The application facilitates learning with a minimal amount of training	1. Buttons on the Mobile screen are easy to identify 2. Layout prompts and fields on each screen is clear, easy to understand and remember 3. The application provides enough options to correct the unintentional human error 4. Sequence of screens is very clear
Accessibility	Self-descriptiveness
1. The user interface layout is easy to distinguish and suitable for visually impaired subjects 2. The auditory and vibrational output helps the users to know where they are in the App and what to do next 3. Going back to the previous screen is easy 4. Placement of the help message is appropriate and clear	Instructions of the application are clear enough to understand Feedback on the completion of sequence of steps is clearer Prompts the users, so that users always know what the application expects them to do next and what their options are 4. The application explains clearly what is required to fill-in on each field the screen

scale was set to 1–7 (1 = Strongly disagree, 2 = disagree, 3 = Somewhat disagree, 4 = neutral, 5 = Somewhat agree, 6= agree, 7=Strongly agree). Figure 2 shows a student is using the application.

5   Results and Discussion

The results obtained for all the usability aspects are discussed in the following subsections.

5.1   Learnability

Learnability aspect was measured against four criteria as stated in Table 2. Figure 3 shows the results obtained on this aspect. It can be seen that the three criteria were measured with a score 6.00 or above out of 7. Third criteria, 'Facilitates learning for the users with no prior smart phone using experience', was evaluated with the maximum score of 6.4 with a standard deviation of 0.55. The lowest score 5.8 was received by second criteria 'Time to learn to use the system is adequate/sufficient' with a standard deviation of 0.45. The evaluation rating on this aspect indicates that the application is easy to learn and facilitate learning Bangla braille more easily and effectively without any assistance.

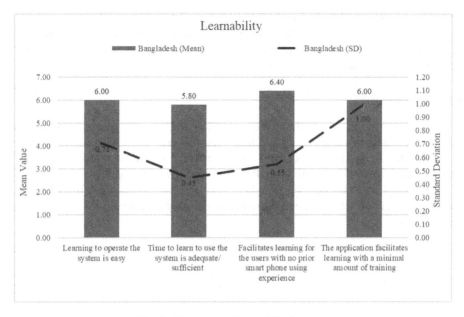

Fig. 3. Results on 'Learnability' aspect.

5.2 Screen/Feature/Interface Evaluation

Results on the evaluation of this aspect is presented in Fig. 4. All four criteria were evaluated with a score 6.2 or above with a standard deviation ranging from 0.55 to

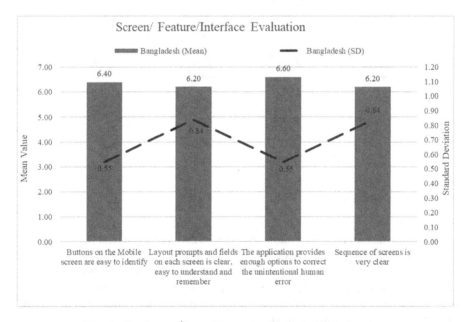

Fig. 4. Results on 'Screen/Feature/Interface Evaluation' aspect.

0.84. Maximum score 6.6 was obtained for the third criteria 'The application provides enough options to correct the unintentional human error' with a standard deviation of 0.55. The results indicate that the features or Interfaces are well designed for the visually impaired users to facilitate braille learning with less errors.

5.3 Accessibility

Evaluation results for accessibility aspect of mBRAILLE application are reported in Fig. 5. Out of four criteria, second and third criteria were scored with a rating 6.0 or above. Highest rating 6.6 was achieved for the criteria on helpfulness of auditory and vibrational feedback of the application. Rest two criteria were evaluated with a score of 5.8. This result indicates that the Bangla braille learning application mBRAILLE is accessible by the visually impaired users due to its' easy to distinguish interfaces and the feedbacks.

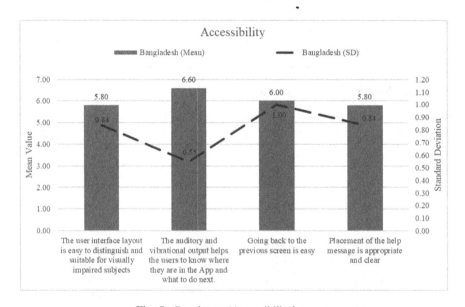

Fig. 5. Results on 'Accessibility' aspect.

5.4 Self-descriptiveness

The evaluation results of this aspect are reported in following Fig. 6. It can be seen from the figure that all the criteria were evaluated with score more than 6.2. A score of 6.4 as the maximum score was achieved for the third criteria; whereas, all rest of the criteria received the same score of 6.2. This aspect is very important, especially for the applications designed to provide self-learning facilities for visually impaired students. Based on the results it can be said that the application is efficiently designed to provide self-learning facilities for the blind students to learn Bangla braille.

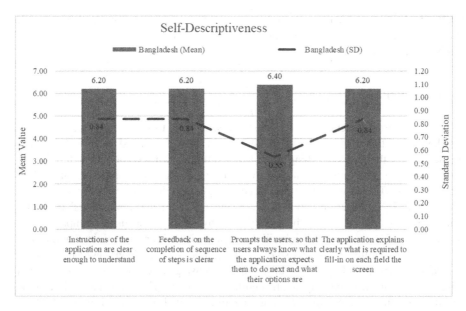

Fig. 6. Evaluation results on 'Self-Descriptiveness' aspect.

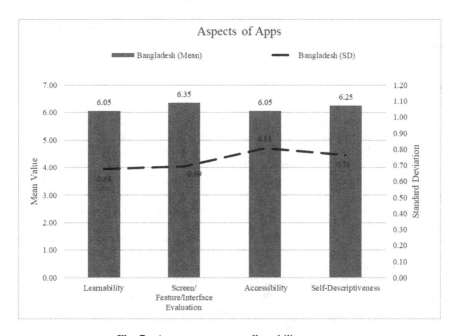

Fig. 7. Average scores on all usability aspects.

Overall, all the aspects were evaluated by the visually impaired students with an average score of above 6.0, as shown in Fig. 7. This result indicates that the mBRAILLE application is a very useful tool for the Bangladeshi visually impaired students to learn Bangla braille more easily without or with minimal assistance of their teacher or parents.

6 Conclusions

Visually impaired students in Bangladesh are struggling to get technological solution for their educational purposes. mBRAILLE has been developed as a first Android application for them to learn Bangla and English braille easily without or with minimal assistance. This article reports the study on different usability aspects (Learnability, Screen/Feature/Interface Evaluation, Accessibility, and Self-Descriptiveness) of the application. The evaluation shows a promising result on the applications' usability. Therefore, this application can be widely used by the blind or visually impaired students to learn Bangla and English braille without assistance or with minimal assistance.

One of the limitations of this study is the number of participants used in usability evaluation; therefore, the future study will be focusing on evaluating the application with a large number of participants from different schools. The application will also be tested for evaluating the actual learning effectiveness of Bangla and English Braille.

Acknowledgements. The authors acknowledge the funding and support provided by Universiti Kebangsaan Malaysia through the Zamalah Research University scholarship. The authors also acknowledge the participation of blind students from Baptist Mission Integrated School in Dhaka for the usability study.

References

1. Nahar, L., Jaafar, A., Ahamed, E., Kaish, A.B.M.A.: Design of a Braille learning application for visually impaired students in Bangladesh. Assist. Technol. **27**(3), 172–182 (2015)
2. EFA Global Monitoring Report. Reaching the Marginalized. United Nations Educational, Scientific and Cultural Organization. OXFORD University Press (2010)
3. Rahman, K.F.: Blindness, 'Vision 2020' and Bangladesh. Financ. Express **20**(436), 10 (2012)
4. Bangladesh Fact Sheet (2019). http://www.seva.org/pdf/Seva_Country_Fact_Sheets_ Bangladesh.pdf
5. Das, A.: Inclusion of student with disabilities in mainstream primary education of Bangladesh. J. Int. Dev. Coop. **17**(2), 1–10 (2011)
6. Alam, K.J.: Country report Bangladesh. In: The 25th Asia-Pacific International Seminar on Special Education, Yokohama, Japan, pp. 37–41 (2005)
7. Nahar, L., Sulaiman, R., Jaafar, A.: "Bangla Braille Learning Application" in smartphone for visually impaired students in Bangladesh. Interact. Learn. Environ. (2019). https://doi.org/ 10.1080/10494820.2019.1619588
8. Hossain, M.J.: Special education in Bangladesh: present trend and future needs. In: 28th Asia-Pacific International Seminar on Education for Individuals with Special Needs, Yokohama, Japan (2008)
9. Mitra, S., Posarac, A., Vick, B.: Disability and Poverty in Developing Countries: A Snapshsot from the World Health Survey. World Bank Sp discussion paper (1109) (2011)

10. Malak, M.S.: Inclusive education reform in Bangladesh: pre-service teachers' responses to include students with special educational needs in regular classrooms. Int. J. Instr. **6**(1), 195–214 (2013)
11. ISO 9241-11: 2018(en) Ergonomics of human-system interaction — Part 11: Usability: Definitions and concepts, International Organization for Standardization
12. Bevan, N., Carter, J., Earthy, J., Geis, T., Harker, S.: New ISO standards for usability, usability reports and usability measures. In: Kurosu, M. (ed.) HCI 2016. LNCS, vol. 9731, pp. 268–278. Springer, Cham (2016). https://doi.org/10.1007/978-3-319-39510-4_25

Early Intervention Through Identification of Learners with Dyscalculia as Initial Analysis to Design AR Assistive Learning Application

Kohilah Miundy[1], Halimah Badioze Zaman[1(✉)], Aliimran Nordin[1], and Kher Hui Ng[2]

[1] Institute of Visual Informatics, Universiti Kebangsaan Malaysia, 43600 Bangi, Selangor, Malaysia
hbzukm@yahoo.com
[2] Nottingham University, Malaysia Campus, Semenyih, Selangor, Malaysia

Abstract. Learners who suffer from dyscalculia are unable to perform in mathematics. Plausible Assistive digital technology that are visual-based fusion technology, particularly Augmented Reality (AR) application, can assist dyscalculia learners perform arithmetic tasks such as addition, subtraction, multiplication, and division more effectively. This paper highlights early intervention through identification of dyscalculia learners in a national elementary school. The identification of dyscalculia learners was done through a screening instrument that combined of Mathematics Learning Ability (MLA) and Mathematics Learning Performance (MLP). The findings categorised the learners based on five main difficulties namely, memory, abstraction, sequencing processing, motor, and visual perception. However, the visual perception category showed most significant difficulty faced by dyscalculia learners in learning mathematics. The findings were used as initial analysis for Systems Requirement Specifications (SRS) that would be used to design and develop a visual-based fusion technology AR application for dyscalculia learners.

Keywords: Dyscalculia · Augmented Reality (AR) · Learning difficulties (LD) · Mathematical difficulty · Invention · Visual-based fusion technology

1 Introduction

We are in exciting times where the digital economy has seen many emerging and disruptive technologies that has benefited societies globally. Malaysia too is experiencing this digital transformation and digital inclusion is important to ensure inclusivity of all sectors of the society including persons with learning difficulties (LD). The dyscalculia learners are also part of the new digital society that needs to be included. Dyscalculia learners are very often lumped into a group of learners with Learning Disabilities known as LD. Learning Disabilities is a term associated with any unexpected difficulties boundary with basic learning skills such as listening, speaking, reading known as Dyslexia, writing known as Dysgraphia and mathematical skills, known as Dyscalculia [1]. Dyscalculia is interconnected to neurologically based

© Springer Nature Switzerland AG 2019
H. Badioze Zaman et al. (Eds.): IVIC 2019, LNCS 11870, pp. 110–122, 2019.
https://doi.org/10.1007/978-3-030-34032-2_11

processing problems with a biological origin which requires specific academic skills that lead to persistent difficulties in the acquisition of specific academic skills [1].

In Malaysia, dyscalculia is a medical phenomenon that is less visible compared to the much-touted autism, dyslexia or attention deficit hyperactivity disorder (ADHD). Thus, a large portion of parents are oblivious of their child suffering from it. It may be difficult to eventually accept the realisation of their child being unable to perform mathematical tasks as other children. Currently, teachers segregate learners afflicted with this disorder from the mainstream, by labeling them as slow learners or assigning them to a less challenging classroom. According to Monuteaux et al. [4], learning mathematics can be an arduous task for dyscalculia learners if they do not have suitable learning materials or intervention tools. However, that does not mean that learners with dyscalculia are unable to be successful in life. With the right support of plausible assistive digital technology, a dyscalculia learner can learn to work around difficulties and use their strengths to their advantage.

2 Literature Review

There are several terms used to define learning difficulties in mathematics such as development dyscalculia [5], mathematics disabilities [6], specific arithmetic difficulties [7], arithmetic learning disabilities [8], specific arithmetic learning difficulties [9], mathematics difficulties [10], number fact disorder [11], mathematics disorder [12], dyscalculia [13], number blindness [13] and many more. These various terms referred to definitions and different origins of the problems ranging from neurological dysfunction to inappropriate opportunities to learn and practice mathematical skills.

Studies indicate that dyscalculia is a learning issue in difficulty of understanding concepts related to numbers such as comprehend basic addition, subtraction, multiplication and division calculations, struggle to memorise mathematical facts and strive to follow mathematical reasoning [14]. The level of brain activation is the same when it involves exact calculation for learners with and without dyscalculia. During tasks involving calculations, both learners with and without dyscalculia have the same level of brain activation [15, 16]. However, when tasks in which the learners have to make approximate calculations are involved, a smaller area of the brain seems to be active for learners with dyscalculia. The parietal lobe of the cerebral cortex in the brain is highly involved with most number operation [14]. When, the parietal lobe is damaged, the learner encounter problems with understanding and grasping numeracy, while oral language skills remain untouched [17]. This reveals that learners with dyscalculia might have some form of damage within this area.

2.1 Learning Skills in Mathematics

A structural disorder of mathematical abilities leading to underachievement in Mathematics, have its origins in a genetic or congenital disorder. There are however further factors that need to be investigated such as visual perception and processing, abstraction in Mathematics, memory in Mathematics and motor in Mathematics.

Visual Perception and Processing in Mathematics. A study was conducted on the interconnection between visual perception and reading disability amongst primary school learners. The results indicate that the correlation between visual perception and reading disability was negative, except for the second hypotheses related to eye-motor coordination and reading disability; and fifth hypotheses related to spatial relations and reading disability, were significant and negative [18]. Thus, a study was conducted to investigate visual, auditory, kinesthetic and tactile known as perceptual abilities which integrates with reading, spelling, and mathematics, known as academic performance. The results showed that academic performance is significantly correlated with the three perceptual abilities. Therefore, reading and spelling were significantly associated with perceptual abilities. Results also showed that mathematics was only significantly correlated with auditory and visual perception [19].

Abstraction in Mathematics. Abstraction in mathematics describes the fundamental ideas that relate to the real world and involve an empirical concept of learning mathematics as abstraction in general. The study represents that the application of mathematical processes is an independent system to solve a problem or is only capable of recalling details but not the main idea as abstraction in apart [20].

Memory in Mathematics. A previous study conducted showed that an early phase identification and treatment is needed on mathematics anxiety because it may lead to interruption on intensive working memory strategies [21]. Investigations reveal that all working memory components are related to mathematical performance, with the highest correlation happens between mathematics and verbal updating [22, 24]. Based on a study by Arsic, et al. [23] there was a significant difference in effectiveness towards cognitive characteristic of attention, working memory and organising abilities between experimental and control group with learners confronted with difficulties in counting ($p < 0.01$). As a result, there was poor effectiveness but positively associated with moderate intensity among assessed attention, working memory and organising abilities characteristic ($p < 0.01$).

Motor Skills in Mathematics. Learners with mathematical learning disabilities, showed significant poor achievement on visual perception, visual motor integration and fine motor coordination which are all related to number fact retrieval or method of calculation [25]. The study revealed that teachers can help stimulate motor skills development such as balance or bilateral coordination and eye-hand coordination in learners. These skills can be improved through continuous physical activity play and have shown to have positive effects on learners' development process, especially when implemented young [26, 27].

2.2 Language in Mathematics

A previous study conducted on the relationship between learners' understanding in mathematical vocabulary and achievement, showed that learners refuse to adapt to new applications and tools in mathematics, because they were not taught in expressing using the explicit mathematical language. However, with the new teaching modeling approach, learners are able to increase their understanding based on specific mathematical vocabulary [28, 29]. Through a previous study conducted by Mercer & Sams

[30], results showed that teachers also have an essential role in effective learning using appropriate mathematical language in problem solving. Larson [31], concluded that learners have better confidence, attitudes, and scores when they have the ability of expressing themselves in mathematical language.

2.3 Diagnosing Dyscalculia Learners

In assisting learners to overcome mathematical difficulties, diagnosing could be the initial step, followed by an intervention process [32]. There are many successful screeners that have been developed by experts to identify dyscalculia learners such as Butterworth Screener [13] available from GL Assessment suitable for learners aged from 6 years-old through fourteen years-old (14). DysCaliUM [33] and Screening Test [34] are available from Tribal 2010, but these screeners are not available for open access, not economical and lack in reporting on their reliability and validity. Teachers preferred to use paper and pencil for testing primary school learners [35, 36]. The current research used a screening test that was designed and developed by Nagavalli & Juliet [37], and adapted by the researchers to identify dyscalculia learners amongst children in a national primary school in Malaysia.

2.4 Early Intervention for Identification of Dyscalculia Learners

The intervention concept is a common term used with various meaning in education. Intervention refers to the intervention programs to support learners in overcoming difficulties [38]. The interventions can vary in terms of target learners, comparison group, aims, setting, duration, mathematical content, conductor and professional developmental support, and instructional design features, which all can have an impact, individually or combined, on the intervention's effectiveness [38] and they can either be classed as remedial or preventive [39]. There are numerous studies currently addressing the use of AR intervention in education with learning difficulties (LD) learners as discussed below:

Augmented Reality (AR) Intervention in Learning Disabilities. Augmented Reality (AR) has an inspiring potential bringing experiential and location-based learning to learners by supplementing existing worlds rather than creating new ones. In keeping up abreast with the fourth industrial revolution (4IR) and moving towards society 5.0, it is important that digital inclusion for persons with special needs are not left out. This digital inclusion can be successfully applied through the use of AR in diverse cases of learning disabilities. AR has a great possibility to enhance the living of those with learning disabilities [40–42].

AR based Dysgraphia Assistive Writing Environment (AR-DAWE) application, was designed to address the spelling mistake issue and provide assistance in spelling to avoid core-writing problem to learners suffering from dysgraphia [43]. Another study focused on the effects of Mobile Augmented Reality (MAR) on word recognition learning Chinese Literacy with interactive effects and corresponding video for ADHD learners was conducted. MAR teaching materials showed significant effects observed in the intervention and maintenance phase by the scores for two (2) students.

3   Methodology

Since this paper highlights on identification of dyscalculia learners for early intervention, the methodology discussed is on the qualitative approach using the questionnaire as a research instrument with selected dimensions namely; visual perception and processing, sequential processing, abstraction, memory, and motor of dyscalculia learners. The design of the study comprised two (2) phases: Phase I and Phase II. Phase I involved the administration of Mathematics Learning Ability (MLA) screening instrument and the Mathematics Learning Performance (MLP) achievement test. Phase II, involved both MLA and MLP again (with different questions and added subfactors), but this time administered on potential dyscalculia learners for the purpose of confirmation.

3.1   Phase I: Identification Study

Aim. The main aim of the Phase I identification study was to identify dyscalculia learners through diagnosis of learners using the Mathematics Learning Ability (MLA) screening instrument and the Mathematics Learning Performance (MLP) assessment test. The diagnosis will help teachers identify learners' specific dyscalculia difficulties, and work on the learners' strengths as the first step to move ahead.

Participants. The MLA screening Instrument and MLP assessment test were administerd to fifty (50) participants from a national elementary school in Klang, Selangor, Malaysia. Based on this total number, 32 were boys (64%) and 18 were girls (36%). They were aged ten (10) years old, and were in Year 4. They learned mathematics at the age of seven (7) years old, in Year 1. Sadock et al. [44], says that a child with mathematics difficulty can be identified when they are at the age of eight (8) years through ten (10) years old. Thus, Dehaene & Wilson [45], explained that dyscalculia learners can be diagnosed when they begin their formal school education. It is based on these previous studies, that, researchers of the current study selected students at the age of ten (10) years-old in Year 4.

Instruments. To verify the framed objectives of the current study, the researchers adapted the instruments, MLA and MLA designed by Nagavalli [46], to suit the Malaysian envionment. The instruments were used for identification of potential dyscalculia learners,
   Phase I: Mathematics Learning Ability (MLA)
   The MLA screening instrument comprises of two parts: demography and screening test with twenty (20) items, which uses two (2) way closed-ended questions using Dichotomy, 'yes' represented by icon ☺; and 'no' represented by icon ☹. Table 1 shows the dimensions and sub-factors of the MLA screening test.
   Phase I: Mathematics Learning Performance (MLP)
   After completing the MLA screening, the students were assessed again using the MLP achievement test. The achievement test had twenty (20) questions. The objective of this test was to identify errors made by the individual learner on the mathematics content. There was no time limit for this assessment but generally, thirty (30) minutes

Table 1. Phase I: MLA screening test dimensions and sub-factors

Dimensions	Sub-factors
Visual perception in mathematical difficulty	• Inability in transpositions, omissions made when writing or copying numbers • Inability in the sense of time and direction • Inability in reversals or isolations made while copying numbers
Sequencing processing in mathematical difficulty	• Inability in number sequences • Inability in reproducing sequential order on demand • Inability in applying rules and formulae were the skills in this dimension
Abstraction in mathematical difficulty	• Inability in application of mathematical process to solve problems • Inability to recall details but not the main idea
Memory in mathematical difficulty	• Inability in inconsistent auditory memory • Inability in inconsistent visual memory • Inability to recall and recognise words
Motor in mathematical difficulty	• Difficulty in drawing • Difficulty in writing • Difficulty in expression

was sufficient for answering the entire questions. Most of the learners could complete the test within the allotted time. MLP measures five dimensions that include: (i) visual perception and processing in mathematical difficulty; (ii) sequential processing in mathematical difficulty; (iii) abstraction in mathematical difficulty; (iv) memory in mathematical difficulty; (v) motor in mathematical difficulty, as indicated in Tables 2 and 3.

Table 2. Phase I: MLA screening instrument

Screening dimensions	Item numbers	Total items
Visual perception and processing in mathematical difficulty	Q1, Q5, Q13, Q18	4
Sequence processing in mathematical difficulty	Q8, Q12	4
Abstraction difficulty in mathematical difficulty	Q3, Q4, Q6, Q14, Q16	5
Memory in mathematical difficulty	Q2, Q7, Q10, Q15, Q17, Q19	3
Motor in mathematical difficulty	Q17, Q18, Q19, Q20	4

Table 3. Phase 1: MLP assessment test instrument

Screening dimensions	Item numbers	Total items
Visual perception and processing in mathematical difficulty	Q1, Q2, Q3, Q4	4
Sequence processing in mathematical difficulty	Q5, Q6, Q7, Q8	4
Abstraction difficulty in mathematical difficulty	Q9, Q10, Q11, Q12, Q13	5
Memory in mathematical difficulty	Q14, Q15, Q16	3
Motor in mathematical difficulty	Q17, Q18, Q19, Q20	4

Phase I: Scoring Procedure

The scoring procedures were key to the tests for data collected. The scoring procedure of MLA screening was crisp and simple: one (1) score was given to every 'yes' responses. No (0) score was given to 'no' responses. On the other hand, the scoring procedure on MLP achievement test gave one (1) score to every 'correct' response. No (0) score was given to any other responses. When the scoring process was completed, all the given scores were added and interpreted based on the total scores obtained.

3.2   Phase II: Identification Study

Aim. The main aim of the Phase II identification study was to confirm dyscalculia learners identified in Phase I using MLA and MLP instruments with different questions and sub-factors. The screening instrument systematically confirm learners with dyscalculia and subsequently propose remedial measures.

Phase II: Mathematics Learning Ability (MLA) Screening Test. The MLA screening test comprised two parts: demography and screening process based on thirty (30) items. This screening instrument was used to screen individual dyscalculia learner on seven (7) components namely: (i) numerical in mathematical difficulty; (ii) sequential in mathematical difficulty; (iii) motor in mathematical difficulty; (iv) language in mathematical difficulty; (v) cognition in mathematical difficulty; (vi) visual and spatial in mathematical difficulty; and (vii) multiple in mathematical difficulty as shown in Table 4 and items of questions based in MLA in screening instrument, indicated in Table 5.

Phase II: Mathematics Learning Performance (MLP) Achievement Test. After completing the MLA screening, the dyscalculia learners were assessed again using the MLP achievement test. The MLP achievement test instrument comprised of twenty (20) questions, used to identify errors made by the individual learners on basic mathematics. Table 6 shows the MLP achievement test with its items based on the screening dimensions.

Phase II: Scoring Procedures. The MLA screening instrument scoring procedures are key to the tests conducted, to ensure quality of the data collected. The scoring

Table 4. Phase II: MLA screening test instrument

Numerical in mathematical difficulty	• Inability in numbers, reading and writing numbers, operation of numbers • Inability in understanding in number sentences or equations • Ability in reading digit but unable to recall their place in a large number
Sequential in mathematical difficulty	• Inability in sequencing the numbers • Inability in sequencing order on activities, events, shapes and colour
Motor in mathematical difficulty	• Inability to perform mathematical operation or calculations • Understand numbers and their relationship to one another, but inability to perform calculations that manipulate numbers and mathematical symbols.
Language in mathematical difficulty	• Inability in talking about the mathematical concepts or relationships • Ability to read and write numbers but inability to talk about them, remember their names or recognise them orally
Cognition in mathematical difficulty	• Inability in understanding mathematical ideas and relationships; such identifying sequence of larger or smaller numbers not limited to oral or written works • Inability in understanding maths and whole numbers • Inability in recalling mathematical ideas after learning them
Visual and spatial in mathematical difficulty	• Trouble with tasks that requires an understanding of visual images and spatial terms in mathematics and relationships
Multiple task in mathematical difficulty	• Inability to perform mathematical operations or calculations • Ability to understand numbers and their relationships; but inability to perform any kind of calculation that requires manipulation of numbers, objects and mathematical symbols

Table 5. Phase II: MLA screening instrument on item numbers based on dimensions

Screening Dimensions	Item numbers	Total Items
Numerical in mathematical difficulty	1, 6, 7, 18	4
Sequential in mathematical difficulty	2, 4, 8, 24, 28, 30	5
Motor in mathematical difficulty	26, 27	2
Language in mathematical difficulty	10, 13, 14, 19, 23	5
Cognition in mathematical difficulty	5, 15, 16, 21	4
Visual and spatial in mathematical difficulty	3,9,11,22,25	5
Multiple Task in mathematical difficulty	12, 17, 20, 29	5

procedures adopted for MLA scores, involved each item corresponding to a three (3) point rating scale with scores: two (2), one (1) and zero (0). The maximum total score for the screening test was 60. Those who scored more than 30 were identified as dyscalculia learner. In the MLP achievement test, one (1) score was given to every

Table 6. Phase II: MLP achievement test instrument on item numbers based on dimensions

Screening dimensions	Item numbers	Total items
Numerical in mathematical difficulty	1, 2, 3, 11	4
Sequential in mathematical difficulty	5, 14, 15, 17, 18	5
Motor in mathematical difficulty	4, 19	2
Language in mathematical difficulty	6, 9	5
Cognition in mathematical difficulty	7, 8	4
Visual and spatial in mathematical difficulty	12, 13, 16	5
multiple task in mathematical difficulty	10, 20	5

correct response. No (0) score was given to any other responses. When the scoring was completed, all the given scores were added and interpreted based on the total scores obtained.

4 Findings

Findings of the study was based on the content analysis of the literature review conducted on previous studies; as well as the initial analysis conducted in an attempt to investigate, analyse and interpret the collected data, based on the analysis of the data related to the objectives formulated for this study. Fifty (50) students from the selected school were screened using the test instruments. The data collected were classified according to the various dimensions and sub factors mentioned earlier. An achievement test administrated includes items tested based on the said difficulties. Category wise mean and standard deviation were used for the study.

4.1 Phase I: Data Analysis

Results of the MLA screening instrument indicates that m = 1.54 (1.313) on memory in mathematical difficulty. The abstraction in mathematical difficulty shows the score was m = 1.24 (1.188). While visual perception and processing in mathematical difficulty and motor in mathematical difficulty experience showed m = 0.52(0.735) and m = 0.52 (0.677), respectively. Therefore, sequencing processing in mathematical difficulty was m = 0.38 (0.602).

Results of the MLP achievement test of the students on visual perception and processing in mathematical difficulty showed the score was m = 3.26(0.723). The abstraction in mathematical difficulty showed m = 2.90(1.474). Hence, sequencing processing in mathematical difficulty was found to be m = 2.84(1.113). Thus, memory in mathematical difficulty showed the score to be m = 2.76(0.916). The motor in mathematical difficulty dimension was found to be m = 2.52(0.677).

In this study too, one-way ANOVA was used to analyse a sample of fifty (50) students to determine whether there was a statistically significant difference between participants in MLA compared to MLP. The investigation was conducted based on five (5) dimensions mentioned earlier. Based on the results obtained in

Phase I, there was statistically no significant difference in identification of participants screened for dyscalculia based on MLA compared to those screened using MLP. Both the instruments had developed items based on dimensions as follows: visual perception and processing in mathematical difficulty with value p = 0.005, sequence processing in mathematical difficulty with value p = 0.000, abstraction in mathematical difficulty value is p = 0.000, memory in mathematical difficulty p = 0.438 and motor in mathematical difficulty value p = 0.004 which were below p = 0.05.

4.2   Phase II: Data Analysis

The two potential dyscalculia learners identified during Phase I were confirmed at Phase II, as they received a score totaled more than 50%. The scoring procedure adopted for MLA screening instrument was that each item corresponds to a three (3) point rating scale and scores included: two (2), one (1) and zero (0). For the MLA achievement screening instrument, learner A scored 48 (80%), and learner B scored 44 (73.3%). Thus, based on the scores obtained by the two (2) students, they were identified and confirmed as dyscalculia learners.

Table 7 shows that the scores on MLA for learners A and B in motor, language, cognition, visual and spatial difficulty, and multiple task difficulty were 100%, 60%, 88%, 50%, and 100%, respectively. Learner A scored 100% and 83% in output of numerical difficulty and organization/sequential difficulty. On the other hand, learner B scored 50% and 67% for the output of numerical difficulty and organisation/sequential difficulty.

Table 7. Scores on MLA screening instrument and MLP assessment test

Dimension	Score on MLA		Score on MLP	
	Learner A	Learner B	Learner A	Learner B
Output of numerical difficulty	100%	50%	100%	100%
Organization/sequential difficulty	83%	67%	40%	40%
Motor difficulty	100%	100%	50%	50%
Language difficulty	60%	60%	100%	20%
Cognition difficulty	88%	88%	50%	50%
Visual and spatial difficulty	50%	50%	33%	33%
Multiple task	100%	100%	100%	100%

5   Discussions and Conclusion

Identification and early intervention of dyscalculia learners is an effort to ensure societal inclusion in the transformation of society 5.0. Identification through diagnosis at an early stage will not only increase dyscalculia learners' confidence level, but will also be able to develop a positive attitude of these children towards mathematics learning. It is known that dyscalculia learners can only be treated but not cured [50]. This study identified seven (7) mathematical difficulties that need serious instructional attention. Significant mathematical deficits have consequences on the management of everyday life as well as on career prospects of the individuals. These deficits affect basic conceptual grasp of mathematics in memory and visual spatial relations. The study found that one of the critical dimensions of difficulty is visual spatial disorganization which most often lead to overall mathematical difficulties with dyscalculia learners.

Based on the intervention conducted to identify dyscalculia learners, two (2) out for fifty (50) students were identified and confirmed to have symptoms of dyscalculia, representing a prevalence of 4% which is also evident previous research conducted [47–49]. The results also showed that the designed screening conducted, described the cluster characteristics associated with dyscalculia and is able to discriminate between learners who display these characters and have similar difficulties. Nations are moving towards society 5.0. Thus, it is imperative to have an optimum level of knowledge to survive in the modern digital world. Contemporary research on dyscalculia are working in this direction with promising results. Research in this field not only provide an understanding of a number of new concepts on dyscalculia for better understanding, it also sheds light on the pedagogical interventions appropriate for them.

Therefore, this identification study conducted provide insightful evidence of difficulty characteristics of individual dyscalculia learners that can be used by stakeholders, particularly teachers and software developers as systems requirements specifications (SRS), to develop an application that will meet specific needs of dyscalculia learners. Societal inclusion in the society 5.0 transformation, is crucial to ensure that all groups of the society are taken care of, including dyscalculia learners.

Aknowledgement. This work was supported by the Universiti Kebangsaan Malaysia (UKM) Grand Challenge Grant (Grant no. AP-2017-0051).

References

1. Giofrè, D., Toffalini, E., Altoè, G., Cornoldi, C.: Intelligence measures as diagnostic tools for children with specific learning disabilities. Intelligence **61**, 140–145 (2017)
2. Kaufmann, L., von Aster, M.: The diagnosis and management of dyscalculia. Dtsch. Aerzteblatt Online **109**(45), 767 (2018)
3. Chinn, S.: The Trouble With Maths: A Practical Guide to Helping Learners with Numeracy Difficulties, vol. **18**(1) (2011)
4. Monuteaux, M.C., Faraone, S.V., Herzig, K., Navsaria, N., Biederman, J.: ADHD and dyscalculia: evidence for independent familial transmission. J. Learn. Disabilty. **38**(1), 86–93 (2005)
5. Kosc, L.: Developmental dyscalculia. J. Learn. Disabil. **7**(3), 164–177 (1974)
6. Geary, D.C.: Mathematical disabilities: reflections on cognitive, neuropsychological, and genetic components. Learn. Individ. Differ. **20**(2), 130–133 (2010)
7. Lewis, C., Hitch, G.J., Walker, P.: The prevalence of specific arithmetic difficulties and specific reading difficulties in 9 to 10-year-old boys and girls. J. Child Psychol. Psychiatry **35**(2), 283–292 (1994)
8. Koontz, K.L.: Identifying simple numerical stimuli: processing inefficiencies exhibited by arithmetic learning disabled children. Math. Cogn. **2**(1), 1–24 (2002)

9. McLean, J.F., Hitch, G.J.: Working memory impairments in children with specific arithmetic learning difficulties. J. Exp. Child Psychol. **74**(3), 240–260 (1999)
10. Jordan, N.C., Montani, T.O.: Cognitive arithmetic and problem solving: a comparison of children with specific and general mathematics difficulties. J. Learn. Disabil. **30**(6), 624–634 (1997)
11. Temple, C.M., Sherwood S.: Representation and retrieval of arithmetical facts: developmental difficulties. Q. J. Exp. Psychol. Sect. A Hum. Exp. Psychol. **55**(3), 733–752 (2002)
12. Association American Psychiatric, Diagnostic and Statistical Manual of Mental Disorders, Fourth Edition: DSM-IV-TR® (2000)
13. Butterworth, B.: Dyscalculia guidance: helping pupils with specific learning difficulties in maths, p. 121 (2003)
14. Sousa, D.A.: How The Brain Learns Mathematics.pdf (2008)
15. Kucian, K., Loenneker, T., Dietrich, T., Dosch, M., Martin, E., von Aster, M.: Impaired neural networks for approximate calculation in dyscalculic children: a functional MRI study. Behav. Brain Funct. **2**, 1–17 (2006)
16. Castelli, F., Glaser, D.E., Butterworth, B.: Discrete and analogue quantity processing in the parietal lobe: a functional MRI study. Proc. Natl. Acad. Sci. **103**(12), 4693–4698 (2006)
17. Lemer, C., Dehaene, S., Spelke, E., Cohen, L.: Approximate quantities and exact number words: dissociable systems. Neuropsychologia **41**(14), 1942–1958 (2003)
18. Baluoti, A.R., Bayat, M.R.: Relationship between visual perception and reading disability in primary students (first, second, third, grade) of Ahwaz city. Int. Res. J. Appl. Basic Sci **3**(10), 2091–2096 (2012)
19. Dhingra, R., Manhas, S., Kohli, N.: Relationship of perceptual abilities with academic performance of children. J. Soc. Sci **23**(2), 143–147 (2017)
20. Mitchelmore, M., White, P.: Abstraction in mathematics and mathematics learning. Psychol. Math. Educ **3**, 329–336 (2004)
21. Ramirez, G., Gunderson, E.A., Levine, S.C., Beilock, S.L.: Math anxiety, working memory, and math achievement in early elementary school. J. Cogn. Dev **14**(2), 187–202 (2013)
22. Friso-Van Den Bos, I., Van Der Ven, S.H.G., Kroesbergen, E.H., Van Luit, J.E.H.: Working memory and mathematics in primary school children: a meta-analysis. Educ. Res. Rev. **10**, 29–44 (2013)
23. Arsic, S., Eminovic, F., Stankovic, I.: The ability of conceptual monitoring and the quality of working memory at children with calculation difficulties. J. Psychol. Res. **1**(1), 12–17 (2017)
24. Pavlin-Bernardic, N., Vlahovic-Stetic, V., Arambasic, L.: Children's solving of mathematical word problems: the contribution of working memory. Rev. Psychol. **15**(1–2), 35–43 (2008)
25. Pieters, S., Desoete, A., Roeyers, H., Vanderswalmen, R., Van Waelvelde, H.: Behind mathematical learning disabilities: what about visual perception and motor skills? Learn. Individ. Differ. **22**(4), 498–504 (2012)
26. Alternatives, E.: Physical acitivity and learning in the Swedish Bunkeflo project evaluation of motor skills training in compulsory school. J. Int. Sci. Publ. Educ. Altern. **11**(2), 1313–2571 (2013)
27. Son, S.-H., Meisels, S.J.: The relationship of young children's motor skills to later school achievement. Merrill. Palmer. Q. **52**(4), 755–778 (2007)
28. Kranda, J.: Precise Mathematical Language: Exploring the Relationship Between Student Vocabulary Understanding and Student Achievement. (2008)
29. Foster, M.E.: Indicators of Mathematics Skill Acquisition in Children with Mild Intellectual Disability: Phonological Awareness, Naming Speed, and Vocabulary Knowledge (2012)
30. Mercer, N., Sams, C.: Teaching children how to use language to solve maths problems. Lang. Educ. **20**(6), 507–528 (2006)

31. Larson, C.: The Importance of Vocabulary Instruction in Everyday Mathematics. Action Res. Proj. Pap. **60** (2007)
32. Issue, S., Gupta, K., Shikha, N., Supriya, S., Nayeem, S.: A review on diagnosis and intervention tools based on, vol. X, pp. 1–5 (2016)
33. Beacham, N., Trott, C.: Screening for dyscalculia within HE. MSOR Connect. **5**(1), 1–4 (2013)
34. Gliga, F., Gliga, T.: Romanian screening instrument for dyscalculia. Proc. - Soc. Behav. Sci. **33**, 15–19 (2012)
35. Geary, D.C., Bailey, D.H., Hoard, M.K.: Predicting mathematical achievement and mathematical learning disability with a simple screening tool: the number sets test. J. Psychoeduc. Assess. **27**(3), 265–279 (2010)
36. Jordan, N.C., Kaplan, D., Locuniak, M.N., Ramineni, C.: Predicting first-grade math achievement from developmental number sense trajectories. Learn. Disabil. Res. Pract. **22** (1), 36–46 (2007)
37. Nagavalli, T., Juliet, P.: Technology for dyscalculic children. SALEM **16**, 1–10 (2015)
38. Mononen, R., Aunio, P.: A Mathematics intervention for low-performing finnish second graders: findings from a pilot study. Eur. J. Spec. Needs Educ. **29**(4), 457–473 (2014)
39. Kucian, K., et al.: Mental number line training in children with developmental dyscalculia. Neuroimage **57**(3), 782–795 (2011)
40. Antonioli, M., Blake, C., Sparks, K., Antonioli, B.M., Blake, C., Sparks, K.: Augmented reality applications in education augmented reality applications in education. J. Technol. Stud. **40**(1), 96–107 (2014)
41. Walker, Z., Rosenblatt, K., McMahon, D.: Teaching the Last Backpack Generation: A Mobile Technology Handbook for Secondary Educators. Corwin Press, Thousand Oaks (2015)
42. Richard, E., Billaudeau, V., Richard, P., Gaudin, G.: Augmented reality for rehabilition of cognitive disable children: preliminary study, no. 2, pp. 102–108. IEEE (2007)
43. Khan, M.F., et al.: Augmented reality based spelling assistance to dysgraphia students. J. Basic Appl. Sci. **13**, 500–507 (2017)
44. Sadock, B.J., Sadock, V.A., Sadock, B.J.: Kaplan and Sadock's Concise Textbook of Clinical Psychiatry, pp. 559–561 (2017)
45. Dehaene, S., Wilson, A.J.: Number sense and developmental dyscalculia. Hum. Behav. Learn. Dev. brain Atyp. Dev. **2**, 212–238 (2007)
46. Nagavalli, T.: A study of dyscalculia primary school children in Salem district and evaluation of applicability of innovative strategies as remedial measures. Indian Educ. **53**, 34 (2015)
47. Butterworth, B.: Handbook of Mathematical Cognition: Development Dyscalcula. no. 22186, pp. 455–468 (2005)
48. Jovanović, G., Jovanović, Z., Banković-Gajić, J., Nikolić, A., Svetozarević, S., Ignjatović-Ristić, D.: The Frequency of the Dyscalculia, vol. 125, no. 2, pp. 170–174 (2014)
49. Miundy, K., Zaman, H.B., Nordin, A.: Review on data driven preliminary study pertaining to assistive digital learning technologies to support dyscalculia learners. In: Badioze Zaman, H., et al. (eds.) Advances in Visual Informatics IVIC 2017, vol. 10645, pp. 233–246. Springer, Heidelberg (2017). https://doi.org/10.1007/978-3-319-70010-6_22
50. Lenz, L., Schuster, K., Richert, A., Jeschke, S.: Are virtual learning environments appropriate for dyscalculic students? A theoretical approach on design optimization of virtual worlds used in mixed-reality simulators. In: 2015 IEEE Games, Entertainment and Media Conference GEM 2015 (2016)

Gamifying Online Knowledge Sharing Environment: A Motivating User Interface Design

Prasanna Ramakrisnan[(⊠)]

Institute of Continuing Education and Professional Studies (iCEPTS),
Universiti Teknologi MARA (UiTM), 40450 Shah Alam, Malaysia
prasanna@uitm.edu.my

Abstract. The way knowledge is shared online is now constantly transforming with the advancement of technology. It is becoming more difficult now to sustain student's attention in online knowledge sharing environment. Students tend to lose their attention quickly and no motivation to participate in the discussion activities posted by the lecturers. The current interface design is lacking of motivation factor to sustain students' participation in online knowledge sharing activities. This paper describes design criteria that apply self-determination theory to self-motivate students in online knowledge sharing activities. The design criteria comprises game and social design elements. There are some typical game design elements used in user interface design are such as the points, badges, leaderboard, level, challenge, reward, progression and etc. These game design elements are now widely used in gamification applications. It was found that those design elements can motivate the students in their online knowledge sharing participation. The aim this paper is to provide the design criteria for a motivating user interface design that can promote students' motivation to share their knowledge online. Previous study had identified a set design criteria based on content validity analysis for designing a motivating user interface. These set of design criteria were designed in a prototype interface called i-Discuss. Our finding reveal that motivation can be designed in user interface for online knowledge sharing activities. Future study will be conducted to evaluate the designed prototype.

Keywords: Online knowledge sharing · Motivating interface · Game design elements

1 Introduction

In traditional learning techniques, knowledge sharing is limited to face-to-face discussions in the classroom. But with the advancement of technology now knowledge sharing can occur regardless of time and place in an online web-based learning environment interface. Labels that always referred to for learning environments are online learning or distance learning. This online environment contains several features that enable learning and communication. Among them are learning modules, communication, testing, assignments and so on. Although there are many features in the online

© Springer Nature Switzerland AG 2019
H. Badioze Zaman et al. (Eds.): IVIC 2019, LNCS 11870, pp. 123–134, 2019.
https://doi.org/10.1007/978-3-030-34032-2_12

learning environment, the use of the discussion interface for communication records the highest use [1].

The platform used by both students and educators as a medium of communication in online learning environments is the discussion interface [2]. The discussion interface is a term used for bulletin boards or discussion boards. It is also known as an internet forum, an online forum or message boards. The discussion interface provides an online environment for students [3], public [4] and employees in organizations [5] to share knowledge. The discussion interface is the communication tool available in the e-learning platform. It is now widely used in higher learning institutions as a medium to assist in the learning and teaching process for blended learning. Mixed learning requires face-to-face sessions as well as online sessions. Face-to-face sessions are in-class while online sessions are usually handled through the discussion interface.

In order to facilitate the implementation of online learning, this discussion interface should be used by students to submit questions related to the course they take. In fact, institutions have taken many steps to encourage students to participate in the discussion interface for learning through contributing and reading discussions [6]. There are many factors such as individual, class, technology, social and motivation that influence the use of discussion interface among students for online knowledge sharing [7–9]. It was found that motivated learners are more committed, maintain better information, and are generally more comfortable in learning [10].

Therefore, the motivating user interface design elements that can nurture motivation among students for online knowledge sharing should be identified. Implementation of the appropriate design elements can involve students while encouraging their activities to turn learning [11]. Design elements such as games [12] and social [13] can motivate students intrinsically in learning. Therefore a set of game and social design elements are recommended for the motivation user interface [14]. This user interface design is expected to increase students' motivation in knowledge sharing activities.

2 Gamification

The concept of gamification can be defined as "the use of game design elements (GDE) in a non-game context" [15]. There are four component identified in the definition (1) game, (2) elements, (3) design, and (4) non-game contexts [16]. The game design elements are the basic building blocks of gamification applications. These game design elements are motivational affordances to produce psychological and behavioural outcomes [12]. The use of different game design elements in the study can lead to changes in user behaviour [17]. So the selection of the appropriate game design elements should be made for each different study. But it is unclear what the element is. In the literature, the game design elements are associated with game mechanics and dynamics [18]. The game mechanics and dynamics are two important tools in gamification [19].

In the context of the game, the game mechanic is a method used by the agent and designed for interaction with the game situation [20]. While in the context of gamification, game mechanic is associated with rules and benefits in game elements that makes it challenging, fun, rewarding or other emotions expected by game designers [21]. According to Brunchball Inc. (2010) this emotion is the result of desire and motivation which is also called as dynamic game. This game mechanic represents the basis of any gamification context. Each game mechanic is characterized by three attributes namely (1) game mechanics type (progression, feedback or behavioural); (2) benefits (engagement, loyalty, time spent, influence, fun, SEO, UGC, vitality) and (3) personality types (explorers, achievers, socializers and killers) [22].

Siexas et al. (2016) gives a detailed description of the game mechanics. Game mechanics are used to gamify an activity. Using individual game mechanics [23] or together [24], it can stimulate user motivation. Some of the common mechanics are points, badges, leaderboards, levels and challenges. Users are driven by game mechanics due to game dynamics. The game dynamics determine individual reactions in response to the applied mechanics [25]. These reactions try to satisfy basic needs and desires such as rewards, self-expression, altruism or competition. By selecting the right set of game mechanics in the website or application, it may be possible to create an experience that stimulates behaviour by fulfilling one or more needs.

3   Online Knowledge Sharing

When literature review is made for knowledge sharing, information sharing terminology is also often discussed. Researchers investigate in the literature whether the sharing takes place in the form of knowledge or information [26]. But there is no distinguish difference between knowledge sharing and information sharing. This is because of the knowledge acquired only when the recipient can interpret the meaning of the information using existing knowledge [27]. Because in literary studies the knowledge sharing terminology is often used in comparison with information sharing, this study will use the term knowledge sharing.

Knowledge sharing is referred to as a process where knowledge is given by one and accepted by another [27]. This knowledge is a subjective thing and is in the mind of one person. The advantages of a student's competitiveness after completing his or her education and entering a job environment are to use the knowledge to innovate new products or processes or services apart from enhancing existing ones efficiently and effectively [28]. The knowledge gained by this student cannot be purchased from anywhere. Therefore, the discussion interface should be built so that it can effectively manage such knowledge.

The discussion interface is used by students to seek or contribute knowledge [29]. In the process of seeking knowledge, students will read the content contributed by other students and this activity is the first step towards a more active participation in the online discussion interface [30]. The researcher has interpreted the activity without giving any contribution (read only) as a lurking or free-rider [31]. While the contributing process is an individual act that adds to joint efforts such as commenting or uploading media into an online site [32].

Both seeking and contributing knowledge in online will only occur when there are conversations between knowledge recipients and knowledge providers within the discussion interface [27]. Usually the form of an online conversation is visual text and illustration [33]. The process of sharing knowledge is an activity that uses appropriate forms of conversation to communicate knowledge to others effectively. It was found that the features and capabilities of an online learning environment support conversations among students [34]. Thus online knowledge sharing for this study is based on the definition of Sharratt & Usoro (2003) and is defined as a process of seeking and contributing knowledge by students in an online environment.

4 Motivation Theory for Online Knowledge Sharing

There are three motivational theories in the literature to explain ways to motivate students in e-learning learning. Among them are Flow Theory [35], Path-Goal Theory [36], and Self-Determination Theory [37]. These three theories explain motivation and how it affects the learning process. But it was found that extrinsic motivation did not affect the behaviour of knowledge sharing and only intrinsic motivation affects knowledge sharing behaviour [38]. Previous study identifies the intrinsic motivation requirement that affects the behaviour of online knowledge sharing at the discussion interface [14]. The Self-Determination Theory was adopted for the motivating design requirement.

Self-Determination Theory mostly used in empirical studies for self-determined and self motivated behaviour [37]. Thus this theory is adopted in this study to enhance student intrinsic motivation leading to self-determined knowledge sharing experience [39]. This theory has been empirically tested in the learning interface design that support the online knowledge sharing activities [40]. It was found that positive feedback increases the students' intrinsic motivation [41] while negative feedback reduces the students' intrinsic motivation [42].

Intrinsic motivation can be design in user interface [43] by using gamification strategies. These strategies can significantly increase students' intrinsic motivation in their online learning [44, 45]. Their use can enhance the students ability to share their knowledge online [46]. Therefore, this intrinsic motivation factor is designed in the user interface by using gamification strategies supported by Self-Determination Theory [47–49].

5 Motivation Design Criteria

Motivation is a theoretical construct used to describe student behaviour. It illustrates the cause of student action, desires, and needs. It can be a challenging job to give students an inner impetus in the process of sharing knowledge online. However, if motivation can be designed in user interface, student's knowledge sharing behaviour can be improved due to the internal encouragement. Understanding this concept, a set of motivation design in user interface were identified [14]. The Table 1 states the 10 identified motivation design criteria.

Table 1. Motivation design criteria

Sub-factor	Motivation design criteria
Autonomy	Option in avatar selection
	Choice in receiving feedback
	Option in media type
Competence	Unexpected response
	Direct response
	Positive response
	Show progress
Relatedness	Connect user interest
	Status visualization
	Show appreciation

6 Designing Motivation in User Interface

The interface is the link between the interface content and the user. The goal is to make sure easily perform their online knowledge sharing activities. While the interface design is a process of detailing a developed interface. This interface design is provided to ensure that interface planning is conducted well with taking into account the motivational criteria.

Once the motivation design criteria were identified, the motivating user interface for online knowledge sharing was developed. The developed user interface was named as "i-Discuss". The i-Discuss was developed based on Motivation Design Methodology [50].

6.1 Motivation Design Criteria 1: Option in Avatar Selection

The designed interface for i-Discuss provides an option for students to upload their avatar. The study adopted recommendations from a study to use his/her own picture as an avatar online [51]. This is for other students or lecturers to identify who contributes to online knowledge sharing.

6.2 Motivation Design Criteria 2: Choice in Receiving Feedback

The i-Discuss interface design allows an option in the receiving feedback in the discussion that a student will engage. With this the student no need to login in to this interface to get that information, instead it is sent to the registered student's email. It coincides with a study stating that students have the opportunity to receive feedback on their assignments immediately [52].

6.3 Motivation Design Criteria 3: Option in Media Type

The i-Discuss interface allows students to choose the appropriate media type for online knowledge sharing. Figure 1 shows the user interface that meets the motivation criteria 3.

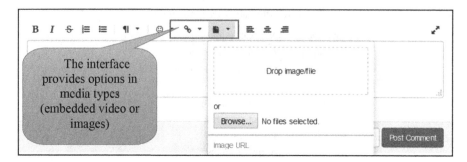

Fig. 1. i-Discuss interface with motivation design criteria 3

6.4   Motivation Design Criteria 4: Unexpected Response

The i-Discuss interface is designed to provide an unexpected response to the students. According to Exton & Murray (2014), efficiency can be enhanced with unexpected awards to the students. Therefore, this study has implemented some badges to provide responses towards their contribution in online discussion. Figure 2 shows the user interface that meets the motivation design criteria 4.

6.5   Motivation Design Criteria 5: Direct Response

The i-Discuss interface is designed to give the students direct responses about their position. This position will show the student's success visually in the leaderboard [53]. This position is based on the experience points gained by the students. Students who are on top the leaderboard are students who earn high experience points.

Fig. 2. i-Discuss interface with motivation design criteria 4

6.6   Motivation Design Criteria 6: Positive Response

The i-Discuss interface is designed to provide students with positive feedback on their knowledge sharing efforts. Although this interface has the option to provide negative feedback, this facility will not be used. This is because the negative feedback reduces intrinsic motivation [54] and it is supported by recent studies [42]. Figure 3 shows the user interface that meets the motivation design criteria 6.

Fig. 3. i-Discuss interface with motivation design criteria 6

6.7   Motivation Design Criteria 7: Show Progress

The i-Discuss interface is designed to display the students progress on their knowledge sharing activities. By highlighting student progress, their sense of competence can be enhanced [55]. Efficiency is one of the components in intrinsic motivation. Figure 4 shows the user interface that meets motivation design criteria 7.

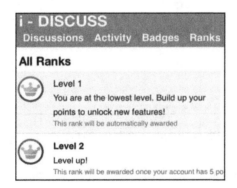

Fig. 4. i-Discuss interface with motivation design criteria 7

6.8   Motivation Design Criteria 8: Connect User Interest

The i-Discuss interface is designed to allow students to connect with other students with similar interests. Figure 5 shows the user interface that meets motivation design criteria 8.

Fig. 5. i-Discuss interface with motivation design criteria 8

6.9   Motivation Design Criteria 9: Status Visualization

The i-Discuss interface is designed to allow students to visualize their social status, reputation and contribution. The visualization of social status and student reputation can be illustrated using levels, badges and leaderboards and has been demonstrated in increased sense of interaction among students [40]. Figure 6 shows the user interface that meets motivation design criteria 9.

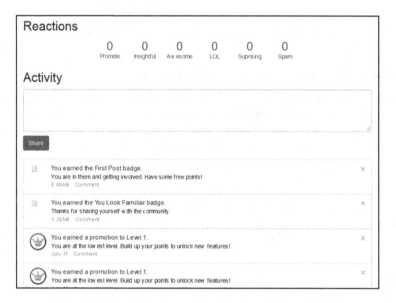

Fig. 6. i-Discuss interface with motivation design criteria 9

6.10   Motivation Design Criteria 10: Show Appreciation

The i-Discuss interface is designed to allow students to show appreciation to other people's contributions. Relatedness can be supported by the evaluation of other students' contributions that connect them with similar interests [40]. Figure 7 shows the user interface that meets the criteria 10.

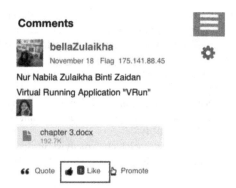

Fig. 7. i-Discuss interface with motivation design criteria 10

7 Conclusion

In review of online knowledge sharing literature, it was identified that not many studies comprehensively study on the design requirement of online discussion interface for knowledge sharing. Based upon the previous studies and Self-Determination Theory, a set of motivating design requirement for online knowledge sharing was identified [14]. Those design requirements were applied in practice by designing a prototype known as i-Discuss. This prototype was designed by applying the motivation design criteria. Future research will focus on evaluating the prototype for the existence of the motivation factor in it.

References

1. Moore, J.L., Dickson-Deane, C., Galyen, K.: e-Learning, online learning, and distance learning environments: are they the same? Internet High. Educ. **14**, 129–135 (2011)
2. Kearsley, G.: Online Education: Learning and Teaching in Cyberspace. Wadsworth, Belmont (2000)
3. Analoui, B.D., Sambrook, S., Doloriert, C.H.: Engaging students in group work to maximise tacit knowledge sharing and use. Int. J. Manag. Educ. **12**, 35–43 (2014)
4. Hsu, C.-L., Lin, J.C.-C.: Acceptance of blog usage: the roles of technology acceptance, social influence and knowledge sharing motivation. Inf. Manag. **45**, 65–74 (2008)
5. Ardichvili, A.: Learning and knowledge sharing in virtual communities of practice: motivators, barriers, and enablers. Adv. Dev. Hum. Resour. **10**, 541–554 (2008)
6. Dennen, V.P.: Pedagogical lurking: Student engagement in non-posting discussion behavior. Comput. Hum. Behav. **24**, 1624–1633 (2008). https://doi.org/10.1016/j.chb.2007.06.003
7. Muilenburg, L.Y., Berge, Z.L.: Student barriers to online learning: a factor analytic study. Distance Educ. **26**, 29–48 (2005)
8. Shoemaker, N.: Can universities encourage students' continued motivation for knowledge sharing and how can this help organizations? J. Coll. Teach. Learn. **11**, 99–114 (2014)
9. Soller, A., Lesgold, A.: A computational approach to analyzing online knowledge sharing interaction. In: Proceedings of Artificial Intelligence in Education, pp. 253–260 (2003)

10. Hanus, M.D., Fox, J.: Assessing the effects of gamification in the classroom: a longitudinal study on intrinsic motivation, social comparison, satisfaction, effort, and academic performance. Comput. Educ. **80**, 152–161 (2015). https://doi.org/10.1016/j.compedu.2014.08.019

11. Raymer, R., Design, E.-L.: Gamification: using game mechanics to enhance elearning. Elearn Mag. **2011**, 3 (2011)

12. Hamari, J., Koivisto, J., Sarsa, H.: Does gamification work?–a literature review of empirical studies on gamification. In: 2014 47th Hawaii International Conference on System Sciences (HICSS), pp. 3025–3034. IEEE (2014)

13. Oldfather, P., Dahl, K.: Toward a social constructivist reconceptualization of intrinsic motivation for literacy learning. J. Lit. Res. **26**, 139–158 (1994). https://doi.org/10.1080/10862969409547843

14. Ramakrisnan, P., Jaafar, A.: Usable, aesthetic, sociable and motivating interface for students' online knowledge sharing. In: Zaphiris, P., Ioannou, A. (eds.) LCT 2016. LNCS, vol. 9753, pp. 550–561. Springer, Cham (2016). https://doi.org/10.1007/978-3-319-39483-1_50

15. Deterding, S., Dixon, D., Khaled, R., Nacke, L.: From game design elements to gamefulness: defining gamification. In: Proceedings of the 15th international academic MindTrek conference: Envisioning future media environments, pp. 9–15. ACM (2011). https://doi.org/10.1145/1979742.1979575

16. Sailer, M., Hense, J., Mandl, H., Klevers, M.: Psychological perspectives on motivation through gamification. IxD&A. **19**, 28–37 (2013)

17. Sailer, M., Hense, J.U., Mayr, S.K., Mandl, H.: How gamification motivates: an experimental study of the effects of specific game design elements on psychological need satisfaction. Comput. Hum. Behav. **69**, 371–380 (2017)

18. da Rocha Seixas, L., Gomes, A.S., de Melo Filho, I.J.: Effectiveness of gamification in the engagement of students. Comput. Hum. Behav. **58**, 48–63 (2016)

19. Law, F.L., Kasirun, Z.M., Gan, C.K.: Gamification towards sustainable mobile application. In: 2011 5th Malaysian Conference in Software Engineering, MySEC 2011, pp. 349–353 (2011). https://doi.org/10.1109/MySEC.2011.6140696

20. Sicart, M.: Defining game mechanics. Game Stud. **8**, 1–14 (2008)

21. Bunchball Inc.: Gamification 101: An Introduction to the Use of Game Dynamics to Influence Behavior. Bunchball white Pap. 14 (2010). https://doi.org/10.1016/j.compedu.2012.12.020

22. Muntean, C.I.: Raising engagement in e-learning through gamification. In: Proceedings 6th International Conference on Virtual Learning ICVL, pp. 323–329 (2011)

23. Hakulinen, L., Auvinen, T., Korhonen, A.: The effect of achievement badges on students' behavior: an empirical study in a university-level computer science course. IJET **10**, 18–29 (2015)

24. Kuo, M.-S., Chuang, T.-Y.: How gamification motivates visits and engagement for online academic dissemination–an empirical study. Comput. Hum. Behav. **55**, 16–27 (2016). https://doi.org/10.1016/j.chb.2015.08.025

25. Zichermann, G., Cunningham, C.: Gamification by Design: Implementing Game Mechanics in Web and Mobile Apps. O'Reilly Media, Inc., Newton (2011)

26. Wang, S., Noe, R.A.: Knowledge sharing: a review and directions for future research. Hum. Resour. Manag. Rev. **20**, 115–131 (2010)

27. Sharratt, M., Usoro, A.: Understanding knowledge-sharing in online communities of practice. Electron. J. Knowl. Manag. **1**, 187–196 (2003)

28. Nonaka, I., Toyama, R., Nagata, A.: A firm as a knowledge-creating entity: a new perspective on the theory of the firm. Ind. Corp. Chang. **9**, 1–20 (2000)

29. Phang, C.W., Kankanhalli, A., Sabherwal, R.: Usability and sociability in online communities: a comparative study of knowledge seeking and contribution. J. Assoc. Inf. Syst. **10**, 721–747 (2009)

30. Nonnecke, B., Preece, J.: Lurker demographics: counting the silent. In: Proceedings of the SIGCHI Conference on Human Factors in Computing Systems, pp. 73–80. ACM (2000)

31. Smith, M.A., Kollock, P.: Communities in Cyberspace. Psychology Press, Abingdon (1999)

32. Preece, J., Shneiderman, B.: The reader-to-leader framework: motivating technology-mediated social participation. AIS Trans. Hum.-Comput. Interact. **1**, 13–32 (2009)

33. Eppler, M.J.: A comparison between concept maps, mind maps, conceptual diagrams, and visual metaphors as complementary tools for knowledge construction and sharing. Inf. Vis. **5**, 202–210 (2006)

34. Ma, W.W.K., Yuen, A.H.K.: Understanding online knowledge sharing: an interpersonal relationship perspective. Comput. Educ. **56**, 210–219 (2011). https://doi.org/10.1016/j.compedu.2010.08.004

35. Mirvis, P.H., Csikszentmihalyi, M., Csikzentmihaly, M.: Flow: the psychology of optimal experience. Acad. Manag. Rev. **16**, 636–640 (1991). https://doi.org/10.5465/AMR.1991.4279513

36. House, R.J.: A path goal theory of leader effectiveness. Adm. Sci. Q. **16**, 321–339 (1971). https://doi.org/10.2307/2391905

37. Deci, E.L., Ryan, R.M.: Overview of self-determination theory: an organismic dialectical perspective. Handb. Self-Determ. Res., 3–33 (2002)

38. Mallasi, H., Ainin, S.: Investigating knowledge sharing behaviour in academic environment. J. Organ. Knowl. Manag. **2015**, 1–20 (2015)

39. Giesbers, B., Rienties, B., Tempelaar, D., Gijselaers, W.: Investigating the relations between motivation, tool use, participation, and performance in an e-learning course using web-videoconferencing. Comput. Hum. Behav. **29**, 285–292 (2013)

40. Shi, L., Cristea, A.I., Hadzidedic, S., Dervishalidovic, N.: Contextual gamification of social interaction: towards increasing motivation in social e-learning (2014)

41. Deci, E.L.: Effects of externally mediated rewards on intrinsic motivation. J. Pers. Soc. Psychol. **18**, 105 (1971)

42. Weidinger, A.F., Spinath, B., Steinmayr, R.: Why does intrinsic motivation decline following negative feedback? the mediating role of ability self-concept and its moderation by goal orientations. Learn. Individ. Differ. **47**, 117–128 (2016)

43. Goldhaber, Tanya S., Langdon, Patrick M., Clarkson, P.John: Designing intrinsically motivating user interfaces for the ageing population. In: Stephanidis, C., Antona, M. (eds.) UAHCI 2013. LNCS, vol. 8010, pp. 68–77. Springer, Heidelberg (2013). https://doi.org/10.1007/978-3-642-39191-0_8

44. Banfield, J., Wilkerson, B.: Increasing student intrinsic motivation and self-efficacy through gamification pedagogy. Contemp. Issues Educ. Res. **7**, 291 (2014)

45. Wilson, D., Calongne, C., Henderson, S.B.: Gamification challenges and a case study in online learning. Internet Learn. **4**, 8 (2015)

46. Mekler, E.D., Brühlmann, F., Opwis, K., Tuch, A.N.: Do points, levels and leaderboards harm intrinsic motivation?: an empirical analysis of common gamification elements. In: Proceedings of the First International Conference on gameful design, research, and applications, pp. 66–73. ACM (2013)

47. Deci, E.L., Ryan, R.M.: Handbook of Self-determination Research. University Rochester Press, Rochester (2002)

48. Deterding, S.: Situated motivational affordances of game elements: a conceptual model. In: Gamification: Using Game Design Elements in Non-Gaming Contexts, a workshop at CHI (2011)

49. Zhang, P.: Technical opinion Motivational affordances: reasons for ICT design and use. Commun. ACM **51**, 145–147 (2008)
50. Ramakrisnan, P., Jaafar, A.: Motivation design methodology for online knowledge sharing interface. In: Badioze Zaman, H., et al. (eds.) Advances in Visual Informatics. IVIC 2017 Lecture Notes in Computer Science, vol. 10645, pp. 224–232. Springer, Cham (2017). https://doi.org/10.1007/978-3-319-70010-6_21
51. Ó'Brolcháin, F., Jacquemard, T., Monaghan, D., O'Connor, N., Novitzky, P., Gordijn, B.: The convergence of virtual reality and social networks: threats to privacy and autonomy. Sci. Eng. Ethics **22**, 1–29 (2016)
52. Brophy, J.E.: Motivating Students to Learn. Routledge, Abingdon (2013)
53. Berger, V., Schrader, U.: Fostering sustainable nutrition behavior through gamification. Sustainability **8**, 67 (2016)
54. Deci, E.L., Ryan, R.M.: Intrinsic Motivation. Wiley, Hoboken (1975)
55. Barata, G., Gama, S., Jorge, J., Gonçalves, D.: Engaging engineering students with gamification. In: 2013 5th International Conference on Games and Virtual Worlds for Serious Applications (VS-GAMES), pp. 1–8. IEEE (2013)

Ascertain Quality Attributes for Design and Development of New Improved Chatbots to Assess Customer Satisfaction Index (CSI): A Preliminary Study

Nurul Muizzah Johari, Halimah Badioze Zaman[(⊠)],
and Puteri N. E. Nohuddin

Institute of Visual Informatics, Universiti Kebangsaan Malaysia,
43600 Bangi, Selangor, Malaysia
halimahivi@ukm.edu.my

Abstract. Chatbots are artificial intelligence applications that are used as tools to communicate and assist humans in any task designed. It uses knowledge that has been provided by the developer and continue to learn on its own through a Natural Language Processing (NLP) approach. This paper highlights a study that aims to investigate quality attributes for a new improved Chatbots to assess customer satisfaction. The preliminary study was conducted to acquire prior understanding on the characteristics and functionalities capable of Chatbots to capture potential customer satisfaction in the tourism domain before a prototype is developed. The findings from this study reveal seven (7) plausible dimensions with several sub-factors of quality attributes that can be applied to new improved Chatbots. These dimensions and sub-factors are useful inputs to the Systems Requirement Specifications (SRS) for the design and development of new improved Chatbots to assess Customer Satisfaction Index (CSI).

Keywords: Chatbots · Quality attributes · Customer Satisfaction Index (CSI)

1 Introduction

Today, computer based Chatbot available for various fields is getting wider attention particularly, in finance and education. Chatbots are applications that imitate human intelligence through a training process, and proposes to reproduce ingenious conversations with humans, using regular natural language [1]. Chatbots are widely used by industries, as it is a method used by the customer services department to measure customer satisfaction [2]. The conversations used in Chatbots are mostly conducted through instant messaging, and accessible to all types of users. With familiar interface, users are comfortable and takes them less time to use the system.

Quality attributes of Chatbots encompasses multidisciplinary areas of engineering, technology, psychology and anthropology. This makes designing an effective new improved Chatbot a complex process. Moreover, today's Chatbots should not only be intelligent in order to study comments made by customers, but learner and provide logical and intelligent answers that best serve the customers' needs. This would be best

© Springer Nature Switzerland AG 2019
H. Badioze Zaman et al. (Eds.): IVIC 2019, LNCS 11870, pp. 135–146, 2019.
https://doi.org/10.1007/978-3-030-34032-2_13

catered by the Chatbots to analyse sentiment of customers. Sentiment is an opinion express by someone upon listening or reading something [3, 4].

As we transform into a digital economy, towards a society 5.0 era, the economic environment has become more competitive, expecting high quality service that is key for a sustainable competitive advantage. This will in turn lead to customer satisfaction, and it has a positive effect on any organisation's profitability. It has been known that satisfied customers generally form the foundation of any successful business, because most times, customer satisfaction leads to repetitive or repeat purchases, brand loyalty, positive word of mouth and sharing of positive sentiments on products or services received through social media. Generally, customer satisfaction is correlated directly to profitability.

On the other hand, Customer Satisfaction Index (CSI) is a tool that measures satisfaction level of customers towards certain product or services rendered. CSI is essential in order to provide a comprehensive insight to the customers' pre and post purchase behaviours [45, 46]. The index will help raise the company's service excellence standard, focus on quality improvement, elevate brand reputation, strengthen long term customer relationship and loyalty. CSI will serve as an indicator of the company's economic health. Thus, the design of a new intelligent Chatbot must study the systems requirement specifications (SRS) carefully, to include specifications that capture customer sentiment for customer satisfaction. This paper highlights the preliminary study on the plausible quality attributes of an effective Chatbot of which the new Chatbot can emulate and improve further, in order to assess Customer Satisfaction Index (CSI).

2   Related Works

2.1   Background on Chatbots

Generally, Chatbots are computer programmes which conduct conversations with humans via text using some form of Artificial Intelligence (AI) technology, particularly conversational AI [20, 22]. Many research have also shown that Chatbots can be built much more effectively without conversations [20, 21]. Typically though, many chatbots are designed with conversations. Whether they are designed with or without conversations, Chatbots in organisations, are normally used in dialog systems for various practical purposes such as e-commerce, customer service and information acquisition [5, 6, 9, 28]. Chatbots available currently, can be simple or sophisticated systems. The former, are built whereby, systems merely scan for keywords within the input, and then pull the most matching keywords or the most similar word pattern, from a database [7, 8]; whilst the latter, are built whereby systems use sophisticated natural language processing technologies [10, 11].

The history of Chatbots can be said to begin since 1950s with the famous Turing Test by Alan Turing, a computer scientist who proposes a test for machine intelligence. The test aimed to decide whether a machine have the ability of human-like intelligence or not [5, 12]. Initially, it was conducted as a game where humans interacted with two parties through textual messages. The respondents had to guess which of the two parties was a machine. If they were unable to guess correctly, then the machine passed the Turing Test. From 1960s onwards, Bots in various forms such as ELIZA, an AI Chatterbot [13, 14]; and other sensory Bots [15, 18, 27]; A.L.I.C.E. with natural language processing was popular for its realistic behavior [16, 26].

Four decades later, the IBM Watson uses Natural Language Processing (NLP) and machine learning to disclose the perception from large amount of data it collected. Watson today has been used successfully to monitor patients with health problems in various hospitals [7, 17, 29, 37, 38]. Search engines, particularly Google has made efforts to also step up their strategy in the field of Artificial Intelligence (AI) field [19, 30, 31, 33, 34]. Today, there are more than 12,000 bots available.

2.2 Chatbot Platforms

Currently, there are many platforms available to for Chatbots. The platforms provide a vast variety of functions for both the administrator and user. Some of the functions of Chatbot platforms include functions such as: assisting administrator in adding more functionalities to the bot by creating a flow, creating machine learning capabilities, and API integration [37, 38]. Chatbot platforms similar to the one listed by the Maruti Techlab [33–35], have also been able to help businesses run more smoothly and efficiently. In some parts of the world, some customers are already experiencing these 'intelligent' Bots servicing them. One example of an interesting Chatbot platform available is Landbot [36, 39]. It is an intuitive tool that allows businesses to create a personalised conversational chatbots to interact with prospective customers and generate leads. This platform also provide businesses to publish their Bots in different formats (landing page, website embed, pop-up, etc.) and on multiple channels (WhatsApp and Facebook Messenger).

2.3 Benefits of Chatbots

The benefits that can be contributed by Chatbots can be considered in many ways. A study conducted by Hill and Farreras [40], found that interaction between Chatbots and humans tend to last longer in a period compared to interactions among humans between strangers. This is because human-Chatbot interactions included shorter messages, and involved less complex vocabulary. Thus, interactions are more précised and practical. This also means that less waste of time on unnecessary small talk and decisions can be made much quicker. Many researchers view Chatbots' benefits as a supporter that aims to assist users to explore the content or services available online [18, 19, 25]. Aishwarya et al. [38]; and Colllum et al. [39], has said that Chatbots are promising in e-commerce [1, 46, 47], whereby customers find Chatbots as a helpful entity that provides them with useful answers to questions asked; provide them with helpful suggestions on purchasing products [3, 32, 41] help make wise orders, and constantly provide updates upon shipping status using natural language processing interface. Most of all, one cannot deny its powerful function in a very dynamic digital shared economy landscape today.

2.4   Chatbots for Tourism Domain

Chatbots especially ones that are embedded with AI technology, are beneficial to all service domains such as finance, healthcare and education. However, its benefits have recently touched the tourism domain, which represents a field with a collection of activities engaged by individuals in a short period of their daily lives, with the purpose of leisure, business, religious as well as for personal reasons [42, 45]. As reported by the Ministry of Tourism, Malaysia, there was 25.8 million of tourist that came to Malaysia in 2018. There has been significant increase in the number of tourists visiting Malaysia in 2018 compared to 2017 [44]. In Malaysia, tourism industry has grown rapidly after automobile and oil sector in terms of profits [44, 46]. There is thus, a need to improve the tourism services in order to increase further the growth of tourism industry in the country and meet the needs of the customers in order to sustain the Customer Satisfaction Index (CSI) in the tourism domain.

The use of Chabots has diversely been introduced to make human's searching activity in any field including tourism easier. This includes a system for providing recommendation to tourism on interesting places that can be visited, hotels and even suggestions on a whole-set of travel plans [44, 45]. Online Chatbots and one travel-accomodation apps have already proved their merits when it comes to bringing in business and providing customer support in the tourism domain. These are factors that the tourism industry heavily relies on today. As players in a competitive field, travel agencies, hotel booking services, and other businesses built around travel and tourism need to keep assessing their offerings constantly, to make sure that they draw and retain enough potential customers. With travel and accommodation Chatbots development becoming more apparent, this would be the way ahead for travel and tourism related businesses [23, 24].

2.5   Customer Satisfaction Index (CSI)

Customer satisfaction is the key to a successful product and services delivered by any organisation or company. Feedbacks by customers upon what has been provided can be given in a positive or negative manner. Customer Satisfaction Index (CSI) is a model used to measure customer satisfaction in a larger economic context, that represent the voice of the customers [46]. In the study conducted, the aim for customer satisfaction index (CSI) is to are categorise sentiments into views in order to: understand the needs of customers better; provide better enforcement for customer satisfaction on the features of the products and services presented; to provide better service and allows good visibility as well as to enforce the senses of customers towards the product and services is needed to be advertised.

2.6   Quality Attributes of Chatbots

Various studies have been conducted to study what are the quality attributes that should be included in new improved Chatbots [51–56]. There are others, but these were studies that placed quality as the central unifying theme to be investigated. Each study showed concern on the lack of guidance for designing quality into new Chatbots developed. Goh [52] called for standard metrics, and Košir bemoaned the lack of them. Content analysis conducted on these studies conducted, revealed that generally, the categories were aligned with the ISO 9241 concept of usability: "The effectiveness, efficiency and satisfaction with which specified users achieve specified goals in particular environments" [57]. Therefore, in this preliminary study we chose findings of a study by Saaty [58], who conducted a quality attributes study using the Analytic Hierarchy Process (AHP), and adapted these attributes to the needs and cultural environment of this country.

The Analytic Hierarchy Process used is a structured approach that involved both qualitative and quantitative considerations. Thus, the approach involved the creation of a hierarchy of quality attributes which were then represented by appropriate metrics, whereby comparisons were made between the quality attributes and one or more product options to assess its relative and global priorities. Various experiments with multiple users were conducted to select the right metrics with the appropriate quality attributes. The categories that were experimented upon were four (4) as follows: Performance, Humanity, Affect and Accessibility. Performance included quality attributes such as 'robustness to unexpected input', 'provides appropriate escalation channels'; Humanity included quality attributes such as 'transparent to inspection', 'able to maintain themed discussion' 'able to response to specific questions'; Affect included quality attributes such as 'provide greetings, pleasant personality', 'entertaining and engaging'; whilst Accessibility included quality attributes such as 'can detect meaning and intent', 'respond to social cues appropriately'. These four (4) categories were used as the fundamental area of categories and based on our detailed study, discussions with experts and past literature we came up with seven (7) dimensions that we felt were crucial in the design and development of new improved Chatbots. We also felt that one obvious category that needed to be included in the technical dimension in this digital economy of industry 4.0 is analytics. Thus, analytics technology, specifically sentiment analytics [12, 13, 17, 39, 41] is a sub-factor that cannot be excluded. Sentiment analytics techniques such as machine learning, lexicon-based, statistical model, rule-based approach, and aspect-based approach are aspects that needed to be taken into consideration in redefining dimension, categories and sub-factors when considering quality attributes of new improved Chatbots.

3   Methodology

The objective of the preliminary study conducted was to come up with initial systems requirements specifications (SRS) based on the plausible quality attributes for a new improved Chatbot to assess Customer Satisfaction Index (CSI) for the Tourism domain. The methodology used was mixed mode approach using the qualitative and development of software evolution-iterative design life cycle [48] in two (2) phases. This paper shall only discuss Phase I of the study, as indicated in Fig. 1, on the needs requirements to acquire the systems requirement specifications (SRS), based on the plausible quality attributes for the design and development of the new improved Chatbot. The requirements shall investigate on the best attributes for quality Chatbots [49–51] adapted and improved on those studied by Saaty [58].

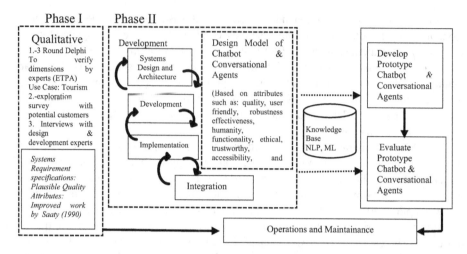

Fig. 1. Phase I mixed mode: qualitative approach to determine quality attributes Source: Adapted from: Zaman [48].

When the specifications are acquired, the prototype will be designed and built by the end of the Phase I. Phase I of the study was the qualitative approach. The qualitative approach began with a three (3) Round Delphi technique to get experts to study the dimensions and sub-factors (quality attributes) of the plausible quality attributes and verify their definitions. Round 1 (R1): questionnaires comprising the dimensions together with the sub-factors were emailed to ten (10) experts with an official letter, invitation and feedback form. The return of the R1 questionnaires within two (2) weeks were analysed and evaluated. Round 2 (R2): suggestions and feedback received were taken into consideration in constructing Delphi Round 2 questionnaire. The feedback were received two (2) weeks later from the ten (10) experts from the multi disciplinary fields of engineering, IT, psychology and anthropology (ETPA). Round 3 was the final round of the Delphi technique. The panel of experts were given the final definitions of the terminologies of the dimensions of the plausible quality attributes and their sub-factors; and they were asked to verify them through a questionnaire. The questionnaire consists also of an open-ended space where they were free to express their opinion on the final definitions provided. They were given two (2) weeks to respond and verify the definitions.

To strengthen the qualitative study, an exploration online survey was sent to thirty-two (32) samples in the tourism industry as a use case study and interviews were conducted with five (5) experts on design and development of intelligent systems including Chatbots. The completed questionnaires were received three (3) – four (4) weeks later. Reliability testing was conducted on the constructs and items of the questionnaires and the alpha cronbach value were all found to be reliable (alpha value for Chatbot exploration survey was 0.906 while the satisfaction level of Chatbot's users was 0.722.

4 Findings

The findings of this preliminary study was crucial in order to come up with the design and architecture of the Chatbot and conversational agents that would help customer satisfaction in the tourism industry and ultimately contribute to the Consumer Satisfaction Index (CSI) of the tourism industry in the country. In summary, the findings of the study was based on the plausible attributes that were verified by the multidisciplinary experts (ETPA) from the three (3) Round Delphi technique; the exploration survey conducted based on the use-case study of the tourism industry and interview with the five design and development experts of intelligent systems including Chatbots. The actual design and development took place in Phase II and will not be discussed in this paper. The results of the findings of the exploration use case study by the 32 samples from the tourism industry are as indicated in Table 1.

Table 1. Phase I exploration survey: plausible quality attributes of Chatbot

Dimensions	Attributes	Frequency (%)
Technical Functionalities	Sentiment analytics: Intelligent (Use AI, NLP, ML, Semantic technology)	27(84)
	User friendly to different cultures of tourists	26(81)
	Automated	1(3)
	Simple interface suitable for the different levels of tourists (educated, young, pensioners etc.)	21(65)
	Interactive (visual, audio) for different groups of tourists	19 (59)
	Multi Lingual to meet needs of multi-lingual tourists locally and globally	18(56)
	General ease of use for tourists	27(84)
Efficiency	Robust to manipulation and unexpected input by tourists	20(62.5)
	Provide appropriate escalation channels for tourists	19(59)
	Quick to answer questions from tourists globally	24(75)
	Can perform damage control easily because good image of country need to be maintained	19(59)
Effectiveness	Interprets statements and commands accurately especially for tourists	27(84)
	Linguistic accuracy in terms of outputs for tourists	23(71.8)
	Execute request/tasks accurately. Very crucial for tourism	23(71.8)
	Contains breadth of knowledge for tourists	20(62.5)
	Can perform simple problem solving for tourists	19(59)

(continued)

Table 1. (*continued*)

Dimensions	Attributes	Frequency (%)
Humanistic	Pleasant Chatbot personality that reflect 'personality of Malaysians'	16(50)
	Transparent and discloses Chatbot identity	17(53)
	Convincing with natural interaction	16(50)
	Able to respond correctly to questions posed by tourists	23(71.8)
	Can maintain themed discussion for example on places of interests, national heritages, global heritages, art, music and theatres	23(71.8)
Ethics	Ethics and cultural knowledge of users (local and foreign tourists)	26(81)
	Protect and respect privacy of tourists	27(84)
	Sensitivity to security of both the tourists and the country	27(84)
	Sensitivity to social concerns of the tourists	23(71.8)
	Trustworthiness	27(84)
	Awareness of social contexts of the tourists	19(59)
Technical Satisfaction	Provide greetings and convey right personality to tourists	14(43.7)
	Exude warmth and authenticity for tourists	15(46.8)
	Provide suitable conversational cues to tourists	16(50)
	Entertaining, fun and enable users (tourists) to enjoy interaction	23(71.8)
	Respond to mood of users (tourists)	20(62.5)
	Provide emotional information through tones and expressions	23(71.8)
Accessibility	Able to detect meaning or intent of tourists	26(81)
	Meet neurodiverse needs such as extra response time & text interface	23(71.8)
	Available 24/7 for tourists who are constantly on the go	23(71.8)

Adapted from: Saaty [58]

It can be observed from Table 1 that there were seven (7) dimensions of plausible quality attributes that can be used to design and develop new improved Chatbots. These dimensions as mentioned earlier, were verified through the three (3) Round Delphi technique with multi-disciplinary experts, the exploration survey sample tourists and interview with development experts. Based on Table 1 too, only one (1) sub-factor (i.e. sub-factor automation under dimension Technical functionalities), that scored very low at 3%; two sub-factors (i.e. under technical satisfaction dimension Technical satisfaction: '*Provide greetings and convey right personality to tourists*' and '*Exude warmth and authenticity for tourists*' that scored 43.7% and 46.8% respectively. The rest of the sub-factors in all the rest of the dimensions all scored above 50%; All dimensions had sub-factors that scored more than 5o%. In fact some even scored above 80%. Overall, the seven dimensions were all useful as indicators of quality attributes for new improved Chatbots.

Interviews conducted with the five (5) development experts also concurred with the dimensions of plausible quality attributes identified.

Designer and Developer Expert 1:

"...... technical functionalities and technical satisfaction is very important in design and development. However aspects on analytics especially sentiment analytics is important for Chabots in order that organisations can make good decision to enhance Customer Satisfaction Index."

Designer and Developer Expert 2:

"....... technical functionalities, Technical satisfaction, ethics and sentiment analyticst are crucial quality attributes of new improved Chatbots"

Designer and Developer Expert 3:

"......technical, humanistic aspects and analytics are important attributes for new improved Chatbots"

Designer and Developer Expert 4:

"Sentiment analytics based on semantic technology is most needed........."

Designer and Developer Expert 5:

"What is essential is technical, ethics, humanity and analytics. They are essential attributes to be considered for new improved Chatbots ...."

Based on the interview conducted with the five (5) intelligent systems development including Chatbots, it can be inferred that all agree that the technical aspects, and particularly analytics has to be included as the plausible quality attributes of new improved Chatbots. However, the other quality attributes and sub-factors identified are also contributory to a good and effective Chatbot that would meet consumers' satisfaction. These plausible quality attributes were useful initial input to the systems requirement specifications (SRS) of the new improved Chatbot for design and development purposes of this study.

5   Conclusion

Customer Satisfaction Index (CSI) is a useful measure on the effectiveness of a Chatbot. In order that customer opinions are collected and analysed in the best manner, quality attributes have to be built and verified. Thus, based on this preliminary study conducted, seven (7) dimensions with their sub-factors of quality attributes of new improved Chatbots were identified and verified through a three (3) Round Delphi technique by multi-disciplinary experts from the fields of Engineering, IT, Psychology and Anthropology (ETPA) and their specific attributes in order to enhance tourist experience in Malaysia and in order to improve the CSI to enhance economic growth in the tourism industry. Through effective and quality Chatbots, the tourism industry particularly, the authorities will gain on understanding the tourists' experiences and needs. This shall result in positive customer satisfaction index (CSI). The data obtained from this preliminary study is significant in helping the researchers to study the seven categories and sub- factors of the quality attributes of Chatbots to be considered for the design and development of the new improved Chatbot in Phase II.

References

1. Ranoliya, B.R., Raghuwanshi, N., Singh, S.: Chatbot for University Related FAQs (2017)
2. Xu, A., Liu, Z., Guo, Y., Sinha, V., Akkiraju, R.: A new chatbot for customer service on social media. In: Proceedings of the ACM Conference on Human Factors in Computing Systems (2017)
3. Delacroix, L.: Longman Advanced American Dictionary. Pearson Education, Edinburgh (2007)
4. Kowcika, A., Gupta, A., Sondhi, K., Shivhre, N., Kumar, R.: Sentiment analysis for social media. Int. J. Adv. Res. Comput. Sci. Softw. Eng. 3(1), 35–56 (2013)
5. Russell, S., Norvig, P.: Artificial Intelligence: A Modern Approach. Prentice Hall Press, Upper Saddle River (2009)
6. Rogers, E.M.: Diffusion of Innovations. Free Press, New York (1995)
7. Peters, H., Vogel, M.: Machine Learning Research Progress. Nova Science, New York (2010)
8. Kashyap, P.: Machine Learning for Decision Makers: Cognitive Computing. Apress, Bangalore (2017)
9. Aube, T., TechCruch: No UI is the new UI (2015). https://techcrunch.com/2015/11/11/no-ui-is-the-new-ui/. Accessed 23 Aug 2016
10. Peirson-Smith, T.: In the age of Artificial Intelligence, can we rise to the challenge of mass unemployment? (2017). http://www.scmp.com/comment/insightopinion/article/2122055/age-artificial-intelligence-can-we-rise-challenge-mass. Accessed 09 May 2018
11. Radziwill, N.M., Benton, M.C.: Evaluating quality of chatbots and intelligent conversational agents. arXiv preprint arXiv:1704.04579 (2017)
12. Rahman, A.M., Al Mamun, A., Islam, A.: Programming challenges of chatbot: current and future prospective. In: 2017 IEEE Region 10 Humanitarian Technology Conference (Project assistant0-HTC), pp. 75–78 (2017)
13. Ray, G., Muhanna, W.A., Barney, J.B.: Information technology and the performance of the customer service process: a resource-based analysis. MIS Q. 29(4), 625–652 (2005)
14. Shah, K.B., Shetty, M.S., Shah, D.P., Pamnani, R.: Approaches towards building a banking assistant. Int. J. Comput. Appl. 166(11), 1–6 (2017)
15. Shawar, B.A., Atwell, E.: Using corpora in machine-learning chatbot systems. Int. J. Corpus Linguist. 10(4), 489–516 (2005)
16. Shawar, B.A., Atwell, E.: Chatbots: are they really useful? In: Ldv Forum, vol. 22, no. 1, pp. 29–49 (2007)
17. Singh, A., Shree, R.: Recognition of natural language processing to manage digital electronic applications. Int. J. Adv. Res. Comput. Sci. 8(5), 1641–1643 (2017)
18. BAM & Conant, P.: Chatbots 101: Practical insights on business of Bots (2016). http://www.slideshare.net/BAM-Mobile/Chatbots101-practical-insights-on-the-business-of-bots. Accessed 20 Aug 2016
19. Beer, A.: Let's Chat! Designing methods for designing Chatbots (2015). http://botdesign.ai/lets-chat-beer-tesis. Accessed 9 Aug 2016
20. BI Intelligence and Business Insider UK. Messaging apps are now bigger than social networks (2016). http://uk.businessinsider.com/the-messaging-app-report-2015-11?r=US&IR=T

21. Charlier, M.: The O'Reilly Design Podcast: designing for the IoT, design's responsibility, and the importance of team dynamics. Interview with Mary Tressler for https://www.oreilly. com/ideas/martin-charlier-on-progrssive-approaches-to-iot-design. Accessed 23 June 2016
22. Connolly, E., Intercom: Principles of Bot design: Inside Intercom. https://blog.intercom.io/ principles-bot-design/. Accessed 29 Aug 2016
23. Debecker, A., VenturaBeat: Three stats that show Chatbots are here to stay. http:// venturabeat.com/2016/08/26/3-ststs-that-show-cahtbots-are-here-to-stay/. Accessed 29 Aug 2016
24. Engadet and Low, C.: Google's 'assistant' is at the core of its new hardware. https://www. engadget.com/2016/10/04/google-assistant-lands-on-new-pixel-phones/. Accessed 5 Sept 2016
25. Huet, E., Bloomberg: The humans hiding behind the Chatbots. http://www.bloomberg.com/ news/articles/2016-04-18/the-humans-hiding-behind-theChatbots. Accessed 29 Aug 2016
26. Huge Inc., van Hoof, P.: The designer's AI Study guide. http://www.hugeinc.com/ideas/ perspective/the-designers-ai-study-guide. Accessed 18 Aug 2016
27. McCarth, J.J., Stanford University: What is Artificial Intelligence? http://www-formal. standford.edu/jmc/whatisai.html. Accessed 5 Oct 2016
28. Kojouharov, S., VentureBeat: Five Tips for building the next great Chatbot. http:// venturebeat.com/2016/07/29/5-tips-for-building-the-next-great-chatbot/?. Accessed 15 Aug 2016
29. Livingston, T.: Bots are better without conversation. https://medium.com@tedlivingston/bots-are-better-without-conversation-fcf9e7634fc4#.z6qvrx8n5. Accessed 20 Aug 2016
30. Livingston, T.: The future of Chat isn't AI. https://medium.com@tedlivingston/the-future-of-chat-isn-t-ai-b07f65bc252#.9d1byI4j0. Accessed 20 Aug 2016
31. Mielke, C., Smashing Magazine: Conversational interfaces: Where are we heading? https:// www.smashingmagazine.com/2016/07/conversation. Accessed 20 Aug 2016
32. Mose, P., Deloitte: Technical trends 2016: Innovating in the digital era. https://www2.deloitte. com/content/dam/Deloitte/ru/Documents/Tehnology/DUP_TechTrends2016.pdf. Accessed 8 Sept 2016
33. Maruti Chatlabs. https://chatbotslife.com/@MarutiTech
34. Mortensen, D.: How we are building our AIs with Machine Learning. https://x.ai/how-to-teach-a-machine-to-understand-us. Accessed 5 Sept 2016
35. Mortensen, D., x.ai: Understanding the Facebook and Microsoft Chatbot revolution. https:// x.ai/understanding-the-facebook-and-microsoft-chatbot-revolution/. Accessed 5 Sept 2016
36. Nicholson, C., Gibson, A.: Artificial Intelligence, machine learning and deep learning Deeplearning4j: Open-source, distributed deep learning for the JVM. http://deeplearning4j. org/ai-machinelearning-deeplearning. Accessed 5 Oct 2016
37. Neilson, J.: 10 Heuristics for user interface design: Article by Neilson. https://www.nngroup. com/articles/ten-usability-heuristics/. Accessed 20 Aug 2016
38. Aishwarya, B., Vijay, G., Sachin, D.: Chatbot for business organization: utility, processes and significance. Int. J. Sci. Res. Comput. Sci. Eng. Inf. Technol. 2(6), 872–881 (2017)
39. Collumn, A., Costea, C., Joyeux, D., Hasan, O., Brunie, L.: A study and comparison of sentiment analysis methods for reputation evaluation. Rapport de recherche RR-LIRIS-2014-002 (2014)
40. Hill, J., Ford, W.R., Farreras, I.G.: Real conversations with artificial intelligence: a comparison between human-human online conversations and human-chatbot conversations. Computer. Hum. Behav. 49, 245–250 (2015)
41. Hippner, H., Rentzmann, R.: Text mining. Informatik Spektrum 29, 287–290 (2006)
42. Kowcika, A., Gupta, A., Sondhi, K., Shivhre, N., Kumar, R.: Sentiment analysis for social media. Int. J. Adv. Res. Comput. Sci. Softw. Eng. (2013)

43. Maruti TechLab: How to develop a chatbot from scratch. https://chatbotsmagazine.com/how-to-develop-a-chatbot-from-scratch-62bed1adab8c. Accessed 9 May 2017
44. MyTourismData: mytourismdata.tourism.gov.my (2019)
45. Nica, I., Tazl, O.A., Wotawa, F.: Chatbot-based tourist recommendations using model-based reasoning. In: Proceedings of the 20th International Configuration Workshop, pp. 27–28, September 2018
46. Poliakova, A.: Application of the customer satisfaction index (CSI) to transport services. Perner's Contact 5(4), 208–215 (2010)
47. Xu, A., Liu, Z., Guo, Y., Sinha, V., Akkiraju, R.: A new chatbot for customer service on social media. In: Proceeding of the ACM Conference on Human Factors in Computing Systems (2017)
48. Zaman, H.B.: Simbiosis Seni, Sains dan Teknologi Berasingan ke Multimedia-fusion. Penerbit Universiti Kebengsaan Malaysia (UKM), Bangi (2009)
49. Radziwill, N., Benton, M.C.: Neurodiversity secrets for innovation and design. SXSW Interactive, Austin TX (2017)
50. Neff, G., Nagy, P.: Automation, algorithms, and politics—talking to bots: symbiotic agency and the case of tay. Int. J. Commun. 10, 17 (2016)
51. Goh, O.S., Ardil, C., Wong, W., Fung, C.C.: A black-box approach for response quality evaluation of conversational agent systems. Int. J. Comput. Intell. 3(3), 195–203 (2007)
52. Vetter, M.: Quality aspects of bots. In: Meyerhoff, D., Laibarra, B., van der Pouw Kraan, R., Wallet, A. (eds.) Software Quality and Software Testing in Internet Times, pp. 165–184. Springer, Berlin (2002). https://doi.org/10.1007/978-3-642-56333-1_11
53. Košir, D.: Implementacija in testiranje klepetalnika. Doctoral dissertation, Univerza v Ljubljani (2013)
54. Coniam, D.: The linguistic accuracy of chatbots: usability from an ESL perspective. Text Talk 34(5), 545–567 (2014)
55. Meira, M.O., Canuto, A.M.P.: Evaluation of emotional agents' architectures: an approach based on quality metrics and the influence of emotions on users. In: Proceedings of the World Congress on Engineering, vol. 1 (2015)
56. Kaleem, M., Alobadi, O., O'Shea, J., Crockett, K.: Framework for the formulation of metrics for conversational agent evaluation. In: RE-WOCHAT: Workshop on Collecting and Generating Resources for Chatbots and Conversational Agents-Development and Evaluation Workshop Programme, 28 May 2016, p. 20 (2016)
57. Abran, A., Khelifi, A., Suryn, W., Seffah, A.: Consolidating the ISO usability models. In: Proceedings of 11th International Software Quality Management Conference, vol. 2003, pp. 23–25 (2003)
58. Saaty, T.L.: Decision Making for Leaders: The Analytic Hierarchy Process for Decisions in a Complex World. RWS Publications, Pittsburgh (1990)

Engineering and Digital Innovation for Society 5.0

Intrinsic Face Image Decomposition from RGB Images with Depth Cues

Shirui Liu[✉], Hamid A. Jalab, and Zhen Dai

University of Malaya, 59200 Kuala Lumpur, Malaysia
liu_shirui@siswa.um.edu.my

Abstract. As a pre-step of reconstructing face attributes technology, the quality of face intrinsic image decomposition result has a direct impact on the sub-operations of reconstructing face attributes detail. There are two challenging problems with the intrinsic face image decomposition methods which are the quality of face-base intrinsic image, and the details of the shading image. In this study a new image model for intrinsic face image decomposition from RGB images with depth cues is proposed to produce high quality results even with simple constraints. The proposed model consists of three main steps: face cropping operation, processing the RGB color normalization, and the super-pixel segmentation. The face image is first cropped to get face area, then a color normalization process for the cropped face image is used to normalize RGB pixels, and finally the super-pixel segmentation based on mean shift algorithm is applied which has a good performance on reduce artifact and shading image's detail retention. To evaluate the proposed model, both qualitative and quantitative assessments be used. The qualitative assessment is based on human subjective visual standards to compare the intrinsic images results, and the quantitative assessment is based on the data analyze of the image information entropy. Qualitative and quantitative results both demonstrate that the performance of the proposed model is better than other techniques in the field of intrinsic face image decomposition.

Keywords: Intrinsic image decomposition · Super-pixel segmentation · Human face · RGB and depth images

1 Introduction

Intrinsic image decomposition is an important problem that targets the recovery of shading and reflectance components from a single image [1]. The initial prototype of intrinsic image was proposed by Barrow and Tanenbaum [2]. The intrinsic image decomposition technology has been developed for more than forty years, the researchers have tried a variety of ways to overcome the difficulties and have contributed their best in getting high-quality results. The problem of intrinsic image decomposition still hasn't been satisfactorily resolved. Not minding whether to use the method of super-pixel, sparse and non-local priors, or L1 norm, is being utilized, the results of intrinsic image decomposition still can be optimized.

© Springer Nature Switzerland AG 2019
H. Badioze Zaman et al. (Eds.): IVIC 2019, LNCS 11870, pp. 149–156, 2019.
https://doi.org/10.1007/978-3-030-34032-2_14

In this study, the intrinsic image decomposition problem based on human faces has been chosen for following reasons: firstly, intrinsic image decomposition has been extensively studied in computer vision and graphics communities, because it can be beneficial to many vision applications and computer graphics such as image relighting and material property editing [3]. Secondly, intrinsic image decomposition is a kind of pre-step for the reconstructing of face attributes like geometry, texture, and illumination [4]. To get a better result of the editing face attributes, it is necessary to process the high-quality intrinsic image decomposition. Therefore, study on the intrinsic image decomposition for face image is very meaningful and essential.

This study aimed at proposing its own intrinsic image decomposition method. The proposed method effectively reduces the artifacts in the intrinsic image decomposition results, and at the same time effectively preserves the details of the shading intrinsic image. The paper is prepared as follows: The critical analysis of previous literature is being described in Sect. 2, while Sect. 3 details the proposed face intrinsic image decomposition algorithm. Section 4 describes the experimented result. Lastly, the paper concludes with Sect. 5.

2 Literature Review

The intrinsic image decomposition is the pre-step of quite amount of image processing applications, such as geometry, texture, and illumination [4]. The intrinsic image decomposition is a kind of reliable algorithm for separating illumination from reflectance in scenes would enable a range of applications, such as image-based resurfacing, texture transfer between images, relighting, material recognition, and other interior design tasks [5]. It is quite necessary and meaningful for us to know how to get the high quality intrinsic image for following reasons: Firstly, intrinsic images are quite effective on address the problems of illumination inconsistency between target and reference images and recolor images [6]; Secondly, intrinsic images also are the pre-step for the reconstructing face attributes like geometry, texture, and illumination, and then edit these attributes to edit the image [4]. In the meantime, artifact problem and shading image's detail lost are two bottlenecks for obtaining high quality intrinsic images. [7–9, 23–26]. There are two reasons can cause the artifact and detail lost: first, the inappropriate super-pixel segmentation [10, 27]; second, the high-frequency surface textures are sometimes factored into the shading image, it is difficult to balance the relationship between reduce the artifacts and keep the detail [11].

As an ill-posed problem, it's necessary to get some priors or additional clues before begin to do the intrinsic image decomposition. These priors include Ritinex, texture cues, color sparsity and depth information [7]. "Retinex" was coined by Land, the term is meant to capture this by combining the word "retina" with "cortex". In [21], the intrinsic image decomposition problem has been formulated as the minimization of a quadratic function and the Retinex theory was incorporated in the function. The Retinex theory has quite widely been used in past research, however, the situation that shading image cause a larger gradient does exist in some extreme conditions. The prior of texture cues is to separate the image to three layers, reflectance layer, shading layer and texture layer [3]. This kind of prior can reduce ambiguity caused by textures, but artifact is quite a problem which exist in the result of decomposition. Color sparsity is based on a simple observation: neighboring pixels usually have the same reflectance if their chromaticity is same or very similar [1]. The advantage of this additional clue is it perform good on intrinsic image decomposition, while the disadvantage is shadow are sometimes factored into the reflectance image. With the commoditization of depth cameras, several methods used depth information for better intrinsic decompose of RGB image [7]. This kind of image can be called as RGB and Depth image. Though it shows good performance on intrinsic image decomposition, it still has the artifact problem and sometimes the result may lose detail [12].

Base on RGB and Depth image, there are amount of method to processing the intrinsic image decomposition. Firstly, [7] use L1-norm to model the direct irradiance component - the main sub-component extracted from shading component, to get the intrinsic scene. [11] Proposed a method which use L1 norm for piecewise image flattening to achieve the intrinsic image results. Secondly, extend the "shape, illumination and reflectance from shading" (SIRFS) model to recovers intrinsic scene properties from a single image. SIRFS model is a kind of intrinsic image decomposition method which was developed by [13–15]. The factor of SIRFS is severely limited by its assumption that input images are segmented images of single objects, illuminated under a single global model of illumination natural images [14]. Thirdly, use the simple linear least squares formulation to decompose the shading component into a number of constituent components that account for different aspects of image formation [16]. Fourthly, use super-pixels in RGB and Depth decomposition. With the use of depth information, low frequency environment light can be represented by spherical harmonics and solved with super-pixels [10].

Super-pixel used in intrinsic image decomposition always represents a cluster of neighboring pixels which is considered to have homogeneous reflectance color, consistent color blocks can usually be found on real world objects [10]. At the same, instead of decompose the intrinsic image base on each pixel, it solves the problem base on each super-pixel and each super-pixel have only one super-pixel reflectance, it means that the amount of calculation will be reduced and then performance will improve a lot.

After forty years' development, the intrinsic image decomposition technology has been greatly improved, but through existing works it can be discover that the artifact problem and shading image's detail lost are still problems in intrinsic image area, are still exist in intrinsic image decomposition. This study focuses on how to reduce the artifacts appear and keep the detail of shading images when processing the intrinsic image decomposition based on face RGB and Depth images and to proposed a face intrinsic image decomposition algorithm to solve the problem we have mentioned.

3   Proposed Method

The proposed methodology of intrinsic face image decomposition from RGB images with depth cues has been described in this section. The proposed method improves on the traditional super-pixel segmentation method to produce high quality intrinsic image results even with simple constraints. The proposed model is given as a flow chart in

Fig. 1 which consists of three main steps: the face cropping operation, the RGB color normalization, and the super-pixel segmentation. The brief explanation of each steps is given in the following subsections.

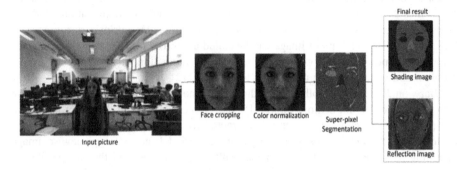

Fig. 1. Flow chart

3.1   Face Cropping

This study concerns images that contain representations of the human face. As processing the information contained in other areas of the image is not only of no use but would also increase the calculation time, cropping the face is a necessary operation. In the proposed method, it employs Viola–Jones framework [17] performs face detection and return the information about target face's position.

3.2   Color Normalization

Basri and Jacobs [18] proved that a pixel's RGB values on the surface can be linearly represented by using the nine-dimensional spherical harmonic basis function. To solve the nine-dimensional spherical harmonic basis function, the method of least squares has been used to solve the nine-dimensional spherical harmonic basis function. The formula of the nine-dimensional spherical harmonics can be express as:

$$I(p) = \sum_{j=1}^{9} \rho(P)l_j h_j(p) \tag{1}$$

Where $h(p)$ represents nine spherical harmonic basis functions, l denotes the coefficient of the spherical harmonic basis function, and $\rho(P)$ denotes normal color at (p).

3.3   Super-Pixel Segmentation

For super-pixel segmentation method can reduce the amount of data processed, the proposed method used super-pixel segmentation to reduce the computation time. In this research, super-pixel segmentation is applied using the mean shift algorithm due to its robustness in term of feature space analysis [22] and also its image segmentation performance [19]. The mean shift algorithm is a kind of mode-seeking algorithm that can be widely used in clustering, image segmentation, and tracking. There are n sample points x_i ($i = 1, \ldots, n,$) in d-dimensional space R_d. The basic form of the mean shift vector at point x can be expressed as:

$$M_h = \frac{1}{k} \sum_{x_i \in S_k} (x_i - x)$$ (2)

Where $(x_i - x)$ is x_i's drift vector relative to x, S_k means that there are k points in the specific area S_h in the sample point set x. S_h is not only a high-dimensional sphere area with radius h, but also the collection of y points. S_h can be expressed as:

$$S_h(x) = \left\{ y : (y - x)^T (y - x) \leq h^2 \right\}$$ (3)

Based on traditional mean shift algorithm, the flow chart of super pixel segmentation in proposed algorithm is shown in Fig. 2.

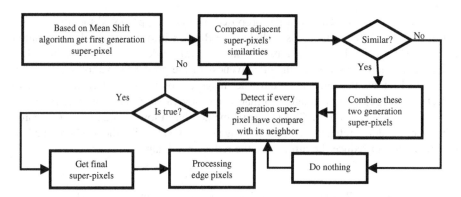

Fig. 2. Flow chart of super-pixel segmentation processing

4 Experimental Results

The dataset for this research comes from IAS-Lab RGB-D Face Dataset [20]. This dataset, representing 55 subjects, provides two different files for every frame: an XYZRGB point cloud (960 × 540 pixels) and an RGB image (1920 × 1080 pixels). For each face, the variations on pose, lighting and expression has provided by the dataset. The main goals of the proposed method are to reduce the artifacts which are caused by inappropriate super-pixel segmentation, and to keep the shading image's detail when processing the face intrinsic image decomposition. Figure 3 illustrate the result of this proposed technique. Where Fig. 3 shows that the proposed method can decompose the human face intrinsic image with different genders and poses. The image entropy is used to measure the performance of proposed method.

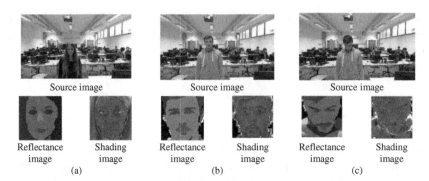

Fig. 3. Intrinsic image result of proposed method

$$\text{Entropy} = -\sum_{i=0}^{L} p(i) \times \log p(i) \qquad (4)$$

Where L denotes intensity levels in the target image, $p(i)$ denotes probability of each L.

To demonstrate the effects of the proposed method, the proposed method is compared with two different methods includes: the Retinex intrinsic image decomposition method [21] and the L1 image transform intrinsic image decomposition method [11]. The experimental results prove the effectiveness of the proposed method.

Table 1 shows the reflectance intrinsic image entropy values of each method. In reflectance image, the low image information entropy value means that more influence of shading has been reduced. The proposed method has a lower value when compared with other method's reflectance intrinsic image entropy value. So, the proposed method has the ability to reduce the artifact on the reflectance image.

Table 1. Reflectance intrinsic image entropy values of each methods.

Image\method	Zhao's algorithm	Bi's algorithm	Proposed method
Figure 3(a)	7.734	6.066	3.578
Figure 3(b)	6.960	7.134	3.517
Figure 3(c)	6.717	6.784	6.609

Table 2 shows the shading intrinsic image entropy values of each method. In shading intrinsic image, the higher image information entropy value shows that more detail has been kept. Table 2 shows that when compared with other methods' shading intrinsic image entropy values, the proposed method has the highest value. So, the proposed algorithm maintains the detail of shading intrinsic image.

Table 2. Shading intrinsic image entropy values of each method.

Image\method	Zhao's algorithm	Bi's algorithm	Proposed method
Figure 3(a)	5.046	5.994	6.246
Figure 3(b)	5.703	5.964	6.019
Figure 3(c)	5.197	5.375	6.385

5 Conclusion

In this research, the problem of intrinsic image decomposition from human face RGBD image have been investigated. Through improving the super-pixel segmentation method, the proposed method has been proven to be effective in reducing artifacts and maintaining the shading intrinsic image details when processing the intrinsic image decomposition based on face RGBD images. But still there are some limitations, the proposed method only focused on solving the artifact and shading intrinsic image detail loss problems caused by the inappropriate super-pixel segmentation. In conclusion, to get a better result of the intrinsic image should be the direction of the researchers' continuous efforts.

References

1. Shen, L., Yeo, C.: Intrinsic images decomposition using a local and global sparse representation of reflectance. In: 2011 IEEE Conference on Computer Vision and Pattern Recognition (CVPR), pp. 697–704. IEEE, June 2011
2. Barrow, H.G., Tannenbaum, J.M.: Recovering intrinsic scene characteristics from images. In: Hanson, A., Riseman, E. (eds.) Computer Vision Systems, 1st edn, 418 p. Academic Press (1978). ISBN 9780323151207
3. Jeon, J., Cho, S., Tong, X., Lee, S.: Intrinsic image decomposition using structure-texture separation and surface normals. In: Fleet, D., Pajdla, T., Schiele, B., Tuytelaars, T. (eds.) ECCV 2014. LNCS, vol. 8695, pp. 218–233. Springer, Cham (2014). https://doi.org/10.1007/978-3-319-10584-0_15
4. Shu, Z., Yumer, E., Hadap, S., Sunkavalli, K., Shechtman, E., Samaras, D.: Neural face editing with intrinsic image disentangling. arXiv preprint arXiv:1704.04131 (2017)
5. Bell, S., Bala, K., Snavely, N.: Intrinsic images in the wild. ACM Trans. Graph. (TOG) **33**(4), 159 (2014)
6. Liu, X., et al.: Intrinsic colorization. In: ACM Transactions on Graphics (TOG), vol. 27, no. 5, p. 152. ACM, December 2008
7. Wang, Y., Li, K., Yang, J., Ye, X.: Intrinsic decomposition from a single RGB-D image with sparse and non-local priors. In: 2017 IEEE International Conference on Multimedia and Expo (ICME), pp. 1201–1206. IEEE, July 2017
8. Yu, J.: Rank-constrained PCA for intrinsic images decomposition. In: 2016 IEEE International Conference on Image Processing (ICIP), pp. 3578–3582. IEEE, September 2016
9. Nie, X., Feng, W., Wan, L., Dai, H., Pun, C.M.: Intrinsic image decomposition by hierarchical L 0 sparsity. In: 2014 IEEE International Conference on Multimedia and Expo (ICME), pp. 1–6. IEEE, July 2014

10. Shi, J., Dong, Y., Tong, X., Chen, Y.: Efficient intrinsic image decomposition for RGBD images. In: Proceedings of the 21st ACM Symposium on Virtual Reality Software and Technology, pp. 17–25. ACM, November 2015

11. Bi, S., Han, X., Yu, Y.: An L 1 image transform for edge-preserving smoothing and scene-level intrinsic decomposition. ACM Trans. Graph. (TOG) **34**(4), 78 (2015)

12. Hachama, M., Ghanem, B., Wonka, P.: Intrinsic scene decomposition from RGB-D images. In: Proceedings of the IEEE International Conference on Computer Vision, pp. 810–818 (2015)

13. Barron, J.T., Malik, J.: High-frequency shape and albedo from shading using natural image statistics, pp. 2521–2528 (2011)

14. Barron, J.T., Malik, J.: Shape, albedo, and illumination from a single image of an unknown object. In: 2012 IEEE Conference on Computer Vision and Pattern Recognition (CVPR), pp. 334–341. IEEE, June 2012

15. Barron, J.T., Malik, J.: Intrinsic scene properties from a single RGB-D image. In: 2013 IEEE Conference on Computer Vision and Pattern Recognition (CVPR), pp. 17–24. IEEE, June 2013

16. Chen, Q., Koltun, V.: A simple model for intrinsic image decomposition with depth cues. In: 2013 IEEE International Conference on Computer Vision (ICCV), pp. 241–248. IEEE, December 2013

17. Viola, P., Jones, M.: Rapid object detection using a boosted cascade of simple features. In: 2001 Proceedings of the 2001 IEEE Computer Society Conference on Computer Vision and Pattern Recognition, CVPR 2001, vol. 1, p. 1. IEEE (2001)

18. Basri, R., Jacobs, D.: Lambertian reflectance and linear subspaces. In: 2001 Proceedings Eighth IEEE International Conference on Computer Vision, ICCV 2001, vol. 2, pp. 383–390. IEEE (2001)

19. Tao, W., Jin, H., Zhang, Y.: Color image segmentation based on mean shift and normalized cuts. IEEE Trans. Syst. Man Cybern. Part B (Cybern.) **37**(5), 1382–1389 (2007)

20. Munaro, M., Ghidoni, S., Dizmen, D.T., Menegatti, E.: A feature-based approach to people re-identification using skeleton keypoints. In: 2014 IEEE International Conference on Robotics and Automation (ICRA), pp. 5644–5651. IEEE, May 2014

21. Zhao, Q., Tan, P., Dai, Q., Shen, L., Wu, E., Lin, S.: A closed-form solution to retinex with nonlocal texture constraints. IEEE Trans. Pattern Anal. Mach. Intell. **34**(7), 1437–1444 (2012)

22. Comaniciu, D., Meer, P.: Mean shift: a robust approach toward feature space analysis. IEEE Trans. Pattern Anal. Mach. Intell. **24**(5), 603–619 (2002)

23. Saini, S., Sakurikar, P., Narayanan, P.J.: Intrinsic image decomposition using focal stacks. In: Proceedings of the Tenth Indian Conference on Computer Vision, Graphics and Image Processing, p. 88. ACM, December 2016

24. Han, G., Xie, X., Lai, J., Zheng, W.S.: Learning an intrinsic image decomposer using synthesized RGB-D dataset. IEEE Signal Process. Lett. **25**(6), 753–757 (2018)

25. Nestmeyer, T., Gehler, P.V.: Reflectance adaptive filtering improves intrinsic image estimation. In: Proceedings of the IEEE Conference on Computer Vision and Pattern Recognition, pp. 6789–6798 (2017)

26. Jiang, X., Pan, Q., Zheng, Y., Feng, X.: Intrinsic image extraction based on deconvolutional neural networks. In: 2017 International Conference on the Frontiers and Advances in Data Science (FADS), pp. 141–146. IEEE, October 2017

27. Jin, X., Gu, Y.: Superpixel-based intrinsic image decomposition of hyperspectral images. IEEE Trans. Geosci. Remote Sens. **55**(8), 4285–4295 (2017)

Haze Removal Algorithm Using Improved Restoration Model Based on Dark Channel Prior

Dai Zhen, Hamid A. Jalab[(✉)], and Liu Shirui

University of Malaya, 59200 Kuala Lumpur, Malaysia
{roycage, liu_shirui}@siswa.um.edu.my,
hamidjalab@um.edu.my

Abstract. In recent years, with the rapid development of social economy and the people's living standard, the awareness of security precaution is becoming increasingly important. However, in severe weather conditions, rain and haze have a large influence on the images obtained by video monitoring like the image contrast information, and it has a bad impact on the security work. So the clarity of images becomes very meaningful, and researchers start to pay attention to the field of image dehazing. Among many studies, the dark channel prior dehazing algorithm is a major breakthrough in the field of image dehazing technology. The advantages of this algorithm mainly focus on solving the problem of over-dependence on the physical model of sky scattering, poor adaptability to images containing sky regions and the problem that the processed images are too dark. Based on the atmospheric physical model, this research proposed a haze removal algorithm based on dark channel prior, which has good robustness to the bright sky regions, and also has a good effect on the edges. Firstly, the haze images were detected to see whether sky regions are included or not. Secondly, haze images that have sky regions were segmented into sky region and non-sky region. Then, the haze images that have sky regions and that have no sky regions were dehazed respectively. Finally, the quantitative assessment is based on NIQE (Natural Image Quality Evaluator), and the qualitative assessment is based on human subjective visual standards to compare the intrinsic images results. Quantitative and qualitative results both demonstrate that the performance of the proposed method is better than other techniques in the field of image dehazing that using dark channel prior. The proposed method can be better applied in the area of video image processing.

Keywords: Image dehazing · Dark channel prior · Restoration model · Image quality assessment

1 Introduction

Among all the bad weather, the frequency of haze is very high, and it can be seen that haze phenomenon has a great influence on human beings. At the same time, the haze has great interference with computer imaging. In the monitoring system and traffic network, whether video systems can work normally or not depends on the correctness

© Springer Nature Switzerland AG 2019
H. Badioze Zaman et al. (Eds.): IVIC 2019, LNCS 11870, pp. 157–169, 2019.
https://doi.org/10.1007/978-3-030-34032-2_15

and completeness of input image information [1]. At present, there are two important methods for haze removal in image processing [2]. One is based on haze image enhancement, and the other one is based on image restoration. The method of haze image enhancement mainly improves the visual effect of images by improving the contrast of haze images and highlight image details, so as to achieve the goal of image dehazing. The researchers combined traditional techniques with a deeper level of enhancing image contrast technology to form a more common technique used image enhancement method, including histogram homogenization [3–5], wavelet analysis [6], Retinex algorithm [7–9], etc. The method of haze image restoration needs to study the physical process of the degradation of haze image quality that based on the physical models in firstly. Then the parameters in the model are estimated to reduce the distortion in the process of degradation, and finally the high quality haze-free image after recovery is obtained. Image restoration technology based on physical model is mainly divided into multiple image restoration technology and single image restoration technology. Multiple image restoration technology is based on multiple images extracted from different weather conditions in the same scene, but time limit is relatively strict. So the researchers proposed a single image restoration technology [10]. There are many researches in haze removal based on single image restoration. For example, Tan used MRF model to construct the cost function of edge strength and used graph cut method to estimate the best illumination [11]. Fattal proposed a method that used independent component analysis to estimate scene irradiance [12]. He proposed a haze removal method based on dark channel prior in 2011 [13]. The focus of this research is to distinguish between sky and non-sky regions in haze images and use an improved restoration model based on dark channel prior for haze removal in single images, so as to realize the image dehazing function quickly and effectively. The study is prepared as follows: Sect. 2 provides a discussion on the existing literature, while Sect. 3 demonstrates details of the proposed haze removal algorithm. Section 4 describes the experimented result. Lastly, the paper concludes with Sect. 5.

2 Literature Review

Researchers propose a single image restoration technology designed to reduce computation time and to avoid environmental restrictions on image restoration. Based on the prior information, haze image restoration method is mainly aimed at the single image with haze, and intends to achieve the purpose of complete dehazing according to the change of the concentration of haze.

2.1 Haze Removal Technology Based on Dark Channel Prior

Currently, in the field of computer vision, the model is commonly used to describe the formation of haze image is [11, 12, 14].

$$I(x) = J(x)t(x) + A(1 - t(x)) \tag{1}$$

where, $I(x)$ is the haze image. $J(x)$ is the haze-free image. A is the atmospheric light. $t(x)$ is the transmittance of medium $(t(x) = e^{-\beta d(x)})$. $J(x)t(x)$ is the damping item. $A(1 - t(x))$ is the atmospheric scattering light. β is the atmospheric scattering coefficient. $d(x)$ is the depth of scene.

Through the observation of a large number of free-haze images, He [13] proposed prior information based on the statistical law of a large number of outdoor haze-free images. That means for most haze-free images of outdoor non-sky regions, there are at least pixels with a very low color channel value.

$$J^{dark}(x) = \min_{y \in \Omega(x)} \left(\min_{c \in \{r,g,b\}} J^c(y) \right) \tag{2}$$

Where, J^c is each channel of the color images. $\Omega(x)$ is a window centered on pixels x. J^{dark} goes to 0 by using the dark primaries principle. And the transmittance is estimated according to the dark channel prior principle and the haze image physical model. The atmospheric light value A is assumed to be known, and the transmittance within a local area is a constant value,

$$\tilde{t}(x) = 1 - \omega \min_{y \in \Omega(x)} \left(\min_{c} \frac{I^c(y)}{A^c} \right) \tag{3}$$

where, $\omega \in [0, 1]$, the parameter ω is introduced to retain a certain depth of field to make the image more natural and realistic. In order to improve the efficiency of haze removal based on dark channel prior, Dr. He used guided filtering instead of soft matting [13].

Then, the image after haze removal is obtained according to the atmospheric light. The first 0.1% pixels in the dark channel map been selected according to the brightness value. And then the value of the maximum brightness points is found in the coordinates of original haze image corresponding to these positions in dark channel image.

Finally, the follow formula is used to get the image after haze removal,

$$J(x) = \frac{I(x) - A}{max(\tilde{t}(x), t_0)} + A \tag{4}$$

2.2   Single Image Haze Removal Using Segmentation of Otsu

In order to solve the issue of low estimated transmittance in the sky regions by dark channel prior, an algorithm for haze removal based on an improved recursive segmentation derived from Otsu algorithm was proposed. Under the thought of image segmentation, the method is accurate to separate sky region via the improved recursive segmentation of Otsu rule [15], which is combined with the normalized gray values of the dark channel map to amend the estimation for the transmission in the sky region. Assuming that the haze image contains L gray values, the probability of gray value appearing in the haze image is $P_i = \frac{n_i}{N}, i = 0, 1, \ldots, L - 1$, where, n_i is number of pixels of gray values i, and N is total number of pixels in haze image. Haze image is divided into sky region and non-sky region by the threshold value x. Sky region $S = \{1,$

2,..., x}, non-sky region B ={$x + 1, x + 2,..., L$}. After obtaining the threshold of sky segmentation, the specific algorithm for haze removal is shown in the Fig. 1.

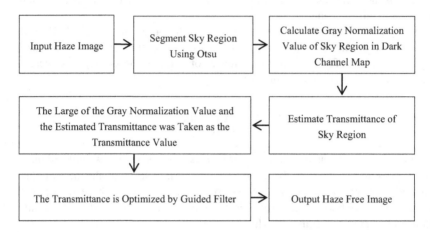

Fig. 1. Steps of method of single image haze removal using an improved recursive segmentation of Otsu

The recovered image preserves the true color and exhibits natural restoration between the boundary regions. In order to effectively deal with the color distortion and halos appearing in the sky region, this algorithm broadens the application of dark channel prior to a certain extent, which has a great prospect for processing outdoor haze images. However, in some specific haze images, the problem of image distortion still exists when this algorithm is used to process [16].

3   Proposed Method

This section presents a haze removal algorithm using improved restoration model based on dark channel prior. The proposed method divides the sky region of haze image, and optimizes the transmittance and the atmospheric light value.

3.1   Sky Region Detection and Segmentation

In the haze removal algorithm process of the dark channel prior, this prior law is not applicable in the sky region of the haze image, and the transmittance estimation in the sky region is not accurate and will be smaller than the actual value. This will result in significant noise amplification and color distortion in the restored dehazing image of the sky region [17]. Therefore, in order to obtain the effect of haze removal on the part of the sky region with good visual effects without affecting the overall haze removal, the sky region should be separated for transmittance correction. The specific steps are shown in Fig. 3.

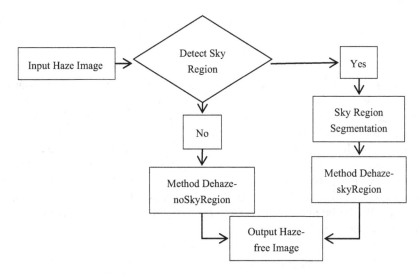

Fig. 2. The steps of proposed dehazing method

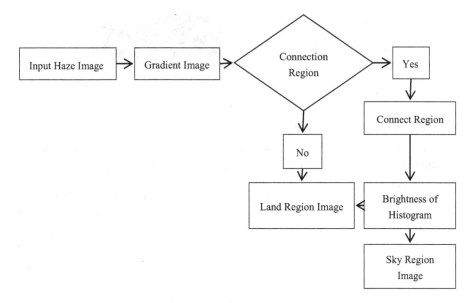

Fig. 3. The method of sky region segmentation

In this section, the gradient and brightness information of haze image are used to segment the sky region. Because the whole sky in the image is smooth, which means there is little change between the adjacent pixels of the image [18]. Therefore, it is easier to identify sky regions by using gradient information. And canny operator has been applied in this research. In the digital image, the simplest gradient expression is shown below:

$$G_y = f(x, y) - f(x - 1, y) \tag{4}$$

$$G_y = f(x, y) - f(x, y - 1) \tag{5}$$

Then calculate brightness histogram of the region that processed by gradient information, and select the threshold of brightness and mark the sky region by following steps, firstly calculate the brightness histogram, mark the mean brightness value as L_{mean}, and mark the max brightness value as L_{max}. Secondly Statistic the maximum frequency of brightness value in the brighter area $[L_{max} - 50, L_{max}]$, and denoted it as L_1. Then Statistic the minimum frequency of brightness value between mean value and maximum frequency brightness value $[L_{max}, L_1]$, and denoted it as L_2. Finally, $L_3 = (L_1 + L_2)/2$, if $L_{max} - L_3 \geq 30$, the brightness threshold is $L_3 + 40$, if $L_{max} - L_3 \leq 30$, the brightness threshold is $L_3 - 20$, others the brightness threshold is L_3. The result shows in Fig. 4.

(a)   (b)

Fig. 4. (a) Haze image, (b) Result after sky segmentation

3.2   Method Dehaze-skyRegion

For haze images with sky regions, this research optimized the value of transmittance and atmospheric light based on the dark channel dehazing theory, and the specific steps shown in Fig. 5.

Compared with method [13], this section optimized the transmittance in firstly, the value of sky region in the haze image is obtained by image segmentation. And the formula of optimized transmittance is shoes as follows:

$$J(t) = 1 - \omega * \frac{(15 * I_{sky} + \omega * J_{dark} * (255 - I_{sky}))}{255} \tag{6}$$

where, J_{dark} is the input dark channel image, I_{sky} is the value of gray scale image of the binary of sky region image, $I_{sky} \in (0, 255)$.

Then, for haze images with large brightness or sky regions, it is not advisable to calculate atmospheric light value in the method [13]. In this section, the average brightness value of the sky region is used to replace the way to calculate atmospheric light value in method [13], which can effectively avoid the problem of color distortion in the sky region after dehazing. Finally, the parameters of transmittance and atmospheric light value are modified, and the filter is optimized. For haze images with sky and large brightness regions, the effect of haze removal is shows in Fig. 6.

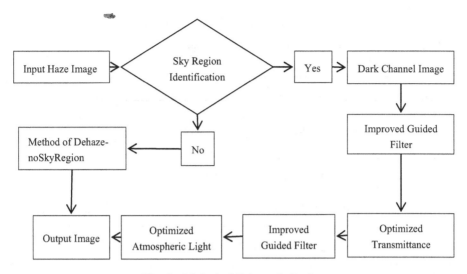

Fig. 5. Method of Dehaze-skyRegion

| (a) | (b) |

Fig. 6. (a) Haze image, (b) Haze-free image using method of dehaze-skyRegion

3.3 Method Dehaze-noSkyRegion

For haze images without sky regions, in this section, bilateral filter was used to replace the guided filter used in the method [13], and inverse filter was applied to the transmittance image. The specific steps are shown in Fig. 7.

In the process of collection, transmission and preservation, the image is often affected by various factors, such as channel interference and the loss of image information. Under the influence of these factors, the image will degrade to some extent. Image restoration method is to use some knowledge of degradation features to reconstruct the degraded image. The image restoration method by degradation function is inverse filtering. Set the Fourier transform before the degradation is $F(x, y)$, the Fourier transform after the degradation is $G(x, y)$, the Fourier transform of degradation function is $H(x, y)$. Inverse filter is the Fourier transform of degradation function divided by the degraded image. Then the estimated value of the Fourier transform of the degraded image is obtained, where $N(x, y)$ is the Fourier transform of noise.

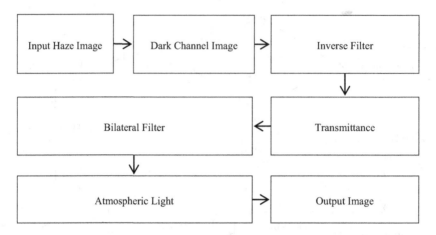

Fig. 7. Method of Dehaze-noSkyRegion

The original image $f(x,y)$ is processed by an image degradation restoration system $H(x,y)$, and then overlapped with noise $N(x,y)$ to obtain the degraded image $g(x,y)$ as is shown in Fig. 8.

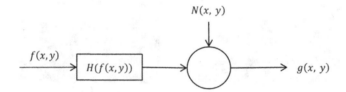

Fig. 8. General mathematical model of image degradation

The mathematical expression for $g(x,y)$ is

$$g(x,y) = H[f(x,y)] + N(x,y) \tag{7}$$

In this section, guided filter used in method [13] is replaced by bilateral filter. Bilateral filter is a non-linear smoothing filter for image, which preserves the edge and reduces the noise of images. It uses the weighted average of intensity values of nearby pixels to take the place of the intensity value of each pixel. The bilateral filter is defined as [18, 20]:

$$I_{filtered}(x) = \frac{1}{W_p} \sum_{x_i \in \Omega} I(x_i) f_r(||I(x_i) - I(x)||) g_s(||x_i - x||) \tag{8}$$

where, the normalization term

$$W_p = \sum_{x_i \in \Omega} f_r(||I(x_i) - I(x)||)g_s(||x_i - x||) \tag{9}$$

Ensure that the filter preserves image energy and $I_{filtered}$ is the filtered image, I refers to the original input image which is to be filtered, X is the coordinates of the present pixel to be filtered, Ω refers to the window centered in x, fr refers to the range kernel for smoothing differences in intensities, gs refers to the spatial kernel for smoothing differences in coordinates. After the weights are calculate, normalize them

$$I_D(i,j) = \frac{\sum_{k,l} I(k,l)\omega(i,j,k,l)}{\sum_{k,l} \omega(i,j,k,l)} \tag{10}$$

where, I_D refers to the denoised intensity of pixel (I, j).

For haze images without sky and large brightness regions, the outcome of haze removal is shown in Fig. 9.

(a)   (b)

Fig. 9. (a) Haze image, (b) Haze-free image using method of dehaze-noSkyRegion

3.4 Color Balance

When a color image is digitized, it often looks a little out of whack. This is due to the different sensitivity of the color channel, the enhancement factor and the offset, and it is called the tricolor imbalance. The color balance algorithm consists of the following three steps.

  i. Select two points color from the screen as gray.

$$F_1 = (R_1, G_1, B_1) \tag{11}$$

$$F_2 = (R_2, G_2, B_2) \tag{12}$$

  ii. Set the G component as reference, and match the R and B components.

$$F_1 = (R_1, G_1, B_1) \; F_1^* = (R_1, G_1, B_1) \tag{13}$$

$$F_2 = (R_2, G_2, B_2) \ F_2^* = (R_2, G_2, B_2) \tag{14}$$

iii. Find out k1 and k2 from $R_1^* = k1 * R_1 + k2$ and $R_2^* = k1 * R_2 + k2$, and find out
    l1 and l2 from $B_1^* = l1 * B_1 + l2$ and $B_2^* = l1 * B_2 + l2$.
iv. use

$$R(x, y)^* = k1 * R(x, y) + k2 \tag{15}$$

$$B(x, y)^* = l1 * B(x, y) + l2 \tag{16}$$

$$G(x, y)^* = G(x, y) \tag{17}$$

The processed image is the one after color balance. The effect of color balance is shown in Fig. 10.

(a)   (b)

Fig. 10. (a) Input image, (b) Output image using color balance

4 Experimental Results

The experiment is test on database which selected on website and database of monitoring system. Different types of images in the database are processed separately. At the same time, in this section, the results of proposed method will be compared with the method of dark channel prior [13] and the method based on Retinex [23]. And in this section, NIQE (Natural Image Quality Evaluator) is selected as the objective evaluation standard of images [21]. The image quality is measured by calculating the distance between the distorted image and the natural image fitting parameters. The specific calculation formula is as follows:

$$D\left(v_1, v_2, \sum\nolimits_1, \sum\nolimits_2\right) = \sqrt{(v_1 - v_2)^T (\frac{\sum_1 + \sum_2}{2})^{-1}(v_1 - v_2)} \tag{18}$$

A smaller score indicates better perceptual quality [19].

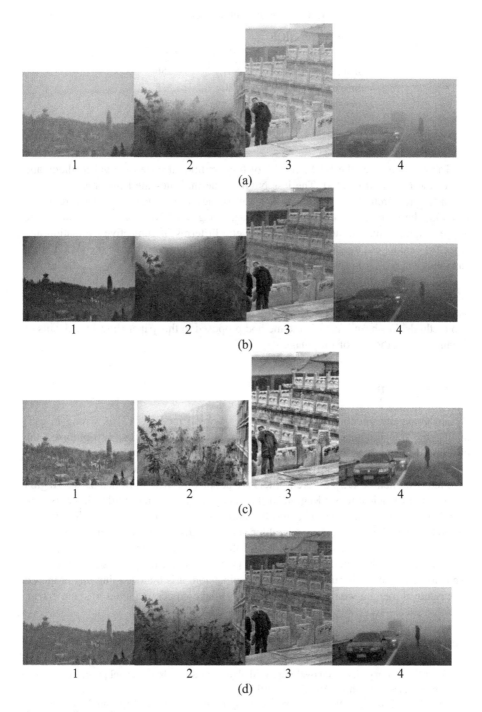

Fig. 11. Effects of two haze removal methods: (a) Haze image, (b) DCP, (c) Retinex, (d) Proposed method

Table 1. Score of result of each method

Haze image	NIQE		
	DCP[13]	Retinex [23]	Proposed
Image 1	4.780	4.861	4.756
Image 2	3.769	3.580	3.518
Image 3	2.595	2.665	2.508
Image 4	5.834	4.634	3.986

Table 1 illustrates the NIQE results of four traditional haze removal methods and that of the proposed method. The less NIQE value indicates the better result.

In this research, haze images in different scenes were selected for haze removal, including haze images with sky region, haze images without sky region, and haze images captured by monitoring equipment, etc. In terms of subjective evaluation and objective evaluation, the proposed method shows the better result than method [13] for haze removal which is shown in Fig. 11 and Table 1.

For the result of haze images with large sky region like image 1, the methods of DCP [13] and Retinex [23] show obvious distortion. For haze image 2, the result that used the proposed method is better in sky and bottom dark regions than that used other two methods. For haze image 3, the method proposed in this paper shows the details of distant view at the top of the image.

5   Conclusion

By analyzing the phenomenon that the haze removal method [13] is wrong in estimating the transmittance of sky and large bright regions, this study optimized the transmittance and atmospheric light value of the haze images containing sky and large bright regions. In order to solve the limitation of edge blur in the image processed by haze removal method [13], different filters are adopted in method of dehaze-skyRegion and method of dehze-noSkyRegion in this study to replace the guided filter used in haze removal method [13]. The results show that the proposed algorithm in this research solves the limitation of edge blur and color distortion in sky and large bright regions, and also improves the robustness of the whole algorithm. And the results have better values in NIQE than that in method [13]. However, the proposed method still needs to be improved in running speed. In conclusion, it is believed that this proposed haze removal method would be beneficial to in image processing areas to some extent.

References

1. Dong, Z.H.: Image haze removal improved algorithm using dark channel prior. M.S. thesis. Lanzhou Jiaotong University, China (2017)
2. Guo, P., Cai, Z.X., et al.: Overview and prospect of image dehazing technology. Comput. Appl. **09**(3), 675–689 (2010)

3. Sheng, H.L., Isa, N.A.M., Chen, H.O., et al.: A New histogram equalization method for digital image enhancement and brightness preservation. Signal Image Video Process. **09**(3), 675–689 (2015)
4. Hitam, M.S., Yussof, W.N.J.H.W., Awalludin, E.A., et al.: Mixture contrast limited adaptive histogram equation for underwater image enhancement. In: International Conference on Computer Applications Technology, pp. 1–5. IEEE (2013)
5. Kim, J.Y., Kim, L.S., Hwang, S.H.: An advanced contrast enhancement using partially overlapped sub-block histogram equation. IEEE Trans. Circuits Syst. Video Technol. **11**(4), 475–484 (2001)
6. Russo, F.: An image enhancement technique combining sharping and noise reduction. IEEE Trans. Instrum. Measur. **51**(4), 824–828 (2002)
7. Tang, L., Chen, S., Liu, W., et al.: Improved retinex image enhancement algorithm. Procedia Environ. Sci. **11**(Part A), 208–212 (2011)
8. Fu, X., Sun, Y., Liwang, M., et al.: A novel retinex based approach for image enhancement with illumination adjustment, pp. 1190–1194 (2014)
9. Zhang, G., Yan, P., Zhao, H., et al.: A survey of image enhancement algorithms based on retinex theory. In The Third International Conference on Computer Science & Education (2008)
10. Wang, Y.C.: Research on haze removal using dark channel prior. M.S. thesis, Dalian University of Technology, China (2011)
11. Tan, R.T.: Visibility in bad weather from a single image. In: Computer Vision and Pattern Recognition (CVPR), pp. 1–8 (2008)
12. Fattal, R.: Single image dehazing. ACM Trans. Graph. **27**(3), 721–729 (2008)
13. He, K.M., Sun, J., Tang, X.O.: Single image haze removal using dark channel prior. IEEE Trans. Pattern Anal. Mach. Intell. **33**, 2341–2353 (2011)
14. Narasimhan, S.G., Nayar, S.K.: Chromatic framework for vision in bad weather. In: Proceeding of IEEE Conference on Computer Vision and Pattern Recognition (CVPR), Hilton Head Island, SC, USA, pp. 1598–1605 (2000)
15. Otsu, N.: A threshold selection method from gray-level histogram. IEEE Trans. Syst. Man Cybern. **9**(1), 62–66 (2007)
16. Wu, Y.H., Pan, C., Wu, N.: Research on improved otsu recursively segmented single image dehazing algorithm. J. XI'an Univ. Sci. Technol. **1**, 438–444 (2017)
17. Mao, T.Y.: Optimizing technology of dark channel prior dehazing based on sky region segmentation. Nanjing University of Aeronautics and Astronautics (2017)
18. Mittal, A., Soundararajan, R., Bovik, A.C.: Making a completely blind image quality analyzer. IEEE Signal Process. Lett. **22**(3), 209–212 (2013)
19. Shanthi, S.A., Sulochana, C.H., Jerome, S.A.: Image denoising using bilateral in subsampled pyramid and nonsubsampled directional filter bank domain. J. Intell. Fuzzy Syst. **31**(1), 237–247 (2016)
20. Papari, G., Idowu, N., Varslot, T.: Fast bilateral filtering for denoising large 3D images. IEEE Trans. Image Process. **26**(1), 251–261) (2017)
21. Xiao, S.B., Li, Y.: Haze removal algorithm based on fast multi-scale retinex with color fidelity. Comput. Eng. Appl. **51**(06), 176–180 (2015)

Initial Investigation on Affective 4D Mathematics Model for Low Vision Learners (AM4LV)

Nurulnadwan Aziz[1]([✉]), Ariffin Abdul Mutalib[2], Siti Zulaiha Ahmad[1],
Sobihatun Nur Abdul Salam[2], and Nur Hazwani Mohamad Roseli[1]

[1] Universiti Teknologi MARA, Shah Alam, Malaysia
nuruln746@uitm.edu.my
[2] Institute of Creative Humanities, Multimedia, and Innovation,
School of Multimedia Technology and Innovation,
Universiti Utara Malaysia, Changlun, Malaysia

Abstract. Towards digital innovation for society 5.0, Mathematics plays roles as a very important subject to trigger critical thinking among students including low vision. Unfortunately, in this digital era, low vision learners still face difficulties in learning Mathematics as they have to adapt the mainstream pedagogical approach, which is totally inappropriate with their learning needs. Most previous studies reveal that low vision learners are lacking in terms of positive interactions that promote two-way communications between teachers and students. The scarcity of this aspect must be challenging for low vision learners because of their limitation in eyesight, which affects their stimulation in learning Mathematics. Therefore, the main aim of this study is to investigate the availability and the needs of affective content particularly in Mathematics specifically for low vision learners. To achieve that, user-centered design approach has been adapted. Mathematics and low vision teachers have been selected as the subjects of this study. Accordingly, the findings of this study reveal that affective content particularly in Mathematics is not yet exist, and that the need for it is urgent.

Keywords: Human computer interaction · Interaction design ·
User-centered design approach · Assistive Technology · Low vision

1 Introduction

The world's population of people with disabilities keeps increasing rapidly. One-third of them are children, younger than 15 years old [1]. In each year, it is estimated that over one-million children in the world are born with disabilities and unfortunately because of afford-less for long term medical cost, most of them are abandoned by their parents. Approximately 90% of them live in developing countries and 90% of children do not attend school [2]. They are disabled differently including physical, hearing, learning, and visual. Visual impairment is one of the disability types suffered by a large percentage of people with disabilities. Roughly, out of the world population, 285 million people are visually impaired. Particularly, 246 million of them are low vision (LV) and 39 million of them are blind [1]. In Malaysia, as at July 2018, there were

© Springer Nature Switzerland AG 2019
H. Badioze Zaman et al. (Eds.): IVIC 2019, LNCS 11870, pp. 170–181, 2019.
https://doi.org/10.1007/978-3-030-34032-2_16

472,228 officially registered disabled people (detailed in Table 1) [3]. Particularly, for visual impairment as recorded in December 2008, 21,204 people were registered, and it increased to 42,184 in June 2018 [3]. This indicates that within 10 years the number of visually-impaired people increased to be doubled. Therefore, research concerning the visually-impaired people as the main target user should be given primary concern since they are also a part of the resources for the country.

Table 1. Registered disabled people according to types of disability, 2008–2018

Types of disability	Year				
	2008	2012	2013	2014	2018
Visual impairment	**21,204**	**40,510**	**46,307**	**50,827**	**42,184**
Hearing impairment	32,850	53,357	58,706	62,153	35,273
Physical impairment	78,036	148,461	162,215	174,795	167,077
Learning Problem	91,303	165,281	178,800	188,911	163,904
Others	10,546	20,673	24,455	27,025	63,790
Total	**233,939**	**445,006**	**470,483**	**531,962**	**472,228**

1.1 Accessibility Among People with Disabilities Towards Digital Society 5.0

Initiatives in assisting the people with disabilities including LV learners to use technologies have been growing in most developing countries. Technologies that are purposely designed for people with disabilities is called Assistive Technology (AT), which is categorized into hardware (such as thermoform) and software (such as screen reader). The advancement of AT has triggered the meaningful impact on the various aspects of people with disabilities' life. The trend is clear that recent devices are designed to be accessible by people with disabilities such as smartphones and tablets [4]. In line with that, the education field is not an exception and has been revolutionary impacted by AT. As an evidence, there is an increasing interest in the usage of AT with educational technologies to promote formal and informal education to the people with disabilities. As an example, special education primary schools have been designed, equipped with computer labs and classrooms with Closed Circuit Televisions (CCTVs), large monitors, and screen magnification tools [5]. Those ATs are utilized as part of the teaching tools to support and improve learning activities in the specific educational setting where the disabled student could acquire knowledge and learn comfortably. However, most of the technologies focus on the technical aspects of hardware and software, which is difficult for LV learners at the primary school level to self-operate. This requires them to have an instructor. On the other hand, AT that specifically focuses in stimulating their active learning experience is highly scarce. Consequently, an Affective 4D Mathematics Model that is specifically designed to cater LV learners learning requirements need to be explored urgently.

1.2   Affective 4D Mathematics Model

Affective 4D Mathematical Model refers to a four-dimensional learning model that evokes (i) feelings, (ii) thoughts, (iii) emotions, and (iv) actions in learning activities of LV learners, particularly in Mathematics. The proposed model will contain specific components and elements that are able to stimulate the LV learners' interest to have positive interactions during their learning activities in Mathematics.

1.3   Mathematics in Education 5.0 Versus LV Learners

Mathematics in Education 5.0 plays an important role to assimilate the necessity of fundamental numerical concept and critical thinking skill among students, including LV learners. Unfortunately, in this digital era, LV learners need to adapt the general students' pedagogical approach in learning Mathematics that is obviously inappropriate with their learning needs and caused them some difficulties. Initial investigation reveals that it is insufficient positive interactivity between teacher and LV learners in promoting effective two-way communications [5]. The scarcity of this aspect must be challenging for LV learners because of their limitation in eyesight, which affects their stimulation in learning Mathematics. The facts also indicate that most of the existing Mathematics models mostly concern on the learning needs of general students, which is unable to make sense to LV learners [5]. Also, most of the existing affective learning models focus on detecting the users' emotions, rather than providing emotions to them particularly for LV learners. Therefore, further study needs to be urgently carried out in proposing a Mathematics model that specifically addresses LV learners as the target users. Consequently, the main aim of this study is to propose an Affective 4D Mathematics Model that is able to stimulate the LV learners to have positive interactions in learning Mathematics, which could then trigger them to have a critical thinking in problem-solving. Prior to develop the intended model, an initial investigation needs to be carried out to determine the availability and the needs of affective content that specifically addresses LV learners. To achieve that, an elicitation of literatures and user centered design approach has been utilized throughout the study as elaborated in the next section.

2   Materials and Methods

There are two phases involved in this study; phase one - elicitation of literature and phase two - user-centered design approach. In the first phase, 15 previous Mathematics models have been reviewed (from year 2013 to 2016) through systematic literature review technique. Specific keywords have been used to search the existing models (i.e. Mathematic Model + low vision) through credible online database; Scopus, ScienceDirect, IEEE, WoS, Emerald, and EBSCO Host. Meanwhile, in the second phase, user-centered design approach has been adapted to complete the study (Fig. 1). As the main target users of this study is LV learners, therefore qualitative method is the appropriate method.

The process of gathering data has been divided into two sessions, which are (i) observation and (ii) interview. They were carried out in Special Education Primary Schools; Integrated Primary School of Pokok Sena (Visual Impairment) and Special

Fig. 1. User centered design approach

Education Primary School of Alma (Visual Impairment). For the purpose of adhering to ethical procedure, this study gathered a formal permission from the school's principles for the purpose of gathering data. Both schools have been selected as they are the sample for learning in suburban area and urban area. Four experts involved in the interview sessions. Two of them are teachers of education for LV and another two are general teachers who are expert at Mathematics. Prior to beginning the interview session, a set of semi-structured interview questions have been prepared and the gathered data were recorded through audio and note taking. Then, data through observation were captured through photography and video. There were six LV learners involved in the observation. Figure 2 illustrates the summary of activities involved in this study.

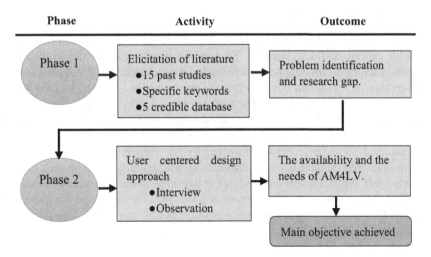

Fig. 2. Summary of research activities

3 Result Analysis and Discussion

This section analyzes and discusses the gathered results based on the research objective and research activities highlighted in the previous section. They are divided into two subsection which are (i) analysis on the previous models and (ii) analysis on observation and interview.

3.1 Analysis on the Previous Models

Table 2 exhibits 15 previous studies that propose Mathematics models as their main result. Eliciting the previous models reveals that some of the available Mathematics' learning materials were provided in the form of application that requires the teachers and students to operate using specific assistive device on their own [6, 16], which is possible for LV learners at primary schools to perform, particularly in developing countries. Combination of learning materials with assistive device is only applicable for certain subjects. This means the actual problem remains unsolved. Therefore, practically, the usage of assistive device is not the best solution to stimulate the LV learners' learning interest in Mathematics [7]. On the other hand, most existing models are incapable to drive an attention to LV learners [9, 11, 12, 14, 17, 18, 20, 22]. Generally, some of them specify the LV learners as the target users, but do not cater their needs in learning Mathematics [8]. They are categorized as generic models.

Also, there are Mathematics models developed for visually impaired students, but the interaction components give minimum focus upon them [19, 21]. In fact, the features are insufficiently tailored for the needs of the LV learners. Besides, it was also found that most existing affective learning models focus on detecting the emotions of the users rather than providing emotions to them particularly for LV learners [10, 13, 23]. Hence, it ought to be noted that this is the research gap that should be the focal point of this study.

3.2 Analysis on Observation

This section analyzes and discusses the data gathered through observation and interview with experts and LV learners. The session began with an observation over classroom teaching to investigate the current teaching practice for LV learners. From the observation, it was found that currently the most-practiced teaching method for LV learners is face to face interaction. The students were divided into small groups subjected to their progress. In school, the standard system for LV learners is similar as the general system. Generally, standard one to standard three are at level one and standard four to standard six are at level two. However, for LV learners the division of standard system is not based on their age as mainstream system, but it is based on their existing knowledge and skills. This means students at age nine is not necessarily in standard three. This study focuses on LV learners at level one. Figures 3 and 4 exhibits the sample of face to face interaction between teachers and students in classroom and computer lab.

Table 2. Existing learning model with their target learners including affective learning model, generic model in Mathematics, and generic models for LV learners.

No.	Author	Name of model	Target learners	Types of model	Justification
1.	[9]	Scratch Math Model	General pupils at primary school	Generic model in Mathematics	Not focus on the needs of LV learners
2.	[10]	Positive Affective Motivational Model	General students	Affective learning model	Only focus on detecting the emotions of the users rather than providing emotions to them
3.	[11]	Students' Affective Characteristics toward Mathematics Model	General students	Affective learning model	Affective learning model but only focus on general students
4.	[12]	Conceptual Design Model of Assistive Courseware	LV learners	Generic model for LV learners	Focus LV learners but the needs of learning Mathematics is insufficiently explored
5.	[13]	Affective Hybrid Deep Model for Audio-Visual Emotion Recognition	General students	Affective learning models	Only focus on detecting the emotions of the users rather than providing emotions to them
6.	[14]	Procedural Model of Mathematics Mobile Game	General children	Generic model in Mathematics	Not focus on the needs of LV learners
7.	[15]	Conceptual Design Model of Instructional Interfaces for Inclusive Courseware	Inclusive learners	Generic model for LV learners	Not focus on Mathematics and not specifically designed for LV learners
8.	[16]	Affective Model for Speech Emotion Recognition	General students	Affective learning models	Need extra device to operate it
9.	[17]	A Model of Labirinto Matematico Game	General children	Generic model in Mathematics	Specific for Mathematics but not for LV learners
10.	[18]	Instructional Learning Object Design Model for Mathematic	Learning disability students	Generic model in Mathematics	Specific for Mathematics but not for LV learners
11.	[19]	The Math Practice Framework	Visually-impaired students	Generic model in Mathematics	Typical model for Mathematics subject. Not address affective elements
12.	[20]	Conceptual Model of Mobile Numerical Application	Children with autism	Generic model in Mathematics	Specific for Mathematics but not for LV learners

(continued)

Table 2. (*continued*)

No.	Author	Name of model	Target learners	Types of model	Justification
13.	[21]	Game-based Model of Learning Mathematics	Visually-impaired students	Generic model in Mathematics	Typical model for Mathematics subject. Not address affective elements
14.	[22]	Conceptual Framework of Digital Learning and Teaching Mathematics	General children at primary school	Generic model in Mathematics	Not focus on the needs of LV learners
15.	[23]	Affective e-Learning Model for Recognizing Learner Emotions in Online Learning Environment	General students	Affective learning models	Only focus on detecting the emotions of the users rather than providing emotions to them

Fig. 3. Face to face interaction in classroom

Fig. 4. Face to face interaction in computer lab

In classroom, the learning activity is carried out in a formal setting, where the LV learners stay in front of the teacher. The teacher teaches then tries to get feedbacks from the LV learners as much as possible. This is to ensure that they are able to grab and understand the learning contents. Meanwhile, in computer lab the learning style is more relaxed and casual. The LV learners stay closed with the teacher (Fig. 4) then both of them keep interact among each other using the typical existing learning materials that are available online.

Due to the limited eyesight faced by the LV learners, the learning concept provided to them is not fixed to formal face to face. The teachers guided them to learn independently by exploring the learning content on their own. When this further investigated, it was found that most of the LV learners prefer to learn with animated materials (Fig. 5).

Fig. 5. Student self-learning

3.3   Analysis on Interview

In the next session, a series of interviews was carried out to support the data gathered through observation. In the interview, a set of semi-structured questions was asked (Table 3). Patton [23] has defined five types of interview questions which are (i) knowledge, (ii) experience, (iii) opinion, (iv) sensory, and (v) feeling. In this study the types of questions were developed based on [23].

Based on the interview, it was found that currently there is no standard design principles proposed by the Ministry of Education to stimulate the LV learners' learning interest in Mathematics through courseware (Q1). Also, it is reported that LV learners have to learn by using the similar learning materials that are provided for general students (i.e. typical textbook, flashcards, and typical online courseware) with the help of speech recognition software called JAWs and AT such as electronic magnifying glass and Closed Circuit Television (CCTV) (Q2). Figure 6 displays the sample of electronic magnifying glass and CCTV that has been utilized in Special Education School in Malaysia.

Table 3. Sample semi-structured interview question

No.	Questions	Types of questions
Q1.	Is there is any standard or design principles of Mathematics courseware specific for low vision learners provided by Ministry of Education?	Knowledge
Q2.	Currently how the low vision learners learn?	Experience
Q3.	How the teachers ensure that the low vision learners able to grasp the knowledge delivered to them?	Experience
Q4.	Is the current teaching method being appropriate to the low vision learners?	Experience
Q5.	Is there are any devices provided by MOE to assist the low vision learners in their learning activities?	Knowledge
Q6.	What are the most critical subject to the low vision learners?	Experience
Q7.	To what extend the AT could assist the low vision learners in their learning activities? particularly in Mathematics subject?	Experience
Q8.	In your opinion, is the Mathematics courseware specific for low vision learners is needed?	Opinion
Q9.	In your opinion, what are lack of existing coursewares?	Opinion
Q10.	How to attract the low vision learners to stay focus on their learning activities?	Sensory
Q11.	What are the appropriate elements of courseware for low vision learners?	Knowledge

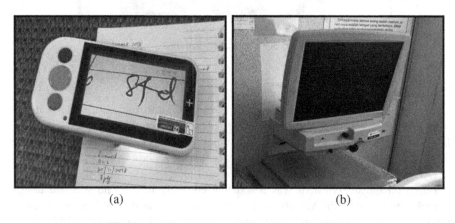

(a)   (b)

Fig. 6. (a) Electronic magnifying glass. (b) CCTV

As they have limited eyesight, it is too difficult for them to adapt the general students' learning styles. This situation triggers the perception that Mathematics is only for visually abled students. In regards to that, the pedagogical approach depends on the teachers' existing knowledge and creativity to ensure the LV learners able to grasp the delivered knowledge (Q3). Based on the interview that has been conducted, the best method for teachers to teach Mathematics to LV learners is by providing them a lot of exercise on A3-sized papers (Q3). However, this method is still difficult to stimulate the LV learners optimally to have positive interactions with teachers or even with their peers (Q4). Another practice is one-way interaction, in which teachers have to speak more because of the limited learning materials particularly in the form of affective learning model for Mathematics (Q3). Again, this method is difficult to inspire the LV learners to have two way of interaction (Q4).

The interview also reported that, in Special Education School, AT tools have been provided by the Ministry of Higher Education to assist teachers in preparing the learning materials for LV learners such as thermoform and embosser (Q5). Others are Closed Circuit Television (CCTV) and electronic magnifying glass particularly to assist the LV learners to learn on their own (Q5). However, the AT tools still not focus on the specific subject in particular Mathematics. Most of the time, the LV learners still need teachers to assist them in using the AT tools. Moreover, the situation becomes worst when the provided tools breakdown or need maintenance. In addition, most of the LV learners hate reading because of getting eyes strain after some reading and the use of LV devices such as electronically magnifying glasses was problematic for them. Psychologically they do not want to look different than their sighted peers.

Next question (Q6), it is reported that Mathematics is the most difficult subjects for LV learners as learning Mathematics need the students to have critical thinking. Moreover, as the LV learners face limited eyesight, it is difficult for teachers to stimulate them to have positive interactions in order to understand their problems as well as to measure their performance even though with the assistance of AT (Q7). Currently simple typical courseware with no multimedia elements has been provided for them (Fig. 7) (Q8). According to the interview, the typical courseware was meaningless to the LV learners as there is only text provided in the courseware (Q9). Combination of multimedia elements with the specific design principles for Mathematics subjects is important (Q8) (Q11). This obviously shows a comprehensive Affective 4D Mathematical Model is a necessity to stimulate the Mathematics' learning interest among the LV learners. Difficulties that faced by them in their learning activities indicates that the need for it is urgent (Q8). This is important to ensure LV learners are facilitated, enjoyed, and motivated them to stay focus on the learning activities similar to general students (Q10).

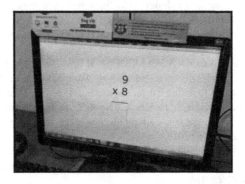

Fig. 7. Typical Mathematics courseware

4 Conclusion

The main objective of this study which is to investigate the availability and the needs of affective content particularly in Mathematics specific for LV learners has been achieved through elicitation of literature and user-centered design approach. The overall findings of this study reveal affective content particularly in Mathematics is insufficiently explored and the need for it is urgent. Particularly, the results from observation and interview indicates that the utilization of typical learning materials is difficult for LV learners as they are special person with unique characteristics. The use of AT provided by MOE also emphasizes on hardware which less interaction and unable to tackle the positive interaction as well as generate the curiosity attitude among the LV learners in learning Mathematics. Therefore, different approach is required to tackle them to have positive interactions in learning Mathematics. In addition, the findings from literatures also exposing that affective 4D Mathematics model specific for LV learners is not yet exist. Even though there are various types of model provided for LV learners, but it means nothing to LV learners as the design principles of the proposed models was inappropriate to LV learners learning needs. With the obtained results, this study intends to propose an Affective 4D Mathematics Model for LV Learners which is called as AM4LV to fulfill the needs of LV learners particularly in learning Mathematics. Hence, this requires more steps that have to be investigated deeply in future.

Acknowledgement. This study is supported by Fundamental Research Grant Scheme (grant number: FRGS/1/2018/ICT01/UUM/02/1) provided by the Ministry of Education, Malaysia. It is registered with SO code 14197.

References

1. World Health Organization. https://www.who.int/disabilities/world_report/2011/report/en/. Accessed 20 May 2019
2. Disabled World. https://www.disabled-world.com/disability/statistics/. Accessed 20 May 2019
3. Malaysia Department of Social Welfare. http://www.jkm.gov.my/
4. Petrovčič, A., Taipale, S., Rogelj, A., Dolničar, V.: Design of mobile phones for older adults: an empirical analysis of design guidelines and checklists for feature phones and smartphones. Int. J. Hum.-Comput. Interact. **34**(3), 251–264 (2018)
5. Ermiza, W.A. Current problem of low vision learners in learning activities. Pers. Commun. (2018)
6. Al-Rajhi, N., Al-Abdulkarim, A., Al-Khalifa, H.S., Al-Otaibi, H.M.: Making linear equations accessible for visually impaired students using 3D printing. In: 15th International Conference on Advanced Learning Technologies, pp. 432–433. IEEE, Washington (2015)
7. Benton, L., Saunders, P., Kalas, I., Hoyles, C., Noss, R.: Designing for learning mathematics through programming: a case study of pupils engaging with place value. Int. J. Child-Comput. Interact. **16**, 68–76 (2018)
8. Tosho, A., Ariffin, A.M., Salam, S.N.: Conceptual design model of instructional interfaces: courseware for inclusive education system (IID4C) distance learning. Int. J. Distance Educ. Technol. **14**(4), 68–82 (2016)

9. Bentona, L., Saundersa, P., Kalasa, I., Hoylesa, C., Nossa, R.: Designing for learning mathematics through programming: a case study of pupils engaging with place value. Int. J. Child-Comput. Interact. **16** (2017)
10. Brom, C., Dechterenko, F., Frollova, N., Starkova, T., Bromova, E., Mello, S.K.D.: Enjoyment or involvement? Affective motivational mediation during learning from a complex computerized simulation. Comput. Educ. **114**, 236–254 (2017)
11. Demir, E.: Testing measurement invariance of the students' affective characteristics model across gender sub-groups. Educ. Sci.: Theory Pract. **17**, 47–62 (2017)
12. Aziz, N., Mutalib, A.A.: Technology for visually-impaired: identifying flaws in assistive courseware. J. Telecommun. Electron. Comput. Eng. **10**(1–11), 83–86 (2018)
13. Zhang, X., Hu, B.Y., Ren, L., Fan, X.: Pathways to reading, mathematics, and science: examining domain-general correlates in young Chinese children. Contemp. Educ. Psychol. **51**, 366–377 (2017)
14. Sutopo, H., Pamungkas, W.: Developing mathematics mobile game to enhance learning for children. In: Proceeding IEEE International Conference on Computational Science and Engineering IEEE/IFIP International Conference on Embedded and Ubiquitous Computing CSE EUC, vol. 1, pp. 191–197. IEEE (2017)
15. Zhou, X., Guo, J., Bie, R.: Deep learning based affective model for speech emotion recognition, pp. 841–846 (2016)
16. Prado, R.T., Yudi Sirakawa, W.Y., Arruda, J.H.S., Pacheco, B.A., Concilio, I.A.S.: Labirinto Matemático: a game to stimulate. In: Proceeding of Latin American Conference Learning Objects and Technology, pp. 1–4. IEEE (2016)
17. Waiyakoon, S., Khlaisang, J., Koraneekij, P.: Development of an instructional learning object design model for tablets using game-based learning with scaffolding to enhance mathematical concepts for mathematic learning disability students. Procedia - Soc. Behav. Sci. **174**, 1489–1496 (2015)
18. Elkabani, I., Zantout, R.: A framework for helping the visually impaired learn and practice math. In: 5th International Conference on Information and Communication Technology and Accessibility, pp. 1–5 (2016)
19. Aziz, N.S.A., Ahmad, W.F.W.: Proposed conceptual model of mobile numerical application for children with autism. In: International Symposium on Mathematical Sciences and Computing Research, pp. 99–103 (2016)
20. Ferreira, F., Cavaco S.: Mathematics for all: a game-based learning environment for visually impaired students. In: Proceedings - Frontiers in Education Conference, FIE, pp. 1–3 (2015)
21. Ahmad, J., Jamaludin, Z.: Embedding interaction design in Wayang Kulit mathematics courseware. In: 3rd Proceeding of International Conference on User Science and Engineering. IEEE (2014)
22. Madurapperuma, A.P., Sandanayake, T.C.: Affective e-learning model for recognising learner emotions in online learning environment. In: International Conference on Advances in ICT for Emerging Regions. IEEE (2013)
23. Patton, M.Q.: Qualitative Research and Evaluation Method, 2nd edn. SAGE Publication Ltd., Thousand Oaks (2015)

Virtual Reality Ideal Learning: A Look into Future Medical Classroom

Mohd Yazid Bajuri[1(✉)], Kamarul Syariza Zamri[1],
Mohammad Nazir Ahmad[2], and Mohd Ismawira Mohd Ismail[2]

[1] Department of Orthopaedics and Traumatology,
Universiti Kebangsaan Malaysia Medical Centre,
Cheras, Kuala Lumpur, Malaysia
ezeds007@yahoo.com.my, geniuskamarul@gmail.com
[2] Institute of Visual Informatics (IVI), Faculty of Information Science
and Technology, Universiti Kebangsaan Malaysia, Bangi, Selangor, Malaysia

Abstract. Virtual Reality (VR) is a new technology and is a convenient way to be used as a teaching method in this era. We presented an innovative way of new teaching methods for undergraduate medical students in learning the anatomy of the human body. Learning anatomy using the conventional method by reading books and lectures only creates a lack of interest and most of the time, students will have problems to enhance their memory due to lack of interactive sessions. In this study, we collaborate with industry which has the experience in developing the VR system module. By using virtual reality, it provides interactive learning sessions during the class and encourages students to participate during the class which helps them to build up their self-esteem in answering the lecturer's questions during the examination. This technology was well received by the medical student and it can fasten their consolidation of knowledge in anatomy of the human body.

Keywords: Virtual reality · Learning · Classroom · Teaching · Medical

1 Introduction

Virtual Reality (VR) is an active and constructive approach which is being widely used in various field such as engineering, architectural, graphic design and as well as in medicine. It provides a great learning experience for the users as they will be actively participating in the VR classroom session by using all the five senses in learning, thus it enhances the students' cognitive function and aid in the memorization process. It is a novel learning environment that is being developed to enhance the students' experience in terms of learning and is the first of its kind to be used in a medical classroom in Malaysia.

From the previous study, students who are involved in learning using virtual reality felt an awesome experience in environment and able to socially interact or discuss with their colleagues in the virtual reality regarding the teaching materials. Specifically, the study significantly shows that learning and doing exercises in Virtual World are more effective. It helps to train the student to work as in the real situation. Particularly, they

© Springer Nature Switzerland AG 2019
H. Badioze Zaman et al. (Eds.): IVIC 2019, LNCS 11870, pp. 182–189, 2019.
https://doi.org/10.1007/978-3-030-34032-2_17

will integrate the theory and learn in virtual environments that gives authentic feeling to the students, and during which they will experience a new way of presence. It will be valuable for any research to analyze which aspects of the visual environment boost the sense of realism for users, whereas detracting from it for others [1]. A literature review has already been conducted regarding the use of Head-Mounted Displays (HMD) and Immersive VR in education. Immersive VR offers good benefits for learning. It allows direct interaction with the object and events that are physically out of our reach, it supports training in a very safe atmosphere avoiding potential dangers. With the help of using this virtual game approach, it attracts the learner's involvement and motivation while increasing a variety of learning styles supported [2].

A systematic review by Kyaw et al. suggesting that VR in education improves knowledge and skills outcome of health professionals when compared with the traditional method of teaching or other types of digital education such as offline and online digital education [3]. Educational institutions will get the advantage by the availability of this virtual technology which can be accessible to the student which are incomprehensible to imagine in the real classrooms mimicking a real environment in the virtual environment. This will make the student more interested and enthusiastic in learning anatomy [4]. This virtual classroom should be accessible to the student in which it creates a new way future teaching method to teach student in the classroom.

The main objectives in developing this module are to help the medical students to increase their knowledge as well as to encourage them to participate in the discussion session during classes plus explore the new method of teaching so that they are eager to learn more.

2 Methodology

2.1 System Development

For the development of this module, we collaborate with the industry which has vast experience in Virtual Reality usage whereby they using Geo Visionary and Visionary Render which allow for the realistic viewing of the anatomy in the module. The VR system is based on a personal computer (PC) environment (Windows 7/10).

The image of the anatomy was converted and translated into a 3D model. In order to stimulate the module, some of the modelings were developed for example class environment, the people in the class, the ambient and many more models using specific modeling software (Fig. 1A). The aforementioned model aid student who never touch the cadaver to be able to feel and immerse with the anatomy parts using virtual reality. After the modeling has been completely rendered, texturing the models play a major role to make it more realistic like a real cadaver which is a process of coloring and add some materials onto the developed model (Fig. 1B). The selection of the color must be realistic and appeared as similar to the real cadaver in reality. After all the models have been developed, the data then imported into the Visionary Render (Fig. 2). All the models were arranged properly according to their anatomical position. Then, the adjustment for color, texture, and material in the software was done simultaneously with shadow, lighting and other realistic features.

The graphical user interface was important in order for the student to be able to interact with the model in the virtual reality system so that they are able to gain knowledge and learn from the interface (Fig. 2).

Fig. 1. (A) Modelling the classroom environment in the VR system. (B) Texturing the model

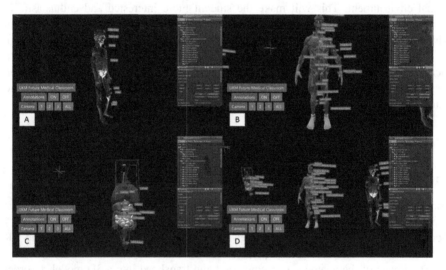

Fig. 2. Importing data into Visionary Render and graphical user interface (GUI) design in Visionary Render (A – Skeletal System; B – Muscle System; C – Organ System; D – Overall System)

Each of the organ and parts of the anatomy were labeled thoroughly. The annotation can be turn on and off according to our preferences. Thus, in the anatomy class using this VR system, the lecturer can make a quiz using this module so that it can enhance the student's memory regarding the anatomy.

2.2 Feedback Form Questionnaire

Once the whole module was successfully developed, 100 medical students of Universiti Kebangsaan Malaysia Medical Centre were recruited to have a hands-on experience on the virtual system that has been developed. They were required to test on the technical aspect of the system and share their experience on how they would see it if it is being practiced in their curriculum. Satisfaction questionnaire was given to assess the level of acceptance and feedbacks regarding usage of VR in anatomy teaching method.

3 Results

A module of anatomy was successfully being developed using virtual reality technology as shown in Figs. 1 and 2. The module has been tested by the medical student at Universiti Kebangsaan Malaysia Medical Centre and was led and guided by the lecturer.

A hundred questionnaires (Appendix) were evaluated by the medical students who did the hands-on and learned anatomy using the VR system module. Based on the result (Fig. 3), the students were very satisfied using this VR system module. Although some commented that little improvement had to be made to ensure that this VR system module is convenient to be used in the future. Out of a hundred medical students, eighty (80%) of them recommends and enjoyed using the VR system module during anatomy class. Fifteen (15%) medical students still preferred using self-study whereas five (5%) students feel comfortable to use conventional teaching methods.

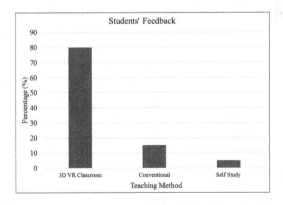

Fig. 3. Students' feedback

Table 1 shows a summary of the students' feedback form questionnaires whereby they all have attended the future medical classroom to learn the anatomy using virtual reality.

Table 1. Summary of the students' feedback form questionnaire

Course Content	Strongly agree (%)	Agree (%)	Uncertain (%)	Disagree (%)	Strongly disagree (%)
Objective were clear	88	12	0	0	0
Workload manageable	64	32	4	0	0
Well Organized	68	32	0	0	0
Student Contribution					
Actively participate	52	44	4	0	0
Student make progression	48	48	4	0	0
Environment and Teaching Method					
Well structured	56	44	0	0	0
Encourage participation	84	16	0	0	0
Conductive environment	68	20	0	12	0
Classroom satisfactory	44	44	4	8	0
Quality of Delivery					
Stimulate interest	88	12	0	0	0
Pace of course appropriate	76	20	0	4	0
Ideas and concepts were presented clearly	80	16	0	4	0
Assessment					
Assessment method reasonable	60	40	0	0	0
Feedback assessment was timely	56	44	0	0	0
Feedback assessment was helpful	60	40	0	0	0
Level of Attendance	<20%	21–40%	41–60%	61–80%	>81%
Student	0	0	4	20	76

4 Discussion

Social interaction and credibility are key parts of situated learning and it seems that Virtual World (VW) exercises will satisfy these criteria effectively. Specifically, evidence significantly indicates that VW exercises offer effective opportunities for situated learning in accident investigation and risk assessment. Particularly, they will facilitate the integration of theory and learning environment that gives an authentic feeling to the students, and during which they will experience a way of presence. It can be valuable for any research to investigate what aspects of the visual environment that is able to boost the sense of realism for the users while detracting it for others [1]. Based on our study, 52% of them are strongly agree and 44% of them agrees actively participate in the classroom which shows a great progression in learning anatomy using virtual reality classroom. It shows that the student felt that using this VW exercises and VR method of teaching gives them an opportunity to fasten the consolidation of knowledge and at the same time actively participate in the learning process.

Regarding the course content; 88% of the student strongly agree that the objective of the course content using virtual reality is clear, 64% students said that the workload to study anatomy is manageable and 68% of them strongly agreed that this course content is well organized and relevant to teach in the class. One of the VR teaching methods by Second Life® SL has been used effectively as a platform for online courses in a graduate distance education program at West Virginia University (WVU), a major university with an in-depth rural place among the state and other areas of the Appalachian region. Course evaluations have shown that almost all students showed satisfaction with this course format, and many students have indicated that they prefer SL for instruction [5].

Based on the environment and teaching methods, 56% strongly agree and 44% agree that this teaching method is well structured supported by 84% strongly agreed and 16% agreed that this module also encourages student participation during the class. Students who are attending the class, 68% strongly agreed and 20% agreed that the teaching was conducted in conductive environment which brings 44% of them are strongly agreed and agreed satisfied with classroom environment. Some instructors who usually use SL in courses report that they were comfortable teaching in SL and have noted that their students seemed to be more focus and engaged in learning activities within the virtual world compared to classes conducted in the desktop conferencing system. The program is committed to using the SL for teaching preparation, and faculty can continue to experiment with new applications of this virtual immersive environment for teaching and learning at a distance [6].

The significant improvement in the teaching method for medical students plays a major role in producing a great doctor in the future. In this study, 100 medical students already evaluated this technology when applying to anatomy class with the lecturers. In terms of teaching quality, 88% strongly agree and 12% agree that this future medical classroom can stimulate interest. Furthermore, 76% strongly agree and 20% agree that the pace, of course, was appropriate which can be accepted by the student. The majority are strongly agreed (80%) that the ideas and concepts were presented clearly. This shows that the VR system module that we developed was practical when we used it during anatomy class. Medical students were all enthusiastic and actively participated in the discussion during the class. It shows that they were all eager to learn anatomy in a different teaching method rather than the conventional way. Using this new teaching method, it can increase students' cognitive function which they can analyze the learning content effectively and organized, can classify the information faster and able to identify important anatomies in the class. A study by Fernandez, shows that people easily understand abstract concepts when learning in three dimensions [7].

Besides, this VR system module also able to make the students become more responsive and participate in learning activities and bring more good competition in their learning's development among themselves. Students can increase their psychomotor function by getting engage in technologically in this collaborative learning using various techniques of information and communication technology (ICT) thus enhancing their knowledge. VR has been used in various fields of study, including construction management [8], surgery [9] and also nursing [10] as a way to motivate and encourage students to improve performance outcomes. De Faria et al. have conducted a study to compare three groups of students using different teaching methods. Group 1 was instructed by conventional methods, Group 2 engaged in interactive nonstereoscopic learning methods and Group 3 students were instructed by interactive stereoscopic lectures. Between these three groups, there were significant differences when Group 2 and 3 were compared with Group 1 ($p < 0.05$) [11]. This literature suggests that using VR in learning can improve students' performance and it is very effective. This technology is now available for use in undergraduate medical school.

5 Conclusion

As technology develops, a VR is a new way of teaching method for undergraduate medical school in learning the anatomy of the human body. To truly transform medical education, it is imperative that medical lecturers use the current technology and related pedagogy to our students' advantage whenever appropriate. This VR system module was well received by the medical students and most of them preferred learning anatomy using VR interactive learning. This study also enhances the understanding of human anatomy and develop knowledge among medical students.

References

1. Falconer, L.: Situated learning in virtual simulations: researching the authentic dimension in virtual worlds. J. Interact. Learn. Res. **24**(3), 285–300 (2013)
2. Michela, O., Laura F.: A literature review on immersive virtual reality in education: state of the art and perspectives. In: eLearning and Software for Education (eLSE) Conference (2015)
3. Kyaw, B.M., et al.: Virtual reality for health professions education: systematic review and meta-analysis by the digital health education collaboration. J. Med. Internet Res. **21**(1), e12959 (2019)
4. Martín-Gutiérrez, J., Mora, C.E., Anorbe-Diaz, B., Gonzalez-Marrero, A.: Virtual technologies trends in education. EURASIA J. Math. Sci. Technol. Educ. **13**(2), 469–486 (2016)
5. Hartley, M.D., Ludlow, B.L., Duff, M.C.: Second Life®: A 3D virtual immersive environment for teacher preparation courses in a distance education program. Rural Spec. Educ. Q. **34**(3), 21–25 (2015)
6. McHugh, M., Farley, D., Maechling, C.R., Dunlop, D.D., French, D.D., Holl, J.L.: Corporate philanthropy toward community health improvement in manufacturing communities. J. Community Health **43**(3), 560–565 (2018)
7. Fernandez, M.: Augmented virtual reality: how to improve education systems. Hig. Learn. Res. Commun. **7**(1), 1–15 (2017)
8. Sacks, R., Perlman, A., Barak, R.: Construction safety training using immersive virtual reality. Constr. Manag. Econ. **31**(9), 1005–1017 (2013)

9. McCloy, R., Stone, R.: Virtual reality in surgery. BMJ **323**(7318), 912–915 (2001)
10. Butt, A., Kardong-Edgren, S., Ellertson, A.: Using game-based virtual reality with haptics for skill acquisition. Clin. Simul. Nurs. **16**, 25–32 (2018)
11. de Faria, J., Teixeira, M., de Moura Sousa Júnior, L., Otoch, J., Figueiredo, E.: Virtual and stereoscopic anatomy: when virtual reality meets medical education. J. Neurosurg. **125**(5), 1105–1111 (2016)

Hybrid Requirement Elicitation Techniques with Lean Six Sigma Methodology for an Enhanced Framework

Narishah Mohamed Salleh[(✉)] and Puteri N. E. Nohuddin

Institute of Visual Informatics, Universiti Kebangsaan Malaysia, 43600 Bangi, Selangor, Malaysia
narishah2@gmail.com, puteri.ivi@ukm.edu.my

Abstract. Requirement Elicitation (RE) is the most important phase in software development life cycle. It is a complex process because it involves the communications between two group of people to get into understanding of what to be built and what need to be delivered from software perspective. The purpose of this paper is to introduce a hybrid framework which combine the RE techniques from analytical and synthetic category with Lean Six Sigma (LSS) method, aimed at improving RE process to produce a quality software requirement. A framework consists of three phases; design, implementation and analysis are proposed where an industry case study is demonstrated for validation. The new framework observed a significance acceptance by analysts where the new hybrid approach is easy to adopt though at absence of users at the early stage of requirement study. The result also shown that the entire RE process cycle time improved tremendously. The limitation of this paper because it only tested in one company and at a specific project. The main contribution of the paper is to provide new knowledge in combining the RE techniques with LSS at absence of end user.

Keywords: Requirement Elicitation · Lean Six Sigma · Combination of elicitation techniques

1 Introduction

RE is the process of acquiring the information from the users implicit and explicitly where it involves finding what is needed for the system to function and translating those into a design specification. One RE technique could not resolve all the requirement challenges at once, thus combination of RE techniques which based on situational background are one of the recommended by most of the literatures [1–3]. However, most of the combination techniques involved extensive communications with end users which lead to rigorous and iterative cycles of RE process that contributes to project failures [4–6].

LSS method also applied a combination of RE techniques with specific tools at specific phases where Survey, Focus Group discussion, interview and questionnaires were practiced in the industrial environment. Voice of Customer (VOC) is utilized with questionnaires and surveys, while SIPOC (Supplier-Input-Process-Output-Customer)

© Springer Nature Switzerland AG 2019
H. Badioze Zaman et al. (Eds.): IVIC 2019, LNCS 11870, pp. 190–201, 2019.
https://doi.org/10.1007/978-3-030-34032-2_18

diagram with focus group discussion to understand current process issues. Both elements still required an extensive two-way communication between requirement engineers and end users.

This paper addressed another new approach in RE framework that combines analytical and synthetic techniques with LSS approach which utilize SIPOC, process mapping and Lean Waste Analysis. The approach initiates from different angle by extracting the information from organization document using SIPOC to explore the problems before solutions were proposed.

The rest of the paper is organized as follows: Sect. 2 describes the motivation, foundation and the reasons behind the combination of RE techniques in a RE process. Section 3 presents an industrial case study of this hybrid technique has been applied. An overall discussion is presented in Sect. 4. Conclusions and future work are described in Sect. 5.

2 Literature Review

Most of the literatures recommended hybrid techniques towards comprehensive requirement engineering where most of the techniques done independently with different purpose of elicitation [3, 7]. The hybrid approach consists of questionnaires, interview and prototype are commonly used in the industry to improve the RE process [7]. The objective of questionnaires to get the overview of information from large group pf peoples before classification and categorization of the requirements. Interview is done to refine the requirements. The prototype is to validate the proposed requirements.

LSS is another scope of SDLC model which utilize the problem solving techniques which aligned with "As-IS" and "To-Be" conceptual approach in standard software requirement procedures. [8] suggested a combination of VOC tools to be applied with focus group discussion to extract the critical quality parameters as part of the requirement process. However, those techniques are highly dependent on the analysts' expertise to conduct requirement study. Next section is to explore the significant techniques for situation where end users were not collaborative and unsure during requirement study.

2.1 Requirement Elicitation Technique

This section will describe the two main techniques that are relevance to this paper.

Content Analysis. Document analysis is categorized as Analytical method which provides ways of exploring expert's knowledge of existing system and acquires requirements from a series of deductions to provide requirements engineer rich information about the product. This method involves exploration into existing documents and facts about a system from organizational documents, policies, literatures, procedures, contracts or products documentations [9]. Still, this procedure required extensive knowledge from the analysts to perform requirement elicitation.

Prototyping. Prototyping is categorized as synthetic method which combine with other RE techniques like conversational, observational and analytical methods [10, 11]. The process usually involved an iterative conversations and discussion with the end users to acquire feedback. It is developed based on preliminary requirements extracted from the brainstorming ideas with the team members or stakeholders. Though, this technique is very costly and time consuming if the scopes were not well defined [12]. There were other alternative types of prototyping such as throwaway prototyping. This system is like a mock-up system where it translates the requirements into a visualize model without any hardcoded programming before the real development were initiated. This approach is not expensive in terms of cost but relatively, it will drag the project timeline if were not handled properly [13, 14].

2.2   Lean Six Sigma in Requirement Engineering

LSS is an integrated principle derived from Six Sigma and Lean Management approach [15, 16]. It is part of continuous improvement process where enhanced performance is obtained through the systematic and structured applications of tools for each phases of its framework [17]. LSS is being increasingly applied not only in manufacturing but also in healthcare [18], software, construction and education [19].

LSS can be integrated with many management theory and methods, such as quality management system, performance excellence model, supply chain management, theory constraints and many others [20]. There is no limit of the scopes to utilize LSS tools and techniques in any of the management theory. However, most of LSS methodology approach is done with the presence of charter team for brainstorming and discussion. Less studies were done by extracting such information utilizing SIPOC and document analysis.

2.3   Lean Six Sigma Framework

The main methodology in LSS is DMAIC. It is an acronym for Define-Measure-Analyze-Improve and Control phase. At each phase, there are specific tools can be applied with specific objectives [21–23]. Define phase is the first step to define objective, to identify the stakeholders and to explore customer's requirement. This is the phase where project leaders will investigate overview of current process [24].

Measure is the second phase where the objective is to collect data and to describe detail mapping of workflows [20]. Analyze phase consists of the tools to determine the root cause of the problems. The fourth phase is Improve which is to implement optimized solutions to solve the problem. The last phase is Control which to sustain the improved results. It is the final phase to implement the final solutions to guarantee the sustainability of the improvement.

2.4   Lean Six Sigma Tools and Technique

This section explains the relevance tools in Define and Measure Phase which associated to requirement elicitation process. The selected tools are SIPOC, Process Mapping and Lean Waste Analysis.

SIPOC. SIPOC is a tool typically used in Define phase of DMAIC framework with the objective to identify process inputs and outputs. There are many advantages such as; it helps to scope the project, to identify the boundaries of the processes, to improve communications among the team members and also provide high level business requirements [25–28]. The main disadvantage involved extensive discussion with the stakeholders. Most of the literatures were done by combining the methods with focus group to conduct discussion or brainstorming session. None of the literatures adopt the concept of extracting the implicit and explicit information of current "As-Is" using document analysis. Figure 1 is the SIPOC diagram:

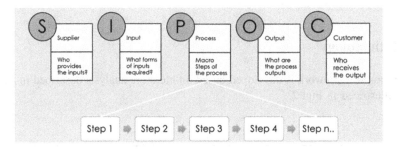

Fig. 1. SIPOC diagram

SIPOC consists of questions to understand the overview of the organizations. Such technique had been demonstrated by many researchers and confirmed the effectiveness of its usage to explore the organization current status before new improvement is proposed [26, 29]. Information collected from SIPOC diagram will be transformed into Swim lane diagram to visualize roles and functions of the workflow. Next sub section will describe the actual activities of Process Mapping.

Process Mapping. Process Mapping is a visualize tool which represent the activities, responsibilities and detail tasks that can be represented by Detail Flow Diagram (DFD), Flow Chart, Business Process Model or Swim Lane Diagram [30–32]. Swim Lane diagram is highly recommended to visualize the main tasks for each role and the integration between the roles.

Lean Waste Analysis. LWA is the significant technique in software engineering to identify non-value add process and to propose software solutions which adopted by many researchers in Lean and Agile [33]. It is known as seven (7) waste theories-MUDA. It consists of comprehensive method to eliminate sources of process waste such as over production, over processing and waiting where leads to identify the important variables of the organization process flow [18, 34–36].

2.5   The Hybrid Techniques

For this paper, document analysis from multiple type of information is vital to be extracted with the right questions and procedures. Introducing SIPOC at the early stage is significant to get to understand the overview of the organization workflow. The boundaries of process scope will be well determined. Transforming such data collected from SIPOC diagram into process mapping using Swim Lane diagram will assist analyst to understand implicitly the tasks at each role. In order to examine the merits of hybrid RE techniques, an industrial case study was conducted to validate the perfor- mance of elicitation processing time and the acceptance level from the analysts. The authors were directly involved in these projects to provide methodological guidance and training for the analysts.

3   Methodology

The proposed framework is developed based on literature analysis described in Sect. 2 which illustrated in Fig. 2.

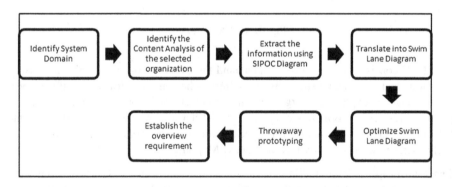

Fig. 2. Combination of RE techniques with LSS approach

The framework initiates from identify the specific domain of knowledge and organization documents. Once the organization document is selected, then requirement will be extracted based on SIPOC diagram where all the relevance data will be mapped into. Table 1 gives a summary of the proposed framework.

The sequential flow is proposed because data collected at each step will be used in the next steps.

Table 1. Summary of the proposed framework

No	Process	Description	Objective
1	Identify System Domain	To select specific area of the system to be build (e.g.: HRMS, Purchasing Request etc.)	This will assist the analysts or requirement engineers to focus the area of knowledge
2	Identify content analysis	Analysts needs to identify the documents that needs to be analyzed (for e.g.: contracts, service agreements, Standard Operating Procedures, Reaction Plans etc.)	To assist analysts to be more specific of the area to be developed
3	Extract requirement using SIPOC	The "As-Is" process is explored using SIPOC structured questions	To understand the overview of the business process, the boundaries of the scope and to identify number of stakeholders
4	Transform into swim lane diagram	Swim lane diagram is applied to describe detail process	This is to identify the roles and responsibilities of each task
5	Lean Waste Analysis	To finalize the right variables	To eliminate non-value or repetitive task
6	Optimize Swim Lane Diagram	Re-design the flow after removed the non-value add processes	To assist analyst to understand the business process flow precisely
7	Throwaway Prototyping	An alternative design to represent the future system	To help the analysts to represent the requirements in visualization mode

3.1   Case Study Demonstration

Case study demonstration is to validate the proposed framework with actual applications in the industry [39, 40].

Project Description. The case study is applied to an industrial project in company X (the name of the company is withheld due to reasons of confidentiality). It is a small size contractor in Oil and Gas industry. The company would like to develop a new enhance application for procurement management system to maximize manpower utilization. However, due to heavy workload and commitment to the current process and customer issues, the company could not afford to spare the employees' time during requirement gathering process. Thus, this study is relevance to confirm its validation.

Experimental Design for Hypothesis Testing. The case study is conducted with two different methods. The first method will be applied a standard company procedure, while the second method will utilize the flow in Fig. 2 (Method B). Tables 2 and 3 are the summary of the process flow for both methods for experimental purpose. Both will be applied on the same system domain to be built.

Table 2. Summary process flow for Method A (Standard Method procedures)

Step	Process	Description	Important points
1	Setup Focus Group Meeting	Application Domain is "Procurement-To-Pay"	No of stakeholders involved
2	Scope the problems and understand the context	Discussion with Focus Group with open-ended interview	Problems were defined precisely
3	Identify Problems Gaps and Opportunity of the system	Understand current "As-Is" process flow	To understand the overview of the business process and to confirm number of stakeholders
4	Observation	Process Mapping to understand detail tasks	To identify detail process map
6	Design the alternative system "To-Be"	Sketch the proposed solutions	To assist analyst to confirm with stakeholders before actual design
7	Iterative Prototyping	System Prototype	To present and to confirm actual design

Table 3. Summary process flow for Method B (As defined in Fig. 2)

Step	Process	Description	Important points
1	Identify System Domain	"Procurement-To-Pay" System	To be specific on the main variables
2	Identify content analysis	Standard Operating Procedures, Contracts with supplier, Current System documentations	To be more specific in terms of Scope and objective
3	Extract requirement using SIPOC	The "As-Is" process is explored using SIPOC structured questions	To understand the overview of the business process, the boundaries of the scope and to identify number of stakeholders
4	Translate into swim lane diagram	To define detail process flow	This is to identify the roles and responsibilities of each task
5	Lean Waste Analysis	To identify input and output variables	To eliminate non-value added or repetitive task, the method is very useful
6	Optimize Swim Lane Diagram	To develop "To-Be" Workflow	To assist analyst to understand the business process flow precisely
7	Throwaway Prototyping	An alternative design to represent the future system	To help the analysts to represent the requirements in visualization mode

Both Methods will be compared based on below variables to quantify based on statistical analysis:

- Requirement Elicitation Processing Time From start till finish
- Number of stakeholders that will be utilizing the system
- Number of iterative activities for each phase till the process completed
- Number of key variables should be displayed at dashboard

The second part of the study is to perform face to face interview with the analyst. The interview questions are constructed in broad view to explore the acceptance level of the analyst towards the propose framework which aligned to organization's environment: [40]:

i. Is Method B cost effective?
ii. Is Requirement generated from Method B is more "complete"?
iii. What are the major benefits of method B in RE process?
iv. What are the major challenges in Method B as compared to Method A?
v. Will method B support complex requirement study? And Why?

4 Data Collection and Analysis

4.1 The Summary of the Result

Method A observed longer cycle time by 48 h compared to Method B. This is due to users' availability. The data showed that to get information from users are highly depending on their availability. Unlike Method B where analyst was in total control of the situation. For Method B, analysts need to extract the information from the documents based on questions from Fig. 1 SIPOC diagram (Table 4).

Table 4. Data summary

Step	Process	Method A	Method B
1	Requirement Elicitation Processing Time	60 h	12 h
2	Number of stakeholders that will be using the system	5 groups	9 groups
3	Number of iterative cycles during the RE process	20 cycles	3 cycles
4	Number of key variables should be displayed at dashboard	3 Parameters	6 Parameters

SIPOC diagram is analyzed based on Five different column which represent Supplier, Type of Input, Major process steps, type of output and lastly the customers. Thus, Method B able to extract detail information based on each stage. While method A is driven by the knowledge of the end users. The users from Method A are: Requestors, Department Head, Purchasing Team, Finance Team and Finance Manager. While Method B produced Requestors, Project Managers, Department Heads, Purchasing and Buyer, Finance Operation, Finance Manager, Division Head and CEO. The difference could occur, because each stakeholder only described based on their specific activities which did not cover end to end process flow.

Number of iterative cycles for Method A is significantly longer compared to Method B, due to ambiguous scope of the requirements. Method B generates less iterative communications because the communication only initiated at throwaway prototyping to perform fine tuning in terms of validation and confirmation between the users and the analysts. However, Method A involve communications at the early stage. The situation gets worst if the end users were not clear of the requirements that need to be built.

Method A showed less parameters where users only need to view number of Purchase Order, Purchase Request and Pending Payment from Finance. While method B proposed more parameters: Pending Purchase Order Approval based on quantity and amount, Purchase Requisition Approval, Pending Request for Payment in quantity and amount. The next section is the data from the interview part.

4.2   Case Study Interview

The case study interview was conducted with an experienced analyst from the selected company. The interview session had taken an hour of half. Table 5 display the interview results:

Table 5. Interview result with the analyst

No	Questions	Respond from analyst
1	Is Method B cost effective?	Yes. The time spent to gather the information is more efficient. Throwaway prototyping is impressive because it will help in assisting the analysts to represent the actual system. The approach has a systematic and standard guideline which easy to adopt
2	Is the overview requirement generated from method B more "complete"?	Yes. It represents a complete overview of the system to be built. The SIPOC diagram with process mapping helped us to determine number of interfaces that related to user roles
3	What are the major benefits of Method B in RE process?	a. The time taken is shorter b. No emotional disturbance compared to typical conversational and prototyping approach where analysts were annoyed by the response of stakeholders Importantly, the preliminary data collection from SIPOC help us to ask the right questions to the end users
4	What are the major challenges of Method B compared to method A?	Lean Waste Analysis concept for requirement. I need more exercise and training for this matter
5	Will method B support complex requirement study? And Why?	Yes, it will. This is due to the comprehensive concept of SIPOC and process mapping

The result showed that Method B is the preferred approach from analyst as compared to Method A.

5   Conclusion

The case study is to handle the situation where collaboration or participation from users were lacking and the actual requirements from end users were ill defined. Though, there were many RE techniques has been evaluated to improve the users' collaboration, increase effective communication during the requirement study and many others, a need of different method should be explored for continuous improvement.

The combination of RE techniques based on situational problem is still not capable to resolve above situation. LSS through DMAIC methodology deploys standard and systematic approach which initiates from exploring and understanding the problems to resolve before solutions were proposed. However, most of the projects were done through collaboration with the experts either internally or externally. The case study had investigated the enhanced framework which combined analytical and synthetic RE techniques with LSS approach. The new framework specifically focused the techniques applied at Define and Measure phase. Extraction of information using SIPOC from current organization documents such as SOP, Customer agreements, workstation procedures and policies observed a significant improvement in the RE process.

6   Future Work

The data collection is limited to a single opinion which did not represent generalize outcome. The next proposed future work should focus to replicate the same method to other analysts on the same domain. The data collections will be analyzed by comparing all the requirement lists to confirm and validate the framework.

References

1. Tiwari, S., Rathore, S.S., Gupta, A.: Selecting requirement elicitation techniques for software projects. In: 2012 CSI Sixth International Conference on Software Engineering (CONSEG), pp. 1–10 (2012)
2. Tiwari, S., Rathore, S.S.: A methodology for the selection of requirement elicitation techniques (2017)
3. Yousuf, M., Asger, M.: Comparison of various requirements elicitation techniques. Int. J. Comput. Appl. **116**(4), 15 (2015)
4. Egas, R.: Requirements elicitation, which method in which situation? Open University of the Netherlands, p. 70 (2015)
5. Jebreen, I., Al-Qerem, A.: Empirical study of analysts' practices in packaged software implementation at small software enterprises. Int. Arab J. Inf. Technol. **14**(4A Special Issue) (2017)
6. Sanaa, H., Afifi, W.A., Darwish, N.R.: The goal questions metrics for agile business intelligence. Egypt. Comput. Sci. J. **40**(2), 24–41 (2016)

7. Zakari, A., Lawan, A.A.: Emerging Trends in Electrical, Electronic and Communications Engineering, vol. 416 (2017)
8. Tenera, A., Pinto, L.C.: A Lean Six Sigma (LSS) project management improvement model. Procedia Soc. Behav. Sci. **119**, 912–920 (2014)
9. Deshmukh, D., More, A.: International Journal of Innovative Research in Computer and Communication Engineering Applying Big Data in Higher Education, pp. 9201–9215 (2017)
10. Iqbal, T.: Requirement elicitation technique: - a review paper. Int. J. Comput. Math. Sci. **3** (9), 1–6 (2014)
11. Bennaceur, A., et al.: Requirements engineering to cite this version: HAL Id : hal-01758502 (2018)
12. Batool, A., et al.: Comparative study of traditional requirement engineering and agile requirement engineering. In: 2013 15th International Conference on Advanced Communications Technology (ICACT), pp. 1006–1014 (2013)
13. Pandey, D., Suman, U., Ramani, A.K.: A framework for modelling software requirements. Int. J. Comput. Sci. Issues **8**(3 3–1), 164–171 (2011)
14. Qurban, M.H., Austria, R.D.: Improving the communication skills of IS developers during requirements elicitation using experiential learning. J. Inf. Syst. Educ. **20**(3), 301–311 (2009)
15. Luo, B., Salmela, H.: How Lean Six Sigma and Agile Principles, pp. 1–89 (2014)
16. Tilk, D.: 5 Steps To Agile Project Success. Intern. Audit **73**(2), 57–61 (2016)
17. Drohomeretski, E., Gouvea Da Costa, S.E., Pinheiro De Lima, E., Garbuio, P.A.D.R.: Lean, six sigma and lean six sigma: an analysis based on operations strategy. Int. J. Prod. Res. **52** (3), 804–824 (2014)
18. Laureani, A., Antony, J., Douglas, A.: Lean six sigma in a call centre: a case study. Int. J. Prod. Perform. Manag. **59**(8), 757–768 (2010)
19. Kumar, M., et al.: Article information. Leadersh. Organ. Dev. J. (2018)
20. Xu, X.Q., Huang, C., Lu, H.: Application of lean six sigma methodology in software continuous integration. Key Eng. Mater. **693**, 1893–1898 (2016)
21. Zasadzień, M.: Application of the six sigma method for improving maintenance processes – case study. In: Proceedings of 6th International Conference on Operations Research and Enterprise Systems, no. Icores, pp. 314–320 (2017)
22. Selvi, K., Majumdar, R.: Applying six sigma techniques to reduce the number of defects of software, no. 02, pp. 319–326 (2014)
23. Pan, Z., Park, H., Baik, J., Choi, H.: A six sigma framework for software process improvements and its implementation. In: 14th Asia-Pacific Software Engineering Conference, vol. 1, no. 3, pp. 446–453 (2007)
24. Kelly, S.: Towards an evolutionary framework for agile requirements elicitation. In: Proceedings of the 2nd ACM SIGCHI Symposium on Engineering Interactive Computing Systems - EICS 2010, p. 349 (2010)
25. Alkinaidri, A., Alsulami, H.: Improving healthcare referral system using lean six sigma. Am. J. Ind. Bus. Manag. **08**(02), 193–206 (2018)
26. Montella, E., et al.: The application of Lean Six Sigma methodology to reduce the risk of healthcare–associated infections in surgery departments. J. Eval. Clin. Pract. **23**(3), 530–539 (2017)
27. Nicolaescu, S., Kifor, C.V., Lobonţ, L.: Design for six sigma applied on software development projects from automotive industry. Acad. J. Manuf. Eng. **12**(4), 76–83 (2015)
28. O'Neill, P.: An exploratory case study analysis of implementation of six sigma in a New Zealand organisation (2018)

29. Sujova, A., Simanova, L., Marcinekova, K.: Sustainable process performance by application of Six Sigma concepts: the research study of two industrial cases. Sustainability **8**(3), 260 (2016)
30. Garza-Reyes, J.A., Al-Balushi, M., Antony, J., Kumar, V.: A Lean Six Sigma framework for the reduction of ship loading commercial time in the iron ore pelletising industry. Prod. Plann. Control **27**(13), 1092–1111 (2016)
31. Kozaczuk, K., Zalewska, M.: Composite testing laboratory performance development based on lean sigma approach - case study. Trans. Inst. Aviat. **245**(4), 60–69 (2016)
32. Krotov, M., Mathrani, S.: A six sigma approach towards improving quality management in manufacturing of nutritional products. In: 2017 International Conference on Industrial Engineering, Management Science and Application, ICIMSA 2017, vol. 1, pp. 225–240 (2017)
33. Poppendieck, M., Poppendieck, T.: Lean Software Development: An Agile Toolkit (2003)
34. Cheng, J.-L.: Improving inventory performance through lean six sigma approaches. IUP J. Oper. Manag. **16**(3), 23–38 (2017)
35. Mahato, S., Dixit, A.R., Agrawal, R.: Process excellence in IT sector in an emerging economic scenario. In: 2016 3rd International Conference on Recent Advances in Information Technology, RAIT 2016, pp. 636–640 (2016)
36. Onsuk, O., Wuttidittachotti, P., Prakancharoen, S., Vallipakorn, S.A.O.: A SDLC developed software testing process using DMAIC model. ARPN J. Eng. Appl. Sci. **10**(3), 1008–1016 (2015)
37. Bennaceur, A., et al.: Requirements Engineering: Handbook of Software Engineering (2018). <hal-01758502>
38. Runeson, P., Host, M., Rainer, A., Regnell, B.: Case Study Research in Software Engineering (2012)
39. García-Borgoñón, L., Barcelona, M.A., García-Garcí, J.A., Escalona, M.J.: Software process accessibility in practice: a case study. In: Dsai 2013, pp. 292–301 (2013)
40. Gaikwad, V., Joeg, P.: A case study in requirements engineering in context of agile. Int. J. Appl. Eng. Res. **12**(8), 1697–1702 (2017)

Longevity Risk Profiling Based on Non-disease Specific Risk Factors Using Association Rules Mining

Nur Haidar Hanafi[1,2(✉)] and Puteri N. E. Nohuddin[1]

[1] Institute of Visual Informatics, Universiti Kebangsaan Malaysia UKM,
43650 Bangi, Selangor, Malaysia
haidar54@uitm.edu.my, puteri.ivi@ukm.edu.my
[2] Faculty of Computer and Mathematical Sciences,
Universiti Teknologi MARA, Seremban 3 Campus,
70300 Seremban, Negeri Sembilan, Malaysia

Abstract. The growing of ageing population causes many major negative impacts especially on pension plans and annuity providers. One of the impacts is on the exposure to longevity risk. There are various methods have been previously developed in order to quantify and classify longevity risk. However, there are some major drawbacks to these methods, especially in long-term mortality risk exposures studies. Therefore, this study is conducted in order to observe the potentiality of Association Rules Mining (ARM) in overcoming these drawbacks. The results show that ARM has an advantage of generating a less complex longevity profile based on the generated association rules; and can be used as an alternative method to the intricated statistical methods in profiling longevity risk exposure.

Keywords: Longevity risk · Association Rules Mining · Risk profiling

1 Introduction

Notable improvements in life expectancy and decrements in mortality rates are considered to be a success story of public health policy providers and socioeconomic legislators. Some believe that this indicates that older people are enjoying better quality of life when compared to previous generations. However, increasing in the number of the ageing population poses various major negative impacts which include higher financial responsibilities for governments and annuity providers [4, 13]. Therefore, it is necessary to better estimate longevity risk for various reasons including for assuring the sustainability of government and other stakeholders, for improving life insurance and annuity pricing, for designing and pricing long term care insurance; and other actuarial practice [7, 10].

2 Longevity Risk

Longevity risk is one of the growing risks across some developing and developed countries as population aged longer than expected. The uncertainty surrounding the quantum by which people are able to survive beyond their life expectancy poses serious

© Springer Nature Switzerland AG 2019
H. Badioze Zaman et al. (Eds.): IVIC 2019, LNCS 11870, pp. 202–213, 2019.
https://doi.org/10.1007/978-3-030-34032-2_19

financial threats to many stakeholders. Living longer than the life expectancy will definitely force people to outlive their available resources in life. Hence, the only option that is available for them is to substantially reducing their standards of living during old ages. Often, the holder of longevity risk is unaware of the seriousness of the financial threats [7, 11, 13].

2.1 Existing Standard Practices

Modelling longevity risk is proven to be a very complicated task, especially when using intricated statistical methods. The most basic tool used in representing longevity risk is life tables [10, 15, 16]. The mortality rates in these life tables are presented as a smooth baseline of the patterns of mortality rates of septuagenarians and octogenarians. The assumption used while developing a life table is that the force of mortality continues to increase exponentially with age. However, it ignores the basic statistical warning that a curve fitted over a particular domain is not necessarily replicated outside of the same domain. Thus, there exist multiple versions of life tables to represent different mortality and morbidity exposures.

Another famous method used by actuaries is stochastic mortality models [4, 8, 18]. Stochastic models incorporate the extrapolative method as in life tables while taking advantage of the time series models that give a probabilistic confidence interval to ease the forecasting process. However, the main major drawback of this method is the limited availability of historical data since it depends too much on past data to project future outcomes. In recent years, some researchers have tried using generalized dynamic factor models and vine-copulae [6]. The methodology consists of two important stages. It starts by fitting the differences in the log-mortality rates using generalized dynamic factor models. The second stage is to construct risk measures using vince copula simulations. However, the models perform worse than models in levels for short forecasting horizons at advanced ages. The model in differences is fitted at the expense of some degree of over-fitting for the advanced ages, thus indirectly ignoring longevity risk.

In order to overcome these drawbacks, this study is conducted with the purpose of observing the potentiality of Association Rules Mining (ARM) as an alternative method in generating a less complex longevity profile, which can be easily understood by actuaries and non-actuaries.

3 Data Mining and Association Rules Mining

Data mining has been suggested by many as an alternative approach to current models of mortality projections [2, 13]. Data mining has the ability of developing analytics-based approaches based on readily available information. This is done with the objective of constructing a more accurate, consistent, and efficient decision-making process. Data mining procedures include various algorithms and techniques like Classification, Clustering, Regression, Artificial Intelligence, Neural Networks, Association Rules, Decision Trees, Genetic Algorithm and Nearest Neighbour method.

ARM model produces knowledge that is more understandable and can be inter-preted easily for the usage of the decision makers, either by actuaries or non-actuaries. It aims to extract interesting correlations, frequent patterns, associations or causual structures among sets of items in the transaction databases or other data repositories [17]. Various attempts have been done in incorporating ARM in longevity studies. For example, in life insurance studies [17] and mortality related to certain diseases such as Alzheimer [5].

The algorithms in ARM is used in finding the frequent itemsets from a given transactional dataset. The itemsets are then been used again in generating the associ-ation rules. The generated association rules allow for prediction of all the possible combination of the given attributes. Different rules express different relationship that lie within the dataset. Many interesting association rules can be derived from even a small amount of dataset.

Apriori algorithm is the most common and widely used by researchers when applying ARM. However, in this study, another ARM algorithm known as the Eclat algorithm is used for generating the association rules. Eclat is an acronym for Equivalence Class Clustering and bottoms up Lattice Traversal. The primary difference between Eclat and Apriori is that Eclat is based on depth-first search algorithm whereby it abandons Apriori's breadth-first search for a recursive depth-first search [9], thus improving the processing time and reducing the memory storage size.

4 Empirical Illustration

The analysis procedures illustrated in this section played a major purpose in high-lighting the potentiality of ARM as an alternative method to the intricated statistical methods as discussed in the previous section. ARM has an advantage of generating a less complex longevity profile based on association rules between longevity risk exposure and an array of risk factors; which can be easily understood by actuaries and non-actuaries. A simpler longevity profile would be a breakthrough in easing a rather complex underwriting process of most longevity products such as pension plans and annuity contracts. More versatile longevity products could be developed to cater to different needs of different levels of a demographic structure.

4.1   Data Selection and Pre-processing

Every year, the US Centres for Disease Control and Prevention (CDC) releases the country's most details report on death amongst Americans under their National Vital Statistics program. The yearly datasets contain information with 77 different attributes as recorded in the death certificate. The death records of those who had died at the age of 70 and above within 2013 until 2015 are used in this study with a total of 3,765,210 recorded deaths. Such datasets are used because they represent real-life risk exposures of people being able to live and die beyond their life expectancy; both typical and extreme ones. Another reason is because of the fact that most nations, public health policy providers, socioeconomic legislators and annuity providers would have in their possession a complete death record system. Taking advantage of these readily available datasets would reduce data acquisition time and storing cost.

The main focus of this paper is on the relationships between non-disease risk factors and longevity risk. Thus, only five attributes have been used which are gender, race, residential status, marital status and education level. These five attributes have been identified as the major non-disease risk factors influencing death in US as suggested in previous studies [1, 3, 4, 11, 14, 19, 20]. To represent the level of exposure to longevity risk, age at death is selected as the response variable. Only deaths that occurred at the age of 70 and above are selected for this study since the size of longevity risk is more significant amongst those within this age group. Any unnatural deaths would disturb the precision of this study, thus only deaths caused by natural events are included; while those caused by suicide, homicide or other unnatural events are removed. The descriptions of the non-disease risk factors along with their codes as coded in R software are presented in Table 1. The R software version 1.1.383 installed in Windows 10 with processor Intel(R) Core(TM) i7-6500U CPU at 2.5 GHz is used in the analysis process.

Table 1. Data descriptions.

Attribute	Description
Age_Death	The age at death; recorded as a single age, was then discretized into 5-year age groups so that it became categorical data {Age Death = "70–74","75–79", . . .,"100+"}
Residential	{Residential = "Residents", "Intrastate NR", "Interstate NR", "Foreign R"}
Education	The education status of the deceased; recoded using the revised 2003 education codes {Education = "Primary", "Secondary", "Diploma/GED", "Degree", "Master", "PHD/Professional"}
Gender	{Gender = "Female", "Male"}
Marital_Status	{Marital_Status = "Single", "Married", "Widowed", "Divorced"}
Race	{Race = "White", "Black", "American Indian", "Asian/Pacific"

Experimental Results. This section presents the empirical results of ARM procedures; along with some key discussions and arguments regarding the practicality of ARM in generating the longevity profile based on non-disease specific risk factors.

4.2   Descriptive Analysis

The correlation between the response variable and each of the risk factors provides some early perception of the possible generated rules. One basic explorative view of such two-way tables can be represented by mosaic plots as shown in Fig. 1. The size of the boxes corresponds to the size of observations within each level of each risk factors. The shading density of each box is based on the Pearson residuals of an independence model fitted to the dataset. The dotted and undotted shading represented the level of the residual for that box. More specifically, dotted region means that there are more observations in that box that would have been expected under the null model; whereas undotted region means there are fewer observations in that box than the one would have been expected. This is known as positive and negative relationships, respectively.

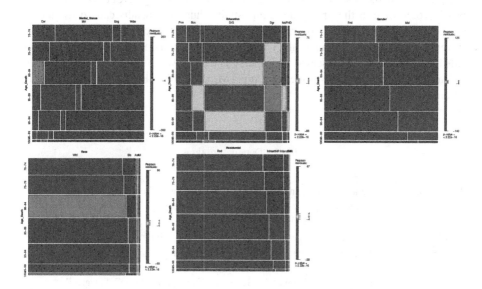

Fig. 1. Classic mosaic plot for correlation between response variable and risk factors.

Theoretically, the p-value of Pearson Residuals indicates the significant departure from the independence of the association between any given two variables. p-value greater than 0.05 means that there is no association between the two variables. All risk factors are significantly associated with age at death based on the values of Pearson Residuals in Fig. 1, since their p-values are less than 0.05. This result shows that all five risk factors are significantly affecting the deceased's life expectancy.

There are a few interesting findings that could be discussed further based on the figure. Even though all attributes are significantly associated with age at death as proven by the p-values, there exist some levels within the Education risk factors that are not associated to age at death. This condition can be seen for boxes with the lightest shading. For example, owning a diploma/GED certificate does not affect those who died between age 80–84 and 90–94.

4.3   Frequent Items

Arranging the risk factors according to the frequency of each level would provide a basic representation of the datasets. As shown in Fig. 2, a basic longevity profile for the datasets is clearly visible for further discussions. Majority of the deceased are widowed white female with diploma/GED qualification, a resident of the States and died between age 85 and 89. One thing that is interesting about this basic profile is it gives an insight peek to the association rules that will be generated later on. It is expected that most of the rules will represent risk exposure of death at the age of 85–89 with relationships to the white race, female, diploma/GED qualification and residents. Furthermore, rules for death occurred at age 100 + will be considered as rare rules and are expected to be difficult to mine due to low support count. However, reducing the threshold for ARM would result in a huge number of uninteresting rules, thus complicating this process. To overcome this problem, the clustering procedure are carried out later on in order to segment the datasets into smaller homogeneous groups.

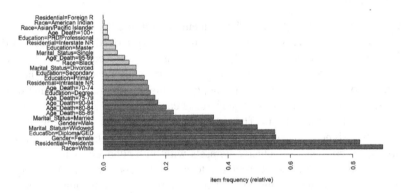

Fig. 2. Frequency of all levels (relative) in ascending order.

Mining frequent itemsets is an important step in mining association rules between attributes, especially when using the Eclat algorithm. Frequent item- sets mining involves tasks of finding all common sets of items having at least a minimum support value to be included in the sets at every possible iteration. There are 3,845 frequent itemsets have been successfully mined by Eclat algorithm with a threshold of 0.08045% and maximum order of six items. The scatter plot for the 3,845 frequent itemsets is shown in Fig. 3. Additional interesting- ness measurement of crossSuppRat is added to the frequent itemsets along with lift measurement.

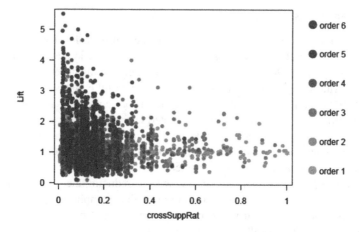

Fig. 3. Scatter plot of 3845 itemsets mined by Eclat algorithm.

4.4 Clustering

Before mining the association rules, the frequent itemsets are first clustered into smaller homogeneous groups to ensure that no rare rules are overlooked. This process is done by using partitioning around medoids (PAM) clustering procedure. The PAM algorithm has partitioned the frequent itemsets into 28 clusters where each itemset is partitioned into exactly one cluster. By applying this algorithm, the average dissimilarity of itemsets to their closest selected itemset can be minimized. Figure 4 shows the silhouette plot of all the clusters. The silhouette width represents how well an itemset belongs to its assigned cluster. Based on the figure, the most compact cluster is cluster 25. This cluster consists of exclusive itemsets with high silhouette widths.

The death records are then clustered into these clusters. By using the uniqueness of each cluster, there are 28 clusters of death records with a homogeneous profile for each cluster. Association rules are mined for each cluster repetitively by applying the Eclat algorithm and any redundant rules are removed. The rules are mined based on the threshold of 100% confidence level, which indicate exact confidence level, and minimum support of 1% to ensure any rare rules are not overlooked. The association rules from each cluster are visualized using paracoord plotting to ease understanding and explanation as shown in Figs. 5, 6, 7 and 8. Based on these figures, it is interesting to found that each cluster produces association rules associated with different levels of the response variable. For example, all 24 rules generated in cluster 1 as in Fig. 5 are for death that occurred at the age between 80 and 84. This has proven that all 28 clusters are highly homogeneous, thus any rare rules would not be overlooked.

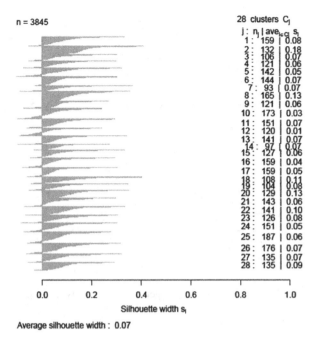

Fig. 4. Silhouette plot of PAM with 28 clusters.

Selecting paracoord plotting to visualize the association rules plays a major role in reducing the complexity of the generated profile. The paracoord plotting shows the interaction between each risk factors in effecting the response variable. Interpreting the rules also proven to be a lot easier when using paracoord plotting. Thicker lines that connecting the response variable and risk factors with each other represent common rules that existed in the cluster. For example, for cluster 5, the most common rules are those who are intrastate non-residents, married, have diploma/GED, white and female having a 100% chance of dying between age 80 and 84.

4.5   Longevity Risk Profiling

There are clusters which generated rules for the same level of the response variable. For example, cluster 6, cluster 27 and cluster 28 are all producing rules for death between age 95 and 99, inclusively. Thus, rules from clusters for the same level of the response variable are combined together and any redundant rules are removed. There are 396 total rules that can be used to profile longevity risk based on different levels of the response variable. A detail profile system can be develop based on these rules. Rules for each combination are visualized using paracoord plotting as shown in Fig. 9.

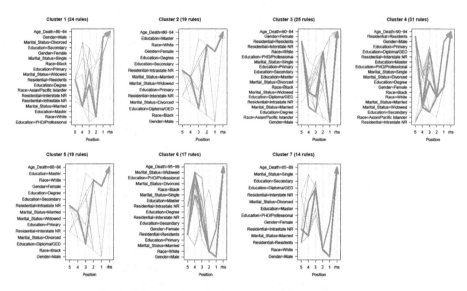

Fig. 5. Visualization of rules generated from cluster [1:7].

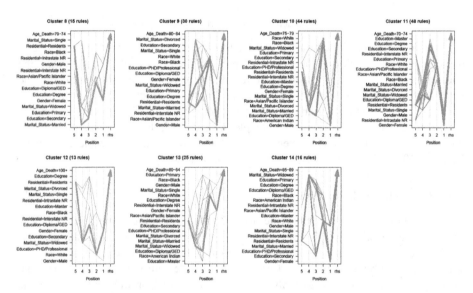

Fig. 6. Visualization of rules generated from cluster [8:14].

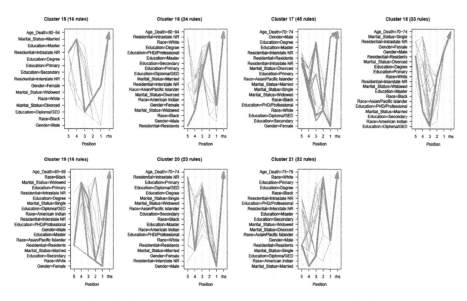

Fig. 7. Visualization of rules generated from cluster [15:21].

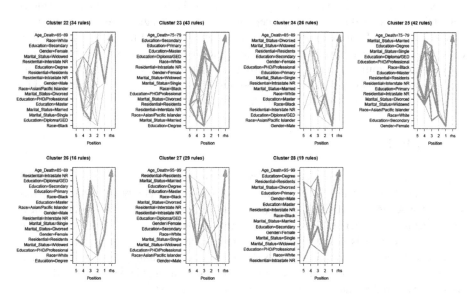

Fig. 8. Visualization of rules generated from cluster [22:28].

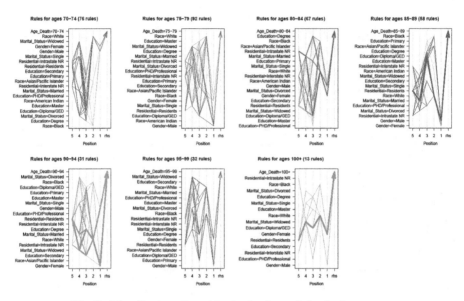

Fig. 9. Visualization of combined rules for each level of exposure.

The most rules are generated for death occurred between age 75 and 79. This is definitely contradicted to the early perception made based on the correlation analysis in Fig. 1. There is only one explanation on this matter. The ARM model has successfully capturing the association between each attribute and the response variable without ignoring any significant rare rules. Interpretation of the rules is similar to the interpretation done in previous section. However, less thicker lines are also interesting to be discussed further when constructing the risk profiling system.

5   Conclusion

In an attempt to find an alternative approach to the existing intricated statistical methods used in modelling, quantifying and classifying longevity risk, this study has shown that ARM is an easily understandable approach in providing an insightful view on the datasets. Reducing the need for an array of clinical longevity biomarkers along with complex models which difficult to communicate to those outside the actuarial practice environment would definitely help the public health policy providers and socioeconomic legislators. Taking advantage of readily available death record datasets would greatly reduce data acquisition time and storing cost.

References

1. Allen, D., Lee, S.: Modeling life insurance risk prudential insurance data set. SAS Student Symposium Forum 2016–2017 (2018)
2. https://support.sas.com/resources/papers/proceedings17/2024–2017.pdf. Accessed 8 Feb 2019
3. Batty, M., et al.: Predictive modeling for life insurance, ways life insurers can participate in the business analytics revolution. Deloitte Consulting LLP (2010)
4. Berry, P., Tsui, L., Jones, G.: Our new 'old' problem–pricing longevity risk in Australia. In: 6th International Longevity Risk and Capital Markets Solutions Conference, Sydney, pp. 9–10, September 2010
5. Bozikas, A., Pitselis, G.: An empirical study on stochastic mortality modelling under the age-period-cohort framework: the case of greece with applications to insurance pricing. Risks **6**(2), 44 (2018)
6. Chaves, R., Ramırez, J., Gorriz, J.M., Puntonet, C.G.: Alzheimer's disease neuroimaging initiative: association rule-based feature selection method for alzheimer's disease diagnosis. Exp. Syst. Appl. **39**(14), 11766–11774 (2012)
7. Chulia, H., Guillen, M., Uribe, J.M.: Modeling longevity risk with generalized dynamic factor models and vine-copulae. ASTIN Bull. J. IAA **46**(1), 165–190 (2016)
8. CRO forum: longevity CRObriefing emerging risks initiative position paper. CRObriefing on longevity (2010)
9. Denuit, M., Trufin, J.: From regulatory life tables to stochastic mortality projections: the exponential decline model. Insur. Math. Econ. **71**, 295–303 (2016)
10. Garg, K., Kumar, D.: Comparing the performance of frequent pattern mining algorithms. Int. J. Comput. Appl. **69**(25), 29–32 (2013)
11. Guo, L., Wang, M.C.: Data mining techniques for mortality at advanced age (2007)
12. Haberman, S., et al.: Longevity basis risk: a methodology for assessing basis risk (2014)
13. Hahsler, M., Gruen, B., Hornik, K.: arules - A computational environment for mining association rules and frequent item sets. J. Stat. Softw. **14**(15), 1–25 (2005). https://doi.org/10.18637/jss.v014.i15
14. Hanafi, N.H., Nohuddin, P.N.E.: Data mining approach in mortality projection: a review study. Adv. Sci. Lett. **24**(3), 1612–1615 (2018)
15. Heron, M.: National vital statistics reports. National Center for Health Statistics (2007)
16. Ibrahim, R.I.: Expanding an abridged life table using the Heligman-Pollard model. Matematika **24**, 1–10 (2008)
17. Lopez, A.D., Salomon, J.A., Ahmad, O.B., Murray, C.J., Mafat, D.: World Health Organization: Life tables for 191 countries: data, methods and results (2001)
18. More, N.P., Patil, S., More, N.P., Patil, S.: Recommending an insurance policy using association rule mining. Int. J. **1**, 70–73 (2014)
19. Piulachs, X., Alemany, R., Guillen, M.: Emergency care usage and longevity have opposite effects on health insurance rates. Kybernetes **46**(1), 102–113 (2017)
20. World Health Organization: Global health risks: mortality and burden of disease attributable to selected major risks. Geneva: World Health Organization (2009)
21. Vinnakota, S., Lam, N.S.: Socioeconomic inequality of cancer mortality in the United States: a spatial data mining approach. Int. J. Health Geograph. **5**(1), 9 (2006)

Ensemble of Deep Convolutional Neural Network for Skin Lesion Classification in Dermoscopy Images

Ather Aldwgeri[1(✉)] and Nirase Fathima Abubacker[2(✉)]

[1] Dublin City University @ Princess Nourah Bint Abdulrahman University, Riyadh, Saudi Arabia
Akaldwighri@pnu.edu.sa
[2] Dublin City University, Dublin, Ireland
nirase.fathimaabubacker@dcu.ie

Abstract. Diagnosis of skin lesions is a very challenging task due to high inter-class similarities and intra-class variations between lesions in terms of color, size, site and appearance. As a result, as is the case with many types of cancer, early detection of skin cancer is vital for survival. Advances in artificial intelligence, in particular, deep learning have enabled to design and implementation of intelligence-based lesion detection and classification systems that are based on visible light images that are capable of performing early and accurate diagnosis of different skin diseases. In most cases, the precision of these methods has reached a level of accuracy that is comparable to that achieved by a qualified dermatologist. This work presents potential skin lesion classification solutions based on the datasets taken from the most recent publicly available "Skin Lesion Analysis Towards Melanoma Detection" grand challenges ISIC 2018. The proposed classification approach leverages convolutional neural networks (CNN) and transfer learning to enhance skin classification. Different pre-trained models were applied, including VGG-Net, ResNet50, InceptionV3, Xception and DenseNet121. Additionally, the heavy class imbalance is examined as a critical problem for this dataset and multiple balancing techniques, such as weight balancing and data augmentation, are considered. Finally, an ensemble approach is evaluated by combining and averaging several CNN architectures to classify the seven different types of skin lesion. The experimental results indicate that the proposed frameworks exhibit promising results when compared with ISIC 2018 challenge live leaderboard.

Keywords: Skin lesion classification · Deep learning · Unbalanced dataset · Convolutional neural network · Data augmentation

1 Introduction

The incidence of skin disease has grown worldwide due to an extended exposure to the harmful radiation from the Sun. Melanoma is the deadliest form of skin cancer; therefore, it has been more extensively researched than other types. Dermoscopy images [1] of skin lesions have proven crucial to improving diagnostic accuracy and

© Springer Nature Switzerland AG 2019
H. Badioze Zaman et al. (Eds.): IVIC 2019, LNCS 11870, pp. 214–226, 2019.
https://doi.org/10.1007/978-3-030-34032-2_20

consequently reducing melanoma deaths. The classification system was first established by dermatologists to improve the diagnostic accuracy of skin disease. Skin cancers often bear similarities to benign and specific lesions associated with other diseases; therefore, distinguishing them is vital importance. The similarity of lesions and patterns among various cancers makes it challenging to determine the exact type of cancer [2]. Automated classification technology can further assist clinicians in their diagnostic decision-making. Recently, deep learning has been used in conjunction with dermoscopy to improve outcomes in the identification and classification of skin disease. The techniques have been applied not only for predicting the presence of disease but also for distinctive the classes of disease [3]. Studies incorporating deep learning algorithms in the process of binary classification have shown remarkable success in predictive capacity, more than when applied to multiclass classification models. The proposed work responds to this discrepancy in performance by investigating an intelligent, dermoscopy-based, multiclass classification system for identifying and distinguishing between various skin lesions, both malignant and benign.

This study is set out as follows: Sect. 2, discussion of background information and related research in the fields of dermatology. Section 3, description of the methodology proposed for this study. Section 4 present the overall technical implementation details. Section 5, evaluation and interpretation of the results of several experiments. Section 6, conclusion of the present study which also identified direction for future.

2   Literature Review

Numerous studies have shown that artificial intelligence has the capability of undertaking classifications for skin cancer at a competence level equal to that of dermatologists [4]. Mobile devices equipped with deep neural networks have the potential to allow dermatologists to undertake consultations remotely. Esteva et al. [5] have demonstrated that their techniques can perform on an equal level with human experts at both extraction and classification employing a single CNN which has only trained with images and disease labels for input. A CNN was trained by these researchers employing a 129,450 clinical images dataset, and its results were compared with those of 21 qualified dermatologists on clinical images for which the results had been found using biopsy; two critical binary classifications were involved [5]. Other research has also shown that machines are capable of outperforming human experts; 58 dermatologists were pitted against a CNN, and most humans did not perform as well as the network. No matter what a physician's level of expertise, they could still be assisted by the image classification capabilities of a CNN [6]. Work by Brinker et al. [4] that comprehensively examines all of the early research using computer technology for dermatology have demonstrated that there are three ways in which CNNs can be employed: firstly to extract features; secondly for end-to-end learning (transfer learning); and thirdly, training models from scratch. An example of the second type of research is undertaken by Han et al. [7] offering a classifier that can analyze the different skin diseases based on clinical imaging. These researchers used a Resnet model and fine-tuned it by using 19,398 training images from Asan dataset. This CNN model achieved the following ROC AUC results: basal cell carcinoma, .96, melanoma

.96, squamous cell carcinoma, .83, and intraepithelial carcinoma .82. Considerable research in the past has demonstrated that there are limitations regarding to both the numbers required for data training with CNN and test data. In general, a model will perform better when huge dataset has been trained, although which is not always available in the field of medical imaging. This problem can be solved by using data augmentation, batch normalization, and regularization with dropout or weight decay [8]. Besides, most of the previous studies were conducted by considered only mela-nocytic melanoma and melanocytic nevus as binary classification. Therefore, they did not consider the imperative need to add multiple skin lesions for classification.

3   Methodological Approach

3.1   CNN Architecture Selection

CNNs are viewed as one of the optimal techniques for interpretation of imaging content and have demonstrated cutting-edge abilities regarding classification, detection, image recognition and retrieval. As CNN is both good at extracting features and discrimi-nating between them, it is widely employed in pattern recognition systems at the stages of feature extraction/generation and model selection. Standard CNN architecture (Fig. 1) is usually made up of alternate convolution/pooling layers, succeeded by one or more fully connected layers. In certain instances, one of the fully connected layers may be substituted with a global average pooling layer.

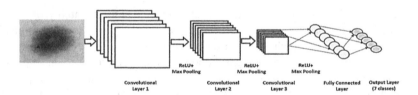

Fig. 1. Example of CNN architecture.

3.2   CNN Pre-trained Models

In recent years many cutting-edge models have come to the market. Five popular convolutional classifier architectures underwent implementation: VGG-Net [9], ResNet50 [10], InceptionV3 [11], Xception [12] and DenseNet121 [13].

3.3   Ensemble Learning

Ensemble learning is becoming increasingly interesting within the context of CNN research. The objective is to foster diversity among the combined models. The outputs of the individual models are merged, for example, by taking the mean outputs, to generate the final prediction. For more clarification, if $\{b\_1,...,b\_k\}$ represents k models of an ensemble and $p(x = y\_i \mid b\_j)$ represents the likelihood that the input, x, is classified as y_i under the model b_j, the ensemble will generate the following prediction Eq. (1) [14]:

$$p(x = y \mid b_1, \ldots, b_k) = \frac{1}{k} \sum_{k=1}^{k} p(x = y_i \mid b_j) \qquad (1)$$

Ensemble learning can achieve more effective generalization and often generates more accurate predictions than individual models in isolation.

4 Implementation Strategy

4.1 Dataset Selection and Preparation

In this work, the dataset created for the ISIC 2018 challenge: "Skin Lesion Analysis Towards Melanoma Detection" workshop is used [15]. Also known as, HAM10000 'Human against Machine' [16]. This dataset is the largest publicly obtainable one, containing 10015 images. The response data established to be categorical classifications which distributed to seven lesions states together. Possible disease categories, shown in Fig. 2 are as follows: MEL: 'Melanoma', NV: 'Melanocytic nevus.', BCC: 'Basal cell carcinom.', AKIEC: 'Actinic keratosis', BKL: 'Benign keratosis', DF: 'Dermatofibroma' and VASC: 'Vascular lesion'.

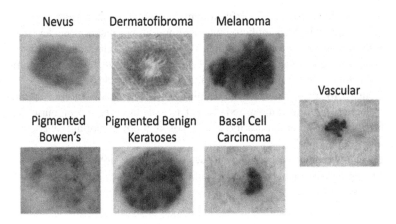

Fig. 2. A simple look at the pictures of skin diseases.

The way in which the disease classified in the given dataset is distributed to a representative of what would typically be observed in clinical practice in that the benign lesions outweigh the malignant lesions. Figure 3(a) shows there is a significant imbalance between the malignant and benign lesions. The model requires the dataset to be splitted into the train, validate and test sets. However, the access provides only the labels of the training set in the ISIC 2018 challenge. Therefore, the dataset divided into three distinct categories of 80% training and 20% test images. For validation, while the model training 20% split to validate the model.

4.2   Dealing with the Unbalanced Dataset

One of the significant problems faced in machine learning is unbalanced training data.

From Fig. 3(a), it is evident that the selected dataset is highly unbalanced and expected to be challenging to solve. Instead of collecting more instances from the real world that is a difficult task, is to develop a technique that enhances the data that already have. To augment existing datasets and produce more robust models, using data augmentation is another way to increase the amount of training data.

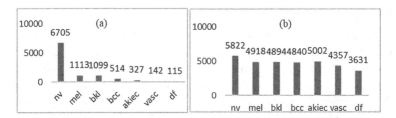

Fig. 3. (a) The dataset distribution illustrates the number of images per-class. (b) Training set after balanced it using data augmentation.

In this work, the popular powerful augmentation techniques were used. Before exploring these methods, for simplicity, one assumption was made: consider no change in the skin lesion shape, colour or texture. The following techniques used as a valid assumption: flip, rotation, shift and zoom. After applying this technique, the number of images in the lower classes increases, excluding the 'NV' class, due to the highest sample. Figure 3(b) illustrates how the training set is balanced. Another approach is applied to dealing with an unbalanced dataset is to apply weights or biases to each output class, especially the minority classes or a more important class, such as 'malignant'.

Overall, to overcome the challenge in dealing with the unbalanced dataset, especially in the medical field; the data augmentation and classes weight was applied to optimize the performance.

4.3   Simple CNN Trained from Scratch

The architecture used in this experiment was designed to be simple, to serve as a baseline. Three convolutional blocks with a 3 × 3 filter window and ReLU activation, followed by a 2 × 2 max pooling layer were created, followed by batch normalization. Feature sizes of 16, 32 and 64 were then specified for each layer. A three dense layer (64, 32, 16 nodes; ReLU activation) with a dropout rate of 0.2 followed the conventional layers. The experiment for this method was conducted in two ways, with balance data and second with unbalance data.

Input images were resized to be 64×64 pixels. Adam [17] was chosen as the optimizer (default learning rate of 0. 001), and categorical cross entropy [18] was implemented as the loss function. The batch size was selected to be 64. The number of epochs was chosen 200 epochs for the balanced, 100 epochs for the unbalanced.

4.4   Fine- Tuning Pre-trained Models (Transfer Learning)

When the indicated models (VGG-Net, ResNet50, InceptionV3, Xception and DenseNet121) were used, a few modifications were necessary to adapt the models to skin lesion classifier. The final output layer must be modified for use as a categorical classifier (7 categories). This can be achieved using softmax nodes and a global average pooling layer followed by a dropout of 0.5. The fully connected layers are then implemented in place of the final classifying block. As these models were more in-depth than a CNN from scratch, the experiment was selected with balance training (data augmentation).

The input images were resized (as referred in Keras [19]) to be 224×244 pixels and 299×299 pixels. Adam [17] was selected as the optimizer (learning rate of 10–4 and decay 10–4), and categorical cross entropy [18] was implemented as the loss function. The batch size was selected to be 32. The number of epochs was chosen 60 epochs.

4.5   Additional Implementation Details

Python was used as the primary programming language. The deep learning framework for all experiments was selected to be Keras [19] with Tensorflow [20]. GPUs (Graphics Processing Units) 'Nvidia GeForce RTX 2070 8 GB' were utilized to meet the demanding workload of training a deep neural network.

5   Evaluation and Results

5.1   Performance Evaluation

The goal matrix is to score predicted responses using balanced accuracy and the area under the receiver operating characteristic curve (ROCAUC) metric. The truth behind the choice of balanced accuracy is due to closeness to the evaluation of dermatologist's performance in classification of digital images.

Balanced Multi-classes Accuracy (B-Acc) [21, 22] (Eq. 2):

$$B - Acc = \frac{1}{l} \sum_{i=1}^{l} \frac{ki}{ni}, \ or \ \frac{1}{l} \sum_{i=1}^{l} Recall \tag{2}$$

where ki is the number of correct predictions in class i, l is the number of classes and ni is the number of examples in class i.

AUC (Area Under the Curve) [23], AUC is a single value that represents the area that appears under a receiver operating characteristic (ROCAUC).

To ensure scientific completeness, the following metrics will also be calculated in terms of the predicted responses versus the ground truth for every one of the categories.

The very useful tool to predict each category is the confusion matrix. There are four outcomes: True Positive *(TP)*, False Positive *(FP)*, True Negative *(TN)*, False Negative *(FN)*.

Sensitivity (Sen), (Eq. 3):

$$\frac{TP}{TO + FN} \tag{3}$$

Specificity (Sep), (Eq. 4):

$$\frac{TN}{TN + FP} \tag{4}$$

Accuracy (ACC), (Eq. 5):

$$\frac{TP + TN}{TP + TN + FP + FN} \tag{5}$$

F1 score, (Eq. 6):

$$2 \times \frac{Precision \times Recall}{Precision \times Recall} \tag{6}$$

Positive predictive values (PPV), (Eq. 7):

$$\frac{TP}{TP + FP} \tag{7}$$

Negative predictive values (NPV), (Eq. 8):

$$\frac{TN}{TN + FN} \tag{8}$$

5.2   Test Set Distribution

The lesions of many skin disorders often have variable distributions. In this work, the dataset shows the real distributions of which lesions appear to be more prevalent than others. Table 1 shows the numbers of each case in each category.

Table 1. The test set distribution.

CLASSES	AKIEC	BCC	BKL	DF	MEL	NV	VASC
	0	1	2	3	4	5	6
CASES*	30	35	88	8	46	883	13

The total number of cases are 1103

5.3 The Evaluation of CNN from Scratch

Table 2 shows that the outcome of B-Acc for the model with balance (0.637) gives better results than the outcome of B-Acc for the model without balance (0.569). For both classes, 'NV' and 'VASC' had a superior sensitivity in the balanced and unbalanced models compared to the other classes due to the easy identification of these types of lesions as benign. For other classes, the CNN with balance had better sensitivity than the CNN without balance.

Table 2. Result of CNN from scratch overall/per-class.

Model	Classes	ACC	Sen	Sep	F1	PPV	NPV	B-Acc
CNN from Scratch With Balance	AKIEC	0.96	**0.43**	0.98	0.40	0.37	0.98	**0.64**
	BCC	0.97	**0.60**	0.98	0.56	0.53	0.99	
	BKL	0.92	**0.67**	0.94	0.56	0.48	0.97	
	DF	0.99	**0.50**	0.99	0.53	0.57	0.99	
	MEL	0.95	0.41	0.97	0.41	0.40	0.97	
	NV	0.91	0.92	0.88	0.94	0.97	0.73	
	VASC	0.99	**0.92**	0.99	0.92	0.92	0.99	
CNN from Scratch Without Balance	AKIEC	0.97	0.33	0.99	0.36	0.4	0.98	0.57
	BCC	0.97	0.51	0.99	0.54	0.56	0.98	
	BKL	0.94	0.45	0.98	0.53	0.65	0.95	
	DF	0.99	0.38	1.0	0.55	1.0	0.99	
	MEL	0.95	0.41	0.97	0.41	0.41	0.97	
	NV	0.93	**0.98**	0.72	0.96	0.93	0.88	
	VASC	0.99	**0.92**	1.0	0.96	1.0	0.99	

5.4 The Evaluation of the Pre-trained Model

Table 3 shows that these six models have better results than the previous experiment (CNN from scratch in Table 2) in terms of all the evaluation matrices. In general, selecting which of these six models is the best approximate results is difficult. On the other hand, the exclusion of MobileNetV2 and NASNetMobile would yield balanced accuracy of ~ 0.70 and 0.69, respectively. The sensitivity of 'NV' and 'VASC' are easily identified compared to other classes. In contrast, the sensitivity values of 'MEL' and 'AKIEC' were the most challenging for the models to identify. Despite the significant differences between the greatest number of cases 'NV' and the fewest cases of 'VASC' both were well classified, which indicates that these six models are not biased.

Table 3 The result of pre-trained models overall and per-class.

Model	No.	Classes	ACC	Sen	Sep	F1	PPV	NPV	B-Acc
VGG19	*1*	AKIEC	0.98	0.53	0.99	0.62	0.73	0.99	**0.79**
		BCC	0.99	**0.91**	0.99	0.85	0.80	0.99	
		BKL	0.96	0.70	0.98	0.74	0.78	0.97	
		DF	0.99	0.63	**1.0**	0.77	**1.0**	0.99	
		MEL	0.96	**0.76**	0.97	**0.64**	0.55	0.99	
		NV	0.95	0.97	**0.88**	0.97	**0.97**	0.87	
		VASC	**1.0**	**1.0**	**1.0**	**1.0**	**1.0**	**1.0**	
ResNet50	*2*	AKIEC	0.98	0.57	0.99	0.67	0.81	0.99	0.74
		BCC	0.98	0.86	0.99	0.74	0.65	0.99	
		BKL	**0.97**	**0.74**	**0.99**	**0.79**	**0.86**	**0.98**	
		DF	0.99	0.63	1.0	0.77	1.0	0.99	
		MEL	**0.97**	0.52	**0.99**	0.57	**0.63**	0.98	
		NV	0.95	**0.98**	0.84	0.97	0.96	**0.92**	
		VASC	0.99	0.92	0.99	0.86	0.8	0.99	
Inception V3	*3*	AKIEC	0.98	0.5	0.99	0.56	0.63	0.99	0.76
		BCC	0.98	0.83	0.99	0.76	0.71	0.99	
		BKL	0.96	0.65	0.98	0.70	0.76	0.97	
		DF	**0.99**	**0.88**	0.99	**0.88**	0.88	**0.99**	
		MEL	0.96	0.57	0.98	0.57	0.57	0.98	
		NV	0.95	0.97	0.84	0.97	0.96	0.89	
		VASC	0.99	0.92	0.99	0.92	0.92	0.99	
DenseNet 121	*4*	AKIEC	**0.99**	0.6	**0.99**	**0.71**	**0.86**	0.99	0.76
		BCC	**0.99**	0.89	**0.99**	**0.89**	**0.89**	0.99	
		BKL	0.96	0.69	0.98	0.74	0.79	0.97	
		DF	0.99	0.63	0.99	0.71	0.83	0.99	
		MEL	0.96	0.57	0.98	0.55	0.53	0.98	
		NV	0.95	**0.98**	0.84	0.97	0.96	**0.92**	
		VASC	**1.0**	**1.0**	**1.0**	**1.0**	**1.0**	**1.0**	
Xception	*5*	AKIEC	0.98	0.47	**0.99**	0.60	0.82	0.99	0.76
		BCC	0.99	**0.91**	0.99	0.85	0.8	**0.99**	
		BKL	0.96	0.72	0.98	0.75	0.78	0.98	
		DF	0.99	0.75	0.99	0.8	0.86	0.99	
		MEL	**0.97**	0.63	0.98	0.62	0.60	**0.98**	
		NV	0.95	0.98	0.85	0.97	0.96	0.92	
		VASC	0.99	0.85	**1.0**	0.92	**1.0**	0.99	
VGG16	*6*	AKIEC	0.98	**0.67**	0.99	0.69	0.71	**0.99**	0.77
		BCC	0.99	0.8	0.99	0.81	0.82	0.99	
		BKL	0.95	0.68	0.98	0.70	0.72	0.97	
		DF	0.99	0.63	0.99	0.71	0.83	0.99	
		MEL	0.97	0.61	0.98	0.60	0.60	0.98	
		NV	**0.96**	0.98	0.87	**0.97**	0.97	0.91	
		VASC	**1.0**	**1.0**	**1.0**	**1.0**	**1.0**	**1.0**	

5.5   The Evaluation of the Ensemble Pre-trained Models

Table 4 indicates that there was a higher outcome for B-Acc (0.801) and the mean average AUC (0.89) after applied the ensemble learning technique for the six pre-trained models.

Table 4. Overall results for the models and the ensemble model.

	1	2	3	4	5	6	Ensemble
B-Acc	0.786	0.744	0.759	0.764	0.757	0.765	**0.801**
AUC	0.88	0.86	0.86	0.87	0.86	0.87	**0.89**

Therefore, melanoma 'MEL', which is the most dangerous type of skin cancer, the ensemble model has achieved high sensitivity of 80.4% (Table 5). In addition, the model for 'NV' (melanocytic nevus), the most widespread disease among all lesions, reached a great of specificity 89% (Table 5).

Table 5. The result for each class for ensemble model.

Model	Classes	ACC	Sen	Sep	F1	PPV	NPV
Ensemble Pre-trained models	AKIEC	0.98	0.6	0.99	0.68	0.78	0.99
	BCC	0.99	0.89	0.99	0.86	0.84	0.99
	BKL	0.96	0.72	0.98	0.75	0.80	0.98
	DF	0.99	0.63	0.99	0.71	0.83	0.99
	MEL	**0.97**	**0.80**	0.981	**0.72**	**0.65**	**0.99**
	NV	**0.96**	0.98	**0.89**	0.97	**0.97**	0.91
	VASC	1.0	1.0	1.0	1.0	1.0	1.0

5.6   Discussion

The results of the first experiment (shown in Table 2) show that the CNN trained from scratch with balance (data augmentation) enhances the results for the test set.

However, training a CNN built from scratch is difficult because it requires a real, sizeable, balanced amount of labelled training data, a requirement that may be difficult to meet in the medical domain, where expert annotation is expensive, and the identification of the diseases (e.g., the types of lesions) is scarce in datasets. Tajbakhsh et al. [24] reported that it is difficult to train a CNN trained from scratch in the medical field, and that is requires a great deal of expertise to ensure proper convergence. For these reasons, the pre-trained models were applied in the second experiment and achieved the results shown in Table 3; these models outperformed CNN trained from scratch. The results of the second experiment performed on several selected pre-trained models (Table 3) were very similar, making it difficult to identify the best model for all types of lesions. As a consequence, concluded that ensemble learning is one of the most successful approaches that can help to combine several models. The last experiment used an ensemble model whose result achieved the best overall balanced accuracy of 80.1%, and a mean average AUC of 0.89. Melanoma 'MEL', the serious and critical type of skin cancer, the ensemble model obtained a sensitivity of 80.4%, which is the highest result qualified dermatologists can reach based on the ABCD rule [25].

Until now, making comparisons among various strategies for skin lesion analysis was basically impossible; this was due to the lack of standardized evaluation metrics and datasets and the difficulties of code and data sharing [26]. Table 6 shows that our proposed method outperforms the other methods in terms of balanced multi-class accuracy and AUC. The results of our method are quite competitive for the ISIC Skin Image Analysis Workshop and Challenge at MICCAI 2018 [15].

Table 6. The previous work shown at the ISIC 2018 workshop and challenge at MICCIA.

References	Experiment	Results	Limitations
Zou et al. [27]	Used two directions First: three step classifiers. Second: whole dataset with augmentation. Used DenseNet -169	Validation with 193 images First: 0.621 B-Acc Second: 0.751 B-Acc	The shortfall of the 3-step process was due to an imbalance; the process conducted be used for one pre-trained model
Pal et al. [28]	Ensemble model created by averaging three pre-trained models (ResNet50, DenseNet-121, and MobileNet) with weight loss to tackle the imbalance problem	Selected 10% of the training for validation; the final result was given after using the ensemble model's B-Acc of 0.775	MobileNet was not a suitable model; this was shown through their results and the limited number of pre-trained models
Xie et al. [29]	Used Multi-level Deep Ensemble (MLDE) model conducted on ResNet-50 networks with an adaptive weight	Randomly selected 10% of the training for validation; the result was an average AUC of 86.5	There was no diversity in the models used

6 Conclusion and Future Work

Skin cancer is a serious medical problem. Early diagnosis for types of cancer like melanoma is vital for survival. Skin lesion classification challenges are more difficult and clinically relevant. In this study, an effective approach was proposed for assisting dermatologists during the diagnosis of skin lesions. The proposed method relied on the International Skin Imaging Collaboration (ISIC 2018) challenge dataset. Additionally, the present reality is that the datasets are highly imbalanced and are not representative of minority skin pigmentations. Regarding the size constraint, data augmentation technique has been approved to be useful for enhancing classification performance. A deep convolutional neural network trained from scratch along with pre-trained models (transfer learning) were investigated. A novel ensemble model that combined several existing CNN architectures was used in order to increase accuracy to help physicians and dermatologists in decision-making. The best performance was achieved by an ensemble model with balanced multi-classes accuracy of 80.1% and mean average 0.89 ROC AUC. The main limitations of this study are the shortage of sufficient amounts of rare skin lesions such as actinic keratosis, dermatofibroma and vascular lesion not only in the ISIC 2018 challenge but in all publicly available datasets. The images used in this study were collected over a period of 20 years; thus, the resolution for these images is directly related to the wavelength used to capture the image which may affect the performance of classification. For future work, more data would need to be gathered from cutaneous skin and dark skin to improve accuracy and generalize the diagnosis network. Also, including demographics data such as (age, race, sex, etc.) could improve the results accuracy by using multiple inputs and mixed data to combine categorical, numeric, and image data into a single end-to-end network. As a result, combining several types of data will make comparable to the diagnoses of dermatologists.

Acknowledgements. This work was supported by the Deanship of Scientific Research (DSR), Princess Nourah Bint Abdulrahman University, Riyadh, Saudi Arabia.

References

1. Kittler, H., Pehamberger, H., Wolff, K., Binder, M.: Diagnostic accuracy of dermoscopy. Lancet Oncol. **3**(3), 159–165 (2002)
2. Yadav, S., Vossaert, K.A., Kopf, A.W., Silverman, M., Grin-Jorgensen, C.: Histopathologic correlates of structures seen on dermoscopy (epiluminescence microscopy). Am. J. Dermatopathol. **15**(4), 297–305 (1993)
3. Pan, S.J., Yang, Q.: A survey on transfer learning. IEEE Trans. Knowl. Data Eng. **22**(10), 1345–1359 (2010)
4. Brinker, T.J., Hekler, A., Utikal, J.S., Grabe, N., Schadendorf, D., Klode, J., et al.: skin cancer classification using convolutional neural networks: systematic review. J. Med. Internet. Res. **20**(10), e11936 (2018)
5. Esteva, A., Kuprel, B., Novoa, R.A., Ko, J., Swetter, S.M., Blau, H.M., et al.: Dermatologist-level classification of skin cancer with deep neural networks. Nature **542**(7639), 115 (2017)
6. Haenssle, H.A., Fink, C., Schneiderbauer, R., Toberer, F., Buhl, T., Blum, A., et al.: Man against machine: diagnostic performance of a deep learning convolutional neural network for dermoscopic melanoma recognition in comparison to 58 dermatologists. Ann. Oncol. **29**(8), 1836–1842 (2018)
7. Han, S.S., Kim, M.S., Lim, W., Park, G.H., Park, I., Chang, S.E.: Classification of the clinical images for benign and malignant cutaneous tumors using a deep learning algorithm. J Invest Dermatol. **138**(7), 1529–1538 (2018)
8. Yamashita, R., Nishio, M., Do, R.K.G., Togashi, K.: Convolutional neural networks: an overview and application in radiology. Insights Imaging **9**(4), 611–629 (2018)
9. Simonyan, K., Zisserman, A.: Very deep convolutional networks for large-scale image recognition. arXiv Prepr arXiv:14091556 (2014)
10. He, K., Zhang, X., Ren, S., Sun, J.: Deep residual learning for image recognition. In: Proceedings of the IEEE Conference on Computer Vision and Pattern Recognition, pp. 770–778 (2016)

11. Szegedy, C., Vanhoucke, V., Ioffe, S., Shlens, J., Wojna, Z.: Rethinking the inception architecture for computer vision. In: Proceedings of the IEEE Conference on Computer Vision and Pattern Recognition, pp. 2818–2826 (2016)

12. Chollet, F.: Xception: deep learning with depthwise separable convolutions. In: Proceedings of the IEEE Conference on Computer Vision and Pattern Recognition, pp. 1251–1258 (2017)

13. Huang, G., Liu, Z., Van Der Maaten, L., Weinberger, K.Q.: Densely connected convolutional networks. In: Proceedings of the IEEE conference on computer vision and pattern recognition, pp. 4700–4708 (2017)

14. Maji, D., Santara, A., Mitra, P., Sheet, D.: Ensemble of deep convolutional neural networks for learning to detect retinal vessels in fundus images. arXiv Prepr arXiv:160304833 (2016)

15. ISIC. Skin lesion analysis towards melanoma detection. https://www.isic-archive.com/#!/topWithHeader/tightContentTop/challenges

16. Tschandl, P., Rosendahl, C., Kittler, H.: The HAM10000 dataset, a large collection of multi-source dermatoscopic images of common pigmented skin lesions. Sci data. **5**, 180161 (2018)

17. Kingma, D.P., Ba, J.: Adam: a method for stochastic optimization. arXiv Prepr arXiv: 14126980 (2014)

18. Keras. Usage of loss functions (2016). https://keras.io/losses/. Accessed 19 Jan 2019

19. Chollet, F., others.: Keras (2015). https://keras.io/applications/

20. Abadi, M., Agarwal, A., Barham, P., Brevdo, E., Chen, Z., Citro, C., et al.: TensorFlow: large-scale machine learning on heterogeneous systems (2015). https://www.tensorflow.org/

21. Carrillo, H., Brodersen, K.H., Castellanos, J.A.: Probabilistic performance evaluation for multiclass classification using the posterior balanced accuracy. In: ROBOT2013: First Iberian Robotics Conference, pp. 347–361 (2014)

22. Kelleher, J.D., Mac Namee, B., D'arcy, A.: Fundamentals of Machine Learning for Predictive Data Analytics: Algorithms, Worked Examples, and Case Studies. MIT Press, Cambridge (2015)

23. Mandrekar, J.N.: Receiver operating characteristic curve in diagnostic test assessment. J Thorac. Oncol. **5**(9), 1315–1316 (2010)

24. Tajbakhsh, N., Shin, J.Y., Gurudu, S.R., Hurst, R.T., Kendall, C.B., Gotway, M.B., et al.: Convolutional neural networks for medical image analysis: full training or fine tuning? IEEE Trans. Med. Imaging **35**(5), 1299–1312 (2016)

25. Argenziano, G., Soyer, H.P.: Dermoscopy of pigmented skin lesions–a valuable tool for early. Lancet Oncol. **2**(7), 443–449 (2001)

26. Fornaciali, M., Carvalho, M., Bittencourt, F.V., Avila, S., Valle, E.: Towards automated melanoma screening: proper computer vision & reliable results. arXiv Prepr arXiv: 160404024 (2016)

27. Zou, J., Ma, X., Zhong, C., Zhang, Y.: Dermoscopic image analysis for ISIC challenge (2018). arXiv Prepr arXiv:180708948

28. Pal, A., Ray, S., Garain, U.: Skin disease identification from dermoscopy images using deep convolutional neural network. arXiv Prepr arXiv:180709163 (2018)

29. Xie, Y., Zhang, J., Xia, Y.: A multi-level deep ensemble model for skin lesion classification in dermoscopy images. arXiv Prepr arXiv:180708488 (2018)

A Comprehensive Review Towards Appropriate Feature Selection for Moving Object Detection Using Aerial Images

Zainal Rasyid Mahayuddin[1] and A. F. M. Saifuddin Saif[2(✉)]

[1] Faculty of Information Science and Technology,
University Kebangsaan Malaysia, Bangi, Selangor, Malaysia
zainalr@ukm.edu.my
[2] Faculty of Science and Technology,
American International University–Bangladesh, Dhaka, Bangladesh
saif@aiub.edu

Abstract. Efficient feature extraction for moving object using aerial images is still an unsolved issue in computer vision, image processing and pattern recognition research domains. Aerial types of images contain various environmental constraints due to capture frames from various altitudes level, i.e. illumination, shadows, occlusion. For this reason, appropriate feature selection for those types of images needs more attention by the researchers to improve detection rate with fast and computationally less complex features extraction method. This research performed comprehensive review with critical analysis for using various features with various methods for moving object detection using aerial images. In this context, three aspects for critical analysis of using various features are identified followed by challenges of using various features. After that, existing methods with advantages and barriers are comprehensively described with various constraints claimed by the previous research. Next, justification for the need of new feature selection is elaborated for optimum detection performance. Later, adequate validation matrics are illustrated to evaluate various features based moving object detection using aerial images performed in the previous research. The overall review performed in this paper have been comprehensively studied and expected to contribute significantly in computer vision, image processing pattern recognition research field.

Keywords: Aerial images · Feature extraction · Segmentation

1 Introduction

Selection of appropriate feature for efficient manipulation within method for moving object detection from aerial types of images is still an unsolved issue in computer vision, image processing and pattern recognition research domains. Previously, various segmentation method within single frame and frame difference method within multiple methods were investigated in order to facilitate computationally fast moving object extraction from aerial images. Image like aerial types have many constrains like lack of features due to unstable camera position, various altitude level, illuminations, structural

© Springer Nature Switzerland AG 2019
H. Badioze Zaman et al. (Eds.): IVIC 2019, LNCS 11870, pp. 227–236, 2019.
https://doi.org/10.1007/978-3-030-34032-2_21

and unstructured shape of objects make the tasks of extracting features more difficult which requires huge amount of processing time during overall detection methodology. This research illustrates comprehensive review of multiple aspects of using various features, constraints of using existing features and existing methods with the usage of various features with advantages and disadvantages for extraction for moving object using aerial images.

Type of features with various constraints and various methods used for extraction is the key factor to increase or decrease computation time and detection rate. Three kinds of features were used previously for moving object detection. i.e., corner [5–8], colour [9, 10, 29], and edge [1, 3, 26] features. Harris corner feature detection is the mostly used for extraction purpose [27, 28]. Besides, several types of edge detectors were used for overall procedure, i.e., Sobel, Canny, and Prewitt [5, 21]. Recently, numerous researchers have started to use corner and edge features together [2, 21, 22].

This research presents comprehensive review with critical analysis of various features which can be categorized as three types, i.e. colour, corner and edge. Section 2 demonstrates previous work on existing features with multiples aspects, Sect. 3 illustrates justification for the need of new feature selection and Sect. 4 depicts various performance parameters which should be used for validation. Concluding remarks is described in the conclusion section.

2   Existing Research on Various Features

Various parameters estimation depending on various sizes is primary concern for motion based moving object detection where types of feature were fertile research concern due to computation time and complexity. In addition, facilitation of fast moving object detection was investigated in previous research based on various methods. Efficient feature selection is an unsolved problem specially for moving object detection for aerial types of image which needs to be integrated with specific method types. For each of the method used previously, researcher considered certain feature for deep manipulation of the overall process. This research found three aspects for critical analysis in previous research for moving object detection from aerial types of images shown in Fig. 1.

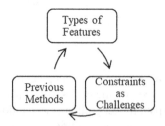

Fig. 1. Three aspects for critical analysis on previous research

Previously, three kinds of features were used by the existing research, i.e. color, corner and edge features. Table 1 shows existing research performed based on various features. Cheng et al. [5] used color features where pixel-wise classification method was used for detection. They preserved relation among neighboring pixels in a region, however due to large parameter constraints, their research lacks in enough reliability. Later, candidate key points of object pixels using color features were identified by Zheng et al. [11]. However, their research did not work well for structural shape. After that, Chen et al. [10] considered color features for complex background in urban environments where they followed the constraints of considering grayscale images in real time which was not a reliable solution.

Table 1. Previous research for moving object detection using various features

Previous research	Colour features	Corner features	Edge features	Colour features + Corner feature
Ibrahim et al. [3]	No	No	No	Yes
Pollard and Antone [6]	No	No	No	Yes
Wang [2]	No	Yes	No	No
Jiang et al. [23]	No	No	Yes	No
Cheraghi and Sheikh [7]	No	Yes	No	No
Luo et al. [8]	Yes	No	Yes	No
Moranduzzo and Melgani [9]	Yes	No	No	No
Chen et al. [10]	Yes	No	No	No
Kembhavi et al. [12]	Yes	No	Yes	No
Wang [2]	No	Yes	Yes	No
Zheng et al. [11]	No	No	Yes	No
Cheng et al. [5]	Yes	Yes	Yes	Yes
Breckon et al. [20]	No	Yes	No	No
Bhuvaneswari and Rauf [15]	No	No	Yes	No
Oreifej et al. [22]	Yes	No	Yes	No
Qian and Medioni [19]	No	No	No	No
Gleason et al. [13]	Yes	Yes (Harris)	No	No
Gaszczak et al. [18]	Yes	No	No	No
Huang et al. [17]	No	Yes (Harris)	No	No

Kembhavi et al. [12] introduced dual selection approach to reduce computation of feature selection where they used corner features by extracting large features set from neighboring pixels. From their research, various issues like unstructured objects, presence of stark contrasts, long shadows constraints, reflection of sunlight, rectangular or triangular structures on the tops of buildings, and occlusion were not considered during validation. Comparing with their research, Gleason et al. [13] improved the solution for various challenges using corner features by considering 3D image orientation, blurring due to unstable vibrations, variations in illumination conditions, and season changes. However, Gleason et al. [13] remove most of the background properties during validation which was unrealistic. Later, frame difference based method considering corner features later introduced by Pollard and Antone [6] where they initialized motion analysis. However, due to usage of only one dataset, research by Pollard and Antone [6] was not validated sufficiently. In addition, Wang [2] and Saif et al. [4] introduced context-aware saliency detection algorithm for attracting human using corner feature where they considered surrounded environment to segment points. Their proposed research provided promising results for constraints like shape resolution and variant appearance of object which overcomes the short-comings of segmentation algorithm for aerial images. However, their research still needs further validation for urban environment scenario.

Wang [2] considered shadows for proposing a new feature extraction framework where edge features were used in conjunction with rotationally invariant shape matching as shape context descriptor. However, Wang [2] could not identify objects for clocked shadows under various lightening condition. Oreifej et al. [22] used edge features for low quality and pose variation issues in the scenario of changing object location and articulation. They assumed that the object position in the next frame should be close to its position in the current frame which results their research exhibited good performance in high frame rate. Later, Luo et al. [8] considered motion estimation by clustering single points from edge features. However, in the context of complexity of shortening environment, real-time changes in background, and inconspicuous features of objects, Luo et al. [8] could not provide expected results. In the context of highly challenging and ambiguous scenario, Jiang et al. [23] and Bhuvaneswari and Rauf [15] used edge features in individual frames for data association. Their research was discriminative for data association where performance of their research across long periods of partial and full occlusion was the challenging issue. Besides, their research was dependent on substantial usage of classifier which increased computation time. In addition, Jiang et al. [23] and Mofaddel and Abd-Elhafiez [16] also considered motion estimation using edge features. However, traditional substantial dependency of huge parameters was not addressed in their research. Previous research based on methods with the concerned features is mentioned in Tables 2 and 3.

Motion detection is closely related with detection of moving object from aerial types of images. So, motion estimation was not addressed adequately in previous research where motion estimation can be described as a function of the image pixel intensity as well as pixel color, corner and edge [24, 25, 30]. Previously, methods proposed by the researcher depend on specific factors, i.e. structural shape of objects, shadows and illumination variation. Besides, existing was not investigated for multiple features which should be an active concern for further investigation. As aerial images are captured from various altitudes level with varieties of constraints, significance of features selection integrating with existing methods should be the basis for further analysis for reliable validation of moving object detection from aerial images.

Table 2. Previous research with various constraints for moving object detection

Previous research	Constrained claimed in previous research	Concerned feature
Cheng et al. [5]	Large parameter estimations	Color
Chen et al. [10]	Complex backgrounds in urban environments	Color
Pollard and Antone [6]	Unstructured objects, the presence of stark contrasts, the presence of long shadows, the reflection of sunlight, rectangular triangular structures on the tops of buildings, and objects in parking spots when the objects were situated in parallel	Edge, Corner and Color
Gleason et al. [13]	3D image orientation, image blurring due to airplane vibrations, variations in illumination conditions, and season changes	Corner
Wang [2]	Shadows	Edge
Oreifej et al. [22]	Pose Variations, high-frame-rate.	Edge
Jiang et al. [23] and Bhuvaneswari and Rauf [15]	Partial and full cclusions, substantial dependencies on a classifier	Edge

Table 3. Previous research with existing methods for moving object detection

Previous research	Method	Disadvantages	Previously used feature for the method used
Cheng et al. [5]	Pixel-wise classification method	Dependent on large parameter estimations	Color
Pollard and Antone [6]	Frame difference method	No motion model proposed	Corner
Kembhavi et al. [12]	Dual selection approach	Did not provide the expected results for unstructured objects	Corner
Wang [2] and Saif et al. [4]	Context-aware saliency detection algorithm	Did not provide sufficient experimental evidence	Corner
Wang [2]	Invariant shape matching	Dependent on lightening conditions	Edge

3 Justification Towards New Feature Selection for Moving Object Detection

Need of significant characteristics selection as feature extraction from scene interpretation of moving object using aerial images has increased tremendously in computer vision, image processing and pattern recognition research domains. The overall reason for significant feature selection is shown in Fig. 2. Details illustrations for each of these reasons are described in the next subsections.

Fig. 2. Overall reason for significant feature selection

3.1 Aspects Towards Efficiency for the Validation Metrics and Motion Features Extraction

Efficiency for the validation metrics, i.e. Detection Rate (DR) and Computer Time (CT) mainly depends on the type of characteristics extracted during execution of the framework for overall detection procedure. Performance of moving object detection has two aspects for validation, i.e. capturing images from moving platform and capturing images from static platform. For the UAV platform where aerial images are mainly captured from various height levels referred as altitude level, extraction of motion features is another crucial part for optimum detection performance. As computer vision mainly focuses on describing the object as scene interpretation before classification, so extraction of motion features surely plays vital role to provide scene descriptor as rich description of object.

3.2 Aspects Towards Challenges on Previously Exists Features

Existing various features based detection, i.e. color based detection, edge based detection and corner based detection could provide reliable solution as suitable feature globally for multiple object detection based on multiple purposes. However, color features are unable to detect multiple objects under same color constraint issues. Besides, adjustment of various parameters during detection causes high computational complexity by corner features. In addition, edges features based detection depends on number of edges detected during overall methodology to provide reliable performance in robust environments.

3.3 Aspects Towards Challenges on Previously Exists Method and Insufficient Features

Commonly, two types of methods exist previously for moving object detection from aerial images, i.e. frame difference based method and static segmentation method applied on single frame. For efficient facilitation of computationally less complex moving object detection, suitable feature extraction plays vital role in the frame achieved from frame difference method or in static segmentation method. The main reason remains behind this fact is that immune validation parameter like Detection Rate (DR) and Computation Time (CT) mostly depends on suitable feature selection and thus demands for fast feature extraction methodology. In addition, as aerial images are captured from various altitudes, this results that these types of images contain less number of features or characteristics to be used for the detection of objects. Thus, insufficient features from aerial images reveals for the selection of unique characteristics with fast feature extraction methodology. Besides, selection of significant features for aerial images are related with selection of important motion features, so the need of fast feature extraction methodology demands to be integrated with selection of significant motion features too for robust detection performance with minimal computation time.

Experimental Validation and Evaluation Parameters. With the usage of previously exist features, researchers experimented moving object detection where robust validation was not available depending on the criteria of features types. Experimental validation using these features with advantages and disadvantages are mentioned below with standard performance metrics demonstrated by the previous research.

3.4 Lack of Experimental Validation in Previous Research

In previous research mostly three types of features were experimented for moving object detection, i.e. corner, color and edge. Breckon et al. [20] achieved detection speed of 6.25 fps using corner features while Chen et al. [10] and Bhuvaneswari and Rauf [15] achieved detection speed of 6 fps and 24.2 fps using color features and edge features respectively. For corner based detection, Harris corner features is the mostly used features whereas using edge feature detection there are three types of edge exists in the previous research, i.e. sobel, prewitt and canny [5, 16, 21, 23]. For significant local variance referred as edge based detection, number of thin and smooth edge plays vital role to decide either the edge is object or not which is more challenging in aerial types of images. In this context, sobel and prewitt edge based detection did not provide reliable object detection performance [14]. In addition, another challenge arises when some of the previous researchers applied canny edge based detection where good performance by using this feature based detection depends on adjustment important parameters which cause high computation time [5, 21].

Besides, combination of using corner and edge features together was initialized before by some researchers [2, 8, 22]. However, in both cases of either using features separately or hybrid methodology, computation time issue did not receive attention by most of the researchers. In addition, selection of motion features for aerial type images was not considered in most of the previous research which should be addressed for moving object detection specially for aerial type images where scene are captured from various altitudes level with significant variation of UAV speed.

3.5   Validation Metrics for Significant Feature Based Moving Object Detection

Evaluation for selection of various features for moving object detection can be performed based on the parameters mentioned in Eqs. (1) and (2) which were illustrated in the previous research [3, 5, 15, 20].

$$DR = \frac{\text{True Positive}}{\text{True Positive} + \text{False Negative}} \times 100\% \tag{1}$$

$$FAR = \frac{\text{False Positive}}{\text{True Positive} + \text{False Positive}} \times 100\% \tag{2}$$

Here, in Eqs. (1) and (2) DR and FAR means Detection Rate and False Alarm Rate respectively. In both equations, True Positive (TP) refers detected region contains targeted moving object in the scene. False Positive (FP) refers detected regions which does not contain targeted moving object in the scene. In addition, False Negative (FN) refers that moving object is not detected for the considered scenario.

4   Conclusion

Moving object detection extracts changed regions from frames either by frame difference method or segmentation method, which is a potential research problem of computer vision, image processing and pattern recognition research domains. In this context, selection of features is still an unsolved issue which influences performance evaluation in terms of detection rate, false alarm rate and computation time. This research performs demonstration of review over existing research about the usage of various features like color features, edge features and corner features. Besides, based on the feature, efficient features extraction technique is one of the vital issues for detection performance especially for aerial images. Later, validation of the selected feature is necessary to evaluate performance robustly for overall detection methodology. For this reason, this research at first illustrates each of the features which were previously used with advantages and disadvantages. Next, justification of the new feature selection and extraction technique is elaborated to influence detection performance. Later, validation criteria are depicted to ensure the best selection of features for optimum detection performance. Based on the illustrated review, it is certain that selection of the correct feature will contribute in the future research in computer vision, image processing and pattern recognition research field.

Acknowledgements. The authors would like to thank Universiti Kebangsaan Malaysia for providing financial support under the GERAN GALAKAN PENYELIDIKAN research grant, GGP-2017-030.

References

1. Yang, Y., Liu, F., Wang, P., Luo, P., Liu, X.: Vehicle detection methods from an unmanned aerial vehicle platform. In: 2012 IEEE International Conference on Vehicular Electronics and Safety (ICVES 2012), pp. 411–415. IEEE (2012)
2. Wang, S.: Vehicle detection on aerial images by extracting corner features for rotational invariant shape matching. In: 2011 IEEE 11th International Conference on Computer and Information Technology, pp. 171–175. IEEE (2011)
3. Ibrahim, A.W.N., Ching, P.W., Seet, G.G., Lau, W.M., Czajewski, W.: Moving objects detection and tracking framework for UAV-based surveillance. In: 2010 Fourth Pacific-Rim Symposium on Image and Video Technology, pp. 456–461. IEEE (2010)
4. Saif, A.S., Prabuwono, A.S., Mahayuddin, Z.R., Mantoro, T.: Vision-based human face recognition using extended principal component analysis. Int. J. Mob. Comput. Multimedia Commun. (IJMCMC) **5**, 82–94 (2013)
5. Cheng, H.-Y., Weng, C.-C., Chen, Y.-Y.: Vehicle detection in aerial surveillance using dynamic Bayesian networks. IEEE Trans. Image Process. **21**, 2152–2159 (2011)
6. Pollard, T., Antone, M.: Detecting and tracking all moving objects in wide-area aerial video. In: 2012 IEEE Computer Society Conference on Computer Vision and Pattern Recognition Workshops, pp. 15–22. IEEE (2012)
7. Cheraghi, S.A., Sheikh, U.U.: Moving object detection using image registration for a moving camera platform. In: 2012 IEEE International Conference on Control System, Computing and Engineering, pp. 355–359. IEEE (2012)
8. Luo, P., Liu, F., Liu, X., Yang, Y.: Stationary vehicle detection in aerial surveillance with a UAV. In: 2012 8th International Conference on Information Science and Digital Content Technology (ICIDT2012), pp. 567–570. IEEE (2012)
9. Moranduzzo, T., Melgani, F.: A SIFT-SVM method for detecting cars in UAV images. In: 2012 IEEE International Geoscience and Remote Sensing Symposium, pp. 6868–6871. IEEE, (2012)
10. Chen, L., Jiang, Z., Yang, J., Ma, Y.: A coarse-to-fine approach for vehicles detection from aerial images. In: 2012 International Conference on Computer Vision in Remote Sensing, pp. 221–225. IEEE (2012)
11. Zheng, Z., Wang, X., Zhou, G., Jiang, L.: Vehicle detection based on morphology from highway aerial images. In: 2012 IEEE International Geoscience and Remote Sensing Symposium, pp. 5997–6000. IEEE (2012)
12. Kembhavi, A., Harwood, D., Davis, L.S.: Vehicle detection using partial least squares. IEEE Trans. Pattern Anal. Mach. Intell. **33**, 1250–1265 (2011)
13. Gleason, J., Nefian, A.V., Bouyssounousse, X., Fong, T., Bebis, G.: Vehicle detection from aerial imagery. In: 2011 IEEE International Conference on Robotics and Automation, pp. 2065–2070. IEEE (2011)
14. Wang, L., Zhao, H., Guo, S., Mai, Y., Liu, S.: The adaptive compensation algorithm for small UAV image stabilization. In: 2012 IEEE International Geoscience and Remote Sensing Symposium, pp. 4391–4394. IEEE (2012)

15. Bhuvaneswari, K., Rauf, H.A.: Edgelet based human detection and tracking by combined segmentation and soft decision. In: 2009 International Conference on Control, Automation, Communication and Energy Conservation, pp. 1–6. IEEE (2009)
16. Mofaddel, M.A., Abd-Elhafiez, W.M.: Fast and accurate approaches for image and moving object segmentation. In: The 2011 International Conference on Computer Engineering & Systems, pp. 252–259. IEEE (2011)
17. Huang, C.-H., Wu, Y.-T., Kao, J.-H., Shih, M.-Yu., Chou, C.-C.: A hybrid moving object detection method for aerial images. In: Qiu, G., Lam, K.M., Kiya, H., Xue, X.-Y., Kuo, C.-C.Jay, Lew, M.S. (eds.) PCM 2010. LNCS, vol. 6297, pp. 357–368. Springer, Heidelberg (2010). https://doi.org/10.1007/978-3-642-15702-8_33
18. Gaszczak, A., Breckon, T.P., Han, J.: Real-time people and vehicle detection from UAV imagery. In: SPIE (2011)
19. Qian, Y., Medioni, G.: Motion pattern interpretation and detection for tracking moving vehicles in airborne video. In: 2009 IEEE Conference on Computer Vision and Pattern Recognition, pp. 2671–2678 (2009)
20. Breckon, T.P., Barnes, S.E., Eichner, M.L., Wahren, K.: Autonomous real-time vehicle detection from a medium-level UAV. In: 24th International Conference on Unmanned Air Vehicle Systems (2009)
21. Teutsch, M., Krüger, W.: Spatio-temporal fusion of object segmentation approaches for moving distant targets. In: 2012 15th International Conference on Information Fusion, pp. 1988–1995 (2012)
22. Oreifej, O., Mehran, R., Shah, M.: Human identity recognition in aerial images. In: 2010 IEEE Computer Society Conference on Computer Vision and Pattern Recognition, pp. 709–716. IEEE (2010)
23. Jiang, Z., Ding, W., Li, H.: Aerial video image object detection and tracing based on motion vector compensation and statistic analysis. In: 2009 Asia Pacific Conference on Postgraduate Research in Microelectronics & Electronics (PrimeAsia), pp. 302–305. IEEE (2009)
24. Saif, A.S., Prabuwono, A.S., Mahayuddin, Z.R.: Motion analysis for moving object detection from UAV aerial images: A review. In: 2014 International Conference on Informatics, Electronics & Vision (ICIEV), pp. 1–6. IEEE (2014)
25. Saif, A.F.M.S., Prabuwono, A.S., Mahayuddin, Z.R.: Real time vision based object detection from UAV aerial images: a conceptual framework. In: Omar, K., et al. (eds.) FIRA 2013. CCIS, vol. 376, pp. 265–274. Springer, Heidelberg (2013). https://doi.org/10.1007/978-3-642-40409-2_23
26. Zebbara, K., Ansari, M.E., Mazoul, A., Oudani, H.: A fast road obstacle detection using association and symmetry recognition. In: 2019 International Conference on Wireless Technologies, Embedded and Intelligent Systems (WITS) (2019)
27. Vasavi, S., Shaik, A.F.: Moving object classification under illumination changes using binary descriptors. In: Optoelectronics in Machine Vision-Based Theories and Applications, pp. 188–232. IGI Global (2019)
28. Wang, Y., et al.: Detection and classification of moving vehicle from video using multiple spatio-temporal features. IEEE Access 7, 80287–80299 (2019)
29. Saif, A.S., Prabuwono, A.S., Mahayuddin, Z.R.: Moment feature based fast feature extraction algorithm for moving object detection using aerial images. PloS one 10, e0126212 (2015)
30. Saif, A., Prabuwono, A.S., Mahayuddin, Z.R.: Moving object detection using dynamic motion modelling from UAV aerial images. Sci. World J. 2014 (2014)

SUFID: Sliced and Unsliced Fruits Images Dataset

Latifah Abdullah Bin Turayki[1([⊠])] and Nirase Fathima Abubacker[2]

[1] DCU @ Princess Nourah bint Abdulrahman University, Riyadh, Saudi Arabia
Laaltraiki@pnu.edu.sa
[2] Dublin City University, Dublin, Ireland
nirase.fathimaabubacker@dcu.ie

Abstract. Given the recent surge in online images of fruit, ever more sophisticated models and algorithms are required to organize, index, retrieve, and interact such data. However, the relative immaturity of the processes in current use is holding back development in the field. The current paper explains how images of ten classes of fruit namely apples, bananas, kiwis, lemons, oranges, pears, pineapples, coconuts, mangos and watermelons, presented both sliced and unsliced, were sourced from the Fruits360, FIDS30, and ImageNet datasets to create a single database, "SUFID", containing 7,500 high-res images. Pre-processing was based on using pixel color distribution to determine whether each image was corrupt, or would fit the database. The paper describes the unique opportunities, principally within computer vision, presented by SUFID's hierarchical structure, accuracy, diversity, and scale, all of which can be of use to food researchers. As the dataset and benchmarks are believed to be of benefit to all researchers in the field, they are offered gratis to support future study.

Keywords: Sliced fruits · Unsliced fruits · Multiclass fruits · Balanced fruits dataset

1 Introduction

Digital imagery is used ever more frequently, with digital images of fruit – in particular, sliced fruit – seeing a surge in number, popularity, and availability. Researchers have therefore proposed increasingly sophisticated algorithms and models to facilitate the use of these images, in particular to encourage better organization, indexing, retrieval of data, and user interaction. Given that fruit is normally traded unsliced, few models or algorithms have, to date, been devised to deal with sliced fruit. Moreover, annotating data to the extent required is costly in terms of time and resources. Therefore, although sliced fruit constitutes a core element of food research, few accurate relevant data are available. A technology which enables the automatic recognition of sliced fruit would thus be of significant use to researchers investigating the causes and treatment of obesity as it would allow them to capture dietary intake, and enable self-recording patients to accurately and easily track their consumption. Fruit trading companies would also benefit from the availability of this type of multiclass dataset [1, 2]. Combined with recent progress in deep learning, it is therefore considered that a good dataset will be of benefit to both researchers and businesses.

© Springer Nature Switzerland AG 2019
H. Badioze Zaman et al. (Eds.): IVIC 2019, LNCS 11870, pp. 237–244, 2019.
https://doi.org/10.1007/978-3-030-34032-2_22

Fig. 1. Sample of the unsliced fruits.   **Fig. 2.** Sample of the sliced fruits.

The SUFID dataset was designed to both reliable and balanced. It offers images of multiclass fruits (ten varieties of fruit), both sliced and unsliced: bananas, coconuts, lemons, oranges, watermelons, apples, kiwis, pears, mangos and pineapples. This is of obvious benefit to researchers seeking to develop robust image-searching algorithms in which understanding is derived from content, and provides training and benchmarking data against which to test such algorithms. Thus, it will reduce both the time and cost of future research in the area of computer vision. Ultimately, it offers significant potential for the creation of a high-performance deep-learning model.

Recent competition in object recognition has further boosted the development of algorithms. Despite these advances, the fact that datasets tend to be collated with a particular purpose in mind has concentrated research in specific areas, such as sliced or unsliced fruit. The present study aims to progress the automated recognition of fruit by making freely available a comprehensive database of images of common varieties of fruit taken in a range of conditions. Furthermore, it is hoped it will foster the development of more advanced methods of fruit production, for example automated harvesting and yield mapping. In the following sections, the paper sets out the research framework underlying the creation of the SUFID balanced fruits dataset: sourcing the images, challenging the derived dataset, and, finally, creating the data collection and pre-processing protocol.

2   Fruit Images Sources

Fruit-related databases tend to suffer from one or both of two limitations: low numbers, or only containing images of whole (unsliced) fruit. The most commonly used datasets are described below.

Fruits-360[1] [3] a dataset of 100×100-sized images of unsliced fruit. Each class is made up of 500–1000 images of a single fruit, pictured from different angles. The Fruits-360 dataset is no has sliced fruits.

Unlike Fruits-360, FIDS30 dataset [4][2] contain images for sliced fruits as well as unsliced. While the database contains 971 images divided into 30 categories, with between 30 to 50 images per category, there is great variety among the images. Some images have white backgrounds, with some having backgrounds that are noisy and

---

[1] https://www.kaggle.com/moltean/fruits#fruits-360_dataset.zip.

[2] https://www.vicos.si/Downloads/FIDS30.

coloured, and image sizes differ greatly. Some images are of just one fruit, while some contain a variety.

ImageNet [5][3] a large database containing approximately 22,000 different categories described by Deng (2009), each with more than 500 images. ImageNet's size and diversity have made it the 'gold standard' for image recognition purposes; however, due to the wide range of objects covered, there is no focus on food research and so fruit images need to be extracted.

After a database was selected from the three sources, the next stage was pre-processing. Pre-processing is a vital part of the process in preparing images, and can be broken down into several steps, as discussed in more detail in the following sections. The quality of images used in this study varied considerably, as did the degree of pre-processing required.

3   Challenges

Several challenges were encountered when building this dataset. Firstly, it was difficult to find sufficient suitable images as far fewer are available of certain types of sliced and unsliced fruit than of others. Secondly, the process of using algorithms to locate the desired data was lengthy and exacting. Thirdly, images were available in a variety of formats, creating noise, which reduced the degree to which they were useful.

Unified image resolution was therefore used to resize images to a predefined resolution, with the standard 224×224 adopted. Table 1 below summarizes the resolutions required for architectures used with transfer learning [6].

Table 1. The Resolution for architectures employed with transfer learning.

Network	Pre-training	Scale
AlexNet	ImageNet	227×227
AlexNet	ImageNet	451×451
VGG16	ImageNet	224×224
VGG19	ImageNet	224×224
GoogleNet	ImageNet	224×224

It has been proven by multiple studies that augmenting data can enhance deep learning as related to image classification. So, when the first stage of pre-processing was complete, the data were augmented by employing traditional elastic and affine transformations, whereby new images were generated by rotation or reflection of the source, or zooming in on certain parts of it.

---

[3] http://www.image-net.org.

Pre-processing is essential with a number of steps needing to be taken for image preparation. Images employed in this study will be of various qualities, and some will require more pre-processing than others.

4 Data Preparation

For an image classification model to be considered 'state-of-the-art', it must have a significant amount of labeled, supervised data which, in turn, depends on a significant investment of human time and effort, given that data are scarce and collating those available is an expensive undertaking. The available fruit-related databases tend to offered limited information about the type and condition of the fruit pictured. Searching existing datasets revealed that they tend to privilege images of whole over sliced fruit, and have too few of the latter for any clear outcome to be generated. Thus, for the new database to be properly balanced, it was necessary to obtain data from several sources.

4.1 Dataset Collection Protocol

Data were sourced from three datasets, namely FIDS30, Fruits360, and ImageNet. The multiclass fruits represented were apples, bananas, coconuts, kiwis, lemons, mangos, oranges, pears, pineapples, and watermelons, selected because they were covered by all three chosen datasets, and a total of 7500 usable images were located. First, approximately 40–60 images per class of fruit were taken from Fruits360; thereafter, a further 47–55 per class were taken from FIDS30, and finally, ImageNet was used to ensure a balance of images of sliced and unsliced fruit for each class.

As ImageNet includes multiple classes of different-sized and-colored fruit images, it is suitable for the detection and classification of objects. First, images were acquired from the ImageNet database by running a crawler (python code) to parse the images of the required classes, forwarding the URLs and unique fruit numbers from the source and downloading copies to the destination, as summarized in Table 2. Thereafter, extraction and pre-processing were carried out as described in the next section.

Table 2. Unique fruit numbers in ImageNet

Class	Apple	Banana	Kiwi	Lemon	Orange
ImageNet fruit number	07739125	07753592	07763629	07749582	07747607
Class	Pear	Pineapple	Coconut	Mango	Watermelon
ImageNet fruit number	07767847	07753275	07772935	07764155	07756951

4.2 Dataset Pre-processing

Inputting the data extracted resulted in a tri-colored matrix described as (L) × (W) (3) where: L = number of pixels in X-axis; W = number of pixels in Y-axis; and 3 = number of channels (blue, green, and red). This study adopted the standard size of matrix used for networks trained on ImageNet, which is 224 × 224 × 3.

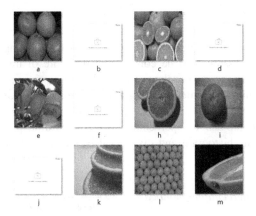

Fig. 3. Sample of images downloaded from ImageNet, (b), (d), (f) and (j) represent invalid images, (a), (c), (e), (g), (h), (i), (k) and (m) represent valid images.

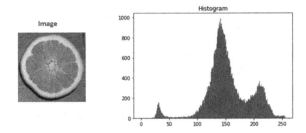

Fig. 4. Pixel colour distribution of a valid image.

Once the images were downloaded, they had to be checked for corruption and to be sure they were valid for the purposes of this study. As can be seen from Fig. 3., it was clear that (b), (d), (f), and (j) were invalid image.

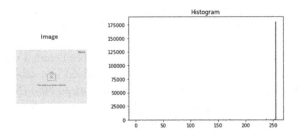

Fig. 5. Pixel colour distribution of a invalid image.

The validity of images was assessed on the basis of distribution of pixel color. Figures 4 and 5 demonstrate how a pixel color distribution plot can determine the fitness or corruption of a given image: if there is too much of a single color within an image, it is generally assumed to be corrupt and therefore of limited use in model training. The filter is designed to evaluate each and every image and then compute the histogram, with the invalidity criterion being a monochrome value of over 0.8. In other words, images which are composed of 80% of more of a single color were excluded as invalid. The filter computes the percentage of monochrome pixels by taking the maximum value of the histogram and dividing it by the size of the image using the formula:

$$percentage\_monochrome = \frac{max\_histogram}{height \times width}$$

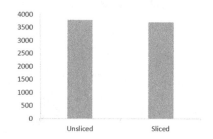

Fig. 6. Number of images of unsliced and sliced fruit.

The next step was to ensure that all imported images had the dimensions required for the extracted database, i.e., 224 × 224 (height x width). After import, filtration, and resizing had been carried out, a balance between images of sliced and unsliced fruit had to be secured to ensure results would be reliable. A thorough manual check revealed that in certain subsets there was an imbalance between the two; therefore, a further search of the source dataset was run in order to extract the necessary number of relevant images. Images of the minority class (sliced or unsliced) were also modified by rotating, cutting, cropping, or zooming as required, and re-inserted into the dataset as an additional balancing step. Figure 6 shows the number of images in the unsliced and sliced fruits.

Once the preparation processes outlined above had been carried out for each and every image in every class of fruit, the dataset was divided into subsets for training, validation, and testing. The first of these, training, comprised 80% (N = 6000) of the total images, with the remaining 20% (N = 1500) assigned to testing. These 1500 images were then withdrawn before the final testing phase.

Despite the laboriousness of the work described above, the set of data ultimately collected is of value as these processes cumulatively balanced out the properties of the images of fruit extracted. This will be of significant help to a range of sections of the research community.

4.3   SUFID Summary

The SUFID balanced fruits dataset comprises a repository of high-quality, 224×224-pixel images of ten classes of fruit (apples, bananas, coconuts, kiwis, lemons, mangos, oranges, pears, pineapples, and watermelons). Each class of fruit is represented by 750 images, of which 600 comprise the training set and the remaining 150 comprise the testing set. A proper balance of sliced and unsliced images of each class of fruit has been maintained. Each image presents one example or multiple examples of a single class of fruit. Sample dataset images are reproduced in Figs. 1 and 2.

5   Experiment Environments

This study used Anaconda Distribution, which employs packages from Python, a programming language that can implement deep learning models using Keras and TensorFlow libraries. TensorFlow was created by Google. It is an-open source deep learning framework that uses data flow graphs to perform numerical computations. The notes in the flow graphs signify mathematical operations, while the edges of the graphs signify the tensors, which are multidimensional data arrays [7]. This study also notably used an Nvidia GPU was used for this study's experiments. The GPU requires CUDA libraries to activate TensorFlow.

6   Conclusions

The current paper has presented the SUFID balanced fruits dataset, which is a high-quality database offering balanced numbers of images of sliced and unsliced examples of ten categories of fruits. The objective of this research is to make this dataset freely and widely available to researchers in relevant fields of computer vision, namely fruit classification, recognition and clustering. The images in the database were sourced from three existing datasets ((Fruits360, ImageNet, and FIDS30) and are of apples, bananas, coconuts, kiwis, lemons, mangos, oranges, pears, pineapples, and watermelons. Images are presented of sliced and unsliced examples of each class of fruit, sometimes appearing singly and sometimes with multiple examples in a single image.

The current research makes three contributions to the field. Firstly, it is our hope that, given its careful balance of images of sliced and unsliced fruits, SUFID will become a valuable resource across computer vision studies, particularly within fruit research, as images of sliced fruit have previously been difficult to source. Secondly, SUFID should be of value in training, as the algorithms currently used for object recognition tend to focus on images of unsliced fruit due to their easier availability. Indeed, future researchers could study the possibilities around transferring knowledge of common objects to models learning rare objects. Lastly, SUFID can serve as a more sophisticated and up-to-date benchmark database for future computer vision research, which it is hoped will encourage more research in the specific field of fruit recognition.

Future work will focus on the following points:

i. Develop an effective systems to classify and clustering multiclass fruits images, including both sliced and unsliced fruit using SUFID.
ii. Extending this study to collect other types of fruits to build a dataset that can be used for other research.

Acknowledgment. The financial support by the Deanship of Scientific Research at the Princess Nourah Bint Abdulrahman University. The authors would like to thank anonymous reviewers for their helpful comments. A version of this dataset with multiclass fruits was presented during in the 6th International Visual Informatics Conference 2019 (IVIC'19).

References

1. Bhargava, A., Bansal, A.: Fruits and vegetables quality evaluation using computer vision: a review. J. King Saud Univ. Inf. Sci. (2018)
2. Zhang, Y., Wang, S., Ji, G., Phillips, P.: Fruit classification using computer vision and feedforward neural network. J. Food Eng. **143**, 167–177 (2014)
3. Fruits 360 dataset. https://www.kaggle.com/moltean/fruits#fruits-360_dataset.zip
4. FIDS30 DataSet. http://www.vicos.si/Downloads/FIDS30
5. ImageNet. http://www.image-net.org
6. Ergun, H., Sert, M.: Fusing deep convolutional networks for large scale visual concept classification. In: 2016 IEEE Second International Conference on Multimedia Big Data (BigMM), pp. 210–213 (2016)
7. Hameed, K., Chai, D., Rassau, A.: A comprehensive review of fruit and vegetable classification techniques. Image Vis. Comput. **80**, 24–44 (2018)

A Combined of Fuzzy TOPSIS with Z-Number and Alpha-Cut for Decision Making Problems

Nurnadiah Zamri$^{(\boxtimes)}$ and Awajan Khaleel Yahia Ibrahim

Faculty of Informatics and Computing, University Sultan Zainal Abidin,
Besut Campus, 22200 Besut, Terengganu, Malaysia
nadiahzamri@unisza.edu.my

Abstract. The most famous method when dealing with decision making is Multi-Criteria Decision Making (MCDM). One of the easiest techniques from MCDM is Fuzzy Technique for Order Preference by Similarity to Ideal Solution (FTOPSIS). However, there are some circumstances in FTOPSIS still needs to be enhanced. Therefore, this paper concentrates on: (1) to develop FTOPSIS with Z-number and α-cut based MCDM problem; the combination of Z-Number and α-cut is seen suitable to solve uncertainty issue due to the additional restriction and reliability parts; (2) to validate the propose method using numerical example. The study presents six steps of FTOPSIS with Z-numbers and α-cut to verify the position of the numerical example; (3) to evaluate the efficiency of the proposed method using ten different number of α-cut. Ten different numbers are 0.1 to 0.9. From the study, this proposed method opens a new revolution in MCDM area to provide different ways when dealing with decision making problems. Thus, give us variety of techniques in decision making area.

Keywords: MCDM · FTOPSIS · Z-Number · A-cut

1 Introduction

In our daily life, one of the most usual tasks for people is making a decision. Usually, to make a precise decision, it is a need to consider every single alternative and criteria to assess which is the best one [1]. One of the ranking processes that involves a group of alternatives and criteria is Multi-Criteria Decision Making (MCDM) method. A Technique for Order Performance by Similarity to Ideal Solution (TOPSIS) is one of the easiest in the calculation of the MCDM method. Fuzzy TOPSIS (FTOPSIS) (developed by Chen [2]) is the expansion of TOPSIS (developed by Hwang and Yoon [3]) with Fuzzy Sets (FSs) method.

FTOPSIS is a method for classifying a group of alternatives using Euclidean distance. FTOPSIS method, also known as a method that easy to handle intangible and less cumbersome mathematical calculations. This method has been explored by many researchers such as Rashidi and Cullinane [4] combined FTOPSIS with Fuzzy Data Development Analysis (DEA). Hajek and Froelich [5] integrated FTOPSIS and Interval-Valued Intuitionistic Fuzzy Cognitive Maps (IVIFCMs) for model the supplier selection task. Gupta [6] proposed FTOPSIS with Best Worst Method (BWM) for

© Springer Nature Switzerland AG 2019
H. Badioze Zaman et al. (Eds.): IVIC 2019, LNCS 11870, pp. 245–256, 2019.
https://doi.org/10.1007/978-3-030-34032-2_23

Green Human Resource Management (GHRM) problem for solving problems in logistics service providers in Sweden. Awajan and Zamri [7] developed FTOPSIS with Z-numbers for assessment on a memorandum of understanding at university. This FTOPSIS with Z-numbers by Awajan and Zamri [7] solved the restriction and reliability issues at rating phase. Hence, able to handle uncertainty in a more proper way. However, this FTOPSIS with Z-numbers by Awajan and Zamri [7] technique is still depended only on the distribution's data at the ranking phase and influenced by thrilling values. Besides, when decision makers' judgment are under uncertainty, it is relatively difficult for them to provide exact numerical values [8].

In this paper, we focus on the ranking phase by Awajan and Zamri [7] by extending FTOPSIS with Z-Numbers and α-cuts. Based on Dymova et al. [9], α-cuts level set based FTOPSIS produce more robust prioritization since more uncertainties can be considered. We also use a real case study on identifying the factors of smoking behaviour among Jordanian to illustrate the propose FTOPSIS with Z-Numbers and α-cuts method. The study presents six steps of FTOPSIS with Z-numbers and α-cut to determine the final classification of each alternative. Next, we used the α-cut from 0.1 to 0.9 to test the effectiveness of the proposed method.

The rest of this study can be traced back as; Sect. 2, detailed out the preliminaries of the study. In Sect. 3, the development of FTOPSIS with Z-Numbers and α-cuts method. Section 4 applied a numerical example on finding the most suitable system analysis engineer. Section 5 concludes.

2   Preliminaries

Definitions that attached to the FTOPSIS with Z-Numbers and α-cut are presented in this section.

Definition 2.1 Fuzzy Sets [10]
Zadeh (the person who introduced Fuzzy Sets (FSs) [10] discussed that a FS can be interpreted as a group of objects that consider grades of membership. The idea of FSs were generalized by classical sets.

Let H be a universe of sets, where $\mu_A(h)$ is a membership function. Each element h in H is a fuzzy number from 0 till 1. Thus, the formula for FSs is as Eq. 1:

$$\tilde{A} = \{(h, \mu_A(h)) \,|\, h \in H\} \tag{1}$$

Definition 2.2 Triangular Fuzzy Number [11]
Next, Zadeh [10] expended FSs into a triangular fuzzy number (TFN). TFN consists of $\bar{A}$ where $\bar{A}$ can be represented as $\bar{A} = (p, q, r)$. Thus, the membership function is given by

$$\mu_{A'}(h) = \begin{cases} h - p/q - 1, & 1 \le h \le q \\ r - h/r - q, & q \le h \le r \\ 0, & \text{otherewise} \end{cases} \tag{2}$$

Definition 2.3 Z-Numbers [12]

A Z-number by Zadeh is an ordered pair of fuzzy numbers denoted as $Z = (\tilde{A}, \tilde{R})$. The first component $\tilde{A}$, a fuzzy restriction on the values, is a real-valued uncertain variable X. The second component $\tilde{R}$ is a measure of fuzzy reliability for the first component.

Definition 2.4 Alpha-Cuts [11, 13]

The α-cut of the fuzzy number $\tilde{A}$ is defined as:

$$\tilde{A}_\alpha = \left\{ x_i : \mu_{\tilde{A}}(x_i) \geq \alpha, \ x_i \in R \right\} \tag{3}$$

Where $\alpha \in [0, 1]$ and $\tilde{A}_\alpha$ is a non-empty bounded closed interval contained in X and it can be denoted by $\tilde{A}_\alpha = [a_\alpha^l, a_\alpha^u]$, and a_α^l and a_α^u are the lower and upper bounds of the closed interval.

We developed steps of FTOPSIS with Z-Numbers and α-cut using Definition 2.1 till 2.4. The rest of the method development will explain in Sect. 3.

3 Proposed Method

This section highlights four different phases in FTOPSIS. In Rating Phase, FTOPSIS is extended with Z-Numbers method. Two different Z-Numbers' linguistic scale are presented in Table 1 and Table 2. Weighting Phase also focusses on two different weighting scale using Z-Numbers which are Table 3 and Table 4. Next, we modified the FTOPSIS and Z-Numbers at the Aggregation Phase with α-cut method. Lastly, conclude it with the Ranking Phase. Therefore, the overall steps are shown as follows:

3.1 Rating Phase

Step 1: Linguistic evaluation and construct a decision matrix.

Basically, linguistic scales are generated suited based on the decision problems. Here, smoking problems are our main target to solve. Therefore, the linguistic scales are scaled from 'Very Poor' to 'Very Good' to suit with the problems. Tables 1 and 2 list all the linguistic evaluation based on Z-Numbers. This linguistic evaluation is used by all experts to classify each alternative rating-based factor.

Table 1. The attributes' linguistic evaluation [14].

Linguistic terms	Z-Numbers' values
Very Poor (VP)	(0,0,1)
Poor (P)	(0,1,3)
Medium Poor (MP)	(1,3,5)
Fair (F)	(3,5,7)
Medium Good (MG)	(5,7,9)
Good (G)	(7,9,10)
Very Good (VG)	(9,10,10)

Table 2. Fuzzy reliability's linguistic evaluation [14].

Linguistic terms	Z-Numbers' values
Not Sure (NS)	(0,0,1)
Quite Sure (QS)	(1,3,5)
Sure (S)	(5,7,9)
Very Confident (VC)	(9,10,10)

Step 2: Normalize the linguistic evaluation.

The matrix of FMCDM problem is formulated as Eq. 4. Then, all these linguistic values are normalized as follows;

$$
Y_p = \left(\tilde{f}_{ij}^p, r\tilde{f}_{ij}^p\right)_{m\times n} =
\begin{array}{c}
 \\
f_1 \\
f_2 \\
\vdots \\
f_m
\end{array}
\begin{bmatrix}
\left(\tilde{f}_{11}^p, r\tilde{f}_{11}^p\right) & \left(\tilde{f}_{12}^p, r\tilde{f}_{12}^p\right) & \cdots & \left(\tilde{f}_{1n}^p, r\tilde{f}_{1n}^p\right) \\
\left(\tilde{f}_{21}^p, r\tilde{f}_{21}^p\right) & \left(\tilde{f}_{22}^p, r\tilde{f}_{22}^p\right) & \cdots & \left(\tilde{f}_{2n}^p, r\tilde{f}_{2n}^p\right) \\
\vdots & \vdots & \vdots & \vdots \\
\left(\tilde{f}_{m1}^p, r\tilde{f}_{m1}^p\right) & \left(\tilde{f}_{m1}^p, r\tilde{f}_{m1}^p\right) & \cdots & \left(\tilde{f}_{mn}^p, r\tilde{f}_{mn}^p\right)
\end{bmatrix}
\tag{4}
$$

$$
Y = \left(\tilde{f}_{ij}, r\tilde{f}_{ij}\right)_{m\times n}, \tag{5}
$$

where $\left(\tilde{f}_{ij}, r\tilde{f}_{ij}\right) = \left(\frac{\left(\tilde{f}_{ij}^1, r\tilde{f}_{ij}^1\right) \oplus \left(\tilde{f}_{ij}^2, r\tilde{f}_{ij}^2\right) \oplus \ldots \oplus \left(\tilde{f}_{ij}^k, r\tilde{f}_{ij}^k\right)}{k}\right)$, $\left(\tilde{f}_{ij}, r\tilde{f}_{ij}\right)$ is a Z-Numbers with FS, $1 \leq i \leq m$, $1 \leq j \leq n$, $1 \leq p \leq k$, and k denotes the number of experts.

3.2 Weighting Phase

Step 3: Form the decision matrix's weighted.

Table 3 is used to form the decision matrix's weighted of $\bar{W}_p$ using Table 3 and Eqs. 6 and 7.

Table 3. Linguistic terms of weights for the attributes and their positive and negative.

Linguistic terms	Fuzzy set with Z-numbers
Very Low (VL)	(0,0,0.1)
Low (L)	(0.,0.1,0.3)
Medium Low (ML)	(0.1,0.5,0.7)
Medium (M)	(0.3,0.5,0.7)
Medium High (MH)	(0.5,0.7,0.9)
High (H)	(0.7,0.9,0.1)
Very High (VH)	(0.9,1.0,1.0)

Construct the weighting matrix $\bar{W}_p$ of the criteria of the experts and construct the pth average weighting matrix $\bar{W}$, respectively, shown as follows:

$$\begin{array}{cccc} f_1 & f_2 & \cdots & f_n \end{array}$$

$$\bar{W}_p = \left(\tilde{w}_i^p, r\tilde{w}_i^p\right)_{1 \times m} = \left[\left(\tilde{w}_1^p, r\tilde{w}_1^p\right) \quad \left(\tilde{w}_2^p, r\tilde{w}_2^p\right) \quad \cdots \quad \left(\tilde{w}_m^p, r\tilde{w}_m^p\right)\right] \tag{6}$$

$$\bar{W} = (\tilde{w}, r\tilde{w})_{1 \times m} \tag{7}$$

where $(\tilde{w}_i^p, r\tilde{w}_i^p) = \frac{\left(\tilde{w}_i^1, r\tilde{w}_i^1\right) \oplus \left(\tilde{w}_i^2, r\tilde{w}_i^2\right) \oplus \ldots \oplus \left(\tilde{w}_i^k, r\tilde{w}_i^k\right)}{k}$, $(\tilde{w}_i^p, r\tilde{w}_i^p)$ is a linguistic value of Z-Numbers with FS, $1 \leq i \leq m, 1 \leq p \leq k$ and represents the number of decision makers. Then, the matrix for decision matrix's weighted is shown as Eq. 8 as follows,

$$\begin{array}{cccc} x_1 & x_2 & \cdots & x_n \end{array}$$

$$\bar{Y}_w = \left(\tilde{v}_{ij}, r\tilde{v}_{ij}\right)_{m \times n} = \begin{array}{c} f_1 \\ f_2 \\ \vdots \\ f_m \end{array} \begin{bmatrix} (\tilde{v}_{11}, r\tilde{v}_{11}) & (\tilde{v}_{12}, r\tilde{v}_{12}) & \cdots & (\tilde{v}_{1n}, r\tilde{v}_{1n}) \\ (\tilde{v}_{21}, r\tilde{v}_{21}) & (\tilde{v}_{22}, r\tilde{v}_{22}) & \cdots & (\tilde{v}_{2n}, r\tilde{v}_{2n}) \\ \vdots & \vdots & \vdots & \vdots \\ (\tilde{v}_{m1}, r\tilde{v}_{m1}) & (\tilde{v}_{m2}, r\tilde{v}_{m2}) & \cdots & (\tilde{v}_{mn}, r\tilde{v}_{mn}) \end{bmatrix}, \tag{8}$$

where $\left(\tilde{v}_{ij}, r\tilde{v}_{ij}\right) = (\tilde{w}_i, r\tilde{w}_i) \otimes \left(\tilde{f}_{ij}, r\tilde{f}_{ij}\right)$, $1 \leq i \leq m$, and $1 \leq j \leq n$.

3.3   Aggregating Phase

Step 4: Verify the PIS distance and NIS distance

A^* is a positive ideal solution;

$$A^* = \{p_1^*, \ldots, p_n^*\}\{(\max_j p_{ij} | i \in I'), (\min_j p_{ij} | i \in I'')\}, \tag{9}$$

A^- is a negative ideal solution;

$$A^- = \{p_1^-, \ldots, p_n^-\} = \{(\min_j p_{ij} | i \in I'), (\max_j p_{ij} | i \in I'')\}, \tag{10}$$

where

I' is referred to as the positive criteria
I'' is referred to as the negative criteria.

where I' is associated with the positive attribute, and I'' is associated with the negative element.

Step 5: Design of PIS distance and NIS distance

PIS distance is calculated using Euclidean distance

$$\left(D_j^*, rD_j^*\right)_\alpha = \left(\sqrt{\sum_{i=1}^{n}(\alpha.\tilde{v}_{ij} - \alpha.\tilde{v}_i^*)^2}, \sqrt{\sum_{i=1}^{n}(\alpha.r\tilde{v}_{ij} - \alpha.\tilde{v}_i^*)^2}\right), j = 1, \ldots, J. \quad (11)$$

and, NIS distance is also calculated by Euclidean distance

$$\left(D_j^-, rD_j^-\right)_\alpha = \left(\sqrt{\sum_{i=1}^{n}(\alpha.\tilde{v}_{ij} - \alpha.\tilde{v}_i^-)^2}, \sqrt{\sum_{i=1}^{n}(\alpha.r\tilde{v}_{ij} - \alpha.r\tilde{v}_i^-)^2}\right), j = 1, \ldots, J. \quad (12)$$

3.4   Ranking Phase

Step 6: The final calculations of relative closeness

Equation 13 is calculated the best of the alternative x_i with respect to f^*,

$$\left(C_j^*, rC_j^*\right)_\alpha = \frac{\left(\dfrac{(D_j^-)_\alpha}{(D_j^* + D_j^-)_\alpha}, \dfrac{(rD_j^-)_\alpha}{(rD_j^* + rD_j^-)_\alpha}\right)}{2}, j = 1, \ldots, J \quad (13)$$

The most influential alternative is ranked based on Eq. 13. The highest value of most influential C_j^* is referred as the best place over the alternative D_j. The highest rank calls as the most effective alternative towards the ideal solution.

4   Numerical Example

Considering an example from Chen [2] where there is a software company desired to hire a system analysis engineer. Three candidates (A1, A2, and A3) are chosen and evaluated based on five different criteria which are emotional steadiness (C1), oral communication skills (C2), personality (C3), past experience (C4) and self-confidence (C5). Three Decision Makers (DMs) are selected based on their expertise to evaluate these three candidates. They were assessed using Z-Numbers linguistic scale where considered both restriction and reliability issues. The hierarchical structure of this example can be seen in Fig. 1.

4.1   Rating Phase

Step 1: Linguistic evaluation and construct a decision matrix for assessing the best suitable to become a system analysis engineer.

Tables 1 and 2 are used to evaluate the uppermost criteria to appoint as a system analysis engineer where all criteria and alternatives are illustrated as in Fig. 1.

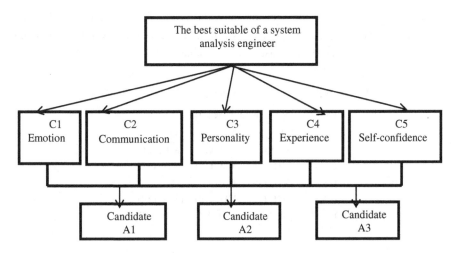

Fig. 1. The ordered arrangement of choosing a system analysis engineer

Step 2: Normalize the linguistic evaluation.

The matrix of FMCDM problem is formulated as Eq. 4. Hence, let's choose $\tilde{f}_{11}$ as an example. Thus, the calculation shows as follows;

$$\tilde{f}_{11} = (MG, S) = ((5, 7, 9), (5, 7, 9))$$
$$(G, VC) = ((7, 9, 10), (9, 10, 10))$$
$$(MG, VC) = ((5, 7, 9), (9, 10, 10))$$

Then, the average for $\tilde{f}_{11}$ is ((0.5667, 0.7667, 0.9333)(0.7667, 0.9, 0.9667)). Then, all these linguistic values are normalized and summarized as follows;

Table 4. Fuzzy decision matrix

	A1	A2	A3
C1	((0.5667, 0.7667, 0.9333), (0.7667, 0.9, 0.9667))	((0.6333, 0.8333, 0.9667), (0.3667, 0.5333, 0.6667))	((0.6333, 0.80, 0.9), (0.2, 0.3333, 0.5))
C2	((0.5, 0.7, 0.8667), (0.3333, 0.4333, 0.5333))	((0.9, 1, 1), (0.1, 0.3, 0.5))	((0.7, 0.8667, 0.9667), (0.5, 0.6667, 0.8))
C3	((0.5667, 0.7667, 0.9), (0.3333, 0.4667, 0.6333))	((0.8333, 0.9667, 1), (0.2333, 0.4333, 0.633))	((0.7, 0.8667, 0.9667), (0.5, 0.6667, 0.8))
C4	((0.8333, 0.9667, 1), (0.2333, 0.4333, 0.6333))	((0.9, 1, 1), (0.1, 0.3, 0.5))	((0.7, 0.8667, 0.9667), (0.5, 0.6667, 0.8))
C5	((0.3, 0.5, 0.7), (0.1667, 0.2333, 0.3667))	((0.7, 0.8667, 0.9667,) (0.5, 0.6667, 0.8))	((0.6333, 0.8333, 0.9667), (0.6333, 0.8, 0.9333))

4.2   Weighting Phase

Step 3: Form the decision matrix's weighted.

Table 3 is used to form the decision matrix's weighted of $\overline{W}_p$ using Table 3 and Eq. 6 and 7. Thus, this weighting matrix $\overline{W}_p$ of the criteria of the experts with the pth average weighting matrix $\overline{W}$, is constructed as Table 5;

Table 5. Weights of criteria evaluated by the decision-makers

Criteria	Decision-Makers (DMs)		
	D1	D2	D3
C1	(H, S)	(VH, QS)	(MH, VC)
C2	(VH, QS)	(VH, QS)	(VH, QS)
C3	(VH, QS)	(H, S)	(H, S)
C4	(VH, QS)	(VH, QS)	(VH, QS)
C5	(M, NS)	(MH, VC)	(MH, VC)

$$\overline{w} = \begin{bmatrix} E & CS & P\,E & SC \\ \tilde{W}_1 & \tilde{W}_2 & \tilde{W}_3\ \tilde{W}_4 & \tilde{W}_5 \end{bmatrix}$$

Let's choose $\tilde{W}_1$ as an example.

$$\tilde{W}_1. = (H, S) = ((7, 9, 1), (5, 7, 9))$$
$$(VH, QS) = ((9, 10, 10), (1, 3, 5))$$
$$(MH, VC) = ((5, 7, 9), (9, 10, 10))$$

Then, the average for $\tilde{W}_1$ is ((0.7, 0.8667, 0.9667), (0.5, 0.6667, 0.8))
Overall, the weighted normalized decision matrix is summarized as Table 6;

Table 6. Weighted matrix

	A1	A2	A3
C1	((0.3967, 0.6644, 0.9022), (0.3833, 0.6, 0.7333))	((0.4433, 0.7222, 0.9344), (0.1833, 0.3556, 0.5333))	((0.396667, 0.6644, 0.87), (0.1, 0.2222, 0.4))
C2	((0.45, 0.7, 0.8667), (0.0167, 0.02889, 0.04267))	((0.81, 1, 1), (0.005, 0.02, 0.04))	((0.63, 0.8667, 0.9667), (0.025, 0.0444, 0.064))
C3	((0.4344, 0.7156, 0.9), (0.0092, 0.0171, 0.02787))	((0.6389, 0.9022, 1), (0.0092, 0.0171, 0.0279))	((0.5367, 0.8089, 0.9667), (0.0138, 0.02444, 0.0352))
C4	((0.75, 0.9667, 1), (0.0045, 0.0112, 0.01951))	((0.75, 1, 1), (0.0019, 0.0077, 0.0154))	((0.63 ,0.8667, 0.9667), (0.0096 ,0.0171, 0.02464))
C5	((0.13, 0.3167, 0.5833), (0.0005, 0.0023, 0.0019))	((0.3033, 0.5489, 0.8056), (0.0016, 0.0029,0.0041))	((0.2744, 0.5278, 0.8056), (0.0020, 0.0034, 0.0048))

4.3   Aggregating Phase

Step 4: Verify the PIS distance and NIS distance

A^* is a positive ideal solution and A^- is a negative ideal solution, thus;

$$A^* = (1,\ 1,\ 1)\quad A^- = (0,\ 0,\ 0)$$

Step 5: Design of PIS distance and NIS distance

PIS distance is calculated using Euclidean distance with α-cuts. Ten different α-cuts which are 0, 0.1, 0.2, 0.3, 0.4, 0.5, 0.6, 0.7, 0.9, 1.0 are tested using Eqs. 11 and 12. Some of the PIS and NIS for α-cuts = 0.2, 0.4, 0.6, 0.8 are detailed as Table 7 as follows;

Table 7. Positive and negative ideal solution

	α-cut = 0.2		α-cut = 0.4		α-cut = 0.6		α-cut = 0.8	
	PIS	NIS	PIS	NIS	PIS	NIS	PIS	NIS
A1	0.4006	0.6582	0.3862	0.6531	0.3748	0.6502	0.3668	0.6493
A1	0.6807	0.4518	0.6751	0.4515	0.6706	0.4523	0.6673	0.4540
A1	0.7141	0.5469	0.7085	0.5464	0.7039	0.5471	0.7007	0.5492
A1	0.7251	0.4675	0.7227	0.4739	0.7209	0.4807	0.7198	0.4878
A1	0.7917	0.4219	0.7908	0.4113	0.7907	0.4025	0.7917	0.3956
A2	0.5164	0.5472	0.5061	0.5419	0.4982	0.5388	0.4928	0.5379
A2	0.6149	0.6184	0.6131	0.6254	0.6119	0.6326	0.6112	0.6399
A2	0.6914	0.5807	0.6873	0.5852	0.6841	0.5903	0.6819	0.5962
A2	0.7446	0.4449	0.7421	0.4541	0.7403	0.4636	0.7393	0.4734
A2	0.7536	0.4487	0.7495	0.4420	0.7466	0.4371	0.7449	0.4338
A3	0.5453	0.6091	0.5386	0.6046	0.5338	0.6017	0.5311	0.6007
A3	0.6435	0.5505	0.6390	0.5539	0.6354	0.5581	0.6327	0.5627
A3	0.7026	0.5279	0.6974	0.5292	0.6933	0.5313	0.6903	0.5346
A3	0.7334	0.4367	0.7297	0.4402	0.7267	0.4444	0.7244	0.4491
A3	0.7435	0.4971	0.7392	0.4891	0.7361	0.4829	0.7346	0.4788

4.4   Ranking Phase

Step 6: The final calculations of relative closeness

Equation 13 is calculated the best of the alternative x_i with respect to f^*, and defined as;

Table 8. Closeness coefficients of the best suitable of a system analysis engineer

	A1	A2	A3
α = 0.0	0.292592938	0.313524214	0.292472161
α = 0.1	0.434109426	0.441646834	0.437004898
α = 0.2	0.434646902	0.442879345	0.437649259
α = 0.3	0.435219037	0.444128576	0.43832625
α = 0.4	0.435825162	0.445391656	0.43903429
α = 0.5	0.436464583	0.446665555	0.439771585
α = 0.6	0.437136587	0.447947118	0.440536124
α = 0.7	0.437840428	0.449233091	0.441325682
α = 0.8	0.438575289	0.450520167	0.442137833
α = 0.9	0.439340204	0.451805023	0.44296996
α = 1	0.319540193	0.335104444	0.338759561

Table 8 discussed on the closeness coefficients of the best suitable of a system analysis engineer. Lastly, results can be summarized in the ranking form as Table 9;

Table 9. Final ranking of a system analysis engineer

	A1	A2	A3
α = 0.0	2	1	3
α = 0.1	3	1	2
α = 0.2	3	1	2
α = 0.3	3	1	2
α = 0.4	3	1	2
α = 0.5	3	1	2
α = 0.6	3	1	2
α = 0.7	3	1	2
α = 0.8	3	1	2
α = 0.9	3	1	2
α = 1	3	2	1

Based on the final ranking, we can summarize that candidate A2 is the best candidate to fill the position as a system analysis engineer. This ranking result obtained from ten different α-cuts which are 0, 0.1, 0.2, 0.3, 0.4, 0.5, 0.6, 0.7, 0.8, 0.9 and 1.0. The results obtained from α-cuts = 0.1 till 0.9 are same, but slightly different for α-cuts = 0 and 1.0. This is because there is none α-cuts process involved for 0 and 1.0. The PIS and NIS values that present the ranking results are obtained directly from the weighted average. Therefore, we can conclude that the overall ranking for choosing the most suitable system analysis engineer position is A2 > A3 > A1. Thus, the same as Chen [2] 's result.

5 Conclusion

FTOPSIS with Z-Numbers created new decision making's environment that considers reliability and restriction. This paper extended FTOPSIS with Z-numbers on the aggregating phase. A new aggregating phase of FTOPSIS with Z-Numbers was constructed to replace the previous euclidean distance. In this proposed FTOPSIS with Z-Numbers, ten α-cuts were built for comparison of ranking values. A numerical example on identifying the most suitable candidate for system analysis engineer position was applied to the proposed method. Three alternatives and five criteria were used to identify this position. Results show that, candidate A2 is the best candidate to fill the position as a system analysis engineer. This ranking result obtained from ten different α-cuts which are 0, 0.1, 0.2, 0.3, 0.4, 0.5, 0.6, 0.7, 0.8, 0.9 and 1.0. The results obtained from α-cuts = 0.1 till 0.9 are same, but slightly different for α-cuts = 0 and 1.0. As a conclusion, the developed method is capable to solve FMCDM cases in a more intelligible due to the α-cuts' benefit. For upcoming works, it is suggested to integrate the α-cuts with the different aggregation method. Properties for the integrated method can be explored.

Acknowledgment. This research was supported by Pusat Pengurusan Kecemerlangan dan Inkubator Penyelidikan, Universiti Sultan Zainal Abidin.

References

1. Urena, R., Kou, G., Wu, J., Chiclana, F., Herrera-Viedma, E.: Dealing with incomplete information in linguistic group decision making by means of interval type-2 fuzzy sets. Int. J. Intell. Syst. **34**(6), 1261–1280 (2019)
2. Chen, C.T.: Extension of the TOPSIS for group decision-making under fuzzy environment. Fuzzy Sets Syst. **114**, 1–9 (2000)
3. Hwang, C.L., Yoon, K.: Multiple Attribute Decision Making: Methods and Applications. Springer, New York (1981). https://doi.org/10.1007/978-3-642-48318-9
4. Rashidi, K., Cullinane, K.: A comparison of fuzzy DEA and fuzzy TOPSIS in sustainable supplier selection: implications for sourcing strategy. Expert Syst. Appl. **121**, 266–281 (2019)
5. Hajek, P., Froelich, W.: Integrating TOPSIS with interval-valued intuitionistic fuzzy cognitive maps for affective group decision making. Inf. Sci. **485**, 394–412 (2019)
6. Gupta, H.: Assessing organizations performance on the basis of GHRM practices using BWM and Fuzzy TOPSIS. J. Environ. Manag. **226**, 201–216 (2018)
7. Awajan, K.Y., Zamri, N.: A fuzzy TOPSIS with Z-numbers method for assessment of memorandu, of understanding at university. Int. J. Eng. Technol. **7**, **3**(28), 149–152 (2018)
8. Zamri, N., Abdullah, L.: Flood control project selection using an interval type-2 entropy weight with interval type-2 fuzzy TOPSIS. In: 3rd International Conference on Mathematical Sciences (ICMS 2013), Kuala Lumpur, vol. 1602, pp. 62–68 (2014)
9. Dymova, L., Sewastjanov, P., Tikhonenko, A.: An interval type-2 fuzzy extension of the TOPSIS method using alpha-cuts. Knowl.-Based Syst. **83**, 116–127 (2015)
10. Zadeh, L.A.: Fuzzy sets. J. Inf. Control **8**, 338–353 (1965)
11. Kaufmann, A., Gupta, M.M.: Introduction to Fuzzy Arithmetic: Theory and Applications. Van Nostrand Reinhold, New York (1985)

12. Zadeh, L.A.: The concept of a linguistic variable and its application approximate reasoning, Part 1, 2, and Part 3. Inf. Sci. 8(3), 199–249 (1975); Inf. Sci. 8(4), 301–357 (1975); Inf. Sci. 9(1), 43–58 (1975)
13. Zimmermann, H.J.: Fuzzy Set Theory and its Applications, 2nd edn. Kluwer Academic Publishers, Boston (1991)
14. Zamri, N., Ahmad, F., Rose, A.N.M., Makhtar, M.: A fuzzy TOPSIS with Z-Numbers approach for evaluation on accident at the construction site. In: Herawan, T., Ghazali, R., Nawi, N.M., Deris, M.M. (eds.) SCDM 2016. AISC, vol. 549, pp. 41–50. Springer, Cham (2017). https://doi.org/10.1007/978-3-319-51281-5_5

Facial Recognition Adaptation as Biometric Authentication for Intelligent Door Locking System

Ahmad Sufril Azlan Mohamed[(✉)], Mohd Nadhir Ab Wahab,
Sanarthana Radha Krishnan, and Darshan Babu L. Arasu

School of Computer Sciences, Universiti Sains Malaysia, 11800 Gelugor,
Penang, Malaysia
sufril@usm.my

Abstract. As field of technology grows, security issues have gained high concern nowadays. Unfortunately, a good access authentication is high in price which had become less affordable. To overcome this scenario, Intelligent Door Locking System is proposed. This system can be divided into 3 parts, which are mobile application, server with web application and microcontroller. The mobile application will be the one in charge of having face recognition process. The face recognition will be carried out using Eigenfaces Algorithm. Users can lock the door using "Normal Lock" mode or "Secure Lock" mode. To unlock the "Normal Lock" mode, user just need to press on unlock button, while to unlock "Se- cure Lock" mode, user would need to pass biometric authentication and passcode authentication process. Once user successfully identified by the mobile application, data will be sent to microcontroller via Bluetooth. At the same time, the microcontroller will retrieve data from server database and check whether the user is having access to enter the room. If yes, the microcontroller will unlock the door. While for the server, it can be easily managed by administration using web application. Users can check their door lock condition from far distance through web application as well. They can lock the door if they realize the door is not locked wherever they are. This bring convenience to the user.

Keywords: Security · Intelligent locking system · Face recognition · Eigenfaces and smart lock

1 Introduction

1.1 Background

In any rooms in the building is using magnetic lock with card access control system. On the aspect of security, normal door lock is not safe enough to secure office's properties and staffs' personal belongings. This is because keys can be easily duplicated, and it is hard to get confirmation whether the keys are taken by other people. The only way is to change the door lock and it is not secure enough as it will be hard to find a technical worker to change the door lock in the midnight. Same as the card access control system. It is hard to prevent card lost accident and we could not know whether

© Springer Nature Switzerland AG 2019
H. Badioze Zaman et al. (Eds.): IVIC 2019, LNCS 11870, pp. 257–267, 2019.
https://doi.org/10.1007/978-3-030-34032-2_24

the card is being misused by other people to get access. To ensure the security, some organizations chose to replace normal door locks with magnetic locks which attached with good access control system. By using access control system, the status of the door can be tracked whether it is locked or unlocked. The access control system technology is improving. From the earliest keypad and password access control system, card access control system, it had now evolved to biometric authentication access control system [1]. However, biometric authentication system seems to be a high-cost investment as it requires hardware, such as fingerprint scanner or camera. To have a good security system, meanwhile able to track the door status and record attendance by capturing the access time which cost lower comparing to existing biometric authentication access control system, it leads to an idea of implementing a mobile biometric authentication for door access.

2 Background Study

2.1 Biometric Authentication Access Control Using Facial Recognition

Face detection is normally done by using Haar-like features [2] while face recognition is done using PCA (Principal Component Analysis) algorithm. Besides, the micro-controller taking place in the system is Raspberry Pi, and Pi Camera is used for capturing the image. This system is a simple and efficient system. This is because PCA algorithm is easy to use and it simplified the analysis being done by narrow down the scope of analysis, which analyses only similar image in the database [16]. The only feature in this system can be improved replacing of the camera with a daily use device installed with a camera, for example, smartphone.

2.2 Automated Attendance Recorder Using Face Recognition

For automated attendance recorder, most of the proposed system are aimed for the lecture hall. Many of the systems are using the same idea where a camera is set up in the lecture hall to capture the image and next process the image to identify all the students in the class for attendance recording [4–6]. These systems will be having higher complexity as it involves several algorithms in face detection, pre-processing, feature extractions and face recognition part. The involvement of several algorithms mainly due to the concept of capturing the picture of whole class and record attendance through face recognition from the image. For example, both systems proposed by Joseph et al. [5] and Chintalapati et al. [7] involved Viola-Jones algorithm for face detection and Histogram equalization for image processing. The high complexity of the system may lead to a high possibility for error to occur. Besides, these systems will be costly as it involved the instalment fee of cameras.

2.3 Mobile Face Recognition

For mobile face recognition system, the solution proposed by Dave et al. [8] involved several steps in face detection, including color segmentation. This is to reduce the computation time of the whole system [9] but somehow raise the complexity of the system. While for the system proposed by Pabbaraju and Puchakayala [10] used Fisherface algorithm for face recognition. The reason for choosing this approach is because of Linear Discriminant Analysis (LDA) able to perform dimensional reduction besides maximizing the class separation [11]. However, comparing to Eigenfaces approach, Fisherface method seems to suffer while handling the case with a variety of facial expression [12].

2.4   Face Recognition and Eigenfaces Approach

A general face recognition has five main steps; which are image or video input, face detection, feature extraction, face recognition and identification/verification (as illustrated in Fig. 1).

Fig. 1. Process of detecting faces.

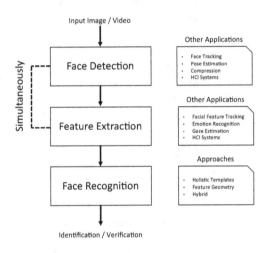

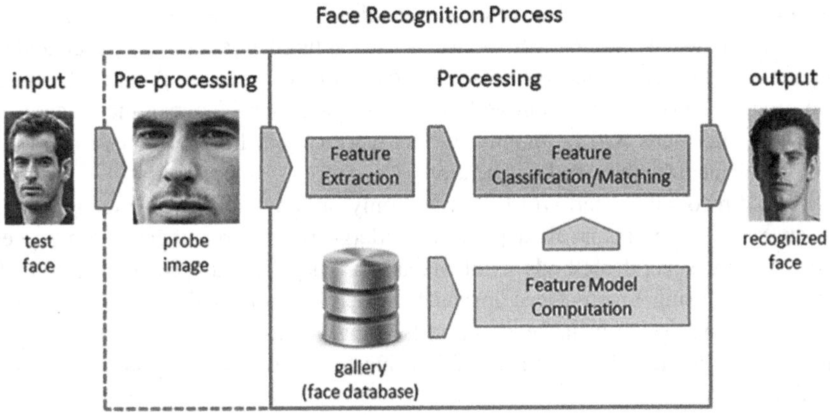

Face Recognition Process

Fig. 2. Illustrative example of facial recognition.

Face recognition is one of the significant applications of image processing [13]. The face is one of the main traits to recognize a person. In the past few decades, automated face recognition using computing capability had slowly get introduced. The very first semi-automated face recognition system was developed in the 1960's. It was considered as "semi-automated" because the process will need the administrator to locate facial features, such as ears, eyes, nose and mouth to complete it. The application of face recognition included face verification and identification (open-set and closed-set) [14]. Both applications have their functions respectively (Fig. 2).

Face identification is the recognizing of a person's identity. It involves a one-to-many matching process with the template database to find the closest match. Face verification is usually applied in cases of deciding whether the person has access. It involves a one-to-one comparison between the captured image on the spot and the biometric template pre-stored in the system database of a person. After the authentication process is done, the system will next decide whether the person has access. For this project, the focus will be mainly on face verification. Figure 3 below shows the difference of identification and verification.

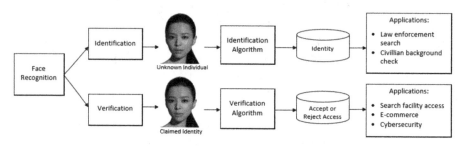

Fig. 3. Difference between identification and verification.

Face identification is the recognizing of a person's identity. It involves a one-to-many matching process with the template database to find the closest match. Face verification is usually applied in cases of deciding whether the person has access. It involves a one-to-one comparison between the captured image on the spot and the biometric template pre-stored in the system database of a person. After the authentication process is done, the system will next decide whether the person has access. For this project, the focus will be mainly on face verification. Figure 3 above shows the difference of identification and verification.

The face recognition part will be applied only on image-based face recognition as users are required to capture their photo to undergo biometric authentication process. Since there are several methods available under image-based face recognition, this system will be using Eigen- faces approach, which is a principal component analysis (PCA) method to do the facial recognition (see Fig. 4). Eigenfaces approach seems to be the suitable method for face recognition due to its simplicity, speed and learning capability [15].

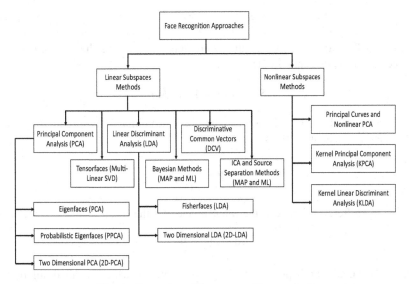

Fig. 4. Examples of face recognition method.

A flowchart of High-level Functioning Principle of the Eigenface-based facial recognition Algorithm was proposed by Pissarenko [15] as illustrated in Fig. 5.

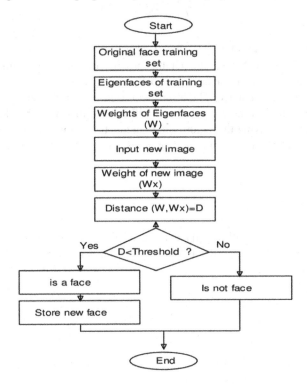

Fig. 5. Flowchart of differences between identification and verification.

The simplified Eigenfaces algorithm proposed by Karande and Talbar [12] is formed by some steps of calculation. The following equations are referred to the work of Turk and Pentland [15]. First, all the training images and the new input image collected are converted into single vectors:

$$S = \{\Gamma_i | i = 1, \ldots, M\} \tag{1}$$

where M is the total number of images. After that, mean image of those training images and the new input image (Ψ) is calculated:

$$\Psi = \frac{S}{M} \tag{2}$$

Next, the difference between the input image and the mean image is calculated:

$$\Phi = \Gamma_i - \Psi \tag{3}$$

After the calculation is done, we will get new images, which is called difference of images. All the difference images are then converted into a column vector i.e. column-wise concatenation of all images:

$$C = \frac{1}{M} \sum_{n=1}^{M} \Phi_n \Phi_n^T = AA^T \tag{4}$$

Where matrix $A = \Phi_n, \Phi_{n+1}, \ldots, \Phi_M$. To get weight vector of each class and the new input image, we will need to get the product of each Eigen image with the difference images. After that, the difference between the weight of new input image and all the images will be calculated. The distance of each class of the images in a database is calculated as well. The new input image will be classified into the class with minimum distance. By applying this algorithm, if an identity of the person in the new input image can be proved to be real and having access. The system will give access to the individual.

3 Method

There are two users that will directly involve with the system, they are the user and administration which here describe as "Use Case". A brief description of the use cases given in the Table 1 below:

Table 1. Use case description

Use case	Description
Face enrolment	User need to capture their picture and store it into database for authentication purpose
Capture user's face with eyelid detection	User will need to have eyelid movement for the system to start recognizing the face
Get door access	Decides who can access a door
Track door status	Keep track of the door lock status so that user can know if their door is locked or unlocked
Record attendance	When user gain access, attendance of the user will be recorded. This attendance can be viewed by administration
Facial recognition algorithm authentication	Eigenfaces algorithm will perform authentication to identify the identity of the user
Set door access rule	Administration can configure the access of each user for each office door
Record date & time	When user gain access, time and date, MAC address of mobile phone and IoT board will be recorded
Track user activity	Administration able to track user's daily activity through the system

When a user request for a door access, user will be requested to capture an image by the mobile application. Then, it will undergo face recognition process. Next, information about the identity will be send to the server for access validation. If the user can access the door, user's attendance will be recorded and stored in the database. At the same time, the permission will be returned to the user by unlocking the magnetic lock and change of door status in the mobile application.

The hardware used for this system are Raspberry Pi 3 model B, 1.2 GHz 64-bit quad-core ARMv8 CPU, 802.11n Wireless LAN, Bluetooth Low Energy (BLE), Micro SD card slot (8 GB), NFC Module (RC522), RFID Card and Samsung Note 3 with 2MP front camera. Meanwhile, the software involved are Raspbian as the operation system, OpenCV, Android Studio, IBM Bluemix/Apache Spark Server and all programming is done on Java (for Android and Raspberry) and PHP (for Server). Eigenfaces Algorithm is used for face recognition. Figure 6 shows the system architecture when combining the hardware and the software.

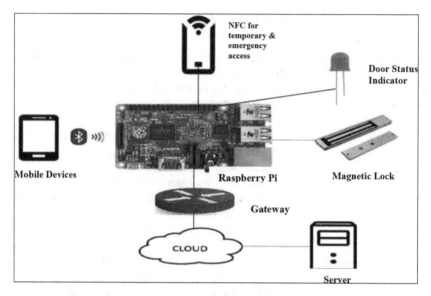

Fig. 6. System architecture diagram of the intelligent door locking system.

4 System Testing and Evaluation

System testing is having important role in a project development. It helps to dictate the performance of the overall system. A good testing strategy is helpful to ensure the functionalities of the system and this may prevent extra expenses in repairing the flaws during future development or maintenance. The testing strategy of this system will be done using the approach shown in Fig. 7.

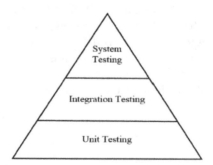

Fig. 7. Testing strategy diagram.

Referring to Fig. 7, it is clearly shown that unit testing is having an important role as it forms the foundation of the other testing process in the development process. Unit testing is done at every stage of development, to do testing on every function involved in the system. This step helps to ensure every unit of the program is functioning well and prevent any unexpected error or outcome which might be difficult to be traces in the following phase of development. As for the development of Intelligent Door Locking system, functions in each classes of mobile application program, functions in microcontroller program and functions in web application program were tested once the development of each function is completed.

Integration is done to ensure all the modules and functions completed previously able to collaborate in harmony and achieve the expected goals of its functionalities. Integration testing also aims to identify if there is any issue when completed modules interact with other modules as well as user interfaces. For Intelligent Door Locking system, the integration in between Bluetooth connection module and user interface module is one of the integration processes which is having high concern. This is because whenever the mobile application receives a message from other parties via Bluetooth connection, it would need to decode the message in order to read the actual content.

System testing is the last step in the overall testing. During the system testing, several aspects such as functionalities, performance, scalability, reliability etc. of the system will be observed. This step meant to test every features and modules in the complete system. For the Intelligent Door Locking system, the testing will be focused on facial recognition module. The testing is carried out within 3 users who are having quite similar features. Table 2 shows the detailed information of test cases and scenarios on facial recognition module.

Table 2. Functionalities of proposed system per attendance recording stages.

Test case	Scenario	Initial state	Event/input	Expected output	Result
TC-01	User with 15 images as trained data	Front camera of mobile device ready for face detection	User capture the image when a green detection box appears	The mobile application able to recognize the user by showing user's registered name	The result meets with the expected output
TC-02	User with 10 images as trained data	Front camera of mobile device ready for face detection	User capture the image when a green detection box appears	The mobile application able to recognize the user by showing user's registered name	The result meets with the expected output
TC-03	User with 5 images as trained data	Front camera of mobile device ready for face detection	User capture the image when a green detection box appears	The mobile application able to recognize the user by showing user's registered name	The result meets with the expected output

Overall accuracy of the face recognition testing is high and constant. This shows that, by having 5 training images during the first sign up for each user is enough for the training process during the initial states. As time pass, user will store more images in the mobile application for training purpose, until a maximum of 15 images. Intelligent Door Locking system aims to raise security level of working environment by using biometric authentication. As the facial recognition authentication process can be functioning well and it is having good stability, therefore, this system able to achieve its' objectives and with extra layer on secure, such as 4-digits passcode authentication, it able to prevent unauthorized party get into a room easily.

5 Conclusion

Intelligent Door Locking system was proposed with the objectives of improving security level of working environment which remain with the conventional key locks or common access control magnetic lock, such as password or card access. The benefits of this system compared to other biometric authentication access control system is that, this system does not need the installation of additional biometric devices. Since smart phone had become part of our lives in recent years, therefore, we should utilize the power of mobile application with the existing front camera which exist in any mobile phones these days.

The main limitations of this system are that it cannot operate when there is out of power situation. Besides that, this system is now implemented for one-to-one condition, where one user can only access one door. All these flaws can be improved in future works. For example, in- stead of magnetic lock, the system can lock the door using a server motor, which can prevent the door from opening easily when theirs is black out situation. Other than that, the system can be improved to handle many-to-many cases, where each user can access several rooms and each room can be accessed by several users. With this feature, the system can be used more widely in working environment, such as meeting room, other than own office. While for mobile application, it can be implemented for other android operation system, such as iOS. By having this, the range of target user can be widened as well.

Acknowledgement. This research is funded under USM RU Grant (PKOMP/8014001) and partly under USM Short Term Grant (PKOMP/6315262) and affiliated with Robotics, Computer Vision & Image Processing (RCVIP) Research Group Lab at School of Computer Sciences, Universiti Sains Malaysia.

References

1. Soyata, T., Muraleedharan, R., Funai, C., Kwon, M., Heinzelman, W.: Cloud-vision: real-time face recognition using a mobile-cloudlet-cloud acceleration architecture. In: 2012 IEEE Symposium on Computers and Communications (ISCC), Cappadocia, pp. 59–66 (2012)
2. Januzaj, Y., Luma, A., Januzaj, Y., Ramaj, V.: Real time access control based on face recognition. In: 2015 International Conference on Network security & Computer Science, Antalya, Turkey, pp. 7–12 (2015)
3. Young, A.W., Burton, A.M.: Recognizing faces. Curr. Dir. Psychol. Sci. **26**(3), 212–217 (2017)

4. Mesni, B.: Authentication in door access control systems. In: Clerk Maxwell, J. (ed.) A Treatise on Electricity and Magnetism, 3rd edn., vol. 2, pp. 68–73. Clarendon, Oxford (2013). http://kintronics.blogspot.my/2013/04/authentication-in-door-access-control.html
5. Joseph, J., Zacharia, K.P.: Automatic attendance management system using face recognition. Int. J. Sci. Res. (IJSR) **2**(11), 327–330 (2013)
6. Turk, M.A., Pentland, A.P.: Face recognition using eigenfaces. In: Proceedings 1991 IEEE Computer Society Conference on Computer Vision and Pattern Recognition, pp. 586–591 (1991)
7. Chintalapati, S., Raghunadh, M.V.: Automated attendance management system based on face recognition algorithms. In: 2013 IEEE International Conference on Computational Intelligence and Computing Research, Enathi, pp. 1–5 (2013)
8. Dave, G., Chao, X., Sriadibhatla, K.: Face recognition in mobile phones. Department of Electrical Engineering, Stanford University, Stanford, USA, pp. 1–7. https://stacks.stanford.edu/file/druid:rz261ds9725/Sriadibhatla_Davo_Chao_FaceRecognition.pdf
9. Saini, R., Saini, A., Agarwal, D.: Analysis of different face recognition algorithms. Int. J. Eng. Res. Technol. **3**(11), 1263–1267 (2014)
10. Pabbaraju, A., Puchakayala, S.: Face recognition in mobile devices. Electrical Engineering and Computer Science, University of Michigan, Ann Arbor, pp. 1–9 (2010). https://pdfs.semanticscholar.org/cc20/0b665f6c446747a48d01e89f6b1e7d7781d4.pdf
11. Mohamed, A.S.A.: Face recognition using eigenfaces. In: MRG International Conference 2006, Salford University, Manchester, United Kingdom, Poster Presentation (2006)
12. Turk, M., Pentland, A.: Eigenfaces for recognition. J. Cogn. Neurosci. **3**(1), 71–86 (1991)
13. Belhumeur, P.N., Hespanha, J.P., Kriegman, D.J.: Eigenfaces vs. fisherfaces: recognition using class specific linear projection. IEEE Trans. Pattern Anal. Mach. Intell. **19**(7), 711–719 (1997)
14. Karande, K.J., Talbar, S.N.: Simplified and modified approach for face recognition using PCA. IET-UK International Conference on Information and Communication Technology in Electrical Sciences (ICTES 2007), pp. 523–526. Dr. M.G.R. University, Chennai (2007)
15. Pissarenko, D.: Eigenface-based facial recognition (2003). http://openbio.sourceforge.net/resources/eigenfaces/eigenfaces-html/facesOptions.html
16. Zhao, W., Chellappa, R., Phillips, P.J., Rosenfeld, A.: Face recognition: a literature survey. ACM Comput. Surv. **35**(4), 399–458 (2003)

Manufacturing Lead Time Classification Using Support Vector Machine

Zhong Heng Lim, Umi Kalsom Yusof[✉], and Haziqah Shamsudin

School of Computer Science, Universiti Sains Malaysia, 11800 Georgetown,
Pulau Pinang, Malaysia
umiyusof@usm.my

Abstract. Product lead time is the indicator of manufacturing controllability, efficiency and performance in most manufacturing industry. The common lead time estimation mostly applied with knowledge-based approaches, but most of them have focused on supervised regression task to predict continuous lead time, which somehow only predicts the product lead time without identifying the critical lengthy manufacturing process. This paper aims to predict the manufacturing lead time of a product with supervised machine learning approach through classification of lead time in time range duration and able to identify the lengthy manufacturing product lead time. The machine learning model are developed with support vector machine algorithm using production and work order data as the model input. The target class is the total duration of product manufacturing time discretized into category attribute with different range of duration. The dataset extracted from work order and production data source and merge into a full dataset. Data preprocessing and feature engineering were applied to clean the dataset and boost the feature set to have 81 features in total. The final feature set was selected using recursive feature elimination approach feature selection technique. The final model applied support vector machine algorithm to perform the classification task and compared with Random Forest and Artificial Neural Network for performance. The final model scored 84.62% of weighted accuracy and able to predict the over-time class with over 65% of accuracy.

Keywords: Manufacturing lead time classification · Support vector machine · Classification · Machine learning · Recursive feature elimination · Discretization

1 Introduction

Product lead time, as the total time to manufacture a unit of production starting from raw material across all the production line processes, is always an important indicator by the manufacturing controllability, efficiency and performance in most manufacturing industry [6]. The production line in a manufacturer organization acquired a combination of rich and high-volume product families that applying mass customization strategy to build customized products module based on clients need, leading to the situation of same product having different manufacturing lead time. However, a promising forecast of lead time estimation is often a difficult challenge to organization

© Springer Nature Switzerland AG 2019
H. Badioze Zaman et al. (Eds.): IVIC 2019, LNCS 11870, pp. 268–278, 2019.
https://doi.org/10.1007/978-3-030-34032-2_25

as it is affected by many factors such as the process needs, batching practices, shop congestion, dispatching rules and custom software and hardware module designs [14]. Most products that have varying process parameters would cause the lead time estimation poor performed even in more sophisticated analytical methods. Even though the engineers of the production line have projected the yield predictability of each manufacturing process, the actual completion time is still way too fluctuated.

The promising lead time estimations are crucial challenges for supply chain planning team to support them in making stocks planning decision. The main problem to tackle is to identify the item that has critical lengthy manufacturing time, so the department could make immediate responses when over-timed manufactured product detected. Most of knowledge-based approaches introduced such as lead time models for analysis in supply chain networks [17], data mining lead time predictive model [14] and statistical learning methods [15] focused on tackling the problem by framing it as supervised regression task with continuous lead time as target class, which somehow only predicts the lead time of the product but does not identify the critical lengthy manufacturing product. The problem could further frame into classification task stating when the product would be finished in a production line within a range of time.

This paper aims to classify the manufacturing lead time of a product with supervised machine learning approach through classification of lead time in time range duration. The lead time classification model also targeted to able to identify the over-time product lead time which is higher than expected lead time estimation. The machine learning model was developed with support vector machine algorithm using production and work order data as the model input. The target class is the total duration of product manufacturing time discretized into category attribute with different range of duration including the over-time duration.

2 Literature Review

2.1 Manufacturing Lead Time

Generally, product lead time is the total time to manufacture a unit of production starting from raw material across all the production line processes, including order preparation time, queue time, run time, move time, inspection time and final delivered as a finished product [6]. Product lead time is always an indicator by the manufacturing controllability, efficiency and performance in most manufacturing industry [6]. Therefore, the main goal of a manufacturer organization is to strive on better minimizing and shortening the manufacturing lead-time in order to ultimately reduce the cost of production and acquiring more competitive advantage against competitors [8].

As manufacturing lead times is one of the most important performance indicators in supply chain production line, the estimation of product lead time is crucial factors to be considered when come to an efficient production schedule planning. The promising estimation of Product Lead Time would project to deliver the assemble-to-order product on time [6], whereby subsequently achieve the shortest possible time milestone and maximize the flow of production line [5].

2.2   Manufacturing Lead Time Classification with Machine Learning

The traditional lead time estimation mostly applied with analytical techniques and continuously improved and enhanced and finally shifted to the knowledge-based approaches to achieve the better estimation model that could fits in the manufacturing environment from time to time.

The literature survey revealed most researches on lead time related analysis have focused on knowledge-based methods, from the static lead time computations model [4] to a more generalized queuing network model [4] and then to a dynamic lead time models for analysis in supply chain networks [2] and finally into data mining methods [14], knowledge-based methods [17], and statistical learning methods [13] for more complex engineered-to-order products.

In particular, the approaches that built through the application of machine learning approaches combined with data analytics techniques and customized for different manufacturing sectors are lead time prediction for semiconductor manufacturer (ensemble method combining nave bayes, decision tree, ANN and multinomial logistic regression) [10], lead times estimation for metallic components in aerospace industry (support vector machine) [5], estimation of production time of steel plates for planning and scheduling (Bayesian network, ANN, SVM) [12] and the lead time prediction in generalized manufacturing environment (ensemble method combining linear regression, support vector machine and decision tree) [7].

These methods are summarized to acquire the strength of being customized for specific environment, designed to enhance the lead time prediction on top of previous studies and providing more fits-into-environment solution for current manufacturing sectors. The more preferable algorithm that widely leveraged in the researches is support vector machine (SVM) [5, 7, 12] as it is being summarized as providing the most promising results in term of model's accuracy and suitability. However, these conducted methods framed the lead time prediction as a regression task, whereby the estimated lead time is projected in numerical values with an probability output. The key question to predict class output as classification task stating when the product would be finished in a production line within a range of time is not addressed.

2.3   Support Vector Machine

Support vector machine (SVM) is the algorithm that can be used for both classification and regression that served as the individualization of hyperplanes parallel to error minimization [3]. In general, SVM plot each data item as a point in N-Dimensional space (where n is the number of feature) and find a hyperplane in the N-Dimensional space that distinctly classifies the data points. The key point of SVM is the algorithm selects the hyperplane which segregates the classes in a better sense, which having the maximum distance from the closest support vector. Hyperplane with larger margin is identified as more robust while low margin hyperplane is tended to higher chance of misclassification [11]. SVM are notoriously difficult to train due to the requirement of normalized inputs and challenging fine tuning of several parameters [11]. However, the ability to segregate the classes with a correct tuning could ultimately achieving most classification task due to the ability of SVM of high tolerance to noisy data, ability to classify untrained patterns and effectiveness in high dimensional spaces problem, which make it an ultimate solution to the classification task with high dimensional features set.

2.4 Feature Selection

As the features retrieved is relatively huge or consists of uncertain relevancy attributes, the feature selection process is to break this curse of dimensionality and efficiently select only the relevant features out from the big dataset. Feature selections aims in reducing the dimensionality to lower the complexity of model, meanwhile reducing the computations, memory and cost of extracting unnecessary input and still maintaining a simpler model that are less susceptible to noise and outliers [9]. The wrapper approach of feature selection technique greedily measures the usefulness of the features based on the classifier performance using either forward selection, backward selection or recursive feature elimination methods. Recursive feature elimination starts with building the model on entire set of predictors, then through computing the importance score for each predictor, the least important predictors are removed and rebuilt again the model until an optimized feature set is selected [1]. Recursive feature elimination method is an effective and efficient technique that used to reduce the model complexity by eliminating the irrelevant features as it applied a greedy approach in selecting the most relevant feature set [9].

3 Methodology

3.1 Research Framework

The methodological approach applied in the use case focuses on three phases, namely data extraction, data preparation and machine learning modelling as illustrated in Fig. 1. The first phase is the data gathering phase where each data source in the production line is extracted accordingly to finally retrieved the work order data, transaction log data, work station data and option configuration data. The second phase involve data preparation and feature engineering. The second phase involve data preparation and feature engineering. This phase consisted of the process of aggregating and merging each dataset gathered by using their primary keys to collect as much attributes as possible. The merged dataset is then cleaned with do-main expert advices for the outliers. The final dataset is produced after the feature engineering session that using One-Hot-Encoding to increase the feature sets with binary feature. The total duration of product lead time is discretized into different time range in this phase for later classification task. Phase 3 is machine learning modelling using support vector machine algorithm. The features set is first being reduced and selected using recursive feature elimination methods. The selected features then trained with support vector machine with fine-tuned parameters. The final output is evaluated using cross validation of k-fold.

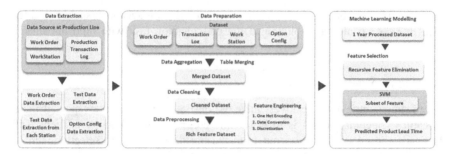

Fig. 1. Research framework of lead time classification model

3.2   Data Source of Manufacturing Production Data

The data source used in current project consist of multiple departments system, namely production transaction data, option configuration data, work station data from the production and work order data retrieved from the production department in electronics test and measurement equipment manufacturing organization. The data source is consisted of at least a year of past production data and word order data with labelling of actual completion time (total duration) of each product family in the production.

The raw dataset is unable to be used directly for classification task as the structure of each data source is not applicable directly with machine learning modelling. Each gathered shattering dataset is first deeply analyzed to explore for more possible features and linking. Table 1 show the basic descriptions of each table extracted from the department.

As the dataset gathered are from 4 different sources, these datatable are merged in a sense of sequential unique product at each product. The work order served as the foundation of the dataset as each product is at unique row that suits as model input. Transaction log table are aggregated to sum up the total duration for each unique product before merging with work order table. The configuration and work station data is merged to acquire total test feature, total test process and work station assignment. After the dataset is merged in sequential form, the full dataset now has rich content of attributes with existing of outliers.

Therefore, data cleaning is performed to remove those outliers in the sense of preparing the instances to be ready for modelling. The outliers are identified and removed by the advises of domain experts which is the process engineers in the plant. The transaction log is first removed with the test status labelled with Incomplete and the process name labelled as Irrelevant Procedure. These label are identified to be invalid be the process engineers as they are mostly caused by human or machine failure. Besides, null values in the dataset such as transaction log, work station is replaced with other and 0, as the nature of the attributes indicated unlabelled data as Others. Features such as test result, rework status, test conducted amount, station downtime is considered irrelevant and unusable as they are not retrievable at the point the input is acquired.

Table 1. Data source of manufacturing production department data

Data Source	Attribute Name	Description	Data Type
Production test transaction log	ProductNumber	Product model	String
	UnitIdentifier	Unique ID specific the product	Numeric
	TestDateTime	The date and time by the test performed	Datetime
	ProcessName	Process name of the product test carry out	String
	TestFeature	Test feature performed	String
	TestResult	Test result (fail, pass, incomplete)	String
	Duration	Duration of test	Numeric
	RunID	Running ID of each batch of test	String
	StationID	Station ID of each test carry out	String
Unit option configuration	ProductNumber	Product model	String
	UnitIdentifier	Unique ID specific the product	Numeric
	OptionConfig	The date and time by the test performed	String
Work order	ProductNumber	Product model	String
	ProductionID	Unique ID specific the product	Numeric
	SoftwareATO	Software module to be included	String
	HardwareATO	Hardware module to be included	String
Work station	StationID	StationID used for mapping	String
	ITStationID	IT station ID	Numeric
	StationName	Station name	String
	Status	Current status of station	String
	DurationHours	Duration of status last	Numeric
	DateUpdate	Date captured for the status updated	String

3.3   Feature Engineering

After cleaning the merged dataset, the features retrieved is still yet to be considered rich and efficient for modelling. One-Hot-Encoding is applied to the multi class feature to create N-dimension of representation for each categorical variable as binary vectors. The categorical attributes applied with One-Hot-Encoding are ProductHardwareMod-ules, TestFeature, StationEntered and ProcessName. The output of the application is an increment of 71 features, boosting the feature set to have a total of 81 features for later modelling uses. The target attribute Time Duration is converted from second to day for ease of interpretation and presentation purpose.

Discretization of Target Class. After boosting the feature set to be richer in content, the target class which is originally real-valued (continuous numerical data type) is being partitioned into a discretized Range of Time Interval for classification task. As the lead time data retrieved is continuous numerical data that only suitable for regression task, current step is important to convert the numerical variables into cat-egorical labels to perform classification. The target class is framed in 8 class of classification with range of [0–2 days], [2–4 days], [4–6 days], [6–14 days], [16–18 days], [18–20 days], [>20 days]. One of the worth pin-point to the uneven range of time interval is due to the nature of time duration of the product end that clustered against 2 wide range, whereby defining just a constant range of time duration would lead to an imbalance class distribution that will weaken the classification task. Figure 2 shows the distribution of Target Class: Total Duration in Days.

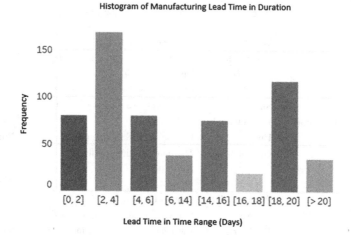

Fig. 2. Distribution of target class (total duration in days)

3.4   Feature Selection

With the processed, cleaned, feature rich dataset produced in previous section, feature selection process is applied to remove the irrelevant features. As the data features that used to train the machine learning models have a huge influence on their performance to be achieved, feature selection session is therefore carried out to remove the irrelevant or partially relevant features that has negative impact to model performance and reduce the model complexity, especially in the high dimensional feature set of current dataset (81 Features).

The feature selection technique used is one of the approaches in wrapper method, namely recursive feature elimination (RFE). RFE aimed to select features by recursively considering smaller and smaller sets of features until the desired number of features to select is eventually reached. With the concept of the RFE, the feature sets retrieved is first into with desired number of features to be used for feature selection, then uses accuracy metric to rank the feature according to their importance and produces its support (True: Relevant feature, False: Irrelevant feature). As the desired number of features could not be just randomly set, a loop function is constructed to iterate across a range of number of features as input and produce the optimum number of features with highest accuracy. The optimum number of features is then feed into the RFE model to get the final set of features given by RFE method. The selected method final produced optimum feature number of 8 and selected 8 features as the subset features to be used in machine learning model for the lead time classification.

3.5 Support Vector Machine

After the features are selected using the RFE, the feature set is used to train to perform the classification task with support vector machine algorithm. As the SVM are generally advised to plotted and tuned to have maximum margin (distance between data points of both classes) so that future data points are classified with more confidence, therefore the constructed SVM is tested accordingly to get the best tuning of parameter that have equivalent trade-off of performance with training time. SKLearn SVC classifier is used as the classifier, while the model is trained and validated with K-Fold cross validation, the performance metrics is collected as in accuracy, precision, recall, F measure score and confusion matrix. The accuracy is evaluated as the measure of ratio between the correctly classified samples to the total number of samples. Meanwhile, precision score and recall score also evaluated as well to indicate the rate of positive samples that were correctly classified and the rate of correctly classified samples to the total number of positive samples. F-measure are last evaluated as the harmonic mean of precision and recall [16]. The training time and testing time is also collected for later model selection evaluation metrics. To further validate the model suitability, another two algorithms namely Random Forest and Artificial Neural Network are used to benchmarking the SVM model constructed applying to the performance metrics.

4 Result and Discussion

The feature set final selected using recursive feature elimination technique consisted of 8 features. According to Table 2, four of the features selected are relevant to production process combined with the hardware module, 2 features are the work station scheduled to the product manufacturing and 1 feature for each test feature procedure and option configuration setting of the product. It is discovered that the combination of hardware module and production processes affects the most lead time of a product. The hardware module is defined as the hardware element within the build of material by the product. The results proved that the combination of certain critical compartment with particular process is prolonging the manufacturing time of the product, leading an impact to forming the over-time lead time. The selected features are summarized in Table 2.

Table 2. Description of top 8 features selected with recursive feature elimination.

Attribute Name	Description	Data Type
EnteredProcessP1_byModuleA	Presence of Process P1 by Hardware Module A	Binary
EnteredProcessG1_byModuleC	Presence of Process G1 by Hardware Module C	Binary
EnteredProcessF1_byModuleA	Presence of Process F1 by Hardware Module A	Binary
EnteredProcessP1_byModuleA _Amt	Amount of Test in Process F1 by Hardware Module A	Numeric
TestFeature_Station1	Test Feature scheduled in Station 1	String
OptionConfig_SetA	Usage of Configuration of Set A	String

The final model constructed is evaluated in the analysis by using Python and Spyder as programming IDE. During the model building and feature selection, cross validation of 10-fold was applied as to evaluate the model performance with the weighted average. To further validate the model's suitability, another 2 algorithms, namely random forest and artificial neural network model are constructed to benchmark the model's performance. Each model is fine-tuned with the optimum parameters to produce the optimum accuracy, giving the result is the best performance of each machine learning model. Table 3 shows the performance comparison of each machine learning model constructed using SVM, random forest and neural network. The results shown SVM ultimately performed 84.66% in accuracy, 84.13% in precision and 84.66% in recall with 10-fold validation. Although the training time and testing time of SVM model is relevantly higher than random forest and neural network model, it still having performance trade-off that worth the long training time. As time component is always an important factor in performance enhancement, the optimization of algorithm is opened as the future research to enhance on top of current approach to the classification problem.

Table 3. Performance evaluation of SVM, random forest and neural network model

Models	Accuracy	Precision	Recall	F Measure	Training time	Testing time
SVM	84.62%	84.13%	84.62%	0.852	7.187 s	303.534 s
Random forest	82.97%	83.42%	82.97%	0.821	0.090 s	4.613 s
Neural network	79.33%	74.78%	79.33%	0.756	5.036 s	167.676 s

As depicted in Fig. 3, SVM model performance outpaced the other two algorithms with significant improvement whether in accuracy, precision, recall and F measure. SVM generally performed better than random forest and neural network in predicting the lead time duration. With feature set selected using RFE, the models tend to generalize better and did not having overfitting issue.

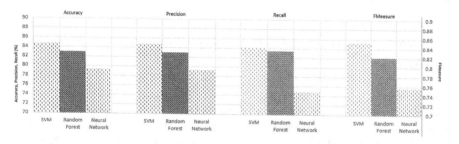

Fig. 3. Bar chart of comparison of performance metrics across SVM, random forest, neural network model.

To further validate on the SVM model trained for its ability to identify the over-time product lead time, the confusion matrix is plotted and analyzed based on the duration of class distribution as depicted in Table 4. The retrieved results shows that the model is strong is classifying over-time class: [18–20 Days] and [over 20 Days], whereby the model able to predict the over-time product with over 65% of accuracy on class of over 20 days and 83% of accuracy on class of 18–20 days. The constructed model fulfilled the main objective to not just predicting the product lead time, but also able to identify the over-time class that is crucial to production stocks issue.

Table 4. Accuracy performance of SVM on cross validation

Day range	Correctly classified	Wrongly classified	Total support	Accuracy (%)
0–2	136	27	163	83.44
2–4	22	16	38	57.94
4–6	481	8	489	98.36
6–14	43	36	79	54.43
14–16	11	22	33	33.33
16–18	10	9	19	52.63
18–20	94	19	113	83.19
>20	23	12	35	65.71
Average accuracy				84.62

5 Conclusion

In a nutshell, the conducted research has successfully built an SVM machine learning model using work order and production data to perform classification task in predicting the product manufacturing lead time and identifying the over-time product with promising performance. The discretization of lead time into time range of duration successfully convert the lead time classification problem into classification problem. The SVM model is validated to be robust enough to perform lead time classification task compared to two other machine learning algorithms, namely random forest and artificial neural network. The final model scored 84.62% of weighted accuracy and able to predict the over-time class with over 65% of accuracy.

Acknowledgment. The authors wish to thank Universiti Sains Malaysia (USM) for the support it has extended in the completion of the present research through the Research University Grant (RUI) (1001/PKOMP/8014084).

References

1. AlNuaimi, N., Masud, M.M., Serhani, M.A., Zaki, N.: Streaming feature selection algorithms for big data: a survey. Appl. Comput. Inform. (2019)
2. Buzacott, J.A.: Commonalities in reengineered business processes: models and issues. Manag. Sci. **42**(5), 768–782 (1996)

3. Bzdok, D., Krzywinski, M., Altman, N.: Machine learning: supervised methods. Nat. Methods **15**, 5–6 (2018)
4. Cohen, M.A., Lee, H.L.: Strategic analysis of integrated production-distribution systems: models and methods. Oper. Res. **36**(2), 216–228 (1988)
5. de Cos Juez, F.J., Nieto, P.G., Torres, J.M., Castro, J.T.: Analysis of lead times of metallic components in the aerospace industry through a supported vector machine model. Math. Comput. Model. **52**(7–8), 1177–1184 (2010)
6. Fahimnia, B., Luong, L., Motevallian, B., Marian, R., Esmaeil, M.: Analyzing and formulation of product lead-time. Ph.D. thesis, Citeseer
7. Gyulai, D., Pfeiffer, A., Nick, G., Gallina, V., Sihn, W., Monostori, L.: Lead time prediction in a flow-shop environment with analytical and machine learning approaches. IFAC-PapersOnLine **51**(11), 1029–1034 (2018)
8. Jaff, T., Ivanov, A.: Manufacturing lead-time reduction and knowledge sharing in the manufacturing sector. InImpact J. Innov. Impact **8**(2), 618 (2016)
9. James, G., Witten, D., Hastie, T., Tibshirani, R.: An Introduction to Statistical Learning, vol. 112. Springer, Cham (2013)
10. Lingitz, L., Gallina, V., Ansari, F., Gyulai, D., Pfeiffer, A., Monostori, L.: Lead time prediction using machine learning algorithms: a case study by a semiconductor manufacturer. PROCEDIA CIRP **72**, 1051–1056 (2018)
11. Loyer, J.L., Henriques, E., Fontul, M., Wiseall, S.: Comparison of machine learning methods applied to the estimation of manufacturing cost of jet engine components. Int. J. Prod. Econ. **178**, 109–119 (2016)
12. Mori, J., Mahalec, V.: Planning and scheduling of steel plates production. Part 1: estimation of production times via hybrid Bayesian networks for large domain of discrete variables. Comput. Chem. Eng. **79**, 113–134 (2015)
13. Mourtzis, D., Doukas, M., Fragou, K., Efthymiou, K., Matzorou, V.: Knowledge based estimation of manufacturing lead time for complex engineered-to-order products. Procedia CIRP **17**, 499–504 (2014)
14. Öztürk, A., Kayalıgil, S., Özdemirel, N.E.: Manufacturing lead time estimation using data mining. Eur. J. Oper. Res. **173**(2), 683–700 (2006)
15. Pfeiffer, A., Gyulai, D., Kádár, B., Monostori, L.: Manufacturing lead time estimation with the combination of simulation and statistical learning methods. Procedia CIRP **41**, 75–80 (2016)
16. Tharwat, A.: Classification assessment methods. Appl. Comput. Inform. (2018)
17. Viswanadham, N., Raghavan, N.S.: Lead time models for analysis of supply chain networks

iFR: A New Framework for Real-Time Face Recognition with Deep Learning

Syazwan Syafiqah Sukri and Nur Intan Raihana Ruhaiyem[✉]

School of Computer Sciences, Universiti Sains Malaysia USM,
11800 Gelugor, Penang, Malaysia
syazwansyafiqah@student.usm.my, intanraihana@usm.my

Abstract. This paper investigates the performance of the real-time face recognition system with machine learning, as well as the performance of each *haarcascade* classifiers that based on accuracy and speed. We employ the subset of machine learning called deep learning to the real-time face recognition system as the deep face recognition technique has improved the state-of-the-art performance. This system uses a pre-trained model named *FaceNet* and employs triplet loss technique to impose a margin between every pair of faces from the same person to other faces. In other words, it minimizes the distance between the anchor and the positive from the same identity and maximizes the distance between the anchor and the negative from different identity. Furthermore, to further investigate the performance of the system, we implement the *Tensorflow* framework to improve the system performance by the usage of Graphics Processing Unit (GPU). This system uses Labeled Faces in Wild (LFW) dataset as the benchmark to test the performance of the face recognition system. Apart from that, we conduct a preliminary experiment to evaluate the performance of *haarcascade* classifiers so that we can choose the best classifier in term of accuracy and speed. Haarcascade_frontalface_default.xml (FD) exhibits best performance compared to haarcascade_frontalface_alt.xml (FA) and haarcascade_frontalface_alt2.xml (FA2) with accurate number of faces detected and shortest average time taken to detect faces.

Keywords: Deep learning · Tensorflow · Face recognition

1 Introduction

1.1 Problem Statement

Traditional attendance management system such as signature method has many flaws especially to the organization such that the attendance can be fabricated where someone else can simply sign the attendance form. Same to the usage of identification card to mark the attendance, someone else may scan the card for his or her friend. Then, the attendance management system has moved to biometric recognition by using face. The traditional facial recognition algorithm such as Principal Component Analysis (PCA), Linear Discriminant Analysis (LDA) and Local Binary Pattern (LBP) have been introduced to replace the manual ways of attendance management. These traditional

© Springer Nature Switzerland AG 2019
H. Badioze Zaman et al. (Eds.): IVIC 2019, LNCS 11870, pp. 279–290, 2019.
https://doi.org/10.1007/978-3-030-34032-2_26

ways are referred as holistic method where the entire face region is used and they relied on hand-crafted features such as edges and texture descriptors [1]. However, these algorithms show low accuracy. In [2], the accuracy result of facial recognition was 70% compared with [3] that exhibited result of 79.65%. With the rapid evolution of facial recognition algorithm, researchers have proposed machine learning techniques in facial recognition to improve the system. A facial recognition system using Convolutional Neural Network (CNN) has been proposed and from the experiment, their system achieved 95% of accuracy [4], is about the same with proposed method of augmentation [5] that achieved 95.02%. Despite the accuracy, speed is also a critical feature to be tackled and from [4], the average prediction time was approximately 0.6 s. Furthermore, the performance of facial recognition also can be affected by spoof attack. Most of the technologies have implemented spoof detection by using external hardware such as infrared sensor (IR) to compute the 3D model of the user's face.

Tensorflow is a machine learning system that runs at large scale and in heterogeneous environment. It also supports large-scale of training. Graphics Processing Unit (GPU) is a computer chip that performs mathematical calculations, especially for rendering images. It has parallel processing architecture. With this feature, it can render images faster than Central Processing Unit (CPU) and performs multiple calculations at the same time.

1.2   Proposed Solutions

In this paper, a real time facial recognition with machine learning is developed which implemented the latest technology of deep learning to train the system with large amounts of data to learn face representation which robust to different variations in the training data. On top of that, the speed of the system is improved by using *Tensorflow* framework that uses GPU instead of CPU. Spoof attack is detected using eye blink detection that requires no external hardware.

2   Background and Related Work

The machine learning implementation in this work of facial recognition is focusing on deep learning method. Deep learning has been explored widely that can be seen through many applications in healthcare, security, entertainment, natural language processing (NLP) and automation. In healthcare, deep learning did help in better diagnosis of life-threatening disease, pathology results and understanding of genetics to predict consequences of diseases. Furthermore, in security deep learning is being implemented in the facial recognition system to make it more robust and achieves better performance in speed and accuracy.

Before face can be detected by the system, face acquisition process is done by using any available camera devices such as webcam and surveillance cameras. After the face acquisition process, face detection process is done since a face need to be located in the input source before it is recognized. Face detection involves two processes which first the whole input source is examined to find the "face" followed by localization procedure to provide more accurate estimation of exact scale and position of the face [6]. Face detection algorithms can be categorized into four categories: (1) Knowledge-based, (2) Feature invariant, (3) Template matching, (4) Appearance-based method.

Spoof detection is a liveness detection of faces that has been introduces as a countermeasure against spoofing attacks [7]. As a user-based access system, a facial recognition system should be robust against spoofing attacks as human face images can be easily obtained from smart phones and social networks. In addition, spoof attacks can be categorized into three categories; print-attack, replay-attack and 3D mask attack. The bad effect of spoof attacks exposure is the system might accept the malicious user as the authenticated user and this will make the reliability of the system in term of its security measure be questioned. According to [8], face spoof detection can be categorized into four categories: (1) motion-based methods, (2) texture-based methods, (3) methods based on image quality analysis, (4) methods based on other cues.

Deep learning in facial recognition has gained attention from many researchers and developers these days, including [9]. The author has stated that the accuracy and efficiency of recognition by using deep learning is par from the traditional approach. *Caffe* framework with nine-layer network is used to develop the facial recognition system and the accuracy achieved by the author is about 80%.

Apart from that, another deep learning approach called *OpenFace* also is used in facial recognition. [10] did a modification on the original *OpenFace* structure where the authors pair the results in closest margin instead of discarding the negative pair that not found in a margin.

3 Methodology

In this paper, the overall face recognition system operated in three processes (Fig. 1). Face detection and spoof detection are two independent processes that work on their own to fulfill their respective function. However, these two processes run concurrently whereas the third process which is face recognition is run and processed after face detection and spoof detection have been completed and passed. Eye blink detection is used as the parameter to detect spoof attacks while *Haarcascade* classifiers are used to detect face and eye blinking. Deep learning is the machine learning approach implemented in this study to develop an intelligent system where *FaceNet* model is used in face recognition process. As *FaceNet* model is a deep learning architecture and deep learning is part of machine learning, *Tensorflow* is used to ease the process of acquiring data, training models, serving predictions and refining future results of the system.

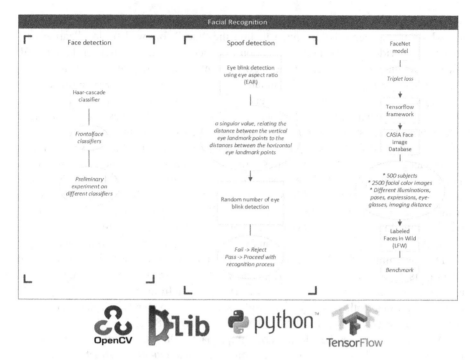

Fig. 1. Overall overview of methodology

3.1   Face Detection

Face detection is the initial step in this work to find the face area in the input source. Figure 2 below shows the steps for face detection process in this paper.

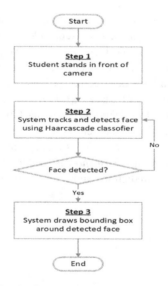

Fig. 2. Steps in face detection process

In face detection process, live video stream is used as the input source, thus a normal web camera attached to the computer is used as the medium to run the live video stream. Based on Fig. 2 above, Step 1 involves a student stands in front of the web camera so that the it can capture the student's face easily and with clear view. Next, the system is using frontal face *Haarcascade* classifier provided by OpenCV; an open-source library to track the movement of student's face (right, left, up, down) and detect the location of the face. In addition, while tracking and trying to detect the location of face, once the system has successfully detected the face, the process continues with Step 3 where a bounding box is drawn around the detected face to clearly show the face region detected in the live video stream.

3.2   Spoof Detection

Spoof detection is an important counter measure to minimize and prevent an attempt to disguise and acquire someone else's access rights by using photo, video or any other substitute for an authorized person's face. In this paper, eye blink detection is used as the method to detect spoofing.

Fig. 3. Steps in eye blink detection for spoof detection

Figure 3 shows the steps involved in eye blink detection for spoofing detection module. After the system has successfully detects face, eye blink detection process is performed. In order to minimize and possibly eliminate the possibility of spoofing, eye blink detection is implemented in this system as the method to identify whether the face detected is/are real face or a photo. Spoofing can be from photo (i.e. static photo), video (i.e. recording video) and 3D model [11]. In this detection function, OpenCV library with Python and *dlib* are used. As this system is using web camera as the input source, the *imutils* library which is a set of convenience functions to make working with OpenCV easier is used to access the web camera. The *dlib* library is using a pre-trained face detector which is based on a modification to the Histogram of Oriented Gradients and Linear SVM method for object detection. There are three steps involved in the eye blink detection process. Step 1 is facial landmark detection which it is applied to localize important regions of the face, including eyes by using *dlib* library. After facial landmark has successfully been detected, the eye aspect ratio (EAR) [12] is computed for both eyes in Step 2. The EAR gives a singular value, relating the distances between the vertical eye landmark points to the distances between the horizontal eye landmark points. After that, a threshold is set to determine if a person is blinking in Step 3. The EAR remains approximately constant when the eyes are open and then will rapidly approach zero during a blink, then increases again when the eyes are open. Figure 4 shows the six facial landmarks associated with the eye that are used for EAR computation.

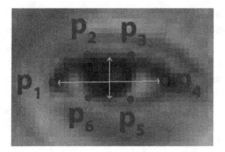

Fig. 4. Six facial landmarks associated with the eye

Based on the Fig. 4, the EAR follows the following equation.

$$EAR = \frac{\|p2 - p6\| + \|p3 - p5\|}{2\|p1 - p4\|} \qquad (1)$$

The facial landmarks of a face are detected by the pre-trained facial landmark detector inside the dlib library called ./shape_predictor_68_face_landmarks.dat. Figure 5 shows the facial landmarks produced by using the dlib library. The position of the numbers is fixed by the facial landmark detector itself and produced automatically. To detect any spoofing attempts, the system is programmed to ask for a random number of eye blink from the user. As this work is mainly focus for attendance system, this proposed method is still applicable. If the user able to give the correct number of eye blink, the system then proceeds to the recognition phase and if not, the system will reject the user and restart the process.

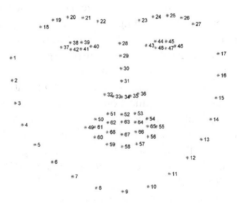

Fig. 5. Facial landmarks produced by *dlib*

3.3   Face Recognition

Once the system has successfully identified the face is real, the process continues with recognition process. I n the face recognition process, deep learning approach with *Tensorflow* framework implementation is used. For deep learning approach, a pre-trained model called *FaceNet* [13] is used in our work. This model directly learns a mapping from face images to a compact Euclidean space which distances are directly corresponding to a measure of facial similarity. The advantage of using this model is it uses deep convolutional neural network trained to directly optimize the embedding itself compare to an intermediate bottleneck layer as in other deep learning approaches before *FaceNet*. It has achieved state-of-art face recognition performance by just using 128-bytes per face. In *FaceNet* model, triplet loss technique is used which it minimizes the distance between the anchor and the positive which both have the same identity, and maximizes the distance between the anchor and the negative which both have different identity (Fig. 6).

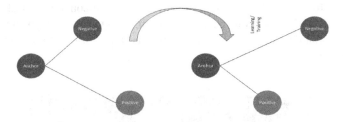

Fig. 6. Triplet loss concept visualization in *FaceNet* model

Together with *FaceNet* model, we implement *Tensorflow* framework [14], a machine learning system that can operate at large scale and in different environments. *Tensorflow* is the second generation of *DistBelief*. *Tensorflow* uses dataflow graphs to represent the computation, shared state and the operations that mutate that state. In traditional dataflow systems, the graph vertices represent the functional computation on immutable data. However, in *Tensorflow*, the vertices are allowed to represent computations that own or update mutable state. Tensors in *Tensorflow* are the dense n-multidimensional arrays which used to represent all data in the computations. Naturally, tensors represent the inputs to and results of the common mathematical operations in most of the machine learning algorithms. The advantage of using *Tensorflow* is it enables the developer to experiment with novel optimizations and training algorithms.

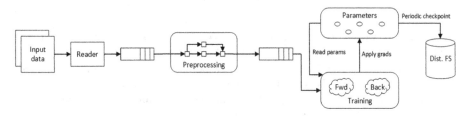

Fig. 7. A schematic *Tensorflow* dataflow graph.

Figure 7 shows the schematic *Tensorflow* dataflow graph for a training pipeline containing subgraphs for reading input data, preprocessing, training and checkpointing state.

Furthermore, we use *Tensorflow* because of its capability of acceleration by supporting both central processing unit (CPU) and graphics processing unit (GPU). We use GPU and this can help to improve the system performance where lots of parallel computations using thousands of cores can be handled by using GPU, and GPU have a large memory bandwidth to deal with the data for the computations. Besides GPU, *Tensorflow* also supports the Cloud TPU that we will do more research on that which might make our system better in performance.

3.4   Dataset

For dataset training selection, we used CASIA Face Image Database Version 5.0 from Institute of Automation Chinese Academy of Sciences. It contains 2,500 color facial images of 500 subjects. All face images are 16-bit color BMP files and the image resolution is 640 × 480. The advantage of this dataset is it contains typical intra-class variations such as illumination, pose, expression, eye-glasses and imaging distance which these variations can give big impact to the accuracy of recognition and learning performance (Fig. 8).

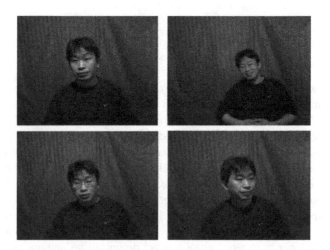

Fig. 8. Sample of CASIA Face Image Database Version 5.0

In addition, we use Labeled of Faces in Wild (LFW) for our benchmark of performance. From the readings, we found that LFW is a popular dataset used for benchmark by other researchers. To compare the performance of our proposed method, we are determined to use the same benchmark. The LFW is intended for studying face recognition in unconstrained images. There are two versions of LFW, one with no alignment and another one with alignment. Hence, we are motivated to use both versions as we want to study the effect of alignment in face recognition algorithms performance.

4 Results

4.1 Preliminary Result

A preliminary experiment was carried out to determine the average time taken of each *Haarcascade* classifiers to detect face(s) in the image. This preliminary experiment was conducted to verify initial hypothesis that the time taken to detect face(s) will affect the speed of overall process of facial recognition. There are five different *Haarcascade* classifiers proposed by Paul Viola and Michael Jones [15] specifically for frontal face of human face which are:

- haarcascade_frontalface_alt.xml (FA)
- haarcascade_frontalface_alt2.xml (FA2)
- haarcascade_frontalface_default.xml (FD)
- haarcascade_frontalcatface.xml (FC)
- haarcascade_frontalcatface_extended.xml (FCE)

Table 1. Summarization of the results based on detection speed

Number of tests	Sample image 1		Sample image 2	
	Fastest	Slowest	Fastest	Slowest
1	FD	FA	FD	FA2
2	FD	FA2	FD	FA
3	FD	FA	FA2	FA
4	FD	FA2	FD	FA
5	FD	FA	FD	FA
6	FD	FA	FD	FA
7	FD	FA	FD	FA
8	FD	FA2	FD	FA
9	FD	FA	FD	FA
10	FD	FA2	FD	FA2

In this preliminary experiment, the range used to identify the fastest and slowest detection process is time difference of before and after detection. The program code below shows the process of calculating the time difference for each classifier.

```
#note time before detection
t1 = time.time()

#call our function to detect faces
haar_detected_img = detect_faces(haar_face_cascade,
test1)

#note time after detection
t2 = time.time()

#calculate time difference
dt1 = t2 - t1
```

From Table 1, the obvious result that we can capture is that the fastest Haarcascade classifier that manage to detect faces was FD (haarcascade_frontalface_default.xml) where it exhibited a constant result of being the fastest classifier in detecting the faces. Motivated by the results shown for both sample images, FD was the fastest classifier in detecting faces within an image. Furthermore, by taking the result from both the accuracy and speed testing, we can conclude that FD was the best classifier to be used in term of accuracy and speed.

4.2   Recognition Result

There are several test cases had been carried out to verify and evaluate the performance of the system. ROC metric had been used to carry out this test.

Table 2. Result of test cases for recognition testing

User	Test 1	Test 2	Test 3
Number 1	Positively recognized	Positively recognized	Positively recognized
Number 2	Not found in database	Not found in database	Not found in database

From Table 2 above, user number 1 was stored in the system while user number 2 was not stored in the system. Training images consist of user number 1 had been trained for the system to recognize the face.

Fig. 9. User is correctly recognized

Figure 9 shows that the user was correctly recognized with higher confidence level compared to other training images stored in the system. Apart from that, the system allowed the recognition process to be done as it can detect eye blink performed by the user. This indicates that the user was not attempting any spoof attack towards the system.

5   Conclusion

In this paper, there are three processes involved in a complete pipeline of facial recognition which are face detection module, spoof detection module and facial recognition module. Inside the face detection module, *Haarcascade* classifier had been chosen as the medium to detect and track the face motivated by widely used by many researchers in face detection. However, there are various types of *Haarcascade* classifiers to choose from. Hence, a preliminary experiment had been conducted to run and test each classifier's performance based on its accuracy and speed. Based on the results obtained, *haarcascade_frontalface_default* (FD) is the best classifier because it had managed to detect faces more accurate in term of correct number of faces and correctly detect faces with shorter time compared to other classifiers. Facial recognition can be exposed to spoof attacks, thus inside spoof detection module, motion-based method which is eye blink detection had been implemented. Eye blink detection is easy to implement as it is considered as non-intrusive approach in this work. With the evolution of technology, deep learning is the latest technique and method for facial recognition. *FaceNet* model had been used in this work together with triplet loss approach and *Tensorflow* framework. *FaceNet* had achieved state-of-the-art facial recognition performance, thus motivated by this result, *Tensorflow* had been added to the process to investigate the performance of facial recognition as *Tensorflow* allows the usage of GPU that can make a system performs more faster and *Tensorflow* is also a machine learning system that can operate at large scale.

References

1. Trigueros, D.S., Meng, L., Hartnett, M.: Face recognition: from traditional to deep learning methods (2018). arXiv:1811.00116v1
2. Sukri, S.S., Ruhaiyem, N.I.R., Mohamed, A.S.A.: Face recognition with real time eye lid movement detection, Lecture Notes in Computer Science (including subseries Lecture Notes in Artificial Intelligence and Lecture Notes in Bioinformatics) (2017). https://doi.org/10.1007/978-3-319-70010-6_33
3. Wagh, P., et al.: Attendance system based on face recognition using eigen face and PCA algorithms. In: Proceedings of the 2015 International Conference on Green Computing and Internet of Things, ICGCIoT 2015, pp. 303–308 (2016). https://doi.org/10.1109/icgciot.2015.7380478
4. Ara, N.M., Simul, N.S., Islam, M.S.: Convolutional neural network approach for vision based student recognition system. In: 20th International Conference of Computer and Information Technology, ICCIT 2017, 2018–January, pp. 1–6 (2018). https://doi.org/10.1109/iccitechn.2017.8281789
5. Arsenovic, M., et al.: FaceTime - deep learning based face recognition attendance system. In: Proceedings of SISY 2017 - IEEE 15th International Symposium on Intelligent Systems and Informatics, pp. 53–57 (2017). https://doi.org/10.1109/sisy.2017.8080587
6. Neeraj, S., Sugandha, S.: Survey of advanced face detection techniques in image processing. Int. J. Adv. Res. Comput. Commun. Eng. 2(1), 22–24 (2014). http://www.ijcsmr.org/vol1issue2/paper26.pdf
7. Bagga, M., Singh, B.: Spoofing detection in face recognition: a review. In: 2016 3rd International Conference on Computing for Sustainable Global Development (INDIACom), New Delhi, pp. 2037–2042 (2016)
8. Kaur, R.: Techniques of face spoof detection: a review. Int. J. Comput. Appl. 164(1), 29–33 (2017)
9. Luo, X., et al.: A deep convolutional neural network model for vehicle recognition and face recognition. In: International Congress of Information and Communication Technology (ICICT 2017) (2017)
10. Santoso, K., Kusuma, G.P.: Face recognition using modified OpenFace. Procedia Computer Science 135, 510–517 (2018). https://doi.org/10.1016/j.procs.2018.08.203
11. Erdogmus, N., Marcel, S.: Spoofing face recognition with 3D masks. IEEE Trans. Inf. Forensics Secur. 9(7), 1084–1097 (2014). https://doi.org/10.1109/TIFS.2014.2322255
12. Soukupová, T., Cech, J.: Real-time eye blink detection using facial landmarks (2016)
13. Schroff, F., Kalenichenko, D., Philbin, J.: FaceNet : a unified embedding for face recognition and clustering. 1, 2014 (2014)
14. Xia, X., Xu, C., Nan, B.: Facial expression recognition based on Tensorflow platform, vol. 01005, pp. 8–11 (2017)
15. Cuimei, L., Zhiliang, Q., Nan, J., Jianhua, W.: Human face detection algorithm via Haar cascade classifier combined with three additional classifiers. In: 2017 13th IEEE International Conference on Electronic Measurement & Instruments (ICEMI) (2017). https://doi.org/10.1109/icemi.2017.8265863

Algebraic-Trigonometric Nonlinear Analytical Inverse Kinematic Modeling and Simulation for Robotic Manipulator Arm Motion Control

Khairul Annuar Abdullah[1,2(✉)], Suziyanti Marjudi[1], Zuriati Yusof[2],
and Riza Sulaiman[2]

[1] Department of Computing, Faculty of Communication, Visual Art and
Computing, Universiti Selangor, 45600 Bestari Jaya, Selangor, Malaysia
{annuar,suziyanti}@unisel.edu.my
[2] Institute of Visual Informatics, Universiti Kebangsaan Malaysia,
43600 Bangi, Selangor, Malaysia
atieyz@gmail.com, riza@ukm.edu.my

Abstract. Robotic manipulator arm has to endure certain challenges of actual applications that regularly affect its motion behavior incorporating end-effector positional accuracy and repeatability, degree-of-freedom constraint, redundant movement, heavy payload uplifting, long reach stretching, and other complications. This study works on finding inverse kinematic (IK) solutions to facilitate the robotic arm motion control with algebraic-trigonometric nonlinear analytical models. The nonlinear analytical models acquired from the extensive manipulation of trigonometric rules, specifically sum-and-difference and Pythagorean identities and algebraic arithmetic in pursuit of determining the reachable actuating joint configurations are experimented for applicability on the fundamental structure of two-segmented manipulator arm. For verification, the precision of the IK solutions yielded by the models are cross-referenced with the manipulator's direct kinematics and tested with the statistical performance measure of minimum squared error while tracking cubic Hermite spline, cubic Bezier, and cubic B-spline curves. For validation, an interactive spreadsheet-based IK application utilizing built-in front-end capabilities including Visual Basic for Applications, Math and Trig Function Library, Name Manager, Data Validation, ActiveX Controls, and Charts is developed to accommodate these models and simulate the feasible joint angles and orientations of robot arm. The application visualizes (1) the robotic linkage motion on xz plane according to the links lengths, end-effector position, and base position specified and (2) the robotic curves trajectory tracking of cubic Hermite spline, cubic Bezier, and cubic B-spline. The algebraic-trigonometric nonlinear analytical models proposed provide alternative practical IK solutions for the two-segmented robotic manipulator arm.

Keywords: Analytical model · Cubic B-spline · Cubic Bezier · Cubic Hermite spline · Geometric motion control · Inverse kinematics · Robotic manipulator arm · Trajectory tracking · Trigonometric rule

© Springer Nature Switzerland AG 2019
H. Badioze Zaman et al. (Eds.): IVIC 2019, LNCS 11870, pp. 291–304, 2019.
https://doi.org/10.1007/978-3-030-34032-2_27

1   Introduction

Robotic manipulator arm constitutes a serial-linked organization that mimics the biological structure of human arm for great agility and versatility while performing tasks [1]. As an indispensable technology in manufacturing automation, the manipulator arm is vastly acknowledged for its winning qualities of speed, agility, accuracy, repeatability, and reliability [2]. The technology is popular as it can be reprogrammed and retooled to execute other tasks at relatively low cost [3]. Jobs in hazardous environment that no human can intervene, tedious manual jobs that are vulnerably exposed to human errors, and jobs of repetitive functions that human operators easily get bored with are competently handled by this automated control technology. The manipulator arm has long become the significant automation enabler to a wide range of processing such as stamping, welding, mounting, casting, spray painting, cutting, grinding, and deburring; assembly such as pick-and-place, palletizing, loading-unloading, packaging, and micro-assembly; and inspection [4]. Safety-critical jobs which corrective repair, preventive maintenance, and unexpected reconfiguration are not possible [5] such as nuclear installation, nuclear waste remediation, and underwater [6] and aerospace [7] explorations also enjoy the benefits as a result of the elegance of manipulator arm technology.

One of the key interests of robotic manipulator arm is related to the science of geometric motion control termed as kinematics, especially inverse kinematics (IK). This is due to the fundamental importance of IK in analyzing the design and control of manipulator arm [8–10]. For instance, instructing the manipulator arm to conform to the target position defined demands its motion to be controlled with the highest stability and accuracy [11]. For the most tasks assigned, the manipulator arm usually requires position and orientation data either via lead through programming applying teach pendant or simulation using computer-aided design and manufacturing systems [12]. For micro-level processing and assembly, end-effector positional sensitivity is extremely crucial [13]. There are occasions in which the manipulator arm is forced to uplift heavy payloads or stretch long horizontal reach within its feasible joint angle limits [14]. Real-life robotic arm applications frequently have to deal with higher degrees-of-freedom (DOF) and redundant motion apart from the naturally serial link-joint chain inaccuracy [15]. All these scenarios demand for the solution of IK, specifically the determination of joint displacements or joint angles effectively and efficiently at any instant of time by the manipulator arm controller.

Despite all the significance and usefulness, the IK of manipulator arm forms a complex optimization problem [16] and is perceived as one of the toughest problems in robotics [14] as it directly dictates accurate motion control for desired trajectory [17, 18]. The complicated IK characteristics as a multi-input multi-output system are substantively reliant on transparent and complete mathematical descriptions for precise representations [19]. The IK complexity originates in the volume of joint variables [20], the diversity of robot configuration [21], the high-nonlinear analytical equations yielded from the transition of workspace to the joint space [22, 23], and the geometric placement of joint axes. The difficulty is also rooted from finding the global optima of multiple optimal local solutions caused by the natural uniqueness of IK problem [24].

The Jacobian matrix was engaged to find the IK solution of 7DOF Mitsubishi PA-10-7C redundant manipulator and the matrix was noticed to possess high precision and rapid convergence [25]. The analytical approach of trigonometric function derivatives and Cramer's rule computed the joint angles of 2R robot respectively on quartic polynomial [26] and cubic Hermite spline curve [15] trajectories. The support vector regression model was more accurately presenting the behavior of 7DOF K-1207 robotic arm than the polynomial model as it could afford to cover the larger partitions of arm workspace [27]. A numerical method, namely New Inverse Kinematics Algorithm was introduced to solve the IK problem of 6DOF robot arms with offset wrist not having nonlinear closed-analytical equations [14]. The FNNs inspired by cerebellar cortex anatomy and function were applied as the IK solution model of two-segmented arm [18]. Contrary to the standard genetic algorithm (GA), the continuous GA displayed faster convergence to the IK solutions of 3R planar manipulator arm in tandem with the minimum execution time and number of generations resulted and the smooth solution curve of joint angles path that minimized the joints net displacement [28]. Generalized reduced gradient algorithm was applied to build a feed-forward neural network well-fitting to predict accurately the joint angles of 2DOF planar manipulator arm [24].

This paper is intended to address the IK problem of robotic manipulator arm with relatively simple yet adequately practical mathematical models resolution.

2   Method

This study emphasizes algebraic-trigonometric nonlinear analytical models to compute the feasible actuator joint angles and end-effector orientations, Θ two-segmented planar manipulator arm, simulate its potential linkage motions, and track several curve trajectories. The development modus operandi commences by solving the second joint angles, θ_2 prior followed by the first joint angles, θ_1. Both divisions of the nonlinear analytical models proposed are originated from the product of transformation matrices, $^{i-1}T_i$ (1):

$$^{i-1}T_i = \begin{bmatrix} c_i & -\gamma_i s_i & \sigma_i s_i & l_i c_i \\ s_i & \gamma_i c_i & -\sigma_i c_i & l_i s_i \\ 0 & \sigma_i & \gamma_i & d_i \\ 0 & 0 & 0 & 1 \end{bmatrix} = \begin{bmatrix} R_i & \mathbf{p}_i \\ 000 & 1 \end{bmatrix} \quad (1)$$

in which $c_i = \cos \theta_i$, $s_i = \sin \theta_i$, $\gamma_i = \cos \alpha_i$, $\sigma_i = \sin \alpha_i$, d_i is link offset, l_i is link length, α_i is link twist, R_i is rotational matrix, and $\mathbf{p}_i$ is positional vector.

$$^0T_1 \cdot {}^1T_2 = P_2$$

in which P is end-effector pose matrix (2).

$$\begin{bmatrix} c_1 & -s_1 & 0 & l_1c_1 \\ s_1 & c_1 & 0 & l_1s_1 \\ 0 & 0 & 1 & 0 \\ 0 & 0 & 0 & 1 \end{bmatrix} \begin{bmatrix} c_2 & -s_2 & 0 & l_2c_2 \\ s_2 & c_2 & 0 & l_2s_2 \\ 0 & 0 & 1 & 0 \\ 0 & 0 & 0 & 1 \end{bmatrix} = \begin{bmatrix} c_{12} & -s_{12} & 0 & l_1c_1+l_2c_{12} \\ s_{12} & c_{12} & 0 & l_1s_1+l_2s_{12} \\ 0 & 0 & 1 & 0 \\ 0 & 0 & 0 & 1 \end{bmatrix}$$

$$= \begin{bmatrix} n_x & b_x & t_x & p_x \\ n_z & b_z & t_z & p_z \\ n_y & b_y & t_y & p_y \\ 0 & 0 & 0 & 1 \end{bmatrix} = \begin{bmatrix} n & b & t & p \\ 0 & 0 & 0 & 1 \end{bmatrix}$$

(2)

in which $p_x = x_{end}$ is end-effector abscissa and $p_z = z_{end}$ is end-effector applicate.

2.1 Development of Algebraic-Trigonometric Nonlinear Analytical Models

The former section of algebraic-trigonometric nonlinear analytical models is aimed at generating the prospective solutions of second joint angles, θ_2. These nonlinear analytical models (4) and (5) are acquired from the manipulation of trigonometric rules, particularly sum-and-difference and Pythagorean identities implementing squaring and addition arithmetic.

Stemming from the end-effector positional vector of pose matrix, apply the trigonometric sum-and-difference identities, $s_{\alpha\beta} = s_\alpha c_\beta + c_\alpha s_\beta$ and $c_{\alpha\beta} = c_\alpha c_\beta - s_\alpha s_\beta$; square and add the equations drawn; and finally adopt the trigonometric Pythagorean identity, $s_\theta^2 + c_\theta^2 = 1$:

$$x_{end} = l_1c_1 + l_2c_{12} = l_1c_1 + l_2(c_1c_2 - s_1s_2) = l_1c_1 + l_2c_1c_2 - l_2s_1s_2$$
$$z_{end} = l_1s_1 + l_2s_{12} = l_1s_1 + l_2(s_1c_2 + c_1s_2) = l_1s_1 + l_2s_1c_2 + l_2c_1s_2$$

$$x_{end}^2 = (l_1c_1 + l_2c_1c_2 - l_2s_1s_2)^2$$
$$= l_1^2c_1^2 + l_2^2c_1^2c_2^2 + l_2^2s_1^2s_2^2 + 2l_1l_2c_1^2c_2 - 2l_1l_2c_1s_1s_2 - 2l_2^2c_1s_1c_2s_2$$

$$z_{end}^2 = (a_1s_1 + l_2s_1c_2 + l_2c_1s_2)^2$$
$$= l_1^2s_1^2 + l_2^2s_1^2c_2^2 + l_2^2c_1^2s_2^2 + 2l_1l_2s_1^2c_2 + 2l_1l_2c_1s_1s_2 + 2l_2^2c_1s_1c_2s_2$$

$$x_{end}^2 + z_{end}^2 = (l_1^2c_1^2 + l_2^2c_1^2c_2^2 + l_2^2s_1^2s_2^2 + 2l_1l_2c_1^2c_2 - 2l_1l_2c_1s_1s_2 - 2l_2^2c_1s_1c_2s_2)$$
$$+ (l_1^2s_1^2 + l_2^2s_1^2c_2^2 + l_2^2c_1^2s_2^2 + 2l_1l_2s_1^2c_2 + 2l_1l_2c_1s_1s_2 + 2l_2^2c_1s_1c_2s_2)$$
$$= l_1^2c_1^2 + l_1^2s_1^2 + l_2^2c_1^2c_2^2 + l_2^2s_1^2c_2^2 + l_2^2s_1^2s_2^2 + l_2^2c_1^2s_2^2 + 2l_1l_2c_1^2c_2 + 2l_1l_2s_1^2c_2$$
$$= l_1^2(s_1^2 + c_1^2) + l_2^2(s_1^2 + c_1^2)(s_2^2 + c_2^2) + 2l_1l_2c_2(s_1^2 + c_1^2) = l_1^2 + l_2^2 + 2l_1l_2c_2$$

(3)

$$c_2 = \frac{x_{end}^2 + z_{end}^2 - l_1^2 - l_2^2}{2l_1l_2} = \frac{(x_{end} - x_{home})^2 + (z_{end} - z_{home})^2 - l_1^2 - l_2^2}{2l_1l_2}$$

accounting for the robot base position is not at the origin, **O**; thus, displacement exists.

$$\theta_2 = \begin{bmatrix} \theta_2^{(1)} & \theta_2^{(2)} \end{bmatrix}^T = c^{-1} \left[\frac{(x_{end} - x_{home})^2 + (z_{end} - z_{home})^2 - l_1^2 - l_2^2}{2l_1l_2} \right] \tag{4}$$

The Pythagorean identity, $s_\theta^2 + c_\theta^2 = 1$ is employed again to trace any remaining candidates of second joint angle, θ_2:

$$s_2^2 = 1 - c_2^2$$

$$s_2 = \pm\sqrt{1 - c_2^2}$$

$$\theta_2 = \begin{bmatrix} \theta_2^{(1)} & \theta_2^{(2)} & \theta_2^{(3)} & \theta_2^{(4)} \end{bmatrix}^T = s^{-1}\left(\pm\sqrt{1 - c_2^2} \right) \tag{5}$$

The latter part of nonlinear models is tasked to find the possible solutions of first joint angle, θ_1. Rooting from the end-effector positional vector and holding the values of second joint angle, θ_2, the models (9) and (11) are established from the usage of trigonometric sum-and-difference identities, $s_{\alpha\beta} = s_\alpha c_\beta + c_\alpha s_\beta$ and $c_{\alpha\beta} = c_\alpha c_\beta - s_\alpha s_\beta$ and the substitution of Eq. (8) derived from Eq. (6), Pythagorean identity, $s_\theta^2 + c_\theta^2 = 1$, and Eq. (3) into Eq. (7):

$$x_{end} = l_1c_1 + l_2c_{12} = l_1c_1 + l_2(c_1c_2 - s_1s_2) = l_1c_1 + l_2c_1c_2 - l_2s_1s_2 \tag{6}$$

$$z_{end} = l_1s_1 + l_2s_{12} = l_1s_1 + l_2(s_1c_2 + c_1s_2) = l_1s_1 + l_2s_1c_2 + l_2c_1s_2 \tag{7}$$

$$s_1 = \frac{l_1c_1 + l_2c_1c_2 - x_{end}}{l_2s_2} \tag{8}$$

$$z_{end} = l_1\left(\frac{l_1c_1 + l_2c_1c_2 - x_{end}}{l_2s_2} \right) + l_2\left(\frac{l_1c_1 + l_2c_1c_2 - x_{end}}{l_2s_2} \right)c_2 + l_2c_1s_2$$

$$z_{end}l_2s_2 = \left(l_1^2c_1 + l_1l_2c_1c_2 - x_{end}\,l_1 \right) + \left(l_1l_2c_1c_2 + l_2^2c_1c_2^2 - x_{end}\,l_2c_2 \right) + \left(l_2^2c_1s_2^2 \right)$$

$$= c_1\left(l_1^2 + l_1l_2c_2 + l_1l_2c_2 + l_2^2c_2^2 + l_2^2s_2^2 \right) - x_{end}\left(l_1 + l_2c_2 \right)$$

$$= c_1\left[l_1^2 + l_1l_2c_2 + l_1l_2c_2 + l_2^2c_2^2 + l_2^2(1 - c_2^2) \right] - x_{end}\left(l_1 + l_2c_2 \right)$$

$$= c_1\left(l_1^2 + l_1l_2c_2 + l_1l_2c_2 + l_2^2c_2^2 + l_2^2 - l_2^2c_2^2 \right) - x_{end}\left(l_1 + l_2c_2 \right)$$

$$= c_1\left(l_1^2 + l_2^2 + 2l_1l_2c_2 \right) - x_{end}\left(l_1 + l_2c_2 \right)$$

$$= c_1\left(x_{end}^2 + z_{end}^2 \right) - x_{end}\left(l_1 + l_2c_2 \right)$$

$$c_1 = \frac{x_{end}\left(l_1 + l_2c_2 \right) + z_{end}\,l_2s_2}{x_{end}^2 + z_{end}^2} = \frac{(x_{end} - x_{home})\left(l_1 + l_2c_2 \right) + (z_{end} - z_{home})\,l_2s_2}{(x_{end} - x_{home})^2 + (z_{end} - z_{home})^2}$$

accounting for the robot base position is not at the origin, **O**; thus, displacement exists.

$$\theta_1 = \begin{bmatrix} \theta_1^{(1)} & \theta_1^{(2)} & \theta_1^{(3)} & \theta_1^{(4)} \end{bmatrix}^T = c^{-1} \left[\frac{(x_{end} - x_{home})(l_1 + l_2 c_2) + (z_{end} - z_{home}) l_2 s_2}{(x_{end} - x_{home})^2 + (z_{end} - z_{home})^2} \right]$$

(9)

The replacement of Eq. (10) exploited from Eq. (7), Pythagorean identity, $s_\theta^2 + c_\theta^2 = 1$, and Eq. (3) into Eq. (6) is correspondingly used to search further the residual candidates of first joint angle, θ_1:

$$c_1 = \frac{z_{end} - l_1 s_1 - l_2 s_1 c_2}{l_2 s_2}$$

(10)

$$x_{end} = l_1 \left(\frac{z_{end} - l_1 s_1 - l_2 s_1 c_2}{l_2 s_2} \right) + l_2 \left(\frac{z_{end} - l_1 s_1 - l_2 s_1 c_2}{l_2 s_2} \right) c_2 - l_2 s_1 s_2$$

$$x_{end} l_2 s_2 = \left(z_{end} l_1 - l_1^2 s_1 - l_1 l_2 s_1 c_2 \right) + \left(z_{end} l_2 c_2 - l_1 l_2 s_1 c_2 - l_2^2 s_1 c_2^2 \right) - l_2^2 s_1 s_2^2$$

$$= s_1 \left(-l_1^2 - l_1 l_2 c_2 - l_1 l_2 c_2 - l_2^2 c_2^2 - l_2^2 s_2^2 \right) + z_{end} \left(l_1 + l_2 c_2 \right)$$

$$= s_1 \left[-l_1^2 - l_1 l_2 c_2 - l_1 l_2 c_2 - l_2^2 c_2^2 - l_2^2 \left(1 - c_2^2 \right) \right] + z_{end} \left(l_1 + l_2 c_2 \right)$$

$$= s_1 \left(-l_1^2 - l_1 l_2 c_2 - l_1 l_2 c_2 - l_2^2 c_2^2 - l_2^2 + l_2^2 c_2^2 \right) + z_{end} \left(l_1 + l_2 c_2 \right)$$

$$= s_1 \left(-l_1^2 - l_2^2 - 2 l_1 l_2 c_2 \right) + z_{end} \left(l_1 + l_2 c_2 \right)$$

$$= -s_1 \left(l_1^2 + l_2^2 + 2 l_1 l_2 c_2 \right) + z_{end} \left(l_1 + l_2 c_2 \right)$$

$$= -s_1 \left(x_{end}^2 + z_{end}^2 \right) + z_{end} \left(l_1 + l_2 c_2 \right)$$

$$s_1 = \frac{z_{end} \left(l_1 + l_2 c_2 \right) - x_{end} l_2 s_2}{x_{end}^2 + z_{end}^2} = \frac{(z_{end} - z_{home}) \left(l_1 + l_2 c_2 \right) - (x_{end} - x_{home}) l_2 s_2}{(x_{end} - x_{home})^2 + (z_{end} - z_{home})^2}$$

accounting for the robot base position is not at the origin, **O**; thus, displacement exists.

$$\theta_1 = \begin{bmatrix} \theta_1^{(1)} & \theta_1^{(2)} & \theta_1^{(3)} & \theta_1^{(4)} \end{bmatrix}^T = s^{-1} \left[\frac{(z_{end} - z_{home})(l_1 + l_2 c_2) \mp (x_{end} - x_{home}) l_2 s_2}{(x_{end} - x_{home})^2 + (z_{end} - z_{home})^2} \right]$$

(11)

3   Results and Discussion

3.1   Verification with Direct Kinematic Model

For verification, the precision of inverse kinematic (IK) solutions by the algebraic-trigonometric nonlinear analytical models is cross-checked with the direct kinematics (DK) of manipulator arm. It is a good practice to double-check the IK solutions procured to the DK formulation for verification [20]. All solutions of IK must be examined to verify whether they may feasibly drive the end-effector to the desired position [8]. Table 1 presents the results obtained from the IK models developed and their comparison with the DK:

Table 1. Fitting of IK models' results to DK.

i	DK								IK			
									(4)	(5)	(9)	(11)
	l_1	l_2	θ_1°	θ_2°	X_{home}	Z_{home}	X_{end}	Z_{end}	θ_2°	θ_2°	θ_1°	θ_1°
1	13.0	5.0	7.0	37.0	0.00	0.00	16.50	5.06	37.0	37.0	7.0	7.0
			27.0	323.0					323.0	143.0	353.0	173.0
									217.0		27.1	27.1
									323.0		332.9	152.9
2	12.0	5.0	20.0	52.0	0.00	0.00	12.82	8.86	52.0	52.0	20.0	20.0
			49.0	308.0					308.0	128.0	340.0	160.0
									232.0		49.3	49.3
									308.0		310.7	130.7
3	25.0	7.0	16.0	34.0	1.00	1.00	29.53	13.25	34.0	34.0	16.0	16.0
			31.0	326.0					326.0	146.0	344.0	164.0
									214.0		30.5	30.5
									326.0		329.5	149.5
4	24.0	7.0	14.0	21.0	1.00	2.00	30.02	11.82	21.0	21.0	14.0	14.0
			23.0	339.0					339.0	159.0	346.0	166.0
									201.0		23.4	23.4
									339.0		336.6	156.6
5	17.0	8.0	19.0	9.0	2.00	2.00	25.14	11.29	8.8	8.8	19.0	19.0
			25.0	351.0					351.2	171.2	341.0	161.0
									188.8		24.7	24.7
									351.2		335.3	155.3
6	15.0	8.0	53.0	23.0	2.00	3.00	12.96	22.74	23.1	23.1	53.0	53.0
			69.0	337.0					336.9	156.9	307.0	127.0
									203.1		68.9	68.9
									336.9		291.1	111.1
7	26.0	10.0	34.0	54.0	3.00	3.00	24.90	27.53	54.0	54.0	34.0	34.0
			63.0	306.0					306.0	126.0	326.0	146.0
									234.0		62.5	62.5
									306.0		297.5	117.5
8	24.0	10.0	12.0	18.0	3.00	4.00	35.14	13.99	17.9	17.9	12.0	12.0
			23.0	342.0					342.1	162.1	348.0	168.0
									197.9		22.5	22.5
									342.1		337.5	157.5
9	50.0	14.0	45.0	25.0	4.00	4.00	44.14	52.51	25.0	25.0	45.0	45.0
			56.0	335.0					335.0	155.0	315.0	135.0
									205.0		55.8	55.8
									335.0		304.2	124.2
10	48.0	14.0	54.0	7.0	4.00	5.00	39.00	56.08	6.9	6.9	54.0	54.0
			57.0	353.0					353.1	173.1	306.0	126.0
									186.9		57.1	57.1
									353.1		302.9	122.9

The italic results in Table 1 proves the efficacy of algebraic-trigonometric nonlinear analytical models (4), (5), (9), and (11) in resolving the IK problem of two-segmented planar manipulator arm. Although slight differences of joint angle vectors, $[\theta_1 \ \theta_2]^T$ occur, the results computed by the models are tolerable due to minimum errors.

3.2 Verifications with Cubic Hermite Spline, Cubic Bezier, and Cubic B-Spline

Apart from the DK matching, the effectiveness of proposed models is experimented against the curve trajectory tracking of cubic Hermite spline (12), cubic Bezier (13), and cubic B-spline (14). The models are found high-performing based on the very low mean squared errors (MSE) (15) illustrated in Table 2 respectively through below and above configurations:

Table 2. Curve trajectory tracking result.

Type of curve	Joint configuration	MSE
Cubic Hermite spline	Elbow-down	4×10^{-4}
	Elbow-up	5×10^{-4}
Cubic Bezier	Elbow-down	5×10^{-4}
	Elbow-up	6×10^{-4}
Cubic b-spline	Elbow-down	6×10^{-4}
	Elbow-up	6×10^{-4}

$$P_{curve}(u) = (x_{curve}, z_{curve}) = P_{ctrl1}\left(2u^3 - 3u^2 + 1\right) + P_{ctrl2}\left(u^3 - 2u^2 + u\right) \\ + P_{ctrl3}\left(u^3 - u^2\right) + P_{ctrl4}\left(-2u^3 + 3u^2\right) \tag{12}$$

$$P_{curve}(u) = (x_{curve}, z_{curve}) = P_{ctrl1}\left(-u^3 - 3u^2 + 1\right) + P_{ctrl2}\left(3u^3 - 6u^2 + 3u\right) \\ + P_{ctrl3}\left(-3u^3 + 3u^2\right) + P_{ctrl4}\left(u^3\right) \tag{13}$$

$$P_{curve}(u) = (x_{curve}, z_{curve}) = P_{ctrl1}\left(\frac{-u^3 + 3u^2 - 3u + 1}{6}\right) + P_{ctrl2}\left(\frac{3u^3 - 6u^2 + 4}{6}\right) \\ + P_{ctrl3}\left(\frac{-3u^3 - 6u^2 + 4}{6}\right) + P_{ctrl4}\left(\frac{u^3}{6}\right) \tag{14}$$

in which P_{ctrl} is control point and $u = [0, 1]$.

$$\text{MSE} = \frac{1}{n} \sum_{i=1}^{n} \left[\left(x_{curve}^{(i)} - x_{end}^{(i)}\right)^2 + \left(z_{curve}^{(i)} - z_{end}^{(i)}\right)^2\right] \tag{15}$$

3.3 Validation with Spreadsheet Computing and Simulation

A spreadsheet-based inverse kinematic (IK) application is constructed for the computation and simulation of algebraic-trigonometric nonlinear analytical models. Simulation is an effective virtual experiment to test diversified models or algorithms for manipulator arm [25]. The application uses inbuilt front-end features such as Visual Basic for Applications for the models programming, Math and Trig Function Library, Name Manager for variables definition and management, Data Validation for incorrect inputs prevention, ActiveX Controls for user-friendly data input, and Charts for data analysis description. This application is able to fulfill the validation purpose, expressly to compute all candidates of joint angles, simulate the feasible ones with orientation, and visualize the linkage motion of manipulator arm on xz plane in accordance with the links lengths, end-effector position, and base position stipulated.

Figure 1 visualizes the simulated linkage motion of two-segmented manipulator arm:

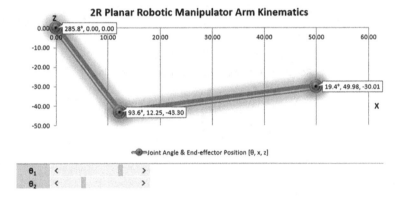

Fig. 1. Linkage motion simulation visual of two-segmented manipulator arm.

Through the validation process, it is learned that two settings of linkage motion are achievable for the two-segmented manipulator arm. For instance, i_8, Fig. 1 is recognized as the elbow-down configuration. In addition to the linkage motion, the validation of algebraic-trigonometric nonlinear analytical models is also conducted via the simulated curve trajectory tracking of cubic Hermite spline, cubic Bezier, and cubic B-spline as depicted in Fig. 2:

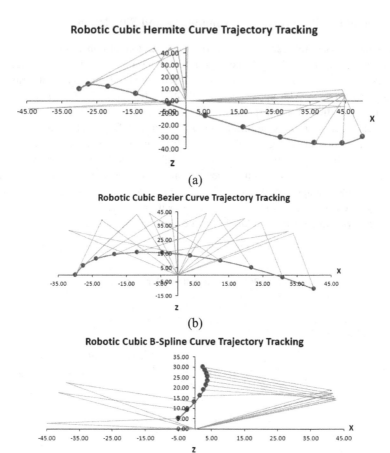

Fig. 2. Trajectory tracking simulation visual of two-segmented manipulator arm.

Figure 2(a), (b), and (c) evidently indicate the models are capable to maneuver the manipulator arm to achieve the cubic Hermite spline, cubic Bezier, and cubic B-spline curve points precisely in both the elbow-down and elbow-up configurations. Figure 3 in the appendix section shows the holistic picture of alternative algebraic-trigonometric nonlinear analytical models undertaken for computing the IK solutions of two-segmented robotic manipulator arm.

4   Conclusion

The sum-and-difference and Pythagorean identities of trigonometric rule are extensively harnessed to realize the algebraic-trigonometric nonlinear analytical models. The inverse kinematic (IK) solutions produced by these models are discovered feasible and precise after verifying with the direct kinematic models and validating with the spreadsheet computing and simulation for the robotic linkage motion and trajectory tracking. The analytical models are also efficient and practical in computation as the nonlinearity is merely the simplified quadratic form.

Advanced studies to add value to this work encompass the development and deployment of new analytical models using transformation matrix or Jacobian matrix inversions for the IK solutions of spatial robotic manipulator arm. Planning to attempt for varied IK solution paradigms with geometrical principles, statistical procedures, numerical methods, and soft computing techniques are also considered in the future works.

Acknowledgement. This research is supported by Geran Penyelidikan Negeri Selangor (GPNS), GPNS-01/UNISEL/18-022. The authors are grateful to Selangor State Government for the approved fund which makes this important research beneficial and viable.

Appendix

See Fig. 3.

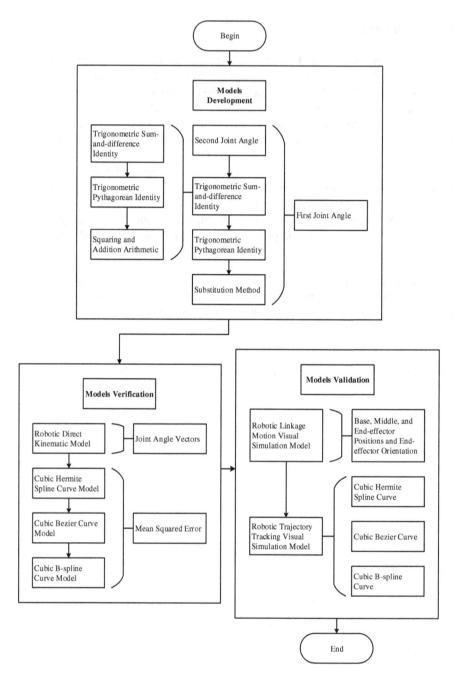

Fig. 3. Development of algebraic-trigonometric nonlinear analytical inverse kinematic models.

References

1. Haughey, B.: Simulation and optimization of a two degree of freedom, planar, parallel manipulator. Unpublished Ph. D. thesis. Victoria University of Wellington, Wellington (2011)
2. Groover, M.P.: Automation, Production Systems and Computer-Integrated Manufacturing. Pearson Higher Education, Boston (2015)
3. Prasanna, K.S., Kar, S.: On the algebraic modeling of planar robots. Ann. - Comput. Sci. Ser. **9**(2), 131–142 (2011)
4. Niku, S.B.: Introduction to Robotics – Analysis, Control, Applications. Wiley, Hoboken (2011)
5. Ben-Gharbia, K.M., Roberts, R.G., Maciejewski, A.A.: Examples of planar robot kinematic designs from optimally fault-tolerant Jacobians. In: ICRA: Proceedings of the 2011 IEEE International on Robotics and Automation, pp. 4710–4715, Shanghai (2011)
6. Sivčev, S., Coleman, J., Omerdić, E., Dooly, G., Toal, D.: Underwater manipulators – a review. Ocean Eng. **163**, 431–450 (2018)
7. Ollero, A.: Aerial robotic manipulators. In: Ang, M.H., Khatib, O., Siciliano, B. (eds.) Encyclopedia of Robotics, pp. 1–8. Springer, Berlin (2019)
8. Kucuk, S., Bingul, Z.: Robot kinematics: forward and inverse kinematics. In: Cubero, S. (ed.) Industrial Robotics - Theory, Modelling and Control - Advanced Robotic Systems, pp. 117–148. InTech, Rijeka (2007)
9. Jha, P.: Novel artificial neural network application for prediction of inverse kinematics of manipulator. Unpublished Master thesis. National Institute of Technology, Rourkela, India (2009)
10. Rocha, C.R., Tonetto, C.P., Dias, A.: A comparison between the Denavit-Hartenberg and the screw-based methods used in kinematic modeling of robot manipulators. Robot. Comput.-Integr. Manuf. **27**(4), 723–728 (2011)
11. Manigpan, S., Kiattisin, S., Leelasantitham, A.: A simulation of 6R industrial articulated robot arm using backpropagation neural network. In: ICCAS: Proceedings of the 2010 International Conference on Control Automation and Systems, pp. 823–826, Gyeonggi-do (2010)
12. Nagata, F., Yoshitake, S., Otsuka, A., Watanabe, K., Habib, M.K.: Development of CAM system based on industrial robotic servo controller without using robot language. Robot. Comput.- Integr. Manuf. **29**(2), 454–462 (2013)
13. Köker, R.: A genetic algorithm approach to a neural-network-based inverse kinematics solution of robotic manipulators based on error minimization. Inf. Sci. **222**, 528–543 (2013)
14. Kucuk, S., Bingul, Z.: Inverse kinematics solutions for industrial robot manipulators with offset wrists. Appl. Math. Model. **38**(7–8), 1983–1999 (2014)
15. Abdullah, K.A., Raja Lope Ahmad, R.M.T., Widyarto, S., Yusof, Z., Sulaiman, R.: Integrated nonlinear-linear analytical models based on trigonometric and Cramer's rules for computing inverse kinematics of robot arm. In: Proceedings of the 4th International Conference on Robotic Automation System (ICORAS 2019), pp. 92–98. Terengganu (2019)
16. Wen, X., Sheng, D., Huang, J.: A hybrid particle swarm optimization for manipulator inverse kinematics control. In: Huang, D.-S., Wunsch, D.C., Levine, D.S., Jo, K.-H. (eds.) ICIC 2008. LNCS, vol. 5226, pp. 784–791. Springer, Heidelberg (2008). https://doi.org/10.1007/978-3-540-87442-3_96
17. Rokbani, N., Alimi, A.M.: Inverse kinematics using particle swarm optimization – a statistical analysis. In: Sreekumar, M. et al. (eds.) Procedia Engineering – Proceedings of the International Conference on Design and Manufacturing (IConDM 2013), pp. 1602–1611. Elsevier, Amsterdam (2013)

18. Asadi-Eydivand, M., Ebadzadeh, M.M., Solati-Hashjin, M., Darlot, C., Abu Osman, N.A.: Cerebellum-inspired neural network solution of the inverse kinematics problem. Biol. Cybern. **109**(6), 561–574 (2015)
19. Pham, D.T., Fahmy, A.A., Eldukhri, E.E.: Adaptive fuzzy neural network for inverse modeling of robot manipulators. In: Proceedings of the 17th International Federation of Automatic Control World Congress, pp. 5308–5313, Seoul (2008)
20. Manseur, R.: Robot Modeling and Kinematics. Da Vinci Engineering Press, Boston (2006)
21. Dutra, M.S., Salcedo, I.L., Diaz, L.M.P.: New technique for inverse kinematics problem using simulated annealing. In: Proceedings of the International Conference on Engineering Optimization, Rio de Janeiro (2008)
22. Cheraghpour, F., Vaezi, M., Jazeh, H.E.S., Moosavian, S.A.A.: Dynamic modeling and kinematic simulation of Staubli© TX40 robot using MATLAB/ADAMS co-simulation. In: Proceedings of the 2011 IEEE International Conference on Mechatronics, pp. 386–391, Istanbul (2011)
23. Hasan, A.T., Al-Assadi, H.M.A.A., Mat Isa, A.A.: Neural networks' based inverse kinematics solution for serial robot manipulators passing through singularities. In: Suzuki, K. (ed.) Artificial Neural Networks - Industrial and Control Engineering Applications, pp. 459–478. InTech, Rijeka (2011)
24. Abdullah, K.A., Yusof, Z., Sulaiman, R.: Spreadsheet-based neural networks modelling and simulation for training and predicting inverse kinematics of robot arm. Int. J. Comput. Aided Eng. Technol. **10**(3), 218–243 (2018)
25. Shen, W., Gu, J., Ma, Y.: 3D kinematic solution for PA10-7C robot arm based on VRML. In: Proceedings of the 2007 IEEE International Conference on Automation and Logistics, pp. 614–619, Jinan (2007)
26. Gouasmi, M., Ouali, M., Fernini, B., Meghatria, M.: Kinematic modelling and simulation of a 2-r robot using solidworks and verification by MATLAB/Simulink. Int. J. Adv. Robot. Syst. **9**(6), 1–13 (2012)
27. Morell, A., Tarokh, M., Acosta, L.: Inverse kinematics solutions for serial robots using support vector regression. In: ICRA - Proceedings of the 2013 International Conference on Robotics and Automation, pp. 4188–4193, Karlsruhe (2013)
28. Momani, S., Abo-Hammour, Z.S., Alsmadi, O.M.K.: Solution of inverse kinematics problem using genetic algorithms. Appl. Math. Inf. Sci. **10**(1), 1–9 (2016)

Combining ARIZ with Shape Grammars to Support Designers

Kok Weng Ng[1], Mei Choo Ang[2(✉)], Dong Theng Cher[3],
Siti Azfanizam Ahmad[4], and Amelia Natasya Abdul Wahab[5]

[1] Department of Mechanical, Materials and Manufacturing,
Faculty of Science and Engineering, University of Nottingham Malaysia,
Semenyih, Malaysia
[2] Institute of Visual Informatics, Universiti Kebangsaan Malaysia,
Bangi, Malaysia
amc@ukm.edu.my
[3] Industrial Centre of Innovation in Smart Manufacturing, SIRIM Berhad,
Kuala Lumpur, Malaysia
[4] Department of Mechanical and Manufacturing Engineering,
Faculty of Engineering, Universiti Putra Malaysia, Serdang, Malaysia
[5] Faculty of Information Science and Technology,
Universiti Kebangsaan Malaysia, Bangi, Malaysia

Abstract. Among TRIZ (Theory of Inventive Problem Solving) methods that are applied to help solve design problems, ARIZ (Algorithm for Inventive Problem Solving) is considered to be the most powerful and is able to solve problems with "minimal changes to the system". However, the potential solutions derived from ARIZ are solution concepts that are general and are dependent on the engineers to further define these solution concepts into specific solutions. Shape grammars have been used to describe the shape of specific solution concepts or products with the intention to allow engineers to explore and generate a variation of specific solutions. This research work explores the application of a novel framework that combines ARIZ with shape grammars to facilitate and help engineers to translate the general solution concepts into a visualisation of specific solution concepts.

Keywords: ARIZ · TRIZ · Support tool · Product design

1 Introduction

Many methodologies have been adopted by enterprises in innovating their products to capture market shares and to be ahead of the competition in the current competitive global market. One of the established methodologies adopted by top enterprises such as Airbus, Rolls-Royce, Samsung, Boeing and many others is TRIZ (also known as "Theory of Inventive Problem Solving") [1, 2]. Although TRIZ is widely used to enhance competitiveness of enterprises, the inventive principles recommended by TRIZ to solve engineering problems are very abstract and requires a significant contribution from designers to derive specific solutions to any problems. Therefore, it is important to explore a generative design systems framework that would be able to

© Springer Nature Switzerland AG 2019
H. Badioze Zaman et al. (Eds.): IVIC 2019, LNCS 11870, pp. 305–317, 2019.
https://doi.org/10.1007/978-3-030-34032-2_28

generate conceptual solutions with physical embodiment features to support designers better. This research work will explore combining ARIZ with shape grammars to derive such a framework.

2   TRIZ or Theory of Inventive Problem Solving

TRIZ is a systematic problem-solving methodology developed by Altshuller [3, 4] that can help designers to be innovative in product development. TRIZ is derived based on decades of study on patent information [3–5]. Although the current TRIZ tools have increased in number in the last few years, the core tools of TRIZ are still the classical TRIZ tools such as Contradiction Matrix, Physical Contradiction Resolving Strategies (Separation, Satisfaction, Bypass), Scientific Effects, System of Standard Inventive Solutions and ARIZ. Different TRIZ methods have different ways to model and solve design problems and these methods suggest general design solutions based on heuristics from successful patents [6]. ARIZ is selected to combine with shape grammars to derive a framework generative design systems based on the investigation by Ang [7] on some of the classical TRIZ methods. Ang [7] found that ARIZ had the most suitable TRIZ tools to work with shape grammars to derive a generative design system to assist designers to generate solution concepts with physical embodiment. Although solution concepts with physical embodiment will inspire better ideas to designers, extensive knowledge and experience are still needed in the detail design solutions. ARIZ is the most suitable TRIZ tool to be linked to shape grammars (refer to Table 1) because ARIZ encourages designers to look for solutions from existing resources or the system. This requirement is necessary in order to be compatible with shape grammars as shape grammars need a shape of an existing system to evolve. Shape grammars are selected to be combined with ARIZ because it is one of the established formal methods that can define and evolve shapes of products [8–12].

3   ARIZ (Algorithm of Inventive Problem Solving)

ARIZ or the algorithm of inventive problem solving is a 9-part algorithm that combines several TRIZ methods for solving a contradiction in sequential step-by-step procedures [13]. ARIZ is considered to be the most powerful TRIZ method because it combines the power of several TRIZ methods and is used for solving "difficult" problems i.e. problems that cannot be solved by other TRIZ methods. There are many versions of ARIZ but only ARIZ-85C is the official version accepted and approved by Altshuller [14]. For this research work, ARIZ-85C is used.

ARIZ specifically considers existing resources available in solving a design problem and explores solutions based on the parameters related to these existing resources [15]. In Part 2 of ARIZ [13], designers are required to identify the parameters of an existing system with a problem to be solved from the aspects of existing substances, fields and resources in a tabular structure. This table, also known as Substance and Field Resources (SFR), will be used to solve the design problem for the existing product or system.

Table 1. Comparing classical TRIZ tools [7]

TRIZ Tool	Model of Problem	Process Flow	Distinct Characteristic(s)	Potential Link to Shape Grammars
1. Contradiction Matrix (40 Inventive Principles)	Engineering Contradiction	Contradiction Matrix (40 inventive principles): Specific design problem → TRIZ General features for the specific problem → Generic design solution (Inventive principles) → Designer's → Specific design solution	Need to map the current contradicting features of the design problem to the 39 TRIZ general features	Difficult – design solution can come from external resources where shape does not exist.
2. Physical Contradiction Resolving Strategies (Separation, Satisfaction, Bypass)	Physical Contradiction	Physical Contradiction Resolving Strategies: Specific design problem → Single contradicting characteristic → Generic design solution (inventive principles) → Designer's knowledge → Specific design solution	Need to identify a single contradicting characteristic of the design problem.	Difficult (same as above)
3. Scientific Effects	Function Model	Scientific Effects: Specific design problem → Generic function terms → Generic design solution → Designer's knowledge → Specific design solution	Need to identify the function terms for the design problem	Difficult (same as above)
4. System of Standard Inventive Solutions	Substance-field Model	System of Standard Inventive Solutions: Specific design problem → Interaction model between substances (subject, object) and a field in zone of → Generic design solution (Standard Inventive Solutions) → Designer's knowledge → Specific design solution	Need to identify interaction between Object and Subject in Zone of Conflict of the design problem and derive design solutions from 76 Standard Inventive Solutions	Difficult (same as above)
5. ARIZ	Engineering Contradiction, Substance-field Model, Physical Contradiction, and Function Model	Specific design problem → Mini problem statement → Substance Field Resource Analysis → Ideal Final Results → Substance and Field Resources (SFR) Table and System of Standard Inventive Solutions → Physical Contradiction Knowledge Base, Effects, Standards, Principles → Generic design solution (Standard Inventive Solutions) → Designer's knowledge → Specific design solution	1. Need to identify 2 alternative engineering contradictions. 2. Need to identify the tool and the product. 3. Define the Ideal Final Result 4. Identify the SFR (from existing resources) 5. Apply Physical Contradiction and other TRIZ tools to solve the design problem	1. Difficult (same as above) 2. No 3. No 4. Yes – parameters of existing resources 5. Difficult (same as above)

The SFR provides the existing parameters that may include the definition of the existing shape of a product. ARIZ consists of sub-steps that will guide designers to solve a contradiction by making minimal changes to the existing system (hence the term "mini" solution was coined but in this context, it does not mean small [15]). This means the designers need to explore and analyse the existing components of the product, the super-systems, and the sub-systems for solutions including their parameters such as the dimensions and properties of the components in the system. Super-systems are defined as elements in the environment external to the system such as air, moisture and sunlight that interact with the system. Parameters such as dimensions can be used to define the shape of an existing component in the system which can then be combined with shape grammars to generate potential design solutions. Most experts in ARIZ apply up to Part 3 or 4 to complete the problem solving and Part 5–9 include experimental steps in development [6].

4   Shape Grammars

Shape grammars were introduced by Stiny and Gips in 1972 [16]. A shape grammar has a set of basic shapes and rules that are applied to govern how shapes can be arranged or manipulated step by step into their final forms. It can be considered as grammars for design and have been used in many different areas such as paintings, decorative art, architecture, product design, and engineering [9, 10, 16–19]. Shape grammars have been applied manually and computationally to create new shapes of products based on shape rules derived from existing products to retain the style or brand identity of the existing product [7, 12, 18–20]. In addition to that, there were some successes in using shape grammars to visualise new shapes of products with the aim to maintain brand identity whilst meeting functional requirements [9, 11]. These successes were achieved by combining optimisation algorithm and shape grammars with the pre-determined functional requirements such as volume and height. Recent works on shape grammars include using shape grammars to generate a customised design of Thonet chair style based on customer preference before optimising the design based on structural requirements [21], investigating computer-based implementation of shape grammars via graph-theoretic representation in architecture [22], and exploring the possibility of shape grammars linking with materials [23]. In this research work, we apply ARIZ as part of a design method to solve design problems and use shape grammars to define the shape of design solution based on solutions recommended by ARIZ to support designers.

5   The Novel Framework that Combines ARIZ with Shape Grammars

ARIZ has been identified to be more suitable to be combined with shape grammars due to two key characteristics of ARIZ. The two key characteristics are that existing resources may include components with shapes which can be a potential source of design solutions and the Substance and Field Resources (SFR) analyses provide crucial linking locations for shape grammars. The novel framework combining ARIZ with shape grammars was derived in our earlier work and it is shown in Fig. 1 [7] where a link to shape grammars is introduced during the SFR analysis in Part 2.0. The resources in SFR with parameters that can be used to define a shape will have their shape rules derived in Part SG.1. It is important to stress that only if a design solution which has parameters that depict a definitive shape will undergo transformation of shape rules to generate new variants of design solutions.

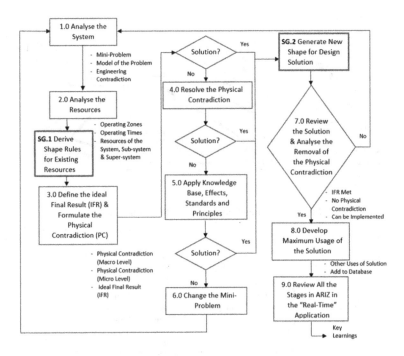

Fig. 1. A novel framework linking ARIZ with shape grammars [7]

At any time, a design solution is found either in Part 3.0, or Part 4.0, or Part 5.0, the designers can proceed to Part SG.2 and then to Part 7.0, 8.0 and 9.0 if required. The efficacy of the novel framework that combines ARIZ with shape grammars is verified via a case study to solve a chemical liquid leakage problem at a hose joint. In this case study, solutions were derived in Part 4.0 to verify the novel framework, thus the case study would not proceed into Part 5.0 - Part 9.0.

6   Illustrative Case Study: Using Novel Framework to Solve the Problem of Hose Joint Leakage

The problem of leakage at hose joint is not new. Many industry appliances use some form of hose joint to transport chemicals or liquids from a source to a container. These joints usually have threaded surfaces to facilitate the connection. The model of the engineering system and the cause-and-effect chain analysis (CECA) for the problem is shown in Figs. 2 and 3.

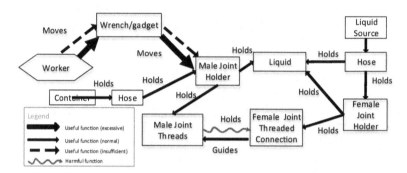

Fig. 2. The function model for the joint leakage

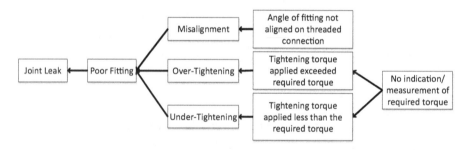

Fig. 3. The Cause-and-Effect Chain Analysis (CECA) for poor fitting problem

Using the novel framework that combines ARIZ with shape grammars to solve the hose joint problem, the problem-solving process started by defining the problem statement and modelling the engineering system from the aspect of the components and functions. CECA is then applied to determine the root cause of the poor fitting. These steps are critical preliminary steps before applying ARIZ to solve any problem. CECA shows that there are several possible root causes that can cause a joint leakage but in this case study, the poor fitting (under-tightening and over-tightening) of the joint is identified to be the root cause. With the root cause determined, the process of applying the new framework (refer to Fig. 1) that combines ARIZ with shape grammars can proceed to Part 1.0 (Table 2), Part 2.0 (Table 3), Part SG.1 (Table 4), Part 3.0 (Table 5), Part 4.0 (Table 6) and finally to Part SG.2 (Table 7).

Table 2. Details of Part 1.0

Part 1.0 Analyse the System	
1.1 There is an engineering system for (indicate the main function)	Stopping liquid leak.
That consists of (to list major parts)	Joint, threaded connection, liquid
Engineering contradiction 1 (EC-1):	If joint threads are over-tightened to joint threaded connection, then liquid leak is stopped, but the joint threads are deformed.
Engineering contradiction 2 (EC-2):	If joint threads are under-tightened to joint threaded connection, the joint threads are not deformed but joint leak happens.
It is necessary to	It is necessary to stop liquid leak without causing deformation of joint threads with minimal changes to the system
1.2 To define the tool and the product	Tool: Joint threaded connection (or female joint threaded connection) Product: Joint threads (or male joint threads)
State 1 (property, feature, parameter)	Joint over-tightened
State 2 (property, feature, parameter)	Joint under-tightened
1.3 Graphic presentation of EC-1 and EC-2	
1.4 To choose a basic contradiction and its graphic interpretation. It is a situation where the main function is delivered better.	Basic engineering contradiction: **EC-1 selected** If joint threads are over-tightened to joint threaded connection, then liquid leak is stopped, but the joint threads are deformed.
Product	Joint threads
Tool	Joint threaded connection
1.5 The aggravated basic contradiction	If joint threads are over-tightened using great force to joint threaded connection, then liquid leak is totally stopped, but the joint threads are severely deformed.
1.6 Indicate the product and the tool from step 1.4 under the condition of step 1.5	Joint threads, joint threaded connection
It is necessary to introduce an X-component that (enables the tool to deliver the main function without any harmful consequences)	It is necessary to introduce an X-component preserves the ability to stop joint leaks without causing deformation of joint threads, with minimal changes and without any harmful consequences.

Table 3. Details of Part 2.0

Part 2.0 Analyse the Resources

To define the operating space (the space where there is a conflict)

The operating space is:	The useful zone is where the joint thread contacts the joint threaded connection, holding each other to close the gaps between them. The harmful zone is where joint threaded connection jams the joint thread. The zone of conflict is where the useful zone interacts or overlaps the harmful zone.
Drawings/ Diagrams of illustrations for operating space	

2.1 To define the operating time	*Do we have T1* (time before the conflict) to improve the situation in advance? Yes. (T1 is when joint threads is about to align with the joint threaded connection). We can make changes to the joint thread design, or add an intermediary prior to the alignment.

2.2 To analyse resources of substances and fields (SFR)

Type	Substances	Parameters	Fields	Consideration of Shape Rules for the Substances
SFR of the system in the operating space	Tool: Joint threaded connection	Diameter, Length, Pitch, Depth, Angle, Toughness	Mechanical	Existing joint threaded connection cannot be modified for solution.
	Product: Joint threads	Length, Diameter, Shape, Weight, Pitch, Depth, Angle, Toughness	Mechanical	Shape rules can be created for the existing joint threads based on length, diameter, depth and angles
SFR of the environment in the operating space	Liquid	Flow rate, Viscosity, Temperature, Volume, Density	Mechanical	Liquid has no shape.
SFR of the super systems	Air	Humidity, Pressure, Temperature, Mass Volume, Density, Flow rate	Pneumatics	Air has no shape.

Table 4. Details of Part SG.1

Part SG.1 Derive Shape Rules for Existing Resources			
Joint Thread Shape Grammar 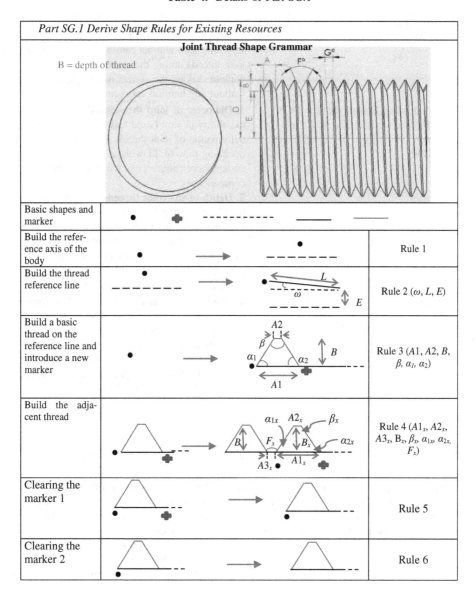			
Basic shapes and marker			
Build the reference axis of the body			Rule 1
Build the thread reference line			Rule 2 (ω, L, E)
Build a basic thread on the reference line and introduce a new marker			Rule 3 ($A1$, $A2$, B, β, α_1, α_2)
Build the adjacent thread			Rule 4 ($A1_x$, $A2_x$, $A3_x$, B_x, β_x, α_{1x}, α_{2x}, F_x)
Clearing the marker 1			Rule 5
Clearing the marker 2			Rule 6

Table 5. Details of Part 3.0

Part 3.0 Define the Ideal Final Result (IFR) & Formulate the Physical Contradiction

3.1. To define IFR	The X-component itself preserves the ability to stop joint leak without causing deformation of joint threads during the operating time of T1 without making the system more complex and without any harmful consequences
3.2. To introduce limitations: it is NOT allowed to use foreign, new fields and substances – use **SFR**	**1. Diameter of joint threads** itself preserves the ability to stop liquid leak without causing deformation of joint threads during the operating time of T1 without making the system more complex and without any harmful consequences **2. Depth of the joint threads** itself preserves the ability to stop liquid leak without causing deformation of joint threads during the operating time of T1 without making the system more complex and without any harmful consequences
3.3. To define the physical contradiction on macro level	**1. Diameter of joint threads** needs to be large to stop liquid leak and the diameter of the joint threads needs to be small to avoid causing deformation of joint threads **2. Depth of the threads** need to be matched with joint threaded connection to stop liquid leak and the depth of the joint threads need to be unmatched to stop over-tightening

Table 6. Details of Part 4.0

Part 4.0 Resolve the physical contradiction

Physical Contradiction	Separation strategies	Principles used and solution
1. Diameter of joint threads (D) needs to be large to stop liquid leak and diameter of joint threads needs to be small to avoid causing deformation of joint threads	*Separation in Space*	Principle used: **Local quality** Solution: Diameter of the joint threads changes from big (inlet) to small (where the back of the joint has smaller diameter while the diameter in front (inlet) is bigger to facilitate easy tightening initially and prevent over-tightening at the end of tightening process)
2. Depth of the threads (B) need to be matched with joint threaded connection to stop liquid leak and the depth of the joint threads need to be unmatched to stop over-tightening	*Separation in Space*	Principle used: **Local quality** Solution: The end threads depth at the back of the joint need to be a different depth to stop over-tightening while the rest of the joint thread depth need to match the thread of the joint connector to stop liquid leak

Table 7. Potential solutions (showing the details of shape rules used for incremental diameter size and modifications on the thread depth) based on local quality inventive principle derived in Part SG.2

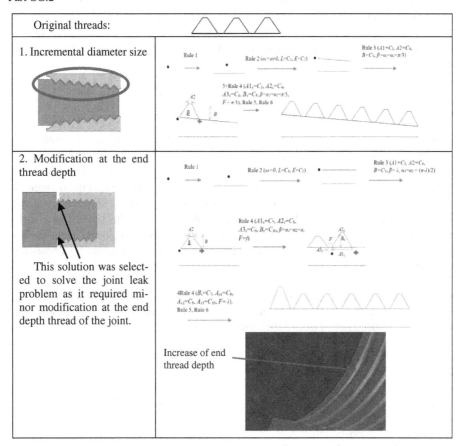

7 Discussion

This research work explores how ARIZ can be combined with shape grammars to derive physical embodiments of the specific solutions from solution concepts derived from ARIZ. A novel framework that combined ARIZ with shape grammars was derived and was verified in a case study to solve joint leakage design problem which cause liquid to leak. The case study on joint leaks has shown that the framework can generate potential specific solutions based on TRIZ inventive principles. The case study also showed that the designers can make better decisions based on the final design solutions due to the improvement in visualisation of the possible variety of specific solutions derived by a shape grammar. The designers in this case study has decided to select specific solutions generated by a shape grammar based on the inventive principle 'Local Quality'. This inventive principle has two potential shape configurations of the thread that could solve the problem of liquid leak due to over and under-tightening of the joint threads. The first shape configuration involved modifications on the joint thread to create incremental diameter size of the thread and the second shape configuration required the end thread of the joint to be made mismatched (refer to Table 7). The final decision was to modify and create a smaller end thread (decreasing the depth of the end thread to act as a stopper) of the joint to solve the problem.

8 Conclusions

The findings from this research work has demonstrated that ARIZ can be combined with shape grammars as a framework to construct shapes of a design solution. ARIZ was chosen because it is the most suitable TRIZ tool to be combined with shape grammars. When ARIZ is combined with shape grammars within a specific domain of a design problem, the conceptual solutions from ARIZ can be transformed by shape grammars to detail out potential specific design solutions. With this novel framework, the designers can visualise the specific solutions better and make better decisions to choose the best solution for a design problem. This framework can also be a basis for generative design systems.

Acknowledgments. The authors would like to thank the Ministry of Education Malaysia (Kementerian Pendidikan Malaysia) and the Universiti Kebangsaan Malaysia for supporting the work through research grant FRGS/1/2018/TK03/UKM/02/6 and GUP-2018-124.

References

1. Gadd, K.: TRIZ for Engineers: Enabling Inventive Problem Solving. Wiley, Singapore (2011)
2. Orloff, M.A.: Modern TRIZ: A Practical Course with EASyTRIZ Technology. Springer, Berlin (2012). https://doi.org/10.1007/978-3-642-25218-1
3. Altshuller, G.: Innovation Algorithm: TRIZ, Systematic Innovation and Technical Creativity. Technical Innovation Center, Worcester (1999)
4. Altshuller, G.: 40 Principles: TRIZ Keys to Innovation. Technical Innovation Center, Worcester (2002)
5. Petrov, V.: TRIZ. Theory of Inventive Problem Solving Level 1. Springer, Heidelberg (2019). https://doi.org/10.1007/978-3-030-04254-7
6. Yilmaz, S., Daly, S.R., Seifert, C.M., Gonzalez, R.: Evidence-based design heuristics for idea generation. Design Stud. **46**, 95–124 (2016)
7. Ang, M.C., Ng, K.W., Cher, D.T., Ahmad, S.A.: Linking TRIZ with shape grammar to support engineers. In: MyTRIZ Conference 2016. Taylor's University Lakeside Campus, Malaysia (2016)
8. Jowers, I., Earl, C., Stiny, G.: Shapes, structures and shape grammar implementation. Comput. Aided Des. **111**, 80–92 (2019)
9. Ang, M.C., Ng, K.W., Pham, D.T.: Combining the Bees algorithm and shape grammar to generate branded product concepts. Proc. IMechE Part B: J. Eng. Manuf. **227**, 1860–1873 (2013)

10. Ang, M.C., Chong, H.Y., McKay, A., Ng, K.W.: Capturing mini brand using a parametric shape grammar. In: Zaman, H.B., et al. (eds.) IVIC 2011. LNCS, vol. 7067, pp. 1–12. Springer, Heidelberg (2011). https://doi.org/10.1007/978-3-642-25200-6_1

11. Ang, M.C., Chau, H.H., McKay, A., de Pennington, A.: Combining evolutionary algorithms and shape grammars to generate branded product design. In: The Second International Conference on Design Computing and Cognition (DCC 2006), pp. 521–539. Technical University of Eindhoven, Netherlands (2006)

12. Agarwal, M., Cagan, J.: A blend of different tastes: the language of coffeemakers. Environ. Plan. B-Plan. Des. **25**, 205–226 (1998)

13. Cameron, G.: TRIZICS: Teach Yourself TRIZ, How to Invent, Innovate and Solve "Impossible" Technical Problems Systematically. CreateSpace Independent Publishing Platform, Scotts Valley (2010)

14. Yeoh, T.S., Yeoh, T.J., Song, C.L.: TRIZ - Systematic Innovation in Manufacturing. Firstfruits Sdn Bhd, Petaling Jaya (2009)

15. Cameron, G.: ARIZ Explored. CreateSpace Independent Publishing Platform, San Bernardino (2015)

16. Stiny, G., Gips, J.: Shape grammars and the generative specification of painting and sculpture. In: Freiman, C. (ed.) Proceedings of IFIP Congress 1971, North Holland, Ljubljana, Yugoslavia, vol. 2, pp. 1460–1465 (1972)

17. Stiny, G., Mitchell, W.J.: The palladian grammar. Environ. Plan. B-Plan. Des. **5**, 5–18 (1978)

18. Pugliese, M.J., Cagan, J.: Capturing a rebel: modeling the Harley-Davidson brand through a motorcycle shape grammar. Res. Eng. Design-Theory Appl. Concurr. Eng. **13**, 139–156 (2002)

19. McCormack, J.P., Cagan, J., Vogel, C.M.: Speaking the Buick language: capturing, understanding, and exploring brand identity with a shape grammar. Des. Stud. **25**, 1–29 (2004)

20. Chau, H.H., Chen, X., McKay, A., de Pennington, A.: Evaluation of a 3D Shape Grammar Implementation. In: Gero, J.S. (ed.) Design Computing and Cognition 2004, pp. 357–376. Springer, Dordrecht (2004). https://doi.org/10.1007/978-1-4020-2393-4_19

21. Barros, M., Duarte, J.P., Chaparro, B.M.: A grammar-based model for the mass customisation of chairs: modelling the optimisation part. Nexus Netw. J. **17**, 875–898 (2015)

22. Strobbe, T., Eloy, S., Pauwels, P., Verstraeten, R., Meyer, R.D., Campenhout, J.V.: A graph-theoretic implementation of the Rabo-de-Bacalhau transformation grammar. AI EDAM-Artif. Intell. Eng. Design Anal. Manuf. **30**, 138–158 (2016)

23. Knight, T.: Shapes and other things. Nexus Netw. J. **17**, 963–980 (2015)

Expert System for Dota 2 Character Selection Using Rule-Based Technique

Mohammad Zaki Azim Zairil Aznin, Norizan Mat Diah[(✉)],
and Nur Atiqah Sia Abdullah

Faculty of Computer and Mathematical Sciences,
Universiti Teknologi MARA, 40450 Shah Alam, Selangor, Malaysia
mzakiazim@gmail.com,
{norizan,atiqah}@fskm.uitm.edu.my

Abstract. Dota 2 is a multiplayer online battle arena strategy-based game developed by Valve Corporation that is currently holding the highest prize money for its international tournament event, which is The International. Due to numerous numbers of characters with each having different strengths and weaknesses, Dota 2 players are having difficulties in selecting a suitable character when playing the game. This research aims to develop an expert system to suggest a suitable character of Dota 2 that can identify the best possibility for Dota 2 character selection using the rule-based technique, to construct an expert system for Dota 2 character selection using the rule-based technique, and to test user evaluation feedback on usability aspects. User evaluation feedback on usability aspects is used as a testing method for this system to retrieve information regarding system performance. Based on the analysis of the testing, this project has passed all the usability levels and usability values required. As a conclusion, the system can help Dota 2 players to select a suitable character for their line-up when playing the game so that they would not face any difficulty as encountered by those who do not know how to select the character properly.

Keywords: Dota 2 · Character selection · Rule-based technique

1 Introduction

In this era of globalization, almost all people are already used to playing games whether it is on mobile phones, laptops or other platforms. This leads to the development of e-sports that are rising in popularity among the young generation [1].

Multiplayer Online Battle Arena (MOBA) is one of the famous genres of e-sports and dominates other games genres at present [2, 3]. Games such as Defense of the Ancient 2 (Dota 2) are one of the famous games in the MOBA area [3, 4]. Dota 2 is a team-based competitive online games in which two teams, called Radiant and Dire, with each team consists of five members fighting against each other to take down the opponent's structure called Ancient [2, 3, 5–8]. Dota 2 is currently the largest e-sports game in terms of the prize money in which even a single event prize pool can exceed $20 m and not only most played, but also the most watched game with million spectating the tournaments live [2, 9].

© Springer Nature Switzerland AG 2019
H. Badioze Zaman et al. (Eds.): IVIC 2019, LNCS 11870, pp. 318–326, 2019.
https://doi.org/10.1007/978-3-030-34032-2_29

[10] found that around 12.4 million unique players are playing Dota 2 per month. Currently, there are 116 characters available in Dota 2 with each character possesses different kind of abilities, skills, strengths, and weaknesses [3, 6, 7, 11].

The players state that the character selection is important because a good selection can ensure the victory of a game and a good line-up can boost the confidence of the players [12]. If a player selects a wrong or unsuitable character to be played, it would be a big disadvantage for the team even before the match begins because the character suitability can affect the strengths and weaknesses of other characters either the opponents or the teammates [11].

Due to numerous numbers of characters with each of them having different strengths and weaknesses, Dota 2 players are having difficulties in selecting a suitable character when playing the game. This research aims to develop an expert system to suggest a suitable character of Dota 2 that can identify the best possibility for Dota 2 character selection using the rule-based technique and construct an expert system for Dota 2 character selection using the rule-based algorithm.

2 Rule-Based Expert System

Nowadays, there are many applications that are developed using Artificial Intelligence (AI) [13]. One of them is an expert system. Expert system (ES) is an interactive computer system decision tool that imitates the decision-making capability of an expert, uses both facts and heuristics to solve tough decision-making problems [14, 15]. Rule-based systems (also known as production systems or expert systems) are the simplest form of artificial intelligence [16]. A rule based system uses rules as the knowledge representation for knowledge coded into the system[16, 17].

Rule-based expert system (RBES) is the earliest type of expert systems being proposed in the early 1970s [15, 18]. An RBES consists of five parts which are knowledge base, database, inference engine, explanation facilities and user interface [18–20].

The RBES employs *IF-THEN* rules (*production rules*) as the major representation paradigm [21]. RBES is defined as a process of collecting information from the expert himself and presenting it in *IF-THEN* statement [13, 15, 22]. Examples of a simple statement containing *IF-THEN* rules:

```
IF      the 'weather' is cloudy
THEN       the act is bringing umbrella
IF      the 'weather' is sunny
THEN       the act is drinking water
```

Every rule consists of two parts which are the antecedent for the *IF* part and consequent for the *THEN* part [18, 22]. The basic syntax of the rule is:

```
IF    <antecedent>

THEN      <consequent>
```

Each of these rules can have numerical, logical or textual values which are called parameters [22]. According to [18], rules might also represent relations, recommendations, and strategies. The main structure of the RBES is formed based on the knowledge base, inference engine, and user interface [13, 18, 21–23].

The advantages of RBES are due to its uniform structure, natural understanding representation, and separation of understanding from its processing, simplicity yet independence [15, 18, 21, 24]. On the other hand, the disadvantages of RBES are due to its opacity, lack of structure, inefficiency, and inability to learn [18, 21].

3   System Development

The system starts when a user asks questions (input data) using a user interface regarding the problem of selecting a suitable Dota 2 character. The user interface then will interact with the inference engine which is the connector between the knowledge base and database. At the inference engine, the comparison will undergo between rules in the knowledge base and facts in the database to produce the most suitable Dota 2 character to be selected. After rules and facts fired and founded, the results will be shown to the user through the user interface. The architecture and process of the system are shown in Fig. 1.

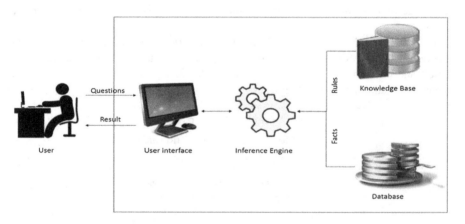

Fig. 1. Architecture and process of the system

3.1   User Interface

There are three user **interfaces** designed for this system which are the main page, criteria page, and result page.

Fig. 2. Main page

Figure 2 shows the main page of the system. When the user first opens the system, a set of Dota 2 wallpapers will appear. Along with a navigation top bar, there are two buttons at the top right of the screen which are 'Home' and 'Counter Pick'. If the user wishes to use the system's counter pick, the user just simply needs to click the 'Counter Pick' button and the system will automatically go to the selection section. The system displays all of the Dota 2 characters. The icons of the characters are clickable for the user to choose which character he wants to know the counter. It should be noted that the user is required to select a character for the system to proceed to the criteria page.

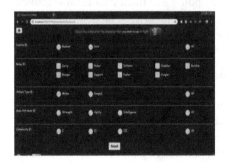

Fig. 3. Criteria page and result page

Figure 3 shows the criteria page and the result page of the system. After the user has picked a character from the main page, this page will be displayed. A set of questions of criteria will be displayed once a character has been selected in the previous session. All questions must be filled in at least one, if there is any unanswered question, an alert will pop out. All answers will then be compared using the rule-based technique to match with any data available in the database. After the user has selected the character that he wants to know about the counter and fill in the criteria of the character that he wants to play, the system will do a comparison between rules and facts. Then, the system will display suggested characters that are suitable to play against the character that has been selected earlier.

3.2   Inference Engine

This system aims to identify the best possibility for Dota 2 character selection is achieved in this process by using the knowledge discovery in database process which will be discussed in this section. The main purpose of this process is to construct a rule-based algorithm for this system, database and forward chaining as the inference engine to construct an expert system for Dota 2 character selection using the rule-based technique.

Knowledge Discovery in Database. Knowledge Discovery in Database (KDD) process is used in this case to transform raw data into facts, hence being imported to the system database. Since the data collected for this project are not large enough, no pattern can be displayed, only confirmed to be a valid fact. The system only requires a confirmation on its data, without a pattern. There are five phases in constructing the database which is selection, pre-processing, transformation, data mining, and knowledge.

Selection. In this phase, the important data to be used in this project are identified first, such as the character's name, character's faction, character's role, character's attack type, character's main attribute, character's complexity, character's image, counter's win-rate and character's total games in a week. Then, verified websites are being selected to be scrapped.

Pre-processing. Pre-processing is a phase for scrapping identified data from identified websites. The data concerning the character's name, character's faction, character's role, character's attack type, character's main attribute, character's complexity, and character's image are scrapped from three websites.

Transformation. Data cleaning is done in this phase to remove noise and anomaly from the selected data from previous phases. Data that are cleaned are not ready for mining as it is not in an appropriate form. Thus, methods such as smoothing, aggregation, and normalization are used to prepare the data for mining. Transformation is the phase of cleaning scrapped data from the Internet. Data that have been scrapped contain noise that is not needed in the database. For this, the cleaning phase is done manually because the data that are scrapped including the noise are not big.

Data Mining. Data mining is a phase of discovering an interesting pattern, however, the data for this project are not big enough to show a pattern. Nevertheless, data mining is used in this phase to confirm that the data are valid to be used as facts. The data mining technique used in this phase is the Association Rule technique while the algorithm being applied is the Apriori algorithm.

The result will prove whether the character is suitable to counter a certain character. This can be seen by the output of the rules of which is more favouring, either win or lose. If the output is a favouring win, the character is valid to be a counter for the other character but if it is favouring lose, the character is not valid to be a counter, thus, confirming the validity of the data that are scrapped from the Internet. The data that are valid and confirmed are then become facts after this process.

Knowledge. After all data of characters have been mined, a set of valid facts are then produced and ready to be imported to the database. Upon the process of obtaining, cleaning, and mining the data, the database is built by creating counters table and information table. Information table list contains the counter's name, counter's faction, character's role, counter's attack type, counter's main attribute, counter's complexity, and counter's image while counters table contains character's name, counter's name, and counter's win-rate. All imported information is already filtered by the data mining process that will be used in the character suggestion process.

Rule-Based Algorithm. The rule-based algorithm used in this system to fulfil the criteria of this system is the Rule-based Expert System. By implementing the generated algorithm from previous KDD process and making some adjustments, a full set of the rule-based algorithm required for this project is constructed.

The rule-based algorithm is constructed in two places which are at the SQL part and PHP part. For the SQL part, the rule-based algorithm is implemented at the selection part to compare the character selected and the role that the user wanted to play while for the PHP part, the rule-based algorithm is implemented at the body part to compare the data on the criteria that have been filled by the user from the previous session. Parts of the rule-based algorithm for both places are shown in Figs. 4 and 5.

```
$sql = "SELECT * FROM counters JOIN counterinformation
WHERE         counterinformation.counterrole         LIKE
'%$role[1]%$role[2]%$role[3]%$role[4]%$role[5]%$role[6]%$role
[7]%$role[8]%$role[9]%' AND counters.heroname = '$id' AND
counterinformation.countername  LIKE  counters.counternames
ORDER BY counters.counterwinrate";
```

Fig. 4. Rule-based algorithm in PHP part

```
if($faction==$row['counterfaction'] &&
$attacktype==$row['counterattacktype'] &&
$mainattribute==$row['countermainattribute'] &&
  $complexity==$row['countercomplexity'])
```

Fig. 5. Rule-based algorithm in PHP part

Forward Chaining. Forward chaining is used as an inference engine to connect rules and facts because the flow of the system is data-driven reasoning which means this technique begins from known data and proceeds with those specific data. Then, only the topmost of the rules will be fired for each time and the rules add a new fact from the database when it is fired. After no rules to be fired, the cycle stops, thus, the result is shown, and for this project, the suggested character that is suitable to be selected is shown.

3.3   Testing

Testing is done by conducting user evaluation feedback on usability aspects in order to get feedback on the system which can lead to a better expert system. User evaluation feedback on usability aspects is conducted based on research done by [25] in which an expert system application to diagnose skin diseases in human is evaluated based on usability aspects.

Questionnaires will be distributed later and will be answered by the respondents based on their experience when performing the tasks. For data analysis, the Likert scale values in questionnaires are interpreted to corresponding merit 0.00 until 5.00. Usability average merit and usability level are depicted in Table 1.

Table 1.   Usability average merit and usability level

Average merit, A	Usability level
$0.00 \leq A \leq 1.00$	Bad
$1.00 < A \leq 2.00$	Poor
$2.00 < A \leq 3.00$	Moderate
$3.00 < A \leq 4.00$	Good
$4.00 < A \leq 5.00$	Excellent

The results obtained from user evaluation feedback on usability aspects are the usability value for each attribute (questions in the questionnaire). Table 2 shows the usability value and usability level for each attribute.

Table 2.   Usability value and usability level for each attribute

No.	Attribute	Usability value	Usability level
1.	Ease of meeting the needs	4.19	Excellent
2.	Ease of time-consuming	4.27	Excellent
3.	Ease of helping to select a character	4.46	Excellent
4.	Ease of information on the system	4.55	Excellent
5.	Ease of trusting the system's information	4.55	Excellent
6.	Ease of expert system application interface for Dota 2 Character Selection	4.00	Good
7.	System design comfortability	4.36	Excellent
8.	Ease of sharing the system with others	4.64	Excellent

Based on Table 2, each question of the questionnaire aims to demonstrate the usability level according to the usability value. As shown in Table 2, the usability value for the attribute "Ease of meeting the needs" is 4.19 which means the usability level is excellent according to Table 1. Based on the attributes, only one attribute achieved the level of good for its usability level which is attribute number 6 while the others achieved excellent. This shows that the system achieved excellent for user acceptance other than attribute "Ease of expert system application interface for Dota 2 Character Selection". From this, the conclusion can be made that the system user interface can be further improved in the future for higher user acceptance.

4   Conclusion

Ruled-Based Expert System is used because it can be manipulated, supporting scrapped data as facts and suitable for recommending purposes. A set of data (facts) that are collected and mined during scrapping and data mining processes are then imported to the database to construct one component of an expert system which is the database. Rules generated from the data mining process are then studied and constructed to become another component of the expert system which a rule-based algorithm is. For the last component of the expert system, a web-based graphical user interface is designed and developed to complete the whole expert system.

User evaluation feedback on usability aspects is conducted to get feedback on the system's performance. Once the data have been collected, the data are analysed to provide the results on the usability value and usability level. Based on the analysis of the testing, this project has passed all the usability value and usability level required. As a conclusion, the project can help Dota 2 players to select a suitable character for their line-up when playing the game so that players in Dota 2 would not face any difficulty as encountered by those who do not know how to select the character properly.

Acknowledgements. The authors would like to thank Faculty of Computer and Mathematical Sciences, Universiti Teknologi MARA, Shah Alam, Selangor, for sponsoring this research.

References

1. Hallman, K., Giel, T.: eSports - competitive sports or recreational activity? Sport Manage. Rev. **21**(1), 14–20 (2018)
2. Summerville, A., Cook, M., Steenhuisen, B.: Draft-analysis of the ancients: predicting draft picks in DotA 2 using machine learning, (Godec), pp. 100–106 (2016)
3. Hanke, L., Chaimowicz, L. A: Recommender system for hero line-ups in MOBA games, pp. 43–49 (2017)
4. Eggert, C., Herrlich, M., Smeddinck, J., Malaka, R.: Classification of player roles in the team-based multi-player game Dota 2. In: Chorianopoulos, K., Divitini, M., Hauge, J.B., Jaccheri, L., Malaka, R. (eds.) ICEC 2015. LNCS, vol. 9353, pp. 112–125. Springer, Cham (2015). https://doi.org/10.1007/978-3-319-24589-8_9

5. Minotti, M.: VB. Comparing MOBAs: league of legends vs. Dota 2 vs. smite vs. heroes of the storm (2015). https://venturebeat.com/2015/07/15/comparing-mobas-league-of-legends-vs-dota-2-vs-smite-vs-heroes-of-the-storm. Accessed 21 July 2019

6. Johansson, F., Wikström, J., Johansson, F.: Result Prediction by mining replays in Dota 2. Master's thesis, Blekinge Institute of Technology, Karlskrona, Sweden (2015)

7. Semenov, A., Romov, P., Korolev, S., Yashkov, D., Neklyudov, K.: Performance of machine learning algorithms in predicting game outcome from drafts in Dota 2. In: Ignatov, D.I., et al. (eds.) AIST 2016. CCIS, vol. 661, pp. 26–37. Springer, Cham (2017). https://doi.org/10.1007/978-3-319-52920-2_3

8. Chen, Z., Sun,Y., El-Nasr M., Nguyen, T.: Player skill decomposition in multiplayer online battle arenas. In: Meaningful Play, October 2016, Michigan, USA, pp. 1–22 (2016)

9. Drachen, A., Yancey, M., Maguire, J., Chu, D., Wang, I. Y.: Skill-based differences in spatio-temporal team behaviour in defence of the ancients 2 (DotA 2), 2 (DotA 2). In: IEEE Games Media Entertainment, Toronto, Canada, pp. 1–8 (2014)

10. Hanke, L., Chaimowicz, L.: A recommender system for hero line-ups in MOBA games. In: Proceedings of the Thirteenth AAAI Conference on Artificial Intelligence and Interactive Digital Entertainment (AIIDE-17), Foz do Igua, Brazil, pp. 43–49 (2017)

11. Conley, K., Perry, D.: How does he saw me? A recommendation engine for picking heroes in Dota 2. Technical report (2013)

12. Hong, E.: Reddit. The Art of Drafting (2017). https://www.reddit.com/r/DotA2/comments/78el10/the_art_of_drafting. Accessed 21 July 2019

13. Hashim, H., Diah, N.M., Kamal, N.A.M: Special Issue based expert system with uncertainty for dengue fever diagnosis. J. Fundam. Appl. Sci. 10(5S), 356–371 (2018)

14. Chakraborty, R.C.: Artificial intelligence: expert systems. ISA Trans. 28(1), 1–74 (2010)

15. Tan, H.: A brief history and technical review of the expert system research. In: IOP Conference Series: Materials Science and Engineering, vol. 242, no. 1 (2017)

16. Grosan, C., Abraham, A.: Rule-based expert systems. In: Grosan, C., Abraham, A. (eds.) Intelligent Systems. Intelligent Systems Reference Library, vol. 17, pp. 149–185. Springer, Heidelberg (2011). https://doi.org/10.1007/978-3-642-21004-4_7

17. Levesque, H., Lakemeyer, G.: The Logic of Knowledge Bases. The MIT Press, Cambridge (2001)

18. Negnevitsky, M.: Artificial Intelligence: A Guide to Intelligent Systems. Artificial Intelligence Systems, 2nd edn. Addison-Wesley, Boston (2005)

19. Aniba, M.R., et al.: Knowledge-based expert systems and a proof-of-concept case study for multiple sequence alignment con-struction and analysis. Brief. Bioinform. 10(1), 11–23 (2009)

20. Tripathi, K.P.: A review on knowledge-based expert system: concept and architecture. IJCA Spec. Issue Artif. Intell. Tech.-Novel Approaches Pract. Appl. 4, 19–23 (2011)

21. Sasikumar, M., Ramani, S., Raman, S.M., Anjaneyulu, K.S.R., Chandrasekar, R.: A Practical Introduction to Rule Based Expert Systems. Narosa Publishing House, New Delhi (2007)

22. Sellitto, M.A., Balugani, E., Gamberini, R., Rimini, B.: A fuzzy logic control application to the cement industry. IFAC-PapersOnLine 51(11), 1542–1547 (2018)

23. Durkin, J.: Research review: application of expert systems in the sciences. Ohio J. Sci. 90(5), 171–179 (1990)

24. Abraham, A: Rule-based expert systems heuristics. In: Handbook of Measuring System Design, pp. 909–919, March 2005

25. Munaiseche, C.P.C., Liando, O.E.S.: Evaluation of expert system application based on usability aspects. In: IOP Conference Series: Materials Science and Engineering, vol. 128, no. 1 (2016)

Preliminary Simulation of Robot on Script Detection from Camera Images

Wydyanto[2(✉)], Norshita Mat Nayan[1], and Riza Sulaiman[1]

[1] Institute Informatics Visual, Universiti Kebangsaan Malaysia,
Bangi, Selangor, Malaysia
norshitaivi@ukm.edu.my
[2] Fakultas Ilmu Komputer, Universitas Bina Darma, Palembang 30264,
Sumatera Selatan, Indonesia
widiwidyanto1969@gmail.com

Abstract. Here is a lot of information is available in a photo images such as advertisement, book cover, banners and many more. Images with text are widely available because of efficiency and low cost of digital portable devices, which provide chances to manual transfers of a document images. Analysis techniques of manually transferred images could serves as a reference and starting point of further technique development but the method cannot be used directly on images captured using cameras. Camera pictures can be problematic with blurry, low resolution, distorted, disorientated images, apart from, complex interaction between content and background. Therefore, *Optical Character Recognition* (OCR) technique was used to change printed text into editable text that is convenient and accessible in various applications. However, OCR accuracy depends on text pre-processing and segmentation algorithm. Hence, this manuscript to introduce OCR Tesseract method and the history of OCR Open Source Tesseract system, its architecture and outcome of trial on various type of images to determine efficiency of OCR Tesseract and accuracy ratio of extracted images from camera.

Keywords: Tesseract · OCR · Camera · Photos

1 Introduction

Script detection test of a camera widely conducted by previous researchers [1] automatic processing of digital images is possible for detection of characters in vehicle license [2, 3]. Disabled people without arms could use the application to write by using ARM 2148 processor which eventually moves the robot arms [4]. Information entries includes printed notes, passport, invoice, bank report, computerized acknowledgement, name card, letter, printed statistical data or appropriate documents [5]. However, words detected from camera images are still considerably difficult.

Usages of Tesseract OCR to detect words are limited to original writing or printed versions. Therefore, this paper is to present preliminary result of script detection on camera images using robots. Tesseract is one of the most suitable literary tools used for

H. Badioze Zaman et al. (Eds.): IVIC 2019, LNCS 11870, pp. 327–342, 2019.
https://doi.org/10.1007/978-3-030-34032-2_30

Optical Character Recognition. Tesseract is an open source engine used to develop OCR systems [6, 9] that is upgraded and managed by Google.

Tesseract is widely used to develop OCR system because of its high portability and accuracy on programming language. Image quality, clear differences between text and background are common factors that influence the accuracy level. Other detailed factor includes complexity of object in photo, illumination, rotation, blurred or degradation, ratio aspects and fonts of the image [7]. Just like OCR system, Tesseract engine depends on input quality of an image.

Preprocessing is a phases of OCR and could be applied on colored or black-and-white images (grayscale). Most of the OCR system uses grayscale or black-and-white images due to high expenses of coloured images [8]. As a result, most of the coloured images will be changed to grayscale images for better quality.

Problem Statement

Camera images will be converted into text, enabling the robot to transcribe the converted version of the images. Images data available in jpg or png will be inserted into controller robot after character detection engine manage to discover the script. Choosing an appropriate and accurate Tesseract OCR characters for robot reading are always problematic in converted word from different technical condition (blurred images, noise, improper illumination, poor background).

1.1   Optical Character Recognition

Optical Character Recognition technology was patented by Gustav Tauschek from German in 1929. Optical Character Recognition is a mechanical machine with template and photodetector whilst, Ray Kurzweil initiated the first program using basic omni font OCR system in 1974. The program used to invent text reader for blind people which help to find out normal and standard fonts. Computer with OCR application directly will manage to detect image sources that are converted into text characters.

There are two automatic system is developed to discover printed characters which includes, OCR (Optical Character Recognition). OCR not influenced by specific formats because it could even detect incomplete stylesheet. It is able to detect characters produced by manual type machine by transfiguring them into computer-readable-characters.

The OCR was used as a turn around accounting documents in purchasing or other related application. Every customer will receive printed voucher book with total payment by rental contract. Scanner will indicate featured matric matching technology to detect, convert and compare characters based on shape, angle and pattern via bitmap images databases. Featured Extraction or Intelligent Character (ICR) method will detect identity of a character from a vacant space, nearby shape, diagonal line, fragmented region etc.

1.2   Tesseract OCR

Tesseract *optic characters recognition* (OCR) works step by steps as shown in Fig. 1. First step involves Adaptive Thresholding [10] which converts images into grayscale images, followed by analysis of large line character extracted from connected components. This method is useful in detecting images which lies on white or black background. Obtained characters will be arranged into line and text for further analyses, referring to parallel text and fixed region. Later, text will be splitted into words using fixed or fuzzy space. Text introduction will be initiated using bypass process as in Fig. 1.

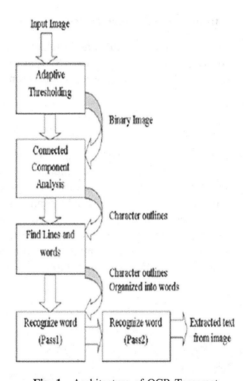

Fig. 1. Architecture of OCR Tesseract

An initial phase includes detection of words from text. Approved words will go though adaptive classification as a practical data which is useful in discovering precise method. Several entries of practical data will be used to resolve problem and extract text from images at the final phase. Efficiency of Tesseract OCR in detecting and extracting words from camera was evaluated in this paper. This preliminary test will be used to prove Tesseract OCR discovers and produces text out of images with different accuracy and presentation (refer Tables 1 and 2). Intermediate grayscale images shows Tesseract was 100% accurate compare to undefined or less accurate reading of Tesseract in coloured images.

2   Script Recognition

2.1   Word Detector

Tesseract OCR engine was connected with Rasberry Pi using Rasbian operating system to determine characters [11]. Web images with words was tested initially to evaluate efficiency of Tesseract OCR machine in detecting word images before camera could be established to capture images. Camera images were used to find out characters of tesseract engine. For example, Tesseract engine was tested for successful rate if inserted with word from normal images, or images with noise.

2.2   Testing of Images from Camera Using Tesseract Engine

Before initiation, open source Tesseract engine was installed into Raspberry Pi with huge memory storage and incorporated with Operating System Rasbian for windows/ GNU/Linux 9 (Strech). After installation, testing was conducted on images with words.

3   Methodology

Optic Characters Recognition was used to extract images which would be written as text by robot with specified methods in every stage. Initiation test using grayscale or black images resulted with 100% accuracy whilst a variated coloured image produces differential accuracy accordingly (Tables 1 and 2). Algorithmic method was used to avoid technical fault of the Tesseract OCR system. Tesseract engine also was used in grayscale (Otsu Thresholding) and segmentation technique. Initiation test resulted with accuracy performance defined from character identification on different inputs using implementation of grayscale or segmentation method. Flow of methodology phases in initiation test is in Fig. 2.

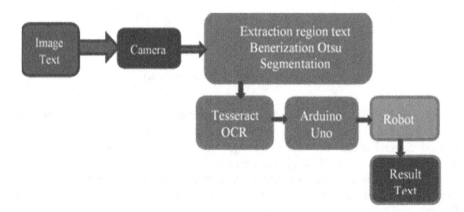

Fig. 2. Method of design

This manuscript mainly focuses on preprocessing phases apart from Tesseract engine. Fundamentally, preprocessing involves several stages such as grayscaling, normalizing, sampling, denoising and thinning [12]. An OCR system uses single or multiple phases of preprocessing which depends on complexity and ability. Initiation of preprocessing involves reading of Tesseract OCR on text region by using grayscale region extraction method. Grayscale (Otsu Thresholding) was used to test accuracy of Tesseract engine with minimized preprocessing. Otsu Thresholding comprises of multiple phases [13] whereas text segmentation involves image changing to black and white. Initially, coloured images were changed into grayscale images by using R, G and B value:

$$l(x, y) = \frac{(R9x, y) + G(x, y) + B(x, y)}{3} \tag{1}$$

Next, is the steps where grayscale distribution probability value was calculated from pixels of coloured images by following, $Pi = \frac{ni}{N}$

where:

N_i = Total pixel at i^{th} grayscale
N = Overall total pixel

Then, pixels will be divided into two classes namely, C0 and C1 by applying initial threshold, k, where C0 and C1 had its own level of grayscale pixels, i.e. [1,...., k] for C0 and [k + 1, ..., L] for C1.

3.1 Improving Output Quality

There are multiple factors that influence reading qualities of Tesseract. Tesseract operates by processing images internally (using Leptonica literature) before Tesseract OCR could extract highly accurate images using algorithm method.

3.2 Method of Grayscale Conversion

Internally, Tesseract converts (Otsu algorithm) coloured into black and white images but sometimes the result could be suboptimal if conversion involves inconsistent background. A value was designated (maybe black or white), if the pixel value is larger than threshold value. Arguement of conversion are image sources which should be converted into grayscale images, followed by definition of threshold value that could classify pixel value, evaluation of pixel value if it exceeds threshold value by using maxVal which could produces black and white images. Tesseract could produces suboptimal images internally (Otsu algorithm) if the background is black and inconsistent. If expected images not obtained, then a different algorithm should be applied such as OpenCV Image Thresholding (Python) that correlates with threshold level of an image.

Reason to Test Images. Average, adaptive and Otsu threshold limit was determined before the implementation of Tesseract. The functions are cv2.threshold, cv2. Adaptive

Threshold. Average threshold level (cv2.threshold) is a pixel value that is larger than threshold level where a single value (black or white) will be fixed. The argument includes essential grayscale images, decide and evaluate pixel value classification if it exceeds threshold value by using maxVal. OpenCV provides different threshold style by determining 4th parameter of the functions. The differential function is:

cv2.THRESH_BINARY
cv2.THRESH_BINARY_INV
cv2.THRESH_TRUNC
cv2.THRESH_TOZERO
cv2.THRESH_TOZERO_INV

Program code used to insert tesseract
Result was as below (Fig. 3):

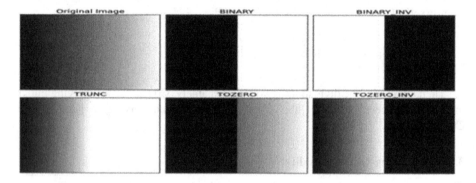

Fig. 3. Absolute adaptive threshold using grayscale mode.

Utilization of a general threshold value is not appropriate due to different illumination on background which could be fixed by electing adaptive threshold. Algorithm was used to calculate the threshold value for small region of images and to obtain different threshold level for same images or images with different illumination. This method only has 3 specific inputs and single argumentative output which gives ideas how threshold value being calculated.

cv2.ADAPTIVE_THRESH_MEAN_C: threshold value in surrounding region. cv2. ADAPTIVE_THRESH_GAUSSIAN_C: the threshold value is a result of total value using Gaussian windows. Block measurement decides surrounding measurement. C- is a reduced constant value used for calculation. Below is the code used to compare general and adaptive threshold value for images with different illumination: result (Fig. 4).

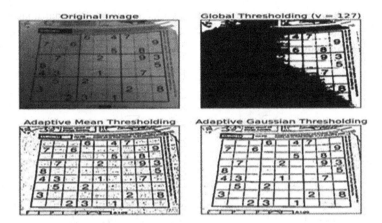

Fig. 4. Differences between Global and adaptiveThreshold level

3.3 Method of Otsu Grayscaling

Otsu grayscaling was performed on images with average threshold values [14]. In Otsu method, calculation of threshold limit is main optimization problem which is used in document images and works well in images with good quality. Digital images produced by a camera have variation in illumination and colour on front or background. Otsu Grayscaling is an effective method in image segmentation with different illumination and minimum colours [4].

Tesseract will calculate threshold value from histogram for bimodal images but grayscaling will be accurate for non-bimodal images. Then, algorithm point out output with optimum threshold value. Noise with different brightness causes text images hard to be read. Tesseract could not neglect noises at grayscaling phase which eventually reduces accuracy later. In general threshold value, arbitrary value was imposed.

Otsu grayscaling will take average value for bimodal images with dual peaks. Fuction cv2.threshold will be used by applying additional flag, cv2.THRESH_OTSU. Then, algorithm determines optimum threshold value and resulted with second output, retVal. If Otsu threshold is not used then retVal which is equal to threshold value was used. General threshold was implemented initially, followed by practisizing threshold Otsu limit directly and images were filtered to nullify noise by using Kernel Gaussian 5×5 (Fig. 5).

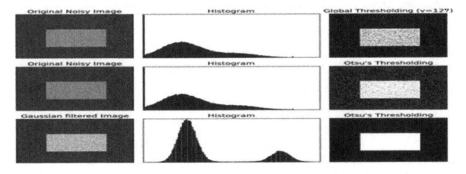

Fig. 5. Result of Otsu Grayscale implementation

Grayscale Otsu incorporated with Python works as below: Bimodal images, Otsu algorithm evaluate threshold value (t) by minimizing variance in worth class as reflected by this relation:

$$\sigma\frac{2}{\omega} = q1(t)\sigma_1^2(t) + q_2(t)\sigma_2^2(t) \tag{2}$$

$$q_1(t) = \sum_{i=1}^{t} P(i) \quad \& \quad q_1(t) = \sum_{i=t+1}^{t} P(i) \tag{3}$$

$$\mu_1(t) = \sum_{i=1}^{t} \frac{iP(i)}{q_1} \quad \& \quad \mu_2(t) = \sum_{i=t+1}^{t} \frac{iP(i)}{q_2} \tag{4}$$

$$\sigma\frac{2}{2}(t) = \sum_{i=1}^{t} [i - \mu_1(i)]^2 \frac{P(i)}{q1_{(t)}} \quad \& \quad \sigma\frac{2}{2}(t) = \sum_{i=t+1}^{1} [i - \mu_1(t)]^2 \frac{P(i)}{q2(t)} \tag{5}$$

T-value is between two variance peaks until second class minimal variance. This could be implemented into Python as follows:

```
img = cv2.imread('noisy2.png',0)
blur = cv2.GaussianBlur(img,(5,5),0)
# find normalized_histogram, and its cumulative distribution function
hist = cv2.calcHist([blur],[0],None,[256],[0,256])
hist_norm = hist.ravel()/hist.max()
Q = hist_norm.cumsum()
bins = np.arange(256)
fn_min = np.inf
thresh = -1
for i in xrange(1,256):
    p1,p2 = np.hsplit(hist_norm,[i]) # probabilities
    # calculates the minimization function
    fn = v1*q1 + v2*q2
    if fn < fn_min:
        fn_min = fn
        thresh = i
# find otsu's threshold value with OpenCV function
ret, otsu = cv2.threshold(blur,0,255,cv2.THRESH_BINARY+cv2.THRESH_OTSU)
print thresh,ret
```

4   Preliminary Test Results

4.1   Test Image

Document images captured using camera had deformative perspective, scattered illumination and blurred images. This technically poor images will produces bad images if inserted into Tesseract OCR machine. Compared to tech images, camera-captured images need different processing such as text localization, segmentation and word detection [15]. There are a lot of variations in handwriting images such as size, style, measurement, colour or italization of a font. Images captured using camera was fixed because it is permanent and placed on a whiteboard. Initial test on images using Tesseract OCR will produces faulty readings because of incomplete or missing characters as shown in Table 2.

4.2   Trial Test

To read word images produces from a camera, objects will be fixed as follows: Images of object will be places at ideal distance, camera will capture the images, and images will be sent to Raspberry then Tesseract will read the scripts (Fig. 6).

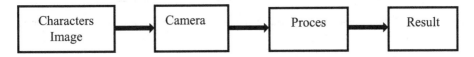

Fig. 6. Word reading process

Image Conversion. Tesseract will process images internally (using Leptonica literature) before real OCR tesseract test could be performed. This process is very effective in producing good output but there are some cases where accuracy level will be reduced significantly. Tesseract had process the images using configuration variable tessedit_write_images.

Image Size Reduction. Tesseract function well on images with minimum 300dpi so that measurement could be changes when trial is conducted.

Noise Removal. Noise with different brightness and colour can make text images hard to read. There is some noise that could not be treated in grayscaling phase by Tesseract which eventually reduces accuracy level.

Rotation or Deskewing. Skewed images are a result of pages transfer that is not done in a straight line technique. Line segmentation Tesseract will reduces if the pages is too skewed and will produce poor images of OCR. To avoid this situation, images of a page will be rotated until horizontal text line was produced.

Background. Transferred images always have dark background which could be noted as additional characters especially when they have different shape and shade. Optical Character Recognition only process text region without background using tesseract *optical character recognition* 3.04.01 Leptonica-1.74.1 engine incorporated in Python (Fig. 7).

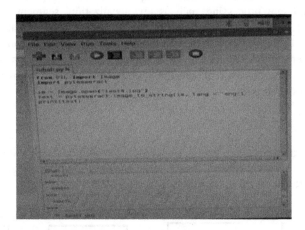

Fig. 7. IDE Python phases with several commands will detect image sources and reflects readings in Tesseract machine

Camera was setup after the phython program opened to undergo testing on complete images.

4.3 Webcam Setup

Before camera is used, its focus point was set up because normally camera possesses fixed focus and not autofocus. Camera was connected and set up for focus point setting before installed with Raspberry Pi.

The focus setting in webcam is shown below:

- i. Webcam was connected on tripod or other suitable mechanism.
- ii. Tripod stand was marked and make sure tripod not easily overlap
- iii. Target word images were placed infront of webcam.
- iv. AMCAP was opened
- v. Webcam lense was adjusted to get sharp images (Fig. 8).

Fig. 8. Camera setting using object

After webcam focus setting, USB cable was connected onto Raspberry pi for installation by typing command: **pi@rasberrypi: ~$ sudo apt-get install fswebcam** (Fig. 9).

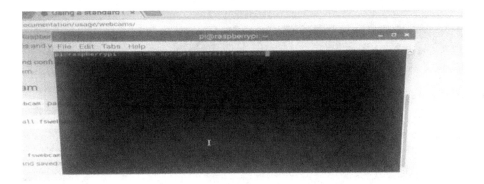

Fig. 9. Raspberry Pi installation

Fswebcam software was installed into raspberry pi by pressing enter by making sure internet line is stable. Command when images was captured by typing; **pi@rasberrypi: ~$ fswebcam - - no-banner Image.jpg** (Fig. 10).

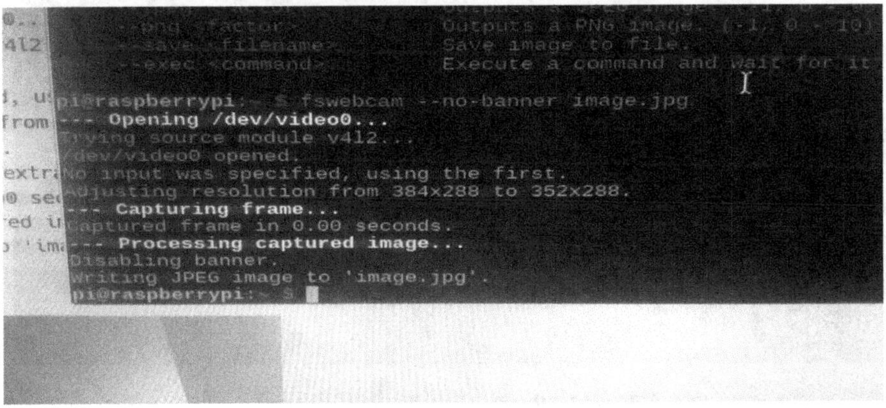

Fig. 10. Image capturing procedures

Above command managed to capture images without banner (information below the images) and save it as file image.jpg. After a few seconds, screenshot from camera was opened. Thonny program was opened to extract text using tesseract engine by typing command in Python as follows;

```
From PIL import Image
Import pytesseract
Im = Image.open("image.jpg")
Text = pytesseract.image_to_string(im, lang = 'eng')
print(text)
```

Above command produces screenshot image.jpg from webcam. When the word detected is in Indonesian language, then lang = 'eng' was replaced into lang = 'ind' (Eng = English, ind = Indonesia) so that a better text image .fswebcam could be capture (Figs. 11, 12 and 13).

Fig. 11. Captured images was inserted into Tesseract for readings

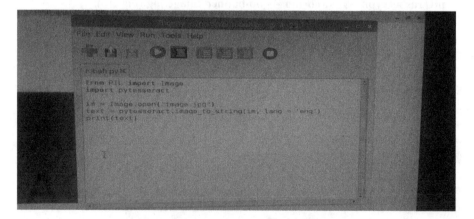

Fig. 12. Reading process by tesseract.

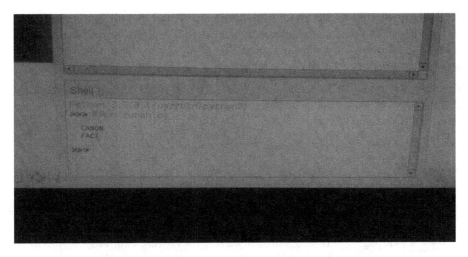

Fig. 13. Text of camera captures.

File Name	: image.jpg
Writing Source	: CANON FACT (red with white background)
Tesseract reading result	: CANON FACT
Ratio (%)	: 100%.

4.4   Adding Buttons to Starts Capture Process on Webcam

Buttons was set up on webcam to starts capture processess using Python language. Captured images were stored in raspberry pi memory once the button is pressed.

Table 1. Initial trial on handwriting images.

source	file name	file measurement	result	accuracy ratio
83ABCO1	test1.jpg	1 cm	BBABCOl	57%
83ABCO1	test2.jpg	2 cm	83ABC01	100%
83ABCO1	test3.jpg	4 cm.	%3ABCO]	71%
83ABCO1	test4.jpg	4 cm	83ABC01	83%

Trial Using Word or Numeral Measurements. Tesseract will not immediately increase its reading ratio as the characters increase but depends on specific measurement to be followed to produce true readings. Above figure shows different style of handwriting which is not fixed or computerized.

Trial on Tesseract OCR Using Image File (Black and White or Coloured).
Tesseract *optical character recognition* was tested using JPG or PNG image file in black, white or coloured.

Table 2. Result of initial test on word images in grayscale or colour

Source	File name	Origin writing	Reading Results	Accuracy Ratio
Noisy image to test Tesseract OCR	noisy.jpg	Noisy image to test Tesseract OCR	Noisy image to test Tesseract OCR	100%
Tesseract Will Fail With Noisy Backgrounds	fail.png	Tesserat will Fail with Noisy Backgrounds	" Tessera'c't will Fail with Noisy Backgrounds	90 %
1234567890	angka.jpg	1234567890	1234567890	100%
05221859	angka.png	05221859	0522I85q	80%
328308	angka5.png	328308	328308	100 %
IVI	IVI.jpg	INSTITUTE OF VISUAL INFORMATICS	ITITUTE OF VISUAL INFURMATI	98%
CAUTION	caution.jpg	CAUTION	TIDAK TERBACA	0 %
doggie	doggie.jpg	Happy Dogs Home I About Us I Services I Contact Us Doggie Daycare	Happy Dogs Home I Aboutus ISerwcss I ContaclUs Doggie Daycare	72%
004200	angka3.jpg	004200	Tidak terbaca	0 %
mobil	mobil.jpg	B 1687 FOM	TIDAK TERBACA	0 %
naufalbuku	naufalbuku.jpg	SERI BUKU PRAKTIS RAHASIA MEMANCING DI EMPANG (Yang Orang lain Tidak Perah Tahu) MOHAMMAD NAUFAL ARFAN	SERI BUKU PRAKTIS RAHASIA MEMANCING DI EMPANG (Vang Orang lain Tidak Pernah Tahu) MOHAMMAD NAUFAL ARFAN	99%
proyek	proyek.jpg	PROYEK LAB KOMPUTER SDN 04 CIKARANG BARAT SUPPORTED : PT. YUTAKA MANUFACTURING INDONESIA	SUPPORTED : _.;g_-' PT.YUTAKA MANUFACTURING INDONESIA W 2 {A , K .\y " /	67 %
PyImageSearch	test2.png	PyImageSearch	PyImageSearch	100%

In Table 2 the results of the preliminary test are conducted to determine the level of accuracy of the OCR tesseract device. Of the 13 images tested there were 4 images with 100% accuracy, this proves the performance of the Tesseract OCR is very accurate for black images. There are 5 images with an accuracy level of less than 100%, this proves that the Tesseract OCR is less accurate in reading images if there are layered letters and lack of lighting. Then there are 4 images that are unreadable or 0% this is because the OCR test cannot read color images with poor lighting.

5 Conclusion

Though Tesseract is command-based engine, it is always available as open source in Dynamic Link Library and accessible in graphical mode. The result of this test are accuracy ratio on different images captured using camera and Tesseract OCR. Tables 1 and 2 show variation in accuracy ratio between black and white or colour script images. This proves that Tesseract method influenced by image sources, tesseract characters, hence, less advisable for coloured images. Optical character recognition by Tesseract is depends on preprocessing of text and algorithm segmentation of images. Future research should be conducted to develop preprocessing method of increasing Tesseract OCR accuracy by cameras. Grayscale and segmented word images captured by camera will be processed into characters by Tesseract OCR, stored and will be written by robots as an information that is necessary for data modification.

References

1. Nakagawa, T., Ozawa, H.: Method of increasing the image character of characters with various background images, p. 50 (2015)
2. Patel, C., Patel, A., Patel, D.: A RRP configuration robot arm for drawing application. J. Chem. Pharmac. Sci. A (2016)
3. Thakkar, A., Shah, P.: Review on tesseract OCR engine and performance Kateryna Zinchenko. Int. J. Innov. Emerg. Res. Eng. 4(12), 4–6 (2017)
4. Pange, D.R., Karwankar, A.R.: Speech recognizing robotic arm for writing process. Int. J. Recent Res. Electr. Electron. Eng. 2(1), 24–31 (2015)
5. Modi, H., Parikh, M.C.: A review on optical character recognition techniques. Int. J. Comput. Appl. 160(6), 20–24 (2017)
6. Smitha, M.L., Antony, P.J., Sachin, D.N.: Document image analysis using imagemagick and tesseract-OCR. Iarjset 3(5), 108–112 (2016). https://doi.org/10.17148/iarjset.2016.3523
7. Hamad, K.A., Kaya, M.: A detailed analysis of optical character recognition technology. Int. J. Appl. Math. Electron. Comput 4, 244–249 (2016). ISSN 2147-8228
8. Zhao, Q.J., Cao, P., Meng, Q.X.: Image capturing and segmentation method for characters marked on hot billets. Adv. Mater. Res. 945–949, 1830–1836 (2014). https://doi.org/10.4028/www.scientific.net/AMR.945-949.1830
9. Patel, C., Patel, A., Patel, D.: Voting models for summary extraction from text documents. In: 2014 International Conference on IT Convergence and Security, ICITCS 2014, pp. 0–3 (2014). https://doi.org/10.1109/icitcs.2014.7021826
10. Juang, J., Tsai, Y., Fan, Y.: Visual recognition and its application to robot arm control. Appl. Sci. 5, 851–880 (2015). https://doi.org/10.3390/app5040851

11. Poovizhi, P.: A study on preprocessing techniques for the character recognition. Int. J. Open Inform. Technol. **2**(12), 21–24 (2014). ISSN 2307-8162

12. Jadhav, K.S., Gaikwad, S.M.: Writing robotic arm by speech recognition. 4983–4990 (2015). https://doi.org/10.15662/ijareeie.2015.0406013

13. Karanje, U.B., Dagade, R.: Survey on text detection, segmentation and recognition from a natural scene images. Int. J. Comput. Appl. **108**(13), 39–43 (2014). https://doi.org/10.5120/18974-0472

14. Kumar, D.: Methods for text segmentation from scene images. Thesis, Department of Electrical Engineering Indian Institute of Science Bangalore – 560 012, India, January 2014

15. Sanchez-Lopez, J.R., Marin-Hernandez, A., Palacios-Hernandez, E.R.: Visual detection, tracking and pose estimation of a robotic arm end effector (2011)

Virtual Lower Limb Stroke Rehabilitation to Assess Post Stroke Patients

Lee Wei Jian and Syadiah Nor Wan Shamsuddin[(✉)]

Faculty of Informatics and Computing, Universiti Sultan Zainal Abidin,
Kuala Terengganu, Malaysia
syadiah@unisza.edu.my

Abstract. Stroke is a disease that causes disability in adults due to the abrupt interruption of constant blood flow to the brain. Most people encounter difficulties with movement after a stroke, which prevents them from moving around. However, patients often show a lessened endurance and motivation in participating in these boring exercises. This may lead to an early termination of stroke rehabilitation, which can cause permanent disability in life. The application of virtual reality in stroke rehabilitation provides an immersive environment to increase the engagement of patients in rehabilitation exercises. In this study, a prototype named virtual lower limb stroke rehabilitation (VRLite) was developed and tested with post stroke patients on the accuracy of measurements and its usability and acceptance. The measurements of knee angles using Kinect and goniometer were compared using Bland-Altman plot to assess the system validity. The upper and lower LoA were 7.2° and −7.5° respectively. The result shows that 95% of LoA were within the upper and lower limit. The result shows that there is no significant difference between the measurements of knee angles using Kinect and goniometer. Hence, the developed program can be used interchangeably with the conventional rehabilitation.

Keywords: Stroke rehabilitation · Virtual reality · Lower limb

1 Introduction

Stroke is one of the main causes of common disabling condition and acquired adult disability in many countries [1]. Stroke can result in severe disability, partial paralysis, and even death. Most stroke survivors encounter difficulties in range of motions, fine motor skills, gross motor skills, reaching, and manipulation. Besides, post-stroke pain is one of the common impairments after stroke that may compromise one's capacity to carry out activities of daily living (ADL) tasks [2]. Patients are more vulnerable and dependent on others in doing personal management such as feeding, driving and ADL tasks, which can cause depression and social isolation. Gait dysfunctions such as hyperextension of the knee during the support phase and the reduction of ankle dorsiflexion during hill contact are the common problems faced by the post stroke patients [3]. Although rehabilitation can effectively improve the motor skills of the patients, they often show lessened endurance and motivation in participating in these

© Springer Nature Switzerland AG 2019
H. Badioze Zaman et al. (Eds.): IVIC 2019, LNCS 11870, pp. 343–352, 2019.
https://doi.org/10.1007/978-3-030-34032-2_31

monotonous and boring exercises [4]. The high therapy expenses is one of the reasons that caused the early termination of stroke rehabilitation [5]. Early withdrawal from stroke rehabilitation can cause permanent disability.

Virtual reality (VR) is described as the stimulation of multiple sensory modalities such as visual, auditory or haptic experiences through the interactions between an individual and a computer-generated environment [6]. The immersive, multisensory, and three-dimensional (3D) environment in VR technology allow the users to have modified experiences of reality. Due to the exciting features of VR, virtual rehabilitation is introduced in the medical sector to increase patient's motivation and engagement in their therapy. VR can improve balance and gait in patients by exploiting the motor learning strategies such as task repetition, multisensory feedback, and motivation [7]. This advanced technology also scientifically validated as a supplemental and stand-alone (e.g., pain distraction) treatment option for a variety of pain and behavioral conditions, and it is emerging as a tool for the detection of neurological disorders [8]. Study show that VR consoles (Kinect system and Nintendo Wii) and robots or exoskeletons are commonly used in virtual rehabilitation [9].

This paper focused on the experiments of Virtual Lower Limb Stroke Rehabilitation (VRLite) prototype with post stroke patients. In addition, it also discussed the analysis of measurements of knee angles using VRLite.

2 Virtual Rehabilitation

The VR is widely used in the medical sector due to its exciting features. The implementation of VR in medical domain helps to engage patients into actively taking part in their therapy. Besides than being useful in the assessment and treatment of patient, this advanced technology also scientifically validated as a supplemental and stand-alone (e.g., pain distraction) treatment option for a variety of pain and behavioral conditions, and it is emerging as a tool for the detection of neurological disorders [8]. While the main area supported by modern technologies in rehabilitation regards the improvement of motor functions of upper limb, the restoration of lower limb function is still being developed [9]. One of the study proposed a motion rehabilitation and evaluation system using a Kinect sensor [10]. The system is able to match skeleton model, control avatar and make rehabilitation evaluation. The results showed that VR intervention completely meets the requirements of rehabilitation due to the short response time and real-time teaching feedback interaction.

Theories of motivation and gamification are also introduced into the virtual rehabilitation to encourage the involvement of patients in rehabilitative training. The concepts of operant conditioning such as positive reinforcement (rewarding game scores for correctly performing the task), positive punishment (reducing the game scores) and negative punishment (restarting the game level) are incorporated into a lower extremity rehabilitation training to produce a positive outcome [11]. López-Jaquero et al. designed a virtual rehabilitation system using theory of influence [12]. During the execution of the exercise, patients gather, share and learn as a group, making them feels they are part of a group. In the virtual environment, tasks are assigned to the patients, which their commitments will be represented by their avatar to let the patients know about their commitments, therefore increases the duration of rehabilitation.

This study focuses on the VRLite, a virtual lower limb rehabilitation program designed based on theories of motivation and gamification approach to increase the engagement of patients [13]. VRLite is consists of three different modules with its own function: Lift Your Leg - tutorial, Collect The Coins – sitting knee extension exercise, Grow The Plants – sit to stand. Researchers also added game mechanics such as gifting system into the program, which helps to create an immersive gameplay by encouraging the social interaction among players.

3 Methods

3.1 Participants

A convenience sample of 30 post stroke patients (age: 59.3 ± 9.8 years, height: 158.1 ± 7.7 cm, mass: 62.1 ± 10.4 kg) with no lower limb injuries or surgeries volunteered to participate in this study. Participants completed informed consent forms prior to testing and all procedures were approved (UniSZA/UHREC/2018/79) by the Universiti Sultan Zainal Abidin Human Research Ethics Committee.

3.2 Procedure

This study is an experimental research to determine whether the conceptual framework designed can increase the motivation and engagement of post stroke patients in lower limb rehabilitation. Kinematic data such as sitting knee extension angle are measured manually using knee goniometer by the physiotherapists before using the Virtual Reality Lower Limb Stroke Rehabilitation (VRLite) application [13]. While participants perform rehabilitation using VRLite, Microsoft® Kinect™ automatically captured the relevant information such as kinematic data. Captured data are recorded into the password-encrypted database during the gameplay. Measurement and calculation on subject's joint angle will be done to compare the accuracy of the system and manual measurement.

Figure 1 shows the login interface in VRLite.

The first module, Lift Your Leg is designed to engage stroke patients into performing sitting knee extension. This game acts as the tutorial for players to develop their skills and get used to the virtual reality environment at an appropriate pace. The humanoid provides real time feedback with the movement performed by the patients. Figure 2 shows the Lift Your Leg gameplay.

In Collect The Coins module, patients are required to collect the coins with a plane in a limited time by performing leg strengthening exercise. The plane will fly autonomously over water and patients will only have to control the altitude of the plane by extending and flexing their knee. Figure 3 shows the Collect The Coins gameplay.

Fig. 1. Login interface for VRLite

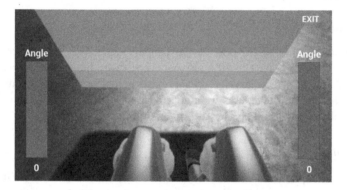

Fig. 2. Lift Your Leg gameplay

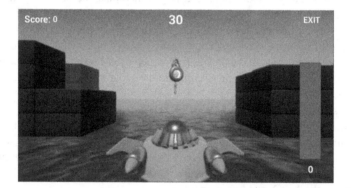

Fig. 3. Collect The Coins gameplay

Grow The Plants requires player to grow the plants by watering them with the water emitted from the plane in a limited time. The altitude of the plane can be controlled by performing sit to stand exercise. Figure 4 shows the Grow The Plants gameplay.

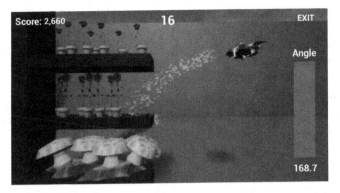

Fig. 4. Grow The Plants gameplay

3.3 Experimental Setup

The Kinect is placed two meters away and facing the subject. Subjects with left defect leg are needed to place their left leg 124° away from the Kinect when performing sitting knee extension, while those with right defect leg are required to place their right leg 142° from the Kinect during sitting knee extension exercise. During the sit to stand movement, subjects are required to sit right in front of the Kinect with their legs facing the Kinect directly.

4 Results

4.1 Kinematic Data

Collect the Coins. Patients are given 30 s to perform sitting knee extension using their defect leg during Collect The Coins gameplay. Figure 5 shows the kinematic data for left and right defect leg in Collect The Coins gameplay.

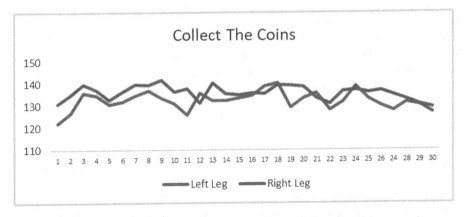

Fig. 5. Kinematic data for left and right defect leg in Collect The Coins gameplay

The lines for left and right defect leg in the graph are plotted using the average knee angle of the patients with the same paretic leg. There are 16 patients (53.3%) with left leg defect and 14 patients (46.7%) with right leg defect. The graph analysis clearly shows that patients with right leg defect has a higher average knee angle in the gameplay compared to the average of those with left paretic leg.

Grow The Plants. During the Grow The Plants gameplay, patients are given 30 s to perform a number of repetitive sit to stand (STS) movement using their defect leg. The number of STS movement performed by defect leg is shown in Table 1.

Table 1. Number of STS movement performed by defect leg

No	Defect leg	N	Mean	Standard deviation	Median	Maximum	Minimum
1	Left	17	4.47	1.546	0.54	7	1
2	Right	13	4.38	2.063	0.55	7	

The result shows that patients with left defect leg performed higher number of STS movement within 30 s. The mean of STS movement performed for 17 patients with left paretic leg is 4.47, which is higher compare to the 4.38 average for patients with right defect leg. The median of STS movement performed for patients left defect leg is also larger than the median of patients with right defect leg.

5 Discussion

The purpose of Bland-Altman analysis is to replace the misleading analyses such as correlation coefficient and regression analysis in the analysis of measurement method comparison data [14]. However, there are a few requirements that needs to be fulfill before using the Bland-Altman analysis. The continuous measurement variables is not necessary to be normally distributed, however, their differences should be normally distributed [15]. In the analysis of Bland and Altman, the difference between measurements are quantified using a graphical method. A scatterplot graph is drawn with X-axis represents the average mean [(K1 + K2)/2], and the Y-axis represents the difference (K1 − K2) of two measurements [15]. The mean bias or the mean difference of the two measurements, $\bar{d}$ and its Limits of Agreement (LoA) or confidence limits are then calculated and plotted in the same graph.

$$LOAs = d \pm 1.96\,\sigma_d \tag{1}$$

The mean of differences, $\bar{d}$ and standard deviation of the differences, σ_d between two methods are used to calculate the upper and lower 95% LoA as shown in Eq. (1) [16].

The knee angle measurements for goniometer and Kinect gathered from the study were tested for normality to determine which statistical test is suitable for analyzing the collected data. Table 2 shows the normality test of mean difference of knee angle measurements for goniometer and Kinect using the Shapiro-Wilk test. The null and alternative hypotheses for this normality test are shown below.

Table 2. Normality test of mean difference between goniometer and kinect knee angle measurements

Item	Statistic	d.f.	Sig.
Mean difference	0.928	30	0.05

- H_0: The mean difference of knee angle measurement for goniometer and Kinect is normally distributed.
- H_1: The mean difference of knee angle measurement for goniometer and Kinect is not normally distributed.

The result shows that the p value for the Shapiro-Wilk test is 0.05, which is equal to the cutoff for significance. The result is significant enough to accept the null hypothesis. Thus, it is concluded that the knee angle measurement for goniometer and Kinect sensor is normally distributed.

The readings of the measurement tools, goniometer and Kinect were compared and validated by calculating the 95% LoA. The highest knee angle achievable by the patients were measured using goniometer and Kinect. The mean of the differences and standard deviation between both measurement tools were computed to obtain the 95% LoA. According to the information provided in Table 2, the calculation for upper LoA is $-0.15 + 1.96 \times 3.75$ and the lower LoA is $-0.15 - 1.96 \times 3.75$ using the Eq. (1) (Table 3).

Table 3. Descriptive Statistics for Mean Difference of Knee Angle Measurements between Goniometer and Kinect

N	Minimum	Maximum	Mean difference, $\bar{d}$	Standard deviation, σ_d
30	-8.10	4.90	-0.15	3.75

The upper and lower LoA were 7.2° and −7.5° respectively. If the 95% LOA were greater than 7.2° or smaller than −7.5°, the differences between the two measurement systems: goniometer and Kinect were considered to be statistically significant. The graph analysis in Fig. 6 clearly shows that over 95% LOA were within the upper and lower limit. Hence, goniometer and Kinect can be used interchangeably or substitute each other in terms of the measurements of knee angle.

This study was to examine the validity of the proposed system VRLite in lower limb stroke rehabilitation. Based on the results of Bland Altman plot, the measurement tool in VRLite can be used to replace the conventional goniometer in terms of accuracy.

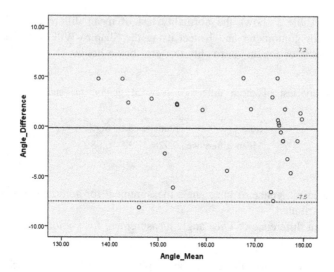

Fig. 6. Confidence intervals on the limits of agreement (LoA) for goniometer and Kinect measurements

All respondents from the study agreed that the interface quality of VRLite is promising. Besides that, all patients agreed that the information provided in this software application are useful, complete and helpful at the same time. All respondents also agreed that this application is useful because it possessed the expected system functionality. Lastly, the results showed that 100% of the patients agree that they are satisfy with the overall of this virtual rehabilitation application.

One of the positive response given by the majority of the respondents is that this rehabilitation software is very enjoyable and fun. Besides that, they think that this virtual reality lower limb stroke rehabilitation is unique and motivating at the same time. One of the patients even suggested that all rehabilitation unit should use this virtual rehabilitation application and is given to the patients more often.

VRLite is highly customizable in terms of features. The rehabilitation module depends on the patient's profile and customize the exercises accordingly to fit the patient's defect leg. Besides that, VRLite captures the kinematic data of the patient during the gameplay automatically and generate reports for assessment. Based on the reports, therapists can evaluate the progress or movement of the patients in a more systematic and simpler manner. Apart from the simple access to the modules as well as uniform navigation buttons in this application, patients can also interact with the others through the gifting system. Patients can access the gifting system through the leaderboards, which enable them to send and receive gifts based on the number of gifts they owned.

Patients can navigate in this virtual rehabilitation software easily and freely because of the uniform use of buttons for each module. The contents and presentation of the information are systematic and organized. All the modules have been compiled from basic to complex and a tutorial module is included for the patients to familiarize themselves in the virtual reality environment. Instructions on how to operate the game are included for each level, which will further enhance the patients' understanding on the mechanisms of the software and how to operate them.

6 Conclusions

The development of this virtual rehabilitation software provides a new dimension in the field of research involving virtual reality, motivation theories, and gamification together with leg strengthening exercises in lower limb rehabilitation for post stroke patients. Post stoke patients are more motivated and have an enjoyable rehabilitation treatment, which will increase their engagement in rehabilitation, thus, regain their gross motor skills in a faster manner.

The study is limited for lower limb stroke rehabilitation. For this study, experiments have been carried with 30 post stroke patients. The results from these testing sessions have produced positive results. The findings demonstrate that VRLite did not only attract the attention and was well-accepted by stroke patients, but it is also able to substitute the conventional knee extension angle measurement method in terms of accuracy.

Acknowledgement. This work is financially supported by the eScience Fund awarded by the Ministry of Science, Technology and Innovation, Malaysia.

References

1. Katan, M., Luft, A.: Global burden of stroke. Semin. Neurol. **38**(2), 208–211 (2018)
2. Lo Buono, V., Corallo, F., Bramanti, P., Marino, S.: Coping strategies and health-related quality of life after stroke. J. Health Psychol. **22**(1), 16–28 (2016)
3. Aqueveque, P., Ortega, P., Pino, E., Saavedra, F., Germany, E., Gómez, B.: Physical Disabilities - Therapeutic Implications. InTech, London (2017)
4. Qiu, Y., et al.: Fun-KneeTM: a novel smart knee sleeve for total-knee-replacement rehabilitation with gamification. In: 2017 IEEE 5th International Conference on Serious Games and Applications for Health, SeGAH, pp. 1–8. IEEE, Heidelberg (2017)
5. Hadning, I., Ikawati, Z., Andayani, T.M.: Stroke treatment cost analysis for consideration on health cost determination using INA- CBGs at Jogja hospital. Int. J. Public Health Sci. **4**(4), 288–293 (2015)
6. Cornick, J.E., Blascovich, J.: Are virtual environments the new frontier in obesity management? Soc. Pers. Psychol. Compass **8**(11), 650–658 (2014)
7. Porras, D.C., Siemonsma, P., Inzelberg, R., Zeilig, G., Plotnik, M.: Advantages of virtual reality in the rehabilitation of balance and gait: Systematic review. Neurology **90**(22), 1017–1025 (2018)
8. Wiederhold, B., Miller, I., Wiederhold, M.: Using virtual reality to mobilize health care: mobile virtual reality technology for attenuation of anxiety and pain. IEEE Consum. Electron. Mag. **7**(1), 106–109 (2018)

9. Bartnicka, J., Herrera, C., Michnik, R., Pavan, E.E., Vercesi, P., Varela-Donoso, E., Garrido, D.: The role of virtual reality and biomechanical technologies in stroke rehabilitation. In: Nazir, S., Teperi, A.-M., Polak-Sopińska, A. (eds.) AHFE 2018. AISC, vol. 785, pp. 351–361. Springer, Cham (2019). https://doi.org/10.1007/978-3-319-93882-0_34
10. Pei, W., Xu, G., Li, M., Ding, H., Zhang, S., Luo, A.: A motion rehabilitation self-training and evaluation system using Kinect. In: 2016 13th International Conference on Ubiquitous Robots and Ambient Intelligence, pp. 353–357. IEEE, Xi'an (2016)
11. Patil, Y.: A multi-interface vr platform for rehabilitation research. In: Proceedings of the 2017 CHI Conference Extended Abstracts on Human Factors in Computing Systems, pp. 154–159. ACM, Denver (2017)
12. López-Jaquero, V., Montero, F., Teruel, M.A.: Influence awareness: considering motivation in computer-assisted rehabilitation. J. Ambient Intell. Humaniz. Comput. 10(6), 2185–2197 (2019)
13. Wei Jian, L., Syadiah Nor, W.S.: The design of virtual lower limb rehabilitation for post-stroke patients. Indonesian J. Electr. Eng. Comput. Sci. 16(1), 544–552 (2019)
14. Bland, J.M., Altman, D.G.: Statistical methods for assessing agreement between two methods of clinical measurement. Lancet 327(8476), 307–310 (1986)
15. Doğan, N.Ö., et al.: The accuracy of mainstream end-tidal carbon dioxide levels to predict the severity of chronic obstructive pulmonary disease exacerbations presented to the ED. Am. J. Emerg. Med. 32(5), 408–411 (2014)
16. Horne, M., Thomas, N., Vail, A., Selles, R., McCabe, C., Tyson, S.: Staff's views on delivering patient-led therapy during inpatient stroke rehabilitation: a focus group study with lessons for trial fidelity. Trials 16(1), 1–8 (2015)

Older Adults' Number Entry Using Touchscreen and Keyboard-Mouse Computers

Zaidatol Haslinda Abdullah Sani[1,2(✉)] and Helen Petrie[2]

[1] Faculty of Computing and Informatics, Universiti Malaysia Sabah,
Kota Kinabalu, Malaysia
linda.sani@ums.edu.my
[2] Department of Computer Science, University of York, York YO10 3GH, UK
helen.petrie@york.ac.uk

Abstract. Touchscreen computers are a rapidly growing sector of the personal computer market and seem to be particularly suitable for older users. However, research has highlighted usability problems with the interaction techniques deployed on these devices for older users. A study was conducted with 12 older users of number entry tasks on a tablet and a PC, comparing three interaction techniques: keypad, plus/minus buttons and number selector (picker on the tablet, pull down menu on the PC). There were no differences in time to enter numbers between the devices, but buttons were fastest and number selectors slowest. Mental workload was also significantly higher with number selectors compared to either buttons or keypad. Older users had a complex pattern of preferences, but overall favoured the keypad for number entry and disliked the picker.

Keywords: Interaction technique · Older adults · Number entry · Input devices · Tablet computer · Desktop computer

1 Introduction

As personal computers have moved from interaction based on the keyboard and mouse to touchscreens, new interaction techniques have emerged. One such interaction technique, which is particularly popular for selecting numbers is a 'picker' or 'spinner'. A picker is a "view that uses a spinning-wheel metaphor to show one or more set of values" [1]. An example of a picker is the DatePicker (see Fig. 1, top left). It allows users to rapidly select date and time values. To select a value, the user place a finger on the appropriate field and spins up or down. The selected value appears in a darker text in the center of the view. The usability of this interaction technique for a wide range of users is important, as it is widely used in modern touchscreen devices.

Although older adults have lower rates of technology usage than younger adults, this user group is now becoming more aware of the advantages of the technology in their daily life. Recent statistics by the Pew Research Center show that 80% of United States adults aged 65 and older are smartphone owners. This value rose by 24% from their last survey in 2013 [2]. Pew Research Center also found that 32% of older adults own tablet computers, double the figure in 2013 [2]. Similar levels of smartphone and

© Springer Nature Switzerland AG 2019
H. Badioze Zaman et al. (Eds.): IVIC 2019, LNCS 11870, pp. 353–367, 2019.
https://doi.org/10.1007/978-3-030-34032-2_32

tablet use by older adults are found in other developed countries such as the UK [3], Australia [4] and New Zealand [5].

Because of the rapid growth of the use of smartphones and tablet computers (henceforth we will refer to them simply as "tablets") by older users, there has been considerable interest in how acceptable and usable they are for older users. Tablets seem to have a number of attributes that make them particularly suitable for older users: their light weight and portability, their interaction techniques which seem more direct than those on PCs (e.g. tapping directly on elements rather than selecting them with a mouse) and their emphasis on leisure applications.

A growing number of studies have investigated the use and acceptability of tablets by older adults [6–12], with mixed results. While these studies generally find that older users are interested in using tablets, studies which involved having them actually use tablets have highlighted a number of usability issues. For example, Jayroe and Wolfram [8] found that older users had difficulties with the "ultra-sensitivity" of an iPad touchscreen and with using the touchscreen keyboard which does not give tactile feedback. Both Werner, Werner and Oberzaucher [11] and Barnard, Bradley, Hodgson and Lloyd [6] also found that older users had difficulties with the touchscreen, not being confident about how long or firmly one needs to tap to select options. Wright [12] found that while older users easily remembered the kinds of gestures used on tablets (e.g. swiping, tapping, pinching), execution of them could be a problem and that inadvertently touching the screen could result in errors and unexpected changes.

Thus, there is a need to investigate in more detail which interaction techniques with tablets are appropriate for older users. Our preliminary research on developing a tablet app for older users highlighted their concern on the use of the touchscreen for entering information, particularly numeric information, and the use of the "picker". Therefore this study investigated older adults' performance and preferences with a number of interaction techniques for number entry on both touchscreen and mouse-keyboard computers, including the picker technique.

1.1 Related Work

There is a considerable body of research on interaction techniques for computers, including touchscreens, that are appropriate for older people. One can divide much of this research into three topics: understanding how changes due to ageing such as visuo-spatial and motor skills affect interaction with a computer [13–16]; innovations to make interaction with a computer easier for older users [17–19]; and comparisons of different interaction techniques, in order to investigate which are the most appropriate for older users [20–27]. It is this last topic that is most relevant to the present work. However, we could find no research which has investigated the use of the picker as an interaction technique and its appropriateness for older users.

Rau and Hsu [27] found that for older users, a touchscreen was better than mouse and keyboard or voice input for keyword search tasks. Wood, Willoughby, Rushing, Bechtel and Gilbert [26] compared the use of a touchscreen, a standard mouse, an enlarged mouse (EZ Ball) and a touchpad as input devices for older adults. Unlike Rau and Hsu, they found that older users performed better with the mouse devices than with the touchscreen devices. Participants raised the issue of the correct and consistent pressure required by the touchscreen as the source of many of their problems. Piper, Campbell and Hollan [24] investigated the use of a large touchscreen by older users, who found it less intimidating frustrating and overwhelming than a PC (in this study actual performance was only with the touchscreen, and users' perceptions of it in comparison with a PC were sought). Chung, Kim, Na and Lee [20] investigated older users' performance and preferences for physical and touchscreen keypads for number entry tasks, in the scenario of using a kiosk, so participants stood in front of an angled display for the tasks. They found that older users were significantly quicker to enter numbers using the touchscreen keypad than with the physical version, but they made significantly more errors with that device. Older users also reported that they found the touchscreen keypad easier to use than the physical one.

Kobayashi, Hiyama, Miura, Asakawa, Hirose, and Ifukube [23] investigated older users' performance with small and large touchscreens (on a smartphone versus on a tablet), focusing particularly on different gestures such as tapping, dragging and pinching. Overall, older users performed more quickly on the larger touchscreen, in spite of it requiring twice the amount of finger movement on the screen.

Jochems, Vetter and Schlick [22] compared performance and preferences of older users for different interaction devices: the mouse, touchscreen and eye-gaze control for pointing tasks. The touchscreen produced fastest performance, followed by eye-gaze control, with mouse slowest. Users also rated the touchscreen as the easiest to use, but rated the eye-gaze as the most difficult. Findlater, Froelich, Fattal, Wobbrock and Dastyar [21] compared older users' performance with a tablet touchscreen and keyboard/mouse on a PC, focusing on pointing, dragging, crossing and steering tasks. Older users were quicker with the touchscreen and made fewer errors than with the PC, and also found the touchscreen generally easier to use than the PC. Zhou, Rau and Salvendy [28] compared older users' text-entry on touchscreens (both smartphone and tablet size) via keyboard and handwriting. Handwriting was faster and preferred by older users on the smaller touchscreen, but there were no differences between the two on the larger tablet touchscreen.

Stobel and Blessing [29] conducted a different kind of study of older users' preferences for different gestures to use with touchscreens. They investigated different gestures that could be used for 34 basic interactive tasks by asking younger and older users to try them out and rate their suitability. Older users' ratings were significantly different from younger users in 50% of the tasks, and in 20 out of the 34 tasks (59%) older and younger users differed in the gesture that was rated most appropriate for the task.

A recent study by Cabeira and Hwang [33] investigates the hands-free point-and-select performance among older adults. This mid-air gesture interaction technique was found to be faster when both visual and audio feedback were used during the point-and-select tasks. The target location on screen also plays an important role in both selection time the accuracy of the point-and-select tasks.

Across these studies, which investigated different interaction techniques, devices and tasks, there is beginning to emerge a picture of touchscreens being faster and easier for older users. However, as mentioned above, no studies could be found which investigated the suitability of the picker for older users on tablets, although this is a popular design option. More detailed research is needed into the suitability of different interaction techniques on tablets for older users. Therefore, this paper presents an investigation of older adults' performance with a number of interaction techniques for number entry on both tablet and desktop computers, including the picker. It also presents results on their opinions and preferences for the different interaction techniques.

2 Method

2.1 Design

A within-participants design was used. The two independent variables were Device and Interaction Technique. Device had two conditions: the desktop computer condition used a personal computer (PC) with a standard QWERTY keyboard and mouse; the touchscreen condition used an iPad with only a touchscreen for interaction (no physical keyboard extension was provided). Interaction Technique had three conditions: the numeric keypad (on the QWERTY keyboard for the PC, and on the touchscreen keyboard for the tablet); plus/minus buttons (henceforth we will refer to these as Buttons, see Fig. 1, top right); Number Selector (a number picker for the tablet, See Fig. 1, bottom left; a pull down menu on the PC, see Fig. 1, bottom right). For the Number Selector condition, we wanted to investigate older adults' use of the picker which is a common feature on touchscreen devices (both tablet computers and smartphones). There is no exact equivalent to the picker on PCs, the closest being a pulldown menu of numbers. So these two interaction techniques were paired as Number Selectors but also investigated separately.

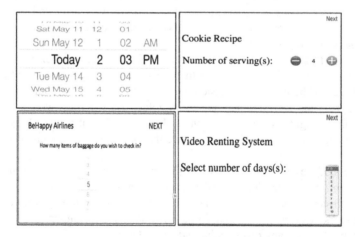

Fig. 1. (Clockwise from top left): DatePicker displaying date and time values; Baking cookies scenario with plus and minus buttons (Buttons for PC); Airline ticket booking scenario with number picker (Number Selector for tablet); Video rental scenario with pull down menu (Number Selector for PC).

Each participant undertook three number entry tasks in each combination of Device and Interaction Technique, one each with an "easy", "medium" and "difficult" number (see Sect. 2.3, below), making 18 tasks in total per participant. The order of tasks was counterbalanced to avoid practice and fatigue effects.

The dependent variables were time to enter each numeric element (digit or decimal point), the number of errors made, participant workload and participant opinions and preferences.

Participant workload was measured using the NASA-TLX [30]. Participant opinions were measured on a series of 10-point rating scales. 10-point rating scales were used to match the rating scales used in the NASA-TLX to create consistency across all the ratings. The opinion ratings were how easy it was to enter numbers with the particular interaction technique, how fast participants thought they were, how accurate they thought they were, how confident they were, and how satisfied they were with the technique. Preferences were also measured by asking participants to rank which interaction technique they would prefer to use, on each device separately and then overall.

2.2   Participants

There were 12 participants, six men and six women. The inclusion criteria were to be 65 years or over, living independently and have some experience with computers. The mean age was 71.5 years with a range from 65 years to 82 years. Four participants had completed secondary school, three had a bachelors' degree, one had a post-graduate degree and four had a professional qualification. Nine participants were retirees and three were working part-time. All 12 participants were web users with experience of using the web from 2 to 30 years (mean = 20 years; SD = 9.9). Five men and five women were computer users with experiences of using computers from 7 to 30 years (mean = 16 years; SD = 9.97). Four men and five women were tablet computer users with experience of using tablets from two weeks to 6 years (mean = 3 years; SD = 1.76).

2.3   Equipment and Materials

The desktop computer condition used a PC with a 21.5-inch LED monitor, a standard QWERTY keyboard, and a 2-button non-scrollable mouse. The PC ran Windows 10 and Internet Explorer 11. The touchscreen condition used an iPad Mini 2 running iOS 9.3.1. Morae[1] software was used to record and analyse the sessions on the PC. ScreenFlow[2] software was used to record and analyse the sessions on the tablet.

A website for the PC and a mobile app for the tablet were created. The first page was an orientation page, the next nine pages consisted of the number entry tasks with a 'Next' button on the top-right corner of each page (see Fig. 1). The last page indicated that the tasks for that device have been completed. The text explaining the tasks was

---

[1] https://www.techsmith.com/morae.html.

[2] https://itunes.apple.com/gb/app/screenflow-6/id1107828211?mt=12.

presented in 18pt, black text on a white background. The button size was 50pt. The screen size of the website on the PC was set to a similar size to the tablet screen, to make for comparable presentations.

The number entry tasks were situated in short, realistic scenarios of use for older adults such as online shopping, purchasing train tickets, borrowing library books, an airline check-in system, and a video renting service. For example, Fig. 1 (bottom right) shows the pull-down menu interaction technique on a PC, for a video renting system. The task requires the participant to enter the number of days they want to rent the video.

The numbers chosen for the number entry tasks were categorized as "easy", "medium" and "difficult". Most of the interaction techniques are designed for use with whole digits (i.e. the Buttons, and the Number Selectors), only the keypad is widely used for input which requires decimal points. Therefore, in order to include the full range of numeric input, the numbers entered on the keypad included decimals, while the numbers entered with the Buttons and the Number Selectors included only whole digits). "Easy" number entry tasks required entering only one digit; "medium" number entry tasks required entering three elements (which might include a decimal point for the keypad entry); and "difficult" number entry tasks required entering five to seven elements (which might include a decimal point). Scenarios in Fig. 1 represent the "easy" number tasks by entering only one digit.

For the NASA-TLX, large print paper versions (18pt) of the dimension pairwise comparison sheets and the task rating sheets were made. Tasks can be rated on 20 or 10 point scales. For ease of rating and consistency for our participants, we used 10 point rating scales for both the NASA-TLX and the opinion ratings of each combination of Device and Interaction Technique.

A perceived usability questionnaire was developed, and presented to participants in large print (18pt). This asked them to rate each combination of Device and Interaction Technique on five 10 point scales:

- how easy it was to enter numbers with the particular technique
- how fast they thought they were with the technique
- how accurate they thought they were with the technique
- how confident they were in using the technique
- how satisfied they were with the technique

The questionnaire also asked participants to rank their preferred interaction technique, within each device (i.e. on the PC and on the tablet) and then across both devices. The questionnaire also collected demographic information about the participants.

2.4   Procedure

The study took place in the Interaction Labs at the University of York, a quiet, private location. Participants were first briefed about the study and completed an informed consent form. Participants were asked to familiarize themselves with the first device they would use in the study (PC or iPad) with one or more practice tasks, as requested by the participant. For each task, a number printed on paper (72pt) was read out loud by the researcher and then placed in clear sight for the participant to consult while entering the number, if they wished.

After the practice task(s), participants completed the first part of the NASA-TLX, the pairwise comparison of dimensions. Participants then performed the nine (3 easy, 3 medium and 3 difficult) entering number tasks with the first device and then completed the second part of the NASA-TLX, their ratings of those tasks, and a questionnaire on their opinions and preferences with those interaction techniques.

The process was repeated with the second device. After completing the tasks with both devices, participants ranked their overall preference of all six techniques for both devices and completed a short demographic questionnaire. Participants were then debriefed about the purpose of the study and invited to ask any questions. Participants were offered a gift voucher worth £20 (approximately USD 29) to thank them for their time and efforts. The study was approved by the Physical Sciences Ethics Committee of the University of York.

2.5   Data Analysis

A Shapiro-Wilks test showed that there was a significant skew in the distribution on majority of the Likert items in the perceived usability questionnaire. Therefore a log transformation [31] was applied to the data before proceeding to further data analysis.

Multilevel linear modeling (MLM) [32] was used to analyze the data. MLM was chosen because examples of interaction techniques used are different for iPad and PC. Thus, it is not a typical repeated measures design. MLM analysis includes analysis for data with several nested levels of independent variables, in this case device (the level 2 outcome variable) and interaction technique (the level 1 outcome variable). All analyses were carried out in the IBM SPSS Statistics Version 25.

3   Results

This study investigated the time to enter each numeric element, the number of errors made, participant workload and participant opinions and preferences. The following Table 1 gives a summary of all of these results. Sections 3.1, 3.2 and 3.3 elaborates the results in detail.

3.1   Time to Enter Numeric Elements and Errors

An analysis of the time to enter individual numeric elements showed that there were significant main effects of Device ($F_{1,60.0} = 9.44$, $p < 0.05$) and Interaction Technique ($F_{2,60.0} = 256.83$, $p < 0.05$) and there was also a significant interaction between these two variables ($F_{2,60.0} = 6.54$, $p < 0.05$). The relationships between the Interaction Technique and the time taken to complete the tasks showed significant variance in intercepts across participants (var (u0j) = 0.11, X^2 (1) = 24.69, $p < 0.05$). Figure 2 shows that, across both devices, the Buttons interaction was fastest, Keypad intermediate and Number Selector was slowest. But for Number Selector and Buttons, the iPad was faster, whereas for the Keypad, the PC was faster.

Table 1. Summary of the time to enter each numeric element, the number of errors made, participant workload and participant opinions and preferences

Devices	iPad			PC		
Interaction technique	Number selector	Button	Keypad	Number selector	Button	Keypad
Time taken (seconds)	4.74	0.76	3.34	4.97	1.21	3.07
Error(s) made	None	None	None	None	None	None
NASA-TLX Mental demand	10.66	5.50	8.25	10.33	8.00	6.33
Physical demand	4.00	2.71	3.85	5.71	5.28	3.57
Temporal demand	11.18	7.45	10.63	9.81	11.27	8.09
Performance	36.41	40.33	40.75	39.41	33.25	37.00
Effort	7.16	4.50	5.16	4.00	5.25	5.58
Frustration	11.57	6.28	10.42	8.57	12.85	8.85
Opinion of ease of number entry	7.66	9.58	9.00	8.41	8.00	9.33
Preferences between devices (no of participants)	2	3	7	4	1	7
Overall preferences (no of participants)	1	0	4	1	1	5

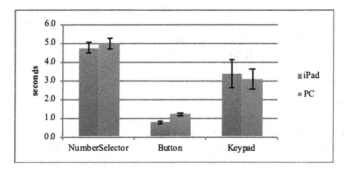

Fig. 2. Mean time per element (seconds) for the three interaction techniques

Participants made no errors in entering numbers, although they did occasionally correct themselves during the process. So no further analyses on errors were conducted.

3.2   Workload: NASA-TLX Dimensions

Of the NASA-TLX dimensions, the relationships between the Interaction Technique and Mental Demand (var (u0j) = 0.1, X^2 (1) = 61.86, p < 0.05) showed significant variance in intercepts across participants. Figure 3 shows that for Number Selector the picker was rated as more mental demanding to use than the pull down menu. Similar

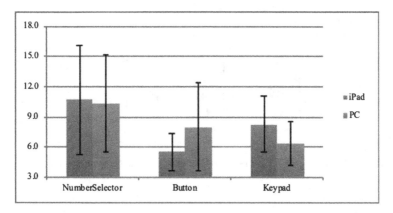

Fig. 3. Mean ratings of NASA-TLX (Mental Demand) for the three interaction techniques for the iPad and PC

result was for the Keypad, where the iPad was rated more mentally demanding than using the PC. For Buttons, the iPad was rated less mentally demanding to use than the PC.

The relationship between the Interaction Technique and Physical Demand (var $(u0j) = 0.2$, X^2 (1) = 8.99, $p < 0.05$) also showed significant variance in intercepts across participants. The Number Selector the pull down was rated as more physical demanding to use than the picker. A similar result was found for the Button, with the PC rated more physically demanding than the iPad. For Keypad, the PC was rated less physically demanding than the iPad (see Fig. 4).

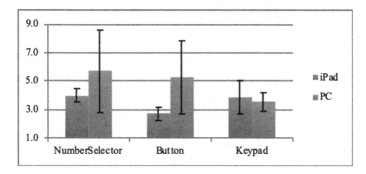

Fig. 4. Mean rating of NASA-TLX (Physical Demand) for the three interaction techniques for the iPad and PC

The relationship between the Interaction Technique and Temporal Demand (var $(u0j) = 0.17$, X^2 (1) = 83.64, $p < 0.05$) also showed significant variance in intercepts across participants. Figure 5 shows that for the Number Selector the picker was rated as more temporal demanding to use than the pull down menu. Similar result was for the

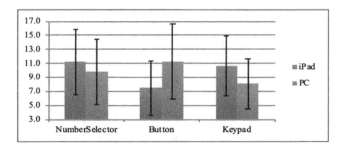

Fig. 5. Mean rating of NASA-TLX (Temporal Demand) for the three interaction techniques for the iPad and PC

Keypad, where the iPad was rated more temporally demanding than using the PC. However, for Button, the iPad was rated less temporally demanding to use than the PC.

The relationship between the Interaction Technique and Performance (var $(u0j) = 0.05$, X^2 (1) = 30.34, p < 0.05) also showed significant variance in intercepts across participants. On the Number Selector participants performed better with the pull down menu than the picker, but on the Buttons and Keypad they performed better on the iPad than on the PC (see Fig. 6).

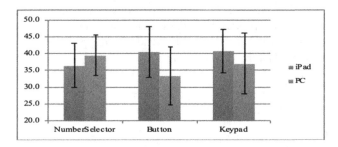

Fig. 6. Mean rating of NASA-TLX (Performance) for the three interaction techniques for the iPad and PC

The relationship between the Interaction Technique and Effort (var(u0j) = 0.19, X^2 (1) = 10.73, p < 0.05) also showed significant variance in intercepts across participants. On Number Selector participants required more effort to use the picker menu than the pull down, but for the Buttons and Keypad they required less effort to use the interaction techniques on the iPad than on the PC (see Fig. 7).

The relationship between the Interaction Technique and Frustration (var $(u0j) = 0.07$, X^2 (1) = 25.46, p < 0.05) also showed significant variance in intercepts across participants. On the Number Selector and Keypad, participants were frustrated more in using the iPad than the PC. However, for the Buttons, participants were frustrated more in PC than iPad (see Fig. 8).

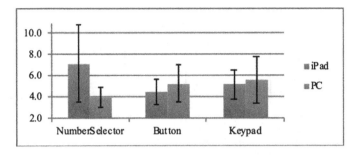

Fig. 7. Mean rating of NASA-TLX (Effort) for the three interaction techniques for the iPad and PC

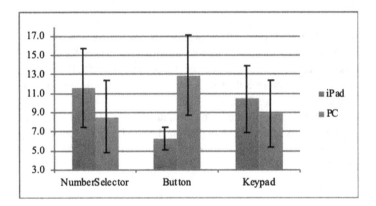

Fig. 8. Mean rating of NASA-TLX (Frustration) for the three interaction techniques for the iPad and PC

3.3   Participant Opinions and Preferences

For the ratings of how easy participants found it to enter the numbers, there were no significant main effects of Device or Interaction Technique nor an interaction between these variables. The relationship between the Interaction Technique and how easy participants found it to enter the numbers showed significant variance in intercepts across participants (var(u0j) = 0.006, X^2 (1) = 9.32, p < 0.05). Figure 9 shows that for Number Selector the pull down menu was rated as easier to use than the picker, for Buttons the iPad was rated easier to use than the PC and for Keypad, there was very little difference in ratings of how easy they were to use on each device.

Finally, participants were asked which interaction technique they would prefer for entering numbers if using an iPad, if using a PC and which was their overall preferred interaction technique. A chi-square test was used to investigate the differences in preferences for the interaction techniques, and between the devices, there was no significance difference (x^2 = 1.67, df = 1, n.s). For the iPad, there was a narrow majority preference for using the Keypad to enter numbers (preferred by 7 out of the 12 participants, 58.3%), with a quarter of participants preferring Buttons

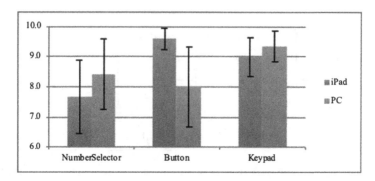

Fig. 9. Mean rating of ease of number entry for the three interaction techniques for the iPad and PC

(3 participants, 25%) and only two participants preferring the Number Selector (16.7%). For the PC, there was also a narrow majority preference for using the Keypad to enter numbers (preferred by 7 out of the 12 participants, 58.3%), with a third of participants preferring Number Selector (4 participants, 33.33%) and only one participant preferring the Buttons (8.3%).

When asked for their overall preference, 5 participants (41.7%) chose the Keypad on the PC, 4 participants chose the Keypad on the iPad (33.3%) and one participant each chose the Buttons on the PC, the Number Selector on the PC and the Number Selector on the iPad.

4   Discussion and Conclusions

This study investigated older users' performance, opinions and preferences for undertaking number entry tasks on two devices, the desktop computer and the tablet computer, using a number of different interaction techniques.

In terms of performance, that was no difference between the devices, in spite of being a keyboard and mouse on one device and the other a touchscreen. This applied to both time taken to enter numbers and perceived workload. However, there were interesting differences between the three interaction techniques. In terms of time taken to enter numbers Buttons were the fastest method, followed by Keypad, with Number Selector slowest.

In terms of older users' opinions and preferences, the pattern across the five opinion rating questions was quite consistent. There were few overall differences between the two devices, although on overall satisfaction, there was a difference, with participants giving highest ratings to the Keypad, intermediate ratings to the Buttons and lowest ratings to the Number Selector. There were no interactions between Device and Interaction Technique on all five questions and the NASA-TLX. However, there were significant variance in intercepts across participants between the Interaction Technique and on all five questions, apart for accuracy, and the NASA-TLX; with participants giving higher ratings to the pull down menus (PC) in comparison to the picker (iPad) for the Number Selector, higher ratings to the Buttons on the iPad in comparison to the Buttons on the PC, and little difference in ratings for the two Keypad versions.

In terms of overall preferences, there was only a narrow overall preference for the Keypad on both devices, with the Number Selector on iPad being the least preferred option.

The current results provide some contrasts with previous research. A number of researchers [20–22, 24, 27] have found that a touchscreen produced faster results than a more physical device (e.g. keyboard and mouse, physical keypad) for older users, whether the current study found no overall difference between the tablet with the touchscreen and the PC. However, only the study by Chung, Kim, Na and Lee [20] used number entry tasks as used in the current research, the other studies used text entry tasks or more basic tasks such as pointing and dragging. Differences may also be due to improvements in touchscreen technologies, which mean that the latest devices only require a short, light taps to select items.

Overall the results show that the current generation of tablet touchscreens do not provide any particular difficulties for older users for number entry if a Keypad or Buttons are used. However, the Number Selector interaction technique was problematic for older users. They were significantly slower with this interaction technique and liked it least.

A number of possibilities might influence the result of this study. It should be highlighted that the participants recruited were all middle-class and quite well educated, and their views and experiences might differ from those of other socioeconomic and educational backgrounds. Therefore, whether these results can be generalized to other older adults from a wider range of backgrounds is not clear and further research to confirm this is required.

There are also a number of other future studies can be done from the results of this study. We are interested in comparing different type of tasks (e.g. text and number entry) across devices. The outcome of this future study might provide a preferable interface design across devices for older adults. Furthermore, it is aware that the number of participants for this study is relatively small. To gain further insights into older adults' performance, opinions and preferences of different interaction techniques for number entry on tablet and PC, more participants are needed to ensure the generalisability of the results. In this study, it was only possible to recruit 12 older adults.

Acknowledgements. This study was part of the first author's PhD research programme. We would like to thank all our participants for their time and effort to take part in the study. The first author would like to acknowledge funding support from Majlis Amanah Rakyat (MARA). A special thank you to Universiti Malaysia Sabah, the first author's current workplace, for providing the funding to attend the 6th International Visual Informatics Conference.

References

1. Apple Inc., Human Interface Guidelines. https://developer.apple.com/library/ios/documenta tion/userexperience/conceptual/mobilehig/
2. Pew Research Center, Technology Use Among Seniors. http://www.pewinternet.org/2017/05/17/technology-use-among-seniors/
3. Of com, Adults' Media Use and Attitudes Report. https://www.ofcom.org.uk/__data/assets/pdf_file/0011/113222/Adults-Media-Use-and-Attitudes-Report-2018.pdf
4. Deloitte, Mobile Consumer Survey 2017 The Australian Cut. https://www2.deloitte.com/au/mobile-consumer-survey?elq_mid=&elq_cid=22689&utm_source=marketo&utm_medium=lp&utm_campaign=tmt-mobile-consumer-survey-2017&utm_content=body&elqTrackId=7018efb652d84958aef44087c37dcfb6&elqaid=180&elqat=2
5. Research New Zealand: A Report on a Survey of New Zealanders' Use of Smartphones and other Mobile Communication Devices (2015). http://www.researchnz.com/pdf/Special%20Reports/Research%20New%20Zealand%20Special%20Report%20-%20Use%20of%20Smartphones.pdf
6. Barnard, Y., Bradley, M.D., Hodgson, F., Lloyd, A.D.: Learning to use new technologies by older adults: perceived difficulties, experimentation behaviour and usability. Comput. Hum. Behav. **29**(4), 1715–1724 (2013)
7. Culén, A.L., Bratteteig, T.: Touch-screens and elderly users: a perfect match. Changes **7**, 15 (2013)
8. Jayroe, T.J., Wolfram, D.: Internet searching, tablet technology and older adults. Proc. Am. Soc. Inform. Sci. Technol. **49**(1), 1–3 (2012)
9. Quan-Haase, A., Martin, K., Schreurs, K.: Interviews with digital seniors: ICT use in the context of everyday life. Inform. Commun. Soc. **19**(5), 691–707 (2016)
10. Tsai, H.Y.S., Shillair, R., Cotten, S.R., Winstead, V., Yost, E.: Getting grandma online: are tablets the answer for increasing digital inclusion for older adults in the US? Educ. Gerontol. **41**(10), 695–709 (2015)
11. Werner, F., Werner, K., Oberzaucher, J.: Tablets for seniors – an evaluation of a current model (iPad). In: Wichert, R., Eberhardt, B. (eds.) Ambient Assisted Living. ATSC, pp. 177–184. Springer, Heidelberg (2012). https://doi.org/10.1007/978-3-642-27491-6_13
12. Wright, P.: Digital tablet issues for older adults'. Gerontechnology **13**(2), 306 (2014)
13. Czaja, S.J., Sharit, J., Nair, S., Rubert, M.: Understanding sources of user variability in computer-based data entry performance. Behav. Inform. Technol. **17**(5), 282–293 (1998)
14. Czaja, S.J., Guerrier, J.H., Nair, S.N., Landauer, T.K.: Computer communication as an aid to independence for older adults'. Behav. Inform. Technol. **12**(4), 197–207 (1993)
15. Siek, K.A., Rogers, Y., Connelly, K.H.: Fat finger worries: how older and younger users physically interact with PDAs. In: Costabile, M.F., Paternò, F. (eds.) INTERACT 2005. LNCS, vol. 3585, pp. 267–280. Springer, Heidelberg (2005). https://doi.org/10.1007/11555261_24
16. Smith, M.W., Sharit, J., Czaja, S.J.: Aging, motor control, and the performance of computer mouse tasks. Hum. Factors: J. Hum. Factors Ergon. Soc. **41**(3), 389–396 (1999)
17. Hourcade, J.P., Nguyen, C.M., Perry, K.B., Denburg, N.L.: Pointassist for older adults: analyzing sub-movement characteristics to aid in pointing tasks. In: Proceeding of the SIGCHI Conference on Human Factors in Computing Systems, pp. 1115–1124(2010)
18. Moffatt, K., McGrenere, J.: Steadied-bubbles: combining techniques to address pen-based pointing errors for younger and older adults'. In: Proceedings of the SIGCHI Conference on Human Factors in Computing Systems, pp. 1125–1134 (2010)

19. Wacharamanotham, C., Hurtmanns, J., Mertens, A., Kronenbuerger, M., Schlick, C., Borchers, J.: Evaluating swabbing: a touchscreen input method for elderly users with tremor. In: Proceeding of the SIGCHI Conference on Human Factors in Computing Systems, pp. 623–626 (2011)
20. Chung, M.K., Kim, D., Na, S., Lee, D.: Usability evaluation of numeric entry tasks on keypad type and age. Int. J. Ind. Ergon. **40**(1), 97–105 (2010)
21. Findlater, L., Froehlich, J.E., Fattal, K., Wobbrock, J.O., Dastyar, T.: Age-related differences in performance with touchscreens compared to traditional mouse input. In: Proceedings of the SIGCHI Conference on Human Factors in Computing Systems, pp. 343–346 (2013)
22. Jochems, N., Vetter, S., Schlick, C.: A comparative study of information input devices for aging computer users. Behav. Inform. Technol. **32**(9), 902–919 (2013)
23. Kobayashi, M., Hiyama, A., Miura, T., Asakawa, C., Hirose, M., Ifukube, T.: Elderly user evaluation of mobile touchscreen interactions. In: Campos, P., Graham, N., Jorge, J., Nunes, N., Palanque, P., Winckler, M. (eds.) INTERACT 2011. LNCS, vol. 6946, pp. 83–99. Springer, Heidelberg (2011). https://doi.org/10.1007/978-3-642-23774-4_9
24. Piper, A.M., Campbell, R., Hollan, J.D.: Exploring the accessibility and appeal of surface computing for older adult health care support. In: Proceedings of the SIGCHI Conference on Human Factors in Computing Systems, pp. 907–916 (2010
25. Snodgrass, J.G., Levy-Berger, G., Haydon, M.: Human experimental Psychology, vol. 395. Oxford University Press, New York (1985)
26. Wood, E., Willoughby, T., Rushing, A., Bechtel, L., Gilbert, J.: Use of computer input devices by older adults. J. Appl. Gerontol. **24**(5), 419–438 (2005)
27. Rau, P.L.P., Hsu, J.W.: Interaction devices and web design for novice older users. Educ. Gerontol. **31**(1), 19–40 (2005)
28. Zhou, J., Rau, P.L.P., Salvendy, G.: Older adults' text entry on smart phones and tablets: investigating effects of display size and input method on acceptance and performance. Int. J. Hum.-Comput. Interact. **30**(9), 727–739 (2014)
29. Stößel, C., Blessing, L.: Mobile device interaction gestures for older users. In: Proceedings of the 6th Nordic Conference on Human-Computer Interaction: Extending Boundaries, pp. 793–796 (2010)
30. Hart, S.G., Staveland, L.E.: Development of NASA-TLX (task load index): results of empirical and theoretical research. Adv. Psychol. **52**, 139–183 (1988)
31. Howell, D.C.: Statistical Methods for Psychology. Cengage Learning, Boston (2009)
32. Snijders, T.A., Bosker, R.: Multilevel Analysis: An Introduction to Basic and Applied Multilevel Analysis. Sage, London (1999)
33. Cabreira, A.T., Hwang, F.: Evaluating the effects of feedback type on older adults' performance in mid-air pointing and target selection. In: Proceedings of the Symposium on Spatial User Interaction, pp. 111–119. ACM (2018)

An Overview and Experiment on Wi-Fi Direct Connection Behaviour with Network Analysing Tools

Thian Seng Lee[1(✉)], Paul Gardner-Stephen[2], Riza Sulaiman[1], and Nazlena Mohammad Ali[1]

[1] Institute of Visual Informatics, National University of Malaysia, 43600 Bangi, Malaysia
thianseng01@yahoo.com, {riza,nazlena.ali}@ukm.edu.my
[2] College of Science and Engineering, Flinders University, Adelaide, South Australia 5001, Australia
paul.gardner-stephen@flinders.edu.au

Abstract. In the context of Wireless Collaboration Network (WCN), mobile devices with the wireless connection capability connect and communicate with each another for data exchange or resource sharing. The wireless technology used in forming the wireless network has been upgraded and improved throughout the years. Wi-Fi Direct is one of the well-established Wi-Fi P2P standards which can be found in almost all Android OS based mobile devices. In this work, the performance and operations of the Wi-Fi Direct standard when forming a P2P connection was reviewed by utilizing the network analysing tools. A systematic review was conducted by comparing the Wi-Fi Direct operations theoretically and practically. An overview of Wi-Fi Direct was presented, followed by experimental testing on the real-time P2P connection using physical mobile phones. The laptops and smartphones with the network traffic analyzer software (Wireshark and Wi-Fi Analyzer) installed were used to record and analyse the performance of the P2P connection activity. Finally, the findings and conclusions were discussed base on the statistical data collected from the experiment. It has been observed that there is a fixed pattern of SSID formed by Wi-Fi Direct framework regardless of the mobile devices brand, and the size of the Wi-Fi probes are device-dependent.

Keywords: Wireless Collaboration Network · Peer-to-peer · Device-to-device · Manet · Ad-hoc network · Android · Wi-Fi Direct · Network analyser · Wireshark

1 Introduction and Background

Every year, mobile devices with improved capabilities and intelligence are introduced to the market. The devices are being used for many purposes such as communication, information searching, entertainment, financial transaction, and many other intelligence functionalities. Most of the functionality of a mobile device required network connectivity, in online or offline mode. Base on the forecast updated by Cisco [1], there

© Springer Nature Switzerland AG 2019
H. Badioze Zaman et al. (Eds.): IVIC 2019, LNCS 11870, pp. 368–379, 2019.
https://doi.org/10.1007/978-3-030-34032-2_33

will be 1.5 mobile device per capita or 12.3 billion mobile-connected devices by 2022. The rapidly growing number of mobile devices in the market is among the factor of innovation in cellular communication technology. The 2G cellular technology has evolved to the latest 5G with higher bandwidth, broader coverage, and ultra-low latency to ensure the eminent quality of network connectivity [2]. The cellular communication technologies required a robust and stable backbone infrastructure with an intermediary agent at a high cost. It is inevitable that such infrastructure-based communication might be unavailable sometimes. For example, during a disaster or when the device is out of the coverage area. Besides, the cost of the data traffic subscription, the availability of the technology in the region, and the compatibility of the mobile devices to the new technology are the other factors where some mobile users could not enjoy the new technology in the short term. [1] reported that the offload traffic generated by mobile devices which connect to the fixed network will be higher than cellular traffic from the mobile devices by 2022. The public Wi-Fi hotspots are expected to grow from 124 million in 2017 to 549 million by 2022, and the Wi-Fi homespots (hotspots at home) is expected to grow from 115 million in 2017 to 532 million by 2022. This shows that the local Wireless Collaboration Network (WCN) as suggested in [3] is a potential supplementary to complement cellular communication technology.

The WCN is an ad-hoc peer-to-peer (P2P)[1] network formed by the end user's mobile devices through common wireless technologies like Bluetooth and Wi-Fi interfaces. For decades, the wireless technologies have been revised and upgraded to support better network connectivity. The new Bluetooth (5.0) standard was introduced to the market in 2016, with the improved bandwidth, connectivity range and the maintained low energy consumption [4]. The Wi-Fi standard was well established and has been upgraded from 802.11a to 802.11aq with device mobility support, broader coverage area and connection stability [5]. Unfortunately, it is not always available in every mobile device. At the point of writing, there is no standard protocol which could efficiently integrate the wireless technologies to form a robust WCN. The main challenges of forming the working WCN has been reported in [3].

As mentioned above, Wi-Fi and Bluetooth are the common wireless interface available in the end user's mobile devices. Comparison of different approaches used to form the WCN has been conducted and presented by [6] and [7]. The outcome from the comparison shows that the Bluetooth standard is more stable and established when forming WCN. However, due to the limitation of Bluetooth standard in terms of range and bandwidth, Wi-Fi standard has become the preferable standard in forming WCN. The term mobile devices in a WCN covers a wide range of mobile products. In this work, the scope of mobile devices was narrowed to focus only on a smartphone, considering the ubiquity nature of mobile phones. There are many brands of the smartphone in the market, with different types of Operating System (OS). All smartphones are equipped with at least one or more Wi-Fi interfaces which support basic Wi-Fi connectivity. However, the implementation of P2P Wi-Fi connectivity function is OS-dependent. For example, Apple Inc. has integrated MultipeerConnectivity

---

[1] Peer-to-peer (P2P) is also known as device-to-device (D2D) by some researchers.

framework[2] (also known as Apple Wireless Direct Link, AWDL) to their proprietary OS (iOS). For the Android OS-based devices, the P2P connection standard is known as Wi-Fi Direct[3]. At the point of writing, the integration of P2P Wi-Fi connectivity between the two abovementioned OS is not possible. We have chosen to focus this research on Android's Wi-Fi Direct standard. This is because Android is an open-source OS, and according to the survey report by [8], Android has been the leading OS since 2011. Wi-Fi Direct has been introduced to the market for many years. However, there is no one standard solution which could efficiently exploit the wireless technologies to form a robust WCN. Therefore, a standardized approach for all mobile devices when forming WCN is needed. But first, the architecture and the functionality of the wireless technology must be explored thoroughly. In this work, comparison was done on the operations of the Wi-Fi Direct connection theoretically as specified in the technical documentation [9], with the connection practically formed by physical devices. The stations (Laptops) with network analyser installed were set-up to analyse the performance and flow of connections.

2   Overview of Wi-Fi Direct Standard and Operations

Wi-Fi Direct, formally known as Wi-Fi Peer-to-Peer certified by Wi-Fi Alliance is a wireless mode which builds upon the Wi-Fi infrastructure mode [9]. However, unlike the common infrastructure mode, Wi-Fi Direct mode does not require an Access Point (AP). The participating devices will negotiate to designate a device to take over the AP-like role. The device with the AP-like role is referred to as the Group Owner (GO), and the devices connected to the GO is referred to as Clients. The clients that connecting to the GO could be a legacy client[4] or a P2P client base on Wi-Fi Direct standard. Figure 1 depicts the P2P topology formed between GO and two clients. The concurrent operation as shown in Fig. 2 is possible if the GO supports multiple Wi-Fi interface either physically or virtually. The GO in the concurrent operation acts as the middle entity between two Wi-Fi groups. In the first group, the GO performs the role as a

Fig. 1. Different types of P2P topology formed by Wi-Fi Direct standard.

---

[2] 'MultipeerConnectivity Framework', *MultipeerConnectivity, Apple Developer Documentation*, Apple Inc., 2019, https://developer.apple.com/documentation/multipeerconnectivity (accessed 1st July 2019).

[3] 'Discover Wi-Fi, Wi-Fi Direct', *Wi-Fi Diect, Wi-Fi Alliance*, Wi-Fi Alliance, 2019, https://wi-fi.org/discover-wi-fi/wi-fi-direct (accessed 1st July 2019).

[4] A legacy client connects to the Wi-Fi Group using conventional 802.11 Wi-Fi standard, as if the client is connecting to an AP in Wi-Fi infrastructure mode.

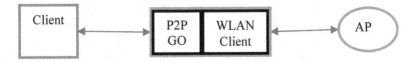

Fig. 2. Concurrent operation of a P2P device (middle).

Wireless LAN Client which connecting to an AP. In the second group, the same GO performs the AP-like role and form a connection with other clients. The concurrent ability of a P2P device allows connectivity expansion for resources sharing and transmission [6].

2.1 P2P Group Formation

The devices will go through several stages when forming the P2P Group. Depends on the pre-condition, the group forming stages normally include Discovery, GO negotiation, Wi-Fi Protected Setup (WPS) Provisioning, and Address Configuration. During the Group formation, the P2P devices communicate by sending network frames such as Beacons, Probe Requests and Probe Responses. Initially, the devices with the Wi-Fi P2P mode enabled will be turned to Listen State. The device in the listen state will randomly pick one of the Listen Channel from the list of Social Channels. The Social Channel include channel 1,6 or 11 for devices operating in the 2.4 GHz band. The minimal period of a P2P Device in the Listen State is at least a contiguous period of 500 ms every 5 s so that other P2P devices can discover it. Figure 3 demonstrates the sample simplified process of forming a P2P Group.

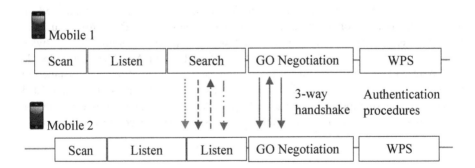

Fig. 3. Sample P2P group formation process.

P2P Devices Discovery. Along the Listen State, the devices will alternate between Scan and Find phases. During the Scan Phase, the devices will scan all Social Channels to collect information about surrounding devices. The objective of the Scan Phase is to find a P2P or P2P Group and fix the channel to establish a P2P Group. During the Find Phase, the device will alternate between the Listen State and the Search State at a random integer N interval of 100 TUs. The device in the Find phase will waits (Listen State) or send (Search State) for Probe Request or Discovery Beacon frames on each of the Social Channels.

GO Negotiation and WPS Provisioning. Assume that it is the first time the P2P devices attempt to form the P2P group; the GO Negotiation stage will begin after the Discovery stage ended and the neighbour P2P devices have been identified. During this stage, the P2P devices will negotiate the GO role using a three-way handshake procedure. The procedure requires the transmission of GO request, response and confirm frames.

After the GO role has been confirmed, the P2P devices will move on to the WPS Provisioning stage. WPS provisioning is compulsory in Wi-Fi Direct standard and normally requires minimal user intervention (e.g. Pressing a button displayed on the screen). The WPS procedure utilizes WPA-2 security and uses Advanced Encryption Standard (AES)-CCMP as cipher and a randomly generated Pre-Shared Key (PSK) to form the authentication credential. The authenticated credential will be used by the P2P devices to skip the GO Negotiation stage and link back to the previously connected GO directly. WPS Provisioning is out of the scope of this work and therefore we do not further explain the details here.

3   Experimental Environment Setup

After the Wi-Fi Direct architecture was reviewed, the experiment was conducted on physical smartphones for comparison between theory and reality. The hardware used in the experimental platform includes two laptops and two smartphones. The software used is the network analyser-Wireshark Desktop[5] and Wi-Fi Analyzer[6] from Google Play. Wireshark was installed in the two laptops and Wi-Fi Analyzer was installed in the two smartphones. The specification details of the hardware and software are listed in Table 1. The smartphones were used to form the P2P connection and the laptops were used as the station to capture the frame transmission between the smartphones.

---

[5] Wireshark download page, Wireshark, 2019, https://www.wireshark.org/download.html (accessed 1st July 2019).

[6] Wifi Analyzer Classic download page, Google Play, 2018, https://play.google.com/store/apps/details?id=com.farproc.wifi.analyzer.classic&hl=en (accessed 1st July 2019).

Table 1. Hardware and software used for experimentation

Hardware	Specifications (model, OS, Wi-Fi interface)
PC 1	HP Pavilion dv4, Ubuntu version 16.04 LTS, Intel Wi-Fi card Pro/Wireless 5100AGN
PC 2	HP Pavilion 14, Ubuntu version 16.04 LTS, USB Wi-Fi dongle TP-Link TLWN727 N
Smartphone 1	Samsung Galaxy J1 mini Android 6.0.1, Wi-Fi b/g/n
Smartphone 2	Lenovo A5000, Android 4.4.2, Wi-Fi b/g/n
Software	Details (name, version, type)
Network traffic analyser	Wireshark, 2.6.6, Third-party freeware (wireshark.org)
Wi-Fi analyser	Wifi Analyzer Classic, 3.11.2, Third-party freeware (Google Play)

3.1 Preliminary Setup

The distance between laptop-to-smartphone and smartphone-to-smartphone were fixed based on the signal strength range within −30 dBm to −67 dBm. This is the reliable Wi-Fi signal strength as suggested by [10]. The signal strength was measured using the Wi-Fi Analyser (Wifi Analyzer Classic) installed in the smartphones. Wifi Analyzer Classic is a free mobile application on Google Play. It is normally used to scan the and display the strength of the Wi-Fi channels surrounding the smartphone. To improve accuracy, both smartphones were used for measurement. A signal broadcast station is needed so that the receiving device(smartphone) can receive the signal for signal strength measurement. To achieve this, the built-in mobile hotspot feature of the HP Pavillion 14 laptop and the tethering feature of the Samsung smartphone were utilized to form the broadcast stations.

To get an ideal distance with good signal coverage between laptop-to-smartphone, the Lenovo phone with the Wi-Fi Analyser was used to measure the SoftAP signal strength based on the broadcast signal by the HP Pavillion 14 laptop. The measurement result's screenshot can be found in Fig. 4a. Referring to the screenshot, The signal with the highest signal strength was transmitted by the Laptop on channel 11, with SoftAP name begin with "DESKTOP". With the signal strength around −50 dBm, the distance between the smartphone and the laptop was approximately 210 cm.

For the smartphone-to-smartphone distance, the Samsung smartphone's tethering service was activated to form the SoftAP name "AndroidAP". Then, the signal strength of the signal transmitted by the SoftAP was measured by the Lenovo smartphone. The measurement result's screenshot can be found in Fig. 4b. Referring to the screenshot, the signal with the second-highest signal strength on channel 6 was transmitted by Samsung's SoftAP named "AndroidAP". Same as the previous measurement, the distance between the two smartphones was fixed at approximately 210 cm, with the signal strength −50 dBm.

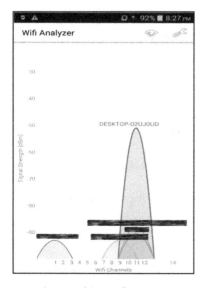
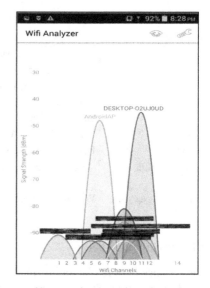

a) smartphone-to-laptop   b) smartphone-to-smartphone

Fig. 4. Wi-Fi signal strength measurement with a Wi-Fi Analyser.

3.2 The Wireshark Analyser

Wireshark is a free and open-source network traffic analyser software under GNU GPLv2 license. It is normally used to capture and analyse the packet flow between network devices. Before we begin the packet capture activity, three initial configuration steps were performed.

Step 1. Wi-Fi Operational Mode Configuration. The type of packets flowing in a network could be either unicast, multicast or broadcast. The default operation mode of a Wi-Fi interface is promiscuous (or managed). In promiscuous mode, only unicast packets can be captured by the Wi-Fi interface. The Wi-Fi interface must be configured into the monitor mode to capture the multicast and broadcast packets. However, unlike the promiscuous mode, which is supported by all Wi-Fi interface, the monitor mode is interface-dependent. That is the reason why we included the external dongle (refer Table 1) in the PC2 package. No additional dongle is required for PC1 as the built-in Wi-Fi interface supports Wi-Fi operations in monitor mode. The Ubuntu terminal command to configure the Wi-Fi operation mode is listed in Table 2.

Step 2. Wi-Fi Channel Configuration. The specific channel in which the Wi-Fi interface operates must be configured so that Wireshark will capture only the packets transmitted on the specific channel. As described in 2.1 the Wi-Fi P2P connection operates on channel 1, 6 and 11. Therefore, we alternated the Wi-Fi interface on both PC1 and PC2 to operates on the three channels, one channel at a time for each test case. Refer Table 2 for the Ubuntu terminal command to configure the Wi-Fi channel. After the monitor mode and the channel has been configured, the Wireshark software was launched in both PCs.

Step 3. Wireshark Capture Filter. The capture filter parameter on the main page of Wireshark was set so that each PC was responsible to record the wireless frame related to a specific smartphone only. In our case, PC1 was configured to capture wireless frame belongs to Lenovo smartphone only and PC2 was configured to capture the wireless frame of Samsung smartphone only. The format of the capture filter has been listed in the third row of Table 2.

Table 2. Commands related to the initial setup.

Purpose	Configuration environment	Command
Configure Wi-Fi operation mode	Ubuntu terminal	*root@username: ~# iwconfig xxx* (interface name) *mode monitor*
Configure Wi-Fi channel	Ubuntu terminal	*root@username: ~# iwconfig xxx* (interface name) *channel n* (channel number)
Configure capture filter	Wireshark front page, with the specific Wi-Fi interface selected	*Capture filter: wlan host xx:xx: xx:xx:xx:xx* (mac address)

After the three initial configuration steps were performed, the "Start capturing packet" button has been clicked to start the capture process.

3.3   Test Cases

Two simple test cases were designed for Wi-Fi Direct connection testing. The two cases included enabling the Wi-Fi Direct feature and forming a connection between the two smartphones. The step by step procedures performed for each test case are listed in the following section.

Enable Wi-Fi Direct. This test case was designed to test the scanning and searching operations. After the initial configuration (explained in Sect. 3.2) steps were performed, begin the step:

  i. Enable Wi-Fi interface for around 5 s.
  ii. Enable Wi-Fi Direct feature for around 10 s.
  iii. Disable the Wi-Fi interface to stop the Wi-Fi connection.
  iv. Switch the Wi-Fi interface channel of both PC with the command listed in Table 2.
  v. Repeat step 1 to 4 until all channel was switched.

The Connection Between the Two Smartphones. This test case was designed to test the GO Negotiation and WPS Provisioning operations. After the initial configuration (explained in Sect. 3.2) steps were performed, begin the step:

  i. Enable the Wi-Fi Direct feature on both smartphones.
  ii. Click P2P device found on the list for Samsung smartphone.

iii. Click accept invitation received on Lenovo smartphone.
iv. Disconnect after the P2P connection was established.
 v. Disable the Wi-Fi interface to stop the Wi-Fi connection.
vi. Switch the Wi-Fi interface channel of both PC (command listed in Table 2)
vii. Repeat step 1 to 6 until all channel was switched.

4   Result and Discussion

The files captured by Wireshark are of the extension ".pcapng". Following the test cases listed in Sect. 3.3, there were a total of 12 PCAPNG files generated. The first 6 PCAPNG files were the Wi-Fi Direct activation session captured on every single channel (ch1,6,11) using both smartphones. The other 6 PCAPNG files were the Wi-Fi Direct P2P connection captured on the 3 channels by the 2 smartphones.

4.1   Wi-Fi Direct Activation Test Case Captured

Figure 5 depicts one of the Wireshark session captured on channel 1, with the capture filter fixed with Lenovo smartphone MAC address only. It was observed that when operating in P2P mode, a temporary SSID labeled as "*DIRECT-*" was generated. The display filter command "*wlan.ssid contains DIRECT*" was applied to the capture session to list only the Wi-Fi Direct frames. Figure 6 shows the result after the display filter was applied.

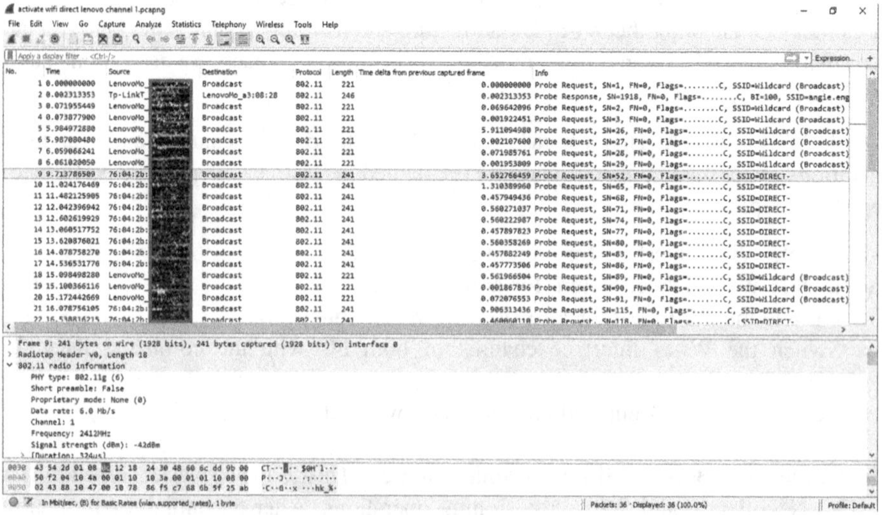

Fig. 5. Screenshot of Wireshark capturing wireless frame.

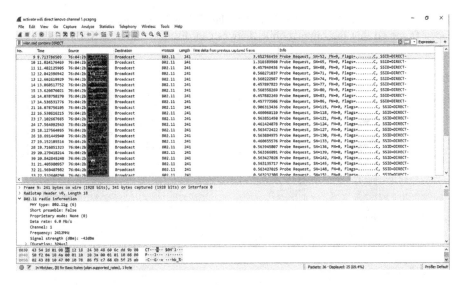

Fig. 6. Screenshot of Wireshark session captured with display filter applied.

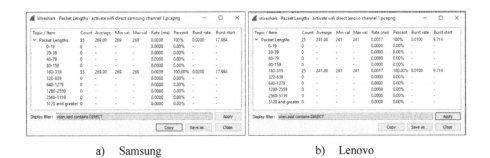

a)   Samsung   b)   Lenovo

Fig. 7. Summary of the packet length captured.

It is also observed that when the Wi-Fi Direct feature was activated, the smartphone started to broadcast a series of probe request with a serial number (SN) labeled. Figure 7 depicts the summary of the total packet captured. The screenshot on the left (a) shows that the probe request size generated by Samsung smartphone was 269 bytes. However, the size of the probe request recorded on Lenovo smartphone was 241 bytes. This shows that the probe request size is not fixed and device-dependent.

4.2   Wi-Fi Direct P2P Connection

Figure 8 depicts one of the Wireshark session captured on channel 1 when forming the P2P connection. The capture filter was to capture frames related to Samsung smartphone MAC address only. It is observed that when the P2P GO was identified; the GO will form a new SSID based on the device name (e.g. DIRECT-kF-Galaxy J1 mini prime). After the new SSID was formed, the GO will continuously broadcast the beacon frame so that the other mobile devices can discover the new SSID.

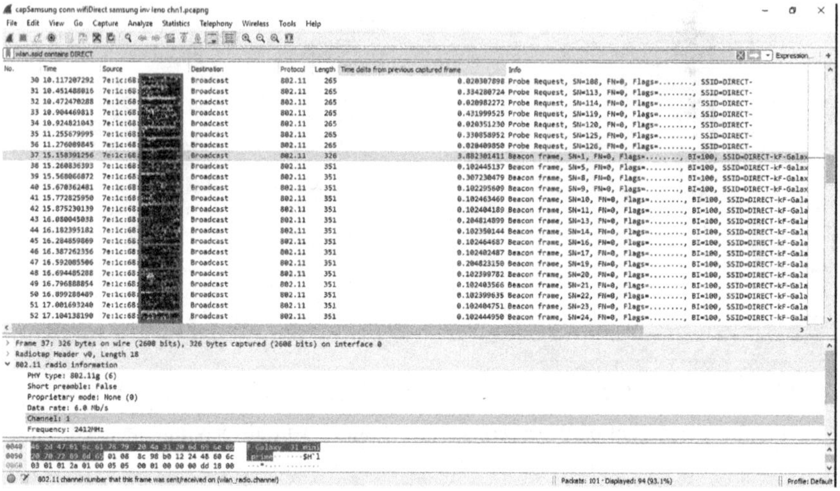

Fig. 8. Screenshot of Wireshark session captured during the P2P connection process.

Figure 9 depicts the summary of the frames transmitted between two smartphones (or known as a conversation between smartphones). When Wi-Fi Direct was activated, the smartphones created a new virtual MAC for the P2P activity. This can be seen in Fig. 9 under the column "Address A", the original MAC address started with "74" and the new MAC address started with "76". A total of 32 frames transmission were recorded between the two smartphones during the P2P group formation and connection.

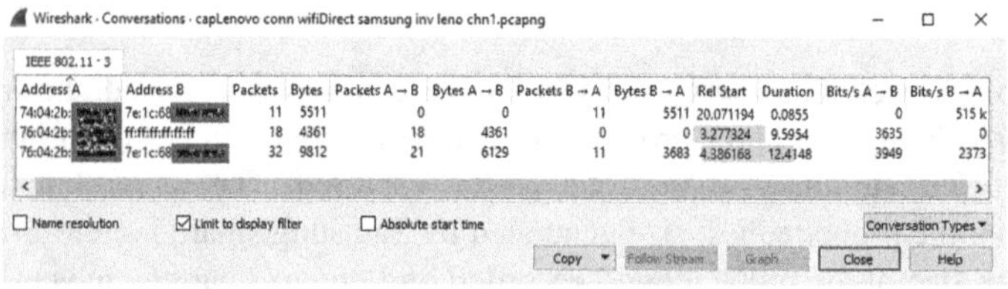

Fig. 9. Summary of the frames transmitted between two smartphones.

5   Conclusion

In this paper, we compared the theoretical and practical group formation operations of the Wi-Fi Direct standard. For the theoretical operations, we presented an overview of the Wi-Fi Direct standard based on the technical documents. Next, we had set up an experimental platform and designed 2 simple test cases for testing. Two smartphones were used for the P2P connection testing and 2 laptops were used as the station to record the frame transmission process. The recording was done using Wireshark Analyzer. When the Wi-Fi Direct was activated, a temporary SSID "DIRECT-" was generated. A new virtual MAC address was issued to the Wi-Fi interface for the Wi-Fi Direct operations. The size of the probe request or response frame is not fixed, and it is device-dependent. The details flow of frames between smartphones are difficult to visualize as the frame was recorded in bundle and we can't rule out the possibility where some frames were dropped or not captured by the Analyzer. However, the pattern of the formation and frame details have been visualized using the analysis tools available in Wireshark Analyzer. The experimental environment has been set up in an ideal and static condition. There are times where Wi-Fi Direct has stopped functioning and the connection cannot be formed. The smartphones were placed on a fixed location which might not reflect the mobility nature of a smartphone. For future work, more devices can be added to collect more sampling data for comparisons. In addition, a better experimental approach could be developed to review the connection between mobilized smartphones.

References

1. Cisco: Cisco Visual Networking Index (VNI) Global Mobile Data Traffic Forecast Update, 2017–2022 (2019)
2. Jiang, D., Liu, G.: An overview of 5g requirements. In: Xiang, W., Zheng, K., Shen, X. (eds.) 5G Mobile Communications, pp. 3–26. Springer, Cham (2017). https://doi.org/10.1007/978-3-319-34208-5_1
3. Lee, T.S., Sulaiman, R.: Preliminary analysis of wireless collaborative network on mobile devices. J. Inf. Commun. Technol. 18(3), 327–343 (2019)
4. Woolley, M., Schmidt, S.: Bluetooth 5 go faster. Go further (2016)
5. IEEE: 802.11aq-2018 - IEEE Standard for Information technology–Telecommunications and information exchange between systems Local and metropolitan area network–Specific requirements Part 11: Wireless LAN Medium Access Control (MAC) and Physical Layer (PHY) Spe. IEEE (2018)
6. Lee, T.S., Sulaiman, R., Ali, N.M.: A peer to peer internet sharing technique on MANET through Wi-Fi interface. In: 4th Visual Informatics International Seminar (VIIS 2018), pp. 1–12 (2018)
7. Shah, N., Abid, S.A., Qian, D., Mehmood, W.: A survey of P2P content sharing in MANETs. Comput. Electr. Eng. 57, 55–68 (2017)
8. Holst, A.: Global smartphone sales to end users from 1st quarter 2009 to 2nd quarter 2018, by Operating System. Statista.com (2019). https://www.statista.com/statistics/266219/global-smartphone-sales-since-1st-quarter-2009-by-operating-system/. Accessed 01 July 2019
9. Wi-Fi Alliance: Wi-Fi Peer-to-Peer (P2P) Technical Specification Version 1.7, Wi-Fi Alliance, P2P Technical Group (2016)
10. Tumusok, J.P., Newth, J.D.: Wi-Fi signal strength: what is a good signal and how do you measure it. EyeSaaS.com (2018). https://eyesaas.com/wi-fi-signal-strength/. Accessed 01 July 2019

Multi-word Similarity and Retrieval Model for a Refined Retrieval of Quranic Sentences

Haslizatul Mohamed Hanum[1]([⊠]), Nur Farhana Rasip[1],
and Zainab Abu Bakar[2]

[1] Faculty of Computer and Mathematical Sciences,
Universiti Teknologi MARA, Shah Alam, Malaysia
haslizatul@uitm.edu.my
[2] Al-Madinah International University, Shah Alam, Malaysia

Abstract. This paper addresses the task of learning sentence similarity on pairs of relevant sentences retrieved from a Quranic Retrieval Application (QRA). With the existing keywords and semantic concepts extraction, a long list of relevant verses (sentences) is retrieved that matches the query. However, as Quranic concepts are repeatedly conveyed on scattered sentences, it is important to classify which of the retrieved sentences are similar not only in word function but in context with subsequence words. Information context on similar sentences is realized with the evaluation of both word similarity and relatedness. This paper proposed a multi-word Term Similarity and Retrieval (mTSR) model that uses the n-gram score function that measures the relatedness of subsequent words. Bigram similarity scores are constructed between every pair of the relevant Quranic sentences, which boost the conventional keyword matched QRA. A similarity score is established to refine the list of relevant sentences aimed to help the user to understand the scattered content of the documents. The results are presented to the user as a refined list of similar sentences, by ranking the first-retrieved results from a keyword search. The ranking is done using a bigram score. When the score is tested on the Malay Quranic Retrieval Application (myQRA) prototype, results show that the refined results accurately matched the manually perceived similar sentences (iS) extracted by the three volunteers.

Keywords: Bigram score · Sentence similarity · Relevant results · Retrieval system · Malay translation of quran

1 Introduction

Text retrieval or categorization methods usually depend on exact matches between words. The documents that match a query are arranged in an ordered list using a term frequency versus an inverse of the document frequency (tf-idf) vector as the term weighting function. The vector helps in determining the most important word in a document. A word is more relevant and important when it appeared or used more often in the document than other words.

A Quranic Retrieval Application (QRA) searches and retrieves a list of relevant Quranic chapters and verses (sentences). Successful retrieval of the relevant Quranic sentences means that results should be semantically related to the user's information

© Springer Nature Switzerland AG 2019
H. Badioze Zaman et al. (Eds.): IVIC 2019, LNCS 11870, pp. 380–389, 2019.
https://doi.org/10.1007/978-3-030-34032-2_34

need presented as a query. However, while an Information Retrieval (IR) application can identify which verse is relevant and which are not, the one central problem is determining which groups of sentences convey related content. This problem arises when the results are ranked according to an ordered list that associates a degree of relevance for each document with the respective query, but unable to group similar sentences.

Identifying the relationship between pair of sentences is important as shown by example on paraphrase applications [1, 2], sentiment analysis [3] and solving word sense disambiguation [4, 5]. Word overlap and word order work as feature vectors to measure similarity value which may perform effectively in some specific domain, but not for others. N-gram language model is commonly used to measure semantic similarity in text documents used for information retrieval, and automatic naturalness evaluation of machine-generated texts [6].

This paper proposes an effective use of bigram on multi-word Term Similarity and Retrieval (mTSR) model to enhance the relevant results based on documents containing multiple topic terms. The model refines the list of retrieved documents by evaluating the bigram similarity score for identifying the content similarity between the quranic sentences.

2   Background

Quranic sentences are written in Arabic and commonly translated into other languages like English and Malay. The Quran contains topics and concepts practiced in the Islam religion and the knowledge are scattered throughout the book. Many types of research were conducted to extract concepts and topics to help users understand the content of the Quran. Recent studies for retrieving unstructured Malay translation of the Quran are limited to development of retrieval application using keyword-matched and semantic relationship [7]. User is presented with a huge list of verses that matches the query but lack of content and term with information. This is due to the lack of extraction tools to evaluate the similarity of verses from scattered Quranic chapters. This project focuses on enhancing the study of Malay unstructured text translated from the Quran and assist the native Malay users with a retrieval application as good as those processing the English [8] and Arabic texts [9, 10].

As a Holy book that contains diverse knowledge, the discovery of concept or topic terms from the Quran is beneficial for improving user acquaintance and wisdom towards understanding the content of the Quran. While processing large vectors of topic or content words offers diverse access to documents, a more efficient content representation using multi-word terms with semantic information offers a more accurate retrieval experience. Semantic information is constructed from a concept not only by considering the meaning of a single word but also by considering other words surrounding it. Representing a document using the n-gram of multi-word terms (or topic terms) has reduced the document vector into a fewer number of meaningful terms that carry information. Retrieving verses of the Quran with similar terms provides a better understanding of the information presented in the Holy document.

A few recent works related to the Quran enhanced retrieval performance using a semantic relational model of topic and concepts from the Quran [9, 10]. Some recent authors labeled the verses from the Quran with a list of pre-defined topics like *iman*, *ibadah*, and *akhlak*, which are the terms that represent the fundamental aspects of teaching in the Islam religion [11]. Another research retrieved Quranic verses using ontology for mapping inter-related concepts and topic terms [12]. By evaluating a keyword, the relevant verses that related to themes, sub-themes, and sub-sub-themes were retrieved [13]. All those works are challenging as it relies on the ability to use the ontology editors to describe the concepts and relationships of a sentence (verse) in scholarly approved and meaningful ways.

A sentence is composed of words and phrases. Unique word in a sentence (referred to term in linguistic and retrieval domains) and their term-frequency (tf) are commonly used as a weight feature to form the data representation of a text document [14]. The similarity of any two sentences is commonly been measured by word similarity and relatedness. Word similarity quantifies closeness of two terms while word relatedness is the degree of how two terms relate to each other. Alphanumeric sequences evaluated using n-gram of words sequences has improved classification task on Malay documents [5, 15]. In those works, bigram models were trained on a training corpus with many documents or sentences, counts all two-word-long subsequence (bigram) that appear on the data, and builds a probability distribution of the bigrams. Bigram combinations of nouns, verbs, or adjectives were extracted as concepts from Malay translated documents using syntactic rule-based approach [16]. Most of the Quranic verses (sentences) were pre-processed and represented as a list of noun terms representing the concepts. These technique of reducing the term vectors into the topic or noun vectors are useful for evaluating the similarity of two documents or sentences.

Sentence similarity identifies how similar the sentences to each other and often defined as a similarity score. Research on semantic similarity on Malay words started with the identification of word variants using stemming method and used of a Malay thesaurus to expand input query in a Malay text retrieval application [17, 18]. In another research, the retrieval performance was evaluated using root words mapped to a thesaurus to observe word correlation in Malay and English translation of the Quran [19]. The similarity between sentences is also calculated using the cosine similarity between the current sentence being investigated and each of its prior sentences [20]. The research adopted the same English-based technique to detect novelty in Malay sentences. Unique words in the sentences and their term-frequency (tf) were used as a weight feature to form the data representation. However, understanding similarity based on single word similarity and relatedness is not enough. Used of n-gram computation for studying multi-word similarity and relatedness are conducted to improve the understanding of sentence similarity.

Dice coefficient measures the degree of similarity between two sets of string, represented as n-gram sequences. The similarity of two strings is measured in terms of the number of common bigrams (bigram is a pair of adjacent words in the string). The Dice Coefficient can be calculated by using the formula shown below:

$$Dice\ Coefficient = 2\frac{|X \cap Y|}{|X| + |Y|} \tag{1}$$

In Eq. (1), the dice coefficient is defined as twice number of common terms, X and Y, in the compared strings divided by the total number of the terms in both strings.

3 Methodology

A two-steps retrieval model is presented in this paper that enhance user experience on relevant documents with visualization of similar sentences. In the first phase, a list of relevant documents is retrieved by using the keyword matching approach. Similar sentences are presented next in the second phase allowing a user to search further within the results. The n-gram similarity score is computed on every pair of sentences and the retrieval performances from each phase are compared using recall and precision. Eight queries are used in the experiments.

3.1 Collection of Quranic Sentences

In order to retrieve documents through a Quranic Retrieval System (QRS), the Malay translation of the Quranic sentences are extracted from the chapters and used as sample dataset for this project. The chosen version of the translation is readily available and recognized by the Department of Islamic Department Malaysia (JAKIM)[1].

The pre-processing step consists of tokenizing, removal of stop-words[2] and stemming processes. Tokenization is the process of parsing the text into a sequence of tokens or terms. Removal of terms that have no meaning to the documents and stemming are the automated procedures to reduce the term sequences into a common form suitable for feature representation.

3.2 Relevant Documents from TF-IDF Vector

After pre-processing the data collection, a list of relevant sentences is first retrieved by using keyword matching. Term Frequency-Inverse Document Frequency (tf-idf) allows the determination of weight for each term (or word) in each document using frequency and ratio of document length. The tf-idf vector is calculated as follows.

$$a_{ij} = tf_{ij}\,idf_i = tf_{ij} * \log_2\left(\frac{N}{df_i}\right) \tag{2}$$

The term a_{ij} is the weight of term i in document j, N is the number of documents in the collection, tf_{ij} is the term frequency of term i in document j, df_i is the document

---

frequency of term i in the collection. This keyword matching approach is implemented as Module 1 in the prototype. Results from this first module are supplied as input to the second module of the prototype.

3.3   Bigram for Similar Sentences

In the second phase of the retrieval process, each sentence from the list of relevant documents is tokenized and estimated into bigram pair of tokens. Then, the system counts the number of bigram pairs in every pair of sentences as bigram score (bscore). The scores are then sorted in descending order; from highest to lowest score. The scores are used in this phase, to retrieve a refined list of similar sentences.

Results from both phases are compared to the manually identified similar sentences (iS) extracted by volunteers using an existing online application[3]. The difference in the number of retrieved sentences was recorded and compared. This is done to ensure that the results retrieved by the prototype match the results from the existing application.

4   Results

Eight chapters are conveniently selected from the first few chapters of the Al-Quran and included as sample documents in a newly developed prototype named Quranic Retrieval Application with Malay translated documents (myQRA). From every selected chapter, each of the verse (sentence) is manually extracted and saved as an individual document. The following Table 1 shows the details of chapters and verses identified as the document collection.

Every document was uniquely named with a combination of alphanumeric codes. For instance, the first sentence of chapter 6 (*Al-An'am*) is stored as A0001. The character 'A' refers to the chapter and the next 4 digits refer to the sentences (or verses). The total number of sentences processed from 8 chapters are 1285 sentences. Each file is pre-processed and the term frequency versus document frequency (tf-idf) vectors are constructed for the prototype.

Table 1. Document collection

Chapter's (*surah*) number, name and code			Number of translated sentences (verses)	File names
6	*Al-An'am*	A	165	A0001-A0165
1	*Al-Baqarah*	B	286	B0001-B0286
3	*Al-Imran*	I	200	I0001-I0200
5	*Al-Ma'idah*	M	120	M0001-M0120
4	*An-Nisa*	N	176	N0001-N0176
9	*At-Taubah*	T	129	T0001-T0129
19	*Maryam*	Y	98	Y0001-Y0098
12	*Yusuf*	F	111	F0001-F0111
Total number of sentences			1285	

---

[3] Al-Quran (Tafsir & by Word) produced by Greentech Apps Foundation, Accessed on 30th July 2018.

The myQRA prototype applied two-steps retrieval modules to allow a user to input a query word and the system will retrieve a list of sentences that match the query. In the first module, a lookup search is conducted on the tf-idf vectors and a list of relevant sentences are retrieved using a word matching approach. Relevant results are presented to the user as ranked documents from the highest value of tf-idf to the lowest value of tf-idf.

The following Table 2 shows the 8 queries used in the experiment and a total number of relevant documents retrieved using the first module. Each of the query words is selected from a list of fundamental topics and concepts in the teaching of Islam. As an example, *pahala* and *dosa*; each represents the concept of reward and penalty for good deeds, while *zakat* and *sedekah; each* distinguishes between a mandatory tax and an alms which is much promoted in Islam. A total of 268 sentences were extracted from the first module as results (relevant documents) to the queries.

Table 2. Relevant documents retrieved from keyword lookup

Query	Number of retrieved relevant documents
1 *Dosa* (sin)	75
2 *Haji* (pilgrimage)	13
3 *Ilmu* (knowledge)	29
4 *Pahala* (reward)	47
5 *Perempuan* (women)	62
6 *Puasa* (an act of fasting)	8
7 *Sedekah* (alms)	12
8 *Zakat* (taxes)	22

Using a matched keyword approach, the query *dosa* (sin) retrieved the highest number of relevant documents (75) as the results, while the query *puasa* (an act of fasting) shows the lowest number of documents (8) retrieved as the relevant documents.

4.1 Similarity Score

Similarity score determines the number of bigrams found on a pair of sentences. Series of experiments were conducted with various counts on the bigram pair as the preliminary study, using 2, 4 and 6 as the bigram score (bscore) values. Table 3 shows the number of relevant sentences retrieved from the first phase (relevant documents retrieved) and after the similarity of sentences is evaluated with using bscore variations of 2 and 4. For each query, the percentage difference (p), is calculated on the number of documents retrieved after a bigram score (bscore) divided with the number of the relevant document (k) as follows.

$$p = \frac{\text{count}_{\text{bscore}}}{\text{count}_k} \tag{3}$$

As results, with a bscore value of 2, the same sentences as using keyword matching approach are retrieved. However, with a bscore value of 4, the system retrieved a smaller number of sentences on most queries, except for the second and sixth queries; *haji* (pilgrimage to Makkah) and *puasa* (fasting).

Table 3. The similarity score for every query

Query		No of retrieved relevant documents k	Results with bscore = 2 n	The difference in retrieved documents p (%)	Results with bscore = 4, n	The difference in retrieved documents, p (%)
1	*Dosa*	75	75	0	71	5
2	*Haji*	13	13	0	13	0
3	*Ilmu*	29	29	0	27	7
4	*Pahala*	47	45	4	45	7
5	*Perempuan*	62	62	0	61	2
6	*Puasa*	8	8	0	8	0
7	*Sedekah*	12	12	0	8	7
8	*Zakat*	22	22	0	21	2

This result shows that the bigram score can be used to eliminate some of the non-similar sentences from the extracted relevant sentences. When we continue the experiment with a higher score than 4, more queries are not affected by the increased score. Percentage of change remained unchanged for the previous two queries (*haji* and *puasa*), plus the fourth and seventh queries; *pahala* and *sedekah*. There is no change in retrieval results observed when bscore = 2 and bscore = 6 are used.

4.2   Evaluation of Similar Sentences

Results of experiments by using bscore = 2 and bscore = 4 for all eight queries are shown in Table 3. Those results (retrieved by myQRA) are compared to a list of similar sentences as perceived by three volunteers. Table 4 shows the number of sentences identified by the volunteers for each query.

Volunteers used an online application[3] and search for relevant sentences using the supplied 8 queries. Then, each volunteer read and evaluated the retrieved sentences and marked the sentences which they perceived as carrying similar information content. Only those sentences which were marked as similar by any two of the volunteers are chosen as identified similar sentences (iS). Each of the retrieved sentence from myQRA (shown in Table 3) and the manually identified sentences (iS) (shown in Table 4) are compared for correctness.

Table 4. Identified sentences for each query

Query		Number of similar sentences perceived by the user (iS)
1	*Dosa*	53
2	*Haji*	13
3	*Ilmu*	19
4	*Pahala*	38
5	*Perempuan*	50
6	*Puasa*	6
7	*Sedekah*	7
8	*Zakat*	15

For prototype testing purposes, the initial relevant documents are shown as a list of verses names, while all contents of the similar sentences are displayed to the user. Developed using the Python scripts, a prototype is developed and tested for the experiment. Figure 1 is the cropped display of the prototype with results from query *dosa*. A total of 75 sentences are extracted in the first module (left) while 71 sentences are extracted in the second module (right). In the second module, sentences are extracted when any pair scored a minimum bigram of 4 and presented to the user as retrieved similar sentences.

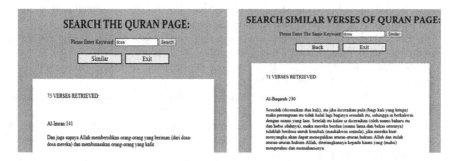

Fig. 1. The myQRA system layout using the mTSR model

From the evaluation, it is observed that a Quranic sentence is not only correctly retrieved but ranked using the bigram-based similarity score. As an example, for the first query (*dosa*), all 53 similar sentences identified by volunteers are retrieved, and the refine search ranked together another 18 sentences that are similar to the identified sentences (iS). The results proved that the system functionality to retrieve similar sentences without compromising the performance of the retrieval system.

5   Conclusion

The experiments show that the bigram score computed on paired sentences can be used to identify similar sentences from scattered chapters of the Quran. The scoring system with bigram similarity is then embedded into the myQRA prototype. Two modules are constructed and combined as a two-steps multi-term Similarity and Retrieval (mTSR) model. In module 1 (left), from a user's query, a list of relevant documents from a conventional keyword search was retrieved. In module 2 (right) the retrieved documents are further ranked using the multi-words similarity score constructed using a bigram language model. Finally, a refined list of relevant documents is retrieved as myQRA final results.

The next step to improve the results would be to re-group the results to either extract different clusters as stories from verses of the Quran or to eliminate some cluster for summarization purposes. Such results would ensure the high performance of the retrieval system can be extended to better usage that benefits users.

Acknowledgment. Special thanks to the members of the MuDIR Research Interest Group for their kind suggestion to improve this paper. The project is supported by Faculty of Computer and Mathematical Sciences, Universiti Teknologi MARA, Shah Alam, Selangor, Malaysia.

References

1. Corley, C., Mihalcea, R.: Measuring the semantic similarity of texts. In: Proceedings of the ACL Workshop on Empirical Modeling of Semantic Equivalence and Entailment, pp. 13–18. Association for Computational Linguistics, Ann Arbor (2005)
2. Islam, A., Inkpen, D.: Semantic text similarity using corpus-based word similarity and string similarity. ACM Trans. Knowl. Discov. Data 2(2), 1–25 (2008)
3. Isa, N., Puteh, M., Kamarudin, R.: Sentiment classification of Malay newspaper using immune network (SCIN), vol. 3 (2013)
4. Abd-Rashid, A., et al.: Word sense disambiguation using fuzzy semanticbased string similarity model. Malays. J. Comput. 3(2), 154–161 (2018)
5. Sazali, S.S., Bakar, Z.A. Jaafar, J.: Word prediction algorithm in resolving ambiguity in Malay text. In: 2016 3rd International Conference on Computing for Sustainable Global Development (INDIACom) (2016)
6. Groves, I., Tian, Y., Douratsos, I.: Treat the system like a human student: automatic naturalness evaluation of generated text without reference texts. In: Proceedings of the 11th International Conference on Natural Language Generation (2018)
7. Zulkefli, N.S.S., Rahman, N.A., Puteh, M.: A survey: framework of an information retrieval for Malay translated hadith document. In: MATEC Web Conference, vol. 135, p. 00073 (2017)
8. Ismail, R., Bakar, Z.A., Rahman, N.A.: Extracting knowledge from English translated Quran using NLP pattern. J. Teknol. 77(19) (2015)
9. AbuShareah, E., et al.: A hybrid approach for indexing and searching the holy Quran (2014)
10. AlMaayah, M., Sawalha, M., Abushariah, M.: A proposed model for Quranic Arabic WordNet. In: Brierley, C., Sawalha, M., Atwell, E. (eds.) LRA, pp. 9–13 (2014)
11. Adeleke, A., et al.: A two-step feature selection method for quranic text classification. Indones. J. Electr. Eng. Comput. Sci. 16(2), 730–736 (2019)

12. Ahmad, N., Bennett, B., Atwell, E.: Semantic-based ontology for Malay Qur'an reader. In: 4th International Conference on Islamic Applications in Computer Science and Technologies, Khartoum, Sudan (2016)
13. Ta'a, A., Abed, Q.A., Ahmad, M.: Al-Quran ontology based on knowledge themes. J. Fundam. Appl. Sci. **9**(5S), 800–817 (2018)
14. Trstenjak, B., Mikac, S., Donko, D.: KNN with TF-IDF based framework for text categorization. Proc. Eng. **69**, 1356–1364 (2014)
15. Sembok, T.M.T., Bakar, Z.A, Ahmad, F.: Experiments in Malay information retrieval. In: 2011 International Conference on Electrical Engineering and Informatics, 17–19 July 2011, Bandung, Indonesia (2011)
16. Husin, M.Z., Saad, S., Noah, S.A.M.: Syntactic rule-based approach for extracting concepts from quranic translation text. In: 2017 6th International Conference on Electrical Engineering and Informatics (ICEEI) (2017)
17. Bakar, Z.A., Rahman, N.A.: Evaluating the effectiveness of thesaurus and stemming methods in retrieving Malay translated Al-Quran documents. In: Sembok, T.M.T., Zaman, H.B., Chen, H., Urs, Shalini R., Myaeng, S.-H. (eds.) ICADL 2003. LNCS, vol. 2911, pp. 653–662. Springer, Heidelberg (2003). https://doi.org/10.1007/978-3-540-24594-0_67
18. Rahman, N.A., Bakar, Z., Sembok, T.: Query expansion using thesaurus in improving Malay Hadith retrieval system, vol. 3, 1404–1409 (2010)
19. Ahmad, N.D., Bennett, B., Atwell, E.: Retrieval performance for malay quran. Int. J. Islamic Appl. Comput. Sci. Technol. **5**(2), 13–25 (2017)
20. Kwee, A.T., Tsai, F.S., Tang, W.: Sentence-level novelty detection in English and Malay. In: Theeramunkong, T., Kijsirikul, B., Cercone, N., Ho, T.-B. (eds.) PAKDD 2009. LNCS (LNAI), vol. 5476, pp. 40–51. Springer, Heidelberg (2009). https://doi.org/10.1007/978-3-642-01307-2_7

Cyber Security and Digital Innovation for Society 5.0

Cyber Security Education Using Integrative Learning Module for an Optimum Learning Experience

Noor Afiza Mat Razali[1(✉)], Khairul Khalil Ishak[2],
Muhamad Aliff Irfan Muhamad Fadzli[1],
and Nurjannatul Jannah Aqilah M. Saad[1]

[1] National Defence University of Malaysia, Kuala Lumpur, Malaysia
noorafiza@upnm.edu.my
[2] Institute of Visual Informatics, Universiti Kebangsaan Malaysia,
Bangi, Selangor, Malaysia

Abstract. Since our world is getting more connected through information technology, home internet users, businesses, and the country's security and defences are prone to threats by cyber-attacks. Therefore, it is important to improve the nation's cyber security preparedness, increase public awareness of cyber security issues, and increase the number of trained cyber security specialists. For these reasons, cyber security education is essential in preparing computer users with the knowledge and skills that will significantly improve security and lower the risks related to the negative effect of digital ecosystems. To deliver an effective cyber security education, it is important to translate conceptual knowledge into practice and promote lifelong learning in cyber security. Scholars have proven that exposure to knowledge and practice is effective in eliminating the gaps between perceived concepts and actual knowledge. Thus, there is a need for a cyber security education system using an integrative learning module for an optimum learning experience from an early age. Therefore, this paper presents a student-centric hands-on system for learning about cyber security. The interactive system was developed based on the ADDIE model to provide lifelong cyber security education using an integrative learning module for an optimum learning experience for secondary students.

Keywords: Cyber security · Cyber security education · Cyber security online module · Integrative learning module · ADDIE model

1 Introduction

With the growth of cyber infrastructure and technological advances in modern society, secure computing and communicating have become critically important. The number of people being threatened by security issues has also increased. People have become more reliant on the Internet, with devices and people always connected. Although network communication makes life more convenient, it also exposes users to cyber security risks, such as malware, hacking, and phishing. Hacking cases are increasing,

© Springer Nature Switzerland AG 2019
H. Badioze Zaman et al. (Eds.): IVIC 2019, LNCS 11870, pp. 393–403, 2019.
https://doi.org/10.1007/978-3-030-34032-2_35

thus more cyber security experts are needed for countering any cyber-attack [1]. There is a high risk of on-going cyber-attacks without the users realising it that could expose organisations to worse cyber-attack. People, nowadays, communicate through the Internet wherever they are quite easily, which allows cyber attackers to easily steal information through anonymous hacking activities. Crucial national information could also become the target of a cyber-attack. Therefore, there is a need for skilled manpower that can stop the attackers from hacking the networks [2].

Cyber security education from an early stage, i.e., secondary school, is important to train students to become ethical Internet users. Students will learn more about cyber security education through cyber-security e-learning as a lifelong learning journey [3, 4]. In the future, more experts and skilled cyber security personnel will be needed to handle the country's critical infrastructure, such as the transportation system, water supply network, health services, agriculture, national defence sector, finance and banking, consulting, education, energy, and manufacturing sectors [5–8].

This paper presents a cyber-security education system that applies an integrative learning module for an optimum learning experience. This system was designed as a lifelong learning method. However, students' motivation and intention for using the proposed cyber security e-learning system should be increased. Therefore, the Motivation Design Methodology [9] was referred to when designing the proposed system. This study used the qualitative analysis method by interviewing experts in cyber security and students to develop this system.

2   Literature Review

The literature review was focused on cyber security education that could be utilised in teaching cyber security to secondary school students using an integrative learning module. Relevant articles and journals were scouted from Google Scholar through eight databases, namely, ACM Digital Library, Springer Link, Elsevier Science Direct, IEEE Xplore Digital Library, ProQuest, Emerald Insight, Taylor & Francis Online, and JSTOR. The keywords used for an enhanced data querying from each database included 'cyber security', 'cyber security education', 'integrative learning module', 'cyber security online module', 'authentication', and 'ADDIE model'. The initial search resulted in 180 related articles and journals on cyber security, integrative module, and learning methodology. A total of 40 articles and journals were chosen as references for this study. Each publication was evaluated based on the title, abstract, keywords, and methodology implemented, with a span of publication year from 2012. This is to ensure that all collected publications were up-to date and relevant for research implementation.

Effective cyber security education and training are important for preparing current and future IT professionals to properly and swiftly deal with real-life security incidents [10], as well as preventing them from unknowingly committing a cyber-attack. A cyber-attack could result in huge financial losses [11] or it could also target a nation's military and national defence system, with the intention of destroying national assets [12–14]. Cyber-attacks on computer systems continue to increase day by day.

Increasing cases of hacking activities have triggered a sudden demand in the job market for cyber security experts and this trend is expected to continue. More than one million job offers are estimated for cyber security expertise throughout the world [18]. Malaysia's National Cyber Security Agency aims to train ten thousand cyber security experts by 2020 [17]. Malaysian educators are beginning to realise the importance of exposure to cyber security knowledge to the students before they further their study at their chosen universities. Exposure to computer technology and cyber security skills will help students to manage their future career as cyber security personnel [4].

According to LeClair, cyber security training plans for the next generations of the cyber security workforce should be carefully developed so that students can see the importance of cyber security education. System and information security courses should be taught in an active learning environment that would enable students to apply the theories that they learned and practice using these lessons through practical enhancement. This method will expose the students to the basis of real cyber security technical requirements [19]. This active learning system offers an e-learning education that ultimately depends on the Internet in its execution, which epitomises computing systems and networks of the Internet generation [20–22].

Innovative educational technologies, such as e-learning, provide unprecedented opportunities for students, trainees, and educators to acquire, develop, and maintain core skills and essential knowledge [23]. The e-learning method could improve the quality of teaching and learning as it supports the face-to-face teaching approaches, and helps learners develop knowledge of using the latest technologies and the Internet [24]. Recent studies have shown that e-learning implementation is not simply a technological solution, but also a process with different factors, such as social factors [25] and individual factors. Salter found that e-learning is more effective in enhancing students' knowledge immediately after various topics and contexts have been taught [26].

Suri and Sharma [27] examined the relationship between students' disciplines and their responses and attitudes towards e-learning. The researchers used the computer and e-learning attitude scale by distributing survey questionnaires to 477 students enrolled in various courses across 6 major disciplines in Panjab University Chandigarh, India. The researchers found a significant relationship between the discipline of a student and his or her background on computer and e-learning usage. Moravec [20] showed how e-learning tools could impact students' achievement. Nearly 2,000 students participated in this study. Moravec [20] compared the results of law-related questions where the e-learning tool was provided in a pilot version, with the results of the same questions where the e-learning tool was not provided. The e-learning tool has definitely affected the students' results. Perrin [28] stated that e-learning systems could improve the communication between and among students, and between students and instructors.

3 Cyber Security Education Using Integrative Learning

Cyber security can be defined as the protection of cyberspace itself, the electronic information, the ICTs that support cyberspace, and the users in their personal, societal, and national capacity, including any of their interests, either tangible or intangible, that are vulnerable to attacks originating in cyberspace [29]. Knowledge comes from learning through education, discovery, experience, and experimentation. Cyber security education should be analysed to capture the essential ingredients that could assist in the development of the conceptual, practical, tactical, and soft skills of cyber security professionals [30]. Effective cyber security education and training are important for preparing current and future IT professionals to properly and swiftly deal with real life incidents. The current cyber security is of major concern among researchers and practitioners, dealing as it does with privacy, confidentiality, and user authentication [31], which need to be addressed to ensure a safer running of organisation systems with higher quality. It is clear that in cyber security, the asset that needs to be protected, extends beyond the boundaries of information, as defined in information security [29].

Integrative learning can be utilised to deliver learning, training, or education programmes using electronic means, such as computers, or other electronic devices [31]. Integrative learning can help learners recollect and apply information longer than other traditional learning situations. It can also be attributed to fostering the ability to make, recognise, and evaluate connections among disparate concepts, fields, or contexts among learners [30]. E-learning is a modern education system and a new method of learning that allows anyone to become a learner without the constraint of time and space. E-learning is an educational management system where the instructor and the learner are at a distance from each other [31]. According to Perrin [28], the adoption of e-learning in education, especially for higher educational institutions, has several benefits because e-learning is considered among the best methods of education. The process of creating an effective learning experience involves effective configuration of curriculum content and the quality of e-learning depends on how well the learning environment is designed and managed [32]. Wong reported that when users perceive e-learning to be useful in acquiring the desired skills and knowledge, they are more likely to use the system [33].

4   Motivation Design Methodology

As stated by Ramakrisnan [9], motivation should be effectively designed in the online discussion interface because the effectiveness of motivation is determined by autonomy, competence, and relatedness with an interface. The elements used to apply motivation in the interface play an important role. Therefore, based on the Motivation Design Methodology, this study proposes the cyber security learning system in five simple steps, as shown in Fig. 1.

4.1   Step 1: Identify Objective of Study

The objective of the study is to enhance students' knowledge on cyber security and its impact in this digital era. It is important to ensure that the students understand and are clear about the goals of learning about cyber security. This objective determines the scope of the modules for student motivational experiences.

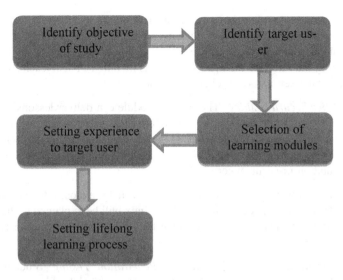

Fig. 1. Proposal of cyber security learning system based on motivation design methodology

4.2   Step 2: Identify Target User

To deliver the best learning experience, it is important to specify the target user. The target users for this learning method are secondary students, who are new to cyber security education. School students are the most addicted to social media and can easily be exposed to cybercrime [34] because cyber security training at schools is not enforced on students. Thus, this proposed system will focus on secondary students, who are studying the Science, Technology, Engineering, and Mathematics (STEM) education curriculum [4].

4.3   Step 3: Selection of Learning Modules

An interactive and understandable learning module is an important aspect of motivational experiences. The purpose for selecting the learning modules is to help educators ensure that they are teaching the appropriate materials to students. A few modules have been established as per student's cyber security learning requirement. We conducted interviews with experts and students to identify the suitable materials for our proposed learning module. Based on the interviews with the experts and students, the modules were developed as described in the following sections:

Module 1: Introduction to Cyber Security. This module is the first teaching process for the target users. It explains the meaning of cyber security and security threats in a computing environment. Students will be exposed to the necessity of cyber security and the type of sensitive data that need to be protected by each person. The cyber security triad, namely, confidentiality, integrity, and availability, can be explained to students as the main elements of cyber security. This module emphasises on the mechanism and the importance of cyber security in our life, with a mix of theory and practical learning.

This module can also explain how cyber security works and how cyber-attacks are launched. This module can expose students to the basic terminology of networks, where several ports, which are usually used in launching cyber-attacks, are located and thus, threatening the safety of the cyberspace. This module can also teach students how to differentiate between a good hacker and a bad hacker.

Module 2: Cyber Security Ethics. The second module can deliver lessons on ethics in cyberspace. Ethics is a moral principle that governs a person's behaviour. Thus, this is an important aspect for students when using social media and online surfing. Students will be introduced to the code of ethics and organisation that focus on the development and implementation of security certification.

Module 3: Introduction to Kali Linux. Students will be exposed to the Kali Linux operating system. The basic commands of Kali Linux will be explained to the students. This module teaches students how to execute the basic commands in the Kali Linux platform.

Module 4: Introduction to Ethical Hacking/Penetration Testing. Students will be exposed to the basic techniques on how to conduct ethical hacking or penetration testing in the networking environment. This module allows students to execute several commands provided by the instructor in the Kali Linux platform to launch the Basic Penetration Testing on the VMware provided. Through this module, students can better understand how to apply the Basic Penetration Testing phase step by step and can differentiate between malicious hacking and penetration testing. This module fully demands hands-on participation from students as they need to complete a series of game-environment hacking processes.

Module 5: Introduction to Digital Forensic. Students will be exposed to the basic knowledge of digital forensics and how to use the processed data in an event investigation. Next, the students will be introduced to tools that can be used in analysing any malicious hacking activity, or crime committed by criminals. From this module, students will learn how to retrieve any document, or file that can be used as evidence to the criminal activity and know that online data will remain there forever. This module can incite fear of cyber-crimes among the students and prevent them from committing any malicious hacking, either intentionally or unintentionally. The tools that will be introduced to the students are EnCase and Tableau for computer-based, and XRY and Cellebrite for mobile-based devices.

Module 6: Career as a Cyber Security Expert. In this module, students will be exposed to career development as a cyber security expert. It is important to educate and enhance students' knowledge on basic elements of cyber-security since secondary school. By exposing students to the field of cyber-security, students would be inclined to choose cyber-security courses in university. They will be more confident in choosing cyber-security as their main choice of study. In the future, a lot of experts and skilled cyber-security personnel would be needed to handle existing cyber-attacks in various sectors. This will answer future demand for skilled and professional cyber security personnel.

4.4   Step 4: Setting the Right Learning Experience for Target Users

Students will be encouraged to play online quizzes to increase motivation. Students can also perform simple hacking tests using the Kali Linux environment to motivate their learning process and to learn how to get along with their friends to solve the test. By including the right type of learning experience, students will continuously maintain their interest in cyber-security.

4.5   Step 5: Setting Lifelong Learning Process

A lifelong learning process should be considered to enhance students' motivation. The lifelong learning process comes with an online learning system. The cyber-security e-learning system was developed as a platform for students to further their knowledge in cyber-security and as an approach to minimise cyber-security risks and threats among secondary students. The ADDIE model is a process of instructional system designs developed by Seel and Glasgow [35] as an instructional learning methodology to develop a curriculum for students. This model takes the initial letter from each of the five components, namely, analysis, design, development, implementation, and evaluation. Figure 2 shows the cycle of the ADDIE model.

Fig. 2. ADDIE model

Phase 1: Analysis. The first phase in ADDIE is analysis, which involves training needs and training plans. It is important to focus on the target audience. Thus, our target is secondary students who have no experience in exploring and learning about cyber-security. In this phase, instructors will try to distinguish between what the students already know and what they should know after completing the training. The factors and elements required for an effective online collaborative learning will also be determined in this phase [36]. We use this phase to gather more information regarding the knowledge and skills the learners need to attain and what needs to be taught to accomplish cyber-security training.

Phase 2: Design. The second phase is where the design of the system is created to be more interactive to attract students. This includes choosing the optimal methods of instruction and creating useful, action-oriented learning objectives to guide the learning process [37]. Graphics and visualisation are a key part of an interactive system. The system has a very user-friendly graphical user interface (GUI). The main window has an interactive design and all the information about the instructors of the system. Interactive design is about the study of user-friendliness and effectiveness of a product. It is committed to understanding the expectations of target users and their potential behaviours and expectations when they use a product [23]. The system consists of elements that are visible to attract users. Even interfaces that are easy to use may require learning, and the more a user uses them the easier it seems.

Phase 3: Development. The development phase consists of developing the system using the Laravel framework. Laravel keeps this process standardised, and it can process non-business logic relationships automatically, allowing programmers to focus on the implementation of business logic [38]. While developing a secure e-Learning system, security authentication needs to be implemented. According to Parikshit, authentication is an identity establishment between communicating parties [39]. Authentication plays an important role in protecting resources against unauthorised use [39]. Authentication and access control are important aspects for establishing secure communications between multiple devices and services. This system has two main users, which are the admin and the students. Hence, the concept of least-privilege of each user role is crucial to maintain data protection and security. This concept restricts the user from accessing data based on the authorisation level. As an example, the admin can access all data related to the students, and create modules and exercises, but students can only view the notes and answer the exercises given. This system consists of the Kali Linux environment, the same as the virtual machine, to make it more interesting to learn and can motivate students' experience.

Phase 4: Implementation. The implementation phase involves effectively delivering the system to the students. A student has to register by clicking the sign-up button before he or she can log into the system. A user can register using his first name, last name, and all the personal details, including an image. Once the student has selected the image, it is displayed in the window for the user to verify when login into the system. Each user login will be authenticated by a different role set in the database. Only authenticated and authorised users can view the existing functions. These functions are all related to the data stored in a database for identifying authorised users, where the selected security credential will return an appropriate object based on security credential. If the identification number and password match the ones stored in the system, then the user is authenticated. Before a student can be authenticated to the system, he or she has to be registered with the system for the first time. This step is called registration. So, for a new user, the student has to register to the system and then, get authenticated before he or she can access it.

Phase 5: Evaluation. The evaluation phase is focused on meeting the goals of the training. In this phase, cyber security education questionnaire will be given to the students to collect feedbacks on every aspect of the course. Based on students' feedbacks, improvement can be done for the content for future cyber security training.

5   Conclusion

Cyber security education needs to emphasise an interdisciplinary approach for learners to think critically and draw connections from disparate disciplines. The need for cyber security education and training as a pervasive element in computing and other related programs is recognised as being an excellent method of building awareness in students. The evolving and dynamic nature of cyber security also requires strong connections with the industry to develop a competent workforce. We find integrative learning approaches to be an effective framework to develop cyber security programmes. The integrative learning approach utilises interdisciplinary approaches and is focused on the application of real-world scenarios. In addition, integrative learning approaches support the development of a community of learners. A holistic approach that emphasises on curriculum, experiential learning, assessment, and community of practice is essential to cyber-security. It motivates students to interact with each other by exchanging and respecting different points of view. It also eases communication and improves relationships that could sustain lifelong learning. Based on the proposed system design in this study, a prototype will be developed and validation of the prototype will be done using the qualitative analysis. Further enhancement of the proposed system will be done based on the validation results.

Acknowledgements. This work was financially supported by the Ministry of Education, Malaysia under KTP grant KTP: LL (R2) – CS/1 (UPNM-17).

References

1. Choo, K.K.R.: The cyber threat landscape: challenges and future research directions. Comput. Secur. **30**(8), 719–731 (2011)
2. Harib, A.R.H., Sarijan, S., Hussin, N.: Information security challenges: a malaysian context. Int. J. Acad. Res. Bus. Soc. Sci. **7**(9), 397–403 (2017)
3. Dutta, S., Mathur, R.: Cybersecurity - an integral part of STEM. In: IEEE 2nd Integrated STEM Education Conference, ISEC (2012)
4. Turner, G.E., Deemer, E.D., Tims, H.E., Corbett, K., Mhire, J.: Cyber value and interest development: assessment of a STEM career intervention for high school students. Electron. J. Sci. Educ. **18**(1), 1–15 (2014)
5. Flatt, H., Schriegel, S.: Analysis of the cyber-security of industry 4.0 technologies based on RAMI 4.0 and identification of requirements. In: 2016 IEEE 21st International Conference on Emerging Technologies and Factory Automation (ETFA), pp. 1–4. IEEE (2016)
6. Conteh, N.Y., Schmick, P.J.: Cybersecurity: risks, vulnerabilities and countermeasures to prevent social engineering attacks. Int. J. Adv. Comput. Res. **6**(23), 31–38 (2016)
7. Carr, M.: Public-private partnerships in national cyber-security strategies. Int. Aff. **1**, 190–209 (2016)
8. Jidiga, G.R., Sammulal, P.: The need of awareness in cyber security with a case study. In: 2013 4th International Conference on Computing, Communications and Networking Technologies, ICCCNT (2013)

9. Ramakrisnan, P., Jaafar, A.: Motivation design methodology for online knowledge sharing interface. In: Badioze Zaman, H., et al. (eds.) Advances in Visual Informatics. IVIC 2017. LNCS, vol. 10645, pp. 224–232. Springer, Cham (2017). https://doi.org/10.1007/978-3-319-70010-6_21

10. Beuran, R., Chinen, K., Tan, Y., Shinoda, Y.: Towards effective cybersecurity education and training. Sch. Inf. Sci. Japan Adv. Inst. Sci. Technol. (April), 1–16 (2016)

11. Kosseff, J.: Defining cyber-security. Iowa Law Rev. **103**(3), 985–1031 (2018)

12. Bogdanoski, M., Peterski, D.: Cyber terrorism – global security threat. Int. Sci. Defence Secur. Peace J. **13**, 59–72 (2013)

13. Goolsby, R., Shanley, L., Lovell, A.: On cybersecurity, crowdsourcing, and social cyber-attack. Office of Naval Research, Arlington, VA (2013)

14. Lu, Y., Da Xu, L.: Internet of things (IoT) cybersecurity research: a review of current research topics. IEEE Internet Things J. **4662**(C), 1 (2018)

15. Pescatore, J.: Securing the internet of things survey. SANS Inst. (2014)

16. Grabosky, P.: Organised crime and the internet. RUSI J. **158**(5), 18–25 (2013)

17. Muniandy, L., Muniandy, B.: State of cyber security and the factors governing its protection in Malaysia. Int. J. Appl. Sci. Technol. **2**(4), 106–112 (2012)

18. Kumar, A.: Malaysia's cyber warfare training targets 10,000 security professionals by 2020 (2016). https://www.mis-asia.com/tech/security/malaysias-cyber-warfare-training-targets-10000-security-professionals-by-2020/. Accessed: 06 Aug 2018

19. LeClair, J., Abraham, S., Shih, L.: An interdisciplinary approach to educating an effective cyber security workforce. Proceedings 2013 InfoSecCD 2013: Information Security Curriculum Development Conference - InfoSecCD 2013, pp. 71–78 (2013)

20. Moravec, T., Štěpánek, P., Valenta, P.: The influence of using e-learning tools on the results of students at the tests. Proc. - Soc. Behav. Sci. **176**, 81–86 (2015)

21. Cheung, R., Cohen, J., Lo, H., Elia, F.: Challenge based learning in cybersecurity education. In: Proceedings of International Conference on Security Management (2011)

22. McCrohan, K.F., Engel, K., Harvey, J.W.: Influence of awareness and training on cyber security. J. Internet Commer. **9**(1), 23–41 (2010)

23. Ning, W.: The key features and applications of newmedia interactive design. In: Proceedings of 2014 IEEE International Conference on Ubiquitous Intelligence and Computing, 2014 IEEE International Conference on Autonomic and Trusted Computing, 2014 IEEE International Conference on Scalable Computing and Communications and Its Associated System, pp. 727–731 (2014)

24. Kattoua, T., Al-Lozi, M., Alrowwad, A.: A review of literature on knowledge management using ICT in higher education. Int. J. Computer Technol. Appl. **7**(5), 754–762 (2016)

25. Tarhini, A., Hone, K., Liu, X.: Measuring the moderating effect of gender and age on e-learning acceptance in England: a structural equation modeling approach for an extended technology acceptance model. J. Educ. Comput. Res. **51**(2), 163–184 (2014)

26. Salter, S.M., Karia, A., Sanfilippo, F.M., Clifford, R.M.: Effectiveness of E-learning in pharmacy education. Am. J. Pharm. Educ. **78**(4), 16–22 (2014)

27. Suri, G., Navkiran, Kaur, G., Sharma, S.: Factors influencing e-learning among university students. Int. J. Mark. Bus. Commun. **5**(1) (2016)

28. Perrin, D.G., Perrin, E., Muirhead, B.: Advantages and disadvantages of adopting e-learning in higher education. Int. J. Instr. Technol. Distance Learn. **12**(1), 29–33 (2015)

29. Von Solms, R., Van Niekerk, J.: From information security to cyber security. Comput. Secur. **38**, 97–102 (2013)

30. Abraham, S., Shih, L.: Towards an integrative learning approach in cybersecurity education, vol. 2, no. 2, p. 1 (2016)

31. Rjaibi, N., Rabai, L., Aissa, A., Louadi, M.: Cyber security measurement in depth for e-learning systems. Int. J. Adv. Res. Comput. Sci. Softw. Eng. **2**(11), 1–15 (2012)
32. Martínez-Caro, E., Cegarra-Navarro, J.G., Cepeda-Carrión, G.: An application of the performance-evaluation model for e-learning quality in higher education. Total Qual. Manag. Bus. Excell. **26**(5–6), 632–647 (2015)
33. Cheok, M.L., Wong, S.L.: Predictors of e-learning satisfaction in teaching and learning for school teachers: a literature review. Int. J. Instr. **8**(1), 75–90 (2016)
34. LeFebvre, R.: The human element in cyber security: a study on student motivation to act. In: Proceedings of 2012 Information Security Curriculum Development Conference (Infosec Cd 2012), pp. 1–8 (2012)
35. Wiphasith, H., Narumol, R., Sumalee, C.: the design of the contents of an e-learning for teaching M.5 English language using ADDIE model. Int. J. Inf. Educ. Technol. **6**(2), 127–131 (2014)
36. Nadiyah, R.S., Faaizah, S.: The development of online project based collaborative learning using ADDIE model. Proc. - Soc. Behav. Sci. **195**, 1803–1812 (2015)
37. Cheung, L.: Using the ADDIE model of instructional design to teach chest radiograph interpretation. J. Biomed. Educ. **2016**, 1–6 (2016)
38. He, R.Y.: Design and implementation of web based on laravel framework. In: ICCSET 2014, pp. 301–304 (2015)
39. Mahalle, P.N., Anggorojati, B., Prasad, N.R., Prasad, R.: Identity authentication and capability based access control (IACAC) for the internet of things. J. Cyber Secur. Mobil. **1**, 309–348 (2013)

CMBlock: In-Browser Detection and Prevention Cryptojacking Tool Using Blacklist and Behavior-Based Detection Method

Muhammad Amirrudin Razali and Shafiza Mohd Shariff[(✉)]

Malaysian Institute of Information Technology, Universiti Kuala Lumpur,
Kuala Lumpur, Malaysia
amirrudinrazali96@gmail.com, shafiza@unikl.edu.my

Abstract. As cryptocurrency fast becoming a popular digital currency, implementation of mining script in browser-based JavaScript has become a worthwhile alternative to the traditional way of mining cryptocurrency. Based on this implementation, a new form of threat, widely called cryptojacking, has become popular on the web. A website that has been affected by cryptojacking abuses its visitor's computing resources to mine cryptocurrency without the machine owner's consent. This paper introduces CMBlock, a web extension for browser we have developed that can detect mining script that runs in the website. This application will be using two different kinds of approach: mining behaviour and blacklist detection technique to mitigate the cryptojacking attack. By implementing the mining behaviour detection, the application is capable of detecting unknown domain that not been listed in the blacklist. This application would be an enhancement of current countermeasure in mitigating the crypto-jacking attack.

Keywords: Cryptojacking detection · Blacklist · Mining behaviour

1 Introduction

A Cryptocurrency is a peer-to-peer digital exchange system in which cryptography is used to generate and distribute currency units. Cryptocurrency process requires distributed verification of transactions without a central authority. Transaction verification will confirm transaction amounts so that payer would not spend twice while spending the currency unit. This verification process is called mining (Mukhopadhyay et al. 2016).

According to Hari et al. (2015), mining is the essential procedure wherein generation, transmission and validation of cryptocurrency are finished. Cryptocurrency guarantees steady, secure and safe propagation of the currency from the payer to payee. Dissimilar to a common currency, where a centralised authority controls and regulate the transaction, digital currencies are decentralised and perform on a peer-to-peer system. Banks that produce physical currency and monitor the transactions require a huge framework to work, function and operate. Cryptocurrencies overcome this need

© Springer Nature Switzerland AG 2019
H. Badioze Zaman et al. (Eds.): IVIC 2019, LNCS 11870, pp. 404–414, 2019.
https://doi.org/10.1007/978-3-030-34032-2_36

by implementing a mining framework where individuals in the framework, called 'miners' or 'nodes', monitor and approve exchanges which creates cash.

Thanks to the decentralised mechanism offer by cryptocurrency, it is now favoured by many industries. Many cryptocurrencies have emerged, such as Bitcoin, Ethereum and Monero. Price of the cryptocurrency has increased since it is getting popular to the world. Huge profits of cryptocurrencies have attracted more hackers to target cryptocurrencies and use various means to implant mining programs in the victims' machine for profit as stated by Liu et al. (2018). Due to the popularity and anonymity features, cybercriminals tend to favour cryptocurrency because they offer a certain level of concealment and can be easily monetised for criminal activity.

This interest has increased in recent years, stemming so much on the far side the need to efficiently use cryptocurrencies as a technique of payment for illicit tools and services. Several actors have conjointly tried to make the most the growing popularity of cryptocurrencies, and sequent rising worth, by conducting various operations aimed toward them. These operations embrace malicious cryptocurrency mining (also known as cryptojacking), the gathering of cryptocurrency wallet credentials, extortion activity, and therefore the targeting of cryptocurrency exchanges (Randi et al. 2018).

Browser-based cryptojacking is growing fast after ransomware trends declining. Cryptojacking works off a user's browser or can be inserted into popular websites, that will then use resources from a user's PC using their browser. Attacker insert low-risk malware by targeting individual computers or take the simpler and more popular route of embedding such malware on large online portals. So far, the simplest and most accessible form of countermeasure for cryptojacking is to install a browser extension that immediately detects and blocks cryptojacking attempts. An example of such a browser extension would be NoCoin, which is a very popular cryptomining malware blocker for Google Chrome. However, the normal browser extensions use the blacklist method only which only the registered or known website will be blocked.

In this work, we propose an application browser extension named as CMBlock that uses two different approaches to block the mining script. The first approach would be a blacklisting method, which is blocking requests/scripts loaded from a blacklist. Blacklist has been traditionally deployed as a key element for any anti-virus and security software suites. Its emphasis on "known" script that already known or developed. Against unknown kind of threat approach, blacklisting approach alone would not be sufficing to prevent the attack. Therefore, we propose to combine the blacklist method with a second method, a mining behaviour detection technique which is detecting potential mining behaviour inside the loaded script that been utilised in pages. Behaviour-based scan for deviations from the standard and has the intelligence to choose whether an anomaly represents a risk or can be ignored. By utilising this method, any new or obscure content that been used in a certain website can be distinguished and keep it from running.

CMBlock is capable of detecting and preventing any mining script from running through user website from cryptojacking attack that will be using user's hardware resources and to prevent any additional threat to the user system. The application will be deployed as a browser extension which can be installed through the browser without needed extra knowledge to handle it. Plus, it does not require additional cost to implement it.

2   Related Work

The review will start with the definition of cryptocurrency and types of it. Then proceed with the crime related to cryptocurrency and finally, the discussion about cryptojacking's current countermeasure and proposed technique.

2.1   Cryptocurrency

A cryptocurrency is a digital or virtual currency designed to work as a medium of exchanges. Dev (2014) also define, in his paper, that cryptocurrency is digital medium exchanges which involves a decentralised network of mutually distrustful parties. The "crypto" part comes from the use of the cryptography technique for verification and security purposes during transactions. According to Houben and Snyers (2018), cryptography is the technique of protecting information by encrypting it into an unreadable format that can only be decrypted by an authorised person who possesses a secret key. Cryptocurrencies such as Bitcoin, are secured via this technique using a unique system of public and private digital keys. Below are the types of cryptocurrency:

Bitcoin. The first cryptocurrency to appear was Bitcoin (BTC), built on the SHA-256 algorithm. This virtual commodity was conceptualised in a whitepaper written in 2009 by a pseudonymous author who went by the name "Satoshi Nakamoto". Bitcoin is currently the most reputable of all cryptocurrency, as it is the oldest, and has been the subject of mainstream media coverage due to rapid market fluctuations and an innovative technical concept (Ahamad et al. 2013).

Litecoin. According to Ahamad et al. (2013), Litecoin (LTC) can be viewed as the 'silver standard' of digital money, as it has been the second most adopted cryptocurrency by miner and trader. The total amount of Litecoin that is accessible for mining and circulation is four times the amount of Bitcoin, which means there will be fourfold the amount of Litecoin available to Bitcoin.

Other Coins. These coins are based on either Bitcoin or Litecoin, meaning the coin make utilisation of SHA-256 or Scrypt encryption algorithms and feature their unique properties. Names of different alternative cryptocurrency range from memorable (Monero, Zcash) to comical (Feathercoin, Terracoin, P2PCoin, BitBar, ChinaCoin, BBQCoin). The profitability of mining and trading altcoin varies daily.

2.2   Crime Related to Cryptocurrency

Cryptocurrency has become the currency of choice for a cybercriminal. Its distinctive characteristics of decentralisation and pseudo-anonymity are also attractive to criminals in general. These criminals value privacy, anonymity, and money, not necessarily in that order, and cryptocurrencies can offer all of those to varying degrees. Recently in 2017, there is an attack related to the use of cryptocurrency, which is known as WannaCry ransomware. According to Paquet-Clouston et al. (2019), WannaCry ransomware infected up to 300,000 victims over 150 countries where the objective of this attack is to extorting money from the victim and demand payment in bitcoin, which is the most famous cryptocurrency. The high amount of cryptocurrency use for crime is because of the rise in value. Even though the cryptocurrency market value has decreased for the first quarter of 2018, but still the value higher compared to the last year. The desire to have these cryptocurrencies has led to the use of illegal ventures.

2.3   Cryptojacking

The prevalence of cryptocurrency has kept on growing over the past decade, and this has attracted attention to cybercriminals. Cybercriminals are presently utilising any way to gain cryptocurrency for their profit. One of the examples is cryptojacking. Cryptojacking is unauthorised use of computational resource to mining cryptocurrency without the consent of the target device's owner. Conventional cryptojacking required user interaction to enable mining software to run on their device. Usually, the cybercriminal would trick the user into downloading their mining software and mine cryptocurrency using their system. However, this conventional cryptojacking proved impracticable for several reasons. Firstly, antivirus installed in the owner's device can easily detect the malicious application use for cryptojacking that run in the system. Secondly, it required user consent whereby the user enable mistakenly installing the cryptojacking application to run on their system (Saad et al. 2018).

A new form of cryptojacking which is using a web browser is more practicable than convenient cryptojacking. In-browser cryptojacking does not require the user to install the mining application or consent to run it on the system. According to Hong et al. (2018), in-browser cryptojacking is where malicious adversaries were utilising web user's CPU resources to mining cryptocurrency by injecting malicious payloads into the compromised websites. This new form of cryptojacking can easily bypass antivirus by hiding in the browser's process, which makes it undetectable. However, the user might be noticing their system performance going slow if they have been infected by in-browsing cryptojacking.

Initially, the in-browser cryptojacking was intended for good use as an alternative way to replace online advertisement. In-browser cryptojacking was made easy by online services such as Coinhive which is provide the cryptojacking template to be implemented in the website owner who would wish to replace annoying online advertisement for their visitor to make income. However, cybercriminal saw this opportunity by exploiting it to mine cryptocurrency illegally.

2.4   Current Countermeasure Technique

The in-browser cryptojacking tool is fairly new. Therefore, there is less attention has been paid to its utilisation, impact and countermeasure. On the browser, current countermeasure includes web extension such as NoCoin and AdBlock plus. Each of these web extensions contains a list of URLs which is known as uniform resource locator to block a website that contains script while surfing. If the user visits a website that already blacklisted by the extension, the user will be notified regarding cryptojacking. Additional information related to current countermeasure, especially as a web extension tool is shown in Table 1.

Table 1. Web extension

Features/Logo			
Name	No Coin	AdBlock plus	Malware bytes
Type	Web Extension	Web Extension	Anti-Malware
Detection method	Blacklist domain	Blacklist domain	Blacklist, Signature and heuristic approach
Domain blacklist	cryptoloot.com, cryptoloot.pro	Coinhive.com, Authedmine.com	Coinhive.com
Cost	Free	Free	39.99 per year subscription
Platform support	Chrome, Mozilla, Opera	Chrome, Mozilla, Opera, Safari, Edge, Explorer	Windows, Mac, Android, IOS

However, there is an issue with the current countermeasure technique, which is the blacklist method on web extension. An attacker could easily evade the web extension that only uses the blacklist method. According to Saad et al. (2018), this blacklisting method is not an effective technique for the countermeasure to in-browser crypto-jacking because of an adaptive attacker can always avoid detection by recreating new URL that is not found in the public list of blacklisted URLs that been used in web extension. In this paper, to counter cryptojacking, we introduce additional technique combining with current countermeasure technique, which is utilising traditional approach blacklisting and detection for potential mining behaviour inside the loaded cryptojacking script.

This additional technique will detect potential mining behaviour inside the loaded script on the website. The detection method will also intercept the cryptomining inline script where the attacker embedded the script inside HTML (known as Hypertext Markup Language for creating web pages and web application) to run the in-browser cryptomining. Also, it intercepts cryptomining script that runs on the proxy network where the proxy network is a dedicated server that acts as an intermediary between two communicating parties, the client and services. According to Wang and Wang (2015), behavioural detection scheme has been used to detect new malware and proved its capabilities to detect new threat along with signature detection. This potential mining behaviour is more efficient than blacklisting because the attacker implements the script with a proxy network an embedded into the inline script that makes it undetectable through blacklisting technique.

3 Methodology

This section describes the methodology that has been using to develop this tool, which is now known as CMBlock. This section shows how the project is fully developed, starting from the first step, such as data collection to the final touch of the project. The understandings of all the activity and process that involve in the development of this project will help to build a good project.

3.1 Development Phase

The CMBlock application is created using react, including user interface based on the google chrome platform as different platform required different application programming interface (API). The user interface will show if the cryptomining script is blocked whenever the user visits the website. In this phase also is where the program is tested. The application is tested to ensure that user interface implemented work and application function working on the intended platform. Figure 1 shows the application interface, architecture and application design flow chart for this project. It consists of an icon of the application that will be located at the right top of the interface. Next is a display for status to show to the user that block miner status is blocked if the website consists of cryptojacking miner script. Below the display, there will be two buttons. The first button is an enable and disable button, while the second button is the 'About' button, describing CMBlock.

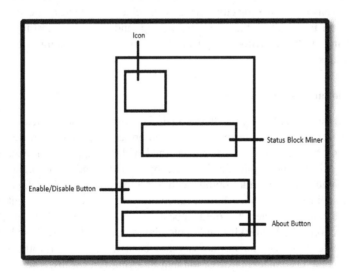

Fig. 1. CMBlock application interface

CMBlock will be installed on the web browser. Whenever the user visited a website that has implemented the script with the domain listed in the blacklist, it would stop the mining process automatically. The element that been used in the blacklist method was the URL pattern with the name of JavaScript mining. For example, like this *://*/ *deepMiner.js where the *://*/* is the URL and deepMiner.js is the JavaScript name. The filter list that been used in this project is from NoCoin web extension where this application is also aiming to block coin miner. However, NoCoin application only works with blacklisting function. The filter list is available through GitHub platform and is available for everyone to use it for their purposes.

Otherwise, it will go to the potential mining behaviour script process to detect it. The potential mining script behaviour works on loaded scripts implemented on the website. This method can detect mining script that has various attributes such as the mining script run through proxies, having a unique domain name or even different way to start the mining process that runs through the inline script of the website. For example, when the mining script consists of the signature behaviour attribute such as *&&typeof this (anyname)* where it can be the function, string, number or undefined text, it will trigger the event to stop and nullified the line. If there is a potential mining script, it will kill the process and end. If there is none, it will straight away end the detection process.

4   Testings and Results

The test results are described in this section. To check whether the actual results match the expected results, software development testing in a project is compulsory. Testing will be done after application implementation to make sure the application works. This testing also to ensure all the objectives have been achieved. The testing consists of two types of testing. First will be the functional testing, and the second testing will be the security testing of the CMBlock application. Results of the testing will be briefly explained in this section.

4.1   Functional Testing

Based on this functional testing result, the analysis shows that the application has been working according to the design specification and project objectives. This test involves primarily black box testing and is not concerned with the application's source code. Each functionality of the application is tested by providing adequate input, verifying output and comparing the actual output with expected outcomes. The functional test starts with enabling and disabling button function; next will be about the buttons, then the status indicator, whether it would appear or not, and lastly the detecting and blocking functions, both blacklist and potential mining behaviour-based detection technique. Table 2 shows that the activity has been done with the outcome, while Table 3 shows the cryptojacking detection and blocking test results. The tool that has been chosen to find the cryptojacking website is PublicWWW. PublicWWW is a search engine that indexes the full source code of the website.

Table 2. CMBlock functional test

No	Test case	Expected result	Result
1	Disable application	Stop the application from running	Successful
2	Enable application	Run the application	Successful
3	About button	Redirected to about page	Successful
4	Status display indicate blocked miner	The display will show blocked miners in whenever a user visits a website that contains crypto miners	Successful
5	Blacklist filter function	The blacklist method would stop the cryptomining process in the website that listed in the filter	Successful

For this project, seven websites infected with cryptojacking and two clean websites have been used to test the detection and blocking process of this application. Five of the websites that have been tested do not require user consent. This type of mining script is most preferred by the attacker because their objective is to steal computing resources to mine cryptocurrency and can be found easily for the testing purpose. The other 2 of the websites requires user consent. This type of mining script usually been used by web administrator to replace advertisement on their website to generate income. This type of mining script will pop up a message to let the user know if they want to donate their resources while browsing the website. The last 2 websites do not contain any mining script. This testing is to ensure that the application would not give any false alarm result.

4.2   Security Testing

For this application, security testing was done by going through source code analysis. The testing was done by using CRXcavator by Duo testing company. CRXcavator is an automatic scanner for chrome extension and produces a quantified risk score based on several factors. These factors include permissions, the inclusion of vulnerable third-

Table 3. Testing for detection and blocking process

No	Domain	Blocking method	Result
	Does not required user consent		
1	http://seriesdanko.to/	Blacklist	Successful
2	http://360eye.cc/indexen.html	Blacklist	Successful
3	http://portaliz.info/	Blacklist	Unsuccessful
4	https://proxtpb.art	Potential mining Behavior	Successful
5	http://sabiduriayciencia.com/	Potential mining behavior	Successful
	Required user consent		
6	https://www.thehopepage.org/	Blacklist	Successful
7	https://authedmine.com/	Blacklist	Unsuccessful
8	https://www.unikl.edu.my/ (clean website)	Both	No false alarm given
9	https://www.facebook.com/ (clean website)	Both	No false alarm given

party JavaScript libraries, weak content security policies and more. Figure 2 shows the results for source code analysis by using CRXcavator. The result shows that this application contains two critical, one medium, two low and one none for the risk assessment by CRXcavator.

Permissions		
Permission	Description	Risk
<all_urls>	Matches any URL that uses a permitted scheme.	Critical
webRequest	Gives your extension access to the chrome.webRequest API.	Critical
storage	Gives your extension access to the chrome.storage API.	Medium
webRequestBlocking	Required if the extension uses the chrome.webRequest API in a blocking fashion.	Low
activeTab	Requests that the extension be granted permissions according to the activeTab specification.	Low
unlimitedStorage	Provides an unlimited quota for storing HTML5 client-side data, such as databases and local storage files. Without this permission, the extension or app is limited to 5 MB of local storage.	None

Fig. 2. CMBlock result for source code security analysis using CRXcavator

5 Discussion

Based on the results obtained in Sect. 4, a discussion of the finding is presented in this section. The result from the testing meets the objective of this application as a cryptojacking detector tool. As for the method used, blacklisting and potential mining behaviour, the results shown in Table 3 positively confirm that the methods proposed for detecting cryptojacking using the in-browser tool are fitting for a cryptojacking security threat. Although the test on different domain consists of the successful and unsuccessful result, we assume this is due to some of the domain that contains cryptojacking mining script already patched by their web administrator by removing it, thus leading to the unsuccessful result. In some cases, other domains infected by cryptojacking is already being taken down, such as an official webpage that provides cryptomining, Coinhive. However, those websites that still infected by cryptojacking is successfully detected and stop by the application that been proposed in this paper.

As for the result of security testing shown, in Fig. 2, the result of the risk assessment level shows that CMBlock contains 2 critical, 1 medium, and 2 low-risk levels. As for the critical risk, it is because of permission <all_urls> and webRequest API. <all_urls> is required for the application to access any website that the user visited. If this permission is disabled, the application would not be able to run on the website that the user visited. The webRequest which that gives the extension access to the chrome. webRequest API where this permission will allow to intercept, block and modify a request coming from the website. As for the webRequest API is required to cancel request to known domain. This permission also required for this application to run properly for the detection of crypto mining script. These two permissions are required as an interception mechanism to cancel request to a known domain.

The one medium risk is from storage permission, which is described as to gives the extension application access to the chrome storage API where the function is to store, retrieve, and track changes to user data. As for storage permission, it is required to be declared for the media type and is strictly validated by chrome. The two low risks are coming from permission webRequestBlocking and activeTab. WebRequestBlocking permission is the permission that required if the extension application uses the chrome. webRequest API in a blocking fashion. This permission is used for the blacklisting method to block the domain that been specified in blacklist filter.

The active tab is permission that request extension application to be granted permission according to the active tab specification. This active tab permission gives an extension temporary access to the currently active tab when a user invokes the extension, example, by clicking its browser. Access to the tab lasts while the user is on that page, and is revoked when the user navigates away or closes the tab. To conclude, some function of the application may come with risk, however, as it is required in order for the application to run smoothly without an error.

6 Conclusion and Recommendation

In this project, we study the occurrence of cryptojacking. Detecting miners utilising blacklists, known domain alone is an ineffective strategy because cryptojacking are actively using obfuscation to evade detection. Instead of the current inadequate measures, this project proposed a detection and prevention application that is using the combination of the blacklist and behaviour-based detection method to mitigate the threat of cryptojacking. The findings show that the proposed solution handle cryptojacking attack better compare to existing mitigation solutions that only use blacklists, which are ineffective in blocking cryptojacking. Finally, the study will encourage the researcher to reconsider existing mitigation technique and propose new solutions against upcoming threats like this.

However, CMBlock also has some weaknesses. As for recommendation and enhancement of the application in the future, this recommendation may help this project to make it more efficient for the user to use it. This project can be improved by adding more potential behaviour traits for detection. Besides that, by implementing more detail notification to the user when the application blocked the cryptomining script such as part of the user system will be affected by the attack. Lastly, CMBlock can auto-add the URL domain into the blacklist database when the user suspected a URL domain of containing cryptomining script.

References

Ahamad, S., Nair, M., Varghese, B.: A survey on crypto currencies. In: 4th International Conference on Advances in Computer Science, AETACS, pp. 42–48. Citeseer (2013)

Dev, J.A.: Bitcoin mining acceleration and performance quantification. In: 2014 IEEE 27th Canadian Conference on Electrical and Computer Engineering (CCECE), pp. 1–6. IEEE (2014)

Hari, K., Sai, S., Venkata, T.V.: Cryptocurrency mining – transition to cloud. Int. J. Adv. Comput. Sci. Appl. 6(9) (2015). https://doi.org/10.14569/IJACSA.2015.060915

Hong, G., et al.: How you get shot in the back: a systematical study about cryptojacking in the real world. In: Proceedings of the 2018 ACM SIGSAC Conference on Computer and Communications Security, pp. 1701–1713. ACM (2018)

Houben, R., Snyers, A.: Cryptocurrencies and blockchain: legal context and implications for financial crime, money laundering and tax evasion. Europe Parliament (2018). http://www.europarl.europa.eu/cmsdata/150761/TAX3%20Study%20on%20cryptocurrencies%20and%20blockchain.pdf

Liu, J., Zhao, Z., Cui, X., Wang, Z., Liu, Q.: A novel approach for detecting browser-based silent miner. In: 2018 IEEE Third International Conference on Data Science in Cyberspace (DSC), pp. 490–497. IEEE (2018)

Mukhopadhyay, U., Skjellum, A., Hambolu, O., Oakley, J., Yu, L., Brooks, R.: A brief survey of cryptocurrency systems. In: 2016 14th Annual Conference on Privacy, Security and Trust (PST), pp. 745–752. IEEE (2016)

Paquet-Clouston, M., Haslhofer, B., Dupont, B.: Ransomware payments in the bitcoin ecosystem. Journal of Cybersecurity 5(1), tyz003 (2019)

Randi, E., Kimberly, G., Bryon, W., Jeremy, K.: How the Rise of Cryptocurrencies Is Shaping the Cyber Crime Landscape: The Growth of Miners, 18 July 2018. (2018). https://www.fireeye.com/blog/threat-research/2018/07/cryptocurrencies-cyber-crime-growth-of-miners.html

Saad, M., Khormali, A., Mohaisen, A.: End-to-end analysis of in-browser cryptojacking. arXiv preprint arXiv:1809.02152. (2018)

Wang, P., Wang, Y.-S.: Malware behavioural detection and vaccine development by using a support vector model classifier. J. Comput. Syst. Sci. 81(6), 1012–1026 (2015)

Systematic Literature Review of Prediction Techniques to Identify Work Skillset

Nurul Saadah Zawawi[1], Ely Salwana[1(✉)], Zahidah Zulkifli[2], and Norshita Mat Nayan[1]

[1] Institute of Visual Informatics, University Kebangsaan Malaysia, 43650 Bangi, Selangor, Malaysia
nurulsaadahzawawi@gmail.com,
{elysalwana,norshitaivi}@ukm.edu.my
[2] Department of Information Systems, Kulliyyah of Information and Communication Technology, International Islamic University Technology, Gombak, Malaysia
zahidahz@iium.edu.my

Abstract. A mismatch of skillsets is a main cause to the unemployment in Malaysia. It is a situation where the level and work skillset that are available do not match the market demands and the individual does not know how to identify the skills that they have. To deal with this problem, prediction techniques is used to assist in identifying work-appropriate skills for individual. Thus, a systematic literature review (SLR) on predicting work skillsets using prediction techniques is proposed. The aim of this study is to give an overview on the prediction techniques that have been used to predict work skillset and the accuracy of the techniques. We use SLR to identify 383 prediction techniques studies for identifying skills published from 2014 to 2019. As a result, 9 studies report adequate information and methodology according to our criteria and apply. From the studies, classification techniques are used for predicting work skillset. The algorithms used is Random Forest with precision is 99%. From this study, a future study will be conducted by developing a prediction model to help identifying appropriate work skillsets to meet current needs and identifying the levels of skills they have. The significant of this study is the researchers are able to understand deeply about the prediction techniques used to identify work skillset and the accuracy of the techniques used.

Keywords: Prediction · Data mining · Work skillset · Skills · Accuracy

1 Introduction

This SLR successfully identify and analyze 383 studies published between 2014 and 2019 that related to techniques used in prediction of work skillset. The analysis investigates existing prediction techniques used and the accuracy. The decision allows the researchers to develop a prediction model based on knowledge and best practices in previous studies. Our results also help researchers make effective decisions on a prediction model that best fits the topic.

© Springer Nature Switzerland AG 2019
H. Badioze Zaman et al. (Eds.): IVIC 2019, LNCS 11870, pp. 415–428, 2019.
https://doi.org/10.1007/978-3-030-34032-2_37

Technology is evolving and Malaysia is experiencing it and what is booming is the 4.0[th] Industrial Revolution (4.0 IR). To meet this challenge, each person must have the skills to meet the job requirements. Therefore, it is important to identify the skills needed while improving existing skills. From the research conducted, emotional intelligence [1], creativity, complex information processing, critical thinking, and decision making are skills needed by the year 2020 [2].

Issues of compatibility are found in the Malaysian job market. A mismatch is a situation where the level and types of skills that are available do not meet the requirements of the job market [3]. Having the right skills and job is important to meet current needs. However, often occurs where existing skills do no match the areas involved. This happens because we are not supplied with the right skills and knowledge as well as the imperfect labor markets [4].

The skills that matches with the job position is very important, but still most people do not clear on how to identify the skills they have. This is because the selection of work is made without the proper advice from professional services and the right way [5]. There are various ways to help individuals identify the skills they have. Data mining (DM) is one of the ways to make predictions.

DM is a technique used for analyzing data to identify useful information from a large database where the information obtained is more accurate and useful. From the research conducted, classification, clustering, and regression are some of the techniques used in DM [6]. Some technique has been developed using this model. This technique has been used in many fields, including human resource management [7] and has become a commonly used techniques in predicting the outcome [8]. To use prediction techniques, we need to know the background of the prediction techniques used in the study to identify which techniques are most appropriate. To identify suitable prediction techniques for use, SLR is proposed to support the objectives of the study, which is:

To investigate the existing prediction techniques for predicting skills and the level of accuracy.

The next section focused on the previous related studies. This section describes prediction techniques and popular algorithms which are generally used in research. In this section, we will get information on prediction techniques. It followed by the research method used in this study in predicting techniques for work skillset. In the next section, the details results about prediction techniques used in identifying work skillset is discussed. The last section is the conclusion, to answer the research question of the study.

2   Prediction Techniques to Identify Skills

In the future, we will rely more on the predictive ability [9] and will be used in the decision-making process and to predict what is uncertain. Company such as Baidu, Google, and IBM is using prediction techniques and algorithm to recruit newcomers, evaluate employees, and forecast career path of staff member [10]. By using prediction techniques, forecasts of predictable skills can help individual to evaluate their skills, as well as to improve those skills. Hereby, in this section, we will describe about existing prediction techniques that used to predict work skillsets.

2.1 DM Techniques in Prediction

DM is defined as the procedure of extracting information from huge sets of data. In other words, we can say that DM is mining of knowledge from data. In DM several techniques are used such as classification, clustering, and regression [6]. DM consists of two types namely supervised learning and unsupervised learning. Supervised learning consists of classification techniques where it uses the decision tree method. It is very important techniques in DM. Algorithms that are often used in the classification are Naïve Bayes, Decision trees, K-Nearest Neighbor (KNN), Support Vector Machine (SVM), and random forest algorithm. While, clustering is unsupervised learning methods. Clustering is one of the DM techniques to group the same data into one set and different data into different groups. Clustering Algorithms used are Density Based Clustering algorithm, Simple K-Means, Hierarchical clustering algorithm [11]. Figure 1 show the techniques commonly used in DM.

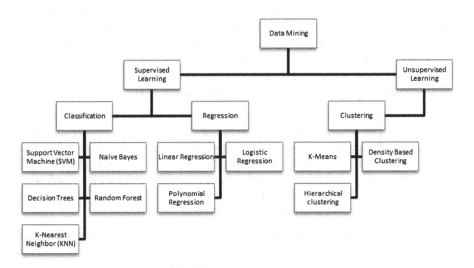

Fig. 1. Data mining techniques and algorithms

2.2 Algorithms

From the SLR, classification techniques are generally used for predicting skill. Thereby, we will discuss about algorithms that used in classification techniques below.

Support Vector Machine (SVM). SVM is one of the classification techniques. The algorithm works by looking for a hyperplane that aims to extend the boundary between two sets of classes. The objective is to separate the data into specific classes. This methods is called linear classifier [12]. SVM are based on statistical learning and work with high dimension data and represents the decision boundaries using a subset of the training set called support vectors [13].

Naive Bayesian. Naive Bayesian is widely used for classification purpose. Naive Bayes are best used if the data obtained is large and use the Bayesian theorem [14]. It is used for classification and returns a score between 0 and 1 of the necessary class abilities by assuming independence of variables [9]. It believes each characteristic to be independent of the others. This algorithm has a strength that is fast and has a high precision outcome [15].

Chaudhari use prediction model that will suggest suitable job position based on a resume and will be used to classify candidate resume [8]. Naive Bayes are also used to predict the potential work of the candidates. The system is designed to offer the jobs based on user profiles [16].

Decision Tree. Classification and prediction methods for returning classes abilities and outputs as flow charts or set of rules to determine class membership [9]. The decision tree is a mathematical model that helps make decision easier [14]. The decision tree consists of several nodes starting from the root node. Since a set of root node attributes is assigned to an attributes that have the smallest entropy. Once the root node has been identified, the algorithm extends the tree by adding the next attribute that has the smallest entropy among of other attributes. The algorithm continues to recourse on attributes which never met so far. The algorithm is terminated then on each node if either every element in the subset belongs to the same class, or there are no more attributes or the node does not meet any training example [17].

Random Forest. Forest is a classification consisting of several decision trees. Each decision tree is constructed using a random vector [18]. Random forests is an idea of the general technique of random decision forests that are combine classification, regression and other tasks that control by constructing a multitude of decision trees at training time and outputting the class that is the mode of the classes (classification) or mean prediction (regression) of the individual trees. Random decision forests accurate for decision trees' habit of overfitting to their training set [13].

K-Nearest Neighbors Classifier (KNN). KNN is the simplest algorithm among the other algorithms. Unknown data point categorization is the basis of the nearest neighbor in which its class is already known. In this algorithm the nearest neighbor is calculated based on the k-value which determines the nearest neighbor number to be considered and therefore specifies the sample data point class. It is used in many areas such as, pattern recognition, marketing of internet, analysis of Image databases cluster [19].

3   Methods

SLR is a secondary study with the objectives to identify, analyze and interpret all available evidences from primary studies related to a specific research question. This study applied the basic SLR method as described by Kitchenham and Charter [20]. The steps used to find information is as follows:

- Define search terms;
- Select sources;

- Application of search terms on sources; and
- Selection of primary studies by application of inclusion and exclusion criteria on search results.

3.1 Research Question

The field of SLR and the specific research questions focuses on identifying key studies, data extraction and analysis of the study. Hence, the research questions must be carefully thought out and expressed [21]. The aim for SLR in this research is to analyze suitable prediction techniques to predict work skillset and the level of accuracy. In this study, the research questions proposed is:

What are the prediction techniques used to predict work skillset and the level of accuracy?

3.2 Search Strategy

We used a few databases, which is electronic libraries to search for primary studies in the related areas. The databases are: ACM Digital Library, IEEE, ISI Web of Science and SCOPUS.

In order to obtain articles that are relevant to this study, the search string is used according to the research question. This search string will be accomplished based on the title as well as the related keyword. Then, the identified search strings will be compiled using logical ANDs and OR to find the right term. The search strings identified are as follows:

("Skills" OR "abilities" OR "ability" OR "aptitude" OR "expertise") AND ("Prediction Techniques" OR "methodology" OR "methods" OR "process" OR "techniques") AND ("Prediction accuracy" OR "forecast" OR "precision" OR "predicts" OR "predictive" OR "Skills Performance" OR "abilities" OR "performance" OR "skills").

3.3 Study Selection

The criteria for studies to be included in our SLR are based on the inclusion and exclusion criteria presented in Table 1.

Table 1. Inclusion and exclusion criteria

Inclusion criteria	Exclusion criteria
• A relevant study with research question • Focused on prediction techniques for predicting work skillset and the accuracy • Conference proceedings or a journal • Year from 2014–2019 • The paper must be in English language	• Book • Duplicate paper • Not on the topic • Review paper

Figure 2 shows the search process of the study. Based on our specified search terms, 383 studies have been found. Based on the publication obtained, the duplicate article was rejected, and this left a total of 326 articles. After that, the article is evaluated based on the title and abstract by taking into account the inclusion and exclusion criteria that have been proposed and the publication reduced to 38 papers for full-text reading. After reading through it, a total of 9 publications meets a study in where 9 publications describes in more detail the prediction techniques used and explain the prediction accuracy for each techniques. Thus, resulting 9 studies in this SLR.

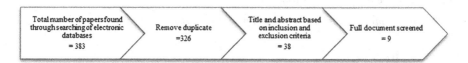

Fig. 2. Selection of the primary studies process.

3.4   Paper Selection

This study was conducted by Mishra to predict the marketability of Master students in Computer Applications and to identify appropriate algorithms for use in making predictions. This study was conducted using several classification techniques such as Naive Bayes, Ensemble Methods and Decision Trees and Multilayer Perceptrons and Sequential Minimal Optimization (SMO). This study aims to help students identify their marketability and by understanding the problems they face, can help management overcome these problems by providing proper training to improve students' learning. This study uses WEKA as a data mining tool. Table 2 show the comparison and the accuracy of the techniques in this research. This study states that the J48 algorithm is suitable for predicting marketability with accuracy of 70.19% and the model building time is 0.02 s which is less than Random Forest [13].

Table 2. Performance comparison of classifier [13].

Algorithm	Accuracy (%)
J48	**70.19**
Random Forest	71.304
Random Tree	63.35
SMO	63.7
Multilayer Perceptron	70.64
Naïve Bayes	62.87

The other studies, using two algorithms, KNN and Naive Bayes to predict student performance and help to improve their performance level. From their predictions, teachers can help the student by paying more attention and taking action in helping improve the students' performance [19]. From the studies conducted, Naive Bayes showed better results than KNN with an accuracy of 93.17%. This research uses Rapid Miner as a DM tool [19] (Table 3).

Table 3. Comparison of KNN and Naïve Bayes [19].

Algorithm	Accuracy (%)
KNN	63.45
Naïve Bayes	93.17

On the other hand, Bharambe use data mining techniques such as classification in research to assessing employability of students [22]. This study aims to identify the skills and suitability of students to meet the needs of the company demand by predicting their employability. The skills are measured using the data obtained from the assessment test survey and the data can identify student's skills such as soft skills, problem solving skills, and technical skills. The data are very useful because students can also identify their weaknesses. Thus, students can take action to meet the needs of the company based on their requirements. Table 4 shows the algorithms used in making predictions such as Random Forest, Decision Tree, KNN, Multi-class Ada Boosted and Quadratic Discriminant Analysis(QDA). The results indicate a Random Forest has the highest accuracy by 99% [22].

Table 4. Comparison of algorithms [22].

Algorithm	Accuracy (%)
Random Forest	99
Decision Tree	97
KNN	91
Multi-class Ada boosted	89
QDA	72

The other study aim to combines clustering and classification techniques for handling big data. The data obtained are large and incomplete. Therefore, to obtain more accurate information the use of unified predictive model techniques was used in this study. This study combines the use of algorithms such as Two-level clustering (K-Means Kernel) as well as four classifiers namely K-Star, Random Tree, simple CART and Random Forest. The combination of these techniques aims to predict student's employability. From the study conducted, student's employability prediction can be improved by using the proposed model. Table 5 shows the four classifiers selected based on their accuracy [23].

Table 5. Comparison of algorithms based on accuracy [23].

Algorithm	Accuracy (%)
Simple CART	**81.11**
Random Forest	**85.96**
Random Tree	**82.9**
K-Star	**82.11**
KNN	80.04
VFI	66.57
VotedPeceptron	56.33
REP Tree	75.43
LMT	80.57
J48 Graft	74.19
J48	73.86
ADT Tree	68.24
IBI	75.41
Ibk	75.43
DTNB	77.09

Next study aims to use data mining, a classification technique to predict employee performance based on their skills. Each employee will be evaluated based on their class of skills to meet the work requirements. This model can assist in deciding what to do with the employees such as providing appropriate training. Employee performance is divided into three classes: class I (good), class II (satisfactory) and class 3 (need improvement). The workers will be evaluated based on those classes. Table 6 shows the accuracy of the algorithm used where the decision tree has a high accuracy of 93.33% [24].

Table 6. Comparison of algorithms [24]

Algorithm	Accuracy
Decision Tree	93.33%
Naïve Bayes	71.67%

Table 7 show that C4.5 algorithm more accurate than other algorithms by 86%. The purpose of this study is to improve accuracy method for predicting. A system for assessing a person's personality is used to help predict the job fit for an individual based on their acquired skills by using classification techniques. The predictions techniques can help students identify their potential based on their skills to suit their chosen occupation [25].

Study [26] aims to assist the university authority have a more accurate knowledge of their computer science and engineering (CSE) under-graduating students by studying various academic, technical and interpersonal factors of the students and predicting an estimated career of them. The ability to predict career using the suggested

Table 7. Accuracy comparison of data mining algorithms [25].

Algorithm	Accuracy (%)
C4.5	86
Naive Bayes	84
K-Star	82
Simple CART	80

method ultimately assisted the university authority in maintaining their collaboration with the industry by providing the sector with properly qualified CSE technicians.

The research also enabled to ensure proper counseling and training sessions for both the prospective students and those who are unaware of their profession. As we can see in Table 8, CART and Multi-Layer Perceptron (MLP) gives us the highest prediction accuracy of 95.24%. Random Forest (RF), the second best classifier gives an accuracy of 95.04%. Other two algorithms, ID3 and Support Vector Classifier give accuracy of 75.46% and 80.41% respectively [26].

Table 8. Accuracy percentage [26].

Algorithm	Accuracy (%)
MLP	95.24
Random Forest	95.04
ID3	75.46
SVM	80.41
CART	95.24

Next related study also aims to predict the students' employability after graduation [28]. Table 9 shows a comparison between the algorithms used to predict student's employability. Among the algorithms used, logistic regression showed higher accuracy than others by 78.4% [27].

Table 9. Comparison of algorithms [27].

Algorithm	Accuracy (%)
Naive Bayes	75.33
J48	74.95
SimpleCart	73.01
Logistic Regression	78.4
Chaid	76.3

The last study proposes a predictive system capable of predicting students' performance. The study was conducted to identify students with poor performance. The study uses classification techniques to classify students based on their grade. From the Table 10 shows a comparison between the algorithms and afterward BFTree is selected for use with a high degree of accuracy with 61.4% [28].

Table 10. Comparison of algorithms [28].

Algorithm	Accuracy (%)
J48	58.3
SimpleCART	59.1
BFTree	61.4
Random Tree	45.7
J48graft	58.3

4 Results and Discussion

This section discusses the analysis of previous work related to prediction techniques used in predicting skills to meet job requirements. This study also looks at the accuracy of the prediction technique used for each previous work. The results of the research conducted on the previous studies found that 9 studies were identified that met this research question. The article contains information on the prediction techniques used and also describes the algorithm selected based on the accuracy of the prediction techniques. Each of the studies will compare the algorithms and will choose the algorithms that have the highest accuracy. From the study, predicting work skillset involves predicting on employability, career and performance involving students and employees. From this analysis, many studies have been conducted involving students and employees. Predicting the skills is necessary to help them find the right job according to their job requirements. It can also help employees evaluate themselves to improve their existing skills.

From the analysis it is found that, the first study used classification technique to predict student's employability. Through the use of this technique, students at risk of being unemployment can be identified. This way, students can take action to improve their performance so that the risk of unemployment was avoided. Predictions are based on parameters such as socioeconomic, academic achievement and emotional skill. This paper compares several algorithms such as Random Forest, Multilayer Perceptron, J48, Random Tree, SMO, and Naive Bayes where each algorithm gets accuracy for each algorithm. From this study, J48 have the highest accuracy by 71.30% [13].

The second paper predict student's performance prediction using KNN and Naive Bayes. This model was developed for students to identify their potential and help improve their performance. Through predictions, teachers can identify student weaknesses and take action to help students. This study used 8 attributes out of 14 attributes. It compares Naïve Bayes and KNN. From the comparison made, Naive Bayes was selected based on a high accuracy by 93.17% [19].

The third study is about student's employability prediction. This study makes predictions based on student skills and job requirements. The purpose of this study is to improve the method of student assessment. It helps students understand the criteria needed to find a job that suits their skills. These skills are evaluated based on soft-skills, problem-solving skills, and technical skills. This study compared Random Forest, Decision tree, KNN, Multi-class Ada and QDA with Random Forest has a high accuracy of 99% [22].

The fourth study used classification and clustering techniques for predicting student's employability and help students improve their performance. Data for this study were obtained from various Universities. However, the data obtained is large and does not provide accurate information. To obtain useful information, unified predictive techniques are used by combining clustering and classification techniques. By using this technique, the accuracy increased to 96.78%. Algorithms for clustering techniques use two-level clustering such as K-Means kernel while for classification techniques using algorithms such as Random forest, Random tree, K-star, and Simple Cart. The data obtained is such as academic records, personal details and skills. The algorithms were compared and Random Forest has a high accuracy by 85.96% [23].

For the fifth study, J48 has high accuracy by 93.33% compared to Naïve Bayes by 71.67%. Sharma said that improving management in the organization is important for retaining motivated and skilled workers. Thus, this study aimed to predict the performance of workers at the Institute of Higher Education. Employee performance is assessed through the various skills available. Through these predictions, they can make decisions about who needs training, promotions and even help choose the right job. [24].

The sixth study compare C4.5, Naïve Bayesian, K-star, and Simple CART to predict career and C4.5 has a high accuracy by 86%. The study makes predictions to assist in the selection of careers based on personal characteristics such as teamwork, honesty, leadership and so on. This study uses C4.5 to predict students' careers [25].

The seventh study use CART and MLP to predict career with high accuracy by 95.24% compared to Random forest, SVM and ID3 which has a lower accuracy. The predictions are made based on features such as academic records, technical skills and interpersonal skills. It aims at predicting appropriate careers while identifying the weaknesses and strengths of the students. This model can help students find careers that fit their characteristics [26].

The eighth study compared Logistic Regression, Chaid, Naïve Bayes, J48, and SimpleCART for predicting IT employability and Logistic Regression get the high accuracy by 78.4%. The study can help provide them with the right skills to meet their job requirements [27].

And the last study intended to predict student performance in academics to see poor student performance by grade as well as identify factors that affect their performance. The study used BFTree with high accuracy by 61.4% compared to Simple CART, J48, and Random Tree [28].

Through the analysis of previous studies, various algorithms have been used. From the results of the analysis performed on the algorithms used, Random Forest has the highest prediction accuracy by (99%), followed by CART and MLP (95.24%), J48 (93.33%), Naïve Bayes (93.17%), C4.5 (86%), Logistic Regression (78.4%) and lastly, the lower prediction accuracy is BFTree by (61.4%). This shows that random forest has the highest precision in making predictions.

5   Conclusion

This paper gives an overview of the existing prediction techniques used in predicting work skillset. From the SLR, 9 publications were obtained to assist in carrying out the study to be undertaken. From the research, it was found that classification techniques were widely used in previous studies. Frequently used algorithms are Random Forest, Decision tree, naïve Bayesian, and SVM. From the research, Random forest is widely used for predicting skills and performance and its accuracy is higher than any other technique.

Appropriate prediction techniques have been identified based on the high accuracy of which have answered the questions of the study. From this study, a prediction model will be developed to predict the skills required in related fields. The model will help to identify their level of skills whether or not they are suitable with the required workplace. It will help to identify skills needed as required. This SLR is only focused on prediction techniques for work skillset as well as accuracy. In the future, studies can be carried out more thoroughly to identify the attributes used in predicting work skillset.

Acknowledgement. This work was supported by the Research University Grant by Universiti Kebangsaan Malaysia: Geran Galakan Penyelidik Muda (grant number GGPM-2018-019).

References

1. Batool, B.F.: Emotional intelligence and effective leadership. J. Bus. Stud. Q. **4**(3), 84–94 (2013)
2. Ballalle, R., Himendra, B.: Fourth industrial revolution and future of workforce. Int. J. Adv. Res. Ideas Innov. Technol. **4**(5), 151–153 (2018)
3. Ibrahim, M.Z., Ab Rahman, M.N., Yasin, R.M.: Ketidaksepadanan Kemahiran dan Kolaborasi Industri-Institusi PLTV di Malaysia: Satu Cadangan Penyelesaian. SkillsMalaysia J. **3**(1), 17–22 (2017)
4. CEDEFOP.: Skill Mismatch: More Than Meets the Eye. Retrieved from European Centre for the Development of Vocational Training (Cedefop) Homepage. http://www.cedefop.europa. eu/files/9087_en.pdf. Accessed 15/21 2019
5. Razak, T.R., Hashim, M.A., Noor, N.M., Halim, I.H.A., Shamsul, N.F.F.: Career path recommendation system for UiTM Perlis students using fuzzy logic. In: 2014 5th International Conference on Intelligent and Advanced Systems: Technological Convergence for Sustainable Future, ICIAS 2014 - Proceedings, pp. 1–5. IEEE, Kuala Lumpur (2014)
6. Sagar, P., Prinima, P., Indu, I.: Analysis of prediction techniques based on classification and regression. Int. J. Comput. Appl. **163**(7), 47–51 (2017)
7. Mallafi, H., Widyantoro, D.H.: Prediction modelling in career management. In: Proceedings - CYBERNETICSCOM 2016: International Conference on Computational Intelligence and Cybernetics, pp. 17–21 (2017)
8. Chaudhari, H., Yadav, N., Shukla, Y.: A predictive analysis on job recruitment. In: International Conference on Recent Trends in Engineering, Science & Technology - (ICRTEST 2016), pp. 1–5. IET (2018)
9. Wimmer, H., Powell, L.M.: A comparison of open source tools for data science. J. Inf. Syst. Appl. Res. **9**(2), 1–9 (2016)

10. Xu, H., Yu, Z., Yang, J., Xiong, H., Zhu, H.: Talent circle detection in job transition networks. In: KDD 2016 Proceedings of the 22nd ACM SIGKDD International Conference on Knowledge Discovery and Data Mining, pp. 655–664. ACM, New York (2016)

11. Parmar, K., Vaghela, D., Sharma, P.: Performance prediction of students using distributed data mining. In: 2015 International Conference on Innovations in Information, Embedded and Communication Systems (ICIIECS), pp. 1–5. IEEE, Coimbatore (2015)

12. Burman, I., Som, S.: Predicting students academic performance using support vector machine. In: 2019 Amity International Conference on Artificial Intelligence (AICAI), pp. 756–759. IEEE, Dubai (2019)

13. Mishra, T., Kumar, D., Gupta, S.: Students' employability prediction model through data mining. Int. J. Appl. Eng. Res. 11(4), 2275–2282 (2016)

14. Putpuek, N., Rojanaprasert, N., Atchariyachanvanich, K., Thamrongthanyawong, T.: Comparative study of prediction models for final GPA score: a case study of Rajabhat Rajanagarindra University. In: Proceedings - 17th IEEE/ACIS International Conference on Computer and Information Science, ICIS 2018, pp. 92–97. IEEE, Singapore (2018)

15. Takci, H., Gurkahraman, K., Yelkuvan, A. F.: Measurement of the appropriateness in career selection of the high school students by using data mining algorithms: a case study. In: 2017 Federated Conference on Computer Science and Information Systems (FedCSIS), pp. 113–117. IEEE, Prague (2017)

16. Choudhary, S.: Collaborative job prediction based on Naive Bayes classifier using python platform. In: 2016 International Conference on Computation System and Information Technology for Sustainable Solutions (CSITSS), pp. 302–306. IEEE, Bangalore (2016)

17. Ciolacu, M., Tehrani, A.F., Beer, R., Popp, H.: Education 4.0-fostering student's performance with machine learning methods. In: 2017 IEEE 23rd International Symposium for Design and Technology in Electronic Packaging (SIITME), pp. 432–437. IEEE, Constanta (2017)

18. Appel, R., Fuchs, T., Dollar, P., Perona, P.: Quickly boosting decision trees - pruning underachieving features earl. In: Proceedings of the 30th International Conference on Machine Learning, Atlanta, Georgia, USA (2013)

19. Amra, I.A.A., Maghari, A.Y.A.: Students performance prediction using KNN and Naïve Bayesian. In: ICIT 2017 - 8th International Conference on Information Technology, Proceedings, pp. 909–913. IEEE, Amman (2017)

20. Kitchenham, B., Pretorius, R., Budgen, D., Pearl Brereton, O., Turner, M., Niazi, M., Linkman, S.: Systematic literature reviews in software engineering - a tertiary study. Inf. Softw. Technol. 52(8), 792–805 (2010)

21. Wohlin, C., Runeson, P., Höst, M., Ohlsson, M.C., Regnell, B., Wesslén, A.: Experimentation in Software Engineering. Springer, Heidelberg (2012). https://doi.org/10.1007/978-3-642-29044-2

22. Bharambe, Y., More, N., Mulchandani, M., Shankarmani, R., Shinde, S.G.: Assessing employability of students using data mining techniques. In: 2017 International Conference on Advances in Computing, Communications and Informatics, ICACCI 2017, pp. 2110–2114. IEEE, Udipi (2017)

23. Thakar, P, Mehta, A.: A unified model of clustering and classification to improve students' employability prediction. Int. J. Intell. Syst. Appl. 9(9), 10–18 (2017)

24. Sharma, M., Goyal, A.: An application of data mining to improve personnel performance evaluation in higher education sector in India. In: 2015 International Conference on Advances in Computer Engineering and Applications, pp. 559–564. IEEE, Ghaziabad (2015)

25. Katore, L.S., Bhakti, S.R., Jayant, S.U.: Novel Professional career prediction and recommendation method for individual through analytics on personal traits using C4. 5 algorithm. In: 2015 Global Conference on Communication Technologies (GCCT), pp. 503–506. IEEE, Thuckalay (2015)
26. Arafath, Y.: Predicting career using data mining. In: 2018 International Conference on Computing, Power and Communication Technologies (GUCON), pp. 889–894 (2018)
27. Piad, K.C., Dumlao, M., Ballera, M.A., Ambat, S.C.: Predicting IT employability using data mining techniques. In: 2016 3rd International Conference on Digital Information Processing, Data Mining, and Wireless Communications, DIPDMWC 2016, pp. 26–30. IEEE, Moscow (2016)
28. Sa, C.L., Hanani, D., Hossain, E.D., Hossin, M.: Student performance analysis system (SPAS). In: The 5th International Conference on Information and Communication Technology for the Muslim World (ICT4M), pp. 1–6. IEEE, Kuching (2015)

Prediction of Learning Disorder: A-Systematic Review

Mohammad Azli Jamhar[1], Ely Salwana[1(✉)], Zahidah Zulkifli[2], Norshita Mat Nayan[1], and Noryusliza Abdullah[3]

[1] Institute of Visual Informatics, University Kebangsaan Malaysia, 43650 Bangi, Selangor, Malaysia
mohammadazli93@gmail.com,
{elysalwana,norshitaivi}@ukm.edu.my
[2] Department of Information Systems, Kulliyyah of ICT, International Islamic University Malaysia, P.O Box 10, 50728 Kuala Lumpur, Malaysia
zahidahz@iium.edu.my
[3] Faculty of Computer Science and Information Technology, Universiti Tun Hussein Onn Malaysia (UTHM), 86400 Parit Raja, Batu Pahat, Johor, Malaysia
yusliza@uthm.edu.my

Abstract. Learning Disorder refers to a number of disorder which may influence the understanding or use of verbal or nonverbal information. The most well-known types of learning disorder involve an issue with reading, writing, listening, and speaking. When we talk about learning disorder, most people only focusing on social development plan. Therefore, in this study, a systematic review was performed to identify, assess and aggregate on the prediction methods used for a predict learning disorder. The main objective of this paper is to, identify the most common prediction methods for learning disorder, in terms of accuracy by using the systematic review technique. From the main objective, we can define the research questions such as, which is the most common and the most accurate prediction methods used for learning disorder. In conclusion, the most common prediction methods for learning disorder which is Decision Tree and Support Vector Machine. For accuracy, Decision Tree, Linear Discriminant Analysis and K-Nearest Neighbor methods have the highest prediction accuracy for a learning disorder. From these findings, this paper can guide others to predict learning disorder by using the most common methods to get the best result in term of accuracy.

Keywords: Learning disorder · Prediction model · Data mining · Systematic review

1 Introduction

Learning disorder are significant difficulty in academic learning that's results in a clinical diagnosis. It can meddle with learning most basic skill, for example reading and writing. There are four most common learning disorders which is, Dyslexia, Attention

H. Badioze Zaman et al. (Eds.): IVIC 2019, LNCS 11870, pp. 429–440, 2019.
https://doi.org/10.1007/978-3-030-34032-2_38

Deficit Hyperactivity Disorder (ADHD), Dyscalculia, and Dysgraphia. Dyslexia is a specific learning disorder in reading. ADHD is a self-focused behavior [1]. A few people suffer from dyscalculia which is a disorder that affects math capabilities. The last type is dysgraphia, related to the physical act of writing. By understanding these disorder, it can help to find the best method in predict learning disorder.

Autism Spectrum Disorder (ASD) is thought to be a cerebral developmental disturbance that limits social communication and interaction behaviors [2]. Individuals with ASD show different attention in real life, especially in social activities [7]. Osman stated that, in his study, he tried to find out whether children have ASD by using classification methods. Two different classification algorithms were used. These are the K-Nearest Neighbor (KNN) algorithm and the Liner Discriminant Analysis (LDA) algorithm.

Currently, there are many method in predict learning disorder such as, K-Neighbor (KNN), Linear Discriminant Analysis, Deep Learning Methods, Support Vector Machine (SVM) and Decision Tree. But the challenges are, we need to identify the best method and technique for learning disorder prediction in term of accuracy. In order to encounter the challenges, a systematic review is proposed. The purpose of systematic review is to support the objectives of this study, which is:

To identify the most common prediction methods for learning disorder in terms of accuracy by using the systematic review

The next section focused on the background of study, related with learning disorder, and predictive model.

2 Background of the Study

Learning disorders are an umbrella term for a wide variety of learning problems. A learning disorder is "not a problem" with intelligence or motivation. Children with learning disorder are not lazy or dumb. In fact, most are just as smart as everyone else, only their brains are simply wired differently. This difference affects how they receive and process information. This can lead to trouble with learning new information and skills, and putting them to use. The most common types of learning disorder involve problems with reading, writing, math, reasoning, listening, and speaking. There are four the most common learning disorder which is, Dyslexia, Attention Deficit/ Hyperactive Disorder (ADHD), Dyscalculia and Dysgraphia. Dyslexia is the most common form of all learning disorder. It is a language based disabilities, in the other words that person has trouble in reading, understanding words, sentences, or paragraphs. Other issues relate generally to fluency, spelling, and comprehension. Second, ADHD. There are three most common characteristics of ADHD, such as inattention, hyperactivity and impulsivity. Student with ADHD have difficulty with paying attention and staying on task. They mostly talking, making noise excessively, running, and having an ability to sit still for calm activities like reading. Third, dyscalculia. People with dyscalculia have difficulty in making arithmetical calculations. They have trouble performing basic math calculations or they may have difficulty with concepts like time, measurement or estimation and high levels of mathematics anxiety. The last types dysgraphia, these can be related to the physical act of writing. Dysgraphia can appear as difficulties with poor handwriting, inability to hold a pencil correctly, trouble putting thoughts on paper and their posture may be tense while trying to write.

Predictive model is a process that uses data mining and probability to forecast outcomes. Each model is comprised of various indicators, which are factors that are probably going to impact future outcomes. When information has been gathered for important indicators, a factual model is figured. The model may utilize a basic straight condition, or it might be a complex neural system, mapped out by advanced programming. The most complex zone of predictive modeling is the neural system. This type of machine learning model independently reviews large volumes of labeled data in search of correlations between variables in the data.

To build predictive modelling, there are a several methods such as, classification, regression and clustering. There a difference between those three techniques. Classification predicts discrete number of values and it sorted under various different names as stated by some parameters. Regression predicts continuous output, used to predict the numeric information. Clustering diving the dataset into own groups.

The next section focused on the methodology of predict learning disorder model. Then a discussion on research question will be described, the detail method on the existing prediction methods are discussed. Lastly, the conclusion and future work are outline in the last section.

3 Research Method

In this paper we followed a systematic literature approach based on the guidelines for performing systematic literature reviews from Kitchenham Barbara. This guideline is able to identify the specific problems from this research. By following this formal method, we want to provide a replicable research review. The aim for systematic review in the current literature is to identify the best method in prediction model. The procedure we undertake is as follows:

- Define search terms;
- Select sources which is digital libraries;
- Application of search terms on sources; and
- Determine of primary studies by use of consideration and rejection.

3.1 Research Question

The purpose of the research question in systematic review is to guide to the results. Determine the research questions is basically what make a systematic review different from a traditional review. Research question is important to understand the current study of prediction model on learning disorder. From the Table 1 below, in structuring the best research questions, we follow a few criteria such as population, comparison, intervention, outcome and context (PICOC).

Table 1. Research question criteria

Criteria	Details
Population	Children with learning disorder
Comparison	Accuracy (Prediction Learning Disorder)
Intervention	Methods prediction
Outcome	Prediction accuracy, the most used prediction method
Context	All types of empirical studies, such as preliminary studies, and case studies

Therefore, we can define the followings as generic the research questions proposed in this study:

What are the prediction methods used for learning disorder?
What are the most accurate prediction methods?

In any case, it is better to start with a small scale preliminary study (small study) or pilot study before going into the depth of this study. The reason for doing the "small study" is to explore the appropriateness of the research questions with the objectives of this study. Next section, the study will explain about search strategy using online database.

3.2 Search Strategy

In systematic review, a well-arranged search strategy is very important so that every piece of information can be found in the search results. So, as to cover the biggest spectrum of relevant publications, we already identified and used the best and significant electronic libraries (online database or search database), such as: IEEE Digital Library, Scopus, ISI Web of Science, Spring Link and Science Direct.

The reason this systematic review chooses this five online database because they give the best result related with prediction of learning disorder in term of accuracy. From the research questions, we already set a few search terms and keywords when using online databases. The following are the search keywords used in the systematic review:

- "Prediction Learning Disorder"
- "Prediction Learning Disabilities"
- "Prediction Model Learning Disorder"
- "Prediction Learning Disorder Plan"
- "Prediction of Autism"
- "Prediction of ADHD".

All the keywords were combined by using the "AND" Boolean operators for example: (Prediction) AND (Learning) AND (Disorder) or (Prediction) AND (Autism). From the five online database, the search items only from Journal Articles and Conference Papers. Moreover, for the publication period, this search limited from year 2014 until 2019.

3.3 Overview of Included Studies

The objective of this paper is to create a systematic review from existing literature related with prediction for learning disorder. From the Fig. 1, the graph shows statistic literature results, between 2011 and 2013 does not provide any relevant literature. But, the results increase in the subsequent years until 2019 related with prediction learning disorder.

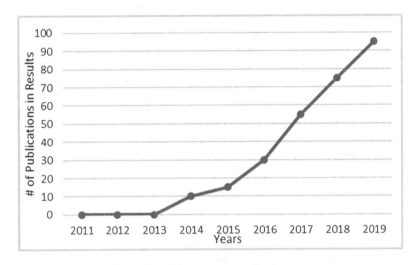

Fig. 1. Resulting primary studies by years

This study started by using the search keywords in each online database separately, a brief summary of the flow of references through this review showed that:

- 6,536 references were found by searching
- 1,278 references were found based on titles and abstracts
- 132 full reports were obtained
- Finally, we go through the full-text of studies in term of quality
- The resulted in 6 studies, which represented final set of primary study.

4   Important Component on Predicting Learning Disorder

This section will be focused and discussed the important factors on predicting learning disorder which is, prediction methods. But before we are going to that section, first we are going to point out all important details from six papers of studies in predicting learning disorder. From the Table 2 it gives a summary of pervious papers such as, objective, models used and the most important the result in term of accuracy.

Table 2. The objectives, algorithms and the outcome for prediction methods

No. of paper	Title	Objectives	Models	Results (Accuracy)	No. of citation
P1	Diagnosis Of Attention Deficit Hyperactivity Disorder Using Deep Belief Network Based On Greedy Approach	Comparing the proposed method and the best method	Deep Belief Network (DBN)	70%	[1]
P2	Prediction Of The Autism Spectrum Disorder Diagnosis With Linear Discriminant Analysis Classifier And K-Nearest Neighbor In Children	To find out whether children have ASD by using classification methods	K-Nearest Neighbor (KNN) Linear Discriminant Analysis (LNA)	89% 91%	[2]
P3	Identification Of Autism Spectrum Disorder Using Deep Learning And The Abide Dataset	To apply deep learning algorithms to identify ASD	Support Vector Machine (SVM) Random Forest (RF) Deep Neural Network (DNN)	65% 63% 70%	[9]
P4	Machine Learning-Based Model For Identification Of Syndromic Autism Spectrum Disorder	To identify syndromic ASD by supervised learning algorithms	Support Vector Machine (SVM) Decision Tree	94% 98%	[10]
P5	Brain-Specific Functional Relationship Networks Inform Autism Spectrum Disorder Gene Prediction	To predict ASD by using a machine learning approach	Random forest Support Vector Machine (SVM)	83%	[11]
P6	Use Of Machine Learning Methods In Prediction Of Short-Term Outcome In Autism Spectrum Disorders	To examine the predictors of outcome with machine learning methods	Decision Tree	71%	[12]

4.1   Prediction Method in Predicting Learning Disorder

This section will discuss about method in prediction model. The systematic review is used to identify the most common prediction model. To build predictive modelling, there are a several method such as, classification, regression and clustering.

Classification. Predicts discrete number of values. It sorted under various different names as stated by some parameters. For example, categorize spam email and non-spam email.

Regression. Predicts continuous output. This technique used to predict the numeric information and also can recognize distribution patterns dependent on the available information and historic information. For example, predicting an individual's salary from their age.

Clustering. Diving the dataset into own groups. The objective is to classify each data into a specific group. For example, survey the performance of smartphones in Australia, and divide the entire country's population into cities.

From the previous research, the most popular task to predict learning disorder is first classification and second regression. Under classification, there are several algorithms have been applied to predict learning disorder, such as Deep Believe Network (DBN), K-Nearest Neighbor (KNN), Support Vector Machine and Decision Tree. For example, [26] they predict learning disability in school, and [12] tested the performance using decision tree algorithm under classification. From the Table 3, it shows a summary from all paper, which paper are using classification, regression and clustering method.

From this paper [1], Deep Belief Networks (DBN) and A Greedy Training Algorithm under classification were used as a deep learning model to predict learning disorder. The proposed method (DBN) was evaluated by two standard data sets of ADHD-200 Global Competitions, including Neuro Image and NYU data sets, and compared with state-of-the-art algorithms. The Linear Discriminant Analysis (LDA) and The K-Nearest Neighbor (KNN) algorithms [2] are used for classification to predict Autism Spectrum Disorder (ASD) at an early age. In the LDA algorithm, the accuracy is 90.8%, whereas the accuracy of the KNN algorithm is 88.5%. In this paper [9], to evaluate the results obtained with deep learning, the performance of the model was compared with results of classifiers trained using Support Vector Machine (SVM) [32], Random Forest (RF) (Ho 1995), and Comparison of Deep Neural Network (DNN). From [10], the standard supervised machine learning techniques decision tree induction, multilayer perceptron and SVM were applied to these data, and a tenfold cross-validation technique was used to estimate their predictive performance. In this paper [11], they trained and optimized five different machine learning models: support vector machine (SVM) with linear kernel, random forest, extremely randomized trees, bagging ensemble of random forests, and AdaBoost ensemble of random forests. The last paper [12], the study the group comprised 433 children (mean age: 72.3 ± 45.9 months) with ASD diagnosis. The ASD symptoms were assessed by the Autism Behavior Checklist, Aberrant Behavior Checklist, Clinical Global Impression scales at baseline (T0) and 12th (T1), 24th (T2), and 36th (T3) months. They tested the performance of for machine learning algorithms (Naive Bayes, Generalized Linear Model, Logistic Regression, and Decision Tree).

Table 3 shows the summary all six paper methods. All of them fall under Classification and Regression technique. No study within the six papers use clustering technique.

Table 3. The summarise papers under classification, and regression

Paper	Technique	Algorithm
[1]	Classification	Deep Belief Network (DBN)
[2]	Classification	**K-Nearest Neighbor (KNN)** **Linear Discriminant Analysis (LNA)**
[9]	Classification	**Support Vector Machine (SVM)** **Deep Neural Network (DNN)**
[10]	Regression	Support Vector Machine (SVM) Decision Tree
[11]	Regression	Support Vector Machine (SVM)
[12]	Regression	Decision Tree

In the next section, the specific explanation in prediction model will be described.

Deep Belief Network. Deep Belief Network (DBN) is one of technique for prediction and a deep architecture that comprise of Restricted Boltzman Machine (RBF). DBN and RBM could be used as a feature extraction method also used as neural network. In this study [1], this algorithm **also** been used to diagnose learning disorder. Firstly, they proposed technique from RBF and converts an enormous number of issue highlights, also FMRI, and diagnosis status. As shown in Table 4 they compare the accuracy the proposed method which is DBN with other methods Support Vector Machine (SVM) and Decision Tree. As the result, the DBN method have significant superiorities accuracy by 70%.

Table 4. Accuracy result using Deep Belief Network with SVM & Decision Tree

Methods	Techniques	Result accuracy
Deep Belief Network (Proposed Method)	**Classification**	**70%**
Support Vector Machine	Regression	61%
Decision Tree	Classification/Regression	54%

K-Nearest Neighbor and Linear Discriminant Analysis. K-Nearest Neighbor (KNN) is one of a popular, simplest and most used algorithms methods for prediction. KNN is a non-parametric method used for classification and regression. For Linear Discriminant Analysis (LDA) algorithm, is one of the most widely used algorithms under classification and it work through the calculation of variance values between classes. From the Table 5 in this article [2] use KNN and LDA algorithm for prediction. Both of algorithm used to calculate five performance evaluation which is, accuracy, sensitivity, specificity, precision and F-measure, but we only focusing on accuracy.

Table 5. Accuracy result using K-Nearest Neighbor and Linear Discriminant Analysis

Methods	Techniques	Result accuracy
K-Nearest Neighbor	Classification	89%
Linear Discriminant Analysis	Classification	91%

Decision Tree. As depicts in Table 6 two papers [10, 12] used Decision Tree method in their research showed that, this algorithm method give the best results in term of accuracy performance compare with others method. Decision Tree one of powerful and popular algorithm for making classification, moreover it can handle high dimensional data [26].

Table 6. Accuracy result using Decision Tree

Methods	Authors	Result accuracy
Decision Tree	Pream Sudha [10]	98%
Decision Tree	Mirac Baris [12]	71%

Support Vector Machine. Support Vector Machine (SVM) one of under classification and regression technique. From the previous research, three papers that have used SVM to predict learning disorder. As shown in the Table 7 all the accuracy results from using SVM. Sembiring using SVM algorithm have faster and good generalization method than others [31].

Table 7. Accuracy result using Decision Tree

Methods	Authors	Result accuracy
Support Vector Machine	Heinsfeld [9]	65%
Support Vector Machine	Pream Sudha [10]	84%
Support Vector Machine	Duda [11]	83%

5   Results and Discussion

In this section, we examine and analyze the outcomes in predicting learning disorder based on the highest accuracy of prediction methods. The analysis shows the prediction accuracy that uses classification and regression method algorithms for predicting learning disorder from previous research.

The analysis shows Support Vector Machine (SVM) is the most popular technique for prediction learning disorder, which is four articles using it when do comparison using other algorithms. The highest accuracy in SVM techniques by (84%) from Pream Sudha [10]. The second highest (83%) from Duda [12]. Next, slightly low by (65%) from Heinsfeld [9]. Lastly, the lowest accuracy in SVM technique by (61%) by Farzi [1].

The second most used technique in prediction learning disorder is Decision Tree. From the analysis for accuracy result shows there are quite a lot of different gaps. The highest accuracy in this technique and this review by (98%) from Pream Sudha and Vijaya [10]. Next, from Usta [12] by (71%) and lastly the lowest prediction accuracy by (54%) from Farzi [1].

The second higher predication accuracy in this review is Linear Discriminant Analysis (LDA) by (91%) of performance accuracy [2] from Altay. Next, when comparing with the first and second highest result which is from Decision Tree and LDA technique, K-Nearest Neighbor (KNN) at the third highest accuracy with (89%) from Pream Sudha [10]. Lastly, Deep Belief Network (DBN) technique accuracy by (70%) [1].

6   Conclusion and Future Work

In summary, prediction for learning disorder can be useful in develop prediction model for learning disorder development plan to help learning disorder children in school to guide and assist them to plan for their skills' development based on their talent and ability. This paper has reviewed previous papers on prediction model of learning disorder with various method from the observation, many researchers have used Support Vector Machine (SVM) and Decision Tree methods for predicting learning disorder. The main objective of this paper is to, identify the most common prediction methods for learning disorder, in terms of accuracy by using the systematic review method. In conclusion, the most common prediction methods for learning disorder which is Decision Tree and Support Vector Machine. For accuracy, Decision Tree [10], Linear Discriminant Analysis [2] and K-Nearest Neighbor [2] methods has the highest prediction accuracy for learning disorder. From this findings, this paper can guide others in predict learning disorder by using the most common methods to get the best result in term of accuracy.

Acknowledgement. This work was supported by the Ministry of Education under Skim Geran Penyelidikan Fundamental (FRGS) (grant number FRGS/1/2018/ICT04/UKM/02/8).

References

1. Farzi, S., Kianian, S., Rastkhadive, I.: Diagnosis of attention deficit hyperactivity disorder using deep belief network based on greedy approach. In: 5th International Symposium on Computational and Business Intelligence (ISCBI), pp. 96–99, Dubai (2017)
2. Altay, O., Ulas, M.: Prediction of the autism spectrum disorder diagnosis with linear discriminant analysis classifier and K-nearest neighbor in children. In: 6th International Symposium on Digital Forensic and Security (ISDFS), pp. 1–4, Antalya (2018)
3. Chamseddine, A., Sawan, M.: Deep learning based method for output regularization of the seizure prediction classifier. In: 2018 IEEE Life Sciences Conference (LSC), pp. 118–121, Montreal, QC (2018)

4. Stefanidis, V., Anogianakis, G., Evangelou, A., Poulos, M.: Learning difficulties prediction using multichannel brain evoked potential data. In: Second International Conference on Mathematics and Computers in Sciences and in Industry (MCSI), pp. 268–272, Sliema (2015)

5. Liu, W., Yu, X., Raj, B., Yi, L., Zou, X., Li, M.: Efficient autism spectrum disorder prediction with eye movement: a machine learning framework. In: International Conference on Affective Computing and Intelligent Interaction (ACII), pp. 649–655, Xi'an (2015)

6. Omar, K.S., Mondal, P., Khan, N.S., Rizvi, M.R.K., Islam, M.N.: A machine learning approach to predict autism spectrum disorder. In: International Conference on Electrical, Computer and Communication Engineering (ECCE), pp. 1–6, Cox'sBazar, Bangladesh (2019)

7. Duan, H.: Learning to predict where the children with ASD look. In: 25th IEEE International Conference on Image Processing (ICIP), pp. 704–708, Athens (2018)

8. Sen, B., Borle, C.N., Greiner, R., Brown, M.R.G.: A general prediction model for the detection of ADHDand Autism using structural and functional MRI. PLOS ONE 13(4), e0194856 (2018)

9. Heinsfeld, A.S., Franco, A.R., Craddock, R.C., Buchweitz, A., Meneguzzi, F.: Identification of autism spectrum disorder using deep learning and the ABIDE dataset. NeuroImage: Clin. 17, 16–23 (2018)

10. Pream Sudha, V., Vijaya, M.S.: Machine learning-based model for identification of syndromic autism spectrum disorder. In: Krishna, A.N., Srikantaiah, K.C., Naveena, C. (eds.) Integrated Intelligent Computing, Communication and Security. SCI, vol. 771, pp. 141–148. Springer, Singapore (2019). https://doi.org/10.1007/978-981-10-8797-4_16

11. Duda, M., Zhang, H., Li, H., Wall, D.P., Burmeister, M., Guan, Y.: Brain-specific functional relationship networks inform autism spectrum disorder gene prediction. Transl. Psychiatry 8 (1), 56 (2018)

12. Usta, M.B., et al.: Use of machine learning methods in prediction of short-term outcome in autism spectrum disorders. Psychiatry Clin. Psychopharmacol. 29, 320–325 (2018)

13. Yahata, N., et al.: A small number of abnormal brain connections predicts adult autism spectrum disorder. Nat. Commun. 7(1), 11254 (2016)

14. Zhou, Y., Yu, F., Duong, T.: Multiparametric MRI characterization and prediction in autism spectrum disorder using graph theory and machine learning. PLoS ONE 9(6), e90405 (2014)

15. Sanders, E.A., Berninger, V.W., Abbott, R.D.: Sequential prediction of literacy achievement for specific learning disabilities contrasting in impaired levels of language in grades 4 to 9. J. Learn. Disabil. 51(2), 137–157 (2017)

16. Baten, E., Desoete, A.: Mathematical (Dis)abilities within the opportunity-propensity model: the choice of math test matters. Front. Psychol. 9 (2018)

17. Mowlem, F.D., Rosenqvist, M.A., Martin, J., Lichtenstein, P., Asherson, P., Larsson, H.: Sex differences in predicting ADHD clinical diagnosis and pharmacological treatment. Eur. Child Adolesc. Psychiatry 28(4), 481–489 (2018)

18. Velki, T., Vrdoljak, G.: Gender as moderator and age as mediator variables in prediction of school adjustment by self-evaluated symptoms of ADHD. Primenjena Psihologija 12(1), 65–83 (2019)

19. Jacobson, L.A., Schneider, H., Mahone, E.M.: Preschool inhibitory control predicts ADHD group status and inhibitory weakness in school. Arch. Clin. Neuropsychol. 33(8), 1006–1014 (2017)

20. Björk, A., Rönngren, Y., Selander, J., Vinberg, S., Hellzen, O., Olofsson, N.: Health, lifestyle habits, and physical fitness among adults with ADHD compared with a random sample of a Swedish general population. Soc. Health Vulnerability 9(1), 1553916 (2018)

21. Haas, S.M., Derefinko, K.J., Waschbusch, D.A.: The use of multi method impulsivity assessment in the prediction of ADHD, conduct problems, and callous-unemotional symptoms. Pers. Individ. Differ. **116**, 289–295 (2017)
22. Wong, H.K., et al.: Personalized medication response prediction for attention-deficit hyperactivity disorder: learning in the model space vs. learning in the data space. Front. Physiol. **8**, 199 (2017)
23. Walker, S.J., Langefeld, C.D., Zimmerman, K., Schwartz, M.Z., Krigsman, A.: A molecular biomarker for prediction of clinical outcome in children with ASD, constipation, and intestinal inflammation. Sci. Rep. **9**(1), 5987 (2019)
24. Julie, M.D., Kannan, B.: Prediction of learning disabilities in school age children using decision tree. In: Meghanathan, N., Boumerdassi, S., Chaki, N., Nagamalai, D. (eds.) ASUC/NeCoM/VLSI/WeST/WiMoN -2010. CCIS, vol. 90, pp. 533–542. Springer, Heidelberg (2010). https://doi.org/10.1007/978-3-642-14493-6_55
25. Laouris, Y., Aristodemou, E., Makris, P.: Prediction of learning abilities based on a cross-modal evaluation of non-verbal mental attributes using video-game-like interfaces. In: Esposito, A., Vích, R. (eds.) Cross-Modal Analysis of Speech, Gestures, Gaze and Facial Expressions. LNCS (LNAI), vol. 5641, pp. 248–265. Springer, Heidelberg (2009). https://doi.org/10.1007/978-3-642-03320-9_24
26. Rosenblum, S., Ben-Simhon, H.A., Meyer, S., Gal, E.: Predictors of handwriting performance among children with autism spectrum disorder. Res. Autism Spectr. Disord. **60**, 16–24 (2019)
27. Chambon, V., Farrer, C., Pacherie, E., Jacquet, P.O., Leboyer, M., Zalla, T.: Reduced sensitivity to social priors during action prediction in adults with autism spectrum disorders. Cognition **160**, 17–26 (2017)
28. Shui, A.M., Katz, T., Malow, B.A., Mazurek, M.O.: Predicting sleep problems in children with autism spectrum disorders. Res. Dev. Disabil. **83**, 270–279 (2018)
29. Sembiring, S., Zarlis, M., Hartama, D., Ramliana, S., Wani, E.: Prediction of student academic performance by an application of data mining techniques. In: International Conference on Management and Artificial Intelligence IPEDR, vol. 6, pp. 110–114 (2011)
30. Kitchenham, B.: Procedures for performing systematic reviews, Technical report. Department of Computer Science, Keele University (2004)
31. Kitchenham, B., et al.: Systematic literature reviews in software engineering - a tertiary study. Inf. Softw. Technol. **52**(8), 792–805 (2010)
32. Vapnik, V.: The support vector method of function estimation. In: Nonlinear Modeling, pp. 55–85. Springer, Boston (1998)

Identifying Fake Account in Facebook Using Machine Learning

Ahmad Nazren Hakimi$^{(\boxtimes)}$, Suzaimah Ramli, Muslihah Wook,
Norulzahrah Mohd Zainudin, Nor Asiakin Hasbullah,
Norshahriah Abdul Wahab, and Noor Afiza Mat Razali

National Defence University of Malaysia, Kuala Lumpur, Malaysia
nazrennasir90@gmail.my,
{suzaimah,muslihah}@upnm.edu.my

Abstract. Nowadays people rely vigorously on online social networks (OSNs) that have attracted cyber criminals' interest in performing malicious acts. Furthermore, with the existence of illicit businesses that provide transactions of fake account services. This study focuses on identifying fake accounts in Facebook which is the most widely used in OSN. The methodology of this study is started with data collection, features identification and learning classifiers. The first process is to collect information on true and fake Facebook accounts. The second process is the use of Facebook user feed data to comprehend user profile activity and to identify a comprehensive collection of 5 characteristics that play a critical role in discriminating against fake users with true users on Facebook. Lastly, we use these characteristics and the identification of main classifiers based on machine learning that perform well in the assignment of identification out of a total of 3 classifiers namely K-nearest neighbour (KNN), support vector machine (SVM) and neural network (NN). The result shows that KNN generate 82% of the highest performing classifiers with classification precision. The findings have revealed that "likes" and "remarks" add well to the job of detection. However, although the precision value is not highly perfect, the findings of this study shows that most fake accounts are able to imitate actual users.

Keywords: Online social network · Fake account · Machine learning · Facebook

1 Introduction

Nowadays, online social networks (OSNs) has been a compulsory tool that every individual needs in their daily live. There are various OSNs platform that have been introduced such as Facebook, Twitter, Instagram and others that are widely used to share about peoples' daily activities pictures and videos (to name a few). With these kind of platforms, one can communicate with other people without boundaries. Based on studies from the Malaysian Communications and Multimedia Commission, until 2018, the rate of online social network usage in Malaysia has reached 87.4% [1]. This

H. Badioze Zaman et al. (Eds.): IVIC 2019, LNCS 11870, pp. 441–450, 2019.
https://doi.org/10.1007/978-3-030-34032-2_39

finding shows that Malaysian citizens are more likely to communicate and interact with each other through OSNs platform.

OSN is commonly associated with someone identity. According to [2], identity is a distinct object connected to a human being. "Name" is a typical instance of an individual. Every individual has a unique name to represent his or her identity. For instance, passport is also typically used to represent individual's identity. Passport normally contains name, date of birth, address, telephone number, nationality, fingerprints and photograph of the person. Although each person may have several identities, he or she must have a unique one in the sense that the identity is only belonging to him or her.

Recently, there are increasing issues regarding the utilisation of false identities in OSNs [3]. A typical situation for using such false identities is to impersonate someone with the goal to perform several criminal activities in the cyber space such as gathering further information for a spear, personal interest and also spread propaganda or campaign. Besides, the false identity is also used for distributing malware such as phishing attack, spamming and scamming [4]. Thus, the promotion of false identity will lead to the creation of fake account in OSNs, which are against the actual goal of the social network platform.

Instagram and Twitter have wealthy and fully functional Application Programming Interfaces (APIs) for acquiring appropriate, real-time and up-to-date user data. While Facebook APIs facilitates access to profile data such as user operations, friends, colleagues, and most fundamental user details (age, birthday, profile status, relationship status, likes, group details, etc.). Typically, the social network profile consists of two primary components of data: static and dynamic. Former is about the data that is statically set by user, while the dynamic one involves demographics and interests of users, and vibrant information refers to user activity and social network position [5]. These type of data can be detected using machine learning techniques such as K-nearest neighbour (KNN), support vector machine (SVM) and neural network (NN) [6].

As Facebook is one of the most popular OSNs[2], and often used by many people particularly in Malaysia [1], this study tends to identify the fake account of Facebook users using machine learning techniques towards data in the Southeast Asia countries. This is mainly due to the fact that most of Facebook users in these countries have identical demographic data such as time stamp, language and culture.

2   Literature Review

In order to use the service, most OSNs require a user to create a network profile containing their fundamental (sometimes private) data such as name, gender, place, e-mail address, etc. The openness of these social networking sites allow opponents to exploit the service by generating various types of fake profiles to perform illegal, adversarial, unlawful, false or malicious actions such as spamming, promotion and marketing, stalking, intimidation, defamation, etc. Specific reasons for setting false profiles, however, usually rely on the sort of social network being targeted. Adversary generates forged identities on networks such as Facebook and Twitter to access users' private data, endorse a specific brand or individual, or defame a user, etc. They strive to monitor members' behaviour or gain the confidence of company experts for specialist locations like LinkedIn and Researchgate. Attackers often target dating websites to take advantage of individuals looking for perfect games and working colleagues by playing with their feelings or stealing private data to obtain cash from these customers. One of the most hazardous fake profiles on OSN dating is called Catfisher, a person who utilizes the websites of internet dating to tempt individuals into a scam romance.

According to [7] fake profiles can be splitted into five classifications, namely compromised profiles, cloned profiles, sybil accounts, sockpuppets, and fake bot profiles, as depicted in Fig. 1. Cloned profiles are divided into inter-site cloning and intra-site cloning. While fake bot profiles are splitted into social bots, spam bots, like bots influential bots and bots nets. On various online social networking sites, the five categories can be regarded as the distinct ways adversaries accomplish their ill goals.

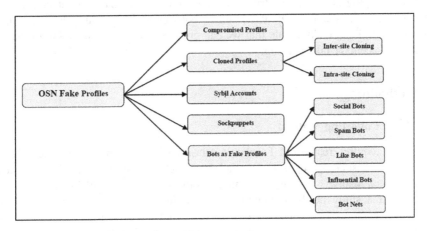

Fig. 1. Type of false online social network profile [7]

There are some attributes for the OSN detection technique that scholars should consider in order to analyse the characteristic that differentiates these profiles from the actual one. Preparation of precise and accurate function set must be prioritised in order to produce an efficient online social network detector. The characteristics can be either manually noted from social network sites or studied using literature study. It is also feasible, however, that some of the characteristics in the literature may not prove to be effective at the moment as opponents continue to change their behaviour to fool and bypass detection systems. Several scientists have recognized various characteristics of internet profiles from time to time in order to train their fake profile detection models [8] and, based on their nature, this study has classified them into 5 groups as follows:

a. **Network-based attributes**

This attributes shows how fake account connect to their contact according to degree of relation such as first degree is their friend and second degree is for their friend of friends.

b. **Content-based attributes**

This attributes tells about how content based can lead us to detect anomalies activities around the Facebook fake profile.

c. **Temporal features**

This features study about time management of Facebook profile such as time-based activities.

d. **Profile-based features**

This features study about profile based activity like following number of other Facebook accounts, post activities and etc.

e. **Action-based features**

This features study on daily activities that has been performed. It includes how many tag has been posted, location sharing, friends tag and etc.

After studying all of these attributes and features, we manage to detect many of malicious activities that is not tally to real Facebook profile behaviour. This factor also can lead to decision-making rule that we can create during implementation of classification of Facebook fake account.

3 Methodology

3.1 Data Collecting Method

This study requires real-world Facebook datasets which are not openly accessible. There are some social graph datasets available which have profile-based feature data, however such datasets are in anonymised form and are unavailable to be used. Therefore, the study needs to obtain data from the Facebook API, although it is restricted to authorised user. These problems are often cited by authors who working on Facebook such as [6]. As Facebook is constantly updating the security policy on privacy, therefore it is hard to access the data without Facebook's permission [9]. Figure 2 shows the type of data collection techniques.

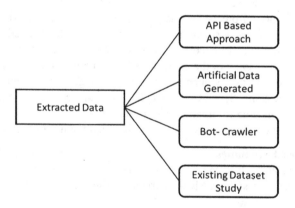

Fig. 2. Data collection technique [7]

According to [7] API-based and bot-crawler approaches are time consuming for data collection techniques and are extremely subject to user privacy and safety environments. To solve a fake account problem in a Facebook, this study utilised an artificial data generated which produce the synthetic data sample based on a network structure or the characteristics of existing datasets. Also, the synthetic data can be produced using different accessible instruments based on any current social network's recognized statistics or parameters. For example, a dummy data set can be generated for analysis purposes if the degree distribution, clustering coefficient, average centrality between the degree and other statistical parameters are known. The generation of artificial or synthetically data can be done by using various online data generators such as GEDIS Studio, Databene Benerator, Mockaroo etc. [10]. This study chooses Mockaroo online generator as the data created is more realistic and similar to the real data [11, 12]. There were 800 sample of data that are successful generated by the Mockaroo which comply with the feature of fake account dataset. Table 1 exhibits the details of the collected Facebook user data.

Table 1. Facebook user data collection

Serial	Description	Value
1	Total user	800
2	Real user	615
3	Fake user	185
4	Assumption real user	560
5	Assumption fake user	240

3.2 Features Identification

Following the collection of the different information characteristics, the next stage is t identify and define a set of characteristics extracted from these data characteristics that would assist as far as possible to distinguish true users and fake users. Finally, a set of 17 characteristics were select out of the different applicants as described in [13], but after a few revision had been done [7, 13–15] the study manage to trace out the most importance characteristics in order to detect fake account as shown in Table 2.

3.3 Learning Classifiers

This study uses monitored machine learning classification algorithms as a final phase in the methodology for detecting false accounts on Facebook. Supervised learners take annotated datasets as input and build predictive models that are used for tasks involving one value prediction using other values in the dataset. In this study situation, the two classes are true users and fake users.

The assumption of using teaching classifiers (as is the strategy followed by many other writers listed in associated work) is that the long-term values of characteristics are likely to differ for true customer accounts and false accounts engaged in multiple anomalous operations.

Table 2. Feature set table with description and intuitive justifications

Serial	Feature name	Feature description	Justification	Measuring methodology
1.	Average Post Likes Received	Average amount of likes a user receives in their own feeds (status, shared messages)	It is anticipated that fake accounts will post and share spam messages that are most likely to have a small count	It is possible to collect information from messages in a user feed like this
2.	Average Post Liked	Average number of posts that the user likes in a user feeds per day	It is anticipated that fake accounts will have a higher activity like ordinary users	This can be gathered from a user's feeds by reviewing the amount of articles where that user contains like information
3.	Average Post Comments Received	Average amount of remarks on the own posts of a user	It is expected that fake accounts will post and share spam messages, with very few comments most likely	Comment information in the feeds of a user can be gathered from the messages
4.	Average Post Comments	Average amount of remarks made by a user in their own feeds on the posts per day	It is anticipated that fake accounts will post and share spam messages, which can take the form of a big amount of comments	This can be gathered from a user's feeds by checking the amount of articles that include the user's comment information
5.	Average Friends	Average amount of friend that connected to user	It is expected that fake account may have huge number of friends rather than normal account	This can be gathered from viewing their friend attribute

K-Nearest Neighbor (KNN). KNN is a technique for classifying objects based on the nearest feature space training examples. One of the simplest of all machine learning algorithms is the k-nearest neighbor algorithm. Training method for this algorithm comprises only of storing the training data 'function vectors and labels. The unlabeled query point is simply allocated to the label of its closest k neighbors in the classification method [16].

Support Vector Machine (SVM). SVM is decision plane ideas that fines a decision's limit. The SVM's objective is to find a hyperplane in the amount of characteristics that clearly classify the data point. It is mainly a classier technique that performs functions in a multidimensional space by building hyperplane that differentiates instances of different class labels. Several constant and different categorical variables can be handled by SVM. SVM supports regression as well as classification [17].

Neural Network (NN). In NN, nodes are linked, sharing their resources to find the most precise outcome, updating the outcome of perception. It is also known as the connecting computer network, which transmits inner values to each other. It has an input, output and hidden layer where input is where we insert the data, output is what is the outcome and hidden is where neural network learn itself about the dataset to generate output [18].

4   Evaluation

This section involves the assessment of the techniques that has been used to determine the efficiency of detecting fake accounts in Facebook. All of the above classifiers were introduced to a blended datasets consisting of a prior recognized real accounts belonging to the first and second stage of users in the social neighbourhood, as well as the Fake accounts. The dataset also includes user accounts that are friends of colleagues in the social neighbourhood, assumed to be real in active accounts and assumed to be Fake in inactive one. In creating projections for unknown user accounts, this study assessed the capacity of different machine learning classification models (KNN, SVM and NN) using Orange tools.

First step is cleaning dataset for learning classifier. In this clustering concept in Orange tool (Linear Projection and Circular Placement) for clustering is apply to the dataset. The combination of features mention in Table 2 is used to determine clustering process and categories the data into four clusters as follows (Fig. 3):

a. Fake account user (G1)
b. Assume Fake account User (G2)
c. Inactive User (G3)
d. Real User (G4).

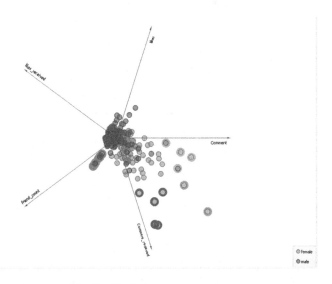

Fig. 3. Clustering process

Second, by using cluster that had been created, the study apply it on classifier learning and use three technique for learning classifier (KNN, SVM and NN) to get the best result of detection. Based on the previous research, the best classifier for detection fake account in Facebook are KNN, SVM and NN [5, 19]. By this it can alleviate the comparison between the three Learning Classifier, which are capable of delivering the best results. Table 3 exhibits the comparison that had been made between these the Classifier:

Table 3. Result of classifier

Serial	Model	Area under ROC curve	Classifier accuracy	Balance of F-score	Precision
1.	KNN	0.967	0.829	0.781	0.760
2.	SVM	0.794	0.729	0.685	0.665
3.	NN	0.958	0.800	0.777	0.772

Based on Table 3, Classifier Accuracy (CA) is the correct fraction of prediction model. If the value is closer to 1, the probability of the model prediction is high. According to the testing dataset, KNN model has the highest CA value (0.829) compared to other models. Figures 4, 5 and 6 depict the results of all the prediction models (KNN, SVM and NN).

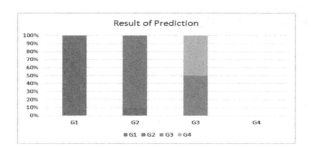

Fig. 4. Prediction result for KNN

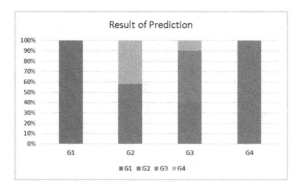

Fig. 5. Prediction result for SVM

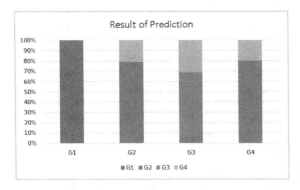

Fig. 6. Prediction result for NN

Figure 4 shows that the prediction of KNN algorithm, which is for G1 group almost all fake account can be detected due to strictly used number of neighbour that had been set. For G2, G3 and G4, up to 70% of detection can be achieved. Referring to Fig. 5, the prediction of SVM algorithm also up to 70% of detection for respective group. Figure 6 explains the result that had been obtain using NN. The result shows that up to 70% detection had been done. In a nutshell, all classifiers provided 70% precision of detection and 30% error rate.

5   Conclusion

Over the years, fake accounts have evolved constantly to avoid their detection. It is therefore essential to create methods to detect the false accounts. Based on the user profile operations and communication with other users on Facebook, this study reveals the fundamentals endeavour to detect the fake accounts in Facebook based on users from Southeast Asia countries. The study used artificial generated dataset for Facebook features as the fine-grained privacy settings on Facebook posed a major challenge to the collection of data. Then, the most frequently used machine learning classification methods are used to identify the highest classifiers. Future research is recommended to utilise hybrid approach on detecting fake account. Other characteristic parameters that can be used to detect fake account such as account ID, location data, devices that is used as a tool to browse social media also should be considered in future research.

References

1. MCMC: Statistic Internet usage survey (2018). https://www.mcmc.gov.my/resources/statistics/internet-users-survey. Accessed 23 July 2018
2. Romanov, A., Semenov, A., Mazhelis, O., Veijalainen, J.: Detection of fake profiles in social media - literature review. In: WEBIST, pp. 363–369 (2017)

3. Kumbhar, A., Wable, M., Nigade, S., Darekar, K., Student, B.E.: A survey on: malicious application and fake user detection in Facebook using data mining. Int. J. Eng. Sci. Comput. **7**(12), 15768 (2017)

4. Guess, A., Nagler, J., Tucker, J.: Less than you think: prevalence and predictors of fake news dissemination on Facebook. Asian-Australas. J. Anim. Sci. **32**(2), 1–9 (2019)

5. Rao, P.S., Gyani, J., Narsimha, G.: Fake profiles identification in online social networks using machine learning and NLP. Int. J. Appl. Eng. Res. **13**(6), 973–4562 (2018)

6. Albayati, M.B., Altamimi, A.M.: An empirical study for detecting fake Facebook profiles using supervised mining techniques. Informatica **43**(1), 77–86 (2019)

7. Fire, M., et al.: A sneak into the Devil's Colony - fake profiles in online social networks. J. Supercomput. **5**(1), 26–39 (2018)

8. Ali, A.M., Alvari, H., Hajibagheri, A., Lakkaraju, K., Sukthankar, G.: Synthetic generators for cloning social network data. In: BioMedCom, pp. 1–9 (2014)

9. Facebook Data Policy: (2018). https://www.digitaltrends.com/social-media/terms-conditions-facebooks-data-use-policy-explained/accessed. Accessed 16 Aug 2019

10. Software Testing Help: Top 10 Best data Generatools in 2019. https://www.softwaretestinghelp.com/test-data-generation-tools. Accessed 14 Aug 2019

11. Generated Data: Generated Data about. https://www.generatedata.com/#t2. Accessed 15 Aug 2019

12. No Title9. Mockaroo Realistic Data Generator. https://mockaroo.com/. Accessed 15 Aug 2019

13. Gupta, A., Kaushal, R.: Towards detecting fake user accounts in Facebook. In: ISEA Asia Security Privacy Conference 2017, ISEASP 2017, vol. 1, pp. 1–6 (2017)

14. Feizy, R.: An evaluation of identity in online social networking: distinguishing fact from fiction (2010)

15. Gheewala, S., Patel, R.: Machine learning based Twitter Spam account detection: a review. In: Proceedings of the 2nd International Conference on Computing Methodologies and Communication, ICCMC 2018, pp. 79–84 (2018)

16. Likhon, A.M., Rahman, A.S.M.M., Choudhury, M.H.: Detection of fake identities on twitter using supervised machine learning. Brac University (2019)

17. Kim, J., Kim, B.-S., Savarese, S.: Comparing image classification methods: K-Nearest-Neighbor and support-vector-machines. Appl. Math. Electr. Comput. Eng. 133–138 (2012)

18. Kudugunta, S., Ferrara, E.: Deep neural networks for bot detection. Inf. Sci. (Ny) **467**, 312–322 (2018)

19. Raturi, R.: Machine learning implementation for identifying fake accounts in social network **118**(20), 4785–4797 (2018)

Internet of Thing (IoT) Smart Home Systems: Conceptual Ethical Framework for Malaysian Developers

Hasnani Hassan$^{(\boxtimes)}$, Robiatul Adawiah Jamaluddin,
and Fadimatu Muhammad Marafa

Department of Information Technology, Faculty of Business,
Information and Human Sciences, Infrastructure University Kuala Lumpur
(IUKL), Kajang, Malaysia
{hasnani, robiatul}@iukl.edu.my,
fadimah.marafa@gmail.com

Abstract. Internet of things (IoT) is an emerging technology that connects 'Things' to the 'Internet' just as implied by its name. The things include our smartphones, smart furniture and electrical appliances. Smart homes are considered the most significant aspect in the field of IoT allowing users to set preferences on their needs, as for example to keep the house in an optimal state and in the case of sick elderly residents resided in the house, to keep track of the medical history according to urine test or blood pressure. Despite these conveniences provided by IoT-based smart home system, the ethical aspect such as data protection and privacy of individuals are violated and thus security issues may arise. Therefore, a conceptual framework has been proposed for consideration in Malaysian context. The purpose of the conceptual framework is as point of reference for IoT developer in the development of smart home system which later can be extended to smart cities development.

Keywords: Internet of Things (IoT) · Smart home · Ethical frameworks · Conceptual framework · Smart cities

1 Introduction

Internet of things (IoT) is known as one of the core technological revolutions of this century. However, there are some important issues about individual data in these technologies [1]. It is obvious that in conventional homes, intruders can just steal or threaten a home if they actually come into the house. But, in the event that a home is connected to the Internet, there is possibility that an intruder or an attacker can access and gain control of your house through Internet connection, from anywhere in the world at any time spying on the home's occupants with closed-circuit television (CCTV) and mobile appliances' cameras connected in the smart home [2].

In another situation, the client probably will not know that their data being gathered by IoT gadgets that automatically share with other applications which allow third parties access for data harvest. This kind of gathering data is turning out to be very common in client's gadgets like intelligent entertainment system such as smart

© Springer Nature Switzerland AG 2019
H. Badioze Zaman et al. (Eds.): IVIC 2019, LNCS 11870, pp. 451–462, 2019.
https://doi.org/10.1007/978-3-030-34032-2_40

television and video game gadgets. These types of devices have voice recognition or vision characteristic that ceaselessly listen to discussions or look for activity in a room and particularly transfer that information for processing to a cloud service, which most of the time involves a third party. An individual may not be aware that his/her conversations and activities are being captured and controlled while being in the presence of these gadgets. However this may have advantage to informed clients, yet can raise issue of individual privacy to uninformed clients who perhaps do not know of the existence of the devices and do not care about how that data collected can be manipulated.

There are even cases in the court that could be instrumental in setting these precedents for all future legal proceeding. For instance, a case presently in the courts includes an Amazon Echo that was present at a homicidal scene, gathered for the proof it may give in convicting the guilty party [3]. So this case, specifically, could turn out to be weighty. Hence, then, individual privacy were not favored by the law written when it comes to these devices.

Therefore, ethical issues such as how data of individual is gathered and shared by third parties are raised. That is on account of there is insufficient legal framework provided that would consider smart home stakeholders in charge for vital failures that harm others. As is often the case, the development of the technology is far faster than policies and regulations. Thus our approach on rules and regulation should be proactive rather than reactive.

2 Literature Review

Ethics is defined as the identification of correct directions for individual's actions towards others and themselves; so the concern of ethics is regarding the conditions to discover what is proper and improper, right and wrong [4]. Ethics is also defined as the study of morality [5]. Morality is originated from Latin word 'mōrālis' meaning character, manner or good behaviour [6]. Scholarly review described morality as "the systems of policies for guiding human behaviour, and principles for assessing those policies.

In IoT-based smart home for instance, there are sensors in and around the environment that capture the temperature and humidity [7]. This application can also gathers all sort of data like human blood pressure and urine or blood ph [8]. The application regulates itself with the utilization of all this environmental data. Anticipate a person who is elderly who lives in smart home. The pre-set appliances could dispense certain amount of medications to this elderly, which triggered by the sensors and indicators that can sense the health issues of this individual.

These IoT applications however raised some ethical concerns [9]. To what extent exactly the usage of IoT will be controlled (usage threshold)? Who will be in charge for possible incorrect medication? What are the impacts of the IoT smart home system faulty? How are these data managed and secured?

Individual data privacy and security posed a genuine concern, particularly in regards of IoT implementation, where possibility such as hacker hacks system remotely for wrong reasons turned out to be cyber invasions. Even though there is increase in the public awareness regarding the risks of privacy in the Internet, due to rapid growth of the IoTs, the relevant of these risks are expected to become more significant owing to the large quantity of data being collected and processed by the 'Things' [10].

3   Methodology

This section explains the methods deployed for this research that involves three main phases. The first phase involves the synthesis of literature review to obtain an understanding of the IoT and smart home system. The second phase is the identification of ethical issues, laws and regulations that contribute to implications of IoT in smart home system. The third part is to analyse the awareness of IoT smart home ethical conceptual framework. These tasks were performed to obtain a wholesome idea of the ethical constraints of IoT and the possibility of applying ethical conceptual framework as a solution. Figure 1 displays the research methodology flow diagram for this research.

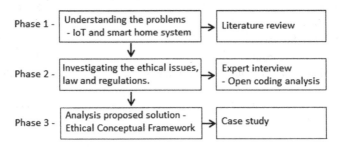

Fig. 1. Research methodology flow diagram

3.1   Phase 1

In the first phase, a comprehensive literature review was conducted to find evidence based on previous studies by relevant authors. This was done to fulfill three particular purposes. Firstly, to develop an understanding about IoT implications, their causes and effects. Secondly, to carry out an investigation on the existing models of ethical conceptual framework with particular emphasis on the smart home system. Thirdly to study about Malaysian laws and regulations in regards of individual data protection and security.

3.2   Phase 2

Next, in the second phase an expert interview session was conducted. The main purpose of the interview session is to have better insights regarding IoT, threats as well as laws regarding data breaches and securities. The interview was carried out with experts from the law enforcements and IoT experts. All of the experts interviewed emphasized on privacy and transparency being the major ethical issue that is not considered by the developers. One of the expert also point out the issue of user awareness, that users are not aware of how these technologies use their data.

According to the expert, there should be a third party between the developers and users such as agencies protecting individual data. However, they gave out some benefits of the smart homes such as convenience, health services for the elderly and people with disabilities. The expert confirmed these issues are as a result of lack of sufficient and clear ethical frameworks laid out for the stakeholders (users, developers and regulators) to take into account. The experts and their positions will be represented in Table 1 below and in addition Table 2 below represents the analysis carried out from the interview session.

Table 1. Experts and positions

Position	Years of Experience
IT Technical Engineer	More than 10yrs
Dean of IT School	More than 10yrs
HOD Network Department	3yrs
Researcher Network Security	3yrs
Researcher in Cloud Computing	4yrs
Consultant in Malaysian Communications and Multimedia Commission (MCMC)	More than 10yrs
Researcher in IoT smart home systems	2yrs
Researcher in Artificial Intelligence	2yrs

Table 2. Open coding analysis.

Theme	Analysis
Strengths and weaknesses	Strengths: Convenience, for the elderly and handicaps by just clicking a button, users can set preferences on their needs as for example to turn on the air conditioning when the weather change, to set alarm or reminder, and to keep medical history according to urine test or blood pressure etcetera. Weakness: Lack of trust, privacy stolen, security and data breach, expensive and power consumption. Data error, loss and tamper can be major issue
IoT technologies in smart homes	Majority of the experts think that the technologies keep changing, so it will be difficult for them to identify the latest technology used in smart homes. Among those identified are: i. biometrics door lock featuring integrated Wi-Fi connectivity. Its Wi-Fi capability allows the door lock to send authorized users push notifications whenever someone attempts entry, and they can also check log history at any

(continued)

Table 2. (*continued*)

Theme	Analysis
	time. ii. Intelligent mirror that served as display where the users can read messages and email while brushing their teeth or taking shower. iii. Robotics and communication between devices, as for example the refrigerator can communicate with other kitchen appliances like washing machine, dishwasher and oven. iv. Energy management, utilization of an environmentally friendly energy supply through use of self-generated solar power v. Voice-controlled furniture that moves about the room, rearranging itself to maximize the living and sleeping spaces in small apartments and condos. vi. Healthcare monitoring such as Smart Medication Dispenser for people with disability and chronic illnesses
Ethical implications of IoT in smart home	The experts argued that security and privacy invasion are the major ethical implications caused by these technologies. According to them, these technologies can affect the functionality of the brain. IoT system can be hacked and the hackers may use the data for criminal activities such as blackmailing and changing the setting of the system without the owner's knowledge
Ethical considerations	Transparency, user awareness, technology migration and security are some of the ethical considerations pointed out by the experts. Trust, integrity and precision are expected by the system especially the one that keeps user profile, behaviour and preferences
Awareness of IoT smart home ethical framework	The entire experts are not aware of any Malaysian ethical framework, but however some of them said they came across for other countries. Most countries have policy and guidelines but no explicit holistic framework especially for the developer
Suggestion and possibility of implementation	Studies need to be done prior to the development including servers maintain by government and contract between users and the agencies. To consider a holistic framework and the compliance of the rules and regulations according to both rule of law and excellent ethical practice

An analysis of Malaysian laws and regulation is also carried out in the second phase in regards of individual data protection and security. This includes criminal activity and its Penalty of Non-Compliance.

Hacking. This type of criminal activity allows unauthorized users to have access to the system. Thus, it is stated under Sect. 3 of the Computer Crimes Act 1987 (CCA), that it is an offense for an unauthorized individual to access the system and intentionally causes the system to carry out any activity in order to gain access to any computer data or program. Anyone found guilty under this Section is entitled to a fine of RM50000 or five years imprisonment or both [12]. In addition, Sect. 4 of the CCA provide further offense individual who are found with hacking offense under Sect. 3 with aim of:

- Commit an offense which involves dishonesty or fraud resulting to injury under the Malaysian Penal Code or
- Enable the commission of that crime, either by himself or assigning it to any other person.

Anyone under this section found guilty will be charged fine of nothing more than RM150000 or 10 year's imprisonment or both.

Denial of Service (DOS). DOS attacks do not have any specific provision [13]. But, under Section 233(1)(b) of the Communications and Multimedia Act 1998 (CMA) [14], anyone who continuously establish a communication with any services of the application purposely to bother, mistreat, threaten or harass anyone, irrespective of whether the communication result and whether or not the individual establishing the communication reveal their identity. Therefore, anyone under this section found guilty will be charged fine of nothing more than RM50000 or one year imprisonment or both and will also be charged RM1000 more for each day that the offense is continued after final judgment [15].

Phishing. There is no particular provision for Phishing attack. However, other legal provisions can be applicable for Phishing offences. Under Section 416 of the Malaysian Penal Code states that any individual is said to 'cheat by personation', if he or she cheats by acting to be someone else, or by intentionally replacing one person with another or pretending that he is a person other than the person he actually is [16]. He or she will be imprisoned for a term, which may extend to seven years and fine.

Infection with Malware. Provision for this offence is provided under the CCA. Under Sect. 5 of the CCA, it is considered an offence for any person to perform any act that he knows can cause content of the computer to be modified. Therefore, anyone found guilty under this section will be charged nothing exceeding RM100000 or ten years imprisonment or both if the action was purposely done to cause damage.

Identity Theft or Fraud. Section 416 of the Malaysian Penal Code make provision for personation which can also be applicable to this criminal activity.

Electronic Theft. Electronic theft such as breach of confidence by an existing or previous employee, or criminal copyright infringement can be brought for copyright infringement either as civil or criminal offence by copyright owners. Section 41 of copyright Act 1987 laid out ranges of copyright offences, including making for sale or hire, disseminating and exhibiting publicly any copy of infringement during the subsistence of copyright in a work.

Other activities that adversely threaten security, integrity, confidentiality and availability of any information technology system, network, data or device are controlled and regulated under the CMA. For instance, to make use of device with the intention of getting details of the contents, sender of any communication with no approval from registered certifying agency (Section 231 of CMA); intercept or attempted interception of any communications (Section 234 of CMA) and extend, adjust, modify, temper with, delete or damage any network devices or any part (Section 235 of CMA). Anyone found guilty with the above mentioned offences will be charged maximum fine from RM50000 to RM300000 or two to three years imprisonment or both.

Section 9 of the Personal Data Protection Act 2010 (PDPA) make provision regarding individual data, organizations should ensure that individual data are secured and should comply with the minimum standard of security laid out by the PDPA standards [17]. Non-compliance to Section 9 will be charged RM100000 fine or two years imprisonment or both and failure to comply with PDPA standards will be charged RM250000 fine or two years imprisonment or both.

All of the mentioned criminal activities are threats to a smart home system which have been discussed in the previous section. Therefore, IoT developers are required to take these laws into consideration to ensure that the right system is developed without any loophole for possible attacks. In addition, users should also be aware of these laws to ensure that they are being provided with the right and safe system. There are many cases where hackers easily get access and control to user's system. For example through open Wi-Fi connection, a user may connect to free Wi-Fi on his mobile phone in which his smart home can be accessed and enter some of his details, these details can be stolen by hackers (i.e. middle man attack) and use it to gain access and control over user's smart home. Regulators will serve as the third party between the users and developers.

3.3   Phase 3

This section discusses the third phase of the research, which is the proposed conceptual framework. Figure 2 displays the proposed conceptual framework and a case study was conducted to analyze its effectiveness. The existing frameworks reviewed are mainly aimed at acknowledging the values of ethic as the basic conduct of business, taking into consideration ethical values in IoT use and comparing it with the GDPR norms. In contrast with the proposed framework, it takes into consideration ethical values specifically in smart homes and then matching it with the Malaysian Regulations.

The framework starts with IoT usage. In consideration, the IoT use is for smart homes implementation with the objectives of smart homes includes comfort, health and security. However, for the ethical issues to be tackled there is need to identify all the stakeholders involved. In this case, researchers will focus on the stakeholders (i.e. developers, users) and regulations. The IoT developers are responsible for developing the "safe" and "ideal" smart homes system. Therefore, it is mandatory for these developers to take into account the ethical consideration when developing these systems. The Regulations provides the laws regarding individual data protections and users need to be aware of these regulations to ensure that they are provided with the right system as well as the safety of their data. In the case of seeking consent, the developer must develop and made aware on End User License Agreement (EULA) [18] that must be accepted by the users in the case of acceptance to give consent or to decline.

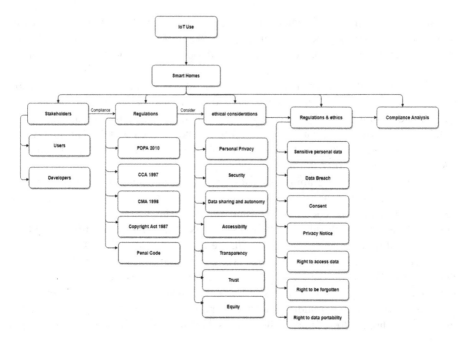

Fig. 2. IoT smart home conceptual ethical framework: Malaysian context.

IoT Smart Home Case and Ethical Framework Explanation. Our proposed framework will be analysed using the case study in the following section:

In IoT-based smart home for instance, there are sensors in and around the environment that capture the temperature and humidity, while for human this application able to gather all sort of data like human blood pressure and urine/blood ph. The smart home regulates itself with the utilization of all this environmental data (such as temperature and humidity). Anticipate a person who is elderly who lives in smart home. The pre-set appliances could dispense certain amount of medications to this elderly, which triggered by the sensors and indicators that can sense the health issues of this individual.

IoT Use. The IoT use from the above case is for smart home systems, where several sensors are installed within the house, the furniture and even attached to the elderly patient in the house to monitor his health. However, all of the data collected about the elderly patient is also transferred to a doctor, and therefore a doctor may intervene if there is the need for system bypass.

Stakeholders. Based on the above case, our stakeholders will be the elderly patient also known as the user, the doctors that provide the medication through the smart home system and the developers of the smart home system as well as the Malaysian regulators.

Regulations. After identifying the stakeholders, there is need to determine the regulations of which these stakeholders need to comply with. In this research, the context is Malaysia; therefore all of these stakeholders need to comply with PDPA 2010 with standard revision 2015, CCA 1997, CMA 1998, copyright Act 1987 and penal code. All of these regulations have been discussed in previous section, together with the punishment and charges in case anyone did not comply with them. These regulations are provided and protected by the MCMC, Royal Malaysian Police, Bank Negara Malaysia, Securities Commission Malaysia and PDPA Department/Commissioner's Office.

Ethical Values. Individual privacy, particularly the data confidentiality in our scenario is very important. Privacy deals with individual whereabouts, while confidentiality deals with individual data protection. That is why personal data protection entails the significance of confidentiality in this case. Therefore, the data confidentiality of the elderly patient such as the blood pressure, the body temperature, etc. should not be tempered with.

In order to ensure the data confidentiality of the patient in the smart home, there is a strong need for proper security. The IoT developers in this case have to ensure that the smart home system is developed in such a way that there will be no room for any malicious attack or breach of data externally. Autonomy is considered to be a prerequisite of privacy, therefore, autonomy and data sharing in our case is the ability of the patient to have control over his communications with other parties involved, or in other words, he should have the right to make decisions regarding his data [19].

In addition, the user of the smart system, that is the patient should have certain level of trust with all the stakeholders involved including the smart home developers, the doctors involved. In order to establish this trust, the developers need not only to provide good security, but also should be very transparent. Transparency in the sense that the users need to know how the smart home system works, what are the processes, how their data is collected, used and shared and also who can access their data. In the case of accessing the data might be the doctors as well as the developers. Once this is established, then there is possibility of the trust to be improved.

Another ethical consideration is equity, in the case of equity could mean equal treatment and handling of the smart home system. The smart home system should be set up by the developers with utmost care, taking into consideration different range of people. For instance, in this case, the elderly patient should be able to make use of the system, however there will be boundaries of which the elderly can be able to use the system. Also, the application should be user friendly enough that the elderly able to apply the device in a reasonable manner equal to their lives. All the stakeholders involved must have a say in this during the process of development.

Regulations and Ethics. This section discussed about the two main principles called regulation and ethical. In addition, each ethics will be matched with the supporting correspondent regulation.

In this case for instance, the regulation supporting personal privacy of the elderly patient is 'sensitive personal data' which is provided by PDPA 2010 that the medical condition of the patient is considered as sensitive data and inappropriate use of this data may lead to discrimination or serious risk to the individual. Therefore, this data should be used in an appropriate manner and only to those that are authorized to access the data. Combining the personal privacy with the supporting law is the 'consent', that is the patient's decision regarding the collection of data. The patient can decide on how he wants his data to be collected [20].

Another regulation associated with the personal privacy is the privacy notice, which entails that the developer should issue a document either electronic, physically or in any format to the data subject (in this case the patient), before processing patient's data, stating to the patient about the terms of personal data collection such as the developer's identity and why the data is being collected and also the techniques for implementing the ARCO (refers to access, rectification, cancellation or opposition) rights. This gives the patient the right to know all of this information about his data [21].

In regards of the security, data breach means that no security breach should take place in any phase of collecting data, usage or storage that may affect significantly in the way of the individual moral rights. Patient's data such as his identity or medical information, if not protected will leave him vulnerable to identity theft.

Regarding the law supporting accessibility is the right to access. Patients should have access to their personal data held by the IoT smart home developers. They also have the right to be forgotten that is they can request for their personal data to be deleted.

But for these regulation compliance to be accessed, going back to our case; the right for patient to request for his personal data to be deleted, specific questions need to be asked. What are processes of the companies concerning these laws and what are the ways in which his data can be erased? Therefore, all of these questions can be addressed in the future research.

4   Discussion and Limitation

The proposed framework is mainly to serve as a guideline for the developers and users on relevant regulations when implementing an IoT smart home system. In order to come up with this framework, researchers try to analyze the ethical and regulation aspect. Thus, it will create awareness to the developers on the regulations and penalties of non-compliance to these regulations and as a result these systems will be developed with utmost care. Also, enabling users to be aware of how their data is being used and shared over the internet.

However, the framework is yet to assess the compliance of the organization with the regulations. In future work, studies can be carried out on assessing organization compliances with regard to regulations laid out. In a case that IoT appliances may requires some kind of communication with electronic payment system, the developers must also comply to guidelines by Security Commission and Bank Negara Malaysia.

Also, the framework is expected to be applicable in all kinds of cases in the Malaysian context. This framework therefore can be applied in many smart home cases in Malaysia conceptually but can lack profundity when used for real life cases. For ethics and regulations during the development, it can be helpful as a guideline, but it may lack profundity as you move to other stages.

Furthermore, the case of the elderly patient, describes that with a good idea of one's ethical viewpoint, can serve as a basis for checklist of related act/laws for enforcement in compliance analysis. Thereby making ethics and regulations to support one another. In an ideal case, a well thought-out guideline about ethical considerations can cover up a considerable part of the regulation.

5 Conclusion

It will be good to find the correlation of smart home system ethical values and the regulation principles with the compliance analysis after the actual implementation. The proposed framework in this paper could be of help for the future development of IoT devices and applications especially in the implementation of smart homes system that can be further expanded to smart cities development in the near future. The matching could help to not only see the regulation as 'some rules imposed from above', but also discover the inner ideas and motivations behind the regulation, which are acted on in software development good practice.

In the future research, the compliance analysis will be added as to map the holistic approach of ethical and legal aspects of IoT development in which although it is considered as non-functional requirements, it will influence other aspects such as security, thus will give huge impact to the usability and acceptance of the technology.

References

1. Christopher, L.O.: Telecommunication, media and technology. In: Guide to Doing Business in Malaysia, Rajah & Tann, Asia, pp.161–162 (2019)
2. Shouran, Z., Ashari, A., Priyambodo, T.: Internet of things (IoT) of smart home: privacy and security. Int. J. Comput. Appl. **182**(39), 3–8 (2019)
3. Amazon Echo Homepage. https://slate.com/technology/2018/11/amazon-echo-alexa-murder-case-new-hampshire-warrant.html. Accessed 30 July 2019
4. Shah, N.: Ethical issues in biomedical research and publication. J Conserv Dent. **14**, 205–207 (2011)
5. Merriam-Webster.: The Merriam-Webster Dictionary, International Edition. Merriam-Webster, Inc. (2016)
6. Collins Dictionaries.: Latin Dictionary. HarperCollins Publishers Limited (2018)
7. IntechOpen Homepage. https://www.intechopen.com/online-first/smart-home-systems-based-on-internet-of-things. Accessed 30 July 2019
8. Kang, M., Park, E., Cho, B.H., Lee, K.S.: Recent patient health monitoring platforms incorporating Internet of Things - enabled smart devices. Int. Neurourol. J. **22**, 76–82 (2018). National Institutes of Health
9. Long, M.: Attack and defend: Linux privilege escalation techniques of 2016. STI graduate student research. SANS Technology Institute (2019)
10. Georgios, M., Dimitrios, L., Nikos, K..: Security in smart home environment. wireless technologies for ambient assisted living and health care: systems and applications. Medican Information Science Reference (2011)

11. Baldini, G., Botterman, M., Neisse, R., Tallacchini, M.: Ethical design in the Internet of Things. Sci. Eng. Ethics **24**(3), 905–925 (2018). https://doi.org/10.1007/s11948-016-9754-5
12. Laws of Malaysia.: Computer Crimes Act 1997. Laws of Malaysia. 9–10. Laws Act 1968 & Percetakan Nasional Malaysia Bhd (2006)
13. ICLG   Homepage.   https://iclg.com/practice-areas/cybersecurity-laws-and-regulations/malaysia. Accessed 30 July 2019
14. Steven, T.: Section 233(1)(a) of the Communications and Multimedia Act 1998 Creates a Chilling Effect on Freedom of Speech and Expression, and Should be Repealed. The Malaysia Bar (2015)
15. Laws of Malaysia.: Communications and Multimedia Act 1998. Laws of Malaysia. Laws Act 1968 & Percetakan Nasional Malaysia Bhd (2006)
16. Laws of Malaysia.: Penal Code. Laws of Malaysia. Laws Act 1968 & Percetakan Nasional Malaysia Bhd (2018)
17. Laws of Malaysia.: Personal Data Protection 2010. Laws of Malaysia. Laws Act 1968 & Percetakan Nasional Malaysia Bhd (2016)
18. Steinberg, J.: Official (ISC)2 Guide to the CISSP-ISSMP CBK, pp. 330–331. CRC Press, Boca Raton (2015)
19. Spyros, G.: Ethics and law in the Internet of Things world. Smart Cities Open Access J. Multi. Digit. Publish. Inst. **1**, 98–120 (2018)
20. Frank, H.: Ethics and legislation regarding Internet of Things and data. Business and decision. Master Thesis. Tilburg University (2017)
21. Galetta, A., de Hert, P.: A European Perspective on Data Protection and the Right of Access. In: Norris, C., de Hert, P., L'Hoiry, X., Galetta, A. (eds.) The Unaccountable State of Surveillance. LGTS, vol. 34, pp. 21–43. Springer, Cham (2017). https://doi.org/10.1007/978-3-319-47573-8_3

Social Informatics and Application for Society 5.0

iPassenger: Smart Passenger Analytics System

Mohd Nadhir Ab Wahab[✉], Ahmad Sufril Azlan Mohamed,
and Kong Chee Chung

School of Computer Sciences, Universiti Sains Malaysia, 11800 Gelugor,
Penang, Malaysia
mohdnadhir@usm.my

Abstract. Automation with intelligence has gradually become the community's talking point around the world. Nowadays, even public transportation such as bus is equipped with video surveillance cameras mainly for monitoring and security purposes. However, they can also be used for other purposes, such as analytics system through passengers counting. This is important to help the bus service provider to improve their fleet management operation by keep tracking of the passenger ridership information. Based on this information, the service provider company can be more flexible with bus scheduling by calculation of lines and stations efficiently. Hence, this paper proposed an analytics system through video footages acquired from daily operation. The incoming and outgoing passengers are tracked based on their head using blob detection and trained MobileNet SSD. The reference line is drawn to make sure that the detected passengers' head crossed the line before it is considered either as incoming or outgoing passengers. Based on this video analysis, the number of passengers is counted concurrent with the location of the bus. This system is tested in several cases and managed to give proper information for the bus service provider. The data is stored in a cloud database for history, graphically visualize the passenger ridership in a day, month or year. Therefore, this system is able to help the bus company to manage their resource efficiently and consequently improving their service quality and lower the cost of transportation.

Keywords: Blob detection · Passengers counting · Analytics system · Passenger ridership · Fleet management

1 Introduction

1.1 Background

Artificial Intelligence (AI) is the ability of a program or machine to understand, apply knowledge and perform a task by like the simulation of human. Recent years, with the development and advancement of artificial intelligence and the Internet, public demand for the smart city has increased exponentially by trying to utilize the available technology. Over the past decade, the number of installed video surveillance cameras has grown exponentially due to reduced cost and increasing public attention to security. This has led to the development of video analytics system with computer vision throughout the entire world in various usages ranging from security to merchant to provide a better lifestyle.

© Springer Nature Switzerland AG 2019
H. Badioze Zaman et al. (Eds.): IVIC 2019, LNCS 11870, pp. 465–476, 2019.
https://doi.org/10.1007/978-3-030-34032-2_41

In public transportation as well, the public is having an increasing demand for smart bus, as part of the smart city [1–3]. In the past, the job of counting the passenger in bus is either done manually by the bus operator (which result in a significant amount of time wastage) or by technology such as infrared (which might not be accurate in crowded and high noise situation). However, public transport companies are always concerned with passenger ridership as it allows them to improve the diagnosis of fraud, optimization of line management, ridership control and forecast, budgetary distribution between the different lines, and improvements in the quality of service [4]. Therefore, the development of passenger counting system has become an important issue in improving the overall fleet management.

Hence, a smart passenger analytics system is proposed. The system will be using technologies such as image processing and machine/deep learning to detect the passenger coming in and going out of the bus and keep track of the number of passengers getting on and off at each stop. Then, the system can extract the information (date, time, latitude, and longitude) from the video frame to determine the arrival and departure of each stop. Lastly, the system can visualize the passenger ridership information graphically to provide useful information to bus companies for better decision making on resources arrangement, service quality, and cost control.

2   Literature Study

2.1   Existing System

The existing systems that are going to be studied and analysed are the Automatic Passenger Counting systems (APC) that have been implemented by some of the bus fleet companies. The two existing APC systems are developed and implemented by using two different methods which are Infra-Red [5, 6] and Radio Frequency Identification (RFID) [7, 10].

The first APC system is implemented by using "Infra-Red motion analyser" based on a passive infra-red technology for people detection and count the people who move through the door. For it to work properly, it requires standard equipment such as infra-red sensors being mounted in the door frame, and an analyser to transform sensor information into counts and transmit it to data collector [5, 6]. It works by having infra-red emitters being set parallelly to one another so that the LED interruption occurs in the direction of crossing when passenger passes door frame for boarding and the entry direction can thus be discriminated from the exit one. It is also known as a "barrier sensors" due to its "bar" configuration at the door frame.

The second ACP system is the one implemented with RFID. This system consists of two parts. The first part will be the installation of receivers or readers capable of managing several data collection antennas in public transportation such as buses. The number of antennas will depend on the size of the vehicle and the number of doors. Then, the second part would be the RFID technology inside the smart cards, storing a single sequential number associated with the individual identification number.

The system works through the antennas, an RFID reader will transmit electromagnetic waves and perform more than 100 readings per second up to seven meters distant from the antennas. Then, when a passenger with smart card approaches for boarding, it will be recognized and identified. The system will then do the counting on the identified cards. The process continues during its trip in the bus, and when it alights the bus until it is carried beyond the reading range (leaving bus) [7].

Furthermore, there is also another system whereby it counts the number of passengers getting on and off when passengers make the payment for the bus fare by using a contactless smart card. The reader equipped at the entrance door will detect the card when it gets near, rebalance the amount of the card in the system and count the number of passengers at the same time. The smart card is equipped with NFC technology which is a subset within the family of RFID technology.

2.2   Features Comparison

The strength of the APC system with infra-red is that it is simpler in term of installation and implementation, easier in replacement and can be installed on any kind of vehicle. While the strength of the system with RFID is it provides better and more systematic public transportation by providing higher quality systems with improved service levels [8, 9]. Besides, it is less susceptible against occlusion, crowding and variating environment compared to the former one.

There are a few weak points in using the APC system with infrared. First, the need to install more than one sensor per door (minimum two), to prevent the infrared ray from being avoided by a passenger and to detect the crossing or passage direction which has led to an increase in cost. Besides, this system has low accuracy while there is occlusion and crowding situation. It will have difficulties distinguishing between a passenger and a group of passengers. Moreover, it is very sensitive to noise, temperature variations, and to dust and smoke which hugely affected its reliability in real-life situations [9].

The weak point of APC system with RFID would be the low feasibility of passengers carrying an RFID card for daily counting and this could also be problematic to people who do not travel frequently as they might not own a smart card [9, 10]. Besides, its performance is highly dependent on the quality of reader (capacity for reading smart-card-embedded tags) being used as it might suffer from huge loss count due to unable to identify those cards that are being kept in bags, packets, shirt pockets, etc. Table 1 compares the APC system with Infra-Red against RFID in terms of way of use, limitations, performance, and cost.

Table 1. Summary of the features comparison.

APC system with infra-red	Aspects	APC system with RFID
Infra-red sensors equipped at door frame to detect and count as passengers cross the line of ray	**Way of use**	Collaboration between RFID readers (equipped on the bus) and smart cards for passenger counting
Susceptible to occlusion, crowding, environments variations	**Limitations**	A must for the passenger to carry the smart card for travel and highly dependent on reader quality
Highly accurate if passengers enter one by one (does not support side-by-side counting)	**Performance**	Accurate if passengers carry card while travel and do not keep it deep in the bag, pocket, etc.
High cost as it requires at least two infra-red sensors to be installed at each door frame for better accuracy	**Cost**	High cost as it requires at least two infra-red sensors to be installed at each door frame for better accuracy

3   System Design and Implementation

3.1   System Architecture

Figure 1 illustrated the overall system architecture for the proposed system. This system consists of a few components which are counting component (passenger counting and information extraction), database (PostgreSQL), server-side (Django) and client-side (passenger ridership monitoring) component. First, by having the video captured by the security cameras equipped in the buses, the video is forwarded to the counting component for video analysis purpose. The video analysis will be responsible for passenger counting and information extraction. This video analysis is done in offline mode where the video footages are acquired after the bus operation is done. The system starts with the information extraction module will constantly extract information such as date, time, latitude, and longitude from the video frame to determine the current location of the bus.

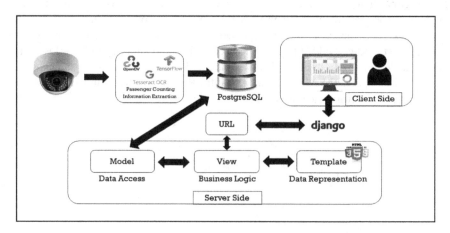

Fig. 1. Overall system architecture.

The details of each stop are stored in the database which their respective latitude, longitude, and range of latitude and longitude (to determine the coverage area of the stop for arrival and departure purpose). Based on the GPS information (latitude and longitude) extracted from the video frame, it will be able to identify whether the bus has arrived or departed from the stop by determining whether the current GPS information drop between the range of each stop's latitude and longitude. Once the bus arrives at a stop station, the system will proceed to passenger counting capability.

3.2   Passenger Counting Process

To perform passenger counting at each stop, there are a total of 6 steps to perform before the result text can be obtained by the system as shown in Fig. 2. As an object detection model (MobileNet SSD is used in the project) accepts inputs as images, to perform object detection on the passenger's head, blobs are created from the images and passed through the net to obtain the detections. Blob is a connected area in an image or image pre-processed and prepared for classification or training purpose. After going through the net, the model will return sets of bounding boxes as results of detections [11, 12].

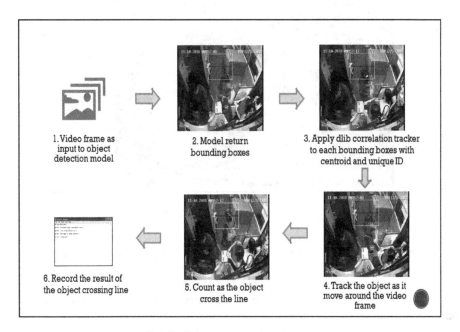

Fig. 2. Passenger counting process.

As object detection is resource consuming, therefore instead of applying detection all the time, the tracker is utilized to track the bounding boxes in between detections. For each of the bounding boxes, dlib correlation tracker is applied to each of the bounding boxes that fulfill the detection confidence level to start tracking it around the video frame. Besides, a unique ID will be assigned to each other the bounding boxes. Centroid tracker is utilized to associate the bounding boxes that are either created from detection or tracker by computing the Euclidean distance between any new centroids and existing centroid. Then, the centroids with minimum Euclidean distance will be associated with the same object ID.

Then, the detected objects are now being tracked around the video frame. To determine whether the tracked object is moving in or out (up or down in this case), the y-coordinate values of all previous centroid locations are obtained. Then, the direction of the object can be computed by calculating the difference between the current centroid location and the mean of all the previous centroid locations. A pre-determined centreline, as shown above, the object can be counted as "in" as long as its direction is negative (which means the object is moving up) and the centroid has passed the centreline. If its direction is positive and the centroid is below the centreline, it is counted as "out". With this, the number of passengers getting on and off at each stop can be counted (Fig. 3).

Fig. 3. Manual annotation for model fine tuning.

To improve the accuracy of existing MobileNet SSD model for our application, model fine-tuning must be done with our own dataset hence it can detect the passenger's head. To do the fine-tuning, around 1500 images have been screenshotted from the video provided by Rapid Penang Bus and for each image, the passenger's heads have been annotated to train it as a new class in the model. Then, the training data is used for model fine-tuning to get the model for our application.

4   Experimental Results and Discussion

4.1   Unit Experiment

In unit testing, each of the individual units/components of a system is tested separately to ensure their functionalities. A unit/component is defined as the smallest testable part of a system which can be an individual program, function, procedure, or method. Through unit testing, errors within each unit are identified and solved as much as possible during this process of testing before it is integrated into the system. Drivers and stubs which are the main unit testing frameworks are used to facilitate the unit testing.

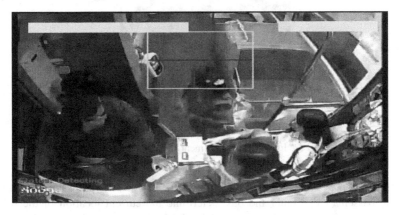

Fig. 4. Unit experiment for passenger detection.

Figure 4 shows the unit testing done for the function of detecting passenger which plays a crucial part in the passenger counting module. Once the video entered the system, each of the video frames will be forwarded through the object detection model net to object localization and classification (object detection). The model should be able to locate and classify the object and return set of bounding boxes indicating the detected objects. Hence, by specifying the detection area in the video, the system should be able to detect the head of the passenger when it enters the range of the area as shown in the figure above.

4.2   Integration Experiment

In the next level of software testing, which is integration testing, the individual units are combined and tested in a group as shown in Fig. 4. The importance of this testing is to expose the faults in the interaction between the integrated units. To discover those errors that usually can't be found during the unit testing such as interface incompatible, parameter values, run-time exception, and unexpected state interaction. Besides, it is more complex than unit testing as it depends on another outside system such as the database. Before proceeding to integration testing, each unit must be unit tested to make sure it functions well beforehand (Fig. 5).

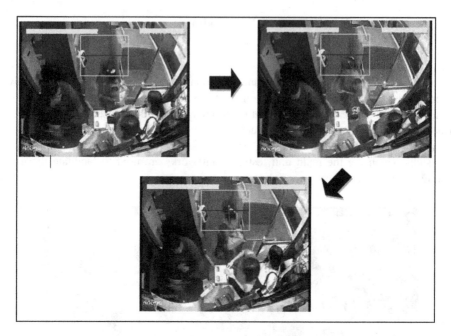

Fig. 5. Integration experiment to detect passenger.

In the system testing, the whole process of the system will be tested which is to count the passenger that enter the bus, determine the current location of the bus by information extraction, save the record to the database and view the data via the web application. First, the system will be entered with the video stream. At the time the video starts streaming, information such as date, time, latitude and longitude should be extracted every n second to determine the current location of the bus.

Then, based on the stop data (range of latitude and longitude that specific the area of each stop) stored in the database, the system should able to constantly determine whether the bus has departed from or arrived at any stop. After that, when the bus arrives at a stop and there are passengers coming in, with the specified detection area (yellow rectangle), the head of the passenger should be detected once it enters the area. Then, the bounding box created should be tracked across the video frame. When the passengers moved in the upward direction and crossed the centreline, the passenger should be counted which increase the total incoming value by one. Based, on the current stop that the bus stops, the ridership data should be stored into the database once the system determines that it has left the stop.

4.3   Summary of Experimental Results

In the next level of software testing which is integration testing, the individual units are combined and tested as a group. The purpose of this experiment is to expose the faults in the interaction between the integrated units to discover errors that usually cannot be found. Tables 2 and 3 show the Detect Passenger, Track Passenger, Count Passenger, and Save Ridership Record Experiments. All these experiments explain the summary, precondition, test steps, expected results, and actual results. Meanwhile, Table 4 summarises the successfulness of each experiment.

Table 2. Detect passenger and track passenger experiments.

Title	Detect the passenger	Track the passenger
Summary	To verify whether the system can detect the head of the passenger that enter or leave the bus	To verify whether the system can track the bounding box of the detected passenger that enter or leave the bus
Precondition	Video input to the system	Video input to the system and passenger detected with the bounding box
Test steps	1. Start running with video analysis 2. When the passenger enters the detection area, observe whether the head of the passenger is detected with the bounding box	1. Start running the video analysis 2. After the passenger is detected in the detection area, observer whether the bounding box of the passenger is assigned with centroid and unique ID and is tracked continuously
Expected result	Passenger is detected, and bounding boxes of detected objects are returned by the model	Bounding boxes of detected passengers are tracked continuously indicating the same object around the detection area
Actual result	Passenger is detected successfully with bounding box indicating the detection of passenger's head	Bounding boxes of detected passengers are tracked successfully

Table 3. Count passenger and save ridership record experiments.

Title	Count the passenger	Save ridership record
Summary	To verify whether the system can count the passenger that enter or leave the bus	To verify whether the system can save the ridership record (incoming and outgoing) of each stop when the bus leaves the stop
Precondition	Video input to the system, passenger detected and tracked in the detection area	Video input to the system, information extracted, current bus location and stop determined, and passengers counted
Test steps	1. Start running the video analysis 2. After the passenger that enters the detection, the area is detected and tracked successfully, observer whether the passenger is counted when its centroid cross the centreline with either direction	1. Start running the video analysis 2. After the information is extracted, determined the current location and the bus arrives at a stop and the passengers are counted, observe whether the system can save the ridership record to the database when the bus leaves the stop
Expected result	Passenger is counted (total in or out value incremented) when its centroid crosses the centreline	The ridership record is saved to the database when the bus leaves the stop
Actual result	Passenger is counted successfully when its centroid crosses the centreline	The ridership record is saved successfully

Based on the experiments of this system (refer to Table 4), it is safe to say that it is feasible to use video footages from public transport to do an automatic passenger counting system. However, this system is not limited to public transport but to any business that requires automatic passenger counting such as restaurants and hotels. Then, the data acquired from this counting system can be analyse based on time, weather, etc. which can help the owner to determine the peak time, non-peak time, and the preference of their customers.

Table 4. Summary of all experiments.

No	Test case	Status
1.	Detect passenger	Success
2.	Track passenger	Success
3.	Count passenger	Success
4.	Save ridership record	Success

An experiment also has been done to evaluate the performance of the passenger counting module which is the combination of the object detection, tracking and counting algorithm. The test has been carried out by randomly selecting 10 front and rear camera videos provided by Rapid Penang. The ground truth values (exact passenger boarding and leaving) are counted manually for each video and recorded as shown in the table above. Then, for each of the video, it is passed as input to the system (iPassenger) to perform the passenger counting. The results have shown the total ground truth for both front and rear videos are 83 (passenger entering and leaving). For the front video, there are 68 passengers counted which give 82% of accuracy. However, there is also a 10 passengers' false error out of the 68 passengers counted which give a 14% of false error.

A false error occurs when the passenger crossed the centreline, counted as in, and left the detection area, but come back in the detection area and crosses the centreline again which cause the same passenger being counted twice. For the rear cameras, out of the ground truth counted value of 83, the system gives a counted value of 59 which gives a 71% of accuracy for the passenger counting at the rear door. Meanwhile, out of the 59 counted value, there is a false error with a value of 4 which contribute to 7% of the total counted value.

The reason that false error occurs is due to the position of the detection area (rectangle) being placed at the centre instead of near the entrance door where there is possibility that passenger might walk back to the driver for an inquiry which creates false error. But, due to the reason that the object detection model is not that accurate and consistent yet because of lack of training data, the poor and inconsistent detection of the model on the passenger queuing at the entrance door will lead to poor tracking. Poor tracking will then cause more false error.

Hence, to improve the passenger counting performance, an important aspect to be given attention would be to improve the accuracy and consistency of the object detection model by fine-tuning the existing model with more training data. With a better detection model, the passenger's head can be detected more consistently without having the problem of redetecting the same object after n second which causes the system to recognize it as a new passenger.

All the footages for this project are acquired from Rapid Penang Sdn. Bhd. and all sensitive information have been taken out for this publication. The snapshots shown are solely for research and academic purposes and are not allowed to be published somewhere else.

5 Conclusion

In a nutshell, all the functional requirements specified for this project are achieved through the successful implementation and integration of the subsystems which are passenger counting subsystem, information extraction subsystem, and passenger ridership monitoring subsystem. With the development of this system, the stated objectives are said to be achieved as it allows the automation of passenger counting with computer vision. Most importantly, the system allows the passenger counting to be done for both front and rear video captured by the camera to automate counting. Besides, the information such as date, time, latitude and longitude can be extracted from the video frame to allow the system to determine the current location of the bus in the video. Based on the GPS information, departure from and arrival to stops can be determined which allow passenger counting to be done at each stop.

By using this extracted information, the analytics system can be developed to provide useful information such as incoming passengers, outgoing passengers, the occupancy rate of the bus for each stop and each bus deploy for a day, a month, or even a year. This information can help the bus provider to arrange the resources efficiently and enhance the passenger experience while using their services.

Acknowledgments. This research is a collaboration between School of Computer Sciences, USM with Rapid Penang Sdn. Bhd. and affiliated with Robotics, Computer Vision & Image Processing (RCVIP) Research Group Lab at School of Computer Sciences, Universiti Sains Malaysia. This project is fully funded by USM Short Term Grant (PKOMP/6315262) and partially funded by USM RU Grant (PKOMP/8014001).

References

1. Allam, Z., Newman, P.: Redefining the smart city: culture, metabolism, and governance. Smart Cities 1(1), 4–25 (2018)
2. Albino, V., Berardi, U., Dangelico, R.M.: Smart cities: definitions, dimensions, performance, and initiatives. J. Urban Technol. 22(1), 1724–1738 (2015)
3. Debnath, A.K., Chin, H.C., Haque, M.M., Yuen, B.: A methodological framework for benchmarking smart transport cities. Cities 37, 47–56 (2014)
4. Sharaby, N., Shiftan, Y.: The impact of fare integration on travel behavior and transit ridership. Transp. Policy 21, 63–70 (2012)

5. Gerland, H., McDonald, I.: bCounted: automatic people counting and people flow management at airports. In: 15th International Conference on Automated People Movers and Automated Transit Systems, pp. 74–81 (2016)
6. Bonyár, A., Géczy, A., Harsanyi, G., Hanák, P.: Passenger detection and counting inside vehicles for ecall- a review on current possibilities. In: IEEE 24th International Symposium for Design and Technology in Electronic Packaging (SIITME), pp. 221–225 (2018)
7. Oberli, C., Landau, D.: Performance evaluation of UHF RFID technologies for real-time passenger tracking in intelligent public transportation systems. IEEE International Symposium on Wireless Communication Systems, pp. 108–112. (2008)
8. Zhou, Z., Chen, B., Yu, H.: Understanding rfid counting protocols. IEEE/ACM Trans. Netw. 24(1), 312–327 (2016)
9. Kulkarni, D.R., Kulkarni, S.H., Nalawade, P.B., Jagtap, S.P.: Passenger counting in bus transport system: a review. Int. J. Innov. Emerg. Res. Eng. 3(3), 101–103 (2016)
10. Ferreira, M., De Gouveia, J., Facchini, E., Pokorny, M., Dias, E.: Real-time monitoring of public transit passenger flows through Radio Frequency Identification - RFID technology embedded in fare smart cards. Latest Trends Syst. 2, 599–605 (2012)
11. De Potter, P., Belet, P., Poppe, C., Verstockt, S., Lambert, P., Van De Walle, R.: Passenger counting in public rail transport - using head-shoulder contour tracking. In: International Conference on Computer Vision Theory and Applications, pp. 705–708 (2012)
12. Li, F., Yang, F., Liang, H., Yang, W.: Automatic passenger counting system for bus based on RGB-D video. In: Proceedings of the 2nd Annual International Conference on Electronics, Electrical Engineering and Information Science (EEEIS 2016), pp. 209–220 (2016)
13. Sojol, J.I., Piya, N.F., Sadman, S., Motahar, T.: Smart bus: an automated passenger counting system. Mathematics 118(18), 3169–3177 (2018)

Investigating the Intentions to Adopt ICT in Malaysian SMEs Using the UTAUT Model

Anis Nur Assila Rozmi[1,2], Mohd Izhar A. Bakar[2],
Abdul Razak Abdul Hadi[3], and A. Imran Nordin[1(✉)]

[1] Institute of Visual Informatics (IVI), Universiti Kebangsaan Malaysia,
Bangi, Selangor, Malaysia
aliimran@ukm.edu.my
[2] Universiti Kuala Lumpur British Malaysian Institute, Gombak,
Selangor, Malaysia
[3] Universiti Kuala Lumpur Business School, Kuala Lumpur, Malaysia

Abstract. Small and Medium Enterprises (SMEs) in today's global competition should establish strong initiatives and strategies to ensure that they can continue to survive. SMEs are now one of the driving engines for job creation and as an economy booster especially in Malaysia. Thus, the application of sophisticated technology in running the business has become necessary. This study aims to predict the intention to adopt the application of Information and Communication Technology (ICT) amongst SMEs in Malaysia. Using the Unified Theory of Acceptance and Use of Technology Model (UTAUT), a survey is conducted with 250 SME owners. A self-reported questionnaire is applied to examine the relationship between factors that influence SME owner's intentions to use ICT, factor that influences action to use ICT, and control factors that mediate the effects of the process of using the ICT in running all the business activities. The findings suggest that three out of five factors in UTAUT affect SME owner's intention to adopt ICT in their business namely effort expectancy, social influence and facilitating conditions. These results are useful especially for the government to plan and to design appropriate trainings to encourage SME owners are willing to adopt ICT in running their business.

Keywords: User intentions · Business IT · ICT adoption · Small and Medium Enterprises (SMEs) · UTAUT

1 Introduction

The applications of Information and Communication Technology (ICT) cover a wide range of areas including health, marketing, finance, medicine, engineering and security among others. In today's 4IR (fourth industrial revolution) era, ICT can assist businesses to collect and store huge amount of data to be used for the analysis, visualization, forecasting and prediction among others of the business patterns. This comprehensive use of ICT forces all businesses especially SMEs to adopt it in their business. Several factors play a role in determining the acceptance of the use of ICT in operating business activities amongst owners of SMEs in Malaysia.

© Springer Nature Switzerland AG 2019
H. Badioze Zaman et al. (Eds.): IVIC 2019, LNCS 11870, pp. 477–487, 2019.
https://doi.org/10.1007/978-3-030-34032-2_42

However, it is not an easy and straightforward task to ensure that all SME owner to adopt ICT in running their business. This issue is not new where Houghton and Winklhofer [13] argue that the technical difficulties and lack of IT knowledge contribute to the decrement of success rate of ICT adoption among SMEs since a decade ago. Indeed, without a proper knowledge and skills, the usage of ICT may be risky and dangerous to the organization [27].

One of the examples of the issues related to lack of ICT knowledge to adopt ICT is the fear of the technology is the fear of using the technology. This feeling occurred because ICT enables several types of threats for the business such as network security threats [18], technical dependency problems [16], and data protection and security [12] among others. Besides, the needs to be equipped with the updated skills and knowledge is important since the rapid advancement of technology can cause a significant loss if the wrong or outdated technology is adopted in the business [14]. Hence, the owners of the SMEs are strongly encouraged to be equipped with the appropriate and necessary ICT knowledge to ensure that the adoption of ICT is beneficial to their businesses. Similarly, Rozmi et al. [28] identify that young entrepreneurs are struggling to fully adopt ICT in operating their businesses for the same reasons which is lack of specific IT knowledge which limit them to fully adopt ICT in their businesses.

Extension to Rozmi [28] study, in this paper we describe a work done using the Unified Theory of Acceptance and Use of Technology Model (UTAUT) to measure the intention among SMEs' owners in Malaysia to adopt ICT. The objective of using UTAUT is to explain factors that influence the intention of the acceptance of ICT. The study aims to provide insights of the current level of acceptance of technology adoption in SMEs in Malaysia. We discuss past research on the benefits of adopting ICT in SMEs, barriers to ICT adoption, the impact of ICT diffusion in SMEs and the UTAUT model in the literature review section. The details of the methodology of the study are described in the methodology section. We present the results on the results section and discuss of findings in the discussion section.

2   Related Work

2.1   Advantages of ICT Adoption in SMEs

There is evidence that ICT plays a crucial role in the operation of SMEs. The use of ICT in the small and medium industries can help entrepreneurs in managing their day-to-day business activities. Sin Tan et al. [29] and Tarutė et al. [32] argue that the use of ICT in SMEs allows businesses to have a broader network of customers around the globe whereby the non-static and geographical distanced type of business environment can be easily accessed. Moreover, the adoption of ICT will facilitate better business transactions between SMEs and their suppliers, increases SMEs productivity, improve their business processes efficiency and provides greater access to market information besides enhancing SMEs entrepreneurial knowledge.

In the latest trend of digital marketing, ICT is argued to facilitate marketing processes and the intelligent marketing systems developed able to assist in the deployment of marketing strategies. ICT allows the introduction of new ideas on mobile applications specifically for business development activities. Besides, ICT also encourages better customer relationship management through better and quicker communication on a stable platform and it becomes a tool to develop stronger customer-business relationships [7]. Braun [9] argues that companies with little cost for digital marketing will be overshadowed by bigger companies that dominate most of the customers over the internet. Not only that, using ICT customers are also able to play their role in influencing the larger population's opinion using the massive social media platforms.

Ashrafi and Murtaza [6] assert the use of ICT in SMEs can provide better and faster customer service and will ensure the company always be in the presence of other companies. Not only that, the adoption of ICT promises positive performance in line with the costs incurred by SME entrepreneurs. Typically, once a company has invested on providing ICT services, SMEs are not only promised with positive work performance, but they can also reduce costs and improve efficiency and provide better customer service. The same opinion was also expressed by Modimogale and Jan [19] where they stated that ICT is a golden opportunity for SMEs to be more commercialized because the availability of ICT increases the motivation of the owner of the enterprise as well as enhancing their management experience and skills. Pires et al. [25] in his study state that the advantages of ICT in SMEs are also to increase the competitive advantage gained from marketing strategies focused on consumer perceptions of value added.

In addition, ICT has a great impact on innovation especially in the areas of management and communication where information and knowledge are easily communicated, accessed and used. This has somehow revolutionized the daily interactions in managing a business. Adding ICT in a business has potentials to generate substantial changes among SME companies by making them more competitive and innovative. This opinion is in line with the study by Ongori and Migiro [21] where they have stated that the impact of globalization has forced SME entrepreneurs to adopt ICT to ensure that they can last long in the market and able to compete with larger companies.

According to a study conducted by Ghobakhloo et al. [11], the modern economic environment monopolized by the power of a huge globalization and competitive competition has led to the use of ICT as important for SME companies in their business dealings. The importance of using ICT includes the revolution of knowledge and how to obtain information. Young entrepreneurs particularly need to leverage ICT power to keep up with other small, medium and global entrepreneurs. This is necessary as a preparation for SME entrepreneurs in an effort to further expand their business to a higher level [19].

2.2 Barriers to ICT Adoption in SMEs

There are still several SME owners who resist to adopt ICT in their company. For example, Ritchie and Brindley [27] list several reasons that influence SMEs owners not to apply ICT which include the complexity of the technology and the complexity of social relationships that occurs internally and externally within an organization after ICT was deployed. Abu et al. [1] add some SME owners are reluctant to improve their business processes and to invest on training because of their own attitudes and fear toward applying new changes in their business. Kapurubandara and Lawson [15] argue that the characteristics of the owners who do not encourage their employees to use ICT and lack of knowledge on how to use technology and concerns over the cost and return on investment are the major factors that influence SME owners not to use ICT in their company.

Low ICT usage among SME entrepreneurs continues to be discussed and amongst the reasons stated is human skills towards the technology, development costs and price issues and concerns over security against these systems. SMEs have limited financial and human resources to adopt ICT in their daily transaction in comparison to larger companies [2]. Moreover, Suhartanto and Leo [30] identify the perceived lack of usefulness of ICT in the business and its resources is considered the most substantial resistance factor for the entrepreneur to adopt the technology. Arendt [5] adds the lack of awareness and high uncertainty about the benefits of ICT as well as concerns over the scarcity of human resources and skills have also contributed to the lack of awareness on the use of ICT among SME entrepreneurs.

2.3 UTAUT Model

Unified Theory of Acceptance and Use of Technology Model (UTAUT) [33] is an extension model from Technology Acceptance Model (TAM) [10]. The current work uses UTAUT Model because it combines both human and social behaviors to illustrate understanding on user's intention to adopt technology. This intention was measured by the behavioral intention to use and the actual usage [22]. UTAUT has grouped 4 main effect and moderating factors which are performance expectancy, effort expectancy, social influence and facilitating conditions. Alwahaishi and Snásel [3] explains that performance expectancy reflects the perceived utility associated with the usage of an ICT and it influences the continuance intention. For effort expectancy, they discover that it reflects the level of perceived difficulty in using the ICT thus affecting user satisfaction. Moreover, social influence has a significant effect on continuance intention to use the ICT because they tend to follow recommendation or other's suggestion. The facilitating conditions is when users have the resources and knowledge useful to explain that the benefit from the usage of ICT is perceived greater than monetary cost which will impact on the intention to use. Hence, UTAUT is suitable to be used to predict the adoption of ICT usage among the SME owners (Fig. 1).

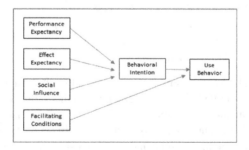

Fig. 1. Theoretical framework of hypotheses. Source: UTAUT model [33].

3 Methodology

3.1 Aim and Hypotheses

We use UTAUT to measure the acceptance of ICT adoption by SME owners in Malaysia. According to UTAUT, five factors influence use of ICT in SMEs include performance expectancy, effort expectancy, social influence, facilitating conditions and behavourial intentions. Hence, the hypotheses are:

Hypothesis 1: Performance Expectancy significantly affect SME owner's intentions to use ICT

Hypothesis 2: Effort Expectancy significantly affect SME owners' intentions to use ICT.

Hypothesis 3: Social Influence significantly affect SME owners' intentions to use ICT.

Hypothesis 4: Facilitating Conditions significantly affect SME owners' intentions to use ICT.

Hypothesis 5: SME owners' behavioral intentions to use ICT significantly affect SME owners' intentions to use ICT.

3.2 Participants

The total number of participants participated in this survey was 250. 84 (33.6%) of them were male and 166 (66.4%) were female. Their age range is from 20 to 74 years old (mean age: 24.71 SD: 8.91). All of them were participants from the digital marketing training. All of them hold either diploma, bachelor's degree or master's degree as their highest level of education. 54.4% of them own a business by selling physical products while 45.6% offers services.

3.3 Instruments

The main design for this study was through self-reported questionnaire. The questionnaire is designed to gather insight on how SME owners in Malaysia adopt ICT and technology in their business. Each element of UTAUT is represented by few questions and participants record their feedback using 5 points - Likert scale (1 = Strongly Disagree and 5 = Strongly Agree). The total number of questions was 54 and the survey was done using physical questionnaire forms. The form consists of three sections. The first section was the informed consent form. The second section was the demographic questions and the third section is the UTAUT questionnaires.

3.4 Procedure

The study was conducted in two sessions. The first session attended by 19 respondents and the other sessions were attended by 231 respondents. During both sessions, participants were requested to gather in the hall after they have completed the final module of the training. They were given the questionnaire and were told to read the informed consent form. After discussing about their participation and there were no other issues about the study, participants were told to sign the informed consent form followed by the other two sections. They were instructed to answer all questions according to their acceptance to adopt ICT in their business. After completed they have completed filling up the questionnaire, participants were debriefed about the aim of the study. Upon completion of the survey, all the survey data collected will be transcript into excel format and the survey data is then analyzed using SPSS version 23.

4   Results

The IBM Statistical Package for Social Science (SPSS) version 23 was used to measure the reliability of the collected data. The construct reliability (Cronbach's alpha) for all the constructs ranged from 0.722 to 0.844 which exceed the recommended threshold value of 0.70. Reliability results are given in Table 1. Table 2 shows the correlation for every item is loaded significantly ($p < .01$ in all cases) on its constructs. The correlation shows that the four items were significantly correlated with the Intention to Use of an ICT. In Table 3, the results of the regression indicated that the three predictors explained 45% of the variance ($R2 = 0.45$, $p < 0.05$). However, the influence between Performance Expectancy was not significant ($\beta = 0.762$, $p > 0.05$). We use regression analysis to investigate the influence of performance expectancy, effort expectancy and social influence on intention to use. The results show that effort expectancy, social influence and facilitating conditions and significantly affect use behavior.

Table 1. Construct reliability (Cronbach's alpha) each constructs.

Construct	Construct reliability (Cronbach's alpha)
Performance Expectancy (PE)	0.759
Effort Expectancy (EE)	0.722
Social Influence (SI)	0.741
Facilitating Conditions (FC)	0.844
Behavioral Intentions (BI)	0.780

Table 2. Correlation of ICT adoption factors.

Constructs	PE	EE	SI	FC	BI
Performance Expectancy (PE)	/	0.659**	0.728**	0.573**	0.684**
Effort Expectancy (EE)	0.659**	/	0.701**	0.706**	0.509**
Social Influence (SI)	0.728**	0.701**	/	0.746**	0.652**
Facilitating Conditions (FC)	0.573**	0.706**	0.746**	/	0.447**
Behavioral Intentions (BI)	0.684**	0.509**	0.652**	0.447**	/

**Correlation is significant at the 0.01 level (2-tailed).

Table 3. Regression of adoption factors on intention to uses.

Construct	β	t-value
Performance Expectancy (PE)	0.762	1.76
Effort Expectancy (EE)	0.108	0.876*
Social Influence (SI)	0.065	1.121*
R^2	0.453	
Adjusted R^2	0.451	

**Significant $p < .05$.

Table 4 shows that Facilitating Conditions explained 52% of the variance ($R2 = 0.52$, $p < 0.05$). It was reported that the influence between Behavioral Intention towards intention to use ICT was not significant ($\beta = 0.064$, $t = 0.77$). Table 5 lists the confirmation of hypothesis which stated that Performance Expectancy and Behavioral Intention are the only factors that has no significant effect on SMEs Owner intention to use ICT. While Effort Expectancy, Social Influence and Facilitating Conditions positively affect the Intention to use ICT among SME Owners.

Table 4. Regression of intention to use on user behavior.

Construct	β	t-value
Facilitating Conditions (FC)	0.064	0.77*
Behavioral Intentions (BI)	3.820	0.39
R^2	0.524	
Adjusted R^2	0.516	

**Significant $p < .05$.

Table 5. The confirmation of hypotheses.

Hypotheses	Confirmed
H1: Performance expectancy positively affects SME owner's intentions to use ICT	No
H2: Effort expectancy positively affects SME owners' intentions to use ICT	Yes
H3: Social influence positively affects SME owners' intentions to use ICT	Yes
H4: Facilitating conditions of ICT in SMEs business transactions positively affects SME owners' intentions to use ICT	Yes
H5: SME owners' behavioral intentions to use ICT positively affect the SME owner's intentions to use ICT	No

5 Discussion

From the results, we can see that two hypotheses were rejected. These factors namely performance expectancy and behavioral intention were not significantly affecting the SME owners' intention to adopt ICT. Possible explanation on why performance expectancy (PE) was not significantly affect their intention to adopt ICT include despite knowing all the benefits from the adoption ICT for their business, SME owners in Malaysia could not relate the use of the latest sophisticated technology to their business. This is like the study done by Marchewka and Kostiwa [17] and Boontarig et al. [8] that suggest users of ICT do not expect much from the ICT and most of them do not bother to use the new technology but rather prefer to keep using the old-fashioned method. Moreover, based on the result, the behavioral intention was not significantly affecting the intention to use ICT because most of the participants do not have any intention to adopt the ICT for their business soon. The reason could be because of the low level on user's excitement to use the technology in the daily activities [17].

The finding suggests three hypotheses were accepted. These factors influence SME owners in Malaysia to adopt ICT in their daily business operation namely effort expectancy, social influence and facilitating conditions. The effort expectancy was significant because when SME owners expect the use of ICT in their business transaction to be easy to use, they increase their intention to use it. This was consistent with findings in the studies conducted by Rahman and Mahmud [26] and Pai and Tu [23] that summarized SME owners are often perceived highly on the ease of use of the ICT for their business activities. They will only use technology is the technology is easy to be used.

Additionally, the social influence significantly affects the intention to adopt ICT because when their peers, investors, shareholders and other entrepreneurs that directly deal with them suggest they adopt the use of ICT, they will increase the intention to adopt. Findings from Mohadis and Ali [20] and Tan [31] show that the social environment has strong interaction to affect SME owners to influence them to use the ICT. It is important to have the ecosystem that encourages the SME owners to be more confident to use the ICT for their business. Moreover, the facilitating conditions significantly affect the intention to adopt because when SME owner receive more facilitating condition to use the ICT, they will adopt them.

There are limitations to this study. Authors conducted the empirical study without exploring the original variance in the theory thus it could influence the final effects. Moreover, the current study did not include the input from business owners that have established their business more than 10 years. The current study was done with business owners who just involved in owning an SME for less than 5 years. In addition, most of the participants are millennials. Their age range is from 20 to 74 years old (mean age: 24.71). The age and the duration of business may have effects towards the intention to use the technology because their experience towards their business and the exposure to the technology would affect their intention to adopt.

Hence, it is crucial to understand on why SME owners in Malaysia do not adopt ICT. Based on our findings, we could use the factors that influence SME owners to manipulate their intention to adopt the technology. Programs conducted by the government should ensure that consider these findings. We understand that the Malaysian government has invested a big amount of investment to improve the living of SME owners under the category of B40 community. There are plenty of government's program and initiatives to increase their living income by improving their lives through business. The government can consider evaluating their successful rate by focusing on our findings. The SME owners are encouraged to use the sophisticated technology in doing business that will assist them to improve business thus to upgrade their life. Technology will enable them to expand and be known by others not only in their current business place but globally.

6 Conclusion

This research attempt to understand the intention of the SME owners to adopt ICT in their business. The study conducted a survey based on the UTAUT theoretical framework. The finding suggests three factors are crucial to influence SME owners to adopt ICT in their business. Effort expectancy, social influence and facilitating conditions significantly affect the intention to adopt ICT. In contrast, performance expectancy and behavioral intention were not. The result is useful to the training provider who work for the Malaysian government to plan and design the interactive way to encourage the SME owners to fully adopt ICT to their business. This is to ensure their business' stability and sustainability. UTAUT model is a suitable approach used in this study because the results predict the intention to use the Information and Communication Technology (ICT) in the Small Medium Enterprises (SMEs) in Malaysia. The suggestion for future study is to include more participants with different group of ages and different number of years of owning a business. By having this, the impact should differ from the current paper.

References

1. Abu, F., Jabar, J., Yunus, A.R.: Modified of UTAUT theory in adoption of technology for Malaysia small medium enterprises (SMEs) in food industry. Aust. J. Basic Appl. Sci. **9**(4), 104–109 (2015)
2. Akomea-Bonsu, C., Sampong, F.: The impact of information and communication technologies (ICT) on small and medium scale enterprises (SMEs) in the Kumasi Metropolis, Ghana, West Africa. Eur. J. Bus. Manag. **4**(20), 152–158 (2012)
3. Alwahaishi, S., Snásel, V.: Acceptance and use of information and communications technology: a UTAUT and flow based theoretical model. J. Technol. Manag. Innov. **8**(2), 61–73 (2013)
4. Apulu, I., Latham, A., Moreton, R.: Issues of ICT adoption amongst SMEs in Nigeria. Int. J. Manag. Pract. **6**(1), 58–76 (2013)
5. Arendt, L.: Barriers to ICT adoption in SMEs: how to bridge the digital divide? J. Syst. Inf. Technol. **10**(2), 93–108 (2008)
6. Ashrafi, R., Murtaza, M.: Use and impact of ICT on SMEs in Oman. Electron. J. Inf. Syst. Eval. **11**(3), 125–138 (2008)
7. Barba-Sánchez, V., Martínez-Ruiz, M.D.P., Jiménez-Zarco, A.I.: Drivers, benefits and challenges of ICT adoption by small and medium sized enterprises (SMEs): a literature review. Prob. Perspect. Manag. **5**(1), 103–114 (2007)
8. Boontarig, W., Chutimaskul, W., Chongsuphajaisiddhi, V., Papasratorn, B.: Factors influencing the Thai elderly intention to use smartphone for e-Health services. In: 2012 IEEE Symposium on Humanities, Science and Engineering Research, pp. 479–483. IEEE, June 2012

9. Braun, P.: Regional tourism networks: the nexus between ICT diffusion and change in Australia. Inf. Technol. Tour. **6**(4), 231–243 (2003)
10. Davis, F.D., Bagozzi, R.P., Warshaw, P.R.: User acceptance of computer technology: a comparison of two theoretical models. Manag. Sci. **35**(8), 982–1003 (1989)
11. Ghobakhloo, M., Hong, T.S., Sabouri, M.S., Zulkifli, N.: Strategies for successful information technology adoption in small and medium-sized enterprises. Information **3**(1), 36–67 (2012)
12. Hallová, M., Polakovič, P., Šilerová, E., Slováková, I.: Data protection and security in SMEs under enterprise infrastructure. Agris On-Line Pap. Econ. Inf. **11**(1), 27–33 (2019)
13. Houghton, K.A., Winklhofer, H.: The effect of website and e-commerce adoption on the relationship between SMEs and their export intermediaries. Int. Small Bus. J. **22**(4), 369–388 (2004)
14. James, O., Nancy, I., Chinazam, K.J., Ogheneovie, E., Israel, A.: Creativity and innovation culture: a prerequisite for sustaining competitive advantage in SMES. Covenant J. Entrepreneurship **1**(3) (2018)
15. Kapurubandara, M., Lawson, R.: Barriers to adopting ICT and e-commerce with SMEs in developing countries: an exploratory study in Sri Lanka. Univ. West. Syd. Aust. **82**, 2005–2016 (2006)
16. Kaufhold, M.A., et al.: Business continuity management in micro enterprises: perception, strategies, and use of ICT. Int. J. Inf. Syst. Crisis Response Manag. (IJISCRAM) **10**(1), 1–19 (2018)
17. Marchewka, J.T., Kostiwa, K.: An application of the UTAUT model for understanding student perceptions using course management software. Commun. IIMA **7**(2), 10 (2007)
18. Mazzarol, T.: SMEs engagement with e-commerce, e-business and e-marketing. Small Enterp. Res. **22**(1), 79–90 (2015)
19. Modimogale, L., Jan, H.: The role of ICT within small and medium enterprises in Gauteng. Commun. IBIMA (2011)
20. Mohadis, H.M., Ali, N.M.: Smartphone application for physical activity enhancement at workplace: would office workers actually use it? In: 2018 International Conference on Information and Communication Technology for the Muslim World (ICT4M), pp. 144–149. IEEE, July 2018
21. Ongori, H., Migiro, S.O.: Information and communication technologies adoption in SMEs: literature review. J. Chin. Entrepreneurship **2**(1), 93–104 (2010)
22. Oye, N.D., Iahad, N.A., Rahim, N.A.: The history of UTAUT model and its impact on ICT acceptance and usage by academicians. Educ. Inf. Technol. **19**(1), 251–270 (2014)
23. Pai, J.C., Tu, F.M.: The acceptance and use of customer relationship management (CRM) systems: an empirical study of distribution service industry in Taiwan. Expert Syst. Appl. **38**(1), 579–584 (2011)
24. Peansupap, V., Walker, D.H.T.: Information communication technology (ICT) implementation constraints. Eng. Constr. Archit. Manag. **13**(4), 364–379 (2006). https://doi.org/10.1108/09699980610680171
25. Pires, G.D., Stanton, J., Rita, P.: The internet, consumer empowerment and marketing strategies. Eur. J. Mark. **40**(9/10), 936–949 (2006)
26. Rahman, A.L.A., Jamaludin, A., Mahmud, Z.: Intention to use digital library based on modified UTAUT model: perspectives of Malaysian postgraduate students. World Acad. Sci. Eng. Technol. **75**, 116–122 (2011)
27. Ritchie, B., Brindley, C.: ICT adoption by SMEs: implications for relationships and management. New Technol. Work Employ. **20**(3), 205–217 (2005)
28. Rozmi, A.N.A., Nordin, A.I., Bakar, M.I.A.: The perception of ICT adoption in small medium enterprise: a SWOT analysis. Int. J. Innov. Bus. Strat. (IJIBS) **19**(1), 69–79 (2018)

29. Sin Tan, K., Choy Chong, S., Lin, B., Cyril Eze, U.: Internet-based ICT adoption among SMEs: demographic versus benefits, barriers, and adoption intention. J. Enterp. Inf. Manag. **23**(1), 27–55 (2010)
30. Suhartanto, D., Leo, G.: Small business entrepreneur resistance of ICT adoption: a lesson from Indonesia. Int. J. Bus. Glob. **21**(1), 5–18 (2018)
31. Tan, P.J.B.: Students' adoptions and attitudes towards electronic placement tests: a UTAUT analysis. Am. J. Comput. Technol. Appl. **1**(1), 14–23 (2013)
32. Tarutė, A., Gatautis, R.: ICT impact on SMEs performance. Procedia-Soc. Behav. Sci. **110**, 1218–1225 (2014)
33. Venkatesh, V., Morris, M.G., Davis, G.B., Davis, F.D.: User acceptance of information technology: toward a unified view. MIS Q. **27**(3), 425 (2003). https://doi.org/10.2307/30036540

Encouraging Correct Tooth Brushing Habits Among Children in the B40 Community Through Gamification

Elavarasi Kuppusamy[1], Farinawati Yazid[1], Murshida Marizan Nor[1],
Chui Ling Goo[1], Muhammad Syafiq Asyraf Rosli[1],
Rohaya Megat Abdul Wahab[1], and A. Imran Nordin[2(✉)]

[1] Faculty of Dentistry, Universiti Kebangsaan Malaysia,
Jalan Raja Muda Abd Aziz, Kuala Lumpur, Malaysia
[2] Institute of Visual Informatics (IVI), Universiti Kebangsaan Malaysia,
Bangi, Malaysia
aliimran@ukm.edu.my

Abstract. Dental caries is one of the serious oral health issues among children in Malaysia especially to those with poor access to healthcare services. According to the national survey, caries prevalence among children in Malaysia are still high at the rate of 74.5%. One of the main preventive strategies that can be applied is through a correct tooth brushing habit with effective plaque control. However, to ensure children can sustain a good practice of oral hygiene is difficult. The repetitive actions performed daily could be boring which could lead to ineffectiveness in the way they brush their teeth. There is a substantial body of literature that suggests gamification strategy can be used to motivate children to perform certain serious activities such as to enhance their healthy life. Hence, this paper describes the work done to apply gamification elements in brushing activities. A total of 73 children from the B40 socioeconomic background (divided into control and intervention group) participated in this study. A self-reported diary is used for children in the intervention group to record their brushing sessions and stickers are added for them to indicate their perception of the level of cleanliness of that brushing session. The result suggests that the post-debris index was significantly lower than pre-debris index for children in the intervention group whereas there was no significant difference for the pre and post-debris index in the control group. This indicates that gamification can be applied in encouraging correct tooth brushing habit among children and the lower cost in the production of the physical diary would be affordable for parents in B40 community to use this strategy with their children.

Keywords: Gamification · Oral health · Tooth brushing habits · B40 community

1 Introduction

Good oral health refers to the ability to speak, smile, smell, taste, chew, swallow and deliver a variety of emotions through the expression of the face with confidence and without pain, feeling of discomfort and free from complex diseases that can occur in

© Springer Nature Switzerland AG 2019
H. Badioze Zaman et al. (Eds.): IVIC 2019, LNCS 11870, pp. 488–497, 2019.
https://doi.org/10.1007/978-3-030-34032-2_43

the mouth. Mouth disease has a serious threat to oral health and consequently affecting the overall health. Frequently reported dental diseases are dental caries, gum disease, dental injury, tumours and oral cancer. A few implications that can be caused by mouth diseases such as caries and gum disease are illness, infections and tooth loss whereby its complications can have a bad effect on the individual and can impair the quality of life of a person [1–3]. The effects of dental caries and gum disease are more serious for children because the formation of untreated caries can affect their quality of life as their teeth and gums can be infected with germs. Moreover, they may not be able to attend school because of illness and can also be hospitalized for serious cases where immediate treatments are needed [4].

Duangthip et al. pointed out that in Malaysia, the current rate of caries prevalence was 75% (refers to 75% of children in Malaysia had caries problems) with an average of dmft (decayed, missing due to caries, filled teeth) index of 3.9 for each child [4]. This number is indeed far from the WHO's oral health goals (50% caries free dentition in this age group) [5]. Also, the indication of treatment requirements associated with high decayed (d) component among Malaysian children [4]. This is an indication of dental caries is a common public health problem among children in Malaysia.

The formation of caries during childhood can be used as an indication that there is a risk of caries in their adulthood. Therefore, it is important to curb the problem of caries formation at a young age to avoid repeating this problem. It has been demonstrated that the problem of early caries development among 5-6-year-old children in Southeast Asia showed that the typical caries formation was high among children when they were at the preschool level. Hence, it is crucial to start a proper oral health care routine especially on the correct tooth brushing activity is taught early to allow the formation of a sustainable habit. Although oral health education on the effective tooth brushing technique can be provided, tooth brushing may not be practised daily by young children. One of the key challenges identified is to ensure they are constantly motivated in performing routine oral health practices and ensuring the frequency of brushing the right tooth for at least 2 min and 2 times a day, which this study aims to tackle using a gamification strategy.

2   Related Work

2.1   Oral Health Care for Children in Malaysia

In Malaysia, oral health care is provided by both public and private organisations. In the public sector, services are largely provided by the Oral Health Division under the Ministry of Health (MOH). For several decades, strategies have been implemented to improve the oral health status of children, with initiatives such as oral health programs for antenatal mothers, pre-school, primary and secondary school children, as well as for children with special needs [6]. The focus of the programs is primarily to provide oral health education and as well as the necessary treatment required by this population. In pre-schools and schools, yearly dental examination and oral health education comprising of information on oral diseases, and prevention of oral diseases are provided. Children are taught by dental health care professionals on the effective techniques of tooth brushing often supported by tooth brushing demonstration. Although this health education is carried out yearly, the number of children affected by preventable oral diseases such as caries and gum diseases is still high. This could be attributed to the failure of adherence to the oral health education provided to the children. A study among 6-year-old pre-school children in Malaysia showed that although their oral health knowledge is good, they demonstrated poor oral health practices [7]. Hence, the application of the knowledge they gain during such oral health promotions is not at a desirable level. As previously stated, one of the factors attributed to this situation is the lack of motivation factors among children to be consistent with their tooth brushing habits. A study which investigated the barriers among school children reported that boredom is one of the factor children shy away from brushing their teeth, hence encouragement in a form fun activities and exercises may help to improve their motivation.

2.2   B40 Community in Malaysia

Population in Malaysia can be categorised economically into three different income groups: Top 20% (T20), Middle 40% (M40), and Bottom 40% (B40). Based on the census conducted by the Department of Statistics Malaysia in October 2017, the B40 category of the population is defined as those with a household median monthly income of below Ringgit Malaysia three thousand eight hundred and fifty (RM3850.00). Several factors such as the removal of fuel subsidies, weakening the global economy, tumbling currency has exacerbated the rising cost of living, which is bound to be the largest concern among the B40 category and Malaysians generally. The cost of living has become a major concern among the B40 household and up to 27% of households living in Kuala Lumpur are earning below the living wage (the level of income needed for a household to afford a minimum acceptable standard of living). Their main concerns are centred on the rising cost of affordable housing, education and healthcare. In terms of oral diseases, low socioeconomic status has been associated with a higher prevalence of preventable diseases such as caries and periodontal disease as well as poor oral hygiene practices [8, 9]. Implementation of oral health education and promotion tailored to the particular target group may act as a strategy to tackle these oral health inequalities.

2.3   Gamification in Healthcare

Gamification refers to the activities that use game elements in non-gaming contexts [10]. Gamification allows users to have full autonomy on the gamified tasks. Each action they take in the activity that has been nominated will provide immediate feedback. This instant feedback makes users more closely connected to the activities that have been dynamically labelled [11]. This instant feedback comes in several forms such as scores, badges, reputations, rewards, and it also could be a form of punishment, fine and many more. Users in the gamified activities are aware that if they do not perform required tasks that have been nominated according to the rules that have been designed, it will affect the under-elements of this gamification such as losing scores, declining reputation and others punishment.

The results from previous research on gamification in the area of medicine have shown that one of the objectives of the application of gamification is to influence patient's motivation in improving health education, preventing and controlling their illness. According to [12], individual motivation can be divided into two namely internal and external motivations. However, motivation differs between individuals. Based on the theory of self-determination or known as "Self-Determination Theory" (SDT), [13] describe internal motivation as an activity undertaken to satisfy the sense of "self-satisfaction" where one's basic psychological needs are filled.

This internal motivation is derived through the autonomy, efficiency and relevance of a person with the ongoing activities. A person with high internal motivation will improve the experience of availability, desire and excitement. While doing activities with high external motivation will produce separate results from the activities itself such as rewards, penalties, and gifts among others that provide an experience of stress, tension, and coercion which in turn gives a sense of satisfaction during autonomy when the activities carried out. [13] argued that many studies have shown that activities with high internal motivation will influence behavioural change over activities that require high external motivation. The reliable gamification can be used as a technique that uses game elements that can enhance one's inner motivation to carry out the activities that are further illustrated, they will be accustomed to continuing to do so.

In addition to increasing the motivation of children with health problems to get better, gamification also has positive effects on healthy children in promoting their active participation in maintaining their health [11]. Furthermore, gamification can be seen as a technique that is practical and easy to use by children [14]. The author also finds that also find that children are more willing to try out home health interventions when interventions are nominated. Some of the results of gamutation namely (1) to enhance internal motivation, (2) easily accessible with modern technological advances, (3) more prominent interventions are more attractive and open to wider community, (4) versatile, (5) tasks that are to be cultivated in daily activities and (6) generate positive experiences through satisfaction of basic psychological needs (through positive emotions, direct involvement, ties with the task, meaning obtained and clear achievement). Furthermore, [15] argue that the use of game elements is suitable in promoting health management among children as it helps children to be engaged with the tasks and to distract them from thinking about the problem. In this study, we aim to assess the effectiveness of gamification in improving tooth brushing behaviour among children in a low socioeconomic background. Gamification refers to the activities that use game elements in the non-gaming contexts [10]. Gamification gives users an opportunity to have full autonomy on the gamified tasks [22]. Each action they take in the activity that has been nominated will provide an immediate feedback. This instant feedback makes users more closely connected to the activities that have been dynamically labeled [11]. This instant feedback comes in several forms such as scores, badges, reputations, rewards, and it also could be a form of punishment, fine and many more. Users in the gamified activities are aware that if they do not perform required tasks that have been nominated according to the rules that have been designed, it will affect the under-elements of this gamification such as losing scores, declining reputation and others punishment.

The results from previous research on gamification in the area of medicine have shown that one of the objectives of the application of gamification is to influence patient's motivation in improving health education, preventing and controlling their illness. According to [12], individual motivation can be divided into two namely internal and external motivations. However, motivation differs between individuals. Based on the theory of self-determination or known as "Self-Determination Theory" (SDT), [13] describe internal motivation as an activity undertaken to satisfy the sense of "self-satisfaction" where one's basic psychological needs are filled.

This internal motivation is derived through the autonomy, efficiency and relevance of a person with the ongoing activities. A person with high internal motivation will improve the experience of availability, desire and excitement. While doing activities with high external motivation will produce separate results from the activities itself such as rewards, penalties, and gifts among others that provide experience of stress, tension, and coercion which in turn gives a sense of satisfaction during autonomy when the activities carried out. [13] argued that many studies have shown that activities with high internal motivation will influence behavioral change over activities that require high external motivation. The reliable gamification can be used as a technique that uses game elements that can enhance one's inner motivation to carry out the activities that are further illustrated, they will be accustomed to continuing to do so.

In addition to increasing the motivation of children with health problems to get better, gamification also has positive effects on healthy children in promoting their active participation in maintaining their health [11]. Furthermore, gamification can be seen as a technique that is practical and easy to use by children [14]. The author also finds that also find that children are more willing to try out home health interventions when interventions are nominated. Some of the results of gamification namely (1) to enhance internal motivation, (2) easily accessible with modern technological advances, (3) more prominent interventions are more attractive and open to wider community, (4) versatile, (5) tasks that are to be cultivated in daily activities and (6) generate positive experiences through satisfaction of basic psychological needs (through positive emotions, direct involvement, ties with the task, meaning obtained and clear achievement). Furthermore, [15] argue that the use of game elements is suitable in promoting health management among children as it helps children to be engaged with the tasks and to distract them from thinking about the problem.

3 Methodology

3.1 Aim and Hypothesis

This study aims to investigate the effectiveness of gamification strategy on encouraging the correct tooth brushing habits among children from a low socioeconomic status background. The design of this study is between subject design where the independent variable is the use of diary and stickers as gamification strategy and the dependent variable is the Oral Hygiene Index (OHI-S). The hypothesis is the OHI-S scores is significantly lower after 21 days of intervention of gamification strategy in comparison to the control group.

3.2   Participants

Seventy-three children from two government pre-schools under KEMAS at *Projek Perumahan Rakyat* (People's Housing Project), Pinggiran Bukit Jalil participated in the study. This low-cost flat is located in a suburb area in Kuala Lumpur which most of the residents are included in the B40 community. 38 of them were female and 35 were male and their age range is 5–6 years old (mean age: 5.55 SD: 0.50). 72 of them were Malay and only 1 was Chinese. All of the participants came from the family in the B40 community where their parent's total household income is below RM 3,850. Seventy of them still required supervision during tooth brushing session and only 3 were allowed to do it unsupervised. Seventy of them used fluoridated toothpaste and 3 of them did not mention the type of toothpaste they used. There were 35 students in pre-school A (intervention group) and 38 students in pre-school B (control group).

3.3   Materials

A self-reported diary and stickers were designed and printed to be distributed to all participants in the intervention group. In this diary, the information about the participants was collected. On each page in the diary, there was a table with a column for date, time and for students to stick the sticker. Three different types of stickers were given to the participants (red colour indicates that students felt unhappy with the brushing session, yellow indicates that students felt neither happy or unhappy and green sticker indicates that students felt happy with their brushing session). To reflect the level of oral hygiene, plaque accumulation on the tooth surface was measured using the Simplified Oral Hygiene Index (OHI-S). Plaque disclosing gel was used to dye the existing plaque debris in the mouth. The index was calculated based on the visibility of the disposing gel on each tooth surface. Dental examination kit and a dental chair were used during the oral examination. All the data was recorded using a dental charting sheet for each pupil.

3.4   Procedure

Before the study started, consents from the parents of the pupils at both pre-schools were obtained through the teachers. Once the consent forms were collected, participants in both pre-schools went through an examination to measure the baseline OHI-S score. Following that, an oral health education session consisting of tooth brushing drills and oral health talks were given by two Paediatric Dental specialists. Then, the pupil in pre-school A (intervention group) was given the diary and the stickers and the researchers inform them on how to use it. They are required to note down in the diary the date, time and to stick the sticker for every time they brush their teeth. This experiment went on for 21 days. The different location of these pre-schools located in two different buildings (approximately 750 metres away between each other) allows us to ensure that participants in the control group did not aware of the diary. Bear in mind, to avoid bias we did this separately to ensure pupils in pre-school B were not aware of this diary. The participants were told that 10 pupils in each group with the most improvement in their oral hygiene will receive a reward at the end of the study. At day 21, another session of dental screening was carried out to measure the post OHI-S score for each participant.

4   Results

Table 1 shows the mean and standard deviation for the pre-debris index and post-debris index for all pupils, participants in control and intervention groups. The overall data in Table 1 were analysed using independent-sample t-test wheres a paired-sample t-test was used to measure the difference for the control and intervention groups. In overall result between all participants, we can see that there was a highly significant difference between baseline OHI-S and at Day 21 $t(144) = 4.593$ $p < 0.01$. The result shows that there was a significant difference between pre and post debris index for intervention group, $t(34) = 1.935$, $p < 0.05$ and there was no significant difference, $t(37) = 1.935$, $p > 0.05$ for the pre and post debris index for participants in the control group. Figures 1 and 2 show the boxplot illustrating the different values of pre and post debris index for both control and intervention groups.

Table 1. Mean and (standard deviation) for the Baseline OHI-S and Day 21 OHI for all pupils, control and intervention group.

Groups	Baseline OHI-S	Day 21 OHI-S
Overall	1.819 (SD: 0.78)	1.225 (SD: 0.78)
Control	1.568 (SD: 0.82)	1.035 (SD: 0.86)
Intervention	2.091 (SD: 0.65)	1.137 (SD: 0.68)

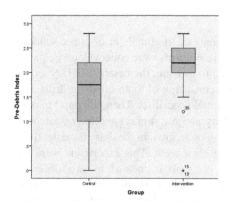

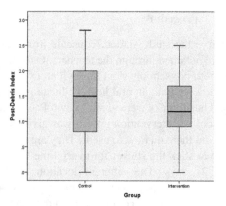

Fig. 1. Boxplot for Baseline OHI-S for control and intervention group.

Fig. 2. Boxplot for Day 21 OHI-S for control and intervention group.

5   Discussion

The risk of many preventable diseases is linked to individual health behaviours, and effective management strategies often require behavioural changes [16]. Pre-school children aged 5–6 years were included in this study due to the high caries prevalence among this group and to emphasise on the formation of the effective tooth brushing habits at a young age as it will lead to the adoption of the habit into their adulthood [11]. However, purposive sampling from one specific location was used in this study to recruit participants, which may not represent the general population. School-based oral health education has been shown to improve children's oral health knowledge and tooth brushing practices [17]. In our study, in addition to school-based oral health education, a self-reported diary was introduced to the children to record their tooth-brushing activities.

In our study, the results show that there was an overall improvement in the level of oral hygiene in both groups after 21 days, indicating a positive oral health behavioural change. One possible explanation for this is because all pupils were introduced to the oral health education slot during our first visit. In the first visit, we conducted an oral health education session to present to all pupils about the oral anatomy, oral health problems and the correct way to brush their teeth. However, the level of improvement in the OHI-S was statistically significant in the intervention group compared to the control group with conventional traditional oral health education alone. Such improvement has also been reported in previous studies, which incorporated game based oral health education to raise oral hygiene among children [18]. Self-rated health is known to have a great effect on the modifiable lifestyle behaviours [19], in our study, we included a simple assessment of the cleanliness of the mouth after brushing as a form of motivation for the children to aim for a high level of cleanliness of their mouth each time they brush. Parental involvement in children's oral hygiene behaviours is undoubtedly important [20], thus this diary is a helpful tool for parents to monitor the tooth brushing habits of their children and take necessary actions to improve their children's tooth brushing habits. In this study, we did not explore the children's perception and experience of using the diary, which would have allowed improving the diary according to the children's feedback. The children in this study were followed up for 30 days, however, a longer duration is more ideal, as according to [21], the average time for the formation of healthy habit formation is 66 days. The sustainability of diary usage by the children could also be evaluated. Future research would focus on this aspect as well as the expansion of the idea of a tooth brushing diary into a virtual version.

6   Conclusion

The incorporation of the gamification elements in tooth brushing practices has shown to improve tooth brushing practices among young children in our study. Initiatives should be implemented by healthcare professionals to integrate various gamification elements into oral health promotions, especially among children to gain their interest and engagement in improving their oral health behaviours. Our long-term goal will focus on the inclusion of tools such as the self-reported diary for pre-school children in oral health promotion programs at national levels.

Acknowledgement. The present study was funded and supported by Universiti Kebangsaan Malaysia through Geran Galakkan Penyelidik Muda (GGPM-2018-046).

References

1. Hegde, R., Awan, K.H.: Effects of periodontal disease on systemic health. Dis. Mon. **65**(6), 185–192 (2018)
2. Zucoloto, M.L., Maroco, J., Campos, J.A.: Impact of oral health on health-related quality of life: a cross-sectional study. BMC Oral Health **16**(1), 55 (2016)
3. Tonetti, M.S., Jepsen, S., Jin, L., Otomo-Corgel, J.: Impact of the global burden of periodontal diseases on health, nutrition and wellbeing of mankind: a call for global action. J. Clin. Periodontol. **44**(5), 456–462 (2017)
4. Duangthip, D., Gao, S.S., Lo, E.C.M., Chu, C.H.: Early childhood caries among 5-to 6-year-old children in Southeast Asia. Int. Dent. J. **67**(2), 98–106 (2017)
5. Ismail, N.S., Ghani, N.M.A., Supaat, S., Kharuddin, A.F., Ardini, Y.D.: The early childhood oral health impact scale (ECOHIS): assessment tool in oral health related quality of life. J. Int. Dent. Med. Res. **11**(1), 162–168 (2018)
6. Ministry of Health. Primary Oral HealthCare (2019). http://ohd.moh.gov.my/v3/index.php/en/the-dental-services/primary-oral-healthcare4. Accessed 27 Aug 2019
7. Ghazali, N., Mohamad Jan, A.S., Shukran, A.S.: Assessment between oral health knowledge, attitude and practice with dental caries among 6-years-old private pre-school children. Int. J. Stud. Child. Women Elder. Disabl. **3**, 184–190 (2018)
8. Cianetti, S., et al.: Dental caries, parents educational level, family income and dental service attendance among children in Italy. Eur. J. Paediatr. Dent. **18**(1), 15–18 (2017)
9. Schwendicke, F., Dörfer, C.E., Schlattmann, P., Page, L.F., Thomson, W.M., Paris, S.: Socioeconomic inequality and caries: a systematic review and meta-analysis. J. Dent. Res. **94**(1), 10–18 (2015)
10. Deterding, S., Dixon, D., Khaled, R., Nacke, L.: From game design elements to gamefulness: defining gamification. In: Proceedings of the 15th International Academic MindTrek Conference: Envisioning Future Media Environments, pp. 9–15. ACM, Finland (2011)
11. Lee, C., Lee, K., Lee, D.: Mobile healthcare applications and gamification for sustained health maintenance. Sustainability **9**(5), 772 (2017)
12. Johnson, D., Deterding, S., Kuhn, K.A., Staneva, A., Stoyanov, S., Hides, L.: Gamification for health and wellbeing: a systematic review of the literature. Internet Interv. **6**, 89–106 (2016)
13. Seaborn, K., Fels, D.I.: Gamification in theory and action: a survey. Int. J. Hum. Comput. Stud. **74**, 14–31 (2015)
14. Jones, B.A., Madden, G.J., Wengreen, H.J., Aguilar, S.S., Desjardins, E.A.: Gamification of dietary decision-making in an elementary-school cafeteria. PLoS ONE **9**(4), e93872 (2014)
15. Hamzah, I., Nordin, A.I., Rasid, N., Alias, H.: Understanding hospitalized pediatric cancer patients' activities for digital games design requirements. In: Badioze Zaman, H., et al. (eds.) International Visual Informatics Conference, vol. 10645, pp. 552–558. Springer, Cham (2017)

16. Sola, D., Couturier, J., Voyer, B.G.: Unlocking patient activation in chronic disease care. Br. J. Healthc. Manag. **21**(5), 220–225 (2015)

17. Singh, H., Kabbarah, A., Singhal, S.: Evidence brief: behavioural impacts of school-based oral health education among children. Ontario Agency for Health Protection and Promotion (Public Health Ontario) (2017)

18. Maheswari, U.N., Asokan, S., Asokan, S., Kumaran, S.T.: Effects of conventional vs game-based oral health education on children's oral health-related knowledge and oral hygiene status-a prospective study. Oral Health Prev. Dent. **12**(4), 331–336 (2014)

19. Zarini, G.G., et al.: Lifestyle behaviors and self-rated health: the living for health program. J. Environ. Public Health **2014**, 9 (2014)

20. Rai, N.K., Tiwari, T.: Parental factors influencing the development of early childhood caries in developing nations: A systematic review. Front. Public Health **16**(6), 64 (2018)

21. Lally, P., Gardner, B.: Promoting habit formation. Health Psychol. Rev. **7**(1), 137–158 (2013)

22. Azevedo, J., et al.: A web-based gamification program to improve nutrition literacy in families of 3-to 5-year-old children: the nutriscience project. J. Nutr. Educ. Behav. **51**, 326–334 (2019)

App4Autism: An Integrated Assistive Technology with Heart Rate Monitoring for Children with Autism

Cheng Yee Yap[1], Kher Hui Ng[1(✉)], Yungen Cheah[2], Suk Yee Lim[2], Jessica Price[2], and Marieke De Vries[2]

[1] School of Computer Science, University of Nottingham Malaysia, Jalan Broga, 43500 Semenyih, Selangor, Malaysia
{kchy6ycy,marina.ng}@nottingham.edu.my
[2] School of Psychology, University of Nottingham Malaysia, Jalan Broga, 43500 Semenyih, Selangor, Malaysia
{khpy6cyy,khpy6lsy,jessica.price, marieke.devries}@nottingham.edu.my

Abstract. Autism Spectrum Disorder (ASD) is a neurological development disorder that affects communication and behavior. Most assistive technologies for children with autistic traits have been designed to support single, targeted activity function such as learning and communication. In this paper, we report the design and development of an assistive mobile application with heart rate monitoring to help children with ASD in their daily life activities. The integrated mobile application, App4Autism was developed using a holistic design approach with the aim of enhancing communication, interaction and learning skills while providing emotion regulation support through music listening and heart rate monitoring. A novel focus of App4Autism is on noise sensitivity; to play music upon automatic detection of loud excessive noise (in decibel) while at the same time, monitoring the user's heart rate using a pulse sensor. The paper focuses on a study to better understand the potential use and incorporation of music listening and heart rate/anxiety level monitoring in the app. The paper provides results of investigation into which music genre is more suitable to keep users calm. Initial experiment involved a general population sample; with results showing that personal music preference might have calming effects on users in environments with excessive background noise. We further expand on the design guidelines for creating an integrated assistive technology.

Keywords: Autism · Early childhood intervention · Mobile application · Heart rate monitoring · Assistive Technology

1 Introduction

For the past decades, Assistive Technology (AT) has been introduced and implemented for people with disabilities [1]. AT can be defined as equipment or software program which maintains or improves the functional capabilities of individuals with disabilities, resulting in improved quality life for them [2]. The design of AT is important as a well-

© Springer Nature Switzerland AG 2019
H. Badioze Zaman et al. (Eds.): IVIC 2019, LNCS 11870, pp. 498–512, 2019.
https://doi.org/10.1007/978-3-030-34032-2_44

designed AT helps increase autonomy and social inclusion for people with disabilities [3]. But, since the disabled experience is made up from a multiplicity of mechanisms, it becomes clear that the possible roles of technologies can be equally diverse [4].

The paper focuses on AT for children with Autism Spectrum Disorder (ASD), a developmental disorder featuring delayed or abnormal development in the aspect of social communication with restricted, repetitive patterns of behavior, interests or activities. Often, autistic children will have difficulty in processing sensory information, causing them to feel overwhelmed. Many individuals with ASD experience hypercacusis, sensitivity to sounds and may get easily distressed due to environmental noises. This may lead to their daily function being disrupted and scenarios of isolation from their caretakers and individuals around them [5]. Technologies are perceived as a promising route for engaging autistic children and to provide therapeutic intervention in order to support them pragmatically with their daily issues. Previous research has suggested that children with ASD have an affinity towards technologies due to their predictable behavior [4].

Currently, most AT and mobile applications children with ASD are designed specifically for single, targeted activity function such as learning and communication. This paper is motivated by the desire to explore the potential of taking a holistic design approach in the design and development of an integrated mobile application, App4Autism, to support learning, interaction and communication as well as musical listening with noise and heart rate monitoring functions. Previous research have shown that music therapy intervention may be an effective method for increasing joint attention skills in some children with autism [6]. Emotional regulation, as supported by the developed mobile app's music listening function, aims to ensure that children with ASD are not affected by sudden loud excessive noises in their surrounding environments. For example, if a loud noise is detected, App4Autism minimises the noise disruption by playing music automatically if the detected noise is above a certain noise-tolerant threshold level of the user (in decibel). The focus of this study is to determine the effects of music in calming down children with ASD and to examine if variation in music genre may affect outcome on their state of emotions.

As a preliminary experiment, we conducted an evaluation of App4Autism with a general population sample to better understand how to incorporate music listening into the mobile application. The aim of the experiment study was to find out if music helps reduce anxiety and which music genre will be better in reducing the heart rate and anxiety level of participants. Participants were required to fill in the following questionnaires; State-Trait Anxiety Intervention (STAI), Short Test of Musical Preferences Revised Version (STOMP-R), Weinstein Noise Sensitivity Scale (WNSS), and the Autism Spectrum Quotient (AQ-10, Adult version). Then, they were engaged in music-listening trials involving different music genres under a simulated real-life noisy environment whereby the participants' baseline heart rate was measured using App4Autism's pulse sensor. Results of the study indicated that personal music preference may have calming effects on users. The finding is essential to help us improve the design of App4Autism to help calm individuals suffering from anxiety, noise sensitivity and ASD. We synthesise our experience into a general design guideline for guiding future designers wishing to develop similar AT.

The paper begins by reviewing related work to provide necessary background and describing the method, study participants and findings. We then propose the design guideline and discuss design implications before concluding.

2 Related Work

2.1 Assistive Technologies for Children with ASD

Assistive Technology is an important topic of research in the area of Human Computer Interaction (HCI). Previous research shows that most children with autism have a high tendency to learn through visual-based platform as visual support is one of the effective tools to enable them to communicate and learn with ease while reducing their dependency on the prompting of adults [7]. There is also research investigating the use of technology in music education for children with ASD. For example, a study engages children with ASD in music making activities using iPad interfaces, which results yield positive response towards the acceptance of technology and music-based classroom. The study further highlights the potential integration of technology and music to improve the focus of children with ASD, increase their educational skills, and reduce their anxiety [8].

Other AT solutions include wearable devices, mainly designed to monitor the state of children with ASD. An example is Empower Me which runs on any smart glasses to prompt users to look up so that they can engage more with their surroundings [9]. Empower Me also uses an emotion recognition software to measure a user's state to determine whether he or she is feeling stressed or anxious based on his/her heart rate or breathing rate. Another similar wearable device is Reveal that detects and provides alert when the anxiety and stress level of a user is rising. It provides data related to heart-rate, body temperature and sweat levels which is useful to determine the cause of meltdowns for their caregivers. The idea behind this device is based on recent studies related to how wearable sensors may be able to assist in the monitoring process of electrodermal and autonomic activity to benefit children with ASD [10].

Mobile applications such as CaptureMyEmotion permits children with ASD to take photos, videos, or sounds, while detecting their arousal level through the use of wireless sensor [11]. It allows children to comment on their emotion at the time of media capture so that they can improve their emotion learning while also provides the caregivers with some insights into their emotions based on the physiological data collected. Researchers at Holland Bloorview have also developed a wearable device, known as the Anxiety Meter, which detects the states of anxiety in children with ASD and helps them manage their symptoms. The app measures the heart rate and then displays them on a mobile device or tablet. The anxiety level of the children with ASD are tracked using the movement of a white bar where if the bar stays on the green range it would indicate that they are in a calm and relax state, while on the other hand if it moves to the red area it would signify that the child requires immediate attention and caregivers would have to calm them down using different calming strategy [12]. There are also mobile applications such as Time-timer that can help children with ASD to manage and schedule their time in an efficient manner [13]. It contains a function whereby it has specific colors to allow autistic individuals to differentiate between the activities they categorised. However, the application is mainly targeted on high functioning autistic individuals.

AACORN is an Alternative and Augmentative Communication (AAC) application that benefits children with autism that are currently facing difficulties in their communication especially among non-verbal children with ASD [13]. The app assists in the development of communication and vocabulary skills of autistic children during the early learning phase. The AACORN is able to predict the words that users may want to use by running an analysis on their behavior and construct a word tree to ease their learning. Another application which could help children with ASD in improving their communication and social skills is Model Me Going Places. Designed for children between the age of 2 to 8, the app displays video of similar aged children interacting and communicating with one another [13]. On the other hand, My Talk Tool Mobile AAC improves the communication skills for children with ASD through words and pictures [13]. This application would be beneficial for verbal and non-verbal children as the non-verbal children may use the pictures or words to express their needs or try to engage in a conversation. This would help them to be more independent. As for children that are verbal, they could use this application to learn and develop more of their speech and communication skills. Finally, Emotions and Feelings Autism Social Story helps children with ASD to express their emotions and feelings. The application contains a social story that displays various types of emotions which could help them learn to identify emotions and express their own feelings too [13].

At present, most AT and mobile apps for children with ASD as reviewed above are specifically designed for a single, targeted purpose or function such as learning, communication or state of emotion monitoring. However, rarely there are AT applications that are designed by taking a holistic, integrated approach in supporting the learning, interaction and communication of children with ASD while at the same time monitoring their state of emotion/anxiety. App4Autism fills in this gap. This paper outlines the design and development of App4Autism as a new concept of an integrated mobile app for children with ASD that uses noise-level and heart-rate monitoring with music listening to keep them calm down as they use the app to learn, play and interact with others in their daily lives.

2.2 Role of Music for Children with ASD

Music has an attention-distraction quality, which can hold one's attention and allow distraction away from the reality of the moment, not to mention modify their emotional state [14]. Hence, cognitive musical engagement such as music listening can provide distraction away from the current stressful situation affecting the targeted individual and regulate their emotional state. This is also applicable in clinical settings, whereby it is found that patients about to undergo a surgery can be effectively calmed down after listening to music [15]. In terms of improving auditory sensitivity issues in ASD individuals, the recommended protocol proposed by Stiegler and Davis is to expose them to an enhanced auditory environment rather than shut them out entirely [16]. With that said, listening to music would be an effective solution to calm down ASD individuals, as well as not shut them out entirely from other auditory stimuli. Not only does music have a structural nature that can promote appropriate and meaningful responses from ASD individuals, it also offers room for development of variability and flexibility to counteract on the rigid characteristics of certain ASD traits [17].

Previous studies also showed that music has an impact on human physiological responses. For example, listening to the music with a faster and irregular tempo will increase the heart rates and blood pressures of listeners [18]. Other than influencing the physiological responses, a study found that the state anxiety scores were significantly lower for the participants who listened to the music compared to those in the control group [19]. This study further aimed to understand the impact of music and its variation in music genre in the presence of background noises by using the App4Autism's heart rate monitoring function.

3   Methodology

3.1   System Design

We developed an integrated mobile application, App4Autism, connecting wirelessly to a pulse sensor for heart rate detection and monitoring. The pulse-sensor is connected to an Arduino UNO board and has the capability of sending data over to App4Autism using Bluetooth services. When powered up, the pulse sensor will display a green LED light whereas the HC-06 Bluetooth module will display a blinking red LED light (Fig. 1).

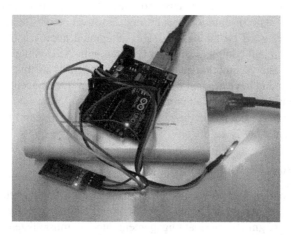

Fig. 1. Hardware setup for heart rate monitoring using pulse sensor and Arduino UNO (Color figure online)

The Graphical User Interface (GUI) design of the mobile app was designed based on research recommendations on suitable colours for children with ASD. The highest color preference for children with ASD are Blue, Red, Green and Yellow rather than Pink and Brown [20]. Therefore, the GUI of App4Autism was designed using the color Blue and Yellow, to be simple and easy to use.

3.2   App Development

The programming language used in developing the heart rate detector was Arduino language with the use of the Arduino IDE and Android Studio. The snippet of Arduino code shows how Arduino is used to power up the board and pulse-sensor [15] (Fig. 2). The output of the pulse-sensor data could be viewed either using a Serial Monitor provided by the Arduino IDE or using the App4Autism's heart rate monitor display function through the use of Bluetooth connection (Fig. 3).

```
void setup() {
    pinMode(blinkPin, OUTPUT);        // pin that will blink to your heartbeat!
    pinMode(fadePin, OUTPUT);         // pin that will fade to your heartbeat!
    Serial.begin(115200);            // we agree to talk fast!
    interruptSetup();                 // sets up to read Pulse Sensor signal every 2mS
    // UN-COMMENT THE NEXT LINE IF YOU ARE POWERING The Pulse Sensor AT LOW VOLTAGE,
    // AND APPLY THAT VOLTAGE TO THE A-REF PIN
    //    analogReference(EXTERNAL);
Genotronex.begin(9600);
    Genotronex.println("Bluetooth On please press 1 or 0 blink LED ..");
    pinMode(ledpin, OUTPUT);
}

void loop() {

    serialOutput();

    if (QS == true) {        // A Heartbeat Was Found
                             // BPM and IBI have been Determined
                             // Quantified Self "QS" true when arduino finds a heartbeat
        digitalWrite(blinkPin, HIGH);   // Blink LED, we got a beat.
        fadeRate = 255;                 // Makes the LED Fade Effect Happen
                                        // Set 'fadeRate' Variable to 255 to fade LED with pulse
        serialOutputWhenBeatHappens();  // A Beat Happened, Output that to serial.
        QS = false;                     // reset the Quantified Self flag for next time
    }
    else {

        digitalWrite(blinkPin, LOW);    // There is not beat, turn off pin 13 LED
    }

    ledFadeToBeat();                    // Makes the LED Fade Effect Happen
    if (Genotronex.available()) {
BluetoothData=Genotronex.read();

}
    delay(20);                          // take a break
}
```

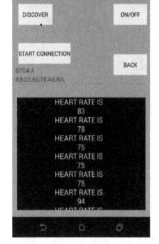

Fig. 2. Snippet of code for pulse-sensor   **Fig. 3.** Heart rate monitor

The integrated mobile app, App4Autism contains 5 primary functions: Pictographs, Quiz, Drawing Board, Music Player, and Heart rate monitor:

- The Pictographs was designed as a gallery which contains different pictures and a text-to-speech function to help children with ASD to accelerate their learning and encourages their oral skills (Fig. 4).
- The quiz function was designed to test the knowledge of what the children have learned through the pictographs.
- The drawing board was designed to enable children to draw and paint freely using their fingers which could help them to improve their kinesthetics skills, which artwork can be saved into the phone gallery once completed (Fig. 5).
- The music player was designed to provide music for children with ASD in order to help them calm down in the presence of loud noise. Users can set the noise threshold level (in decibel) according to the noise tolerance level of each child (Fig. 6). When the app detects a loud noise above the pre-set threshold level, music will be automatically played by the music player. Users were recommended to wear

noise cancelling headphones to listen to the music to minimise or block out the external, disruptive noise.

- Finally, the heart rate monitor was designed to display the live heart rate data of the users using the pulse sensor.

Fig. 4. Pictograph

Fig. 5. Drawing board

Fig. 6. Music player

3.3 Participant Selection

The preliminary study focuses on testing the App4Autism with a general population sample, before deploying the app to children with ASD in the next phase of research. Two experiments were conducted: (1) to evaluate the effectiveness of music therapy and impact of music genre towards reducing anxiety level of users when placed in a background with excessive noises, and (2) to perform a Mobile Usability Scale (MUS) test to determine the usability of the mobile application. A total of 60 under-graduate students from The University of Nottingham Malaysia (UNM) were recruited to take part in the first experiment. Among them a total of 31 were females and 29 of them were males, all in the age range of 18 to 24 years old (M = 21.08, SD = 1.45). For the MUS testing, a total of 10 participants were recruited to include 2 females and 8 males in the age range of 19 to 22 years old (M = 21.9, SD = 1.04).

3.4 Evaluation Process

The first experiment was conducted under a controlled setting which reflects a real-life situation of being in an environment filled with loud background noises. The loud excessive noise was replicated by playing a babble audio stimulus in the background through the use of speakers. Two different genres of music were selected for use in this experiment: classical music and metal music. The experiment used a between-group design where participants were assigned under three different categories of music randomly: classical music, metal music, or silence. The experiment also comprised of different covariables such as noise sensitivity scores, characteristics of autism, and music preference, whereas the dependent variable would be the distinction in pulse rate before and after the music stimulus (babble) was played.

The music experiment consisted of two components: questionnaires and music-listening user trials. Initially, participants were required to fill in the State-Trait Anxiety Intervention (STAI), Short Test of Musical Preferences Revised Version (STOMP-R), Weinstein Noise Sensitivity Scale (WNSS), and the Autism Spectrum Quotient (AQ-10, Adult version). Next, participants were required to wear a headphone and the app's pulse sensor, both connected to the App4Autism app. The participants' heart rate was measured in 3 different phases during the music listening trial: at the start after placing the headphone, when babble was played, and when a different category of music was played (only one). Each phase lasted for 2 min and 30 s. When the babble was played using a speaker, participants were required to fill in the anxiety part of the STAI. When a category of music was selected and played, while the babble was still playing in the background, participants would fill in the STAI completely. The heart rate of the participant was measured throughout each phase and a debrief session was provided for the participants before they leave. Further data analysis was conducted on the heart rate collected data through the use of IBM SPSS Statistics.

For the usability testing of mobile app, participants filled in a Mobile Usability Scale (MUS) questionnaire. The score of each scale would be 1 to 5 where 1 being 'Strongly Disagree' and 5 being 'Strongly Agree'. The average score of each question was then calculated for interpreting the usability scale score.

4 Results

4.1 Experiment Results

After analyzing the data obtained from the first experiment, the means and standard deviations of each variables are displayed in Table 1. Differences in pulse rate are obtained by calculating the baseline and condition phase average pulse rates.

Table 1. Result of means (and Standard Deviations) of WNSS Scores, AQ-10 Scores, number of participants (N) and pulse rates

Noise Sensitivity[a]	87.70 (13.10)				
Autistic Traits[b]	23.16 (3.09)				
Pulse Rates	Baseline	Babble	Condition	Difference	N
Classical	77.83 (8.65)	77.07 (8.46)	78.11 (7.77)	0.28	19
Metal	76.18 (16.88)	76.09 (14.16)	76.78 (12.32)	0.60	19
Silence	76.07 (9.36)	77.86 (9.80)	77.65 (9.77)	1.58	18

Note. Four participants' data were excluded due to corrupted pulse rate data.
a: Weinstein Noise Sensitivity Scale
b: Autism Quotient (AQ-10)

In order to determine the effectiveness of each music genre in helping individuals to calm down when placed in a background with excessive noises, the music conditions with pulse rate differences were compared and presented in Fig. 7. A one-way analysis of variance (ANOVA), conducted using IBM SPSS showed that there is no significant difference in pulse rate differences for all three conditions, $F_{(2,53)} = 0.404$, $p = 0.670$.

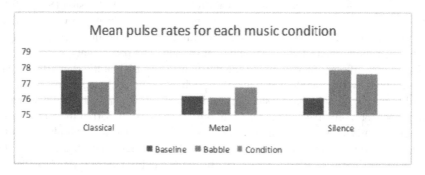

Fig. 7. Mean pulse rates for each music condition during the three phases of trials

In order to determine whether individual music preferences could influence calming effects, a comparison was made between music conditions and music preferences along with pulse rate differences. For music preference, the average STOMP-R scores of the "Sophisticated" (classical music) and "Intense" (metal music) categories were compared for each participant and grouped into the category where a higher score was obtained. One participant was excluded from this analysis due to the same average scores for both STOMP-R categories. The total number of participants in "Sophisticated" group in each music condition would be Classical:15, Metal: 11, Silence: 15, whereas in the "Intense" group would be Classical: 4, Metal: 8, Silence: 2. The mean pulse rate differences for the "Sophisticated" group is displayed in Fig. 8 while the pulse rate differences for the "Intense" group is displayed in Fig. 9. A 2 × 3 ANOVA showed that there was a trend towards the significance of pulse rate differences in all three conditions, $F_{(2,49)} = 2.727$, $p = 0.075$.

In order to determine whether the mobile application might be useful for noise sensitive and individuals with ASD, the correlation between noise sensitivity traits were explored in order to determine whether these factors could affect pulse rate differences. Correlational analyses results are displayed in Table 2 and none of the findings were statistically significant.

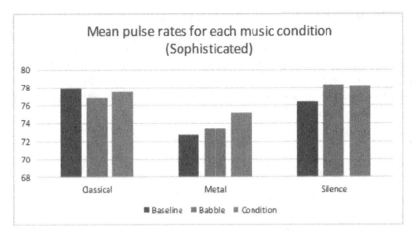

Fig. 8. Mean pulse rates of "Sophisticated" group for each music condition during the three phases of trials

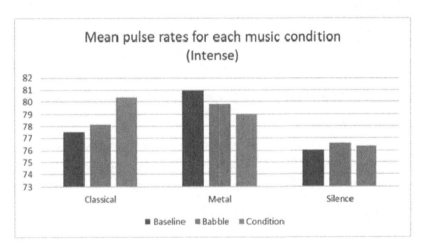

Fig. 9. Mean pulse rates of the "Intense" group for each music condition during the three phases of trials

Table 2. Result of correlations between WNSS Scores, AQ-10 scores and pulse rate differences

	WNSS	AQ-10
Pulse rate differences	0.173	−0.045

However, a significance was found between music genre and state anxiety score, F $(2,52) = 0.466$, $p = 0.007$. In order to determine how music genre affects the anxiety score, a post hoc test (Bonferroni) was conducted. Results revealed that the reduce in state anxiety score is higher with classical music compared to metal music ($p = 0.012$), whereas silence condition had a significant lower state anxiety score compared to metal music (p = 0.030). However, no significant difference was found between classical music and silence condition (p = 1.000). In general, there were slight differences in state anxiety scores across the three different music conditions (Fig. 10). Classical music holds the largest effect in decreasing heart rate, followed by silence condition and metal music. The means and standard deviations of heart rate and state anxiety scores are shown below in Table 3.

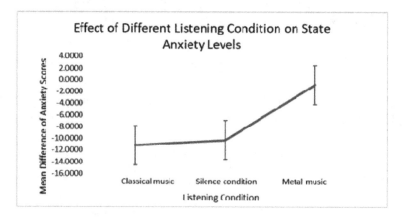

Fig. 10. Effect of classical music, silence condition, metal music on state anxiety scores

Table 3. Result of means (and Standard Deviations) of state anxiety scores

Anxiety Scores	Babble	Condition	Mean Difference Scores	N
Classical	48.00(7.79)	36.79(9.57)	−11.21(8,65)	19
Metal	48.68(9.46)	47.84(12.28)	−0.84(9.87)	19
Silence	45.65(9.23)	35.35(9.58)	−10.29(12.39)	17

4.2   Results of Mobile Usability Scale (MUS)

The Mobile Usability Scale, adapted from the standard System Usability Scale (SUS), was used to evaluate the usability performance of the application, which average score is shown in Table 4.

Based on the calculation for interpreting the SUS score, the final MUS score for the mobile application, App4Autism was 71.8, within the rating of 'Good'. Results indicated that the app's functionalities were usable and acceptable, and participants were clear with the objective of the app. This would allow the mobile application to be tested and used by children with ASD in future.

Table 4. Results of mobile usability scale test

No.	Usability scale questions	Average score
1	I think that I would like to use this mobile application frequently	3.3
2	I found the mobile application unnecessarily complex	2.2
3	I thought the mobile application was easy to use	3.2
4	I think that I would need the support of a technical person to be able to use this mobile application	2.1
5	I found the various functions in this mobile application were well integrated	4.2
6	I thought there was too much inconsistency in this mobile application	2.1
7	I would imagine that most people would learn to use this mobile application very quickly	4.2
8	I found the mobile application very cumbersome to use	2.1
9	I felt very confident using the mobile application	3.8
10	I needed to learn a lot of things before I could get going with this mobile application	1.5

5 Discussion

Based on the results obtained from the first music experiment, when participants were placed in a situation with excessive loud background noises, they did not calm down when music was played as indicated by the heart rate data of the participants. However, when state anxiety and music preferences were included in the analysis, there were significance in pulse rate differences between each music condition. The "Sophisticated" group calmed down when classical music was being played but becoming more distressed when metal music was being played. In contrast, for the "Intense" group they managed to calm down when metal music was played but becoming more distressed as classical music was being played. Thus, these findings indicated that music preference plays an important role in determining the heart rate of the participants as when listening to music within their preferred genre, it could result in the participant being more excited instead of being calmed.

Each individual perceives music in a different manner as not all music genre could calm a person down or excite them [21]. Positive effects are possible with music which may have conflicting results for the experiment conducted. However, since this experiment was tested on participants without developmental disorder, when used on children with ASD it could have a different result. In previous research, most music therapy involves interaction with the children and not just only with the presence of music. In the experiment conducted, there was an absence of interaction as participants were sitting down while filling up questionnaires and having their heart rate measured.

At present, the results of the study suggested that heart rate may not be a suitable option for measuring the emotional state of individuals with ASD. However, there are many other physiological responses that could be considered for use such as Galvanic Skin Response (GSR), blood pressure and cortical activity. However, other similar study found that one's heart rate would increase significantly with familiar music [22] and depends on factors such as preference, current mood and music training [23]. Music is an influential cue that can generate emotional experiences from the episodic memory, and is a pervasive element of social life and accompanies many significant events in an individual's life [24]. As such, from the results of the study, we have learned that when designing and incorporating musical listening into App4Autism, we need to obtain relevant data based on the music preference of the children from the primary caregivers. Playing music of their own choice will be more effective to calm them down and reduce their anxiety level in the presence of loud noise.

We propose an integrated design framework with several factors to be considered by future designers when designing suitable AT for children with ASD as shown in Fig. 11. The important factors include education/learning interest, communication and social interaction, and the center of them all would be emotion. Emotion plays a significant role because if a child is having an anxiety attack or meltdown, he/she could temporarily lose control of their emotion. Inadvertently, this would have a negative impact towards their social, learning and interacting skills. As such an important concept feature behind the App4Autism is its ability to help regulate the state of users so that they can pay attention and carry out other activities such as learning and communication well, with minimal disruption. In the future, testing can be done by providing parents the application so that they can monitor the state of their children and provide feedback on the usability and effectiveness of the application. Primary caregivers will monitor the children under daily basis as the breakdown of children with ASD is unpredictable.

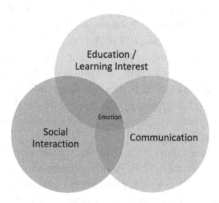

Fig. 11. Design guidelines when creating an integrated assistive technology application for children with ASD

6   Conclusion

In conclusion, the paper presents a new AT concept of an integrated mobile application with heart rate monitoring to help researchers and primary caregivers monitor the emotional state of children with ASD. Other integrated functions of App4Autism include a pictograph with a text-to-speech function which could be used as a form of communication by nonverbal children with ASD, a quiz test to measure their learning gains, a drawing board to help them express their creativity, a music player to play music intended to calm them down, adjustable based on the noise sensitivity of the children, and finally a heart rate monitor to determine the emotional state of the children. Results from the music experiment suggested that music preference plays an important factor in regulating the emotion of users. Thus, future design iteration of the App4Autism should allow users to select and pre-assign their music of choice to be played when loud noise is detected. The potential benefit of the mobile app is tremendous as the holistic and integrated functionalities supported by the app may improve the ability of children with ASD to learn, communicate and interact while maintaining their calmness. Future work will involve studying the mobile app with actual children with ASD in a special need childcare centre.

Acknowledgements. We would like to thank Miss Rani from the SCSOA for allowing us to conduct ethnographic studies and interviews at the childcare centre to help understand the needs of children with autism and by providing valuable suggestions and insights.

References

1. Ossmann, R., et al.: AsTeRICS, a flexible assistive technology construction set. Procedia Comput. Sci. **14**, 1–9 (2012)
2. Liffick, B.W.: Introducing assistive technology in an HCI course. In: 9th Annual SIGCSE Conference on Innovation and Technology in Computer Science Education, pp. 232–232. ACM New York (2004)
3. Chandra, P., Jones, J.: Assistive technology and autonomy in a cyborg world. In: 7th International Conference on Information and Communication Technologies and Development. ACM, New York (2015)
4. Frauenberger, C.: Disability and technology – a critical realist perspective. In: 17th International ACM SIGACCESS Conference on Computers & Accessibility, pp. 89–96. ACM, New York (2015)
5. Sensory integration and therapy in sensory room. https://novakdjokovicfoundation.org/sensory-integration-and-therapy-in-sensory-room/. Accessed 26 Sept 2018
6. Geretsegger, M., Holck, U., Gold, C.: Randomised controlled trial of improvisational music theraphy's effectiveness for children with autism spectrum disorders (TIME-A): study protocol. BMC Pediatr. **12**(1), 536 (2012)
7. Kamaruzaman, M.F., Rani, N.M., Md Nor, H., Azahari, M.H.H.: Developing user interface design application for children with autism. Procedia – Soc. Behav. Sci. **217**, 887–894 (2016)
8. Hillier, A., Greher, G., Queenan, A., Marshall, S., Kopec, J.: Music, technology and adolescents with autism spectrum disorders: the effectiveness of the touch screen interface. Music Educ. Res. **18**(3), 269–282 (2016)
9. This Emotionally Intelligent Device is Helping Kids with Autism Form Bonds. https://www.vice.com/en_us/article/9kz49d/this-emotionally-intelligent-device-is-helping-kids-with-autism-form-bonds. Accessed 11 Dec 2018
10. Kushki, A., et al.: Investigating the autonomic nervous system response to anxiety in children with autism spectrum disorders. PLoS ONE **8**(4), e59730 (2013)

11. Leijdekkers, P., Gay, V., Wong, F.: CaptureMyEmotion: a mobile app to improve emotion learning for autistic children using sensors. In: Proceedings of the 26th IEEE International Symposium on Computer-Based Medical Systems, pp. 381–384. IEEE, Porto, Portugal (2013)

12. New Tool Measures Anxiety in Children with Autism Spectrum Disorder Could Lead to New Treatments. http://caho-hospitals.com/new-tool-measures-anxiety-in-children-with-autism-spectrum-disorder-could-lead-to-new-treatments/. Accessed 11 Dec 2018

13. Mobile Apps to help individuals on the Autism spectrum 2018 Edition. https://disabilitycreditcanada.com/mobile-apps-individuals-with-autism/. Accessed 11 Dec 2018

14. Brown, C.J., Chen, A.C.N., Dworkin, S.F.: Music in the control of human pain. Music Ther. **8**(1), 47–60 (1989)

15. Miluk-Kolasa, B., Matejek, M., Stupnicki, R.: The effects of music listening on changes in selected physiological parameters in adult pre-surgical patients. J. Music Ther. **33**(3), 208–218 (1996)

16. Stiegler, L.N., Davis, R.: Understanding sound sensitivity in individuals with autism spectrum disorders. Focus Autism Other Dev. Disabil. **25**(2), 67–75 (2010)

17. Wigram, T., Gold, C.: Music therapy in the assessment and treatment of autistic spectrum disorder: clinical application and research evidence. Child: Care Health Dev. **32**(5), 535–542 (2006)

18. Bernardi, L., Porta, C., Sleight, P.: Cardiovascular, cerebrovascular, and respiratory changes induced by different types of music in musicians and non-musicians: the importance of silence. Heart **92**(4), 445–452 (2006)

19. Moss, V.A.: The effect of music on anxiety in the surgical patient. Perioper. Nurs. Q. **3**(1), 9–16 (1987)

20. Grandgeorge, M., Masataka, N.: Atypical color preference in children with autism spectrum disorder. Front. Psychol. **7**, 1976 (2016)

21. Hanser, S.B.: Controversy in music listening/stress reduction research. Arts Psychother. **15**(3), 211–217 (1988)

22. Fontaine, C.W., Schwalm, N.D.: Effects of familiarity of music on vigilant performance. Percept. Mot. Skills **49**(1), 71–74 (1979)

23. Rickard, N.S.: Intense emotional responses to music: a test of the physiological arousal hypothesis. Psychol. Music **32**(4), 371–388 (2004)

24. Cochrabe, T., Fantini, B., Scherer, K.R.: The Emotional Power of Music: Multidisciplinary Perspectives on Musical Arousal, Expression, and Social Control. Oxford University Press, Oxford (2013)

Review on Preliminary Study on Student's Motivation in Learning History

Muhammad Baderi[✉], Wan Fatimah Wan Ahmad,
and Muhammad Ridhuan Tony Lim Abdullah

Faculty of Science and Information Technology, Universiti Teknologi Petronas,
32610 Seri Iskandar, Perak, Malaysia
muhammad_17007663@utp.edu.my

Abstract. Learning history is compulsory to every student in Malaysia. However, most of the students are not interested in this subject. This study aims to gather the preliminary data to investigate student's motivation in learning history and their perspective on integrating technology into the classroom. This study used convenience sampling technique (n = 83 students) and collected data through an instrument distributed among the students. The results indicate that the current materials for learning history are not sufficient and satisfactory. Therefore, this study proposed a new technology namely Virtual Reality technology in learning history and positive feedbacks received in incorporating this technology in learning history subject into the classroom.

Keywords: Learning history · Student's motivation · Integrating technology

1 Background Study

Malaysia is on track towards developed and High-Nation Income (HNI) country status. In order to progress and achieve the objectives, the Government of Malaysia has to equip its young generation with the required skillsets to meet the demands of future markets. Malaysia has allocated 3.8% of its Gross Domestic Product (GDP) income into the education sector. This is in par with the top-performing countries in education like Singapore, South Korea and Japan [1] (pg. E–3). However, Malaysian student's performances are far-lagged with its peers and even their performances are lower than the countries that have spent lesser in education [1] (pg. E3–15). Aware of these problems, the Ministry of Education (MoE), has initiated Malaysia Education Blueprint 2013–2025 to transform the education system. One of the elements that has and will be transformed is by leveraging Information and Communications Technology (ICT) to scale up the quality of learning [1] (MEB;20).

Malaysia is a multi-racial county literally lives in harmony. Majority of Malaysian are Malay and then followed by Chinese and Indian. However, there are a few incidents happened that spark the racial tension to the country. Learning and understanding history are necessary for racial integration and to keep the peace amongst the races. Learning history subject is a medium of social integration and it is one of the compulsory subjects for the students in Malaysia. Students have to pass the subject in order to get the Malaysia Certificate of Education (SPM). History teachers are facing

© Springer Nature Switzerland AG 2019
H. Badioze Zaman et al. (Eds.): IVIC 2019, LNCS 11870, pp. 513–522, 2019.
https://doi.org/10.1007/978-3-030-34032-2_45

challenges in the process of teaching this subject due to most of the students considered learning history subject as an invaluable, outdated, mundane and dull subject [2, 3]. Another factor that also contributed to this problem is the relevancy of the contents. Most of the students cannot relate historical contents with today's world. The nature of the subject required students to memorize a lot of historical events, figures and dates and it is one of the contributing factors of the less motivation of the students [3]. This is also worsened by the unattractiveness and passive of the content that mostly delivered by paper-based materials [4]. The learning environment has to be shifted to improve the motivation and perception of the students on this subject. Embracing digital transformation is necessary to improve the education sector. Currently, an initiative towards Society 5.0 to resolve various social challenges and ageing population, virtual reality is one of the technologies that can help. There are lots of studies that help an ageing population such as stroke rehabilitation, traumatic treatments and medical training and education.

2 Literature Review

2.1 Overview of Educational Technology

Educational technology plays a huge role in improving student's motivation and performances. Studies showed that students who learn through technology were more effective than the conventional method which used paper-based [3, 4]. It makes the learning environment funs and stimulate motivation and focus on learning [5]. Educational technology also reduces the workload of teaching in term of saving times on providing materials, monitoring class attendance, progress and performance and on-demand support for teacher on aiding slow-leaner [6]. There are a lot of educational technologies available as a medium of learning, but the recent trend is focused on Augmented Reality and Virtual Reality. There a lot of study needs to discover these new technologies.

2.2 Virtual Reality

Virtual reality (VR) is a human-computer interface that simulates user's eye with the artificial world display by a headset [7]. The headset contains computational hardware and distortion lenses that create a stereoscopic view to the user. Virtual reality is a technology developed circa 1960 by Martin Helling. At that time, this technology was used for military training purposes. Due to some limitations of technological hardware, this technology did not thrive back then. However, it was revitalized by the Kick Starter Campaign initiated by Palmer Luckey that developed Head Mounted Display (HMD) that offers fully immersive Virtual Reality (VR) experiences to the users in 2012. To connect to a virtual world, users have to obtain VR resources. VR resources were divided into two categories; (i) visualization and (ii) interaction devices. Virtual reality is in a completely virtual environment [7]. The continuum of the virtual environment and real environment explained by the following figure.

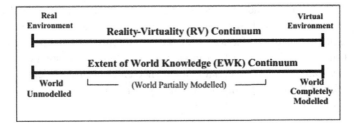

Fig. 1. Reality-virtuality continuum [8]

Figure 1 showed the continuum of the real environment with the virtual environment. There are two separate entities. Virtual environment is completely an artificial environment, modelled by computer software [8] and meanwhile, the real environment is the completely unmodelled environment. The middle ground between the virtual environment and the real environment is an Augmented Reality.

2.3 Virtual Reality as a Learning Tool and Improving Motivation

Virtual reality has been studied its implementation in many areas of education likes in science and technology courses, medical and health courses, architecture, engineering and even art and social sciences courses. With the advent of computer hardware such as Graphical Processing Unit (GPU) in the personal computer as one of the core hardware to develop the Virtual Reality application and its easily available for mass markets, it attracts and stimulates the participation from the industrial players, re-searchers and indie developers. Many software engines such as Unity, Unreal, Amazon Sumerian and Open Sim are free, and they facilitate indie developers and researchers to develop Virtual Reality applications. According to the study by [9], VR capable in simulates an authentic and relevant scenario and it can be leveraged to tap the user emotion. The multimodal interaction in VR promotes rich engagement to the VR users. This attribute that involves student's participation promotes the active learning environments and thus students are more concentrate on the learning environment. The interactive design of a virtual world also increases the attention span of the user. The sense of presence of a user in a virtual world provides engaging experiences. Inside the virtual world, students are free to interact, manipulate and roaming around the virtual world thus it leads to an active learning environment. These inter-actions improve the student's motivation in learning. VR can simulate something that beyond the capability of human vision such as animate molecules and outer space. Well-design VR that eye-catching intrigues and attracts student's engagement to the materials. It stimulates student's motivation into the learning materials [10]. Virtual reality encourages students learning by doing. A study from [19] has been conducted to compare a traditional teaching method and Virtual Reality. From that study, student's motivation scores higher in term of interest towards the subject, giving them the freedom to enjoy the learning process according to their pace (personalize learning experience) and attention to the Virtual Reality is longer than the conventional teaching method. Results from the study [20] showed that students who have received the exposure in learning Virtual Reality tend to continue using it again and regards this technology is being more friendly to them rather than the conventional method. These results indicate that students are comfortable, confidence and satisfaction with Virtual Reality and it contributed to the elements of motivation based on [16] model that emphasizes on attention, relevancy, confidence and satisfaction of material that enhance and improve student's motivation. Moreover, Virtual Reality is giving the autonomy to learn with the facilitates of virtual agents as a guide in the virtual world [10].

2.4 Challenges of Using Virtual Reality

Although virtual reality offers tremendous amounts of benefits as an assistive tool in teaching and learning however implement it in the classroom faces a few challenges. Firstly, the cost of Virtual Reality headset or Head-Mounted Display (HMD) is costly. Most of the HMDs are tethered with a computer and it required a sophisticated graphics card to run the application [11]. However, there are new products produced by the Oculus Company that produces fully mobile HMD like Go and Quest. There is also a mobile-phone Virtual Reality that embedded mobile phones with a headset. However, the problems with the mobile-phone VR are the refresh rate of the mobile are low, it causes a lag display between the virtual world and eye movement and the users are easily prone to get nausea. Mobile-phone VR also has another limited capacity. It did not provide a fully immersive experience [12]. Interactions in the mobile-phone VR are limited to navigation level only (visual, audio and navigation) [7]. Users could not control and manipulate inside the virtual environment. Another challenge with the current VR's technology is users can only use it in a limited time because it can cause nausea. Despite the improvement of refresh rate and LED technology in HMD's lenses, the effect of using the HMD still causing nausea to the users. Locomotion in the Virtual Reality tricks user's brain they are one point to another point, but the body of the users are not moving. The conflict between vision and other sensory channels also contribute to motion sickness [12]. However, there are few developments to improve the locomotion such as using the omnidirectional treadmill to improve the locomotion in the virtual world. Another challenge of using virtual reality, it couldn't provide photo-realism in the virtual world yet. Although there are current developments in ray tracing technology in graphics card, however the quality of the visualization is not on par with the photo-realism. Furthermore, there is lack of expertise of VR developers and if there is a problem occurred in the app, it will impede the learning process. Another potential challenge in integrating this technology also the teacher's acceptance of the new technology. Most of the teacher still comfortable with the traditional methods and integration of new technology might be a burden to them [3]. Virtual Reality in education is more commonly to the concrete subject such as science, physic, chemistry, astronomy and medical subject. There is a lack of study of Virtual Reality in an abstract-concept subject such as history.

2.5 Virtual Reality in Learning History

Virtual Reality has the capability to simulate historical events with the visualization of 3D environments. Students get the first-hand artificial experience inside the virtual world thus it will improve student's understanding of historical events. VR can reconstruct ruin and lost monuments by modelling in 3-Dimensional format [13]. Virtual environments can be navigated, and it leads to active learning to the students. Students have the liberty roam around the virtual world and manipulate the elements or objects inside the virtual world and they can learn from their experience in the virtual world [7]. These interactions are in line with the constructivism theory that promotes a student-centric approach to knowledge. Immersive experience also increases the attention to the learners. The richness of graphics and audio surrounded inside the virtual world stimulates the attention span to the learners [9]. According to the [9], VR in some instances accurately illustrate some features and students tend to spend more time observing the elements and interact with the virtual world. This leads to the learner to be an active participant. Multi-sensory interaction with virtual environments creates rich engagements with virtual environments. However, a combination of audio-visual exhibits to the students must be limited to avoid the overload information in multimedia learning. According to the Multimedia Learning Theory [14], humans have a dual-channel for processing information; visual information and auditory information and each channel has limited information capacity (p. 63). Developers of the contents able to create an interactive design and student's centric design before creating the VR content. Based on the study from [10], students' performed very well in term of the academic performances versus videos and textbooks approaches According to that study, student's attitude towards the virtual reality are positive and student's engagement with the Virtual Reality material are longer than the others. Presumably, the longer the engagements with material the more motivated students to the learning process.

3   Methodology

This study used a questionnaire as a tool for gathering the preliminary data. The preliminary data is necessary to evaluate the feasibility of the research results from the preliminary study can be used as a reference in the future works. There are 3 steps involved.

3.1   Selection of the Sample

The sample size of this study involved 83 students from undergraduate studies at Universiti Teknologi Petronas who were studying Tamadun Islam dan Tamadun Asia which comprises of History. The sample size for this study is not been calculated, base on [17] that stated, the sample not be required as long as it must be the representative of the target population. However, researchers adopted a general rule of thumb from [18] that considered more than 30 persons is enough for sampling size for a pilot study. 83 students out of 513 students based on students who undertake subject for that semester. The sampling of this study used convenience sampling in conducting this study to provide useful information.

3.2   Instruments

A questionnaire was used as an instrument to get the data from the students. The questionnaire was crafted according to the research questions as aforementioned in the previous section. The questionnaire consisted of nominal, ordinal and 5 points Likert's Scale and it was adapted based on the [15]. This questionnaire is based on the theory of ARCS model regarding student's motivation.

3.3   Procedure of Study

The enumerators distributed the questionnaire to every student in the class. Students were instructed to answer the questionnaire based on their perceptions and not influence by other people. Students were given the autonomy to answer it and there is no limit of times given to complete the questionnaire. Results from the questionnaire the results were analyzed and summarized and later on displayed in infographic format.

4   Result and Discussion

4.1   Result of Student's Motivation to Current Materials

This study comprises of 83 students in tertiary education. 59 students are male and 24 students are female. The ethnicity of the students are Malay (n = 51), Chinese (14), Indian (n = 11) and others (n = 6). The age of students are 20-year-old (24), 21-year-old (n = 46), 22-year-old (n = 11), 26-year old (n = 1) and 27-year-old (n = 1) year Fig. 2 exhibits a result from the preliminary study in term of student's motivation to the current materials. This questionnaire is adapted on the theory of Keller's ARCS Motivational Model [16] that measured 4 parameters to evaluate student's motivation in learning. ARCS is abbreviation of A = Attention; R = Relevance; C = Confidence

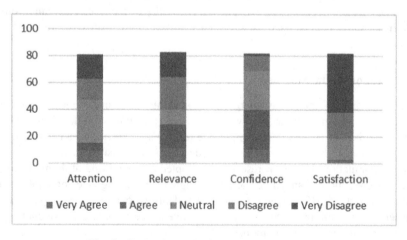

Fig. 2. Student's motivation to current materials

and S = Satisfaction. In Attention parameter section, the questions asking on learning environments, utilizing material/tools in learning, the content and organization of the current material. Most of the students find that the current material could not keep their attention into learning (Disagree = 16; Very Disagree = 18). Students find that current materials are full of textual facts to be memorized. This result is supported by the past studies from Munirah 2013 and Syazwani 2016 [3, 4] that stated current materials are passive and couldn't attract and hold student's attention. In term of the relevancy of the material, students were questioned about the value and relevancy of the materials into their daily life. From the result, 43 out of 83 students (Disagree = 24; Very Disagree = 19). find that the current materials are irrelevant to them. Most of the students are hard to relate historical events with today's world. The result showed that most of the students find that learning from past events will not be benefitted to the modern world. The current materials contain did not relates the information on how students can be utilizing the information to their daily's live. In term of confidence, the findings are contradicted. Most of the students (Very Agree = 10; Agree = 30) find that they are very confident in the current materials. Students are able to revise the materials independently without any aid from other people. In term of satisfaction, the majority of the students (Very Disagree = 44; Disagree = 19) find the current materials are not satisfying. Students find the current materials are full of text, lack of pictures, inorganize and unattractive. There are few strategies can be taken to mitigate these issues. Shifting the paper-based materials to the multimedia platform can be one of the ways to promotes student's motivation in learning this subject [4]. According to [4], intervention of educational technologies is able to improve the learning environment for this subject and stimulates interest of the students thus indirectly will improves the student's performance based on the study from Keller that stated one of the factors to enhance and improves cognitive of students by improving the motivational factors to study the subject [16]. There are a lot of technologies have been offered to incorporate it into learning history subject. However, there is not enough information on how Virtual Reality technology can be utilized into learning history. The next sub-section discusses the student's perception on integrating Virtual Reality with History subject.

4.2 Perception on Integrating VR in Learning History Subject

A survey was conducted on the student's perception in incorporating Virtual Reality into the History classroom. The same students as a previous subsection were required to answer the questionnaire. All of the students (n = 83) are aware of this technology and the majority of them (n = 48), have experience of using Virtual Reality. Either it is semi-immersive and fully-immersive Virtual Reality. The questionnaire measured 3 parameters of student's perception on integrating Virtual Reality (i) acceptance; (ii) motivation and (iii) performance. Students are required to answer all of the questions provided. In the first parameter which is to measure the acceptance level of Virtual Reality, students were asking whether they will embrace and use Virtual Reality as a learning tool if it will be provided in the classroom. Most of the respondents (Very Agree = 19; Agree = 44; Total = 63) are positive to the idea of incorporating Virtual Reality in learning history subject as shown in Fig. 3. Next is a motivation parameter. Students were asking whether incorporating Virtual Reality will change the learning environment from passive to active and thus increase their motivation in learning history. their perspectives are mostly positive towards the idea of incorporating Virtual Reality (Very Agree = 24; Agree = 28; Total = 52). Finding from the data, students presumably thinks that technological intervention such as incorporating Virtual Reality in the classroom creates a fun environment for them and it will lead them to be motivated in learning history subject. Their perception also in line with the study from [4] that stated of educational technology intervention sparks fun and stimulates motivation to the students. However, in term of performances, the outcomes of learning history in VR are ambiguous. Students were asking whether the usage of the Virtual Reality will improve their cognitive performance and thus increase their scores in learning history subject. Majority of the students answered in neutral (n = 32), however, the combination of Agree and Very Agree (n = 34) constitutes the majority. Students are vague in the potential of Virtual Reality in learning and the effectiveness of Virtual Reality in improving the performances in scoring this subject.

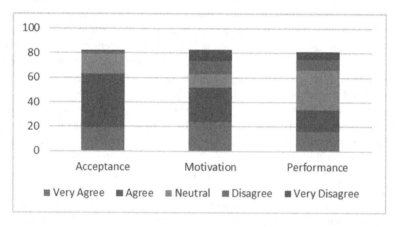

Fig. 3. Finding on student's perspectives incorporating VR in learning history subject

5   Conclusion and Future Work

This preliminary study was designed to identify the problems of current material in learning history and viability of incorporating Virtual Reality to increase the motivation of the students in learning history subject. In summary, this paper described the student's motivation in learning history subject for the current materials are unattractive and affected student's motivation in learning history and perceptions toward history subject are not in a good condition. Students are hard to keep their attention in the current learning environment due to the passive environment and heavily dependent on paper-based materials. On another point, findings showed that there are needs of integrating Virtual Reality into learning history subject. The student is very welcoming to Virtual Reality as a new way of learning history. However, there is a result that shown students are not too optimistic on the capability of Virtual Reality as a medium to learn history. Students are sceptical toward the effectiveness of Virtual Reality as a contributing factor in enhancing and improving scores in learning history subject.

This paper has a few limitations whereby this study used a convenience sampling method in selecting respondents. Results from the convenience sampling technique cannot be categorized as a general finding from the population. Secondly, this study is not in-depth on discussing the motivational factors of current materials in learning history. Although it was adapted from the Keller's ACRS Model, a prominent scholar for the motivational model, this study only used a descriptive analysis rather than a statistical analysis in finding the students motivation on current materials as suggested by the author. Data from the preliminary study will be contributed as a part of justification in selecting an educational technology for learning History.

References

1. Malaysia Education Blueprint 2013–2025. Education **27**(1), 1–268 (2013)
2. Ahmad, A., Rahman, S.H.A., Abdullah, N.A.T.: Tahap Keupayaan Pengajaran Guru Sejarah dan Hubungannya dengan Pencapaian Murid di Sekolah Berprestasi Rendah (The relationship between history teachers' level of capability and students' performance in low performance schools), Pendidik **34**(1), 53–66 (2009)
3. Munirah Husna, B., Abdul Razaq, A., Noria Munirah, Y.: Pengajaran dan pembelajaran Sejarah Abad Ke-21; Isu dan cabaran. In: Proceeding 7th International Seminar on Regional Education, vol. 1, pp. 5–7 (2015)
4. Talib, N.S.B.A., Ghani, K.B.A., Yusoff, N.A.B., Awang, M.M.: Kaedah Pembelajaran Sejarah Dengan Mengambil Kira Minat Dan Peningkatan Prestasi, no. 1984 (2016)
5. Sung, Y.T., Chang, K.E., Liu, T.C.: The effects of integrating mobile devices with teaching and learning on students' learning performance: a meta-analysis and research synthesis. Comput. Educ. **94**, 252–275 (2016)
6. Selwood, I., Pilkington, R.: Teacher workload: Using ICT to release time to teach. Educ. Rev. **57**(2), 163–174 (2005)
7. Vergara, D., Rubio, M., Lorenzo, M.: On the design of virtual reality learning environments in engineering. Multimodal Technol. Interact. **1**(2), 11 (2017)
8. Milgram, P., Colquhoun, H.: A taxonomy of real and virtual world display integration. In: Mixed Reality, pp. 5–30 (1999)
9. Pantelidis, V.: Reasons to use virtual reality in education and training courses and a model to determine when to use virtual reality. Themes Sci. Technol. Educ. **2**(1), 59–70 (2009)
10. Ijaz, K., Bogdanovych, A., Trescak, T.: Virtual worlds vs books and videos in history education. Interact. Learn. Environ. **25**(7), 904–929 (2017)
11. Anthes, C., García-Hernández, R.J., Wiedemann, M., Kranzlmüller, D.: State of the art of virtual reality technology. In: IEEE Aerospace Conference Proceedings, June, March 2016
12. CAICT and Huawei: Virtual Reality/Augmented Reality White Paper, December 2017
13. Younes, G., et al.: Virtual and augmented reality for rich interaction with cultural heritage sites: a case study from the Roman Theater at Byblos. Digit. Appl. Archaeol. Cultural Herit. **5**, 1–9 (2017)
14. Mayer, R.E.: Cognitive theory of multimedia learning. In: Mayer, R. (ed.) The Cambridge Handbook of Multimedia Learning, 2nd (edn.), vol. 58, no. 12, pp. 43–71. Cambridge University Press, Cambridge (2014)
15. Amin, A.M., Corebima, A.D., Zubaidah, S., Mahanal, S.: Pre-motivational study based arcs (attention, relevance, confidence, and satisfaction) at biology education students at physiology animal lecture, November 2017, pp. 116–124 (2016)

16. Keller, J.M.: Motivational Design for Learning and Performance: The ARCS Model Approach. Springer, Heidelberg (2010)
17. Thabane, L., Ma, J., Chu, R., Ismaila, A.: A tutorial on pilot studies: the what, why and how. Med. Res. Methodol. **10**, 1 (2010)
18. Lancaster, G.A., Dodd, S., Williamson, P.R.: Design and analysis of pilot studies: recommendations for good practice. J. Eval. Clin. Pract. **10**(2), 307–312 (2004)
19. Kaewprapan, W., Suksakulchai, S.: Student motivation and attitude towards virtual versus traditional learning based on cognitive styles. Kaewprapan, Wacheerapan, pp. 19–21, November 2008
20. Moreno, R., Mayer, R.E.: Virtual reality and learning: cognitive and motivational effects of students' sense of presence. In: Human-Computer Interaction Proceedings, pp. 1–3 (2001)

Factors in Personal Information Management Evaluation

Mohammad Rustom Al Nasar[1(✉)], Masnizah Mohd[2],
and Nazlena Mohamad Ali[3]

[1] Faculty of Economics and Administrative Sciences, Jadara University,
Irbid 21110, Jordan
mis.nassar@yahoo.com
[2] Faculty of Information Science and Technology,
Universiti Kebangsaan Malaysia, 43600 Bangi, Malaysia
[3] Institute of Visual Informatics, Universiti Kebangsaan Malaysia,
43600 Bangi, Malaysia

Abstract. Personal Information Management (PIM) is the domain that involves methods and procedures to study how people keep, manage, maintain and re-find information. Related studies show that re-finding could be a difficult and time-consuming task due to many factors involves during the re-finding time. Even though, many innovative PIM systems have been designed and published, little existing works have focused on several factors that people face and the time taken to perform the re-finding process. This paper aims to investigate the efficiency of performing the re-finding process using a recently developed personal photographs management system called PHOTO REFINDER. Accordingly, twenty participants performed 100 re-finding tasks using PHOTO REFINDER and Baseline systems. Subsequently, quantitative data were collected through a pre-study questionnaire and a screen recorder system to calculate the time taken to perform given tasks. The results showed that PHOTO REFINDER supported users significantly with less time during the re-finding process with respect to each factor. This study contributes to the PIM domain by describing the methodology used to design the evaluation experiment and considering all factors that could affect the re-finding process.

Keywords: Personal Information Management · Information re-finding · Evaluation · PHOTO REFINDER

1 Introduction

Due to the availability of smartphones and digital cameras, personal photographs systems received growing research attention recently. Specific emphasis has been placed on developing and improving systems (e.g. PhotoMemory [1], EasyAlbum [2] and Miaow [3]) to assist people with locating personal photographs that they have previously kept. Many studies have suggested that people require re-finding photographs they have kept before [4–6]. Therefore, re-finding considers the heart of PIM, if people are not able to successfully re-find their photographs, then keep decisions and

© Springer Nature Switzerland AG 2019
H. Badioze Zaman et al. (Eds.): IVIC 2019, LNCS 11870, pp. 523–536, 2019.
https://doi.org/10.1007/978-3-030-34032-2_46

management activities will end in futile. Hence, the question arises is what are the factors that make re-finding photographs difficult.

Previous works have shown that refinding personal information can be difficult, time-consuming and frustrating tasks due to many factors [1, 5, 7]. The factors have been widely studied, the previous researches indicated that people tend to keep and store too many photographs [5, 8, 9]. However, when managing photographs, people tend to use general labeling methods to organize and manage their photograph, which results in stacks of files [1, 7, 8]. Whittaker et al. [7] have shown that people face problems when they try to re-find the information which has been changed (moved, modified or deleted). Computer literacy has also considered, where novice users lack the sharp strategies that more experienced users had developed over time and how that could affect re-finding [10, 11]. The limitations of human memory have another starring role in PIM, where people forget a lot of details about their old photograph collections [1, 5]. Finally, the literature showed that retrieving strategies (searching vs. browsing) play a role to make re-finding easier, people who use search-based strategy face less difficulty compare to who used browse-based strategy [1, 5, 12].

However, it is noteworthy that most PIM systems have been not evaluated due to the difficulties of performing the evaluation in the context of PIM [5, 12]. One of the core difficulties is produced by the nature of PIM. People keep information in order to complete other tasks. The information that people keep are unique to them and the information within a collection basically belong to the owner's personal familiarities. Therefore, as personal information is unique, researchers face difficulty to create evaluation tasks that are appropriate to all participants in one evaluation. Secondly, the privacy issue that makes participants avoid and uncomfortable to share their information with researchers. Finally, researchers know little about the tasks that make people re-find their information [13].

In this paper, the most affecting factors in re-finding personal photographs are considered in order to enhance the re-finding process. The rest of the paper is organized as follows. Section 2 discusses the related works. Section 3 discusses the evaluation methodology that is used in a user-controlled evaluation. Section 4 discusses the results obtained from the experiment and followed by the discussion of the results in Sect. 5. Finally, the conclusions are reported in Sect. 6.

2   Related Works

PIM research is still growing where one of the focuses now is on improving re-finding personal information and this work is in this direction. PIM researchers have attempted to build better visualization techniques and features in order to give good insight for the users during the re-finding process [14]. This led to a poor of research efforts that concentrated on improving re-finding by focusing on few factors in system design [1, 2, 6] and involving the users in the final stage of evaluation [17, 18]. The reviewed works on PIM systems help to identify the gaps in previous works to design a new PIM system.

Most of the previous systems that supporting PIM processes have focused more on their design about algorithms (fully automatic) [6, 19] or semi-automatic [20] to help users to perform some activities such as tagging, annotation, and classifications which are mainly used to support managing process for better retrieval. One critical problem is that users fundamentally do not trust fully automatic and semi-automatic features. People are concerned that important photographs might be misfiled or wrongly tagged. It is clear that despite large improvements in fully automatic and semi-automatic systems, however, these systems are still not effective [5]. Thus, there is an increasing need in terms of evaluation in the PIM domain for user interfaces and the features used to help the users to re-find their photographs effectively. Based on the works reviewed, the user aspect was rarely involved to measure the effectiveness of their approach and features. Most of it reported on the effectiveness of the system performances were used poor user evaluation methodology.

Considering all the factors that affect re-finding is also considering one of the most important limitations of previous works. Most of the works are mainly focused on enhancing the searching strategy in comparison with browsing strategy [6, 18] and other systems focusing to enhance memory role during re-finding [1].

Therefore, PHOTO REFINDER system has been developed to support PIM processes (keeping, managing, maintaining) in general and re-finding in particular [16]. The system is considered one of the rare PIM systems which focus on the early user's evaluation to improve the main functionality of performing PIM processes [15]. In this paper, we try to highlight the efforts which have been done to consider the above limitations with evaluation methodology to control factors to get the best possible results.

3 Evaluation Methodology

This section discusses the control lab based-user procedures to evaluate PHOTO REFINDER system with consideration to factors that affect re-finding personal photographs.

3.1 Evaluation Procedures

All participants were asked to bring their own photographs collections to the lab. A set of methods used to avoid limitations of evaluation as mentioned. Firstly, participants brought the photographs which they found suitable to be shared with the researchers, thus avoiding the privacy issue. Secondly, some re-finding tasks that suit the participants' collections were given to confirm that all participants perform the same tasks based on their photographs collections. Finally, researchers created tasks based on real tasks, meaning that the experiment and the tasks were familiar to participants based on their own photographs collections.

To establish the degree of efficiency of re-finding personal photographs, the PHOTO REFINDER system was tested against the Baseline system. The Baseline system offers a few options like the standard operating system. When using the Baseline system, retrieving the photographs was performed by browsing the album collections, changing the album view size option, sorting the albums based on (date, name), changing the thumbnails view size option, sorting the thumbnails based on (date, name) and labeling the collection manually. Using baseline as standalone systems during the evaluation is a common technique in previous works [1, 17].

Participants had a chance to perform random re-find tasks using PHOTO REFINDER and Baseline systems in a training session before the final evaluation took a place to familiarize themselves with the systems and the experiment's tasks. The final experiment was divided for three main sessions, the first session was to keep and manage the photographs, the second session is maintaining the photographs (moving and updating), and the last one was re-finding tasks. Each session took approximately 30 min - 1 h. Participants were also offered a short break (5 to 10 min) after each session. In the last session, the tasks and systems were assigned according to a Greco-Latin square design to minimize possible learning effects and the tiredness factor [21]. The time taken to complete each task was calculated based on the screen recorder software. Finally, all participants were rewarded at the end of the evaluation as a token of appreciation for their efforts in this experiment.

3.2 Re-finding Tasks

Participants were required to perform five different re-finding tasks. These tasks were adopted from [7, 8] based on Participants' photograph collections, like the following:

- **Task 1:** Find photographs from a particular event in the collection.
- **Task 2:** Find an individual photo from the collection.
- **Task 3:** Find photographs that spanned across different events such as birthdays or New Year photographs.
- **Task 4:** Find photograph(s) which have been moved.
- **Task 5:** Find photograph(s) which have been modified.

3.3 Participants

20 participants (10 Females) were invited using class advertising, email invitation, and college advertising to participate. The population consisted of two groups of participants; undergraduate and postgraduate, each group contained 10 participants. The two groups were different as they came from different faculties (the postgraduates came from the faculty of information science and technology (FTSM) and the undergraduates from other faculties). All undergraduate students came from non-computer science backgrounds and had low-levels of computer literacy; this was obvious during the evaluation and from the questionnaire. The postgraduate students were selected from the master and Ph.D degrees, therefore, they had much more experience with computers. Table 1 shows the differences between participants statistically in terms of computer literacy based on the pre-study questionnaire given. The participants answered on a scale from 1 to 5 (years of using the computer, hours of using the computer/day and how they rate themselves as an expert to use the computer), where 1 meant 'no' and 5 meant 'a lot'.

The results showed that the postgraduate group is statistical significance difference using the computer (in years) as compared to the undergraduate group (Mann-Whitney U test, p = 0.005). The results showed a statistically significant difference in using the computer (in hours/day), which is more than the undergraduate group (Mann-Whitney U test, p = 0.036). There is also a statistically significant difference in participants' responses (Experts using a computer) across groups (Mann-Whitney U test, p = 0.0002). The postgraduate group had high computer literacy (familiarity with using a computer) compared to the undergraduate group.

Table 1. Result of participants' answers for computer literacy questions

Participants	Year of using computer		Hours of using computer/day		Expert	
	Under-graduate	Post-graduate	Under-graduate	Post-graduate	Under-graduate	Post-graduate
Mean Std	3.80 (sd = 1.229)	5.00 (sd = 0.00)	3.50 (sd = 0.850)	4.30 (sd = 0.675)	2.60 (sd = 0.699)	4.30 (sd = 0.675)
Median	4.00	5.00	3.50	4.00	3.00	4.00

4 Results

The following sections present the findings of the user study methodology outlined in Sect. 3. The focus here is on how each factor affects re-finding tasks and how much time participants need to complete each. Again, previous studies drew attention to a number of factors that may impact the personal photographs re-finding and, accordingly, how participants go about re-finding that requested photographs based on each. This section examines six factors to determine the time of re-finding and how participants were able to perform re-finding tasks based on (1) Amount of personal photographs (A lot or A few), (2) Labelling strategies, (3) Maintaining photographs (if photographs moved or updated), (4) Re-finding strategies (Searching vs. Browsing), (5) Computer literacy (Expert Vs. Novice) and (6) Human memory role (Frequent of seeing photographs).

4.1 Performance Across Amount of Photographs Groups

The number of photographs was controlled before the experiment took place, the participants were asked randomly to bring personal photographs based on it, Table 2. The idea is that the number of photographs was one of the factors involved in the experiments. Therefore, understanding how the new system able to support different photograph groups (a lot and a few) are required. The control was balanced between postgraduate and undergraduate students where each group assigned photographs under 'a few' and 'a lot' categories. The results are presented below:

Table 2. Controlled number of photographs used in the experiment.

Groups	No. of photographs	No. of postgraduate	No. of undergraduate
A few	<1000 photographs	5	5
A lot	≥ 1000 photographs	5	5

The result of the Mann-Whitney U test reveals that there is a significant difference that exists between 'A lot' photograph group in terms of the number of photographs used in the experiments (mean = 1361.30, sd = 248.040, median = 1296) and 'A few' photograph group (mean = 433.40, sd = 233.108, median = 393.50), p = 0.000011.

A lot of photographs group performed with reasonable consistency regardless of the system they were using compare with a few photographs group. On average, they take more time (secs) (mean = 13.52, sd = 4.869) compare with a few photographs group (mean = 12.76, sd = 3.802) to perform all re-finding tasks using PHOTO REFINDER.

Moreover, A lot of photographs group also take more time (secs) (mean = 31.72, sd = 4.869) compare with a few photographs group (mean = 29.30, sd = 12.676) to perform all tasks by using Baseline system. Figure 1 shows the previous results graphically; both groups (A lot and A few) take more time to complete all given tasks using the Baseline system compare with PHOTO REFINDER. A Wilcoxon signed-rank test showed that participants from a lot group of photographs did elicit a statistically significantly different in time to perform overall re-finding tasks using PHOTO REFINDER, where (p = 0.005). Moreover, the same test showed that participants from a few photographs group of photographs did elicit a statistically significantly different in time to perform overall re-finding tasks using PHOTO REFINDER, where (p = 0.005). The results confirmed statistically that PHOTO REFINDER help both groups to perform the tasks faster.

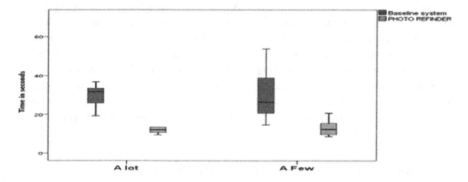

Fig. 1. The time taken in seconds to complete re-finding tasks for types of amount of photographs

4.2   Performance Across Labelling Strategies

Another factor that has been tested in the evaluation is labeling strategies which participants used in the Baseline system to descript their photographs collections. This factor has been tested across two different tasks (Task 1 and Task 2). Each label has applied four times (20% from the total tasks) in each take to make a control to this factor and make sure that there is a balance between all label types.

Participants from different labeling strategies get more benefit while using PHOTO REFINDER to perform the tasks with less time compare to the Baseline system. Time-base labels were the worst label which participants used in the Baseline system which took on average (mean = 22.00, sd = 17.607) to complete Task 1 and (mean = 60.75, sd = 53.804) for Task 2. Meanwhile, PHOTO REFINDER supports this task by helping participants finish the task with (mean = 12.50, sd = 3.109) and (mean = 15.25, sd = 3.304) respectively. Surprisingly, the Baseline system supported participants who used mixed labels more compared with PHOTO REFINDER. While they spent on average (mean = 9.50, sd = 5.916) to finish Task 1 and (mean = 32.25, sd = 33.270) to finish Task 2 compare with PHOTO REFINDER (mean = 15.50, sd = 3.873) and (mean = 34.25, sd = 20.123) respectively. This is because participants were more familiar with their mixed label than the one PHOTO REFINDER generated.

Moreover, Figs. 2 and 1 show the previous results graphically. Friedman test shows that there was a statistically significant difference in time spent to perform Task 1 between both systems depending on which type of label was used to complete the task, where (p = 0.042). The Same test also proves that there was a statistically significant difference in time spent to perform Task 2 between both systems depending on which type of label was used to complete the task, where (p = 0.037) (Fig. 3).

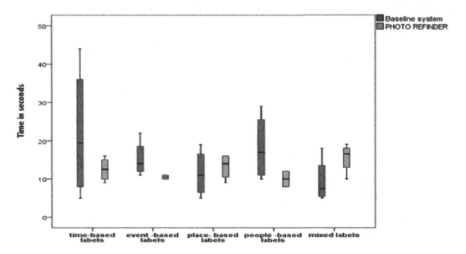

Fig. 2. Time taken to re-find one album for different labeling strategies used in baseline system, note: PHOTO REFINDER always = mixed labels

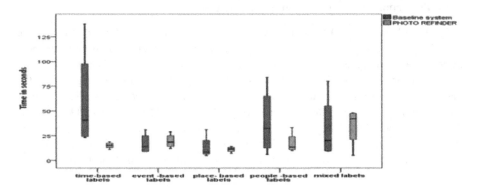

Fig. 3. Time taken to re-find single photograph for different labeling strategies used in baseline system, note: PHOTO REFINDER always = mixed labels

4.3 Performance Across Maintaining Factor

The next factor which has been tested is how PHOTO REFINDER supported the photographs which have been maintained (moved and updated). Participants were performing 20 tasks to re-find the photographs which have been moved and 20 tasks for photographs that have been updated. PHOTO REFINDER supported participants in both tasks, where the participants on average finished Task 4 (mean = 11.25, sd = 7.152) and (mean = 8.70, sd = 3.935) for Task 5. Meanwhile, participants completed Task 4 on average (mean = 41.35, sd = 36.504) and (mean = 25.70, sd = 19.219) for Task 5 by using Baseline system. Figure 4 shows the previous results graphically.

A Wilcoxon signed-rank test showed that there is a statistical significant difference in time to re-find moved photographs between both systems, where (p = 0.000252), and statistically significantly different in time re-find updated photographs between both systems, where (p = 0.000188). The results confirmed statistically that PHOTO REFINDER help participants to complete both tasks with less time.

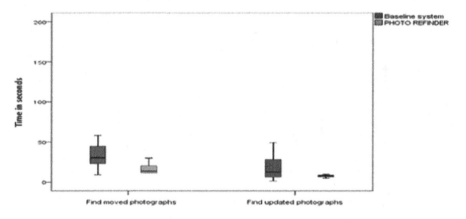

Fig. 4. Time taken to re-find maintained photographs (moved and updated) across systems

4.4 Performance Across Re-finding Strategies

Since PHOTO REFINDER is mainly about searching instead of browsing and the Baseline system is more about browsing, the different strategies used between both systems were compared. The searching strategy was clearly better than the browsing strategy to perform all re-finding tasks. On average, the searching strategy helps the participant to perform tasks with less time (secs) (mean = 13.17, sd = 4.272) compare with browsing strategy in the Baseline system (mean = 30.51, sd = 13.300).

On the other hand, Fig. 5 shows the previous results graphically; participants took more time to complete re-finding tasks using the Baseline system. A Wilcoxon signed-rank test showed that there is statistical significant difference in time to perform re-finding tasks between both systems, where (p = 0.000088).

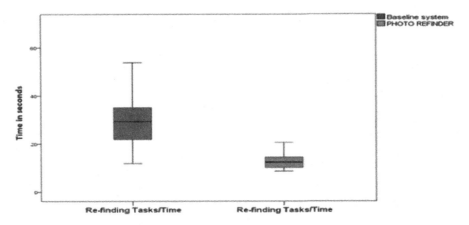

Fig. 5. The average time to perform re-finding tasks/Seconds across systems

4.5   Performance Across Computer Literacy Groups

The postgraduate group used to be an expert in using a computer and undergraduate group consider as a novice one (Sect. 3.3). The postgraduate group takes on average less time (mean = 12.26 secs, sd = 3.268) to complete all re-finding tasks compared with undergraduate (mean = 14.080, sd = 5.100) using PHOTO REFINDER.

Surprisingly, the undergraduate group took on average less time (mean = 27.28, sd = 7.690) to complete re-finding tasks compared with a postgraduate group (mean = 33.74, sd = 16.701) using the Baseline system. During the evaluation, it was clear that the photographs of the postgraduate group are old collections. Some of these collections were captured more than 10 years ago. The undergraduate group had new collections, where some of the participants used newly captured photographs to use them in the experiment. This could be one of the reasons why the undergraduate group performed better compared with the postgraduate group.

Figure 6 shows the previous results graphically; both groups took more time to complete re-finding tasks using the Baseline system. A Wilcoxon signed-rank test showed that participants from the undergraduate group did elicit a statistical significant difference in performing overall re-finding tasks using PHOTO REFINDER, where (p = 0.008). Moreover, again A Wilcoxon signed-rank test showed that participants from the postgraduate group did elicit a statistically significantly different in performing overall re-finding tasks using PHOTO REFINDER, where (p = 0.005).

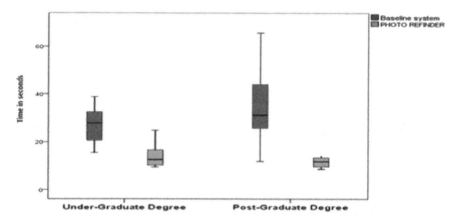

Fig. 6. Time taken to perform re-finding tasks based on computer literacy groups

4.6   Performance Across Frequent of Seeing the Photographs

Another factor that has been tested in the evaluation is frequently seeing the photographs by participants. Again, this factor has been tested across two different tasks (Task 1 and Task 2). In the total 40 tasks, 2 were seen by participants "Every day", 5 were "Once per week", 7 were "Once per month", 6 "Every three months" and 20 were "More than three months". Accordingly, although the way evaluation was created meant that the experimenter only had limited control over the frequency of seeing photographs. However, the result shows that the participants do not see their photographs frequently.

Participants who do not see their photographs frequently (more than three months) get the benefit while using PHOTO REFINDER to perform both tasks with less time compared to the Baseline system. Photographs which are not seen frequently (more than three months) were commonly performed and with reasonable consistency in a team of the time taken to perform the tasks. On average PHOTO REFINDER helped participants to perform Task 1 with less time (mean = 12.40, sd = 3.169) and (mean = 21.20, sd = 13.298) for Task 2 compared with Baseline system (mean = 14.90, sd = 10.867) and (mean = 46.00, sd = 43.079) to perform both tasks respectively. Moreover, Figs. 7 and 8 show the previous results graphically.

Friedman test shows that there was a statistical significant difference in time spent to perform Task 1 between both systems depending on which frequently of seeing photographs to complete the task, where ($p = 0.004$). The Same test also proves that there was a statistical significant difference in time spent to perform Task 2 between both systems depending on which frequently seen photographs to complete the task, where ($p = 0.039$).

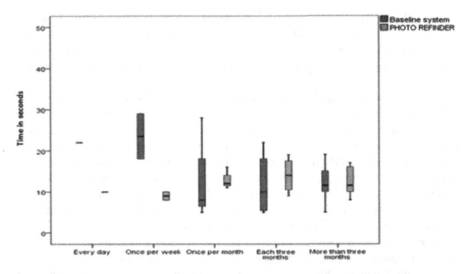

Fig. 7. Time taken to perform re-find one album based on frequent of seeing photographs

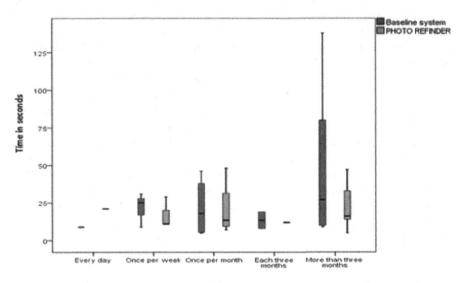

Fig. 8. Time taken to perform re-find single photograph based on frequent of seeing photographs

5   Findings Discussion

In the previous section, the performances of participants have been analyzed across experimental systems (PHOTO REFINDER and Baseline systems). The performance of the participants using both systems was examined for different factors that affect re-finding personal photographs.

Overall, the Baseline system offered inferior performance to perform re-finding tasks compare with PHOTO REFINDER. However, the performance of participants changed effectively for different re-finding tasks, which suggested that participants need different features when performing different tasks based on a different factor they faced.

It was discovered that different participants groups of computer literacy performed differently with the different systems used. As an example, the undergraduate group (as a novice) achieved their best performance when using the Baseline system compared with the postgraduate group (an expert). The postgraduate group performed better once they used PHOTO REFINDER compared with the undergraduate group. Based on the characteristics of photographs that each group has, possible explanation for these findings is that the Baseline system does not help well the participants who have old photographs collections. Further, features provided in PHOTO REFINDER help the postgraduate group more than the undergraduate group.

When participants' performance with the two systems was analyzed for tasks of different frequencies of seeing photographs factor, it was revealed that often tasks that involved re-finding for non-frequently seeing photographs were well supported by PHOTO REFINDER. With respect for the human memory role in the context of PIM, as the period of frequently seeing the photographs increased, it seems that the participants needed more time to complete the tasks with the Baseline system. Participants' behavior and performance when using the Baseline system were also influenced by the labeling they used to describe their albums. Participants who labeled their albums collections very well tended to finish the task faster, while other participants took more time to complete the task (especially those who used time-based labels).

When participants used PHOTO REFINDER, the mutual practice was to start re-finding with some tags related to the photographs which they requested to retrieve, utilizing semantic key-words (events name, people associated with the photographs or place that the photographs captured in). This differed from the Baseline system as it provides few options to exploit the visual preview. Re-finding with keywords filter "Search by Free-Text" was also used, although, not as frequently as faceted metadata (events, people and places). One possible explanation for this could be that the participants do not like to write any word to filter their photographs. It was discovered that the undergraduate group used "Search by Free-Text" feature more (10%) than the postgraduate group, where they just used this feature with less than (1%) from total interactions. This could be another reason why the postgraduate group finished their tasks faster compared with the undergraduate group.

Moreover, when using PHOTO REFINDER, there was clear evidence that participants interacted well with the systems' features to re-find the requested photographs. For example, the participants started their re-finding journey by using one tag the represent photographs they wish to find. Through interaction with the PHOTO REFINDER, additional tags were generated to reduce the results that participants have on the main screen. For example, if a participant was asked to re-find a photograph with a particular friend in a specific place, he or she used the "Search by People" feature to filter the albums. When this process returns many albums (particular friend associated with many albums), the participants apply another filter "Search by Places" to reach his or her target directly. This also was a common behavior between both participants groups. This was different from the Baseline system. The re-finding strategies for most of the participants were as resemble trial and error (except those who have small photographs collections (less than 500 photographs)). Participants were cycled through their albums collections by opening the albums to see whether they contained the requested photograph(s), moving on to other albums if they did not. This scenario of re-finding has involved some options such as "Albums SIZE options" and "Thumbnails SIZE options". Although, these features helped participants to understand more about their photographs collection they are looking for, nevertheless, these options do not support the participants enough to complete their tasks fast, where they were not always helpful or meaningful.

6   Conclusion

This study has increased the understanding of the PIM community about what is the role of the factors that affect re-finding personal photographs. It has shown how PHOTO REFINDER system can help participants to re-find their photographs with significantly less time using the Baseline system. The user-controlled evaluation mythology used in this study is also considered as a guide for other researchers to control the factors and get the best possible results. However, the study has been limited to one type of information (personal photographs). More efforts are needed to understand the role of these factors with different types of information such as email messages, web pages, music files, and computer files. Increasing the understanding of these factors and the PIM processes will provide the researchers and designers with a better idea of the systems that should be designed and the necessary features that could be added to them. Moreover, other issues researchers need to focus on how some technologies (Facebook, WhatsApp, Flickr, and Google+) affect re-finding processes. Another domain that researchers need to focus on is the cloud computing area and how it affects the ways that people use to keep, manage, maintain and re-find their information in general and personal photographs in particular.

References

1. Elsweiler, D., Ruthven, I., Jones, C.: Towards memory supporting personal information management tools. J. Am. Soc. Inf. Sci. Technol. **58**(7), 924–946 (2007)
2. Cui, J., Wen, F., Xiao, R., Tian, Y., Tang, X.: EasyAlbum: an interactive photo annotation system based on face clustering and re-ranking. ACM (2007)
3. Gomi, A., Itoh, T.: MIAOW: a 3D image browser applying a location-and time-based hierarchical data visualization technique. ACM (2010)
4. Dumais, S., Cutrell, E., Cadiz, J.J., Jancke, G., Sarin, R., Robbins, D.C.: Stuff I've seen: a system for personal information retrieval and re-use (2016)
5. Whittaker, S.: Personal information management: from information consumption to curation. Ann. Rev. Inf. Sci. Technol. **45**(1), 1–62 (2011)
6. Li, Y., Geng, M., Liu, F., Zhang, D.: Visualization of photo album: selecting a representative photo of a specific event. In: Li, G., Yang, J., Gama, J., Natwichai, J., Tong, Y. (eds.)

DASFAA 2019. LNCS, vol. 11448, pp. 128–141. Springer, Cham (2019). https://doi.org/10.1007/978-3-030-18590-9_9

7. Whittaker, S., Bergman, O., Clough, P.: Easy on that trigger dad: a study of long term family photo retrieval. Pers. Ubiquit. Comput. **14**(1), 31–43 (2010)
8. Rodden, K., Wood, K.R.: How do people manage their digital photographs? ACM (2003)
9. Kirk, D., Sellen, A., Rother, C., Wood, K.: Understanding photowork. ACM (2006)
10. Elsweiler, D., Baillie, M., Ruthven, I.: What makes re-finding information difficult? A study of email re-finding. In: Clough, P., et al. (eds.) ECIR 2011. LNCS, vol. 6611, pp. 568–579. Springer, Heidelberg (2011). https://doi.org/10.1007/978-3-642-20161-5_57
11. Aula, A., Khan, R.M., Guan, Z.: How does search behavior change as search becomes more difficult? ACM (2010)
12. Al Nasar, M.R., Mohd, M., Ali, N.M.: Factors in re-finding the personal photographs: review and possible research directions. Res. J. Appl. Sci. Eng. Technol. **7**(4), 857–869 (2014)
13. Elsweiler, D., Ruthven, I.: Towards task-based personal information management evaluations. ACM (2007)
14. Al Nasar, M.R., Mohd, M., Ali, N.M.: Personal information management systems and interfaces: an overview. IEEE (2011)
15. Al Nasar, M.R., Mohd, M., Ali, N.M.: Personal information management: evaluation of the PHOTO REFINDER system. Adv. Sci. Lett. **24**(2), 1090–1094 (2018)
16. Al Nasar, M.R., Mohd, M., Ali, N.M.: Evaluation on personal information management processes. Asian J. Inf. Technol. **16**(8), 660–666 (2017)
17. Graham, A., Garcia-Molina, H., Paepcke, A., Winograd, T.: Time as essence for photo browsing through personal digital libraries. ACM (2002)
18. Robbins, D., Dumais, S., Sarin, R., Cutrell, E.: Fast, flexible filtering with Phlat—Personal search and organization made easy (2006)
19. Sinha, P., Jain, R.: Classification and annotation of digital photos using optical context data. ACM (2008)
20. Mota, J., Fonseca, M.J., Gonçalves, D., Jorge, J.A.: Agrafo: a visual interface for grouping and browsing digital photos (2008)
21. Voorhees, E.M., Harman, D.K.: TREC: Experiment and Evaluation in Information Retrieval. MIT Press, Cambridge (2005)

The Factors that Influence the Reading Habit Among Malaysian: A Systematic Literature Review

Ahmed Sedik Hassan Mohammed[1], Zahidah Zulkifli[1(✉)], and Ely Salwana Mat Surin[2]

[1] Kulliyyah of Information and Communication Technology, International Islamic University Malaysia, P.O. Box 10, 50728 Kuala Lumpur, Malaysia
sediq269@gmail.com, zahidahz@iium.edu.my
[2] Institute of Visual Informatics (IVI), Universiti Kebangsaan Malaysia, 43600 Bangi, Selangor, Malaysia
elysalwana@ukm.edu.my

Abstract. Reading is an action that a person does to obtain a wider knowledge through his or her experience and this process may lead that person into a very eye-opening self-discovery. In Malaysia, reading habits rate is still at a lower level, Malaysian on average read only two books per year. About 80% of Malaysian university students are reluctant readers. They can read but choose not to read. Therefore, the objective of this study is to identify the factors affecting the reading habit among Malaysia. To answer the research question of this study we performed a systematic literature review (SLR). We defined a mapping study process adapted from existing guidelines to categorize and to structure the research evidence that has been published in the area of reading habits among Malaysian and world-wide. Twenty-Four papers were used in our synthesis of evidence, and five factors were identified. The results of this SLR showed the five factors that can affect the reading habits among Malaysian: (1) Internet (2) Environmental influence (3) Lack of motivation (4) Peer pressure (5) Entertainment. The findings of this SLR would be beneficial for understanding the needs of Malaysian towards the reading habit by looking at the factors, that might be a measurement of reading habit environment in other specific scopes.

Keywords: Reading · Reading habit · Reading habit issues · Systematic literature review · Malaysian · University students

1 Introduction

Reading is considered as a way of getting new information and gaining knowledge. It enables us to progress and expand our minds and thoughtfully share views in order to improve our personal performance in the areas of career or life [1]. In other words, reading is the main source transferring experiences to the individual which in return influence the reader's way of thinking and sharing thoughts [2].

© Springer Nature Switzerland AG 2019
H. Badioze Zaman et al. (Eds.): IVIC 2019, LNCS 11870, pp. 537–549, 2019.
https://doi.org/10.1007/978-3-030-34032-2_47

To some extent, as an ineluctable activity, reading has always been seeing a source of both mental and personal development for a human being. And according to an Islamic point of view, the revelation that our prophet Muhammad (SAW) has received was to read, which would lead us to consider reading as a compulsory activity. In many situations such as gaining knowledge, sharing thoughts, expressing feelings, etc. have become reality by the act of reading [3]. In a broad way, the more we read the more our reading habit gradually enhances [4]. Shen [5], defines a reading habit as how often, how much, and what the readers read. For Sangkaeo [6], reading habit refers to the behavior, which expresses the likeness of reading and tastes of reading. A good reading habit and by reading books regularly can make the readers to analyze and scrutinize others' idea which makes one think more critically [7]. In addition, reading benefits readers in many ways. It empowers to become critical and analytical readers who are capable to cope and understand things in a deep perspective [8]. Thus, the objectives of this study is to identify the factors that affect the reading habits among Malaysian. The study used a systematic literature review to identify the factors affecting the reading habits among Malaysia. Parsifal SLR has been used as a tool to support SLR process. Parsifal SLR is a website that helps you planning, conducting, and reporting the review. We followed the procedures of Kitchenham and Ebse [9].

2   Background of Problems

The non-reading problem has been a major issue existing in Malaysian society [10]. Many studies have been conducted regarding reading trends in Malaysia and have consistently shown different strong reports. The results of a survey conducted by Frank Small & Associates [11] on Malaysians' reading habits reliably indicated that they read an average of two books a year which would be very surprising. This fact indicates that reading trends in Malaysian society are desperately dissatisfying. However, following the some concept, in 2005 another survey has been administrated on 60,441 Malaysians in which the results have shown that trends had not changed so far: 98% of people aged 10 years old and above still read only two books a year [10]. A further international study conducted by the Central Connecticut State University (2016) on 61 countries, found Malaysia ranked sixth from the bottom in the list of World's Most Literate Nation (WLMN) ranking. This regular issue is very upsetting and would importantly need prompt solutions from teachers, school administrators, educational practitioners, parents and to some extent government to discuss further this persistence alarming matter.

Numerous studies have gone to understand Malaysians reading habit. The study carried out by Baharuddin et al. [12] on three things such as understanding reading habits and reading interests among students in Malaysia. Later, the study aimed to investigate the factors leading or encouraging students to read or not to read. Moreover, Khairuddin [13] have conducted a research to carefully identify factors influencing the reading habit and choice of reading materials among form one boys of SS17 Secondary School in Subang Jaya. Therefore, the results have displayed that the lack of encouragement and the Length of time given to the students to read are the factors which influence the reading habits among the students. Straightforwardly, this study mainly focuses on identifying the factors that affect reading habits among Malaysians.

The results of literacy statistics in 2016 indicated that 85 of Malaysians were found to have regular reading habits. Seventy-seven percent of them were found to prefer newspaper, 3% (each) were found to be interested in magazines and books and 1.6% were the comic readers. Dato Sri Michael Manyin, Minister of Education, Science and Technological Research, stated that from the statistic it is clear that Malaysians are more interested in reading light material while people from more developed countries like the US prefer books. This needs to be solved as soon as possible as it can prevent the development of knowledge, intelligence, and maturity in an individual. It is important that reading habits need to be present from a very young age [4].

3   Method

This section describes the systematic literature review method that we applied in this study. The details of review planning and conduct are also discussed in this section.

3.1   Introduction

A systematic literature review can be defined as a method to inquiry, regain by evaluating carefully all existing research evidence with the purpose to provide the reliable answers to particular research matters or questions [14]. Systematic literature review aims to generate a scientific summary of the evidence in an area. In contrast to "traditional" narrative review, systematic literature review helps us to go in depth by retrieving useful fact-based evidences questions [14]. To this regard, this method of inquiring has become a popular research methodology since the 1990s and it was widely used in medical research and within that field, there are several well-documented standards to support its use [15]. The three main phases conducting in this SLR study are planning, conduct review and reporting. The SLR method of the present study follows the procedures of Kitchenham and Ebse [9] (Fig. 1).

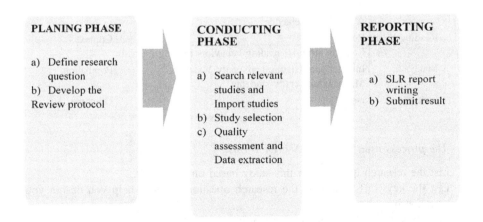

Fig. 1. Mapping study process

Planning Phase. The Planning review is the initial phase of the SLR which focuses on specifying the mapping study protocol which defines systematic activities to gather and collect information [16]. The starting point of SLR is identifying the research question. The research question is formulated and presented in the review protocol.

Research Questions. The principle objective of generating the research question is to direct the identification of relevant literature, to identify data that need to be mined from these selected studies, and the parameters to be evaluated. The primary focus of this SLR study is to principally find or figure out the factors affecting the reading habits among Malaysians. Therefore, this study needs to overtly detect previous contributions of studies on reading habits reported within the period of 2014 to 2018.

RQ: *What are the factors that affect reading habits among Malaysians?*

Develop the Review Protocol. After the research question was formed for the SLR, the PICOC criteria were used to define the research question. The researcher used PICOC to Separate the terms using commas. This will make it possible to save them separately as keywords so it can help us to design our search string (Tables 1 and 2).

Table 1. Summary of PICOC

Population	Malaysian
Intervention	Reading habit model
Comparison	N/A
Outcome	Factors
Context	Reading habit

Table 2. Keywords and synonyms

Keyword	Synonyms	Related to
Model	A framework A framework behavior A modeling behavior	Intervention
Reading habit	Reading Reading attitudes reading behaviors reading interests	Context
Malaysia	International Islamic University Malaysia Malaysia university students	Population
Factors	Issues	Outcome

The process used to Derive Search Terms:

- List the research question for this study based on the PICOC.
- List the keywords based on the research question that can help you design your search string.
- Identify synonyms and alternative words.

- Use Boolean "OR" to Join the synonyms.
- Use the Boolean "AND" to link major term.

Conducting Phase

A. Searching Relevant Studies. According to Kitchenham and Ebse [9], in order to figure out all the necessary previous relevant studies, researcher's process of inquiry must be exhaustive and in-depth, thoroughly comprehensive to address the RQs and that need to be included in the SLR. Straightforwardly, this section describes the strategies of the review that are designed, to retrieve the aforementioned relevant studies. For the automatic procedure, this study uses the following search string with proper search terms:

("Malaysia" OR "International Islamic University Malaysia" OR "Malaysia university students" OR "students") AND ("reading habits" OR "reading" OR "reading attitude" OR "reading behaviors" OR "reading interests") AND ("Model" OR "A Framework" OR "A Framework Behavior" OR "A Modeling Behavior") AND ("Factors" OR "issues").

This study uses three digital libraries to find similar studies in reading habits research fields, special combinations of keywords were generated and searched through well-known databases such as Scopus, Google scholar, and Science@Direct. We chose those three online databases because they are well-established, multidisciplinary study platforms, holding a broad variety of peer-reviewed journals, and they are being kept up to date. Table 3 below shows imported studies.

Table 3. Imported studies

Database	Number of imported studies
Scopus	322
Google Scholar	46
Science@Direct	98

B. Study Selection. In order to answer this study research question and to identify relevant primary studies in the existing reading habit papers. This identification process is performed with study selections criteria which include both the inclusion and exclusion criteria. This criterion is based upon the research question.

The researcher defined the following selection criteria:

- **Inclusion criteria:**
  - Studies about reading habits among Malaysian
  - Studies about reading habits among Malaysian students
  - Both qualitative and quantitative method
  - Studies published within the period of 2014–2018.
- **Exclusion criteria:**
  - Papers not written in English
  - Papers that do not relate to reading habits
  - Papers not related to Malaysian reading habits.

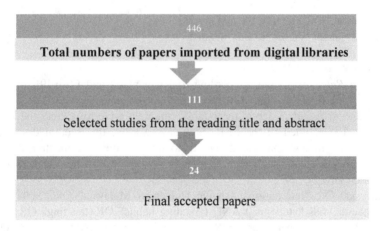

Fig. 2. Paper selection process

Figure 2 shows the paper selection process. The number of papers imported from the digital libraries was a total of 446. After applying the inclusion and exclusion criteria at the title and abstract level, a total of 111 papers remained only. The next filtration was applied at the content level with the inclusion/exclusion criteria being used to remove (i) papers not written in English and (ii) papers that do not relate to reading habits (iii) papers not related to Malaysian reading habits. After these exclusions, 24 papers were only considered as final.

C. Quality Assessment and Data Extraction. In order to easily enable the data extraction process, a form was designed which was used to compile evidence relating to the research question and measure the quality of the primary studies. The assessment checklist was comprised of four general questions to measure the quality of both quantitative and qualitative studies according to the following ratio scale: Yes = 1 point, No = 0 points, and Partially = 0.5 point. The resulting total quality score for each study ranged between 0 (very poor) and 4 (very good) (Table 4).

Table 4. Study quality checklist

Item	Answer
1. Were the aim(s) of the study clearly stated? [14]	Yes/No/Partial
2. Were the data collection carried out very well? For example, discussion of procedures used for collection, and how the study setting may have influenced the data collected [14]	Yes/No/Partial
3. Is the data analysis process appropriate? [9]	Yes/No/Partial
4. Were the findings of the research clearly stated?? [17]	Yes/No/Partial

D. Data Extraction Result and Quality Checklist. For each of the paper, we identified: the author's name, publication year, paper type (journal/conference), source (Scopus/ScienceDirect/google scholar), and the total quality score. These 24 papers were published in the time period of 2014 to 2018. Among the 24 papers, 21 papers were published in journals and the remaining 3 papers were published in conference proceedings. The average quality score across all paper is 3.29 out of 4.0. For journals, the average quality score of the studies is approximately 3.6 out of 4.0. Conferences, by comparison, have a slightly lower average quality score of 2.8. Hence, all 24 papers are accepted for the next phase.

Reporting Phase

A. SLR Results. This section presents the synthesis of evidence by performing the analysis of extracted data from the literature search results. This SLR study found the factors that have a clear impact on reading habits among Malaysians. Table 5 shows a list of the factors that influence Malaysians reading habits.

RQ: *What are the factors that affect reading habits among Malaysians*

Table 5. List of factors

No	Factors	Studies (S)	Total # Studies
1	Internet	S2, S3, S5, S6, S9, S11, S12, S13, S15, S17, S19, S20, S21, S24	14
2	Lack of motivation	S7, S8, S10, S18	4
3	Environmental influence	S1, S4, S5, S14, S16, S22	6
4	Social pressure (Peers Pressure)	S4, S19, S20	3
5	Entertainment	S16, S17, S20	3

The study found that most of the authors agreed that the internet has the highest impact on the reading habit. "Internet" is the most studied factor that believed it affects the reading habit (14 papers), followed by "Environmental influence" and "lack of motivation" respectively 6 papers and 4 papers, and "peer pressure" and "entertainment" are the least studied: covered by 3 papers. Table 6 shows the definition of each factor.

Table 6. Factors definitions

No	Factors	Definition
F1	Internet	The rapid growth of technology has been very significant in the 21st century in almost every field. The Internet is one of the factors that exercise impacts reading habits. Since then, plenty of societies have become more and more reliably dependent on it. The number of Internet users in Malaysia is soaring faster. The internet of thing (IoT) has affected Malaysians reading behavior; 93% of those aged between 12–29 use the online system, while those aged between 29 years and above nearly (74%) of them use the internet. Majority of Malaysians prefer surfing the Internet as their main activity during leisure time [18]

(continued)

Table 6. (*continued*)

No	Factors	Definition
F2	Lack of motivation	It is very obvious almost in every society. People are getting more and more disconnected from buying books. The real encouragement is badly weak and therefore, none of us does not intend to buy tangible books to read
F3	Environmental influence (Lack of Facilities and services/internal and external environment)	The environment itself whether it is internal or external has a constant influence on ones reading habits. The lack of facilities and services are seeing as the main factors having effects on Malaysians. Since then, no many important people visit the least of libraries that are available. It was asserted that Malaysian students do not really believe that libraries are not really well-equipped with good reading materials. However, their main purpose to visit libraries would only be to study inside for exam preparations rather than reading leisure. In this case, it is highly suggested that libraries should offer free access to books and be able to conduct a variety of programs or workshops to the community [19]
F4	Peers pressure	The fourth factor that affects reading habit is peers influence. Peer pressure is a quite strong factor when it comes to reading habits and most of the time this factor affects the students [20]. Negative peer pressure is when friends or a group of people decides to pressure another person from stopping them something they were doing or pressure them into doing something they do not want to do
F5	Entertainment	With the help of technology, many entertaining activities had emerged such as movies, music, social media and computer game. People do entertain and read through their gadgets, which causes to forget step by step the importance of the library. Many studies indicated that students become less and less interested in reading. Many different factors are involved but social media and technology development are believed to be the two strongest factors. Technology development has proven to strongly affect reading habits. Technology and electronic media are the reasons why the students are more interested in watching TV shows and playing online games during their free time. It is also believed that electronic materials have played an important role in changing the way people perceive reading and how printed publications are being used for reading [21]

B. List of Selected Papers. As mentioned in the study selection part, the total number of papers that were imported in the digital library was 446 papers and the total number of papers included in the data extraction phase was 111. The final accepted papers are 24 studies after inclusion/exclusion criteria being used to remove papers are not written in English, papers that are not related to the reading habits, and the papers that are not related to Malaysian reading habits (Table 7).

Table 7. List of selected papers

Code	Papers	Factors
S1	An Exploratory Study of the Reading Habits of Urban Malaysians	F1,
S2	A Correlational Study of Foreign Language Anxiety and Library Anxiety	F1,
S3	A Cross-Cultural Comparison of Media Multitasking in American and Malaysian College Students	F1,
S4	An Assessment of Physical Factors that Influencing Reading Habits of Secondary School Students in Gombak District, Kuala Lumpur, Malaysia	F3, F4,
S5	Bibliotherapy in the Malaysian Public Libraries A Conceptual Framework	F3
S6	Digital Literacy Do Undergraduates Read More or Less	F1,
S7	Exploring perceptions on ESL students' reading habits	F2, F3
S8	Factors that influence the reading habit among form one boys: A case study of SMK SS17 Subang Jaya	F2, F3
S9	Qiraahbot's prototype development for an extensive reading activity	F1,
S10	Re-thinking a literacy: when undergraduates surrender their reading choices	F2,
S11	Reading Habits and Attitudes of UMSKAL Undergraduates	F1, F2,
S12	Reading movies, watching novels	F1
S13	Reading Trends and Perceptions towards Islamic English Websites as	F1
S14	Systematic Tracking of Malaysian Primary School Students' ESL Reading	F1, F3
S15	The Impact of Digital-Based Materials on Undergraduates'	F1
S16	The Integration of Interactive Display Method and Heritage	F1, F5, F3
S17	The Online Reading Habits of Malaysian Students	F1, F5
S18	The Relationship Between Parenting Styles and Students' Attitude Toward Leisure Time Reading	F1, F2, F3
S19	The Determination of Reading Habits among Students	F1, F4
S20	Transformative Higher Education Teaching and Learning Using	F1, F5
S21	Uncovering Print and Digital Literacies What Matters to Undergraduates	F1
S22	Understanding e-book acceptance through Technology Acceptance Model	F1, F3, F4
S23	Understanding of Reading Habits among Students in Malaysia: A Review	F1
S24	Use of the internet for academic purposes among students in Malaysian institutions of higher education	F1

4   Discussion

The purpose of this systematic literature review (SLR) was to identify the factors affecting the reading habits among Malaysians. To do this, we selected 24 papers related to the reading habit among Malaysians that were published between 2014 to 2018. Altogether, five factors were identified by a total of twenty-four studies which investigated how these factors affected the reading habit.

The result of the SLR shows that most of the researchers focused on the impact of the internet on the reading habit. Almost 14 study's findings reported that Malaysians reading is affected by the Internet. The Internet has been discussed in various studies as one of the factors affecting the reading habit. Previous studies have shown that the Internet had become the most used media among Malaysians and it is one of the frequently used sources by the students when looking for information, which changed the behavior of students reading habits. Saaid and Wahab [19] conducted a survey about The Impact of Digital-Based Materials on Undergraduates Reading Habit and the respondents were from Universiti Teknologi MARA (UiTM). 103 UiTM students participated in this study and the result showed that the majority of UiTM students (69.2%) read digital-based materials for leisure rather than research (18.1%) and study (12.7%). From this result, it shows us that digital-based materials are more useful for students than printed materials. Malaysian students spend nearly 20 h per week on the internet. Among these users, 66% had stated that their reason to go online is to learn. Most of Malaysian citizens depend more on the internet for finding books or information because of the internet more accessible and more cost-effective and less time consuming [18]. The advancement of technology does not help the students to read more regardless of types of reading materials [22].

Lack of motivation has a significant impact on reading habit. motivation or encouragement to read is one of the most important things that Malaysians needs in order to increase the interest of reading books. Lack of motivation is affecting the reading habit among Malaysian, especially the students, because they don't get encouragement and have low motivation to read. As suggested by Baharuddin et al. [12] in their paper, students need encouragement to read and the Encouragement to read should come from multiple sources such as from the university, home, and also community.

The third factor that affects Malaysia reading habits is Environmental influence. Our SLR showed that six studies investigated Environment influence on reading habit. Environment influence is the physical factor that affecting the reading habits among Malaysian. The main reasons for this problem are lack of positive role models in the home, lack of reading materials at home and library, and lack of facilities and services at the library. The library environment or the university environment can have an influence on some students reading habits. for example, the students moved from rural schools to universities may have an influence on their affective behavior toward the university and library environment [23]. The environment can influence the students reading habit in a way how they have been taught to read because in this world we are surrounded by people, and the attitudes can be learned from people by just looking and feeling interested about it [20]. Most of the students nowadays prefer the informal environment of a reading place where they can have some other activities performed while they are reading such as eating food, chatting with friends, listening to music and watching movies [19].

Our SLR found that peer pressure is one of the factors affecting the reading habits among Malaysians. The SLR result showed that 3 studies investigated peer pressure and our SLR proofed reading habits can be influenced by peers. Peer pressure can be good and bad when it comes to reading habits. A study conducted by Rosli et al. [20] stated that most of the students got recommended by their friends for the books they read, which has a more significant percentage than teachers. Positive peer pressure is important because it can encourage to read more but negative peer pressure can influence our attitude towards reading habits and makes them reluctant readers.

Malaysian peoples today read very little and no longer find pleasure in reading, they favor the digital entertainments [24]. Youth and adults of Malaysian are now more towards hedonism and digital-based entertainment [24]. Jafre et al. [21] conducted a survey about The Online Reading Habits of Malaysian Students. the result showed that 83.7% of the respondents went online daily. the result also revealed that the majority of the respondents go online for entertainment purpose. Our SLR found that Malaysian students favored digital entertainment rather than reading.

5 Conclusion

In this paper, we perform a systematic literature review to investigate the factors affecting the reading habit among Malaysian. The result was combined automatic search. A total of 446 papers from three online databases were analyzed and went through three filtration steps. A total of 24 studies were used in our SLR to answer the research question, from which five compatibility factors potentially affecting the reading habits were identified. this study answers the Research Question acknowledging that reading habits are greatly influenced by the internet, environmental, Lack of motivation, peer pressure, and entertainment. The outcome of this study can be used by the Malaysians to be aware of these factors that are affecting their reading habits and helps them to increase their reading habits.

As part of our future work, it suggested for future studies to conduct another SLR and select a bigger sample to find out the world wide reading habit issues and compare them with Malaysian reading habits. we are also working on another paper which is related to this paper and the study is about testing the factors we found on this SLR paper. The paper is about finding out the relationship between the selected factors (internet, lack of motivation, environmental influence, peer pressure, and entertainment) and the reading habits among Malaysian university students. The paper will show if there is a relationship between the factors we found on this SLR and the reading habits among the university students.

Acknowledgement. This work was supported by the FRGS project funded by the Ministry of Education Malaysia, Grant No. FRGS/1/2018/ICT04/UIAM/02/2. This project is a collaborative project between Kulliyyah of ICT, IIUM and Kulliyyah of IRKHS, IIUM.

References

1. Mat Yatin, S.F., Sulaiman, S.T.M., Shuhaimi, H., Ibrahim, M., Murad, M.: Reading habits and reading activities: a bibliometric study. Aust. J. Basic Appl. Sci. **8**, 163–170 (2014)
2. Green, P.: Teachers intervention in children's reading. J. Child Hood Educ. **46**(3), 147–149 (2002)

3. Edizer, Z.Ç.: Relationship between the attitudes of turkish prospective teachers on reading habits and their perceptions of the uses of metacognitive reading strategies. Kastamonu Educ. J. **23**(2), 645–658 (2014)

4. Ponnudurai, P., Irawan, M.K.: An exploratory study of the reading habits of urban Malaysians and its impact on academic achievement. Int. J. Eng. Technol. **7**(3.25), 263–267 (2018). https://doi.org/10.14419/ijet.v7i3.25.17559

5. Shen, L.: Computer technology and college students' reading habits. Chia-Nan Annu. Bull. **32**, 559–572 (2006)

6. Sangkaeo, S.: Reading habit promotion in Asian libraries. In: Paper Presented at 65th IFLA Council and General Council and General Conference, Bangkok, Thailand (1999)

7. Cunningham, A.E., Stanovich, K.E.: What Reading does for the mind **1**(2), 137–149 (2001)

8. Cook, A.E., Halleran, J.G., O'Brien, E.J.: What is readily available during reading? A memory-based view of text processing. Discourse Process. **26**(2–3), 109–129 (1998). https://doi.org/10.1080/01638539809545041

9. Kitchenham, B., Ebse, C.: Guidelines for performing systematic literature reviews in software engineering executive summary (2007)

10. Mansor, N.: Exploring perceptions on ESL students' reading habits. J. Bus. Soc. Dev. **5**(2), 19–24 (2017)

11. Frank Small & Associates: Study of Reading Habits in Malaysia. Perpustakaan Negara Malaysia, Kuala Lumpur (1996)

12. Baharuddin, M.F., Hasnol, W.M.H.W., Ramsi, M.F.M., Kadir, M.R.A.: Understanding of reading habits among students in Malaysia: a review (2015). https://doi.org/10.13140/RG.2.1.3075.8482

13. Khairuddin, Z., Shukry, A.S.M., Sani, N.A.: Reading trends and perceptions towards Islamic English websites as teaching materials. Engl. Lang. Teach. **7**(8), 124–133 (2014). https://doi.org/10.5539/elt.v7n8p124

14. Salleh, N., Mendes, E., Grundy, J.C.: Empirical studies of pair programming for CS/SE teaching in higher education: a systematic literature review. IEEE Trans. Softw. Eng. **37**(4), 509–525 (2011). https://doi.org/10.1109/TSE.2010.59

15. Babar, M.A., Zhang, H.: Systematic literature reviews in software engineering: preliminary results from interviews with researchers. In: 2009 3rd International Symposium on Empirical Software Engineering and Measurement, pp. 346–355 (2009). https://doi.org/10.1109/ESEM.2009.5314235

16. Vale, T., de Almeida, E.S., Alves, V., Kulesza, U., Niu, N., de Lima, R.: Software product lines traceability: a systematic mapping study. Inf. Softw. Technol. **84**, 1–18 (2017). https://doi.org/10.1016/j.infsof.2016.12.004

17. Guinea, A.S., Nain, G., Le Traon, Y.: A systematic review on the engineering of software for ubiquitous systems. J. Syst. Softw. **118**, 251–276 (2016). https://doi.org/10.1016/j.jss.2016.05.024

18. Saaid, S.A., Wahab, Z.A.: The impact of digital-based materials on undergraduates' reading habit. Int. J. Soc. Sci. Hum. **4**(3), 249–253 (2014). https://doi.org/10.7763/ijssh.2014.v4.357

19. Murad, M.B., Ibrahim, M.B., Hashim, K.S., Mat Yatin, S.F.B., Sulaiman, S.T.M.: An assessment of physical factors that influencing reading habits of secondary school students in Gombak. Adv. Sci. Lett. **23**(4), 1–14 (2017)

20. Rosli, N.A., Razali, N.F., Zamil, Z.U.A., Noor, S.N.F.M., Baharuddin, M.F.: The determination of reading habits among students: a concept. Int. J. Acad. Res. Bus. Soc. Sci. **7**(12), 791–798 (2018)

21. Abidin, M.J.B.Z., Pourmohammadi, M., Varasingam, P., Choon Lean, O.: The online reading habits of Malaysian students. Read. Matrix © 2014 **14**(2), 164–172 (2014)

22. Yaacob, Z.: Digital Literacy : Do Undergraduates Read More or Less? pp. 7–10 (2016)

23. Sinnasamy, J., Karim, N.H.A.: A correlational study of foreign language anxiety and library anxiety among non-native speakers of English: a case study in a Malaysian public university. J. Acad. Librariansh. **40**(5), 431–435 (2014)
24. Hashim, A.F., Taib, M.Z.M., Alias, A.: The integration of interactive display method and heritage exhibition at museum. Procedia - Soc. Behav. Sci. **153**, 308–316 (2014). https://doi.org/10.1016/j.sbspro.2014.10.06

Student's Perception on Entrepreneurial Education Programs for Graduate Startups in Selected ASEAN Universities

Md. Sum Sarmila[1], Shamshubaridah Ramlee[2], Akmal Sabarudin[3],
Norhana Arsad[4], Murshida Marizan Nor[6],
Zainebbeevi Kamal Batcha[3], Nurul Asmaa Ramli[2],
and A. Imran Nordin[5(✉)]

[1] Faculty of Social Sciences and Humanities, Universiti Kebangsaan Malaysia,
Bangi, Selangor, Malaysia
[2] Center for Entrepreneurship & SME Development (UKM-CESMED),
Universiti Kebangsaan Malaysia, Bangi, Selangor, Malaysia
[3] Faculty of Health Sciences, Universiti Kebangsaan Malaysia, Jalan Raja Muda
Abdul Aziz, Kuala Lumpur, Malaysia
[4] Faculty of Engineering and Built Environment, Universiti Kebangsaan
Malaysia, Bangi, Selangor, Malaysia
[5] Institute of Visual Informatics (IVI), Universiti Kebangsaan Malaysia, Bangi,
Selangor, Malaysia
[6] Faculty of Dentistry, Universiti Kebangsaan Malaysia, Jalan Raja Muda
Abdul Aziz, Kuala Lumpur, Malaysia
aliimran@ukm.edu.my

Abstract. Entrepreneurship education plays a crucial role in higher education to increase student's interests and capability of having an entrepreneurial mindset. This study aims to evaluate student's perception of their institution, instructors and themselves towards entrepreneurship education to inform gamification design of entrepreneurship education in the 4IR era. Through knowledge transfer programs, a self-reported questionnaire was distributed to 3 participating universities in 3 ASEAN countries namely Malaysia, Indonesia and Vietnam measuring their perception of the current entrepreneurship education at their respective institutions. In total, 209 responses were received, comprising students from Malaysia (27.3%), Indonesia (42.6%) and Vietnam (30.1%). The results suggest that the combination of student's perception of the institutions that provide necessary supports, the instructors' abilities to deliver teaching materials in an engaging way and students' openness to learn entrepreneurship influence the student's openness to entrepreneurial education in higher education. These results imply useful inputs to design gamification strategies where the gamified teaching and learning within the institution, instructors and the students would influence better acceptance of entrepreneurial education courses.

Keywords: Entrepreneurship education · Knowledge transfer · ASEAN · Student · Fourth industrial revolution (4IR) · Gamification

© Springer Nature Switzerland AG 2019
H. Badioze Zaman et al. (Eds.): IVIC 2019, LNCS 11870, pp. 550–559, 2019.
https://doi.org/10.1007/978-3-030-34032-2_48

1   Introduction

Recent development in the job market where jobs have transformed due to the advancement of technology have indeed forced institutions of higher learning to embrace entrepreneurship education and programs. According to [19] Siemieniak & Rembiasz in 2019 recent trend in education suggest that entrepreneurship education must be taught in the tertiary education to allow students to grasp all the necessary knowledge and skills to have an entrepreneurial mindset before they leave the institution. According to the Online Cambridge dictionary defines entrepreneurship as a skill in starting a new business, especially involves seeing new opportunities[1]. In addition, The Network for Teaching Entrepreneurship defines the entrepreneurial mindset as the set of attitudes, skills and behaviors that students need to succeed academically, personally and professionally[2]. These include: initiative and self-direction, risk-taking, flexibility and adaptability, creativity and innovation, critical thinking and problem solving. This entrepreneurship mindset will help unemployment among the youth and graduate.

Despite the importance of entrepreneurship education in higher education, there are a lot of questions on the most appropriate method of delivering the contents. According to [20], knowledge transfer is one of the strategies that can be implemented to enhance the delivery of entrepreneurship education. In addition, in the 4IR era, it is argued that gamification in education enables students engagement with courses in higher education [21]. However, little is known on how to design gamification for entrepreneurship education via knowledge transfer program.

Countries in ASEAN are learning from each other the best way in propagating entrepreneurship knowledge and mindsets to ensure students are industry ready upon graduation. In this study we take that a well structured policy on entrepreneurship teaching, training and program will influence the success of transferring entrepreneurship knowledge at institutions of higher learning. The entrepreneurship ecosystem and collaboration as well as educator's ability to deliver knowledge and their entrepreneurship experiences are factors that influence the success of knowledge transfers. However, what is more important is students' perceptions on educators' abilities and their readiness to learn entrepreneurship are vital to ensure the success of entrepreneurship knowledge transfers among them. This study is organized in 6 sections; Sect. 2 discussed the related works in entrepreneurship education. Section 3 discussed the methodology employed; Sects. 4 and 5 presents and discuss results and findings while Sect. 5 concludes.

1.1   Entrepreneurship Education

Entrepreneurship has emerged over more than a decade as it is seen as an economic force in the world that can increase a country's gross income. The same can be seen in the field of entrepreneurship education with the growth in curriculum development among universities. The number of colleges and universities that offer courses related to

---

[1] https://dictionary.cambridge.org/dictionary/english/entrepreneur.

[2] https://entrepreneurship.msu.edu/the-entrepreneurial-mindset/.

entrepreneurship has grown from a handful in the 1970s to over 1,600 in 2005 [5]. This imply that entrepreneurship plays a major role in developing mindsets among students.

Teaching people about the realities of entrepreneurship may increase their entrepreneurial self-efficacy [1]. In addition, the top seven criteria that help entrepreneurship programs include courses offered, faculty publication, impact on community, alumni exploits, innovation, alumni startup and outreach to scholars [2]. Entrepreneurship education is important to help expose the student to the real situation in the world [3]. Theoretical disciplines have become one of the greatest challenges facing educators [4] where the entrepreneurship education are exposed to innovation and creativity. These attributes need to be identified, nurtured and freely expressed in the classroom. To realize this goal, the educator must be able to focus on innovation in an entrepreneurial classroom [5]. A research form Central and Eastern European Universities showed that great opportunity to capitalize on the market economy will be achieved if they are advances in innovation, new product development and new management thinking by companies in the global economy. This will help the business educators create new entrepreneurship programmes that can prepare and educate students for a new world.

In general, entrepreneurship education in higher education focuses more broadly on student's personal development in terms of changing their mindset, enhancing their skills (communication, negotiation, social, etc.) and developing the entrepreneurial attitudes and behaviour to ensure that they are fully equipped with necessary skills to compete when they graduated from the higher institutions [15]. In addition, the term entrepreneurship education has been defined to focus more on the specific context of setting up a venture and becoming self-employed [13]. It is argued that the opportunity identifications at the institutional level, available resources and student's motivation on entrepreneurship are the central role of entrepreneurship training [16].

1.2   Entrepreneurship Education in the Malaysian Context

Malaysia is seen as one of the counties that very much emphasize entrepreneurship to prepare students to either be employed or become employers themselves. Malaysian government supports and utilize limited resources to develop entrepreneurial activities [6]. The Malaysian government have successfully provided programs that include financial support in terms of grants, eco-systems within and outside institutions the academic circle. In addition, implementation of entrepreneurial education at tertiary level and entrepreneurship training are done to enhance students entrepreneur skills. Malaysian is seen as the early stages of entrepreneurship development with very dynamic and volatile. The number of early-stage entrepreneurial activities in Malaysia is still lower than in other parts of developing countries [6].

Entrepreneurship in Malaysia is encouraged through entrepreneurship education. Students are exposed in entrepreneurship education at tertiary level and university for entrepreneurial skills and activities. This shows that the Ministry of Education, Malaysia is focused on strengthening the entrepreneurship culture among youth. Building the interest of our young generation is a step that is taken by the Malaysian government to help expose them in entrepreneurship. The policy makers should take an appropriate measure with current trends of entrepreneurship education programs at universities in Malaysia [7].

The Malaysian government has made a lot of efforts in promoting entrepreneurship education by improving the current policy on entrepreneurship education, providing various entrepreneurship programs to increase the number of young entrepreneurs, and highlighting the need to empower entrepreneurship education among graduates of Higher Education Institutes (HEIs) [8]. Currently, there are six (6) thrust which is implemented to empower entrepreneurship education. The six thrust are to empower the Entrepreneurship Center in every HEIs, to provide a holistic and well-planned entrepreneurial education and programs, to enhance the competency of HEIs' entrepreneurship trainers and facilitators among educators, to increase the outcome and effectiveness of the implemented HEIs' entrepreneurial education programs. to empower entrepreneurial development programs, and to provide a conducive environment and ecosystem for entrepreneurship development [8].

One of the factors that influence entrepreneurship education in Malaysia is how the government policy embed entrepreneurship education among the youngsters. Second is by enforce support on business environment such as agencies, Ministry of Higher Education (KPM) corporate sector, NGOs, society and funding institutions. Third is to create a centre of entrepreneurship for all university, which is led and operated by the Ministry of Higher Education (KPM). In Malaysia, entrepreneurship education in higher education aims to promote the development of student's attitude, behaviour and mindset to compete and solve the problem of unemployment after they graduate. The Ministry of Higher Education in Malaysia (KPM) has taken the initiative so that entrepreneurship subjects becomes compulsory for all students at the Malaysia's public universities. This action will encourage entrepreneurship activities at their respective universities. Trainings, seminars, short courses, conferences and entrepreneurship events were introduced as fun activities for students to learn entrepreneurship. Besides that, entrepreneurship education is also a platform for university to improve the learning ecosystem for promoting the innovative thinking for future generations.

Entrepreneurship education ecosystem in Malaysia is divided into two main elements, external and internal to the academic institutions. The external factors include support from the business environment, from government (agencies and Ministry of Higher Education) corporate sector, NGOs, society and funding institutions. In contrast, the internal factors include the support from HLIs' top management, academic and non-academic staff's mindsets, effectiveness of ECs, education programs, development of student entrepreneurs, competency of educators and readiness of students. The challenges faced by entrepreneurship educators in universities is how to embed entrepreneurship education for both business and non-business students. Meanwhile, student's priority to focus on academic grades while venturing into business is an added challenge [14]. On the educator's part, they too argued that they are burdened with academic tasks and for them to commit to entrepreneurship education, they need more time to be trained on the delivery of entrepreneurship curriculum.

1.3 Knowledge Transfer Among Higher Education

Knowledge transfer among business practitioners or industries to learning institutions is becoming increasingly important in higher education. Practitioners or trainers are agent of transfer knowledge process. The relationship between knowledge characteristics and knowledge transfer is the main source for recipient learning intent and source of learning attractiveness [9]. The practitioners or trainers need to polish their delivery skills to bring their practice closer to both students and educators. The framework that is used for knowledge transfer is the interactions of people, tools, and tasks provide as a basis for competitive advantage.

The framework to help improve knowledge transfer process among the learners [10] include 3 (three) main categories of knowledge transfer barriers [11]. The three main categories are personal knowledge, organizational knowledge sharing and technology knowledge sharing. Personal knowledge includes lack of time, fear of sharing, low of awareness and realization, lack of experience, hands of learning, observation, interactive problem solving, insufficient capture, feedback and communication, lack of time and interaction between knowledge sources and recipients, poor verbal/written communication and interpersonal skills; age differences, gender differences, lack of social network, differences in education levels and others. The second category is an organizational knowledge that is unclear goals and strategic, lack of leadership, lack of recognition system, lack of support and sharing practices, lack of sharing opportunities and resources, size of business is to small and others. The third is technology barriers which indicates lack of integration of IT systems and processes, lack of technical support (internal and external), lack of technology knowledge and the training and lack of familiarity and experience. In addition, results have implications for course designs in the traditional classroom context and the more innovative online environment [12].

2   Methodology

2.1   Aim and Hypothesis

This study aims to design of an entrepreneurial knowledge transfer program for students who are interested in the technology-based startups among ASEAN universities. The objective of this study is to identify factors that influence how students perceive entrepreneurial education and how they accept the module. Three factors are identified to influence the student's openness to entrepreneurial education in higher education, namely the perception of the institutional readiness to deliver entrepreneurial education modules, the perception of the instructors and teaching materials used and student's openness to learn entrepreneurship. Given that only Malaysia has a policy on entrepreneurship education, we hypothesized that students in higher education in Malaysia significantly perceived that the prepared entrepreneurial education module designed by universities and commissioned by the Ministry of Education is easy to use and follow in comparison to students in Indonesia and Vietnam.

2.2   Participants

The total number of participants recruited in this study was 209 (57 from Malaysia, 63 from Vietnam and 89 from Indonesia). 144 of them were female and 65 of them were male. Their age ranged from 18-year-old to 45-year-old (mean age: 21.06 SD: 3.49). The level of education for students who participated in this study was 44 undergraduates and 13 postgraduates from Malaysia, 60 undergraduates and 3 post-graduates from Vietnam and 87 undergraduates and 2 postgraduates from Indonesia. All of them were recruited through convenience sampling strategy. 46 Malaysian students (80.7%), 14 Vietnamese students (22.2%) and 31 Indonesian students (34.8%) have taken entrepreneurship courses at their university. All of the participants were recruited from several faculties namely Faculty of Economic, Business and Management, Faculty of Engineering and Built Environment, Faculty of Information Science and Technology, Faculty of Science and Technology, Faculty of Health Sciences, Faculty of Medicine, Faculty of Social Sciences and Humanities, Faculty of Islamic Studies, Faculty of Education and Faculty of Law.

2.3 Materials

The survey was conducted using both physical paper questionnaire and online questionnaire (through Google form). The questionnaire is divided into two sections: Section A focuses on the demographic information; Section B contains 44 questions focuses on measuring the factors that influence their acceptance of the entrepreneurial education at their respective institutions measuring the entrepreneurship development in teaching and learning which include entrepreneurship learning ecosystem and student pathways to become entrepreneurs. A 5-point Likert-scale was used to allow participants to represent their agreement towards the statements in the questionnaire.

3   Results

Table 1 shows the descriptive results for student's perception of the institutional readiness to deliver entrepreneurial education modules, student's perception of the instructors and teaching materials used and student's openness to learn entrepreneurship in Malaysia, Vietnam and Indonesia. These factors are identified through EC-OECD Entrepreneurial Universiti Framework focusing on student and institutional towards Entrepreneurship learning ecosystem[3].

Using One-Way ANOVA, there was a significant effect of the factors that influence student's perception of entrepreneurial education in their institutions. Using the benchmark of the p-value of $p < 0.05$, student's perception of the institutional readiness to deliver entrepreneurial education modules was significantly different [F (2, 206) = 4.412, p = 0.013]. Post-hoc comparisons using the Tukey HSD test indicate that only the mean score for Malaysia (M = 36.75, SD = 7.00) and Indonesia (M = 32.62, SD = 10.53) was significantly different. In addition, there was a significant effect on student's perception of the instructors and teaching materials used [F (2, 206) = 3.585, p = 0.029], Post hoc comparisons using the Tukey HSD test indicated that only the mean score for Malaysia (M = 21.68, SD = 4.30) was significantly different than Vietnam (M = 19.56, SD = 4.27).

---

[3] https://www.oecd.org/site/cfecpr/ECOECD%20Entrepreneurial%20Universities%20Framework.pdf.

Table 1. Mean and (standard deviation) for the factors that influence the entrepreneurship learning ecosystem

Factors	Country	Mean (standard deviation)
Student's perception of the institutional readiness to deliver entrepreneurial education modules	Malaysia	36.75 (7.00)
	Vietnam	35.57 (7.21)
	Indonesia	32.62 (10.53)
Student's perception of the instructors and teaching materials used	Malaysia	21.68 (4.30)
	Vietnam	19.56 (4.27)
	Indonesia	20.57 (4.44)
Student's openness to learn entrepreneurship	Malaysia	6.65 (1.93)
	Vietnam	6.13 (2.03)
	Indonesia	7.47 (2.02)

Moreover, there was a significant effect on student's openness to learn entrepreneurship [$F_{(2, 206)} = 8.683$, $p = 0.000$], Post hoc comparisons using the Tukey HSD test indicated that the mean score for Malaysia ($M = 6.65$, $SD = 1.93$) was significantly different than Indonesia ($M = 7.47$, $SD = 2.02$). The mean score for Indonesia was also significantly different than Vietnam ($M = 6.13$, $SD = 2.03$). However, the mean scores for Malaysia and Vietnam were not significantly different. Taken together, these results suggest that student's perceptions of their institution, instructors and themselves really do influence the success of entrepreneurial education in the higher education institution. Specifically, our results suggest that when students perceive the institutions provide necessary supports, the instructors are fully equipped with complete teaching materials to deliver the entrepreneurial education modules and when students are open to learning, they will do better in the entrepreneurial education courses. However, it should be noted that these factors come together to ensure the success of the course.

4   Discussion

The hypothesis is accepted except for the third element. The analysis emphasizes three major findings that are considered important to understand the degree of acceptance among students about their perceptions on the entrepreneurship education conducted in their university. This survey shows that students from different ASEAN countries view the entrepreneurship education differently. We measured student's perception of the institutional in terms of entrepreneurship modules and contents used, student's perception towards the educators and teaching system, as well as student's perception on themselves (their self-openness towards entrepreneurship knowledge). We argue that these perceptions have a significant effect the students' acceptance towards entrepreneurship education. Our findings are consistent with [16] that suggest these three factors namely opportunity identifications at the institutional level, available resources and student's motivation on entrepreneurship are the central role of entrepreneurship training.

The results also revealed that there is a reasonable level of consensus among groups of students in Malaysia and Vietnam on institutional readiness to deliver entrepreneurial education modules. There were too much expectations on the institution for the students to learn about entrepreneurship. The participating universities (Malaysia and Vietnam) have obtained their accreditation and molded their entrepreneurship modules according to industrial needs. The programs offered by these universities are relevant and parallel to the advancement of technology in entrepreneurship or also known as techno-preneurship. This is to ensure that they can face the rapidly changing economy and dynamic market [17]. Hence, graduates from these two countries expect their institutions to give well-prepared entrepreneurship skills and knowledge regardless of their disciplines. On the other hand, Indonesia has developed their entrepreneurship curriculum way advance to cater the student's needs without any controlling body or authorities to monitor and accredit their curriculum. The entrepreneurship programs in the participating university in Indonesia were very much involved with community engagement.

In terms of instructors and teaching material used, the survey shows that most students in Vietnam disagree on being mentored by academics to help them to nurture interest in learning entrepreneurship. Although Vietnam has its own incubator for students' startup, the programs are mostly engaged with experts from the industries. This is argued to be the key entrepreneurship education ecosystem enablers for knowledge commercialization and engagement with entrepreneurial communities [18]. Thus, the students are likely to appreciate university as a platform to learn entrepreneurship but not holistically involve academics and support staff in the ecosystem. In Indonesia, most of the university lecturers who involved in teaching entrepreneurship students are entrepreneurs themselves. The lecturers enjoy teaching entrepreneurship using 'learning by doing' approach during class teaching. Unlike Vietnam and Indonesia, Malaysian, entrepreneurship educators are encouraged to have appropriate credentials or undergo professional entrepreneurship training conducted by the Ministry of Education such as business mentorship and educators' enhancement programs before conducting entrepreneurial programs in the university.

Our study asserts that Malaysian and Vietnamese students are significantly less open to learn entrepreneurship. This is due to multiple factors such as comfortable with existing learning curriculum prepared by the lecturers and almost zero risk of failing the subjects. In Malaysia, almost all 22 public universities, polytechnics and college communities have made fundamental entrepreneurship course compulsory. It is very challenging to find those who are really interested and passionate about learning entrepreneurship even when the course is compulsory. This study also showed several factors affecting the openness of the students to learn entrepreneurship education such as self-reliance, resilience, entrepreneurial mindset and personal experience. Indonesian students have all these factors hence making it easier for them to embrace entrepreneurship knowledge and education. In spite of not having a structured entrepreneurship modules or curriculum, their educators are accepted as a role model in business as they too have micro business ventures themselves.

It is important to ensure that the design for gamification on entrepreneurship education includes all three main players namely the institution, the educators and the students. The design of the gamified teaching and learning on entrepreneurship must be consistent at all levels in higher education where the combination of efforts will ensure a broader acceptance of this program.

5 Conclusion

Entrepreneurship education plays a crucial role in higher education in ASEAN to increase student's interests and capability of having an entrepreneurial mindset. In an effort to transfer the entrepreneurial knowledge to prepare students for the industry be it to be employed or be an employer themselves, the students' perception on the knowledge transfers need first to be identified. This study revealed that having a well structured policy on entrepreneurship is essential but at the same time acceptance of entrepreneurship education depends on the students' readiness to embrace the subjects and knowledge. However, this readiness also depends on the delivery abilities of educators. This is also influenced by educators' personal experiences in entrepreneurship activities which we argue can be done via gamification.

Acknowledgement. The authors would like to thank Universiti Kebangsaan Malaysia for supporting this project under Dana Cabaran Perdana (DCP-2017-017/1), Foreign Trade University, Hanoi, Universitas Eka Sakti, Padang, Indonesia and Universitas Muhamaddiah Sumatera Utara, Indonesia for the collaborations in making this research possible.

References

1. Izquierdo, E., Buelens, M.: Competing models of entrepreneurial intentions: the influence of entrepreneurial self-efficacy and attitudes. Int. J. Entrepreneurship Small Bus. **13**(1), 75–91 (2011)
2. Vesper, K.H., Gartner, W.B.: Measuring progress in entrepreneurship education. J. Bus. Ventur. **12**(5), 403–421 (1997)
3. Fayolle, A., Gailly, B., Lassas-Clerc, N.: Assessing the impact of entrepreneurship education programmes: a new methodology. J. Eur. Ind. Training **30**(9), 701–720 (2006)
4. Collins, L., Hannon, P.D., Smith, A.: Enacting entrepreneurial intent: the gaps between student needs and higher education capability. Educ. + Training, **46**(8/9), 454–463 (2004)
5. Boyle, T.J.: A new model of entrepreneurship education: implications for Central and Eastern European universities. Ind. High. Educ. **21**(1), 9–19 (2007)
6. Zamberi Ahmad, S., Xavier, S.R.: Entrepreneurial environments and growth: evidence from Malaysia GEM data. J. Chin. Entrepreneurship **4**(1), 50–69 (2012)
7. Din, B.H., Anuar, A.R., Usman, M.: The effectiveness of the entrepreneurship education program in upgrading entrepreneurial skills among public university students. Proc.-Soc. Behav. Sci. **224**, 117–123 (2016)
8. Shamsudin, S.F.F.B., Al Mamun, A., Nawi, N.B.C., Nasir, N.A.B.M., Zakaria, M.N.B.: Policies and practices for entrepreneurial education: The Malaysian experience. J. Dev. Areas **50**(5), 307–316 (2016)
9. Pérez-Nordtvedt, L., Kedia, B.L., Datta, D.K., Rasheed, A.A.: Effectiveness and efficiency of cross-border knowledge transfer: An empirical examination. J. Manag. Stud. **45**(4), 714–744 (2008)

10. Argote, L., Ingram, P.: Knowledge transfer: a basis for competitive advantage in firms. Organ. Behav. Hum. Decis. Process. **82**(1), 150–169 (2000)
11. Riege, A.: Three-dozen knowledge-sharing barriers managers must consider. J. Knowl. Manag. **9**(3), 18–35 (2005)
12. Nemanich, L., Banks, M., Vera, D.: Enhancing knowledge transfer in classroom versus online settings: the interplay among instructor, student, content, and context. Decis. Sci. J. Innovative Educ. **7**(1), 123–148 (2009)
13. Lackéus, M.: Entrepreneurship in education: What, why, when, how. Entrepreneurship 360. Background Paper (2015)
14. Rahim, H.L., Kadir, M.A.B.A., Abidin, Z.Z., Junid, J., Kamaruddin, L.M., Lajin, N.F.M., Bakri, A.A.: Entrepreneurship education in Malaysia: a critical review. J. Technol. Manag. Bus. **2**(2), 1–11 (2015). http://penerbit.uthm.edu.my/ojs/index.php/jtmb/article/download/1162/779
15. Binti Othman, N., Othman, S.H.: The perceptions of public university students of entrepreneurship education in Malaysia. Int. Bus. Manag. **11**(4), 865–873 (2017)
16. Olugbola, S.A.: Exploring entrepreneurial readiness of youth and startup success components: entrepreneurship training as a moderator. J. Innov. Knowl. **2**(3), 155–171 (2017)
17. Dao, C.T.: A proposal for improving entrepreneurship education for engineering students in Vietnam. Rev. Integr. Bus. Econ. Res. **7**, 12–19 (2018)
18. Belitski, M., Heron, K.: Expanding entrepreneurship education ecosystems. J. Manag. Dev. **36**(2), 163–177 (2017)
19. Siemieniak, P., Rembiasz, M.: Importance of knowledge in the process of shaping the entrepreneurial attitudes of young people. In: MATEC Web of Conferences, vol. 290, p. 13010, EDP Sciences (2019)
20. Foo, H.Y., Turner, J.J.: Entrepreneurial learning'–the role of university led business incubators and mentors in equipping graduates with the necessary skills set for industry 4.0. Int. J. Educ. **4**(30), 283–298 (2019)
21. Ruiz-Alba, J.L., Soares, A., Rodríguez-Molina, M.A., Banoun, A.: Gamification and entrepreneurial intentions. J. Small Bus. Enterp. Dev. (2019). https://doi.org/10.1108/JSBED-09-2018-0266

Enhance Multi-factor Authentication Model for Intelligence Community Access to Critical Surveillance Data

Wan Nurhidayat Wan Muhamad[1], Noor Afiza Mat Razali[1(✉)],
Khairul Khalil Ishak[2], Nor Asiakin Hasbullah[1],
Norulzahrah Mohd Zainudin[1], Suzaimah Ramli[1], Muslihah Wook[1],
Zurida Ishak[3], and Nurjannatul Jannah Aqilah MSaad[1]

[1] National Defence University of Malaysia, Kuala Lumpur, Malaysia
noorafiza.matrazali@gmail.com
[2] Institute of Visual Informatics, Universiti Kebangsaan Malaysia, Bangi,
Selangor, Malaysia
kkishak@gmail.com
[3] Management and Science University, Shah Alam, Malaysia

Abstract. Protection of critical data is one of the greatest challenges in any organization around the globe, especially for the intelligence community. Managing data, assets and resources require strong security method such as the authentication process that can guarantee only designated person will be receiving the required information. Any breach of information and assets could risk in the nation's sovereignty and give significant impacts in social, political, economy and diplomacy or even lives. Authentication method enables intelligence data to be transferred covertly and the access to the system by a legitimate user is guaranteed, hence the elements of confidentiality, integrity, and availability of the data is assured. This study analyzed various authentication methods used to secure multiple platforms of data and system. This study serves as theoretical analysis on multi-factor authentication model for intelligence community access to critical surveillance data. This study aims to propose the enhance model that could be used as a basis to build a framework of the secured authentication system to avoid common attack on authentication and access management.

Keywords: Multi-factor authentication · Intelligence community ·
Identity verification · Biometric

1 Introduction

New technology has brought changes in analytical skills and techniques for data collection and analysis including in the intelligence community. Digital revolution nowadays had urged the intelligence community to shift the dimension of intelligence gathering from the conventional Human Intelligence (HUMINT) method, to the latest and sophisticated intelligence data gathering methods of Signal Intelligence (SIGINT) [1]. Big data analytics can help to accurately predict the situation that can be useful for

© Springer Nature Switzerland AG 2019
H. Badioze Zaman et al. (Eds.): IVIC 2019, LNCS 11870, pp. 560–569, 2019.
https://doi.org/10.1007/978-3-030-34032-2_49

decision making to protect national interests. Data analysis at the national level by the intelligence agencies often provides additional tactical intelligence to the team on the operational ground [2, 3]. Intelligence analyst relies on the accuracy of the data gathered to support the decision making regarding national security. Source of data that's being fed for analysis is varying and the data could originate from devices and sensors that are sending the data continuously to an intelligence center.

Protection of intelligence data, assets and resources could be the greatest challenges. Risk of leakage and espionage of confidential information about the intelligence agencies need to be avoided. Any breach or corruption of important information and assets could risk in the nation's sovereignty and significant implications in social, political, cultural, economy and diplomacy or even lives [4]. Processes of orchestrating and disseminating intelligence data and analysis are complex and difficult. Securing sensitive information is the key element for any intelligence organizations in protecting its assets and interest. Data that is analyzed will be shared among the intelligence community. The protection of the data is crucial because if the data can be accessed by non-intelligence party, the potential of exploitation is enormous [4]. One way of the protection is by controlling access to the data itself by applying a multi-factor authentication technique.

Researchers are proposing various techniques for authentication, however, study on how the multi-factor authentication for application in intelligence communities that are more discrete in nature is yet to be addressed. Thus, this research aims to propose a model for the enhanced multi-factor authentication technique for the intelligence community. This study will attempt to investigates/identify the current multi-factor authentication technique exist and propose enhanced multi-factor authentication model for the intelligence community to ensure the security of the data. The result shall create a enhanced model that is expected to improve authentication to guarantee that only designated person in the intelligence community will have access to the intelligence information for intelligence purposes. Thus, this study can assist response personnel (in intelligence agencies) maintain the discretions access of the intelligence data.

1.1 Intelligence Community

Intelligence community refers as government and other public or private agencies involved in intelligence cycle including planning, collection, analysis and dissemination of intelligence information related to international and internal security. According to Office of the Director of National Intelligence the term "intelligence community" in United States includes the following: the Office of the Director of National Intelligence, the Central Intelligence Agency (CIA), the Defense Intelligence Agency (DIA), other offices within the Department of Defense for the collection of specialized national intelligence through reconnaissance programs, and the intelligence elements of the Army, the Navy, the Air Force, the Marine Corps, the Coast Guard, the Federal Bureau of Investigation, the Drug Enforcement Administration, and the Department of Energy [5]. The intelligence community also includes companies and individual handling intelligence support and services to the government or private sectors in intelligence cycle [5].

In Malaysia, intelligence community refers as government agencies and organization handling intelligence cycle involved the Defence Intelligence Staff Division (DISD) of Malaysian Armed Forces (MAF), the intelligence elements of the Malaysian Army, the Royal Malaysian Navy and the Royal Malaysian Air Force, the Special Branch of Royal Malaysian Police, the Intelligence Branch of Malaysian Maritime Enforcement Agency, the Intelligence Division of Malaysian Anti-Corruption Commission and few other agencies. The intelligence community does not only limit to government agencies but also include corporate organization such as the Financial Intelligence and Enforcement Department of Bank Negara Malaysia Anti-Money Laundering & Counter Financing of Terrorism Regime and private contractor companies handling intelligence related projects or systems with the government intelligence agencies. This research will focus on the DISD as the main military intelligence agency which responsible in fulfilling the need of defence intelligence for MAF operations and for national defence.

1.2   Protection of Intelligence Data

Protection of the intelligence data, assets and resources could be the greatest challenges for any intelligence community. Securing sensitive information is the key element for any intelligence organizations in protecting its assets and interest. Managing data, assets and resources require strong security method that can guarantee that only designated person in the intelligence community will be receiving the intelligence information. Communication process linked to various intelligence agencies in intelligence community must be carefully designed with emphasize on the most secure identity verification. Traditionally, identity verification is using password as the method of authentication. However, researchers pointed out that using single authentication such as username and password for authentication is vulnerable to attacks and security risks. A study on password attack [6] found that password vulnerable to attack such as dictionary attacks, brute force attacks, video recording attack, spyware, shoulder surfing, phishing etc. Few study also found that password can be easily attack by intruders online and offline [6, 7]. Meanwhile weak password management is one of the main common information security risks faced by individuals in Malaysia [8].

1.3   Identity and Access Management

According to NIST [9], identity management described as the process of managing the identification, authentication, and authorization associated with individuals or entities (devices, processes, etc.). Identification is the process of claiming an identity. An identity is a range of unique characteristic belong to a device, entity, or person within a predefined set. Process of proving a given identity claim is known as authentication. Authentication is performed by an individual or entity claiming an association with a specific identity and providing an authenticator or token (e.g., password, PIN, smartcard, biometric) as proof of that association. Authorization is a process of deciding and authorizing access of systems and information by an individual or devices.

Authentication, authorization, administration of Identities and audit will be the focus of Identity and Access Management (IAM). Its primary concern is verification of identity of entity and grating correct level of access for resources researchers [10]. In this study, we are focusing on authentication techniques.

1.4 Authentication Techniques

Authentication is proven as a more secure and efficient method in identity verification [11]. Authentication enables intelligence data to be transferred covertly and the access to the system by a legitimate user is guaranteed, hence the elements of confidentiality, integrity and availability of the data is assured. Traditional authentication technique used elements such as something you know such as password and pin, something you have such as token and smart card, and something you are such as fingerprint and voice [7]. Opris [12] found that the multi-factor authentication increases the security and reduces the risk of a forger to cracks the security through addition of an obstruction to entry, making difficult for forger to login into the stolen account even if he knows the password. Nwabueze, Obioha, and Onuoha [13] recommend that to increase security and to avoid attack due to authentication factors, Information Technology (IT) professional and industry should implement enhanced multi-factor authentication in their upcoming products.

2 Related Works

A multi-factor authentication is an authentication using two or more different factors to authenticate the legitimate users. Factors include something you know (e.g., password/PIN); something you have (e.g., cryptographic identification device, token); or something you are (e.g., biometric) [14]. Multi-factor authentication includes usage of combination of username and password with token or smart card to authenticate users. The usage of smartcard namely as Common Access Card (CAC) is an example of 'something you have' factor and widely used for the Department of Defense(DOD) of United States [15]. Another approach [16] is combination of username and password with biometric-based authentication for instance iris authentication, thumbprint or fingerprint authetication, and also facial recognisation. Biometric-based authentication use 'something you are' factor which identifies user using unique physical traits of the user. Few previous studies on the usage of multi-factor authentication in military or intelligence community such [17] study on usage of multi-factor authentication on military logistic, [18] development of multi-factor authentication system using Common Access Card (CAC) by the Defense Advanced Research Projects Agency's (DARPA) High-Assurance Cyber Military Systems (HACMS) program for Department of Defense of United States, [19] Authentication and Authorization of Users and Services in Dynamic Military SOA Environments focusing on authentication and authorization of web services etc.

[20] proposed an authentication approach using a multi-faceted authentication scheme that continuously authenticating user's connected devices. Using few inference of the user, such as often place visited, physical vicinity with the gadget (conveying in

the pocket or device put on the table), and walking styles are recorded and used for authentication. [21] proposed usage of multi-factor authorization from server to authenticate flash drive. This protocol uses server's generated secret key as ad hoc factor of the multi-factor authentication process. Connection of the flash drive to the internet will authenticate the flash drive to the server side thus enabling file system in flash drive.

[22] propose that two-factor authentication will reduce the chances of authenticator to provide fake evidence of its identity in case of identity fraud. There are more element to acknowledge in ensuring the accuracy and integrity level of identity proofing. [23] propose combination of the usage of biometric authentication together with token ID and passcode. Using multi-factor authentication core, token ID and passcode is generated by a proposed specific algorithm. Meanwhile, for usage in military where cognitive load need to be minimum, [24] propose application of face recognition algorithm which works wells in variable condition. [25] propose authentication technique using threshold cryptography based on user's encrypted password or PIN number. [26] propose combination of an optical authentication technique based on two-beam interference with chaotic maps. In this approach, user password represented by a chaotic map as what user know factor and optical authentication technique represented by interferogram as what user have factor. [27] proposed system using user's cognitive responses of selected stimuli as an authentication method. To evaluate cognitive responses, brain activity are used as biometric signals. [28] propose using time-based onetime password (TOTP) technique. Author propose system logging process which require user to provide username and password as first factor and second factor require user to include virtually generate TOTP as a token. [29] propose a multi-factor authentication technique of secure electronic voting system using fingerprint as biometrics factor and smart card secured cryptographically. Proposed system use combination of an improved Feistel block cipher and feature extraction technique for securing voters' smart card confidential data and voters' fingerprint template.

In [30], using multi-factor authentication author propose a user-centered data backup approach to authenticate a user. Proposed design required user to choose symmetrical key before it is divides into three segment and key is destroyed afterward. By combining shares previously stored in user's smart card and laptop, the key will be rebuilt. The key can still be reconstructed by using biometric and password in case of lost key or laptop. Author found this approach meets it's security objective, stronger and user friendly. [31] propose two-factor authentication using smart cards to improve security and practicality. In the study, author suggested the use of strong password combined with physical token such as cell time-based hardware identity device and cell phone to increase security and practicality of proposed authentication approach. Based on [32] study on cloud computing authentication, author propose a new multi-factor authentication scheme which can be integrated with existing authentication system to provide adequate and practical solution. Based on few factors, Cloud Access Management (CAM) is used to authenticate the user. Arithmetic captcha and secret-splitting will also be used to authenticate user in cloud computing scenario. To produce effective, robust, and renewable biometric templates for users' verification, research by

[33] propose an authentication framework using combination of random biometric data to present what user is factor using and secure keys using passwords to present what user know factor. Research also study the deployment of proposed framework by using user passwords chosen and dynamic handwritten signatures as authentication process. [34] propose an improved of bio-hashing based three-factor authentication scheme for telecare medical information systems using two phases include fuzzy verifier utilizing local password verification to avoid password guessing and offline identity attack and secondly authentication phase. propose authentication approach using re-identification of accelerometer data generated from mobile devices on web-based and low-effort system.

The techniques and approaches used in the literature review can be summarized into few main approach including combination of password and biometric based approach [23, 24, 26, 30, 33], combination of password and time based authentication approach [28, 31], combination of location based and biometric authentication approach [20], combination of password and token authentication approach [21], and other techniques and approaches in [22, 25, 27, 29, 34, 35]. Using multi-factor authentication had been proven way to improve authentication in literatures mentioned.

Researcher pointed out studies on multi-factor authentication in MAF especially for intelligence community are still lacking. Multi-factor authentication however, comes with the overhead of employing multiple authentication programs to complete the process. For the intelligence community, the right amount of overhead need to be implemented while not jeopardizing the security. Thus, this research proposes enhance multi-factor authentication for intelligence community with consideration of processing power for efficient intelligence community access to critical surveillance data. This proposed model designed to achieve Intelligence Community Information Environment (IC IE) Data Strategy mission to make IC data discoverable, accessible, and usable at the speed of mission [36].

3   Enhance Multi-factor Authentication Model for Intelligence Community Access to Critical Surveillance Data

3.1   Conceptual Model Development

Base on the researches in literature, this study suggests a conceptual model of enhance multi-factor authentication for intelligence community access to critical surveillance data using a combination of username and password, biometric authentication, IoT devices authentication, and one-time authorization code (see Fig. 1.). The development of this model will adapt the prototyping model of Software Development Life Cycle (SCLC) as per suggested by [37] which will include determining user requirement, developing an initial prototype, user review, and evaluation on the prototype, and delivery of final improved and revised prototype.

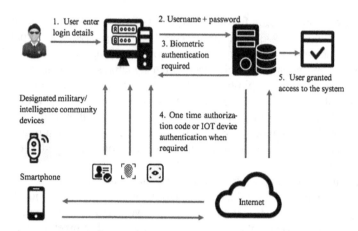

Fig. 1. Enhance multi-factor authentication model for intelligence community

The proposed model strengthens authentication security of critical surveillance data access by using an adaptive authentication. Using a combination of both static and dynamic authentication methods, the user from intelligence community personnel/organization required to provide username and password as the first step and the next authentication will be followed by biometric authentication, authentication using designated intelligence community devices or one-time authorization code from the smartphone. In step 1 and 2 of Fig. 1, the user login process can be done on designated work-station or mobile devices which will act as a client while the authorization process executed on the authentication server. Characteristic of required username and password is pre-determine to require the user to provide a secure password. The server will authenticate the user using username and password given and decided required further authentication including smartcard or biometric authentication.

In step 3 of Fig. 1, the smartcard or also known as common access cards (CAC) specially provided and only limited to intelligence community will contain user's identity information and public key infrastructure (PKI) certificate. The smartcard reader attached directly to the system using the direct or serial port and remote network access using Secure Shell, which will be authenticated using Kerberos authentication concept. Biometric authentication may vary from fingerprint (involving the use of optical, capacitive or ultrasonic fingerprint scanner), retinal scanning or facial recognition. Pre-captured biometric will be registered in the database of the system. This variety of biometric method will reduce the false-negative chances for the user to access the system and implementation will adapt the Trusted Execution Environment (TEE) using TrustZone from ARM.

In step 4 of Fig. 1, one-time authorization code (OTAC) or IoT device authentication is needed only when required. In case of further authentication due to abnormality and suspicious login, this further authentication step will be involved. For OTAC authentication, a per session used short message services (SMS) representing a ciphered digital certificate will be sent to mobile phone connected to

2G/3G/4G cellular network and user is required to provide code to access the system on a challenge page which will be displayed. The server will decide whether to authenticates or denies the user based on OTAC provided. A designated military or intelligence community IoT device will be used as device-to-server identity authentication. The proposed IoT device use PKI digital certificates to enable the authentication process using proximity-based protocols connection i.e. Wi-Fi and Bluetooth or GPS and can be attached to compulsory traditional military identity tag such as dog tag. This proposed model adapts user-friendly authentication and at the same time enhance the security of the system from the possible attack which is required by the intelligence community. Despite all the authentication factors proposed, the agencies will also promote and implement policies and best practices to protect stored critical surveillance data.

4   Discussion and Future Works

Model of enhancing multi-factor authentication for intelligence community access to critical surveillance data is needed by stakeholder in order to authenticate user identity with different multiple factors defined by the system. This model can be integrated with existing authentication systems in stakeholder by adding enhanced authentication factors without the need of replacing existing systems. It can ensure secured access of a system used by stakeholder thus avoiding use of single password and access card authentication and crucial to face today's threat pattern. Based on the theoretical finding about the enhanced multi-factor authentication in this paper, empirical analysis will be done by adopting the systematic data gathering and the content analysis method. After that, validation in real scenario will be done to determine the acceptance and feasibility of the proposed model, as well as potential scenarios of using multi-factor authentication interfaces with the intelligence community. The validation also will be done in the intelligence community by implementing a proof of technology by setting up multi-factor authentication pilot program on a prototype intelligence data system based on proposed conceptual model. This validation will involve small group of users and will provide needed feedback on this proposed conceptual model. Future work includes further research of the enhanced model and also research in adaptive multi-factor authentication method.

References

1. Pomerleau, M.: How technology has changed intelligence collection – Defense Systems (2015) https://defensesystems.com/articles/2015/04/22/technology-has-changed-intelligence-gathering.aspx. Accessed 20 June 2019
2. Van Puyvelde, D., Coulthart, S., Hossain, M.S.: Beyond the buzzword: big data and national security decision-making. Int. Aff. **93**(6), 1397–1416 (2017)
3. Odom, W.E.: Intelligence analysis. Intell. Natl. Secur. **23**(3), 316–332 (2008)

4. Gandhi, P., Sharma, A., Mahoney, A., Sousan, W., Zhu, W., Laplante, P.: Dimensions of cyber-attacks: cultural, social, economic, and political. Technol. Soc. Mag. IEEE **30**, 28–38 (2011)
5. National Security Act of 1947. https://www.dni.gov/index.php/ic-legal-reference-book/national-security-act-of-1947. Accessed 20 June 2019
6. Raza, M., Iqbal, M., Sharif, M., Haider, W.: A survey of password attacks and comparative analysis on methods for secure authentication. World Appl. Sci. J. **19**(4), 439–444 (2012)
7. Arjun, G.S., Rashmi, P.D., Arjun, G.S., Rashmi, P.D.: One Time Keyboard (OTK) Authentication. Int. J. Innov. Res. Sci. Technol. **4**(1) 173–177 (2017)
8. Ong, L.: Awareness of information security risks : an investigation of people aspects (a study in Malaysia), pp. 1–256 (2015)
9. Hastings, N., Dempsey, K., Paulsen, C.: Considerations for identity management in public safety mobile networks. US Department of Commerce, National Institute of Standards and Technology (2015)
10. Sharma, D.H., Dhote, C.A., Potey, M.M.: Identity and access management as security-as-a-service from clouds. Proc. Comput. Sci. **79**, 170–174 (2016)
11. Ferrag, M.A., Maglaras, L., Derhab, A.: Authentication and authorization for mobile IoT devices using bio-features: recent advances and future trends 2019 (2019)
12. Opris, V.N.: Biometric multi-factor authentication scheme in cloud computing. Sci. Bull. Nav. Acad. **19**(1), 472–475 (2016)
13. Nwabueze, E.E., Obioha, I., Onuoha, O.: Enhancing multi-factor authentication in modern computing. Commun. Netw. **06**(03), 172–178 (2017)
14. J. Task Force Transformation Initiative, "NIST Special Publication 800-53 Security and Privacy Controls for Federal Information Systems and Organizations
15. Libicki, M.C., Jackson, B.A., Rudavsky, R., Webb, K.W.: Influences on the adoption of multifactor authentication. J. Natl. Cancer Inst. 92(23), 1872(2000)
16. Lal, N.A., Prasad, S., Farik, M.: A review of authentication methods. Int. J. Sci. Technol. Res. **5**(11), 246–249 (2016)
17. Waters, T.: Multifactor authentication – a new chain of custody option for military logistics. Cyber Def. Rev. **2**(3), 1–14 (2017)
18. Lee, J.: Defense department developing multifactor authentication system—Biometric Update (2017). https://www.biometricupdate.com/201706/defense-department-developing-multifactor-authentication-system. Accessed 20 June 2019
19. Jasiul, B., Sliwa, J., Piotrowski, R., Goniacz, R., Amanowicz, M.: Authentication and Authorization of Users and Services in Federated SOA Environments-Challenges and Opportunities
20. Shila, D.M., Srivastava, K., O'Neill, P., Reddy, K., Sritapan, V.: A multi-faceted approach to user authentication for mobile devices—using human movement, usage, and location patterns. In: 2016 IEEE Symposium on Technologies for Homeland Security (HST), pp. 1–6 (2016)
21. Soimart, L., Mookdarsanit, P.: Multi-factor authentication protocol for information accessibility in flash drive. In: 9th Applied Computer Technology Information System (2016)
22. Singh, S.: Multi-factor authentication and their approaches. Int. Res. J. Manag. IT Soc. Sci. **4**(3), 68–81 (2017)
23. Mihailescu, D.M.I., Racuciu, C., Grecu, D.L., Nita, L.S.: A multi-factor authentication scheme including biometric characteristics as one factor. Mircea cel Batran Nav. Acad. Sci. Bull. **17**(1), 348–352 (2015)

24. Podilchuk, C., Barinov, W., Hulbert, W., Jairaj, A.: Face recognition in a tactical environment. In: 2010-MILCOM 2010 Military Communications Conference, pp. 900–905 (2010)
25. Venukumar, V., Pathari, V.: Multi-factor authentication using threshold cryptography. In: 2016 International Conference on Advances in Computing, Communications and Informatics (ICACCI), pp. 1694–1698 (2016)
26. Souza, D.F.L., Burlamaqui, A.M.F., Souza Filho, G.L.: A multi factor authentication approach based on biometrics, optical interference and chaotic maps. IEEE Lat. Am. Trans. **15**(9), 1700–1708 (2017)
27. Kim, S.-P., Kang, J.-H., Jo, Y.C., Oakley, I.: Development of a multi-modal personal authentication interface. In: 2017 Asia-Pacific Signal and Information Processing Association Annual Summit and Conference (APSIPA ASC), pp. 712–715 (2017)
28. Taher, K.A., Nahar, T., Hossain, S.A.: Enhanced cryptocurrency security by time-based token multi-factor authentication algorithm. In: 2019 International Conference on Robotics, Electrical and Signal Processing Techniques (ICREST), pp. 308–312 (2019)
29. Oke, B.A., Olaniyi, O.M., Aboaba, A.A., Arulogun, O.T.: Developing multifactor authentication technique for secure electronic voting system. In: 2017 International Conference on Computing Networking and Informatics (ICCNI), pp. 1–6 (2017)
30. Liu, Y., Zhong, Q., Chang, L., Xia, Z., He, D., Cheng, C.: A secure data backup scheme using multi-factor authentication. IET Inf. Secur. **11**(5), 250–255 (2016)
31. Theofanos, M., Garfinkel, S., Choong, Y.-Y.: Secure and usable enterprise authentication: lessons from the field. IEEE Secur. Priv. **14**(5), 14–21 (2016)
32. Banyal, R.K., Jain, P., Jain, V.K.: Multi-factor authentication framework for cloud computing. In: 2013 Fifth International Conference on Computational Intelligence, Modelling and Simulation, pp. 105–110 (2013)
33. Khan, S.H., Akbar, M.A., Shahzad, F., Farooq, M., Khan, Z.: Secure biometric template generation for multi-factor authentication. Pattern Recogn. **48**(2), 458–472 (2015)
34. Jiang, Q., Chen, Z., Li, B., Shen, J., Yang, L., Ma, J.: Security analysis and improvement of bio-hashing based three-factor authentication scheme for telecare medical information systems. J. Ambient Intell. Humaniz. Comput. **9**(4), 1061–1073 (2018)
35. Ray, P.P., Mukherjee, M., Shu, L.: Internet of Things for disaster management: state-of-the-art and prospects. IEEE Access **5**(i), 18818–18835 (2017)
36. Intelligence Community Information Environment (IC IE) Data Strategy 2017-2021 (2017). https://www.dni.gov/files/documents/CIO/Data-Strategy_2017-2021_Final.pdf
37. Ben-Zahia, M.A., Jaluta, I.: Criteria for selecting software development models. In: GSCIT 2014 - Global Summit on Computer and Information Technology, pp. 1–6 (2014)

Disaster Management Support Model for Malaysia

Hasmeda Erna Che Hamid[1], Nurjannatul Jannah Aqilah MSaad[1],
Noor Afiza Mat Razali[1(✉)], Mohammad Adib Khairuddin[1],
Mohd Nazri Ismail[1], Suzaimah Ramli[1], Muslihah Wook[1],
Khairul Khalil Ishak[2], Zurida Ishak[3], Nor Asiakin Hasbullah[1],
Norshahriah Wahab[1], Norulzahrah Mohd Zainudin[1],
and Putri Nurshamiera Natasha Azizan Shah[1]

[1] Universiti Pertahanan Nasional Malaysia, Kuala Lumpur, Malaysia
noorafiza@upnm.edu.my
[2] Institute of Visual Informatics, Universiti Kebangsaan Malaysia, Bangi,
Selangor, Malaysia
[3] Management and Science University, Shah Alam, Malaysia

Abstract. In accordance to the National Security Council (NSC) Directive concerning the coordination between responsible agencies and committee, the Malaysian government has established a national disaster management agency with the sole purpose to cater matters related to disaster in a fast, orderly, systematic and coordinated manner. Furthermore, coordination also involves the integration of technologies and modules from all relevant parties such as police, fire departments, civil defence, welfare and public health. Due to the lack of studies addressing the suitable design for disaster management support model that could complement disaster management policy, this research intends to present a solution, with Malaysia as the case study. This paper starts by identifying issues related to disaster management support and thoroughly reviews the coordination policy of disaster management globally and locally in Malaysia. Qualitative method was chosen as the main methodology and been implemented throughout this study in determining the accurate process of disaster management in Malaysia by expert personnel. As for disaster management related policy, a content analysis method has been done through existing documentation. For conclusion, this paper will then propose a design for disaster management support model that complements the policy of disaster management, specifically for Malaysia.

Keywords: Disaster management · Disaster management policy · Support system

1 Introduction

Disaster has been classified into two categories, man made and natural causes: Sudden occurrence of disaster demand fast and highly coordinated manner of dissemination and this include information concerning the situation [4, 5]. Information collected not only can be used during a disaster, but such information is crucial for pre-disaster phase

© Springer Nature Switzerland AG 2019
H. Badioze Zaman et al. (Eds.): IVIC 2019, LNCS 11870, pp. 570–581, 2019.
https://doi.org/10.1007/978-3-030-34032-2_50

where it can provide an adequate preparation and information on possible disaster strike to authority [4, 6, 7]. Information dissemination has been included under Malaysia Disaster Management (DM) process, liable to Malaysia National Security Council 20 (MNSC 20) under Communication. MNSC 20 have been revised to complement to global DM policy [8–10]. Aside of Communication, there are other policies stated in MNSC 20 as the guideline of DM process in Malaysia including on the involvement of multi-agency, fund management, organization management etc. [8, 9]. Various initiatives have been used to mitigate the risks and impacts before, during and after the disaster. For mitigating risk, during current and post-disaster, the process itself involved a vast amount of manpower, placement and vary resources [4]. Due to this, many agencies, organizations and bodies came forward to give a hand for rescue and rehabilitation operations during and post-disaster [5]. However, it is undeniably a bit challenging in managing all resources, simultaneously in an orderly manner which concerning to coordination of the responsible party for an effective DM process [11, 12]. Hence, managing disaster is a hassle if there is inadequate resource availability with current restraint on a DM process where little implementation of compliance towards MNSC 20.

By exploiting the advantages of the current growth of technology, a systematic information system for information sharing purposes, which cover broad aspects that compliments to MNSC 20 can be developed. The advantages of an organization that has a good information system can increase the trust of consumers to the management and processing of data that is accurate and secure [2]. By taking count each aspect of MNSC 20, this paper proposed a design of disaster management support (DMS) model by integrating modules aligned with disaster management in Malaysia. It is purposely to give an overview about the implementation of MNSC 20 policy in context of information system. To understand the process in dealing with DMS in Malaysia, qualitative method was used for information gathering. Interviews with experts in the National Disaster Management Agency (NADMA) had been done and we performed the analysis base on the result of the interviews. Meanwhile, the content analysis method has been used to study disaster management related policy through existing documentations. Base on the findings from the interview and content analysis method, we propose the disaster management support for Malaysia.

2 Global Disaster Management Policy

The UN World Conference on Disaster Risk Reduction discusses policies related to disaster risk reduction. At the first session in 1994, The Yokohama Strategy, which consists of ten principles, is developed to make a safer world. In 2005, the Hyogo Framework for Action (HFA) consists of five priorities for action is formed to build disaster resilient communities. The Priority Act 2 is to identify, assess and monitor disaster risks and enhance early warning. Priority Act 3 is addressing the usage of knowledge, innovation and education to build a culture of safety and resilience at all levels. While Priority Act 4, is involving the reduction of underlying risk factors for disaster. Priority Act 5 was aimed to strengthen disaster preparedness for effective response at all levels [13]. However, there is an obstacle in deploying HFA wholly.

According to [14], only Priority Act 2, which is to identify, assess and monitor disaster risks for early warning is likely to be the only have high rate of successful implemented. On the other hand, Priority Act 3, usage of knowledge, innovation and education for resilience and Priority Act 4, to reduce underlying factors, are said to be the most difficult act to be implemented. Identifying and assessing disaster have resulted in better preparation of the nation towards disaster strike which saved countless lives. However, to reduce underlying factors and to find the root case are undeniably complex [14, 15]. To address the gap in HFA, the Sendai Framework for Disaster Risk Reduction set seven global targets in coordination with the Sustainable Development Goals (SDGs) [14, 15].

Japan is the world leader in disaster readiness where disaster risk reduction (DRR) has been a cultural norm in society. In Japan, the Cabinet Office is responsible to correspond to the risk of disaster [16]. However, when large scale disasters occur, Emergency Response Team together with the Prime Minister makes the policies and provides overall coordination regarding disaster emergency measures. Japan has developed role-specific disaster prevention plans to strengthen the policy at three-tiered; national, prefectural and municipal governments, where the jurisdiction is performed at each stage. This enables a prompt and accurate emergency response [17, 18]. United States is also strongly supporting DRR Program not only to reduce the impact of disaster but also for a faster recovery. The Federal Emergency Management Agency (FEMA) is the responsible agency to support citizens and be the first responders towards all hazards. Through FEMA 2018-2022 Strategic Plan, the focus is to build a culture of preparedness and readiness for catastrophic disasters. The other mission of FEMA is helping people before, during and after disasters [19, 20].

In Malaysia, disaster is managed by NADMA under the Directive 20 of the National Security Council that acts as the focal point in managing disaster that has three (3) levels of disaster management at district level, state level and national level [3, 8]. Each level consists of specific agencies that will deploy relief operation during disaster. Any disaster that involves local incidents which have potential to spread, will be managed by District Disaster Management and Relief Committee (DMRC) and considered as level one. In level two, disaster will be managed by State Disaster Management and Relief Committee (SDMR) and on level three; Central Disaster Management and Relief Committee (CDMRC) are responsible in managing disaster management that includes forming a central, state and district level of disaster management. Base on the framework and policies discussed above, the culture of preparedness and readiness are vital to be induced to the society in order to act fast, orderly, systematic and coordinated manner when disaster strike. Processes and procedures related to disaster management need to always be improved and communicated among all the related parties that involve with disaster management and relief committee.

3   Malaysia Disaster Management Coordination and Policy

Malaysia is often considered as a country less prone to major disasters. However, as an equatorial climate country, Malaysia is vulnerable to risks such as flooding, landslides and mudslides. In 1997, the MNSC has formulated a national policy, management mechanism and disaster aid known as the Directive No. 20. MNSC, as the leading agency, was given a mandate under the Directive No. 20 to coordinate and execute appropriate actions during disasters. The federal government had established a special agency, National Disaster Management Agency (NADMA) in October 2015, dedicated to disaster risk management (DRM). Under the Malaysia DM structure, seven service themes were established, including; (1) search and rescue, (2) health and medical services, (3) media, (4) support, (5) security control, (6) welfare, and (7) warnings and alerts. There are 79 agencies have been identified responsible for carrying out activities related to DRM both from a top-down and bottom-up perspective. This long list of agencies contained, among others, 38 federal agencies, 21 state agencies and 17 district agencies and 2 NGOs. These agencies might have their own and/or work together with other agencies to execute DRM projects at various levels. The following section discusses three main issues and challenges faced by agencies in DRM derived from the review of the literature. Figure 1 shown disaster management structure in Malaysia.

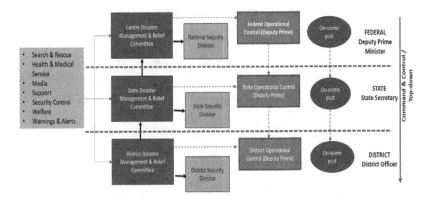

Fig. 1. Disaster management structure in Malaysia

3.1   National Disaster Command Centre (NDCC)

NDCC is the National Disaster Control Center aims to be the Center for Disaster Operation Control (PKOB) when the disaster in Malaysia. Coordination of NDCC is shown in Fig. 2. The system used in NDCC is National Disaster Information Management System (My DIMS). It is a Disaster Management System developed for assisting in disaster management activities in Malaysia. My DIMS encompass four phases of Disaster Management Activities I.e. Mitigation, Inventory, Reaction and Recovery. This system also works in providing real-time disaster warning and alarm monitoring and real-time information dissemination through 4 different ways i.e. SMS, FAX, Phone Calls (ACS) as well as the Disaster Portal. The task of the NDCC in

National Disaster Management Agency is very import for coordinating the information from various sources especially from technical agencies. Following Figs provided in this section are representing the workflow of NDCC based on interview done with NDCC staff. Figure 3 shows the process of the decision-making process in Malaysia DM.

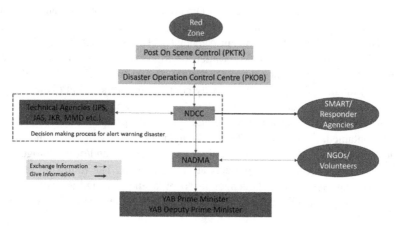

Fig. 2. NDCC coordination flow

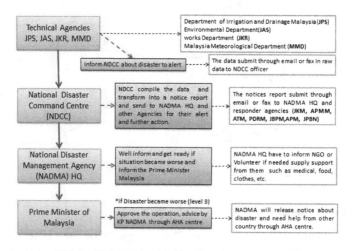

Fig. 3. DM decision making flowchart – Malaysia

Base on the Malaysia disaster management decision making flow and process, coordination and policies discussion above, we suggest the establishment a DM Support model that can integrate process and information for fast, orderly, systematic and coordinated manner that involves the integration of technologies and modules from all relevant parties including police, fire departments, civil defence, welfare and public health at federal, state and district level. The technology integration can contribute to fast information sharing and decision making during the disaster. It also will assist on the coordination of the most required action for the affected group during the disaster. Parallel to the growth of IT convergence, and preparation towards global 4th Industrial Revolution, it is essential for Malaysia to establish a technology integrated disaster management (DM) model.

4 Disaster Management Support (DMS) Model

Concisely, IT convergence is undeniably causative to the huge change of society in term of information sharing [21]. Hence, technology integrated DM or alleged, as DM information system, is reasonable in managing disaster in a systematic manner and could raise disaster awareness through efficient information sharing [22].

Based on the literature review and interview with experts about DM globally and in Malaysia, this paper discussed and proposed a design for Disaster Management Support (DMS) model for Malaysia. As discerning to DM policy, a document analysis method was employed as the validity tool of research based on credible resources of expertise in Malaysia DM. Consequently, it enables researcher to count on specific reliable resource [23]. Taking into consideration of related policies on disaster risk reduction by the UN World Conference on Disaster Risk Reduction, DMS attempt to provide a DM system model that could be executed as helping hand in managing disaster in Malaysia. This model will be fully established by implementing associated attributes from Yokohama Strategy Principles, the Hyogo Framework for Action and Sendai Framework for Disaster Risk Reduction that is compatible with Malaysia environment.

Based on literature review, a DM model could emphasize each DM phase and management process clearly [24]. A DM model is indeed convenient for DM management process execution as it provides (i) simplification of critical and complex events, (ii) better understanding of the current disaster situation, (iii) provide the essential element needed for DM process and (iv) could help establish a base that can make better integration of relief operation [25]. In addition, for an effective DM process to be executed, the ability of participating actors (agencies, volunteers etc.) to work together whilst promoting information sharing process between them, said can enhance the decision making process [26]. Thus, taking into consideration of these expediency traits of DM model and the importance of information sharing for DM process, this study designed a DM support model focusing on DM information sharing system interface. This model also has been validated by expert respectively from NADMA and NDCC staff. It shows that this module is suitable to be implemented in Malaysia DM. Figure 4 shows the proposed model for disaster management support (DMS) for Malaysia.

Fig. 4. Disaster management support model (DMS)

This model attempt to enhance and improved DM process in Malaysia by providing step for DM in Malaysia by considering suitable criteria for international and of course to comply towards national DM policies in context of DM information sharing system development. Elaboration on each step shown in the model will be explained in the next subsection.

4.1   Step 1: Identify Objectives

The objective of the study is to enhance current DMS according to international and national DM policy. It is important to ensure DMS is liaised to outline national DM policy as well as complimenting national DM policy to improve the overall disaster management environment in Malaysia. However, with international DM policy, going with its nature, to cover broad aspects that might incompatible to the Malaysia DM environment, hence, this objective helps to determine scope of study, while adhere to both international and national DM policy. In addition, clear objectives and scope will help in providing a better understanding in developing improved DMS. Therefore, this study will develop an interface of DMS align to outline objectives.

4.2   Step 2: Understanding Context of Study and Target User

Understanding context of study in DM domain is nevertheless crucial. In MNSC 20, DM is focusing on preparedness, prevention, response and recovery. By taking count these aspects, this research analyzes and mapped each aspect that will comply to MNSC 20 traits. It starts by defining and understanding each DM phase and its linking to each other for a better DM management process execution. Its help in outline the AP Respective agencies, voluntary bodies, private sectors and other relevant agencies are expected to be the targeted user in DMS. This is significant to MNSC 20 in emphasizing for involvement of multi-agencies and bodies in DM of Malaysia.

4.3   Step 3: Development and Selection of Modules

Development of modules was done according to Malaysia's DM structural themes and MNSC 20 directives. The modules are resulted from several interview session carried out with expert in NADMA and NDCC respectively. This is to ensure that developed modules are suitable to be executed in Malaysia. The modules are mapped to MNSC 20 in complying towards DM policy. Developed modules that are mapped to MNSC 20 are as follows:

Module 1: Management of Volunteer and Training. In most developed countries, emergency and disaster management highly rely on the workforce of professional personnel and volunteers that affiliated with local authorities or agency [18, 27], same goes to Malaysia. A volunteer management system is doubly needed to be designed effectively to avoid a scenario that can distract responders from delivering their duties and create problems such as security, safety and health problem to the disaster area [28]. Plus, this module was developed accordingly to interview result with Malaysia DM expert, on current problems in managing the vast number of agencies, non-governmental organizations (NGOs) and non-governmental individual (NGIs) in DM. Hence, this module aims to assemble and identified all NGOs, NGIs and agencies involved under one organization systematically. Through this, management of organization during DM will be more efficient with an appointed government agency, such as NADMA, as the head of the organization. Therefore, it complies to MNSC 20 on directive of (i) Identification and involvement of multi-agency in DM and (ii) DM organization structure mechanism of 'chain-of-command'. This module allowed any NGOs, NGIs or any other organization whom wish to take part in DM, to register legally under government. This is to ensure the security and to avoid any unwanted incident during DM. Aside that, registered party can attend any training provided by government or appointed agency for skills enhancement, expedient to government mandate. This will indirectly smoothen the disaster relief process.

Module 2: Management of Donation for Disaster. This module established align to Fund Management policies. It states where donations should be managed by federal and state government during disaster, including of collection and allocation of fund for the national DM process. This module allowed any individual to donate money or goods for disaster relief through a trusted party which is from selected government agency. As an example, NADMA.

Module 3: Management of Asset and Logistics. According to MNSC 20, capability of requesting assistance and equipment needed from any agency or organizations, are crucial during DM [29]. Consequently, having a system of asset and logistics management will be more convenient for any DM process. This is due to the module itself, aims to provide an integrated database on every asset and logistics available in Malaysia. This will provide a request and demand flow where it will locate and suggest nearest asset and logistics available for better access. For instance, if a disaster happened, needed assets and logistics is one click away by making a request.

Module 4: Management of Evacuation Centre. This module's flow is most likely the same with Module 3. It will provide a database of information on each evacuation centre in Malaysia such as maximum capacity of the centre. It focusses on placing disaster affected people to evacuation centers in an orderly manner meanderingly avoiding the overcrowded center. It worked on, either, affected victims themselves can search which evacuation centers are nearest to them and checked in, or officer in charge directly locate the number of people affected by disaster and laced them to evacuation center based on the maximum capacity. This module can be mapped to MNSC 20 of preparedness for disaster.

Module 5: Analysis of Data Collected by Sensors or Satellites for Disaster Decision Making. Decision making in DM is nevertheless crucial for fast response [30, 31]. Usually, a collection of real-time data will be analyzed in predicting the disaster occurrence. Consequently, will assists in any decision making upon disaster strike. However, decision making in DM does not only applied during disaster strike, but also vital in pre-disaster phase [4, 12, 32]. As an example, identifying linking data resource to be run with current data for a disaster strike simulation [4]. When disaster happens, it is the most crucial phase, where necessary action needs to be taken immediately in minimizing damage or saving lives. On the other side, real-time data collected from sensors and satellites are, however complicated to begin with as it comes with a vast amount of data [33, 34]. Hence, analyzing these data might consume more time and thus deliberately decision-making process. Thus, a system with an enhanced data analysis technique is indeed highly needed. By integrating with current AI technology, it could escalate time needed for disaster decision making. Hence, the purposes of Module 5 establishments.

Module 6: Communication and Information Sharing during the Disaster. The heart of the entire DM process can be said about communication where it connects all respected, responsible agencies to take appropriate action [5, 11, 35]. There's several approaches initiate by scholars in dissemination of information during disaster such as website and mobile application with vary functions embedded [35–37] and not to mention on the exploitation of social media usage [6, 38, 39]. Technology advancement in information and communications technology enable the deployments contain information that can be used across the organizations such as government bodies, rescue teams, disaster management teams, military, volunteers, citizens and media [18, 27, 28]. Integrating of current advance technology of networks with multi-domain such as AI, information should be more systematically and effectively disseminated and parallel to its target audience. Hence, this module attempts to provide an idea on information dissemination during the most critical phase of DM. In addition, it complements to MNSC 20 under communication policies, in term of using current technology.

4.4   Step 4: Prototype Development Through RAD

Following the establishment of modules, a system with integration of all modules should be developed. Hence, for development process, a Rapid Application Development (RAD) model can be used as the methodology approach. RAD model is chosen due to its process by involving end users directly during development. This can avoid any misunderstanding occur between developer and end user, hence minimize the risk of changes [40]. In addition, RAD model is suitable in developing new systems with broad aspect. The table below shows some of the characteristics of the RAD model emphasizing on the advantages of the model according to [40] (Table 1).

Table 1. RAD model characteristic

Feature	Description
Cost consuming	Low
Risk involvement	Low
Changes incorporated	Low
Flexibility	High
Maintenance	Low
Integrity and security	Vital
Time-frame	Short

Hence, a system with multi modules that compliment to MNSC 20 directives and align to Malaysia DM themes can be developed though this model. Figure 5 shows the mapped relation between developed modules with MNSC 20.

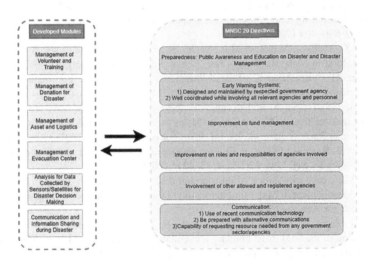

Fig. 5. Mapped developed modules and MNSC 20

5 Conclusion

Disaster management (DM) is inevitably vital in managing disaster from each phase – pre-disaster, during the disaster, post-disaster, to avoid any undesirable incidents. However, designing DM process flow that will complement to each aspect on MNSC 20 is nevertheless complicated. Hence, this paper proposed a model design, focusing on DM Support System that hopefully will contribute to efficient DM in Malaysia. Each established module is focusing on DM handling and to improve current DM restraint. As future work, a metamodel on model-driven approach will be developed. Validation will be done through prototype testing by related DM agencies to determine the effectiveness of the proposed model.

Acknowledgements. This research is supported by the Ministry of Education, Malaysia under RACER FRGS grant.

References

1. Mohamed Shaluf, I., Ahmadun, F.: Disaster types in Malaysia: an overview. Disaster Prev. Manag. Int. J. **15**(2), 286–298 (2006)
2. Sundar, I., Sezhiyan, I.: Disaster management (2007)
3. Chan, N.W.: Impacts of disasters and disaster risk management in Malaysia: the case of floods. In: Aldrich, D.P., Oum, S., Sawada, Y. (eds.) Resilience and Recovery in Asian Disasters. RGS, vol. 18, pp. 239–265. Springer, Tokyo (2015). https://doi.org/10.1007/978-4-431-55022-8_12
4. Meissner, A., Luckenbach, T., Risse, T., Kirste, T., Kirchner, H.: Design challenges for an integrated disaster management communication and information system, Fraunhofer IPSI - Integrated Publication and Information Systems Institute, Darmstadt, Germany Fraunhofer FOKUS - Institute for Open Communication Systems, Ber, no. Diren (2002)
5. Azmani, S., Juliana, N., Idrose, A.M., Amin, N.A., Saudi, A.S.: Challenges of communication system during emergency disaster response in Malaysia: a review. J. Fundam. Appl. Sci. **9**(4S), 890–904 (2017)
6. Aisha, T.S., Wok, S., Manaf, A.M.A., Ismail, R.: Exploring the use of social media during the 2014 flood in Malaysia. Proc. - Soc. Behav. Sci. **211**(September), 931–937 (2015)
7. Seppänen, H., Virrantaus, K.: Shared situational awareness and information quality in disaster management. Saf. Sci. **77**, 112–122 (2015)
8. Khairilmizal, S., Hussin, M.F., Hussain, A.R., Jusoh, M.H., Sulaiman, A.A., et al.: Implementation of disaster management policy in Malaysia and its compliance towards international disaster management framework. Int. Inf. Inst. (Tokyo). Inf. **19**(8A), 3301–3306 (2014)
9. Khairilmizal, S., et al.: Policy on disaster management in Malaysia: the need of supporting governance. Adv. Sci. Lett. **22**(12), 4213–4215 (2016)
10. Hussin, M.F., et al.: Evolution of disaster and disaster management policy in Malaysia. In: Disaster Management in Malaysia International Disaster Risk Reduction Framework Hyogo Framework for Action (2014)
11. Saab, D.J., Tapia, A., Maitland, C., Maldonado, E., Tchouakeu, L.M.N.: Inter-organizational coordination in the wild: trust building and collaboration among field-level ICT workers in humanitarian relief organizations. Voluntas **24**(1), 194–213 (2013)
12. Lee, J., Bharosa, N., Yang, J., Janssen, M., Rao, H.R.: Group value and intention to use - a study of multi-agency disaster management information systems for public safety. Decis. Support Syst. **50**(2), 404–414 (2011)
13. Strategy, I.: Hyogo Framework for Action 2005-2015 , *, no. January 2005 (2015)
14. Briceño, S.: Looking back and beyond Sendai : 25 years of international policy experience on disaster risk reduction, pp. 1–7 (2015)
15. Pearson, L., Pelling, M.: The UN Sendai framework for disaster risk reduction 2015–2030: negotiation process and prospects for science and practice. J. Extrem. Events **2**(1), 1–12 (2015)
16. Quarantelli, E.L., Boin, A., Lagadec, P.: Studying future disasters and crises: a heuristic approach. In: Rodríguez, H., Donner, W., Trainor, Joseph E. (eds.) Handbook of Disaster Research. HSSR, pp. 61–83. Springer, Cham (2018). https://doi.org/10.1007/978-3-319-63254-4_4
17. Fuse, A., Yokota, H.: An analysis of Japan Disaster Medical Assistance Team (J-DMAT) deployments in comparison with those of J-DMAT's counterpart in the United States (US-DMAT). J. Nippon Med. Sch. **77**(6), 318–324 (2010)

18. Johnson, T.R.: Disaster Volunteerism, IIGR Working Paper. Ser., p. 31, December 2014
19. Cutter, S.L., et al.: Disaster resilience: a national imperative. Environment **55**(2), 25–29 (2013)
20. Roberts, P.S.: FEMA after Katrina. Policy Rev. **1**(July), 15–33 (2006)
21. Li, J., Li, Q., Liu, C., Ullah Khan, S., Ghani, N.: Community-based collaborative information system for emergency management. Comput. Oper. Res. **42**, 116–124 (2014)
22. Jung, H., Chung, K.: Ontology-driven slope modeling for disaster management service. Cluster Comput. **18**(2), 677–692 (2015)
23. Bowen, G.A.: Document analysis as a qualitative research method
24. Asghar, S., Alahakoon, D., Churilov, L.: A comprehensive conceptual model for disaster management. J. Humanit. Assist. **1360**(0222), 1–5 (2006)
25. Kelly, C.: Simplifying disasters: Developing a model for complex non-linear events. Aust. J. Emerg. Manag. **14**(1), 25–27 (1999)
26. Bodeau, D., Fedorowicz, J., Markus, L., Brooks, J.: Characterizing and improving collaboration and information-sharing across emergency preparedness and response communities. In: International Conference e-Government, pp. 192–200 (2009)
27. Whittaker, J., McLennan, B., Handmer, J.: A review of informal volunteerism in emergencies and disasters: definition, opportunities and challenges. Int. J. Disaster Risk Reduct. **13**, 358–368 (2015)
28. Afiza, N., et al.: Volunteer management system for disaster management. Int. J. Recent Technol. Eng. **7**(5), 569–576 (2019)
29. Center for excellence in disaster management and humanitarian assistance, Malaysia: disaster management reference handbook 2016, 7 January 2016 (2016)
30. Pearce, L.: Disaster management and community planning, and public participation: how to achieve sustainable hazard mitigation. Nat. Hazards **28**, 211–228 (2003)
31. Wex, F., Schryen, G., Feuerriegel, S., Neumann, D.: Emergency response in natural disaster management: allocation and scheduling of rescue units. Eur. J. Oper. Res. **235**(3), 697–708 (2014)
32. Islam, M.S., Lim, S.H.: When 'nature' strikes: a sociology of climate change and disaster vulnerabilities in Asia. Nat. Cult. **10**(1), 57–80 (2015)
33. Kaisler, S., Armour, F., Espinosa, J.A., Money, W.: Big data: issues and challenges moving forward. In: 2013 46th Hawaii International Conference System Science, pp. 995–1004 (2013)
34. Scholar, J.S.I.P.G., Shanmugapriya, E.: Big data in disaster management, vol. 1, no. December, pp. 86–108 (2016)
35. Park, C.H., Johnston, E.W.: A framework for analyzing digital volunteer contributions in emergent crisis response efforts. New Media Soc. **19**(8), 1308–1327 (2017)
36. Fiedrich, F.F., Burghardt, P.: Agent-based systems for disaster management. Commun. ACM - Emerg. Response Inf. Syst. Emerg. Trends Technol. **50**(3), 41–42 (2007)
37. Raman, M., Dorasamy, M., Muthaiyah, S., Kaliannan, M.: Web-based community disaster management and awareness system (CEMAS) in Malaysia. In: ISCRAM 2014 Conference Proceedings - 11th International Conference on Information Systems for Crisis Response and Management, May 2014, pp. 384–393 (2014)
38. Adam, N.R., Shafiq, B., Staffin, R.: Spatial computing and social media in the context of disaster management. IEEE Intell. Syst. **27**(6), 90–97 (2012)
39. Houston, J.B., et al.: Social media and disasters: a functional framework for social media use in disaster planning, response, and research. Disasters **39**(1), 1–23 (2015)
40. Sabale, R.G., Dani, A.R.: Comparative study of prototype model for software engineering with system development life cycle. IOSR J. Eng. **02**(07), 21–24 (2013)

Investigating Relationships Between Roads Based on Speed Performance Index of Road on Weekdays

Bagus Priambodo[1,2(✉)], Azlina Ahmad[1], and Rabiah Abdul Kadir[1]

[1] Institute of Visual Informatics, Universiti Kebangsaan Malaysia,
Bangi, Malaysia
azlinaivi@ukm.edu.my
[2] Faculty of Computer Science, Universitas Mercu Buana, Jakarta, Indonesia
bagus.priambodo@mercubuana.ac.id

Abstract. Traffic congestion or traffic jam occurs as a ripple effect from a road congestion in the neighbouring area. Previous studies show that spatial correlation is exist between roads in neighbouring roads. There is similar traffic pattern observed between roads in a neighbouring area with respect to day and time. Nowadays, various machine learning model have been developed to predict traffic flow to provide traffic information. However, studies on relationships between road segments in a neighbouring area are still limited. It is important to investigate these relationships because they can assist drivers in avoiding roads which are impacted by road congestion or by a roadblock in a neighbouring area. Hence, this study investigates relationships of roads in a neighbouring area based on similarity of traffic condition. Traffic condition is influenced by number of vehicles and average speed of vehicles. In our study we determine traffic condition based on speed performance index of road in interval time. We used k-means clustering method to cluster condition of traffic flow on road segments. The experiments show that relationship roads can be revealed by clustering traffic condition in interval time.

Keywords: Relationship between roads · Roads clustering · Speed performance index · K-Means clustering

1 Introduction

The increasing number of vehicles in urban areas lead to worsen traffic congestion. Not only it causes environmental pollution, traffic congestion also causes stress and economic losses [1]. Thus, it is important to provide traffic information to drivers which can assist their driving plans and at the same time improve their driving habits [2]. Furthermore, the availability of traffic information can affect changes in flow of traffic in an area.

Traffic congestion is a situation where the vehicle exceeds capacity of the road. Some indications that a road is congested include low average speed, longer travel time than usual, and long queue of cars. Therefore, effective methods or models need to be developed to identify congested links, to analyse the relationship between the

© Springer Nature Switzerland AG 2019
H. Badioze Zaman et al. (Eds.): IVIC 2019, LNCS 11870, pp. 582–591, 2019.
https://doi.org/10.1007/978-3-030-34032-2_51

occurrence of congestion and increasing traffic flow, and to find congestion distribution in a road network. Some research used neural network for prediction of traffic flow based on speed of traffic in neighbouring links using all day's data [3]. A research by Zhou & Huang [4] used neural network to predict traffic flow on road intersections using all day's data.

Other studies revealed that on the same day (working day or weekends), traffic on the road has similar pattern at the same time interval [5]. During working days or weekend, adjacent roads have similar road traffic condition based on historical data [6]. Investigating similar traffic conditions at adjacent roads can lead to traffic flow patterns of the neighbouring roads. Discovering relationships between roads in a neighbouring area can provide information on roads that are impacted by congestion thus can be a guide to drivers in avoiding congested roads.

2   Related Work

Neural network models [2–4] and time series [1], are commonly applied to forecast traffic flow and traffic congestion. Some studies used probability method such as Bayes classifier [5, 6]. Others used k-NN as non-parametric model to predict short-term traffic flow [7–10]. However, studies on relationship between road segments in a neighbouring area are relatively new and certainly need to be explored further.

Research on relationships between road segments used extracted historical data of taxi GPS trajectory to study the correlation between two roads segments [11]. In their study, they defined congestion correlation from road segment A to segment B with a certain distance d as: If congestion occurs in road segment A at time t and at time $t+T$, then congestion occurs at road segment B. Another research applied data from sensors using correlation method to find relationships between roads segments [12]. Visualization method was also used in several studies to investigate traffic flow patterns in neighbouring roads [13–15].

3   Problem

One of the complexities related to predicting traffic congestion is unpredictability. Another related complexity is the behaviour of traffic congestion that is dynamic and interrelated. Many factors affecting traffic flow such as speed of vehicle, weather, special days or events and also occurrence of accidents. These complexities may influence the prediction of traffic flow on neighbouring roads that are affected by a congested road segment in the same area.

Congestion in an urban area, generally will spread through road networks due to the increase in traffic volume. Many types of research on traffic flow produced promising results based on historical traffic data. Unfortunately, spatial-temporal propagation of traffic congestions in an urban area is still unclear [16]. Monitoring and understanding traffic congestions are complex and unpredictable. Sometimes traffic congestions occur, and sometimes they do not. Furthermore, traffic congestions affect traffic flow in the same area because they will propagate to neighbouring roads in the same area [14, 16].

Determining relationships between roads in a neighbouring area can provide information on the propagation of traffic congestion to traffic management offices. This information will assist them in performing traffic flow engineering. From Fig. 1, we anticipate that traffic flow on road 158324 will be influenced by traffic flow on surrounding roads such as road 158446. This means that traffic flow on surrounding roads will be affected by the traffic condition on road 158324.

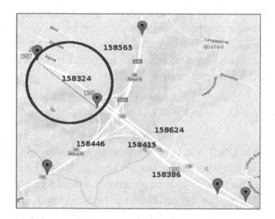

Fig. 1. Road 158324 and its surrounding roads.

Traffic condition is influenced by the number of vehicles and the average speed when passing by the roads (See Table 1). Previously, we have conducted experiments to find correlation value between neighbouring roads using the correlation method. However, using the correlation method, correlation value vary from one area to another area [4, 12]. There exists a relationship between road A to road B if traffic condition in road A and road B have the same traffic condition from time t+T. Road A and road B are in the same area within a certain distanced d. K-means method can be used for clustering traffic flow in neighbouring roads. However, using an unsupervised method like k-means can produce results that vary for each road in the neighbouring area. Therefore, it would be difficult to determine if the traffic condition in road A at time t is similar to traffic condition in neighbouring roads. To address this issue, we calculate speed performance index of each road. In this experiment, we considered data on weekdays (Monday to Thursday) only. We cluster similarity of speed performance index of each road using k-Means clustering method. Then, we search the best k by using Bayes and Chi-square to evaluate the result of clustering by adjusting k value.

4 Dataset and Method

4.1 Dataset

In this study, the data set that we used are collected from IoT traffic sensor in Aarhus, Denmark [17–19]. A total of 449 sensors were installed, as shown in Fig. 2.

Fig. 2. Map of the location of 449 IoT traffic sensors in the city of Aarhus, Denmark.

For example, the name of the sensor at location A is 173225. This sensor is placed from Hinnerup Street Nordjyske Motorvej 0 Aarhus, Aarhus 15 Aarhus Denmark, the distance between the two sensors 3253 m. We conduct experiment using average speed and time for calculating speed performance index. More details of this sensor are present in Tables 1 and 2.

Table 1. Details of traffic data taken from sensor 173225.

Start	End	Point 1	Point 2	Observation
10/1/2014 1:45:00 AM	11/13/2014 10:40:00 AM	Coordinates (lat, long): 56.2348975970264, 10.125013142824, City: Hinnerup Street: Nordjyske Motorvej 0 Postal Code: 8382	Coordinates (lat, long): 56.2138565106957, 10.144907008598. City: Aarhus Street: 15 0 Postal Code: 8200	Distance between two sensors (meters): 3253 Duration (seconds): 100 Organization: COWI Road type: STREET NDT in KMH: 117 EXT ID: 192

Table 2. Details of traffic data taken from sensor 173225.

Avg measured time	Avg speed	Median measured time	Time stamp	Vehicle count
376	14	376	2014-08-01T08:30:00	4
225	23	225	2014-08-01T08:40:00	3
285	18	285	2014-08-01T08:50:00	2

4.2 Methodology

To determine the relationship between roads, we need to find similarity of traffic condition in neighbouring roads. Traffic flow condition is influenced by traffic speed of vehicles passing through and a number of vehicles. In this paper, traffic condition are determined based on the speed performance index [20]. We cluster neighbouring roads based on speed performance index using k-Means. We consider road A as a neighbouring road to road B if the distance between them is approximately four (4) kilometers. Details of our methodology are represented in Fig. 3.

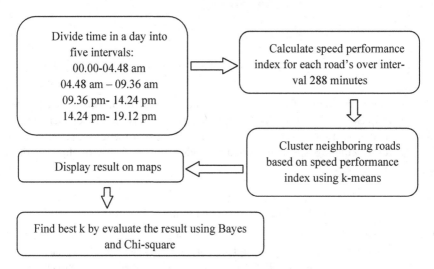

Fig. 3. Methodology to determine relationships of neighbouring roads based on speed performance index using k-means

We follow the speed performance index based on the travel speed from [20], with some adjustments. Beijing Traffic Management Bureau (BTMB) gave two thresholds (25, 50) as criterion of classification of urban traffic state. We define maximum speed limit as 160 km/hour. Instead of calculating speed performance index hourly, we calculate speed performance index for every 288 min defined in (0). This study uses the speed performance index to measure the road traffic state but adopt one threshold only that is 0–33 for congestion. The speed performance index is calculated for neighbouring roads every day from February 2014 until October 2014.

$$R_v = \frac{v}{V_{max}} \times 100 \tag{0}$$

Rv : the speed performance index;
v : the average travel speed, km/h;
$Vmax$: the maximum permissible road speed, km/h.

K-means is one of the best and simplest clustering algorithm [17] available today. It is a method of grouping data which divides the existing data into two or more cluster. The k-means method attempts to cluster the existing data into more than one cluster. Data in one cluster has the same characteristics with each other but has different characteristics from the data in the other clusters. In other words, this method seeks to minimize variations between existing data within a cluster and maximize variation with existing data in other clusters [21]. The procedure used in performing optimization using k-means is as follows:

1. Specify k = n, as we would like to adjust similarity result based on k.
2. Randomly select distinct data points as initial cluster means.
3. Then, calculate the distance between each of cluster means and all other points using Euclidean distance formula.
4. Assign each point to the cluster having the closest mean.
5. For each of the k clusters, recalculate the cluster centroid (means) by calculating the new mean value of all the data points in the cluster.
6. Repeat steps 3 to 5 until the centroids do not change or the maximum number of repetitions is reached (we set the maximum number of repetitions as 1000).

The total within sum of square or the total within-cluster variation is defined (1) as:

$$\sum_{k=1}^{4} W(C_k) = \sum_{k=1}^{4} \sum_{x_i \in C_k} (x_i - \mu_k)^2 \tag{1}$$

Where:

x_i is data point belonging to the cluster $C_k \mu_k$ is the mean value of the points assigned to the cluster C_k

5 Results and Discussion

We calculate the speed performance index from February 2014 until October 2014. In this study, we present and discuss the results of road 158324 and road 193294 with their neighbouring roads. For road 158324 we use interval II (04.48 am–09.36 am), and for road 193294 we use interval III (09.36 am–2.24 pm). This is because congestion occurred over these time intervals.

Results of clustering for neighbouring roads of 1584324 are shown in Table 3 and the results of clustering neighbouring roads of 193294 are shown in Table 4. There are different number of neighbouring roads for road 158324 and road 193294. For road 158324, there are 21 neighbouring roads, whereas for road 193294 there are 60. The number of k clusters are determined by the number of neighbouring roads. The higher the number of neighbouring roads, the higher the number of k clusters. Thus, road 193294 has higher k (k = 15) compared to road 158324 (k = 5) since road 193294 has more neighbouring roads than road 158324. Adjusting k cluster influences the number of similar roads with destination roads namely road 158324 and road 193294. A higher number of k clusters will show roads which have higher relationships with destination

roads. As seen in Table 4, results of clustering for neighbouring roads of 1584324 with
k = 8 filtered only three (3) roads that have high Bayes and Chi-square result (p-value
less than 0.05) compared with when k = 3. Similarly, as seen in Table 4, results of
clustering for neighbouring roads of 193294 with k = 15 filtered five (5) roads that
have high Bayes and chi-square result (p-value less than 0.05) compared with when
k = 5.

Table 3. Clustering results of neighbouring roads for road 158324

K-3	Bayes	Chi square P Value	K-8	Bayes	Chi square P value
158386	0.96	0.00000095	158386	0.96	0.00000095
158415	0.82	0.21	158415	0.82	0.21
171572	0.65	0.77	173011	0.70	0.01
173011	0.70	0.01			
173118	0.66	NA			
173225	0.66	NA			

Table 4. Clustering results of neighbouring roads for road 193294

K-5	Bayes	Chi square P value	K-15	Bayes	Chi square P value
182875	NA	NA	193322	0.62	0.31
193268	1.00	0.41	193430	0.69	0.012
193322	0.63	0.32	194878	0.82	0.0000114
193430	0.69	0.01	195015	0.62	0.68
194878	0.82	0.0000114	195150	0.70	0.012
194905	0.65	0.56			
194960	0.64	0.16			
194986	0.74	0.00			
195015	0.62	0.68			
195041	0.57	0.21			
195070	0.88	0.00			
195096	1.00	0.24			
195150	0.70	0.01			
195259	0.78	0.23			
195286	0.64	0.03			
195312	0.70	0.00			
195923	0.50	0.77			
197274	0.73	0.33			
197355	0.67	0.30			
197408	0.70	0.47			
197434	NA	NA			

For further observation, the results are shown on the map. Results for neighbouring roads of road 158324 are shown in Fig. 4 and results for neighbouring roads of road 193294 are shown in Fig. 5. From Fig. 4, the black line shows roads that are having similar traffic condition with road 158324 based on 288-minute interval of traffic flow. We can see the black lines are near and connected with road 158324. Different results are obtained for road 193294 as seen in Fig. 5. With k = 5, the result shows several black lines are disconnected from road 193294. But with k = 15, the black lines are filtered. Black lines that are disconnected from road 193294 are removed. Only high relationship roads with road 193294 are shown on maps.

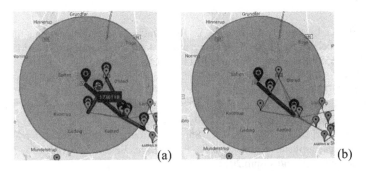

Fig. 4. Relationship of road 158324 with neighbouring roads using k-means (a) k = 3 (b) k = 8.

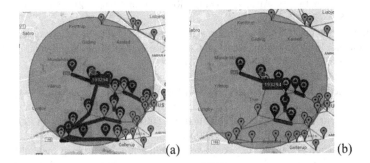

Fig. 5. Relationship of road 193294 with neighbouring roads using k-means (a) k = 5 (b) k = 15

6 Conclusion

Our main objective is to investigate the impact of road congestion on neighbouring roads. Our approach is to study the relationship between roads in a neighbouring area. The results of our experiments show that there exists a relationship between a road and its neighbouring roads. Neighbouring roads with high relationship with target road (road having a congestion), can be used to predict the propagation of traffic congestion.

Our experiments show that relationship of roads can be revealed by clustering traffic condition during certain time intervals. The time interval can be adjusted for one hour, or more as need. Furthermore, by adjusting k to a higher value results in stronger relationship between roads in a neighbouring area. The experiment shows that by adjusting k to a higher value results in clustered neighbouring roads which have higher relationship with target road (using Bayes and chi-square) if compare to using smaller k value. Our next plan is to apply findings of the experiments with probability method to predict propagation impact of road congestion.

References

1. Dong, H., Jia, L., Sun, X., Li, C., Qin, Y.: Road traffic flow prediction with a time-oriented ARIMA model. In: NCM 2009 - 5th International Joint Conference on INC, IMS, and IDC, pp. 1649–1652 (2009). https://doi.org/10.1109/NCM.2009.224
2. Lee, E.-M., Kim, J.-H., Yoon, W.-S.: Traffic speed prediction under weekday, time, and neighboring links' speed: back propagation neural network approach. In: Huang, D.-S., Heutte, L., Loog, M. (eds.) ICIC 2007. LNCS, vol. 4681, pp. 626–635. Springer, Heidelberg (2007). https://doi.org/10.1007/978-3-540-74171-8_62
3. Kumar, K., Parida, M., Katiyar, V.K.: Short term traffic flow prediction for a non urban highway using artificial neural network. Proc. - Soc. Behav. Sci. **104**, 755–764 (2013). https://doi.org/10.1016/j.sbspro.2013.11.170
4. Priambodo, B., Ahmad, A.: Traffic flow prediction model based on neighbouring roads using neural network and multiple regression. J. Inf. Commun. Technol. **17**, 513–535 (2018)
5. Kim, J., Wang, G.: Diagnosis and prediction of traffic congestion on urban road networks using bayesian networks. Australas. Transp. Res. Forum **2016**, 1–21 (2016). https://doi.org/10.3141/2595-12
6. Aung, S.S., Naing, T.T.: Naïve Bayes classifier based traffic detection system on cloud infrastructure. In: 2015 6th International Conference on Modeling, Simulation, pp. 193–198 (2015). https://doi.org/10.1109/ISMS.2015.45
7. Kindzerske, M.D., Ni, D.: Composite nearest neighbor nonparametric regression to improve traffic prediction. Transp. Res. Rec. 30–35 (2007). https://doi.org/10.3141/1993-05
8. Yu, B., Song, X., Guan, F., Yang, Z., Yao, B.: k-nearest neighbor model for multiple-time-step prediction of short-term traffic condition. J. Transp. Eng. **142**, 04016018 (2016). https://doi.org/10.1061/(ASCE)TE.1943-5436.0000816
9. Pang, X., Wang, C., Huang, G.: A short-term traffic flow forecasting method based on a three-layer k-nearest neighbor non-parametric regression algorithm. J. Transp. Technol. **6**, 200–206 (2016)
10. Wu, Y., Tan, H., Jin, P., Shen, B., Ran, B.: Short-term traffic flow prediction based on multilinear analysis and k- nearest neighbor regression. In: 15th International Conference of Transportation Professionals, pp. 557–569 (2015). https://doi.org/10.1061/9780784479292.051
11. Wang, Y., Cao, J., Li, W., Gu, T.: Mining traffic congestion correlation between road segments on GPS trajectories. In: 2016 IEEE International Conference on Smart Computing SMARTCOMP 2016 (2016). https://doi.org/10.1109/SMARTCOMP.2016.7501704

12. Priambodo, B., Ahmad, A.: Predicting traffic flow based on average speed of neighbouring road using multiple regression. In: Badioze Zaman, H., et al. (eds.) Advances in Visual Informatics IVIC 2017. LNCS, vol. 10645, pp. 309–318. Springer, Cham (2017). https://doi.org/10.1007/978-3-319-70010-6_29

13. Petrovska, N., Stevanovic, A.: Traffic congestion analysis visualisation tool. In: Proceedings of the IEEE Conference on Intelligent Transportation Systems, ITSC, October 2015, pp. 1489–1494 (2015). https://doi.org/10.1109/ITSC.2015.243

14. Wang, Z., Lu, M., Yuan, X., Zhang, J., Van De Wetering, H.: Visual traffic jam analysis based on trajectory data. IEEE Trans. Vis. Comput. Graph. **19**, 2159–2168 (2013). https://doi.org/10.1109/TVCG.2013.228

15. Anwar, A., Nagel, T., Ratti, C.: Traffic origins: a simple visualization technique to support traffic incident analysis. In: IEEE Pacific Visualization Symposium 2014, pp. 316–319 (2014). https://doi.org/10.1109/PacificVis.2014.35

16. Jiang, Y., Kang, R., Li, D., Guo, S., Havlin, S.: Spatio-temporal propagation of traffic jams in urban traffic networks. Phys. Soc. (2017)

17. Syed Azimuddin, S., Desikan, K.: A simple density with distance based initial seed selection technique for K means algorithm. J. Comput. Inf. Technol. **25**, 291–300 (2018). https://doi.org/10.20532/cit.2017.1003605

18. Wang, G., Kim, J.: Prediction of traffic congestion and incidents on urban road networks using naive bayes classifier (2016)

19. Bischof, S., Karapantelakis, A., Sheth, A., Mileo, A.: Semantic modelling of smart city data description of smart city data. In: W3C Workshop on the Web of Things Enablers and services for an open Web of Devices, pp. 1–5 (2014)

20. He, F., Yan, X., Liu, Y., Ma, L.: A Traffic congestion assessment method for urban road networks based on speed performance index. In: Green Intelligent Transportation System and Safety, pp. 425–433 (2016). https://doi.org/10.1016/j.proeng.2016.01.277

21. Kesumawati, A., Setianingsih, D.: A segmentation group by Kohonen Self Organizing Maps (SOM) and K -means algorithms (case study: malnutrition cases in Central Java of Indonesia). Int. J. Adv. Soft Comput. Appl. **8**, 110–115 (2016)

Social Network Sites (SNS) Issues in Learning Landscape – Systematic Literature Review

Nani Amalina Zulkanain[1]([✉]), Suraya Miskon[2],
Syed Norris Syed Abdullah[2], Nazmona Mat Ali[2], Mahadi Bahari[2],
and Norasnita Ahmad[2]

[1] Faculty of Computing, Universiti Teknologi Malaysia, 81310 Johor Bahru,
Johor, Malaysia
amalinanan94@gmail.com
[2] Azman Hashim International Business School, Universiti Teknologi Malaysia,
81310 Johor Bahru, Johor, Malaysia
{suraya,norris,nazmona,mahadi,norasnita}@utm.my

Abstract. The education platform today has evolved in align with the development of information technology. Social Network Sites (SNS) appears to be one of the many famous platforms applied in numerous fields, such as business and education. With that, this paper lists the present types of SNS employed for the education arena and the issues involved. Hence, the Systematic Literature Review (SLR) methods was performed to comb through publications that contained studies pertaining the types of SNS and their relevant issues. Based on qualitative analysis, Facebook, Twitter, YouTube and WhatsApp emerged as the present trends of SNS applied by students and instructors for their learning session. The related issues are distraction, lack of guidelines, low internet connectivity, professional boundaries, unnecessary statements and low response.

Keywords: Social Network Sites · Education · Systematic Literature Review

1 Introduction

Social Network Sites (SNS) has been adopted as learning tool in line with this digital era. SNS is defined as a platform for sharing information expressed through texts, videos, images, documents and music [1]. SNS generate a sense of engagement within the educational settings as it offers a sense of presence even with distance or time constraints [2]. They also discovered that instructors use SNS as a tool for communication, collaboration and encouraging students to make friends. In addition, many educational institutes have adopted SNS platforms to extend the benefits of learning purpose. The structure of this study focusing with the aim to explore the current SNS used in education with the recent issues facing by both instructor and students specifically in learning perspective. Several of data gather through a few of publications. Then, all the data are sorted using thematic analysis which consist of two phases of filtration (first-level coding and second-level coding). All results indicate the current SNS and the respective issues discussed.

© Springer Nature Switzerland AG 2019
H. Badioze Zaman et al. (Eds.): IVIC 2019, LNCS 11870, pp. 592–600, 2019.
https://doi.org/10.1007/978-3-030-34032-2_52

2   SNS in Learning Landscape

As such, numerous studies have proven the effectiveness of SNS in enhancing the academic performance amongst the students [3–5] apart from exerting a positive impact on their academic experience. The functions include overall activities carried out by the students or instructors in providing the ability to upload and download any media, share, copy and forward text or media to others as well as the ability to generate comfortable informal conversation. These functions offer vital advantages to both instructors and students for the purpose of learning [6]. Generally, SNS has been well-accepted within the education arena, as adopted by both instructors and students for learning [7], thus leading to encouragement of further development in utilizing new approach for learning. The accessibility of SNS using internet connections further motivates [4] and enhances effective communication [8] that facilitate distance learning involving various courses, materials design and teaching methods [9]. The use of SNS nevertheless, has certain drawbacks. With that, this study investigated the issues around SNS implemented for learning platform. This research discovered the types of SNS adopted in the learning platform and several issues related to the learning session using SNS. The study outcomes are bound to assist instructors and students in selecting the suitable SNS types, apart from preparing well to address the issues unravelled.

3   Methods

This section focusing to data collection and analysis. Further description explained below.

3.1   Data Collection

This research began with review of literature contributed by prior studies concerning the use of SNS platforms. In order to discover the types of SNS and related issues in learning landscape, the first step in this research process was to collect papers from selected databases, which were Web of Science, Scopus, Emerald and Ebscohost. The first main inclusion part of publications was filtered between year 2006 (ranked according to the number of SNS released to market) and year 2018, which includes journals and conference proceedings based on "social media" and "social network" context. After that, the outcomes were categorized and identified based on education perspectives only.

3.2   Data Analysis

All the selected publications were sorted using NVIVO program, by applying the thematic analysis methods. NVIVO refers to a software program that provides tools for qualitative analysis or mixed-method research. Thematic analysis is a method used to identify categories to uncover meanings [10]. This part of the research is aimed in finding justification in other researches pertaining to the use of specific SNS type based on their specific function. Therefore, the systematic literature review (SLR) is deemed essential to easily review all related studies and to analyze the gathered data in a manageable way via thematic analysis. All the attributes were coded with first-level coding based on five inclusive criteria of categories (types of SNS, reasons for use of social network, patterns based on year, gaps and issues) to easily comprehend the patterns of topics. Based on the reading, all the content selected according to these categories. The first-level coding displayed the overall statements of the categories. Next, the statements were reviewed and revised to develop themes for the second-level coding [11, 12]. In this research, second-level coding focused on the types of SNS and the issues subcategories. The subcategories (types of SNS and issues of SNS for learning purpose) are discussed in the next section.

4   Findings and Discussions

This study identified the present SNS used widely in the learning platform. The following delineates the results regarding the types of present SNS.

4.1   Types of Social Network Sites (SNS)

Based on the review of the literature through SLR and several phases of coding, there are several types of SNS that has been studied and validated, higher rank used as learning platform.

Facebook. The use of Facebook as a learning platform has received attention from many researchers and it has been used widely to test and validate the purpose [2, 13], the impacts [14] and the benefits for both students and instructors. In a study that looked into the roles of SNS, which involved 489 students, 84.7% reported using Facebook for learning purposes [15]. In another study that involved 160 students, 59.8% of the students stated that they chose Facebook to connect with other students to learn [16]. In a study that compared Facebook and Twitter, the highest ranked choice by students with 93.8% was Facebook. This portrays the high popularity of Facebook that can be adopted as a platform for both communication and learning. In a study that investigated the applications of SNS amidst three institutions with involvement of 138 students, 93.48% of the respondents rated Facebook as their main preference for intellectual social interaction [17].

Twitter. This platform offers a limited number of words for its users to write and update. Retweet function provides the ability amongst users to copy status from other tweets and share it in their Twitter wall for information sharing purposes [18]. Twitter is also famous for its hashtag (#) function; which eases search for trending topics discussed by the Twitter community across the globe [18]. Twitter has been vastly evaluated to comprehend its functions and impacts learning purposes due to its functionality that supports learning sessions [3, 19]. Additionally, its functionality and interface are highly suitable for mobile technology within the learning environment. However, a number of studies related to the types of SNS used for learning have asserted that Twitter is not match with Facebook in term of ranking. A study showed that Twitter only received 47.83% of attention for learning purpose, when compared to the top ranking Facebook [19].

YouTube. This platform contains unlimited videos that ease comprehension and offer support in learning materials [20]. Recent studies concerning the use of YouTube for learning purposes showed that YouTube is one of the best teaching tools [21] that allow social relationships based on uploaded video as well as through finding and sharing information [22]. Apart from its interactive function, it gives brief information based regarding the vast types of video that contain the graphical information or real life instance from multiple sources [23, 24]. A study that examined the impact of YouTube as learning platform showed that 78% of students used YouTube as their main source of learning [25]. However, YouTube cannot outrank Facebook as it only recorded 43.6% of users [15].

WhatsApp. This platform adapts instant messaging applications which are trendy at present times [26]. WhatsApp has already been part of a recent study regarding its use as a learning platform [4]. WhatsApp has been reported to enhance academic performance [8, 27], besides assisting students for assessment preparation [28]. A recent study concerning the impact of using WhatsApp found that 57% of students chose WhatsApp for learning purposes [26], another study revealed that 89.9% of students used Twitter and WhatsApp frequently in their daily communication [29]. The study also showed that the participants were comfortable using WhatsApp for communication and sending images or media. In a study regarding the use of for dental education, WhatsApp was ranked higher when compared to Facebook instant message as a communication strategy among students [30], mainly due its effectiveness and its unique feature in the ability of determining the recipients have received and read the message sent.

4.2   Issues of SNS for Learning Purpose

Some studies show that users were uncomfortable using SNS as a learning platform due to several shortcomings. These issues can be categorised into distraction, low internet connectivity, lack of guidelines, professional boundaries, unnecessary statement and low response.

Distraction. Neither all instructors nor students can accept the use of SNS platform for learning purpose due to dependency on text books [4] and low trust issues towards online information. In a study that focused on Facebook group discussion, students display tendency to focus on trivial social interaction instead of learning which led to less attention paid to class session in SNS virtual environment [17]. This solely means, wasting time and less chance for engagement with other members and instructor [15]. Surprisingly, a study showing that distraction can also occur if many unnecessary knowledge is shared by others instead of forming an effective collaborative group to carry out activities [31]. This is because, an active group discussion for learning surely can increase learning performance, while shallow conversations during learning session in SNS cause delay and wavered concentration [32]. The presence of advertisement provided by SNS also distracts student due to exposure to unnecessary information [33]. Another issue is that students tend to perform multitasking by concentrating in learning replying to message immediately. Not all conversations are dense with quality information. This scenario leads to poor learning performance [34]. This reflects the effect if no specific instruction or pedagogy is applied in SNS learning platform.

Low Internet Connectivity. This seems to be the most common issue faced in learning via SNS. Poor internet connectivity causes complication that highly relies on reliable network for communication and learning [35]. High internet connectivity demand high budget that is necessary for networking purpose. Nonetheless, utility budget for learning via SNS is a waste if the internet connection is unstable [36]. One barrier regarding the internet issue affects students who are unsubscribe to any internet plan at their home or mobile, hence making them unable to participate in learning session via SNS. Thus, issues related to internet connectivity should be addressed prior implementing learning through SNS.

Lack of guidelines. Pedagogy is applied primarily in physical learning and Learning Management System (LMS), but lacking for application in SNS [37]. Several problems may occur when students or instructors are unclear about learning within SNS environment [38]. They tend to question the possibility of learning to actually take place and the flow of information without facing any distraction. Technically, SNS provides many functions and a variety of interfaces. However, some of students have expressed the difficulties in managing communication channel due to lack of guidelines or facilitation from the instructor [35, 39]. Several functions in SNS tend to become useless during learning if the students fail to adapts and gain academic performance. It is easy to collaborate in physical learning since it adapts face-to-face interaction however, it difficult to adapt collaborative learning in SNS due to distance and time constraint. Additionally, they facilitate on their own without any specific guideline from instructor. A number of students or instructors, hence prefer formal learning since it remains the professional boundaries although, it is difficult to remain the privacy border as they can directly communicate via personal chat [40]. Next, those familiar with learning via SNS can easily collaborate and adapt with SNS learning, while students who are unfamiliar with the SNS environment are bound to experience difficulties in terms of communication and technical skill. Therefore, it is crucial to list down all the steps as preparation for novice students so as to ensure that they gain understanding in each learning session [41]. Some students may face difficulties in ways of responding and engaging with the instructor. They definitely need some basic ideas prior to SNS learning [42]. Ethical issues may rise in the absence of strict rules or guidelines in education [43]. A few students may post inappropriate or unrelated statements with the learning topics. In a study related to WhatsApp use, lack of knowledge in accurately using WhatsApp for learning and teaching led to some challenges in knowledge delivery [27]. Thus, rules and guidelines must be established first prior to implementing SNS in education.

Professional Boundaries. Boundaries between students and instructors have emerged to be an issue linked with information privacy. In a study that investigated the application of Facebook, some instructors were comfortable sharing personal information with their students [40], while some highlighted the in appropriate friendly relationship between students and instructors. Next is the interaction channel that concerns professional ethical behaviour [41]. In a study that examined learning using Twitter, the students are uninterested in their instructor's life story [44] and wished to place focus on learning. However, a few instructors are satisfied with the use of SNS and only prepare assignments and notes through SNS that are meant to give a positive impact on students' intention [45]. In this way, the instructors can retain their professionalism as an educator in SNS as well as in the physical class. In a study related to Twitter use, the students were unaware of privacy issues as Twitter is less restrictive when compared to Facebook [46]. This is because Twitter does not offer a platform for group discussions, but instead focuses more on personal statements in the timeline. It depends on one's perspective to accept and to judge the level of professionalism towards others.

Unnecessary Statements. The present millennial students use technology almost every day. Hence, they tend to share their personal feelings in SNS and receive unnecessary comments by their followers [47]. In some cases, students tend to critic and manipulate information that leads to cyber-bullying [17]. This is because, they use harsh words and dare to say anything for they do not meet physically. Since many learning resources are easy-to-search, some end up evaluating and criticising without true facts [47]. In a case of using Facebook for chatting, most unnecessary conversation can cause low level of motivation in learn especially when the topic of discussion deviates from that of the subject [48]. Therefore, students and instructors should be more serious and retain professionalism in their posting so as to ensure that all statements only indicate their opinions or answers in line with the learning topics and nothing related to personal statements.

Low Response. Every learning platform is concerned about interaction during learning hence, making responses an essential aspect in valuing interest and concentration amongst students during learning session. SNS is primarily created for socialisation and communication [46]. Low response may reflect less interest or low motivation. Some students only response to initiate discussion [49] while some become supportive depending on the topic of discussion. Low response leads to dull conversation. Distance learning without facing each other may cause massive problems if the students do not interact with each other. The sense of engagement is absent between the students and the instructors. Generally, YouTube promotes video sharing and most students use videos to initiate discussion [21], while less response is received in the comment section as it is not a platform for chatting or discussion.

5 Conclusion and Future Work

Most of the issues discussed are linked with Facebook and Twitter. WhatsApp, in specific has issues with the guidelines that are required as a main concern in education platform whereas YouTube generates low responses during learning session. This research discovered that the present SNS is actively used as a learning platform to support learning purpose. From the types of SNS that has been analysed, the emerging issues associated with the use of SNS are distraction, lack of guidelines, low internet connectivity, professional boundaries, unnecessary statements and low response. This research is significance for researcher to understand the SNS issues in education platform. The description of these information will be valuable for current educators to applied SNS according to trends of current technology. In conclusion, most SNS appear to share similar issues in adapting SNS as an education platform. Hence, future studies would need to focus on quantitative data gathered from specific target groups to probe into the uprising issues faced by millennial students within the SNS environment for learning purposes.

Acknowledgement. The authors would like to thank the Ministry of Higher Education (MOHE) and the Universiti Teknologi Malaysia (UTM) for the Research University Grant Scheme (GUP) (vote number: I6H76) that had supported this research.

References

1. Brooker, P., Barnett, J., Cribbin, T.: Doing social media analytics. Big Data Soc. **3**, 1–12 (2016)
2. See, J., Lim, Y., Agostinho, S., Harper, B., Chicharo, J.: The engagement of social media technologies by undergraduate informatics students for academic purpose in Malaysia. J. Inf. Commun. Ethics Soc. **12**, 177–194 (2014). https://doi.org/10.1108/jices-03-2014-0016
3. Al-Rahmi, W.M., Zeki, A.M.: A model of using social media for collaborative learning to enhance learners' performance on learning. J. King Saud Univ. - Comput. Inf. Sci. **29**, 526–535 (2017). https://doi.org/10.1016/j.jksuci.2016.09.002
4. Dar, Q.A., et al.: Use of social media tool "Whatsapp" in medical education. Ann. King Edward Med. Univ. **23**, 39–42 (2017). https://doi.org/10.21649/akemu.v23i1.1497
5. Tezer, M., Taspolat, A., Sami, K., Fatih Sapanca, H.: The impact of using social media on academic achievement and attitudes of prospective teachers. Int. J. Cogn. Reseach Sci. Eng. Educ. **5**, 75–83 (2017). https://doi.org/10.5937/ijcrsee1702075t
6. Maleko Munguatosha, G., Birevu Muyinda, P., Thaddeus Lubega, J.: A social networked learning adoption model for higher education institutions in developing countries. Horiz. **19**, 307–320 (2011). https://doi.org/10.1108/10748121111179439
7. Cao, Y., Hong, P.: Antecedents and consequences of social media utilization in college teaching: a proposed model with mixed-methods investigation. Horiz. **19**, 297–306 (2011). https://doi.org/10.1108/10748121111179420
8. Wong, C.-H., Tan, G.W.-H., Loke, S.-P., Ooi, K.-B.: Adoption of mobile social networking sites for learning? Online Inf. Rev. **39**, 762–778 (2015). https://doi.org/10.1108/OIR-05-2015-0152
9. Moghavvemi, S., Sulaiman, A., Jaafar, N.I., Kasem, N.: Social media as a complementary learning tool for teaching and learning: the case of youtube. Int. J. Manag. Educ. **16**, 37–42 (2018). https://doi.org/10.1016/j.ijme.2017.12.001
10. Fereday, J., Muir-Cochrane, E.: Demonstrating rigor using thematic analysis: a hybrid approach of inductive and deductive coding and theme development. Int. J. Qual. Methods. **5**, 80–92 (2006). https://doi.org/10.1177/160940690600500107
11. Bandara, W., Miskon, S., Fielt, E.: Association for information systems. AIS electronic library (AISeL). A systematic, tool-supported method for conducting literature reviews in information systems. In: European Conference on Information Systems, pp. 1–14 (2011)
12. Bandara, W., Furtmueller, E., Beekhuyzen, J., Gorbacheva, E., Miskon, S.: Achieving rigour in literature reviews: insights from qualitative data analysis and tool-support. Commun. Assoc. Inf. Syst. **34**, 154–204 (2015)
13. Hamade, S.N.: Perception and use of social networking sites among university students. Libr. Rev. **62**, 388–397 (2013). https://doi.org/10.1108/LR-12-2012-0131

14. Burbules, N.C.: How we use and are used by social media in education. Educ. Theory. **66**, 551–565 (2016). https://doi.org/10.1111/edth.12188
15. Singh, K.P., Gill, M.S.: Role and users' approach to social networking sites (SNSs): a study of universities of North India. Electron. Libr. **33**, 19–34 (2015). https://doi.org/10.1108/EL-12-2012-0165
16. Bialy, S.El, Ayoub, A.R.: The trends of use of social media by medical students. Educ. Med. J. **9**, 59–68 (2017). https://doi.org/10.21315/eimj2017.9.1.6
17. Fasae, J.K., Adegbilero-Iwari, I.: Use of social media by science students in Public Universities in Southwest Nigeria. Electron. Libr. **34**, 213–222 (2016). https://doi.org/10.1108/EL-11-2014-0205
18. Merrill, N.: Higher education administration with social media for social research: applications for higher education communications. Cutting-edge Technol. High. Educ. **2**, 25–48 (2015)
19. Waycott, J., Thompson, C., Sheard, J., Clerehan, R.: A virtual panopticon in the community of practice: Students' experiences of being visible on social media. Internet High. Educ. **35**, 12–20 (2017). https://doi.org/10.1016/j.iheduc.2017.07.001
20. Saw, G., Abbott, W., Donaghey, J., Mcdonald, C.: Social media for international students – it's not all about Facebook. Libr. Manag. J. Serv. Manag. Iss Qual. Mark. Res. An Int. J. **34**, 156–174 (2012)
21. Neier, S., Zayer, L.T.: Students' perceptions and experiences of social media in higher education. J. Mark. Educ. **37**, 133–143 (2015). https://doi.org/10.1177/0273475315583748
22. Mansour, E.A.H.: The use of Social Networking Sites (SNSs) by the faculty members of the School of Library and Information Science, PAAET. Kuwait. Electron. Libr. **33**, 524–546 (2015). https://doi.org/10.1108/EL-06-2013-0110
23. Pacheco, E., Lips, M., Yoong, P.: Transition 2.0: digital technologies, higher education, and vision impairment. Internet High. Educ. **37**, 1–10 (2017). https://doi.org/10.1016/j.iheduc.2017.11.001
24. Rueda, L., Benitez, J., Braojos, J.: From traditional education technologies to student satisfaction in management education: a theory of the role of social media applications. Inf. Manag. **54**, 1059–1071 (2017). https://doi.org/10.1016/j.im.2017.06.002
25. Barry, D.S., Marzouk, F., Chulak-Oglu, K., Bennett, D., Tierney, P., O'Keeffe, G.W.: Anatomy education for the YouTube generation. Anat. Sci. Educ. **9**, 90–96 (2016). https://doi.org/10.1002/ase.1550
26. Jaafar, A.: The impact of using social media and internet on academic performance: case study Bahrain Universities. **4**, 1–12 (2017). https://doi.org/10.4108/eai.28-6-2017.152748
27. Altaany, F.: Usage whatsapp application for e-learning and its impact on academic performance in irbid national university in Jordan. Int. J. Appl. Eng. Res. **10**, 39875–39879 (2015)
28. Smit, I.: WhatsApp with learning preferences? In: Proceedings - Frontiers in Education Conference, FIE (2015)
29. Asiri, A.K., Almetrek, M.A., Alsamghan, A.S., Mustafa, O., Alshehri, S.F.: Impact of Twitter and WhatsApp on sleep quality among medical students in King Khalid University. Saudi Arabia Sleep Hypn. **20**, 247–252 (2018)
30. Khatoon, B., Hill, K.B., Walmsley, A.D.: Instant messaging in dental education. J. Dent. Educ. **79**, 1471–1478 (2015). https://doi.org/10.5958/2393-8005.2016.00013.9
31. Alt, D.: College students' perceived learning environment and their social media engagement in activities unrelated to class work. Instr. Sci. **45**, 623–643 (2017). https://doi.org/10.1007/s11251-017-9418-0

32. Badri, M., Alnuaimi, A., Al Rashedi, A., Yang, G., Temsah, K., Temsah, K.: School children's use of digital devices, social media and parental knowledge and involvement – the case of Abu Dhabi. Educ. Inf. Technol. **22**, 2645–2664 (2017). https://doi.org/10.1007/s10639-016-9557

33. Nicolai, L., et al.: Facebook groups as a powerful and dynamic tool in medical education: mixed-method study. J. Med. Internet Res. **19**, 408–4081 (2017). https://doi.org/10.2196/jmir.7990

34. Wu, J.: University students' motivated attention and use of regulation strategies on social media. Comput. Educ. **89**, 75–90 (2015)

35. Poellhuber, B., Roy, N., Anderson, T.: Distance students' readiness for social media and collaboration. Int. Rev. Res. Open Distance Learn. **12**, 102–125 (2011)

36. Dumpit, D.Z., Fernandez, C.J.: Analysis of the use of social media in Higher Education Institutions (HEIs) using the technology acceptance model. Int. J. Educ. Technol. High. Educ. **14**, 1–16 (2017). https://doi.org/10.1186/s41239-017-0045-2

37. Dabbagh, N., Kitsantas, A.: Personal learning environments, social media, and self-regulated learning: a natural formula for connecting formal and informal learning. Internet High. Educ. **15**, 3–8 (2012). https://doi.org/10.1016/j.iheduc.2011.06.002

38. Minocha, S.: Role of social software tools in education: a literature review. Educ. + Train. **51**, 353–369 (2009). https://doi.org/10.1108/00400910910987174

39. Lisbet, P.S.: How social-media enhanced learning platforms support students in taking responsibility for their own learning. J. Appl. Res. High. Educ. J. Appl. Res. High. Educ. J. Inf. Commun. Ethics Soc. **5**, 261–272 (2014)

40. Towner, T.L., Lego Muñoz, C.: Facebook and education: a classroom connection? In: Educating Educators with Social Media, pp. 33–57 (2011)

41. Benson, V., Morgan, S.: Social university challenge: constructing pragmatic graduate competencies for social networking. Br. J. Educ. Technol. **47**, 465–473 (2016)

42. Rambe, P., Nel, L.: Technological utopia, dystopia and ambivalence: teaching with social media at a South African University. Br. J. Educ. Technol. **46**, 629–648 (2015). https://doi.org/10.1111/bjet.12159

43. Foley, N.M., Maher, B.M., Corrigan, M.A.: Social media and tomorrow's medical students - how do they fit? J. Surg. Educ. **71**, 385–390 (2014). https://doi.org/10.1016/j.jsurg.2013.10.008

44. Degroot, J.M., et al.: Twitter use and its effects on student perception of instructor credibility twitter use and its effects on student perception of instructor credibility. Commun. Educ. ISSN. **64**, 419–437 (2015). https://doi.org/10.1080/03634523.2015.1014386

45. Merle, P., Freberg, K.: All about that tweet: student perceptions of professors' social media use in the classroom. J. Res. Interact. Mark. **10**, 124–136 (2016). https://doi.org/10.1108/JRIM-01-2015-0008

46. Liu, D., Kirschner, P.A., Karpinski, A.C.: A meta-analysis of the relationship of academic performance and social network site use among adolescents and young adults. Comput. Hum. Behav. **77**, 148–157 (2017). https://doi.org/10.1016/j.chb.2017.08.039

47. Gammon, M.A., White, J.: (Social) media literacy: challenges and opportunities for higher education. Educ. Educ. With Soc. Media. **1**, 329–345 (2015)

48. Keles, E.: Use of Facebook for the community services practices course: community of inquiry as a theoretical framework. Comput. Educ. **116**, 203–224 (2018). https://doi.org/10.1016/j.compedu.2017.09.003

49. Kelly, N., Antonio, A.: Teacher peer support in social network sites. Teach. Teach. Educ. **56**, 138–149 (2016). https://doi.org/10.1016/j.tate.2016.02.007

Proposed UX Model for Children Educational Mobile Application

Kiranjeet Kaur[(✉)], Khairul Shafee Kalid, and Savita K. Sugathan

Department of Computer Information Sciences,
Universiti Teknologi PETRONAS, Seri Iskandar, Malaysia
kiranjeetkaurssks@gmail.com,
{khairulshafee_kalid, savitasugathan}@utp.edu.my

Abstract. The evolution of mobile learning is robustly popular among children these days since the engagement is portable and owns unique interactive specialties that tends to attract more users. User experience (UX) is one of the potential approaches in designing mobile applications to deliver a complete experience for utilizing a technology. However, this concept of UX has not been adopted while designing educational mobile application for children even when researchers have claimed that children's experience differs from adults. Therefore, the inadequate experience of mobile learning leads in affecting children's cognitive skills in learning perspective. The problem statement argued in this paper is children's cognitive skills on solving educational critical thinking problems are diminishing due to lacking of adequate elements while designing educational mobile application. To support the problem this paper aims to develop EduMobile UX Model for children when designers are developing educational mobile application for them. This study conducted a literature review to develop EduMobile UX Model. This model will be referred by designers when designing children educational mobile application.

Keywords: User Experience · Children educational application · Cognitive skills

1 Introduction

Mobile devices are trending in the current technological era among the modern generation [1] as it advances in interactivity as well as promotes friendly features. Mobile devices are easily portable, educational contents can be accessed anytime and anywhere, and material presentation would be beyond the traditional classroom settings learning. Several researchers believe that mobile learning gives the opportunity to the students and teachers to facilitate an interactive plus innovative teaching and learning process. Furthermore, learning is easy through mobile devices like mobile phones, handheld computers and tablets. The usage of mobile while learning is becoming a part of the children life but their cognitive skill on the other hand is getting affected [1]. This is due to the poorly designed interface as well as neglecting children's experience while using a mobile application when learning. Technological development has introduced latest resources but at the end the user is who that decides to accept or reject the service.

© Springer Nature Switzerland AG 2019
H. Badioze Zaman et al. (Eds.): IVIC 2019, LNCS 11870, pp. 601–610, 2019.
https://doi.org/10.1007/978-3-030-34032-2_53

Thus, UX plays the core concepts in mobile application even though the consent is uncertain. UX converges information, visual, web and content design, application architecture, visual rhetoric (image and branding), content creation and writing, and analysis (business, web, and "big data" analytics), among others [2]. Several ventures of defining, understanding and scoping UX has been done yet, there is no specific consensus which reached this concept [3]. The manner which perceive the surrounding of a user and adapts the usability into the application delivers a complete experience. Hence, it is important to understand children's experience in using a mobile application while learning because of their divergent perception compared to adults. Problem supporting this research content is children's cognitive skills on solving educational critical thinking problems are diminishing due to lacking of adequate elements while designing educational mobile application. Hence, this paper aims to develop and validate EduMobile UX model for children educational mobile application which could be adopted as well adapted by designers while designing the application. This objective considers to answer the research question, "what are the identified elements of UX in designing children educational mobile application?".

2 Literature Review

2.1 User Experience

Introduction to UX. UX is a well-defined consequence of presentation, functionality, system performance, interactive behavior, and assistive capabilities of an interactive system for hardware as well as software [4]. UX has evolved into one of the core concepts of HCI where wide range of disciplines' researchers and practitioners daily work on these concepts. According to ISO 9241-210 [5] UX is a person's perceptions and responses resulting from the use and/or anticipated use of a product, system or service. Furthermore, UX is also a consequence of brand image, presentation, functionality, system performance, interactive behavior and assistive capabilities of the interactive system, the user's internal and physical state resulting from prior experiences, attitudes, skills and personality, and the context of use. Despite several attempts of understanding, defining and scoping UX, no secured consensus has been reached on this concept [2]. Donald Norman was the first author who used the term "User Experience" to describe all the person's experience aspects with a system and he claims his introduction to the term UX as he believed "usability" to be narrowed deeply for representing a holistic vision of HCI [2]. According to Jacob Nielsen and Don Norman, UX encompasses "all aspects of the end-user's interaction with company, its services and its products" [3] yet not all associated with UX have agreed on this definition [6].

Generally, developers who are interested in UX design, not only focuses on what the product does but on how the users tend to interact with it. Thus, a positive experience requires substantial benefits to users and a negative experience entails frustration and failure [7]. Section below describes the existing designs when designing mobile application.

Theories Involving Software Design for Children. According to [1], there are many theories which concerns designing software for children which are: (1) user-centered design (UCD), (2) contextual design, (3) participatory design, (4) cooperative inquiry,

(5) informant design, (6) learner-centered design, (7) constructional design, and (8) interaction design. UCD involves user indirectly in the software design but only the designer is allowed to control the design process. Contextual design refers on the required information, users daily activities and software goals. This model is suitable to design child-centered context [1]. Participatory design was not used for children because designers think children cannot deliver useful ideas and opinion when designing [8]. Cooperative inquiry refers to the methodologies carried out which are observation, questionnaires and children involvement in the design but it is best to be applied with students aged 7-10 years old [1]. Informant design appreciates the involvement of children in the design because designers believe that it leads to a funny and intuitive design [1]. Constructional design allows users to build their own preferred design based on the allocation of the application. Thus, this model is also controlled by the designer at the end. Interaction design defines the behavior of certain products and systems in response with the users [1].

Fadel had developed a model called Experienced-Centered Web Design Model [9], where he has done a comparative study on UX's axes then, associated with the similarities between categories and dimensions and finalized it into three dimensions which are emotional, aesthetic and functional. The emotional dimension defines the emotional responses and interaction which occurs when a user is using the system [10]. The functional dimension defines the interface role (features) in the general context of the system [11]. Aesthetic dimension defines about the visual and interaction design principles, where the interface planning, creation, evaluation, and communication takes place [12]. Even though the model name represents web but it is easily adaptable in mobile application designs. International Organization for Standardization (ISO) has produced many usability models but none covers all the aspects of usability [13]. Thus, all these above models discussed above does not include and utilize all the required elements which are needed to provide best user experience for children while using educational mobile application. Next session discusses on the importance of including all the user experience aspects.

Elements of UX. This study compares the elements of UX discussed by several authors to address the importance of including cognitive dimension in designing mobile application. Each of the elements play an unique role in their respective fields. The user interface design or aesthetic plays a role of best interaction of beauty [14] for users in order for them to accept the application because their dislikes could lead to anxiety or discomfort [15]. A fun as well as engaging interface design has motivated more students in learning [16]. The importance of functional dimension has been claimed as the clients' needs in relation towards the interface [9]. It is necessary to anticipate the use of a product or a system through a user's perception and responses [17] towards engaging as well as fun experience [16]. Functional elements are able to compare and contrast the users' convenience, features and design of product [18] to attract targeted group of users for sustaining their loyalty [19].

On the other hand, the emotional elements creates its importance in UX by character interactivity users towards an interface and to what extend they can react to a user's interventions [9]. It is crucial to stress on this element due to users' complex and mixed feelings of emotions [17] during the interaction with the system or product [20]. The interaction between a user and the system may lead to unique experience in different context of use [21] which includes users perceptual and emotional aspects [4]. Cognitive defines level of ability which demands to master a specific information and technology literacy creatively as well as using innovative skills [22]. The representation of cognitive element in designing a system is important because it portrays a paradigmatic shifts of how a user anticipates about the interface [6] and the results will then represent usability of a system, product or service [17]. Nevertheless, cognitive helps to reduce complexity of an experience [4] by directing them to a right path of using the system [23]. Nevertheless, cognitive inclusive enhances users imagination and improves their behavior [24]. A systematic literature review was conducted to identify the UX elements required to be included in designing educational mobile application for children aged 10–12 years old. Table 1 describes the researchers who have highlighted the elements and its importance to be included in designing mobile application.

Table 1. UX elements supported by researchers

Elements	Researcher
Effectiveness	[15, 17, 21, 24–26]
Efficiency	[15, 17, 19, 21, 26–28]
Satisfaction	[15, 18, 19, 21, 26, 28–33]
Gesture Interaction	[11, 26, 30, 34–36]
Learnability	[21, 22, 26, 31, 32, 37, 38]
Memorability	[19, 21, 26, 34]
Convenience	[6, 18, 19, 24, 26]
Responsive	[6]
Animation	[6, 17, 24, 26, 27, 33, 35, 39, 40]
Discoverability	[6, 19, 26, 34, 35, 38]
Colours	[6, 16, 17, 27, 33, 35, 36, 39–41]
Enjoyment	[17–19, 21, 26, 28, 42]
Attractiveness	[17, 24, 26, 28]
Text	[16, 17, 26, 27, 30, 39–41]
Audio	[16, 17, 26, 27, 33, 35, 39–42]
Complexity	[17, 21, 22, 24, 26–28, 33, 37–39]
Engaging	[16, 21]
Motivation	[16, 18, 21, 25, 26, 37, 39, 41]
Usefulness	[16, 18]
Comfortable	[19]
Technology fit	[11, 18, 19, 24, 26, 30, 39]
Pleasure	[19, 23, 28, 36]
Simplicity	[27]
Collaborative	[24]
Interactive	[2, 24]
Innovative	[37]
Conceptual	[39]
Flexibility	[11]

The elements were chosen based on number of researchers highlighted it in their study and which could be adopted while designing a standard educational mobile application for upper primary school children. The elements chosen are later discussed in the next chapter.

2.2 Children of Children Mental Development

Cognitive development initially was introduced by Jean Piaget, developmental psychologist. He explains that there are four basic concepts to elaborate the individual's cognitive structure activity process which are schema, assimilation, adaption and balance [43]. Cognitive development refers to the lifespan development of thinking. Thinking has unclear boundaries which differs from other mental activities yet it involves higher mental processes such as problem solving, reasoning, creating, conceptualizing, categorizing, remembering and planning [44]. One of the most influential theory of cognitive development are Piaget's Theory of Cognitive Development.

Piaget's theory often focuses on the children's progress by referring to the development stages qualitatively [44]. According to Ellin Kotsky, Piaget's Theory occupied middle ground of two-level psychological function explanation. However, many researchers claim that Piaget and his challengers deliver different, pending perspective of the similar issues which has to be incorporated into cognitive development model [45]. In cognitive development, Jean Piaget's theory describes that children undergo through four mental development stages [46]. This theory not only focuses on understanding the way children obtain knowledge yet understanding the nature of intelligence. The stages in Jean Piaget's theory are sensorimotor stage (birth – 2 years), preoperational stage (2–7 years), concrete operational stage (7–11 years) and formal operational stage (12 years - adult). This research focuses on children ages 10–12 years old thus, concrete operational stage is discussed in this paper. This stage goes through logical thought of development [46]. It is discussed that children at this stage are concrete, their thinking involves logical and sophisticated in their thinking in this stage. Normally, children practice solving logical problems in their mind. Hence, the feedback from the application is the key that indicates performance changes in children and provides more interest in using it.

3 Methodology

The methodology will be implementing in three sequential stages. The Fig. 1 illustrates the stages with the following outcome.

Stage 1: Define and Design. Several research papers have been reviewed for developing UX model. This research has looked into the importance of UX elements and dimensions (functional, aesthetic, emotional and cognitive) which needs to be considered while designing an educational mobile application for children. After reviewing all the studies in previous chapter, this research develops EduMobile UX Model which incorporates all the relevant aspects of usability, user experience and ISO9241-210. This model has all the necessary elements which needs to be incorporated when

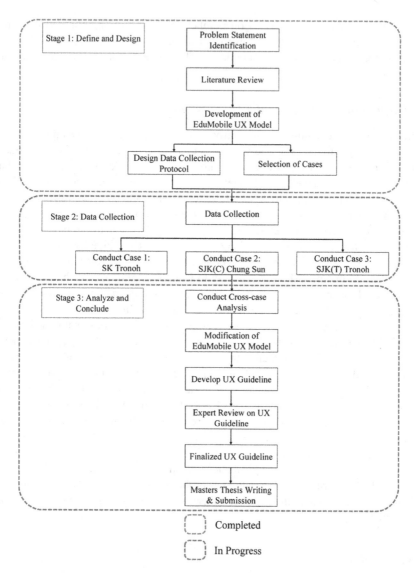

Fig. 1. Research activity

designing educational mobile application especially for children aged 10–12 years old. Figure 2 describes the elements and dimensions included to complete the experience of a user.

Stage 2: Data Collection. The research will be using a qualitative exploratory case study method by Robert Yin [47] to conduct the research. The research adopts purposive sampling where some criteria has been developed in order to select the sample or cases. The criteria are (a) similarity in Science syllabus, (b) government funded schools (sekolah kebangsaan), (c) each schools should teach lessons in different

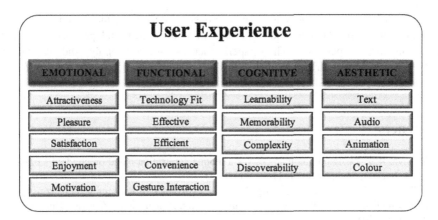

Fig. 2. EduMobile UX model

language since, Malaysia is a multi-national country and, (d) school population should be less than 30. Thus, the schools (cases) chosen for this research are SK Tronoh, SJK (C) Chung Sun and SJK(T) Tamil. This study's unit of analysis will be the mobile application used in schools during observation session. The mobile application version used is Android and the mobile application is "Environment Current Affairs 2018 (offline)". The application used in this research is selected accordingly where the content in the app contributes with the "Kementerian Pendidikan Malaysia" syllabus, English language settings, Google Play ratings and this app is poor in user experience design. The data collection method will be conducted through semi-structured interviews based on the model developed and observation. Students will be the respondents of the interview as well as the observation session since, they are the audience who will be engaging to the mobile application. Since, children participate fully in designing the technology, they have the most privileges as design partners. Furthermore, children have many positive ideas that can support the process of the application design. The result from the data collection will be validating the EduMobile UX Model.

Stage 3: Analyze and Conclude. This session will be analyzing the respondents results through Atlas.ti. The outcome from the analysis will used to develop the UX guideline by adapting the final version of EduMobile UX Model. The guideline will then be evaluated by mobile application expert. Later, the guideline will be presented to the designers for referral purpose while designing educational mobile application for children. The guideline will be contributing in researchers master's thesis.

4 Conclusion and Future Work

Mobile learning practice is growing tremendously among children but similarly children's cognitive skills tends to be unpleasant. Therefore, designing an appropriate mobile application for children while improving and maintaining their thinking skills is crucial. User Experience of a child differs from an adult experience thus, providing the accurate elements for designers as a guide to design educational mobile application is important for them to understand children's thinking ability and produce sufficient mobile learning experience. This papers focuses on developing and validating EduMobile UX Model for children educational mobile application which tends to focus on solving the problem statement above.

References

1. Kraleva, R.S.: Designing an interface for a mobile application based on children's opinion. Int. J. Interact. Mob. Technol. **11**(1), 53 (2017)
2. Lallemand, C., Gronier, G., Koenig, V.: User experience: a concept without consensus? Exploring practitioners' perspectives through an international survey. Comput. Hum. Behav. **43**, 35–48 (2015)
3. Norman, D., Nielsen, J.: The Definition of User Experience (UX). Nielsen Norman Group (2016). https://www.nngroup.com/articles/definition-user-experience/. Accessed 02 June 2018
4. Pucillo, F., Cascini, G.: A framework for user experience, needs and affordances. Des. Stud. **35**(2), 160–179 (2014)
5. International standard: International standard, vol. 2010 (2010)
6. Mullins, C.: Responsive, mobile app, mobile first: untangling the UX design web in practical experience. In: Proceedings of 33rd Annual International Conference on Design Communication (SIGDOC 2015), pp. 22:1–22:6 (2015)
7. Park, C.-H., Jang, G., Chai, Y.-H.: Culturability in mobile data services: a qualitative study of the relationship between cultural characteristics and user-experience attributes. Int. J. Hum. Comput. Interact. **20**(3), 285–303 (2006)
8. Nesset, V., Large, A.: Children in the information technology design process : a review of theories and their applications. vol. 26, pp. 140–161 (2004)
9. Fadel, L.M.: Experience-Centered Web Design Model. In: Marcus, A. (ed.) DUXU 2014. LNCS, vol. 8518, pp. 92–103. Springer, Cham (2014). https://doi.org/10.1007/978-3-319-07626-3_9
10. Law, E.L.: The measurability and predictability of user experience. pp. 1–9 (2011)
11. Inostroza, R., Rusu, C., Roncagliolo, S., Rusu, V.: Usability heuristics for touchscreen-based mobile devices: update. In: Proceedings of the 2013 Chilean Conference on Human-Computer Interaction - ChileCHI 2013, no. 2241, pp. 24–29 (2013)
12. Vorvoreanu, M., Gray, C.M., Parsons, P., Rasche, N.: Advancing UX Education. In: Proceedings of 2017 CHI Conference on Human Factors in Computing Systems - CHI 2017, pp. 1441–1446 (2017)
13. Tahir, R., Arif, F.: A measurement model based on usability metrics for mobile learning user interface for children. Int. J. E-Learn. Edu. Technol. Digit. Media **1**(1), 16–31 (2015)
14. Wong, C.Y., Chu, K., Pauzi, M.A.M.: Advocating UX practice in industry: lessons learnt from UX innovate bootcamp. In: Proceedings of 2016 4th International Conference on User Science and Engineering i-USEr, pp. 204–209 (2017)
15. Al-Khalifa, H.S., Garcia, R.A.: Website design based on cultures: an investigation of saudis, filipinos, and indians government websites' attributes. In: Marcus, A. (ed.) DUXU 2014. LNCS, vol. 8518, pp. 15–27. Springer, Cham (2014). https://doi.org/10.1007/978-3-319-07626-3_2

16. Ariffin, S.A.: Needs and potentials for studying local malaysian culture through mobile learning. In: Proceedings of the 3rd International Conference on Human-Computer Interaction and User Experience in Indonesia - CHIuXiD 2017, no. Mcmc, pp. 60–66 (2017)

17. Nagalingam, V., Ibrahim, R.: A review of user experience (UX) frameworks for educational games, pp. 134–143 (2015)

18. Seol, S.H., Ko, D.S., Yeo, I.S.: UX analysis based on TR and UTAUT of sports smart wearable devices. KSII Trans. Internet Inf. Syst. **11**(8), 4162–4179 (2017)

19. Hussain, A., Mkpojiogu, E.O.C., Fadzil, N.M., Hassan, N.M.: The UX of amila pregnancy on mobile device. In: AIP Conference Proceedings, vol. 1891, p. 020061 (2017)

20. Mahlke, S., Thüring, M.: Studying antecedents of emotional experiences in interactive contexts. In: Proceedings of the SIGCHI Conference on Human Factors in Computing Systems - CHI 2007, p. 915 (2007)

21. Nagalingam, V., Ibrahim, R.: Finding the right elements user experience elements for educational games. In: Proceedings of 2017 International Conference on E-commerce, E-Business and E-Government, vol. Part F1296, pp. 90–93. ACM (2017)

22. Zhu, Z.-T., Yu, M.-H., Riezebos, P.: A research framework of smart education. Smart Learn. Environ. **3**(1), 4 (2016)

23. Patil, M.S., et al.: UX design to promote undergraduate projects to products: case study. In: Proceedings of - 2016 IEEE 4th International Conference on MOOCs, Innovation and Technology in Education MITE, pp. 302–307 (2017)

24. Yilmaz, R.M.: Educational magic toys developed with augmented reality technology for early childhood education. Comput. Hum. Behav. **54**, 240–248 (2016)

25. MacDonald, C.M., Rozaklis, L.: Assessing the implementation of authentic, client-facing student projects in user experience (UX) education: insights from multiple stakeholders. Proc. Assoc. Inf. Sci. Technol. **54**(1), 268–278 (2017)

26. Masood, M., Thigambaram, M.: The usability of mobile applications for pre-schoolers. Procedia - Soc. Behav. Sci. **197**(February), 1818–1826 (2015)

27. Park, J., Han, S.H., Kim, H.K., Oh, S., Moon, H.: Modeling user experience: a case study on a mobile device. Int. J. Ind. Ergon. **43**(2), 187–196 (2013)

28. Ibrahim, N., Fatimah, W., Ahmad, W., Shafie, A.: User experience study on folktales mobile application for children's education. In: Proceedings of - NGMAST 2015 9th International Conference on Next Generation Mobile Applications, Services and Technologies, pp. 353–358 (2016)

29. Sugiyama, Y., Kato, T., Sakamoto, T., Science, A.I.: A proposed quantitative UX analysis method based on a psychometric, no. 2008, pp. 434–443 (2018)

30. Hoehle, H., Venkatesh, V.: Mobile application usability : conceptualization & instrument development, vol. 39, no. 2, pp. 435–472 (2015)

31. Chau, C.L., Bers, M.U., Pott, M.: Positive technological development for young children in the context of children's mobile apps a dissertation submitted by Clement L. Chau in partial fulfillment of the requirement for the degree of Doctor of Philosophy in Child Development Tufts Unive (2014)

32. Patwardhan, M., Stoll, R., Hamel, D.B., Amresh, A., Gary, K.A., Pina, A.: Designing a mobile application to support the indicated prevention and early intervention of childhood anxiety. In: Proceedings of the Conference on Wireless Health - WH 2015, pp. 1–8 (2015)

33. Moreno, H.B.R., Ramirez, M.R., Rojas, E.M., Soto, M.D.C.S.: Digital education using apps for today's children. Iberian Conference on Information Systems and Technologies, vol. 2018-June, pp. 1–6 (2018)

34. Chuan, N.K., Sivaji, A., Loo, F.A., Ahmad, W.F.W., Nathan, S.S.: Evaluating 'Gesture Interaction' requirements of mobile applications for deaf users: discovering the needs of the hearing-impiared in using touchscreen gestures. In: 2017 IEEE Conference on Open Systems ICOS, pp. 90–95 (2018)

35. Fernandes, L., et al.: Bringing User Experience empirical data to gesture-control and somatic interaction in virtual reality videogames : an exploratory study with a multimodal interaction prototype (2015)

36. Ting, J., Jing, Y., Jianbo, X.: The application of multi-perception user experience in emotional design characteristics parameter models, pp. 424–427 (2018)

37. Dow, S., Gerber, E., Wong, A.: A pilot study of using crowds in the classroom. In: Proceedings of the SIGCHI Conference on Human Factors in Computing Systems - CHI 2013, p. 227 (2013)

38. Bano, M., Zowghi, D., Kearney, M., Schuck, S., Aubusson, P.: Mobile learning for science and mathematics school education: a systematic review of empirical evidence. Comput. Edu. **121**, 30–58 (2018)

39. Laine, T.H., Nygren, E., Dirin, A., Suk, H.J.: Science spots AR: a platform for science learning games with augmented reality. Educ. Technol. Res. Dev. **64**(3), 507–531 (2016)

40. Faily, S., Lyle, J., Flechais, I., Simpson, A., Fléchais, I., Simpson, A.: Usability and security by design: a case study in research and development. In: Proceedings of 2015 Workshop Usable Security (USEC 2015), p. 10 (2015)

41. Figueiredo, M., Solmaz, A., Rodrigues, J.: An interactive app for stem learning in mobile. Eurasia Proc. Educ. Soc. Sci. **4**, 465–470 (2016)

42. Heintz, M., Law, E.L.C.: Challenges and resolutions for engaging teachers and students in participatory design of online science learning resources. CEUR Workshop Proc. **1776**, 42–48 (2016)

43. Ni, Q., Yu, Y.: Research on educational mobile games and the effect it has on the cognitive development of preschool children. In: Third International Conference on Digital Information, Networking, and Wireless Communications, pp. 165–169 (2015)

44. Feldman, D.H.: Cognitive development in childhood. Handb. Psychol. **6**, 197–213 (2013)

45. Ellin Kotsky, S.: New Trends in Conceptual Representation: Challenges to Piaget's Theory - Google Books. Psychology Press (2013). Theory of cognitive development co. https://books.google.com.my/books?hl=en&lr=&id=24NqhCnc-hkC&oi=fnd&pg=PP1&dq=piaget%27s+theory+of+cognitive+development+comparison&ots=0iajXJa0yP&sig=FfjY5RWeeCmBr3KBw6Ni9TJZWO4&redir_esc=y#v=onepage&q=piaget's. Accessed 07 June 2018

46. Cherry, K.: Piaget's 4 Stages of Cognitive Development Explained (2018). https://www.verywellmind.com/piagets-stages-of-cognitive-development-2795457. Accessed 02 June 2018

47. Yin, R.K.: Case study research - design and methods. Clin. Res. **2**, 8–13 (2006)

eRMS for Research Management and Monitoring at Universiti Pertahanan Nasional Malaysia (UPNM)

Syahaneim Marzukhi[1]([⊠]), Hasmeda Erna Che Hamid[1],
Hafizah Ariff[2], Mohd Hakimi Ahmad Zainudin[1],
Nur Shazwani Abdul Latif[3], Nurul Fatehah Roslan[1],
and Ayuni Akmal Ramlee[1]

[1] Centre for Research and Innovation Management, Universiti Pertahanan
Nasional Malaysia, Kem Perdana Sungai Besi, 57000 Kuala Lumpur, Malaysia
syahaneim@upnm.edu.my
[2] Faculty of Defence Science and Technology, Universiti Pertahanan Nasional
Malaysia, Kem Perdana Sungai Besi, 57000 Kuala Lumpur, Malaysia
[3] Centre for Tropicalization, Universiti Pertahanan Nasional Malaysia, Kem
Perdana Sungai Besi, 57000 Kuala Lumpur, Malaysia

Abstract. Research and innovation development has become an important element besides teaching and learning for every university in Malaysia. Hence, the research activities carried out at NDUM need to be recorded and managed more efficiently on a regular basis. To date, managing of research at NDUM is conducted manually by the Research Management and Innovation (CRIM) staffs starting from research grant application until research completion. Therefore, Research Management System (eRMS) is developed to assist the process of managing and monitoring research activities and output at NDUM. eRMS consists of several modules including: grant application, grant registration, research monitoring, research reporting (i.e. financial, assets, budget), research output (i.e. publication, intellectual property and human capital) and dashboard of research project's achievement. The system is expected to enhance the performance and quality of research management effectively, as well as to reduce cost and time in managing research project at the CRIM.

Keywords: eRMS · CRIM · NDUM · Research activities

1 Introduction

Recently, research and development (R&D) and innovation has become an important element besides teaching and learning in every university in Malaysia. Moreover, apart from teaching and learning, research and development (R&D) and innovation is one of the main performance indicator for the university. Due to this circumstances, most universities and research institutes in Malaysia have established Research Management Centre to manage their research and development (R&D) and innovation activities. In addition, the management of research and development (R&D) and innovation has emerged as a specialized area within both funding agencies and higher education

© Springer Nature Switzerland AG 2019
H. Badioze Zaman et al. (Eds.): IVIC 2019, LNCS 11870, pp. 611–619, 2019.
https://doi.org/10.1007/978-3-030-34032-2_54

institutions [1]. Basically, research management will include activities as follows: attracting funding, managing funds, liaising with funding bodies, project planning, monitoring project implementation, budget and performance, and evaluating project. These activities are mostly arising on top of research activities itself in order to meet the research output and target such as publications, product, human capital and commercialization.

Thus, in order to execute this role, the Centre for Research Management and Innovation (CRIM) has been established at National Defense University of Malaysia (NDUM) as an entity that responsible in managing and monitoring research activities. Some of the activities include: grant applications, financial management and procurement for each research project, preparing progress report for each research project, maintaining and updating data of every research project (i.e. research graduates, publications and intellectual properties), and many others. Historically, NDUM was awarded with research grant since 2008, where the first research grant was the Sciencefund. From there, the research and development activities keep growing each year with more than 320 research projects were granted to NDUM until today. Here, information regarding the research projects is recorded and maintained by the CRIMs' staff to ensure the outputs and outcomes of the research activities are up to date. Regardless of advancement in current technology, some of the activities are still not adopting the latest technology to enhance the work performance. For example, some of the research management activities including registration of research proposal, reviewing, monitoring and reporting activities related to research projects are still perform manually using Microsoft Excel. Thus, the process become a daunting task for CRIMs' staff as the method is less effective and prone to errors [3]. Besides, the researcher for each research project needs to fill in various forms according to its purpose manually using pen and paper, where the chances of the forms might be missing and misplaced are high. Worst case scenario, when the information needed by the top management cannot be accessed immediately and efficiently. Thus, details report and achievement for each research project cannot be presented effectively.

With rapid advancement in technology, Management Information Systems (MIS) have been used globally to improve the daily work and manage task efficiently. MIS is the development and the use of information systems that help businesses achieve their goals and objectives [3]. Using MIS, the development of new and rich system which represents and meets requirement of different stakeholders is at ease [7]. Here, the system should be able to translate user requirement systematically and produced the results effectively. According to [1], MIS can provide a quick and efficient way on information collection, transmission, processing, storing, updating and maintenance. Some initial studies shown that implementation of management information systems have delivered impressive benefits to the organization in which the information can be access in a faster and easier way, provides better processing procedures and delivers accountability for effective corporate management [2].

Based on the above scenarios, there is a need to develop as system in order to assist the administration process of monitoring and managing research project more effectively and efficiently at NDUM. Thus, an initial system for managing and monitoring research project at NDUM has been developed. However, the system is not yet complete as there are many more modules are required. Therefore, the system will be further developed and tested as a platform in understanding the processes involved for managing and monitoring research activities at NDUM.

This paper gives an overview of the main design and implementation of Research Management System (eRMS) for managing and monitoring of research projects and activities at NDUM. The Research Management System (eRMS) was developed with the aim of addressing the issues described above. Some illustrations are also provided based on the systems' design.

2 Methodology

Structure, planning, and process of designing and developing eRMS concerned a detail and systematic approach to ensure that the system is successfully designed follows the outline objectives. The system development process follows the Rapid Application Development (RAD) model as a guideline. RAD is an approach to develop information system that promises better and cheaper systems, and more rapid deployment by having system developers and end users work together jointly in real-time to develop systems [5, 6]. RAD is chosen as a method to develop the research management system namely eRMS, as it requires minimum planning for rapid prototyping development. Based on [4], the author stated, RAD can offer faster development and give high quality system compared to traditional software development lifecycle such as SDLC. RAD consist of 4 main phases of RAD: (1) Requirement Planning Phase, (2) User Design Phase, (3) Construction Phase, and (4) Cutover Phase (see Fig. 1) [6, 9, 10].

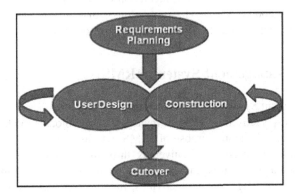

Fig. 1. Rapid Application Development (RAD) model [10].

Phase 1, is also known as the Concept Definition Phase, where this phase defines the business functions and data subject areas that the system will support and determine the system's scope. During this phase, the developers, the clients (e.g. the users), and the team members communicate to determine the goals and expectations for the project, as well as current and potential issues that would need to be addressed during the build [8]. The basic process of this phase involves: (1) investigating the current problem, (2) defining the requirements for the project, and (3) finalizing the requirements based on the team member's approval [8].

Phase 2, is also known as the Functional Design Phase. This stage uses workshops to model the system's data and processes, in order to build a working prototype of critical system components. During this phase, the clients work hand in hand with the developers to ensure their needs are being met at every step in the design process. The process is like a customizable software development, where the user can test each prototype of the product, at each stage, to ensure it meets their expectations. Here, the developer designs a prototype and the client tests it [8]. Next, they come together to communicate on what worked and what didn't, where this process worked out in an iterative process until they reach a satisfactory design.

Phase 3 takes the prototypes and beta systems from the previous phase and converts them into the working model. Phase 3, is also known as the Development Phase, this stage completes the construction of the physical application system, builds the conversion system, and develops user aids and implementation work plans. As the majority of the problems and changes were addressed during previous phase, thus, the developers can construct the final working model more quickly compared following a traditional project management approach. The process of this phase involves several smaller steps as the following: (1) preparation for rapid construction, (2) application and program development, (3) coding and (4) system integration and system testing [8]. Here, the software development team of programmers, coders, testers, and developers work together during this phase to ensure the system is working successfully and the end result satisfies the client's expectations and objectives.

Finally, Phase 4, takes the prototypes and beta systems from the design phase and converts them into the working model. This phase includes final user testing and training, data conversion, and the implementation of the application system. In short, RAD is the best method that can produces a system with dramatic savings in cost, time, and human efforts that is suitable for the development of eRMS.

3   Research Management System (eRMS)

Research Management System (eRMS) describes a solution that lets an enterprise level of the university especially the CRIM to manage and monitor research activities and resources efficiently. The main purpose of eRMS is to improve the work processes of managing research activities at the university through the web-based system. Here, eRMS is a complete web-based customized solution for the CRIM that enable the centre to effectively manage research activities, funding and grants, research projects, researcher's publications and ranking, and many others. The system has powerful-reporting tool to track all research activities that can be break down from all faculties and departments, and research projects of the university.

The system makes it easy for the CRIM to monitor and keep track of the information regarding research grants including activities, input and output, financial, assets, publications, and many others that is recorded accordingly in order to keep the information up-to-date following the university and Ministry of Education compliances. Generally, eRMS consists of several working modules including grant applications, grant registration, research monitoring, reporting (i.e. financial, assets, budget), research outputs (i.e. publications, intellectual property and human capital) and dashboard of full report of research's performance. eRMS lets the users sign-in to different enterprise modules and applications within his or her privileges. Further, eRMS is a highly versatile centralized system that enables user to build reports, carry out performance assessments, manage researcher profiles, enable research networking, and many more, while reducing administrative burden, cost and duration of a work process at the CRIM.

Figure 2 illustrates the main interface of the system that comprises of few modules. The interface is simple and easy to use. The system has two main users, either the CRIM staffs or the NDUM researcher. In order to access the system, every researcher needs to be registered to the system. Here, the researcher needs to provide all related information about the research project. The researcher is required to fill-in and complete the essential information (i.e. award, professional services, publication, supervision, intellectual property, gift, grant, networking, membership, knowledge transfer and joint research) and provides the evidence. On the other hand, the researcher can also view details of his or her research project (i.e. grant details, votes allocation and expenditure) and the research project's asset (i.e. name, serial number, price, invoice date, registration date, acceptance date) in order to monitor their research project closely (see Figs. 2, 3 and 4).

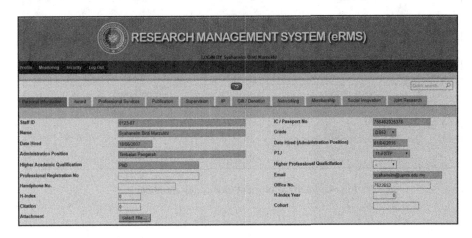

Fig. 2. Interface of research information for each researcher - by output.

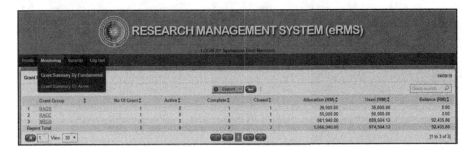

Fig. 3. Interface of research information for each researcher - by grant.

Based on these information, the CRIM staffs can monitor the output of each research project and generate report to give an overview of the university's performance in research and development. Figure 3 shows a reporting of the university's performance in research and development using a dashboard. Further, the CRIM staffs can monitor the status and the allocation of the research project effectively and efficiently. The dashboard displays the latest information regarding the status and the allocation of the research project for each faculty as the system is automatically linked to the treasurer's database for latest information (i.e. allocation and expenditure). Further, all the information (i.e. grant's allocation, grant's balance and expenditure) can be printed and saved using the system. Moreover, the CRIM staffs can also view details of the expenditure for each research project based on the selected criteria (see Figs. 5 and 6). Apart from that, the CRIM staffs can update and monitor the records of the assets for each research project using the system (see Fig. 7). Details of the asset can be recorded and uploaded using the system for proper documentation.

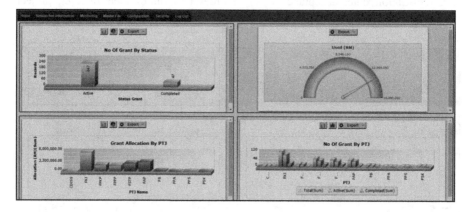

Fig. 4. Interface of grant monitoring dashboard.

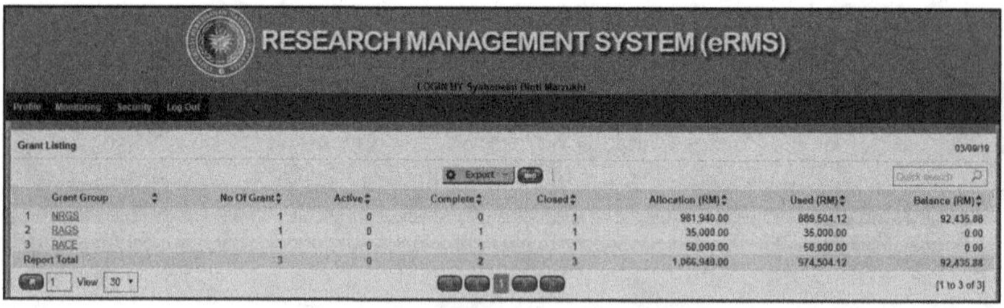

Fig. 5. Interface of research project expenditure by vote.

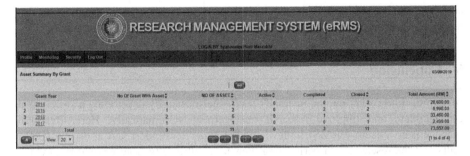

Fig. 6. Interface of research project asset by year.

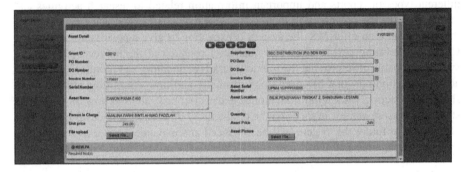

Fig. 7. Interface of asset registration for project research.

4   Discussion

Research Management System has been widely used by other universities and other higher education institutions in Malaysia to monitor research activities and output. Managing extremely complex research processes has been an important and crucial task in most research management centre. In NDUM, the research activity is moving at a fast pace, such that monitoring research activities and output become a challenging task to the CRIM staffs. This is due to the task of managing and administrating research activities and output has been carried out manually since 2008. Based on this scenario, the CRIM has taken an initiative to improve the research management process at NDUM through the web-based system known as eRMS. Findings show that the system be able to record, manage and monitor all research activities and output at NDUM effectively. Once the researcher has completed and fill-in his or her research project information (i.e. award, professional services, publication, supervision, intellectual property, gift, grant, networking, membership, and joint research) successfully, the system be able to collect the information related to the output of each researcher project and generate various types of report automatically. Besides that, the CRIM staffs and the researcher also have a privilege for an easy access to researcher project details including financial and asset for monitoring purposes. Thus, research achievement and performance (i.e. publication, intellectual property and human capital, project performance and activities) can be monitored throughout the research duration effectively.

5   Conclusion

An approach to overcome the manually task is performed by developing a system that can facilitate and improve research management systematically. Here, Research Management System (eRMS) is developed in order to support and assist the CRIM staffs and the researcher in performing their tasks efficiently from anywhere, anytime and any pace. The system enables the CRIM staffs to manage and monitor research activities and output including financial, effectively and efficiently. The generation of different types of reports and important information related to research activities and output, benefits the university in monitoring research progress and achievement. With the implementation of eRMS, the system is expecting to give a positive impact on the CRIM by elevating performance and quality of research at the university level. The system is capable of improving the previous task (i.e. updating and monitoring research activities and output) that has been done manually and time consuming efficiently. In short, the system gives a relief from a once exhausting task, as from now on the CRIM staffs and the researcher can focus on the productivity of research and development task effectively. In future the system will be enhanced and expanded into a more complete research management system where many other task can be performed strategically.

Acknowledgement. The authors would like to thank the National Defence University of Malaysia for the continuous support in financial, technical advises and the use of research facility in making eRMS come to reality.

References

1. Effectiveness of Research Innovation and Management at Policy and Institutional Levels: Cambodia, Malaysia, Thailand, Vietnam. https://www.oecd.org/sti/. Accessed 07 Aug 2017
2. Li, C., Wang, Z.: Research on the applications of information technology in sport management. In: Qu, X., Yang, Y. (eds.) IBI 2011. CCIS, vol. 268, pp. 247–252. Springer, Heidelberg (2012). https://doi.org/10.1007/978-3-642-29087-9_37
3. Kroenke, D.: Experiencing MIS, 7th edn. Pearson, Edinburgh (2016)
4. Abdul Kadhim, H., Bahari, M., Bakri, A., Ismail, W.: A research framework of electronic document management systems (EDMS) implementation process in government. J. Theor. Appl. Inf. Technol. **81**(3), 420–432 (2015)
5. Hoffer, J.A., George, J.F., Valacich, J.S.: Modern System Analysis and Design, 8th edn. Prentice Hall, Upper Saddle River (2017)
6. Martin, J.: Rapid Application Development. McMilan Publishing, New York (1991)
7. Poger, S., Schiaffino, R., Ricardo, C.: A software development project: a student-written assessment system. J. Comput. Sci. Coll. **20**(5), 229–238 (2005)
8. Rapid Application Development Methodology. https://www.lucidchart.com/blog/rapid-application-development-methodology. Accessed 01 Aug 2018

9. Beynon-Davies, P., Carne, C., Mackay, H., Tudhope, D.: Rapid application development (RAD): an empirical review. Eur. J. Inf. Syst. **8**, 211–223 (1999)

10. Naz, R., Khan, M.N.A.: Rapid application development techniques: a critical review. Int. J. Softw. Eng. Appl. **9**(11), 63–176 (2015)

The Importance of the Psychomotor Factors for Effective Learning Management System Use in TVET

Nor Azlan Ahmad[1], Nur Fazidah Elias[2(✉)],
and Noraidah Sahari@Ashaari[2]

[1] Universiti Islam Malaysia, Cyberjaya, Selangor, Malaysia
azlan@uim.edu.my
[2] Universiti Kebangsaan Malaysia, Bangi, Selangor, Malaysia
{fazidah,nsa}@ukm.edu.my

Abstract. This study discusses on psychomotor factors in the use of learning management system (LMS) at polytechnic institutions in Malaysia. The use of LMS system in conventional education focuses more on cognitive and effective factors. This is different in the technical and vocational education which emphasizes on affective and psychomotor factors. This study will investigate the important of these two factors by conducting a literature review using terms such as practical training, vocational training, and technical education. Findings from this study will provide an insight for policy makers, software developers and related agencies to improve existing LMS systems for effective education and teaching using LMS in the field of TVET.

Keywords: Psychomotor · LMS · TVET · Technical and vocational

1 Introduction

Technical and vocational education training (TVET) plays an important role in providing skilled manpower needed by the country. To become a developed nation by 2020, Malaysia is targeting 50% of its workers are skilled workers to be at par with Singapore, Korea and Taiwan [1]. The Malaysia Education Blueprint 2013–2025 states the importance of future technical and vocational learning development. One of these plans is to change the perception of the community towards technical and vocational education and training [2]. In addition, highly skilled and experience instructors in the field of TVET is extremely poor in the national education system [3]. Great emphasis on improving the quality of education and skill-based training, increasing the awareness as well as improving the perception of TVET and strengthen the collaboration with industries for better recognition were among the further steps to be taken. In realising these steps, Malaysian government has allocated RM30 million of the 2019 budget through Dana Wibawa Pendidikan TVET, 20 million for Boot camp TVET programme and RM400 million to strengthen research activity among university in Malaysia.

© Springer Nature Switzerland AG 2019
H. Badioze Zaman et al. (Eds.): IVIC 2019, LNCS 11870, pp. 620–627, 2019.
https://doi.org/10.1007/978-3-030-34032-2_55

This paper will discuss the implementation of learning management system (LMS) and it uses at polytechnic in Malaysia. Currently, there is no guidelines in designing effective LMS for TVET use. Many available standard or models focus on cognitive domain which is not suitable for TVET in Malaysia. In this study, psychomotor element is consider as the education that relates to practical-centred teaching and as a foundation for lecturer in developing existing techniques and skills. The lecturer can share and facilitate students in understanding the theory element and learned skills [4]. Vocational education is more focused on knowledge and skills. Teaching and learning in vocational education involves psychomotor aspects where it provides students with physical activity [4].

2 Research Background in TVET LMS

Implementation of LMS in TVET in Malaysia has started in December 2012 by the Department of Polytechnics Malaysia through the introduction of the CIDOS System at all polytechnics in Malaysia. Unlike conventional teaching and learning, technical and vocational education training emphasizes on technical aspects with at least 70% of vocational training and 30% of theory [4]. It involves learning technological knowledge and technical skills simultaneously [5].

A study conducted by Romli [6] with the accountancy student at POLIMAS polytechnics found that the students were satisfied with LMS and also suggested further studies to investigate the effectiveness of LMS use among students in engineering. Some researchers also agree most student seem to have sufficient internet experience and this could help them to use LMS without facing many problem [7].

The online learning method use Learning Management Systems (LMS) targeting the students and lecturers. Implementation of LMS at technical and vocational institutions is different from other conventional educational institutions as the technical institution's education not only emphasizes on cognitive skills but also emphasizes on technical skills (psychomotor) and self-help factors [8]. Based on the survey conducted at Politeknik Seberang Perai, there were evidence of decreasing use of LMS from the year 2015 to 2018 (Table 1).

Table 1. Student Using Learning Management Systems (LMS) in Politeknik Seberang Perai, Penang

(2015–2018)	
Year	Total access by user
2018	301,633
2017	182,275
2016	199,243
2015	231,033

Based on Table 1, usage of LMS at the polytechnic is still not sufficient. Studies on LMS in polytechnics was carried out by earlier researchers to study on system use by either the lecturers or the students [6, 9, 10]. However, there are not many studies that were conducted in identifying the effective elements of LMS. LMS learning in TVET differs from conventional LMS learning because in the technical and vocational fields technical aspects of learning are more emphasizes [11]. Elements such as system quality, quality of information and the quality of service should be looked at in the context of learning in the field of TVET. This will then affect the user's satisfaction and increase the benefits of TVET as educational institutions as a whole. A study by Pireva, Imran and Dalipi [12] found that despite many improvements that have been made in the development of the LMS, there are still a number of shortcomings involving the content and selection of course materials, better material content arrangements, frequent exchange and adaptation syllabuses ontology. This is a bit of a nuisance to those who have limited time and those who lack the skills in ICT.

3   Measuring Effective Use of LMS TVET

Although there have been many studies conducted on the use of Learning Management Systems (LMS), only a few have listed important elements and are somewhat underdeveloped involving institutions technical and vocational education [3, 13–15]. According to Ramírez-correa et al. [16] the high level of user's satisfaction will ensure that the systems is maximized and provides overall benefits continuously.

In this paper, important psychomotor factors were identified by conducting a literature review using terms that are relevant in the area of interest of this study such as TVET, LMS, information system, system quality, practical education, training information system and vocational learning system. The searching process was conducted in a wide range of online databases such as IEEE Xplore digital library, Wiley Online Library, Science Direct, Google scholar, Citeseerx, ResearchGate, and Springer link.

The study conducted by Muhammad and Cavus [17] states that accessibility, appropriateness, evaluation tools, learning, multilateral support, mobile, reliability, safety, support, sustainability, usability and user satisfaction should be considered in evaluating effective LMS to meet the needs of users (i.e. students, lecturers, or educational institutions). Among these features, learning, reliability, usability, and user satisfaction should be given the highest priority in evaluating effective LMS. Moreover, current LMS need to be updated from time to time because user's needs changed in parallel with the changes and advances of technology [18].

Accordingly to Markova et al. [19], challenges such as inferiority, lack of control over lecturers, less effective interactions and sense of separation reduce the level of users satisfaction with online learning experience. This is supported by a study on 286 students regarding factors affecting the user to use the LMS using the Technology Acceptance Model (TAM) that users feel unhappy in using LMS and consequently affect their interest in using LMS [20].

There is also a study stating that the elements of system quality and information quality are important elements that influence users in using the LMS [21]. The biggest challenge of e-learning implementation in technical and vocational education is the development of technology, human resource development, infrastructure development, economic issues, management and policy [3].

4 Psychomotor Aspects in TVET

According to Yasak and Alias [3], previous researches focused more on cognitive aspects and paid less attention to psychomotor aspects. Teaching in vocational education should focus not only on knowledge and but also on skills. Psychomotor is an important aspect that should be emphasized in teaching competency in vocational education. Teaching based on psychomotor is a way to provide students with the hands on skills [4].

Finding from a study [22] shown that the implementation of LMS in vocational education has increased student knowledge and technical skill. Student would independently use the technology, completing or performing tasks more obediently, more creative, disciplined and responsible. This is in contrast to Direct Learning Method (DLM) students who were more dependent on teachers and tend to be less developed.

Many previous studies indicated that the conventional education ignores two importance domain which is psychomotor and effective domain [23]. The study by Olivos et al. [24] states that the practical activities and facilities provided at educational institutions are the best aspects of training and identify the extent to which theoretical explanations are understood by the students. Students who are involved with physical activity and assisted by instructors and quality media materials further encourage good relationships and enhance their satisfaction in the use of e-learning systems [25]. This will fulfill the needs of local industries that require graduates with technical skills and not looking for competent workers from overseas [26, 27].

There is also a researcher that states rather than the psychomotor domain, the integration of information technology in education is more focused on cognitive domain [3], though previous study also noted that for those involved in more complex technical fields such as aviation and surgery will also affect the development of their psychomotor domain. Moreover, a study by De Compos et al. [28] has stated that the psychomotor domain are closely related to the motor characteristics and that the movement-mind relationship is related to basic activities. Therefore, the understanding of the psychomotor needs in TVET is necessary to be done.

Knowledge of technical skills is also necessary for TVET lecturers, those with training and skills that are capable for teaching well. Among the key challenges faced by TVET lecturers are lack of exposure to teaching, lack of experience and workload that leads lecturers to have less approach in teaching. Teaching methods are the same as conventional teaching in the classroom but lecturers need to play an active role and strategy [29]. Another study also stated that TVET lecturers need to have cognitive behavior, pedagogy and psychomotor competence [30]. This view is also supported by Yasak and Alias [3], which states that the use of ICT in TVET education will stimulate students to actively use cognitive and psychomotor domains. One of the studies made reference to the Taxonomy Psychomotor Harrow (1972) which explained the psychomotor aspect clearly (see Fig. 1). This taxonomy model is related to mastery of physical skills ranging from reflexive movement to exhibiting appropriate body language [31].

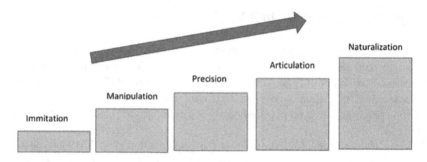

Fig. 1. Taxonomy Psychomotor Harrow (1972) [31].

The study conducted by [32] shows that imitation, manipulation, accuracy, articulation and naturalization with the support of proper teaching and learning strategies can provide more impact to students learning. Detailed description of various elements of psychomotor learning domain descriptors is depicted in Table 2.

Table 2. Psychomotor Learning Domain Descriptor

Level	Category of level	Behaviours descriptor
1	Imitation	Copy action of another; observe and replicate
2	Manipulation	Reproduce activity from instruction or memory
3	Precision	Execute skill reliably, independent of help
4	Articulation	Adapt and integrate expertise to satisfy a non-standard objective
5	Naturalization	Automated, unconscious mastery of activity and related skills at strategic level

There are two other factors that are considered to be important for effective LMS.

4.1 Motivation

Motivation is an important factor in ensuring the success of the LMS [32]. Motivation can be divided into intrinsic and extrinsic, where intrinsic motivation refers to motivation that comes internally and is done without expecting rewards and interests [33]. Extrinsic refers to external factors affecting users such as grades and rewards that provide satisfaction and enjoyment to the user even though the information technology element itself does not give satisfaction as expected [34]. A study done by Kuo et al. [35] states that the effectiveness of computer systems use is one of the key factors in achieving sustainable ICT learning. Harandi [36] conducted a study at the University of Tehran Alzahra, Iran found that the use of e-learning has increased student's motivation in learning. According to Olivos et al. [24] motivation has a significant impact on the transfer of learning gained through the practice of laboratories. Furthermore, a study that was conducted on the use of smartphones by UTHM engineering students, also found that student's motivation for online learning was high which improved the skill of compiling, making students more responsible. Yilmaz [37] suggested that motivation, computer systems, internet and online communication independently, is an important predictor of student satisfaction.

4.2   Self-discipline

Motivation and self-discipline are two important factors that influence success [34, 38, 39]. Self-discipline means the ability to control feelings and overcome weaknesses (Oxford 2016). Self-discipline can also be defined as self-control, the ability to avoid any negative in the treatment [38]. Those students with a much better level of self-discipline are able to control their daily activities, avoid problems, overcome tasks and overcome possible difficulties in tasks. They are trying to find solutions and the ability to control themselves. Research is also intended to examine the motivation and self-discipline of lecturers and students in online teaching and learning. According to Ogrizek et al. [32], there is a high level of rejection of interest and motivation in online learning and teaching.

5   Conclusion

This paper discussed the important of psychomotor and other factors for effective use of LMS in technical and vocational education training (TVET) fields. Previous works have suggested that psychomotor factors are important as well as other quality factors such as information quality, system quality and service quality. Moreover, other factors such as motivation and self-discipline can increase the effectiveness of LMS in TVET. This research is a part of ongoing research that focuses on identifying important factors for effective implementation of LMS that will not just emphasize on the IS success factors but will incorporate the psychomotor factors. The factor presented in this paper will be tested with other success factors (i.e. DeLone & McLean, Davis) to provide an overarching view of what an effective LMS TVET should be.

References

1. Jalani, N.H.: TEVT di Malaysia: Cabaran dan harapan. In: Seminar Kebangsaan Majlis Dekan-Dekan Pendidikan Awam 2015, pp. 340–346 (2015)
2. Yunos, J.M., Lai, C.S., Hamdan, N.H.: Changes and challenges in sustainability of technical and vocational education and training – teacher education programme: a case study. In: IEEE 8th International Conference on Engineering Education (ICEED), Langkawi, pp. 80–85 (2016)
3. Yasak, Z., Alias, M.: ICT Integrations in TVET: is it up to expectations? Procedia – Soc. Behav. Sci. **204**, 88–97 (2015)
4. Mohamad, M.M., Bakar, N.A., Sulaiman, N.L., Salleh, K.M., Sern, L.C.: Applying standard competency assessment in vocational teaching practices. Can. Center Sci. Educ. **11**(24), 216–223 (2017)

5. Ismail, A., Hassan, R., Masek, M., Hamzah, N., Ismail, I.M., Subramaniam, T.S.: Implementation of vocational training into TVET teacher program for national core standard. In: IEEE 8th International Conference on Engineering Education (ICEED), Langkawi, pp. 28–31 (2016)

6. Romli, R.: Implementation of CIDOS (E-Learning) among diploma in accountancy students in politeknik Sultan Abdul Halim Mu 'adzam Shah, Jitra Kedah. In: National Innovation and Invention Competition Through Exhibition (iCompEx 2016), Kedah, pp. 1–8 (2016)

7. Baleghi-zadeh, S., Ayub, A.F.M., Mahmud, R., Daud, S.M.: An assessment of task-technology fit, subjective norm and internet experience of learning management system in views of Malaysian higher education students. Int. J. Inf. Commun. Technol. Res. 4(4), 142–146 (2014)

8. Azlim, M., Amran, M., Rusli, M.R.: Utilization of educational technology to enhance teaching practices: case study of community college in Malaysia. Procedia – Soc. Behav. Sci. 195, 1793–1797 (2015)

9. Makzin, N.: Pelaksanaan pembelajaran melalui Curriculum Information Document Online System (CIDOS) dalam memperkasakan pengajaran pensyarah di Politeknik. MSc. Thesis, Universiti Tun Hussien Onn, Batu Pahat, Johor (2016)

10. Shida, N., Osman, S., Halim, A., Sultan, P.I.: Students' perceptions of the use of asynchronous discussion forums, quizzes, and uploaded resources. Int. J. Eng. Technol. 7, 201–204 (2018)

11. Buntat, Y., Sihes, A.J., Hassan, W.N.M.W., Jabor, M.K., Aziz, A.A.: A review of transforming TVET education in Malaysia: issues and challenges, pp. 1–4. American Scientific Publishers, Valencia (2015)

12. Pireva, K., Imran, A.S., Dalipi, F.: User behaviour analysis on LMS and MOOC. In: IEEE Conference on e-Learning, e-Management and e-Services, pp. 21–26. IEEEXplore, Melaka (2015)

13. Abdelhak, A., Mohammed, T., Mohammed, R., Khalid, S., Abderrahim, T.: Quality management in vocational training: evaluation of a specialized institution in ICT. Procedia – Soc. Behav. Sci. 191, 1928–1933 (2015)

14. Aydin, S., Arpaz, E., Koparan, B.: Online learning in vocational school: focus on students' perceptions. Procedia – Soc. Behav. Sci. 174, 3663–3667 (2015)

15. Musid, N.A., Affandi, H.M., Husain, S.H., Kamal, M.F.M., Abas, N.H.: The development of on job training assessment constructs and elements for construction technology students in Malaysian vocational college. J. Tech. Educ. Train. 11(1), 26–35 (2019)

16. Ramírez-correa, P.E., Rondan-cataluña, F.J., Arenas-gaitán, J., Alfaro-perez, J.L.: Telematics and informatics moderating effect of learning styles on a learning management system's success. J. Telematics Infom. 34, 272–286 (2017)

17. Muhammad, M.N., Cavus, N.: Fuzzy DEMATEL method for identifying LMS evaluation criteria. Procedia Comput. Sci. 120, 742–749 (2017)

18. Almarashdesh, I., Elias, N.F., Sahari, N., Mat Zin, N.: Development of an interactive learning management system for Malaysian distance learning institutions. Middle-East J. Sci. Res. 14(11), 1471–1479 (2013)

19. Markova, T., Glazkova, I., Zaborova, E.: Quality issues of online distance learning. Procedia – Soc. Behav. Sci. 237, 685–691 (2017)

20. Al-gahtani, S.S.: Empirical investigation of e-learning acceptance and assimilation: a structural equation model. Appl. Comput. Inform. 12(1), 27–50 (2016)

21. Mohammadi, H.: Computers in human behavior investigating users' perspectives on e-learning: an integration of TAM and IS success model. Comput. Hum. Behav. 45, 359–374 (2015)

22. Joko, Wulandari, G.S.: The development of learning management system using Edmodo. In: IOP Conference Series: Materials Science and Engineering, vol. 336. IOP Publishing, Surabaya (2018)
23. Ahmad, A., Latib, N.A.: Teaching in automotive practical task: practices in vocational colleges. Procedia – Soc. Behav. Sci. **204**, 290–299 (2015)
24. Olivos, P., Santos, A., Martín, S., Canas, M., Gómez-lázaro, E., Maya, Y.: The relationship between learning styles and motivation to transfer of learning in a vocational training programme. Suma Psicologica **23**, 25–32 (2016)
25. Stănescu, M., Musat, N.: Quality analysis model of the e-learning training system for sports occupations. Procedia – Soc. Behav. Sci. **180**, 1351–1356 (2015)
26. Buntat, Y., Jabor, M.K., Lenni, L., Ahmad, A.S., Rahman, R.A.: Technical Skills Valued by Employers: A Review, pp. 14–17. American Scientific Publishers, Valencia (2015)
27. Mukhtar, M.I., Ahmad, J.: Assessment for learning: practice in TVET. Procedia – Soc. Behav. Sci. **204**, 119–126 (2015)
28. De Campos, P.R.B., Neto, E.D.B.C., Moreno, U.F.: Proposal of a new taxonomy of the psychomotor domain for the engineering laboratory. In: 3rd International Conference of the Portuguese Society for Engineering Education (CISPEE), pp. 1–8. IEEEXplore, Aviero (2018)
29. Yusof, Y., Roddin, R., Awang, H.: What students need, and what teacher did: the impact of teacher's teaching approaches to the development of students' generic competences. Procedia – Soc. Behav. Sci. **204**, 36–44 (2015)
30. Cakrawati, D., Handayani, S., Handayani, M.N.: Model of learning implementation in preparing vocational teachers. In: 3th UPI International Conference on Technical and Vocational Education and Training (TVET), pp. 50–53. Atlantis Press (2016)
31. Reeves, T.C.: How do you know they are learning? The importance of alignment in higher education. Int. J. Learn. Technol. **2**(4), 294–309 (2014)
32. Ogrizek, I., Lackovi, S., Jurina, K.: Successful and proactive e-learning environment fostered by teachers' motivation in technology use. Procedia – Soc. Behav. Sci. **174**, 3656–3662 (2015)
33. Fabito, B.S.: Exploring critical success factors of mobile learning as perceived by students of the College of Computer Studies - National University. In: International Conference on Soft Computing, Intelligent System and Information Technology, pp. 220–226. IEEE (2017)
34. Mohamad, S.N.M., Salleh, M.A.M., Salam, S.: Factors affecting lecturers motivation in using online teaching tools. Procedia – Soc. Behav. Sci. **195**, 1778–1784 (2015)
35. Kuo, F.Y., Tseng, F.C., Lin, C.I.C., Tang, W.H.: Critical success factors for motivating and sustaining women's ICT learning. Comput. Educ. **67**, 208–218 (2013)
36. Harandi, S.R.: Effects of e-learning on students' motivation. Procedia – Soc. Behav. Sci. **181**, 423–430 (2015)
37. Yilmaz, R.: Computers in human behavior exploring the role of e-learning readiness on student satisfaction and motivation in flipped classroom. Comput. Hum. Behav. **70**, 251–260 (2017)
38. Gorbunovs, A., Kapenieks, A., Cakula, S.: Self-discipline as a key indicator to improve learning outcomes in e-learning environment. Procedia – Soc. Behav. Sci. **231**, 256–262 (2016)
39. Copriady, J.: Self-motivation as a mediator for teachers' readiness in applying ICT in teaching and learning. Turk. Online J. Educ. Technol. **13**(4), 115–123 (2014)

Identifying Suitable Icon Button for Museum Application Interface Using Online Card Sorting Method

Fasihah Mohammad Shuhaili$^{(\boxtimes)}$, Suziah Sulaiman,
Dayang Rohaya Awang Rambli, and Saipunidzam Mahamad

Universiti Teknologi PETRONAS, 32610 Seri Iskandar, Perak, Malaysia
{fasihah_g03599, suziah, dayangrohaya.ar,
saipunidzam_mahamad}@utp.edu.my

Abstract. A good interface is made up of components that allow users to readily comprehend the conceptual model and know what interacting on an interface is like. There are many graphical components in an interface to help user interacts which include icon buttons. The countless number and range of icon buttons comes with a need to define the most appropriate set for the interface of museum implementation. This paper presents a card sorting method that uses feedback from users to obtain an efficient classification of possible navigation structure icon buttons. It interprets the exploratory analysis of a histogram matrix related to the final categories of cards used in the study. It focuses on the details of making a decision about the final categories and associated labels. It also helps in making an informed judgment when multiple interpretations of data are possible. The study findings suggest that "play, pause and stop", "speaker", and "video", the icon representation on the buttons could be a set of potential signifier for a museum interface.

Keywords: Signifier · Icon button · Card sorting · Museum application · Exploratory analysis

1 Introduction

A good interface consists of elements that enable users to understand the conceptual model easily, and to know what it is like to interact on an interface. It involves the best way of presenting information on the screen, thus enabling users to perform their tasks, including determining how structure menus make navigation options, designing icons and other graphical elements to be easily recognized and understood [1]. There are various graphical elements that should be in the interface include input controls, navigational and information components to support user interaction on the interface. These graphical elements include signifier, previously known as perceivable affordance.

Signifier shows the possible actions that users can take with it that is simply put what the object can afford to the users. It is regarded as a key priority for interfaces that provide meaningful information for better understanding on the displayed information, thereby help to improve interaction. Several researchers [2–4] have reported that a

© Springer Nature Switzerland AG 2019
H. Badioze Zaman et al. (Eds.): IVIC 2019, LNCS 11870, pp. 628–639, 2019.
https://doi.org/10.1007/978-3-030-34032-2_56

common signifier used within a museum application is icon buttons. There are many variations of icon buttons for interfaces but identifying the most suitable set for the museum applications is still required. Such an identification could be done using card sorting method, which in this case employs users' input to help derive an effective classification of possible icon buttons for navigation structure.

In this paper, suitable icon buttons will be determined to be applied into a museum application. Icon button is an important signifier for the interface. It will assure a user will handle the device accordingly and acknowledge interaction to happen. The signifier is a basic element needed in designing interface. Good signifiers literally keep the users' focus on learning. Weak interface design could affect process of learning by lagging the progress, causing complication and problem in navigating the interface [5].

Throughout this paper, card sorting technique will be used to determine the suitable icon buttons for the museum environment. The technique provides an insight into the participants' categorization and idea of the items represented on the cards [6]. Open card sorting is applied in which participants are to sort items into the categories that make sense to them, and label each category by themselves. Percentages are calculated for the presumed categories before decision could be made on the chosen icon buttons. Besides, card sorting also reveals the intuitiveness of the information architecture [7].

2   Background

2.1   The Importance of Signifier in Interface Design

Signifier is a term used by researchers to point out the perceivable signal of input interaction in an interface. Signifier refers to any mark, sound or perceivable indicator that signal possible action that should be done. In virtual environment, signifier is fundamentally far important principle than affordance to manifest a good design [8]. Moreover, signifier should be something that is easily to discover. The ability to discover the signifier illustrates a good interface design. Some common signifiers come in the form of drawings, labels, and signs such as the signs labelled "push," "pull," or "exit" on doors, or arrows, and diagrams. The display helps in considering what is to be acted upon or in which direction to gesture, or other instructions [9]. Signifier should have the ability to make users discover and assist them on what should be done next.

Signifier is considered as a critical part in designing interface as it will assure a user to handle the device accordingly and acknowledge interaction to happen. The signifier is a basic element needed in designing interface whereas good signifiers literally keep the users' focus on learning while weak interface design could affect process of learning by lagging the progress, causing complication and problem in navigating the interface. There are a few typical signifiers that are likely to be used by users which are; (1) clickable buttons; sometime user tend to waste time looking for object to click because the button did not indicate the ability to click properly; (2) underlined text for linked content; it is encouraged by usability expert for interface designer not to simply underline text for other purposes, otherwise it will create wrong expectation [5].

2.2   Card Sorting

Card sorting is a popular research method that helps to derive an effective information representation [10]. It is a tool that helps user to understand well the contextual of the information and also gives insight to designer on how the users might think. Card sorting enable user to explore the various ways the card items could be categorized and identify the best possible category.

Card sorting can be conducted in two ways, open or closed card sorting. In an open card sorting, users will be given a set of cards with some contents written on it. Users will be then asked to sort the cards into groups according to what's similar and describe the group they make. For a closed card sorting, a set of contents card and categories are given to the users, then they are required to sort the cards into the predetermined categories. A minimum of 30 contents items is sufficient to prevent overlap while creating the groups [11]. It may sound easy yet a strong approach when choosing the best categorization for information representation. A minimum number of participants needed to produce an effective organization is estimated in the range of 20 to 30 persons. A graph proves the reasonable correlation obtained from the range of 20 to 30 are very similar to that derived from the full set of participants [12].

Although the technique is simple to conduct, the preparation of cards and consecutive analysis of the data may seem endless and time consuming [6]. There are two methods of analysis that can be used: exploratory, and statistical. Both approaches help to track the key patterns in the data and acquire useful observation for the research. Exploratory analysis acquires small amount of data while statistical method particularly useful when huge of data being involved [11]. This paper practices exploratory analysis due to its small data involved.

Before carrying out an exploratory analysis, the details collected should encompass all the different areas that are being explored. These include analyzing the groups, card placement, labels, organizational schemes, how accurately people have grouped content and participants' comments. By the end of the analysis, a percentage of how often a card was placed in a category could be obtained. The analysis will identify potential high confidence icon button (75% agreement), moderate confidence icon button (50%–75% agreement) and low icon button agreement (less than 50% agreement) too [13]. One might see the difference of what they thought and what the participants actually did. Besides, one could determine the content if it is evenly distributed between categories or being clumped in a few.

Statistical analysis is useful when huge data is involved. This approach is able to identify the existence of a particular pattern in the data as well as to determine the most consistent pattern. There are several statistical methods that could be used to analyze the card sorting data, for example, K-means cluster analysis, hierarchical cluster analysis (HCA) and multidimensional scaling (MDS). These three approaches are widely available in statistical software where the output can be presented visually [11]. Statistical analysis may look tricky but it can highlight trends and connection that may not be noticed during exploratory analysis. The analysis should be run more than once to find similarities and differences of the results.

3   Methodology

3.1   Participants

Twenty-one students from a few local universities in Malaysia participated in the card sorting study. The participants were from adult group and have experiences using touch-operated devices. Nine of the participants were involved in industrial field. All of them were range between 18 to 28 years old and were randomly picked.

3.2   Materials

Thirty icon buttons selected for this study were extracted from literatures that involve multi-touch applications. There are three main fields created which are medical, education, and leisure and entertainment [14]. For medical part, there is a total of four icon buttons being derived. Education field consists of eighteen icon buttons, while leisure and entertainment have eight.

The online card sorting is being conducted through Optimal Workshop (www.optimalworkshop.com) that offers suite of tools to find out how people think the content should be organized. This website was chosen based on its friendly features and various options offered. However, there are limitations of ten users per survey allowed. Thus, the survey may have to be divided into three surveys. By that, a total of 30 participants will be collected. However, the challenge is to present the overall result since the result can display ten surveys only. To overcome this problem, another website (www.usabilititest.com) was used. This website is able to support up to hundred participants.

3.3   Online Card Procedure

Card sorting can be done either using physical card or online version. This is because there is no difference in utilizing either one of the methods with respect to the reliability of the results. However, the online version of card sorting technique is capable to save time and effort for the researchers and practitioners [6]. In this study, the participants were required to access into the card sorting web. When they accessed into the website, a brief of explanation was displayed as general instructions to the study. In general, the study took less than ten minutes to complete. The participants were advised to take their time and carefully decide on the category of the card. They were informed that there were no correct or wrong answers on the card sort, and they just need to do it naturally.

The participants were later given some instructions which required them to look at a list of 30 icon buttons on the left pane of the web. Figure 1 shows an illustration of the instructions while Fig. 2 shows a small part of the interface consisting of several icon buttons on the left pane and three predetermined groups. The participants were asked to drag and sort all the 30 icon buttons into three different fields on the right side of the interface. They are required to sort the icon buttons based on the given description of each field. They have been informed that one field might have more than one icon button. The participants were also given an opportunity to create labels with no restrictions. The sorting is dependent on participants' decision on which field that they feel the icon button should be.

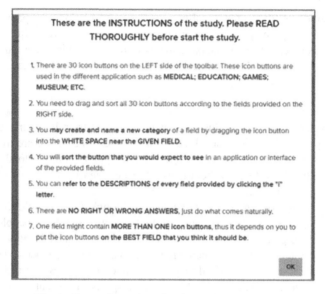

Fig. 1. Instructions given for the card sorting activity

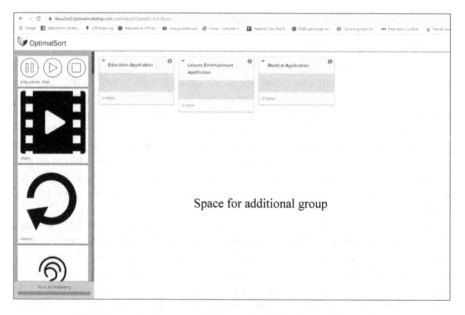

Fig. 2. Icon buttons on the left pane and the given field groups

4   Result and Discussion

Card sorting is a method that generates a whole structure of information and suggestion of topic agreement for navigation, menus and any possible taxonomies. Heuristic guideline for topic agreement suggested to use spreadsheet to interpret the card agreement.

	card index	card label	category label
1			
2	4	play, pause, stop	Leisure Entertainment Application
3	27	restaurant	Leisure Entertainment Application
4	15	home	Leisure Entertainment Application
5	28	go	Leisure Entertainment Application
6	26	taxi	Leisure Entertainment Application

Fig. 3. Card index, card label and category label

Figure 3 shows some samples of the card index, card label and category label being the input for the first, second and third column, respectively. It presents the data collected of one participant. Card index represents the card number in the queue of card sorting online while category label is either the existing predetermined categories or the categories that the participants created.

Figure 4 shows the tabulated data collected from some of the participants. Findings from each participant are presented in the respective columns after card index and card label columns. In this example, column called sort 1, sort 2, and sort 3 consist of results from participants 1, 2, and 3, respectively. With this tabulated data, it is possible to view all the categories created by each participant and see how the cards being distributed. The collected categories that bring a same meaning were then being group and change into a consistent category label. It were created based on similar word and idea. This is because, participants tend to create a different categories although they referred to a same subject. For example, most participants sorted card index number 29 into a same category that is leisure entertainment application. One participant, however, created a new category called 'movie' for this card instead. This example shows the need to standardize the label name so that identification of co-occurrence of the cards in one category could be made.

card index	card label	sort 1	sort 2	sort 3
4	play, pause, stop	Leisure Entertainment Application	Leisure Entertainment Application	Leisure Entertainment Application
27	restaurant	Leisure Entertainment Application	Leisure Entertainment Application	Leisure Entertainment Application
15	home	Leisure Entertainment Application	Education Application	medical application
28	go	Leisure Entertainment Application	Leisure Entertainment Application	Leisure Entertainment Application
26	taxi	Leisure Entertainment Application	Transportation application	transportation
3	snowflake	Leisure Entertainment Application	Nature	nature
8	image	Leisure Entertainment Application	Leisure Entertainment Application	Leisure Entertainment Application
11	information	Leisure Entertainment Application	Education Application	education application
7	search	Medical Application	Education Application	medical application
14	ear	Medical Application	Medical Application	Leisure Entertainment Application
25	delete	Medical Application	Education Application	education application
29	first aid	Medical Application	Medical Application	medical application
30	cut	Medical Application	Medical Application	education application

Fig. 4. Examples of data collected from the participants

The co-occurrence of a card could be displayed in various visualization method. There are many qualitative and quantitative analytical methods that could be used such as dendrograms, similarity matrix, word frequency cloud, and histograms matrix. Different methods resulted in different analysis for display based on their purpose. In this study, histogram matrix is applied to display the participant's card agreement in specific subject areas. The co-occurrence of the card is used to show the card agreement across participants. The value of the co-occurrence is used to measure the confidence level that will assist to determine the strength of the relationship between two cards or the validity of a card or subject [13]. Higher confidence shows higher agreement between participants. Table 1 shows the co-occurrence of a card within the related fields.

The analysis started by analyzing the groups that participants have created. This is to figure out how the participants thought and categorized the cards. Table 1 shows how often a card was placed in a category. The first column presents all 30 cards used in the study. The second, third, and forth are the pre-defined categories i.e. *medical*, *education*, and *leisure entertainment*, given to the participants for the card sort activities. Seven new groups were created by the participants. These new groups were quite diverse which indicate that they are many ways the card content could be grouped. The seven new groups are: *transportation, nature, information, navigation, users support, software and editing* and *education and leisure entertainment*.

Table 1. The co-occurrence of the card in a category

	Medical	Education	Leisure entertainment	Transportation	Nature	Information	Navigation	Users support	Software & editing	Education, leisure entertainment
play, pause, stop	0	1	28	0	0	0	0	0	0	1
speaker	0	5	25	0	0	0	0	0	0	0
video	1	6	23	0	0	0	0	0	0	0
eraser	0	29	0	0	0	0	0	0	1	0
print	1	26	1	0	0	1	0	0	1	0
copy	3	24	2	0	0	0	0	0	1	0
search	9	14	4	0	0	0	1	1	1	0
delete	3	14	7	0	0	2	3	0	0	1
help	8	13	4	0	0	1	3	1	0	0
information	5	13	6	0	0	0	3	0	2	1
ear	18	8	4	0	0	0	0	0	0	0
cut	15	9	1	0	0	0	0	0	5	0
home	8	7	8	0	0	1	4	0	1	1
up arrow	5	7	10	2	0	2	4	0	0	0
go	11	1	13	1	0	0	3	0	0	1
back arrow	0	8	13	3	0	2	3	0	0	1
lock	3	5	13	2	0	1	2	3	0	1
forward arrow	3	6	12	3	0	2	3	0	0	1
save	1	22	5	0	0	1	0	0	1	0
attach	3	22	1	0	0	0	1	0	3	0
satellite	2	16	12	0	0	0	0	0	0	0
bookmark	0	20	7	0	0	1	2	0	0	0
reread	2	18	8	0	0	1	1	0	0	0
recycle	5	15	3	0	0	0	1	0	5	1
restaurant	1	0	22	0	0	3	2	2	0	0
taxi	4	0	18	7	0	0	1	0	0	0
image	3	10	15	0	0	0	0	0	1	1
avatar	2	9	16	0	2	1	0	0	0	0
snowflake	6	6	15	0	3	0	0	0	0	0
first aid	29	1	0	0	0	0	0	0	0	0

Based on the groups created, transportation group consists of seven participants who consistently sort "taxi" into the group. In most cases, participants created similar groups that consist of similar cards. This shows that everybody understands and have similar expectations on the groupings. New groups emerged because participants might have thought that they need to create a group to make the card strongly fit into its own category. Besides that, twenty-nine participants consistently sort "eraser" into education group and "first aid" into medical groups. It was observed that the "first aid" card and the "eraser card" are sorted based on the nature of the objects within their respective fields. One participant suggested a combination of groups: education and leisure entertainment (refer to Table 1) could fit the card that he or she wants. Within the focus of leisure entertainment field, there were four cards whose number of sorts was over twenty which are "speaker", "play, pause, stop", "video" and "restaurant" cards. Before the data collection, it was predicted that with the exception of "speaker" card, all other three cards will be sorted under leisure entertainment category. The study findings have confirmed this prediction. This finding indicates that participants'

Table 2. Corresponding histogram matrix visualization

	Medical	Education	Leisure entertainment	Transportation	Nature	Instruction & information	Navigation & directory	Users support	oftware & editing	Education, leisure entertainment
play, pause, stop	0.00%	3.33%	93.33%	0.00%	0.00%	0.00%	0.00%	0.00%	0.00%	3.33%
speaker	0.00%	16.67%	83.33%	0.00%	0.00%	0.00%	0.00%	0.00%	0.00%	0.00%
video	3.33%	20.00%	76.67%	0.00%	0.00%	0.00%	0.00%	0.00%	0.00%	0.00%
eraser	0.00%	96.67%	0.00%	0.00%	0.00%	0.00%	0.00%	0.00%	3.33%	0.00%
print	3.33%	86.67%	3.33%	0.00%	0.00%	3.33%	0.00%	0.00%	3.33%	0.00%
copy	10.00%	80.00%	6.67%	0.00%	0.00%	0.00%	0.00%	0.00%	3.33%	0.00%
search	30.00%	46.67%	13.33%	0.00%	0.00%	0.00%	3.33%	3.33%	3.33%	0.00%
delete	10.00%	46.67%	23.33%	0.00%	0.00%	6.67%	10.00%	0.00%	0.00%	3.33%
help	26.67%	43.33%	13.33%	0.00%	0.00%	3.33%	10.00%	3.33%	0.00%	0.00%
information	16.67%	43.33%	20.00%	0.00%	0.00%	0.00%	10.00%	0.00%	6.67%	3.33%
ear	60.00%	26.67%	13.33%	0.00%	0.00%	0.00%	0.00%	0.00%	0.00%	0.00%
cut	50.00%	30.00%	3.33%	0.00%	0.00%	0.00%	0.00%	0.00%	16.67%	0.00%
home	26.67%	23.33%	26.67%	0.00%	0.00%	3.33%	13.33%	0.00%	3.33%	3.33%
up arrow	16.67%	23.33%	33.33%	6.67%	0.00%	6.67%	13.33%	0.00%	0.00%	0.00%
go	36.67%	3.33%	43.33%	3.33%	0.00%	0.00%	10.00%	0.00%	0.00%	3.33%
back arrow	0.00%	26.67%	43.33%	10.00%	0.00%	6.67%	10.00%	0.00%	0.00%	3.33%
lock	10.00%	16.67%	43.33%	6.67%	0.00%	3.33%	6.67%	10.00%	0.00%	3.33%
forward arrow	10.00%	20.00%	40.00%	10.00%	0.00%	6.67%	10.00%	0.00%	0.00%	3.33%
save	3.33%	73.33%	16.67%	0.00%	0.00%	3.33%	0.00%	0.00%	3.33%	0.00%
attach	10.00%	73.33%	3.33%	0.00%	0.00%	0.00%	3.33%	0.00%	10.00%	0.00%
satellite	6.67%	53.33%	40.00%	0.00%	0.00%	0.00%	0.00%	0.00%	0.00%	0.00%
bookmark	0.00%	66.67%	23.33%	0.00%	0.00%	3.33%	6.67%	0.00%	0.00%	0.00%
reread	6.67%	60.00%	26.67%	0.00%	0.00%	3.33%	3.33%	0.00%	0.00%	0.00%
recycle	16.67%	50.00%	10.00%	0.00%	0.00%	0.00%	3.33%	0.00%	16.67%	3.33%
restaurant	3.33%	0.00%	73.33%	0.00%	0.00%	10.00%	6.67%	6.67%	0.00%	0.00%
taxi	13.33%	0.00%	60.00%	23.33%	0.00%	0.00%	3.33%	0.00%	0.00%	0.00%

image	10.00 %	33.33 %	50.00 %	0.00%	0.00%	0.00%	0.00%	0.00%	3.33%	3.33%
avatar	6.67%	30.00 %	53.33 %	0.00%	6.67%	3.33%	0.00%	0.00%	0.00%	0.00%
snow-flake	20.00 %	20.00 %	50.00 %	0.00%	10.00%	0.00%	0.00%	0.00%	0.00%	0.00%
first aid	96.67%	3.33%	0.00%	0.00%	0.00%	0.00%	0.00%	0.00%	0.00%	0.00%

opinions in terms card sorting were not much different from each other. Besides, the cards that were used in this card sorting activity were quite familiar to what the participants had experienced previously when interacting the interface except for a few cards such as "snowflake", "satellite" and "taxi". The cards used need to be similar enough to assist participants to suggest potential grouping [11]. This helps in categorizing the cards easily.

Table 2 shows a histogram matrix containing percentages of the card placement in a category. It is obtained by converting the frequency of co-occurrence of a category in Table 1 into percentage. The percentage of the card represents the value of confidence level in terms of user agreement. The three main categories i.e. medical, education, and leisure entertainment have several groups of cards that are being highlighted with color fill. These categories consist of three different color fill that represent three different level of confidence. The blue fill represents a high level of confidence, yellow represents moderate level, and white indicates lower level. Potential high confidence means $\geq 75\%$ agreement on the icon buttons, moderate confidence is between 50% and 74% agreement, and low confidence is $\leq 49\%$ agreement.

The analysis of *medical* category in Table 2 shows high potential cards with 75% of cards agreement being the "first aid" card. This is highlighted with blue fill. The analysis shows moderate level confidence cards between 50% to 75% which are the "ear" card and "cut" card. The cards that obtained less than 49% fall under the lower level of confidence cards agreement. For the *education* category where the analysis shows high confidence of cards agreement being the "eraser", "print", and "copy" cards. Whereas "save", "attach", "satellite", "bookmark", "reread" and "recycle" cards were identified under moderate level of confidence cards agreement. *Leisure entertainment* category have "play, pause and stop", "speaker" and "video" cards as the high level of confidence card while "restaurant", "taxi", "image", "avatar" and "snowflake" cards fall under moderate confidence cards. A number of cards with low level of cards agreement were also identified, but they were possibly indicating ambiguous or problem cards.

In this study, the analysis of cards within the *leisure entertainment* category is being focused. This is because museum environment has been categorized as leisure entertainment. Leisure entertainment is a form of activities that hold the attention and interest of the audience or gives pleasure through leisure activities [15]. Based on the result obtained for high level of confidence, three cards were identified i.e. "play, pause and stop", "speaker" and "video" cards. All three cards obtained between 76 to 94% of co-occurrence which indicate that more than half of the participants sorted the same card into the *leisure entertainment* category. This shows that most of them had the same idea or interpretation of which category the card would be in. The cards that have been sorted into the *leisure entertainment* category were basically consisting of entertainment element; thus, a reason for most of the participants' choice.

It would be interesting to find out if implementation of the icon buttons on these three selected cards into a museum application could attract user's attention. It is believed that people tend to be attracted to video and audio where the mechanism of attention could also improve performance [16]. Previously, one tends to read all the information on the display board when they went to a museum that has no audio supporting the exhibits. Several years now, museum has started to integrate these elements through games, video and even virtual reality technology in disseminating information to the public. Thus, able to grab and sustain the visitor's interest while visiting the museum. Overall, the exploratory analysis from the study is able to identify potential high confidence, moderate, and low agreements on icon buttons in each application category.

5   Conclusion

It is important for a user to understand the information on the interface of the environment they deal with. By understanding the information being displayed, with the assistance of the visible cues, will enable users to navigate the surface more efficiently. The study shows how card sort technique can be used to determine suitable icon buttons for museum environment. The findings reveal that "play, pause and stop", "speaker" and "video", the labels representing icon buttons on the cards could be a set of potential signifiers for a museum interface. For future recommendation, more studies could be done in examining how best these icon buttons be useful as signifiers when interacting with museum application interface.

Acknowledgements. We would like to thank all participants who took part in this study. This research has received financial support from Universiti Teknologi PETRONAS, and Ministry of Higher Education, Malaysia.

References

1. Preece, J., Sharp, H., Rogers, Y.: Interaction Design: Beyond Human-Computer Interaction. Wiley, Hoboken (2015)
2. DeVane, B., Dietmeier, J., Miller, B.J., Missall, K., Nanda, S.: Dropping in to Game Design: Iterations of a Skatepark Physics Game for a Children's Museum Exhibit. International Society of the Learning Sciences, Inc. (ISLS) (2018)
3. Steier, R., Pierroux, P., Krange, I.: Embodied interpretation: gesture, social interaction, and meaning making in a national art museum. Learn. Cult. Soc. Interact. **7**, 28–42 (2015)
4. Patsoule, E.: Interactions around a multi-touch tabletop: a rapid ethnographic study in a museum. In: Marcus, A. (ed.) DUXU 2014. LNCS, vol. 8520, pp. 434–445. Springer, Cham (2014). https://doi.org/10.1007/978-3-319-07638-6_42
5. Peters, D.: Interface Design for Learning: Design Strategies for Learning Experiences. Pearson Education, London (2013)

6. Petrie, H., Power, C., Cairns, P., Seneler, C.: Using card sorts for understanding website information architectures: technological, methodological and cultural issues. In: Campos, P., Graham, N., Jorge, J., Nunes, N., Palanque, P., Winckler, M. (eds.) INTERACT 2011. LNCS, vol. 6949, pp. 309–322. Springer, Heidelberg (2011). https://doi.org/10.1007/978-3-642-23768-3_26
7. Albert, W., Tullis, T.: Measuring the User Experience: Collecting, Analyzing, and Presenting Usability Metrics. Newnes, Boston (2013)
8. Interface Design for Learning: Basic Principles A–Z, Accessibility. Peachpit (2018). http://www.peachpit.com/articles/article.aspx?p=2164586
9. Norman, D.: The Design of Everyday Things: Revised and, Expanded edn. Basic Books, New York (2013)
10. Righi, C., James, J., Beasley, M., Day, D.L., Fox, J.E., Gieber, J., et al.: Card sort analysis best practices. J. Usability Stud. **8**, 69–89 (2013)
11. Spencer, D.: Card Sorting: Designing Usable Categories. Rosenfeld Media, New York (2009)
12. Tullis, T., Wood, L.: How many users are enough for a card-sorting study. In: Proceedings UPA (2004)
13. Paul, C.L.: Analyzing card-sorting data using graph visualization. J. Usability Stud. **9**, 87–104 (2014)
14. Piper, A.M., Hollan, J.D.: Tabletop displays for small group study: affordances of paper and digital materials. In: Proceedings of the SIGCHI Conference on Human Factors in Computing Systems, pp. 1227–1236 (2009)
15. Entertainment definition and meaning. Collins English Dictionary (2018)
16. Yao, L., Torabi, A., Cho, K., Ballas, N., Pal, C., Larochelle, H. et al.: Video description generation incorporating spatio-temporal features and a soft-attention mechanism. arXiv preprint arXiv:1502.08029 (2015)

Understanding Instant Messaging in the Workplace

Jason Ariel Rajendran[1], Hanif Baharin[1(✉)],
and Fazillah Mohmad Kamal[2]

[1] The National University of Malaysia, 43600 Bangi, Selangor, Malaysia
jasonariel4@gmail.com, hbaharin@ukm.edu.my
[2] Universiti Utara Malaysia, 06010 Sintok, Kedah, Malaysia
fazillah@uum.edu.my

Abstract. In the workplace, effective communication plays a vital role. Many work tasks require communication which includes planning, organizing, motivating and controlling. Communication establishes relationship between superiors and their subordinates, and it determines the quality of relationship between colleagues. Currently, computer mediated communication such as Instant Messaging (IM) is used in complimentary to or as a replacement of e-mails to complete tasks. This paper discusses how IM has evolved and being adapted at work. Reviews conducted from previous studies show the impact and how people practice IM in workplaces to create a better communication and relationship in areas such as education, health care, business and others. Research shows that communication through IM applications can support or improve the quality of communication, work task and the relationship between colleagues. Based on the current trend of IM usage is the workplace, the paper proposes a qualitative method to study WhatsApp mobile application usage in the workplace. This approach will be used to observe how IM is adapted in WhatsApp group conversation in the workplace. The goal of this proposed study is to observe the use of WhatsApp at work using the existing framework, develop an IM usage model at the workplace and test and validate the IM model to make it more workplace-friendly that encourages to full implementation as a medium of communication in the workplace.

Keywords: Instant messaging · IM · Mobile instant messaging ·
Social messaging · Workplace communication · CMC

1 Introduction

The adoption of new communication technologies such as Instant Messaging applications has allowed people in the world to overcome geographic and time limitations to interact with each other [30]. These applications are also being adopted in the working environment. With that, this study will focus on one chosen application which is WhatsApp. WhatsApp is a new technology that people has adopted in the workplace in

H. Badioze Zaman et al. (Eds.): IVIC 2019, LNCS 11870, pp. 640–652, 2019.
https://doi.org/10.1007/978-3-030-34032-2_57

lieu of or to replace email as the main and formal communication channel. How do people adapt to using WhatsApp in workplace and what are the elements or theme that can be identified that shows work related interactions? This is the main reason of this upcoming research to identify how people use WhatsApp in the workplace and by using this application does it help in completing tasks or maintaining a good relationship in the organization. The role of Human Computer Interaction (HCI) and User Experience (UX), is to understand how people adopt, adapt and use of IM such as WhatsApp in the workplace and improve the design of such technology so that it fits to the work context and culture, to maximize the benefit of technology and minimize its negative impacts on work and people. In previous research and study as stated in the literature reviews, it was viewed on the adoption of WhatsApp in family environment and how familial bonding is created. Through that we will view how those tradition and culture in the family environment can be brought to the workplace in terms of bonding. It shows that bonding is important a for social interaction in the workplace [36].

2 A Brief History of Instant Messaging

Instant Messaging (IM) is a form of Computer Mediated Communication (CMC) which enables various users to send text-based messages or chat privately with other users in real-time communication over the internet. The requirements to send an instant message are two end users must download and install an IM application have access to the internet. IM has become so sophisticated, which enables communication through more than text-based messages. Some of the example IM applications are WhatsApp, WeChat, Telegram, Skype, etc. These applications allow user to share information in the form of text formats, photos, videos, audio, documents, location sharing, contact sharing, voice calling and video calling. In 2015, the number of worldwide IM accounts, not including mobile messaging, totals over 3.2 billion. This figure is expected to grow at an average annual rate of about 4% over the next four years and reach over 3.8 billion by the end of 2019 [1]. Furthermore, the use of IM in business is growing since IM use in the workplace can be tightly monitored and controlled [1]. On the consumer perspective, IM is used more for reaching friends and family.

The number of mobile messaging applications usage recorded in 2016 was 1.58 billion. Today, in 2019, there are about 2.18 billion users using mobile messaging applications to communicate and that number is expected to increase to 2.48 billion in 2021 [34]. Mobile Messaging (also referred to as Mobile IM or Mobile Chat) has shown explosive growth particularly with consumers and young users, however, in time strong adoption of Mobile Messaging among business users is expected due to its simplicity and immediacy (Fig. 1).

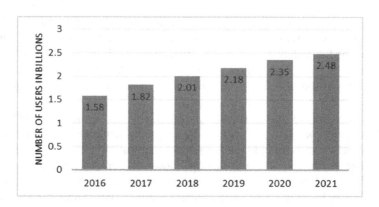

Fig. 1. Number of mobile phone messaging app users worldwide from 2016 to 2021 (Source: Statista 2019, https://www.statista.com/statistics/483255/number-of-mobile-messaging-users-worldwide/)

While messaging is commonplace today, it was only decades ago that chatting with friends and strangers online was a revolutionary. In 1961, MIT's Compatible Time-Sharing System (CTSS), along with other multi-user operating system helps to pioneer instant messaging by allowing up to 3 users to chat in real-time [4]. Internet Relay Chat (IRC) allows users to connect to networks with client software to chat with groups in real-time also known as internet text messaging [5]. IRC peaked in popularity in the 1990s, but still has millions of users. In December 1992, the first message, "Merry Christmas", is sent over the Vodafone GSM network in the U.K. As the 20th century ends, the first major IM platforms ICQ, AIM, MSN and Yahoo all battle for market share in the new instant messaging market [6].

Israeli company Mirabilis launches ICQ in 1996, which allowed users to chat one-on-one or groups, exchange files, and search for other users. In the mid-2000, ICQ had over 74 million accounts registered users with a high new subscription on 80, 000 in a day [7]. The following year, 1997, AOL launches AOL Instant Messenger (AIM), which pioneers the "Buddy List" concept. By the mid-2000s, social media has grown rapidly. Yahoo! Messenger launches in 1998, allowing users with Yahoo! ID to connect. Across the Pacific Ocean, Tencent Holdings launches its first successful application in 1999. It's called QQ, and it is initially a near-exact clone of ICQ. QQ is a multi-platform instant messaging that enables its users to text voice and video chat, file sharing, email, games and more [8]. In the same year, Microsoft releases Messenger, competitor to AIM and Yahoo.

The year 2000 is the era for the flourishing of instant messaging. Apple launches iChat for its Mac OS X operating system which is compatible with AIM. Every year IM start to evolve. In the year 2003, Skype allows Internet users to communicate with others through video, voice and instant messaging. In 2004, Facebook was launched and started gaining popularity [5]. As of July 2010, Facebook has more than 500 million active users. [5]. The year 2005 was the era of social network such as Yahoo! 360, Youtube and Facebook. Yahoo! Inc. also launched Yahoo! 360 in 2005 where people could create profiles with photo albums and interact with people of the same interest. Google Talk, available within Gmail itself, is launched to allow easy communication between email contacts in 2005.

By 2006, 159 billion SMS text messages were sent in the United States [10]. In the same year, Myspace became the most popular social networking website with approximately 43.2 million users visit MySpace monthly. At the same time, another social media giant called Twitter was founded. Twitter became popular as a micro blogging platform and most celebrity uses it [5]. MySpace than launches the first instant messaging platform built within a social network called MySpaceIM. By then, instant messaging application users has grown. Google Talk recorded around 0.9 million users following by Yahoo Messenger totaling 22 million, MSN reaching 27 million users and AIM over 53 million users.

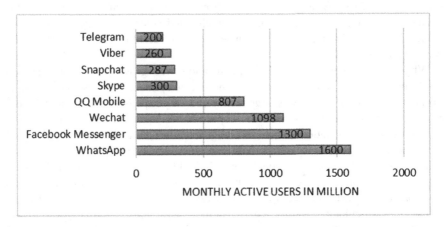

Fig. 2. Most popular mobile messaging apps worldwide as of April 2019, based on number of monthly active users (Source: Statista 2019, https://www.statista.com/statistics/258749/most-popular-global-mobile-messenger-apps/)

Two years after on 2008, Facebook Chat is released, allowing Facebook users to message friends or groups of friends on the social network. Now known as Facebook Messenger, the application was effectively decoupled the main Facebook application in 2014. This move accelerated the growth of Messenger's users base.

Above all these applications available in market for users, as an upstart, a mobile instant messaging (IM) called WhatsApp was launched in 2009 which allows users to send texts, pictures, video and audio. These features were all for free, appealing to consumers who are tired of paying for SMS and MMS. By the time in 2010, instant messaging undergoes a renaissance, as new apps like Snapchat, WhatsApp, and WeChat changed the concept of messaging entirely to a different level. Prior to the evolution, many newborn IM application start to merge the market. WhatsApp application with currently more than 1.6 billion monthly active users, as shown in Fig. 2, top them all following by Facebook Messenger, WeChat, QQ Mobile, SKype, Snapchat, Viber and Telegram as of April 2019 [33].

Gradually, these messaging applications are implementing new features and most of the applications accounts now are linkable which allows user to have a single account and connect to other applications. IM application are being integrated with features such as virtual and augmented reality, instant translation, chatbots, e-commerce and end-to-end encryption security. These applications have a huge impact on our daily routine where we just need them every time.

When IM was first introduced, it was only accessible in desktop. The first messaging program invented was IRC, an IM like program. Followed by ICQ (I Seek You) and AOL (America Online), which was made public and downloadable that enables users to communicate real-time. Then came along Microsoft's MSN Messenger, Google Talk and Yahoo Messenger (YM). At that time, MSN Messenger and YM allow users to talk just like the telephone using microphones and speakers equipped by both users [9]. In 2003, Skype was introduced, a telecommunication software, that provides users with instant messaging, video chat and voice chat, followed MySpace, Twitter, Facebook and others. This are the examples of desktop apps that were used to communicate in real-time.

While instant messaging and communication was growing through desktops, mobile phones were being evolved from normal telephone. The first mobile phone appeared in the late 1940s, it was large, heavy and very expensive and commonly used inside vehicles and by a few numbers of people. As years goes by, mobile phones evolved from first generation (1G) to second generation (2G) and third generation (3G) where mobile phones begin to incorporate internet connection [11]. Mobile devices such as hand-helds, tablets personal computers (PC) and internet enabled cellular telephones can communicate via instant messaging systems [9]. These devices are moveable, easy to use, and accessible from anywhere comes with simple applications such as clock, calculator, calendar, games and more. Originally, smartphones were used for communication through calling and messaging functions only [12]. In 2006, Blackberry changed the usage paradigms of smartphones. It came up with Blackberry operating system. In the following year on 2007, the Apple company came up with the first iPhone operating on iOS. In 2008, Andy Rubin developed a mobile operating system called Android and then was bought over by Google [13]. These smartphones operating system was a game changer [14].

As Wi-Fi (Wireless Fidelity) and high-speed mobile networks hits the market, chatting applications quickly became the source to share multimedia contents as videos, photos, stickers, games, articles, live streams and more. In most countries, Short Message Service (SMS) is expensive and it appears that via mobile internet texting or calling is cheaper [14]. By then, every social messaging companies started to mobilize their applications so that mobile device users could download them for free from the internet also known as AppStore or Play Store. For example, Facebook Messenger, Telegram, WhatsApp, WeChat, Skype, and YM. By January 2015, WhatsApp alone hosted 30 billion messages per day compared to 20 billion for SMS [14].

Today's IM has evolved tremendously. IM users are facilitated with built-in features that can make their daily routine easier. All information is accessed and received through IM. Earlier, instant messaging was used on desktops for at the workplace. It is then slowly evolved and became a tool for socializing purposes through smartphones.

Now these mobile IM applications that was meant for socializing has entered workplace environment where it eases the communication and task management.

From this brief history of IM, it can be postulated that the development of IM application technology has a great impact in the field of communication and contributes to communication facilities due to its synchronous role, the low cost of its usage, and the ubiquity of smartphone use coupled with the availability of 4G internet. This paper proposes a study to understand how mobile IM, WhatsApp in specific, as a tool of communication and collaboration in the workplace, since the usage of WhatsApp has already been adapted to manage tasks in the workplace. Early observations show that there are disruptions to work processes and social interactions in the workplace, despite its ease of use and synchronicity which allows a more efficient communication to coordinate work. This paper will next review the current literature on the use of mobile IM in the workplace, and then will propose a research to study workplace mobile IM usage in order to propose design improvement to minimize work disruptions and enhance social cohesion.

3   Literature Review

Organizations now have modern technology that allows tasks to be completed using electronic tools to ensure productivity among lower, higher and professional management [3]. Computer mediated communications such as Instant Messaging (IM) are used at work other than email, fax, voicemail, mobile phone, conference-based web and digital private assistant with networking. IM is one of the fastest growing communications technologies in today's workplace due to its speed and real-time accessibility [15]. There is a connection between the use of IM and employee engagement within the organization. A study was conducted that is the work of two departments comprising 200 people where almost everyone uses the IM application [16]. IM is used either for personal or work purposes. Although the data collected shows a low percentage IM usage, the researchers believe that the use of IM among employees will grow where employees have backgrounds of various groups, roles, knowledge and culture [17].

Research on mobile IM in the workplace covers many aspects. For example, according to studies conducted of the usage of IM in the workplace can increase productivity and improve communication quality [18]. The same study also recommends the use of IM as a major and official application in the workplace that is believed to enhance the effectiveness and efficiency of communication within the organization because it can reduce costs and employees feel more comfortable communicating with IM applications [18]. Research conducted in the workplace on the importance of IM applications and its content analysis shows that chats are used for discussion or give orders to streamline projects and meetings as well as to negotiate availability [19]. In addition, the results of the study [18] show that the use of IM applications

The usage of IM application as a communication tool in the workplace has not been officially accepted yet. This is because the IM application is only used for informal communication and as a replacement apart from the formal communication medium such as telephone, e-mail (e-mail), or face-to-face meeting [20]. Informal communication is mostly brief, unplanned, and frequent. It supports several different functions such as execution of work-related task, co-ordination of group activity, transmission of office culture, and social functions such as team building [31]. Formal communication methods have weaknesses and interruption occurs during work. Among the most common causes of interruptions are phone calls and face-to-face conversations [21]. IM is believed to assist in interruption management. For example, a person who wants to send message to a person on the other end need not to be concerned when to initiate a conversation. On the other side, the recipient can choose to ignore the notification or give an early explicit indication of their unavailability. Although the notification that pops up on the screen might be disruptive, it is not as disruptive as the unexpected visit or telephone calls. Research also states that it is acceptable socially to ignore an incoming IM as it means that the recipient is either away or busy [21]. Research shows that employees are more likely to gossip at the workplace during face-to-face conversation [19]. The asynchronous nature of email is also a disadvantage in communication and ineffective because there is no immediate and real-time response [9]. There is a small expectation that the user will respond immediately to the email [19]. In addition, the same study also found that the availability of individuals at the workplace is also difficult to be known and the time taken to determine the availability of a person through phone calls or face-to-face meeting takes longer time [19].

Other reasons IM is used at workplace by employers is to give instruction, get information, maintain relationships in the organization [3]. The same study also states that distance, time and geographical factors affect the way of communication when an employee is outside the working area. The way instructions are given also affects the feelings and emotions of employees to carry out the task [3]. Modern workplace is inherently collaborative, and this collaboration relies on effective communication among co-workers. Earlier, IM applications are reported to be preferred as informal face-to-face (FTF) conversation because it is less intrusive and allows multitasking [2]. Other than that, research shows that the use of IM workplace can maintain a mutual relationship among co-workers [3]. This is a key element in a healthy communication and relationship where conversation which includes the usage of symbols and emoticons helps in creating a better emotional feeling in the workplace environment. These can be taken as an advantage to implement IM applications in the workplace by changing and developing new features to the current applications, so it can be more workplace friendly. This study believes that by implementing IM applications to the workplace according to its demand could bring changes on how communication between employers and employees.

Analysis shows that chats are widely used for work or job conferencing to coordinate projects and meetings as well as to negotiate availability [19]. Another reason IM is used at work by an organization's employers is to give employees instructions, to get information, to keep in touch with the employee and create feelings [3]. The same study also states that the distance, time, and geographical factors affect the mode of communication when an employee is out of work. The way messages are conveyed also affect the employees' emotions to follow the instructions given [3].

3.1   Usage of WhatsApp in Different Work Context

In this section, this paper will analyze current research on the use of WhatsApp conducted in the different contexts of workplace, namely, in education and healthcare.

Usage of IM such as WhatsApp in education work field also has many advantages [32]. According to Church and De Oliveira [22], WhatsApp is used to create a shared group among teachers and students. They found that the teachers learn a lot about their students as they know in which area their students are weak and the areas they excel. Additionally, the group also contributes to a positive mood in the classroom when students share the fun-facts in the group. WhatsApp allows outdoor classroom learning where students and teachers can communicate with each other. It allows easy and fast sharing of materials. The results of this research say that IM has the advantage over the technology used by the education system, such as low cost, simplicity, flexibility, efficiency and use of native language.

WhatsApp application is also used as one of the mobile learning techniques to develop students writing skills and determining the effectiveness of using WhatsApp [23]. Experimental quasi-experimental designs are used where several students are distributed into two groups, experimental groups using WhatsApp technology to develop their writing skills and controlled group that learn writing skills through books. Then the students were given pre and post-test. Test results indicate that the experimental group student performs better than the student from the controlled group. It can be concluded that IM tools can help students to participate in the classroom and build relationships between teachers and students so that the learning process works smoothly [23].

IM has become a priority in communication for social life, but its educational value is not well understood [24]. Thus, tests on student perceptions on the usage of IM in the classroom and the impact on student's engagement has been done. The tool used to examine students is the WeChat app which is a popular application in Hong Kong [24]. As a result, students can do academic-related topics in the IM group and the group is very helpful in planning task activities that require immediate decision [24]. It can be summarized that IM does not only makes communication efficient but also creates a healthy relationship between teachers and student which is vital to assist teachers to understand their students and help their students to do better.

The same concept goes to the use of IM in healthcare. IM application and other app-based messaging technologies are being used by doctors and nurses to communicate between them to transfer patient-related clinical information in England [25]. Although, in terms of data security, it is not secured, yet it seems to be ignored by the practitioners. A key development in April 2016 saw WhatsApp release a white paper detailing a new end- to-end encryption features [25]. Upon the implementation of this security feature in WhatsApp, messages were encrypted between users and prevention of the third party and WhatsApp itself from accessing the messages. They also stated that, if IM tools can be adopted in the healthcare area, it also requires the National Health Service bodies to negotiate whether such tools can reach a critical mass required for widespread use. A research on WhatsApp use in the evaluation of haematuria resulted using the IM tool, urologists can differentiate normal urine and any form of haematuria with 100% accuracy [26]. 212 haematuria patients were evaluated by two groups of urologists where one group had face-to-face evaluation and another group received pictures via WhatsApp. The aim of the research is to make use of the advancement in telemedicine to provide the possibility to send photos of haematuria cases to professionals for further evaluation remotely and reduce unnecessary costs of services. They believe that WhatsApp can provide valuable aid to tertiary hospitals where the urologist is not always present as well as in rural areas [26].

The use of mobile and wireless technologies to support the achievement of health objectives (mHealth) has the potential to transform the face of health service delivery across the globe [27]. The relationship between specialists, doctors, nurses and patients can improve the quality of the patient's healthcare and it has been proven that mobile health application and instant messaging tools for communication purposes have saved many lives due to its efficiency and real-time communication.

Earlier research has focused on the adoption of family connecting communication technology in the family circle. This technology allows family members to communicate with each other more diversely. Massive adoption of IM such as WhatsApp has been noted [28]. Studies on family connecting technology (FCT) indicated the role of "kinkeeper" who keeps the interactions active in a family group. This "kinkeeper" is identified as a person who initiates the interactions in a group and plays a vital role in creating a familial bonding by drawing in family members participation. Nowadays family members are forced to live apart due to the modern and busy lifestyles which has changed the family interaction [28]. It can be clearly seen that although family members have difficulties in interacting physically and spending time together, with the help communication technology such as WhatsApp and the "kinkeeper", bonding within the family circle is still possible. They can preplan activities and celebrate special occasions without being missed out and get updates on each members of their well beings, and this keeps relationship between families even stronger. Through these procedure or theory, it can be utilized in the same way in the workplace to help people from different background, cultures, traditions, communities, and disciplines to create a bonding in the working environment and adapt the digital transformation more effectively and to create a better working environment.

Based on the studies that have been done, the usage of IM helps create a healthy relationship between employers and employees. The nature of IM that assist a sender to convey a message in an interactive way where symbols and icons can be included in the message so that when the receiver reads the message it helps to understand the message better and creates a positive feeling to improve the performance of any activity in any field of work, whether in industrial organizations, education, health care and other fields. The social understanding and healthy communication are important in a workplace so that daily task will be more efficient.

4   Research Question

- How do people adapt to using WhatsApp in workplace?
- What are the design implications of WhatsApp?

5 Future Works

For future work, we plan to observe how WhatsApp as communication tool is adopted, adapted and used in the workplace using an existing framework, Table 1, which has been used to observe the usage of WhatsApp in terms family bonding [29]. This is because there are very few studies and less information of usage of WhatsApp in the workplace in Malaysia. Then, a model of IM usage in the workplace will be developed based on the analysis of the observation. WhatsApp application is chosen to be studied because according to the percentage of user in Fig. 3, WhatsApp has the highest value of 91% among the other Messenger/VoIP applications as of January 2019 [35].

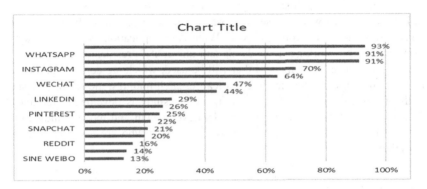

Fig. 3. User percentage of social media platforms in Malaysia (Source: DataReportal, Digital 2019: Malaysia, https://datareportal.com/reports/digital-2019-malaysia?rq=malaysia)

Table 1. Existing Framework to observe familial bonding

Element	Characteristics	Observation
(Virtual family assembly) Shared Context	Types of settings	What it is that users do together
	Continuance	Repetition of occurence
	Involvement	Representation of user's attendance
(Virtual boundary) Privacy	Framing	The environment in which the events are carried out
	Recognition	Users' capability to recognize others
(Mutual focus of attention) Reciprocity	Engagement	Users' temporal patterns of action within experience to show their commitment
	Focus	What is the focus of their social actions intended to be.
(Shared emotion) Expression	Affectual	What is the common mood
	Shared reflection	How users express coordinated mood

Each element in the framework helps in understanding how a group of people interact in terms of shared context, privacy, reciprocity and expression. Shared context element allows us to observe what the users in the WhatsApp group do and this can be identified through the conversation. We can also see how frequently people interact and the involvement of the members in the group and it can be a conversation about a physical event going on or about the memories shared. In the Privacy element, we can see events taking place virtually such as discussions on certain topics either past or present within a group of people focused who they recognize. On the other hand, in some events that occurs where members engage together to show commitment and share experience for mutual reciprocity. Through this relationship created, the expression towards the interaction can be observed on how members communicate and express themselves through sharing photos, music, emoji, video, emoticons and text. This is how the framework is used to observe interactions. Data will be collected by observing recorded chats from groups in WhatsApp application and the targeted participants are people working in academia and university's residential colleges.

There are four research method that will be used, which are conceptual modelling done through reviewing theories of empirical research findings, the research design of the ethnomethodologically informed ethnographic study is developed, iterative data collection and analysis for theoretical model development and model validation. The analysis will be validated by interviewing participants who are involved during the observation.

6   Conclusion

IM usage has many benefits in the workplace. Although the IM is not used formally but this platform provides many benefits in terms of multi-tasking, timesaving, efficient, reliable, free and the most vital part is to create a better social relationship in the working environment. This study will be conducted to prove that the IM can be applied as the formal use in the workplace with the help of new features implemented. This technology is believed to be more developed in the future. Users can perform multi-tasking at work and at the same time completing other tasks outside of work. The focus now is to study on how IM is adapted and used in the workplace and to develop a model that can help in its use. This technology can help employers and employees create a better relationship and make communication between them more efficient.

Acknowledgement. This research was conducted under the support and funding from the Malaysian Ministry of Education's Fundamental Research Grant Scheme (FRGS) no: FRGS/1/2017/ICT04/UKM/02/3.

References

1. Group TR: Instant Messaging Statistics Report, 2015–2019 (2019)
2. Maina, T.M.: Instant Messaging an effective way of communication in workplace. Kenya Murang's University College (2013)

3. Aripin, N., Mustafa, H., Hussein, A.: Instant Messaging (IM) used in the workplace. J. Techno-Soc. **3**(1) (2011)

4. Corbató, F., Daggett, M., Daley, R., Denning, P., Grier, D.A., Mills, R., Roach, R., Scherr, A.: Compatible Time-Sharing System (1961–1973) Fiftieth Anniversary Commemorative Overview. IEEE Computer Society (2011). https://doi.org/10.1007/s10584-009-9672-5

5. Edosomwan, S., Prakasan, S.K., Kouame, D., Watson, J., Seymour, T.: The history of social media and its impact on business. J. Appl. Manag. Entrep. **16**(3), 79–91 (2011)

6. Desjardins, J.: The evolution of instant messaging (2016). http://www.visualcapitalist.com/evolution-instant-messaging/

7. Leung, L.: College student motives for chatting on ICQ. New Media Soc. **3**, 483–500 (2001)

8. Rong, M.: WeChat impact on social and economic in China. Bachelor's thesis, Autumn 2016, Business Information Technology Oulu University of Applied Sciences (2016)

9. Bhagyavati: Computer network popular application and future directions: email and instant messaging. In: Bidgoli, H. (eds.) Handbook of Computer Networks: Distributed Networks, Network Planning, Control, Management, and New Trends, pp. 733–740. DeSales University, Pennsylvania, USA (2008)

10. Richter, F.: Here's what Facebook gets for $19billion. The Statistical Portal (2014). www.statistica.com/chart/1804/whatsapp-user-base/. Accessed 06 June 2014

11. Cerdeno, E.: Phone Evolution and Revolution. MAPFRE RE (2013)

12. Rashedul, I., Rofiqul, I., Mazumder, T.A.: Mobile application and its global impact. Int. J. Eng. Technol. IJET-IJENS **10**(06), 72–78 (2010)

13. Conti, J.P.: The androids are coming. Eng. Technol. **3**(9), 72–75 (2008). (Comms)

14. Barot, T., Oren, E.: The Dawn of the Social Messaging Era (2015). https://towcenter.gitbooks.io/guide-to-chat-apps/content/introductionthe_dawn_of/

15. Rennecker, J., Godwin, L.: Theorizing the unintended consequences of instant messaging (IM) for worker productivity. Sprouts: Work. Pap. Inf. Envir. Syst. Organ. **3**(3), 137–168. https://doi.org/10.1021/ie202796u

16. Ariffin, Z., Omar, S.Z.: Usage of Whatsapp in relation to employee engagement in a telecommunication company. Int. J. Acad. Res. Bus. Soc. Sci. **8**(1), 434–452 (2018). https://doi.org/10.6007/IJARBSS/v8-i1/3818

17. Ou, C.X.J., Davison, R.M.: The impact of instant messaging in the workplace. In: Americas Conference on Information Systems, vol. 5, pp. 3782–3792 (2010). https://www.scopus.com/inward/record.uri?eid=2-s2.0-84870365478&partnerID=40&md5=0f09d3b87af33b0e8c6fbff7113dcba5

18. Pi, S.M., Liu, Y.C., Chen, T.Y., Li, S.H.: The Influence of Instant Messaging Usage Behavior on Organizational Communication Satisfaction, pp. 1–9 (2008)

19. Handel, M., Arbor, A., Herbsleb, J.D.: What Is Chat Doing in the Workplace?, pp. 238–247 (2002). https://doi.org/10.1145/587078.587080

20. Cameron, A.F., Webster, J.: Unintended consequences of emerging communication technologies: instant messaging in the workplace. Comput. Hum. Behav. **21**(1), 85–103 (2005). https://doi.org/10.1016/j.chb.2003.12.001

21. Garrett, R.K., Danziger, J.N.: IM = Interruption management? Instant messaging and disruption in the workplace. J. Comput.-Med. Commun. **13**(1), 23–42 (2007). https://doi.org/10.1111/j.1083-6101.2007.00384.x

22. Church, K., de Oliveira, R.: What's up with whatsapp?: comparing mobile instant messaging behaviors with traditional SMS. In: MobileHCI, p. 352 (2013). https://doi.org/10.1145/2493190.2493225

23. Fattah, S.F.: The effectiveness of using WhatsApp messenger as one of mobile learning techniques to develop students' writing skills. J. Educ. Pract. **6**(32), 115–127 (2015). https://doi.org/10.1111/j.1365-2729.2005.00129.x

24. Tang, Y., Hew, K.F.: Examining student participation and perception of mobile instant messaging: an exploratory study. Int. J. Learn. Teach. **3**(4), 264–271 (2017). https://doi.org/10.18178/ijlt.3.4.264-271

25. Chari, A., Gane, S.B.C.: Instant messaging applications in healthcare: are we harnessing their potential? BMJ Innov. (2018). https://doi.org/10.1136/bmjinnov-2017-000197

26. Sener, T.E., et al.: WhatsApp use in the evaluation of hematuria. Int. J. Med. Inform. **111**, 17–23 (2018). https://doi.org/10.1016/j.ijmedinf.2017.12.011

27. Burns, C.: WHO international standards/reference reagents. Glob. Obs. eHealth Ser **3**, 99 (2011). https://doi.org/10.4258/hir.2012.18.3.231

28. Kamal, F., Noor, N., Baharin, H.: "Silence is golden no more" in family digital environment: understanding the Kinkeeper role through mobile social messaging system. In: Twenty-Fourth European Conference on Information Systems (ECIS), June (2016)

29. Kamal, F.M., Noor, N.L.M., Baharin, H.: Digital ritualized interaction: towards conceptualizing mediated familial bonding via family connecting technology. Jurnal Teknologi **77**(4), 127–133 (2015). https://doi.org/10.11113/jt.v77.6053

30. Chang, H.-J., Ian, W.-Z.: Instant messaging usage and interruptions in the workplace. Int. J. Knowl. Content Dev. Technol. **4**(2), 25–47 (2014). https://doi.org/10.5865/IJKCT.2014.4.2.025

31. Whittaker, S., Frohlich, D., Daly-Jones, O.: Informal workplace communication: what is it like and how might we support it? In: Adelson, B., Dumais, S., Olson, J. (eds.) Proceedings of the SIGCHI Conference on Human Factors in Computing Systems (CHI 1994), pp. 131–137. ACM, New York (1994). https://doi.org/10.1145/191666.191726

32. Bouhnik, D., Deshen, M., Gan, R.: WhatsApp goes to school: mobile instant messaging between teachers and students. J. Inf. Technol. Educ.: Res. **13**, 217–231 (2014)

33. Statistica: Most popular mobile messaging applications worldwide as of April 2019, based on number of monthly active users (2019). https://www.statista.com/statistics/258749/most-popular-global-mobile-messenger-apps/. Accessed 30 Jun 2019

34. Statistica: Number of mobile phone messaging app users worldwide from 2016 to 2021 (2018). https://www.statista.com/statistics/483255/number-of-mobile-messaging-users-worldwide/. Accessed 2 July 2019

35. DataReportal: Digital 2019: Malaysia (2019). https://datareportal.com/reports/digital-2019-malaysia?rq=malaysia. Accessed 4 July 2019

36. Nardi, B.A., Whittaker, S., Bradner, E.: Interaction and outeraction: instant messaging in action. In: Proceedings of the 2000 ACM Conference on Computer Supported Cooperative Work, December 2000, Philadelphia, Pennsylvania, USA, pp. 79–88 (2000). https://doi.org/10.1145/358916.358975

Usability Evaluation of Heart Disease Monitoring Mobile Applications: A Comparative Study

Muhammad Sobri[1,2](✉), Mohamad Taha Ijab[2], and Norshita Mat Nayan[2]

[1] Universitas Bina Darma, Palembang, South Sumatera, Indonesia
sobri@binadarma.ac.id
[2] The National University of Malaysia, Bangi, Selangor, Malaysia

Abstract. Heart disease is one of the most prominent silent killers in the world. Further, treating the heart disease problems is considerably costly. In the era of the Fourth Industrial Revolution (4IR), many heart disease monitoring mobile applications are available on Google Play and Apple App Store. These applications enable the patients to carry out self-monitoring of their heart conditions practically easy. This study aims to conduct usability evaluations of selected heart disease monitoring mobile applications from the perspective of the heart patients. The compared applications are: (i) Cardiag Diagnosis, (ii) iCare Health Monitoring Full, and (iii) Heart Rate Plus. These applications were evaluated and compared based on the features offered by the applications as well as their common usability elements: (i) learnability, (ii) efficiency, (iii) memorability, (iv) error, and (v) satisfaction. This comparative study adopted the Post-Study System Usability Questionnaire (PSSUQ) in evaluating heart disease monitoring mobile applications. The study recruited twenty heart patients in a hospital in Palembang, Indonesia. From the participants' assessments, the study found that the applications: (i) offer peripheral features unnecessary to the users, (ii) slowness in providing results (i.e., measurement and/or feedback), (iii) unmemorable features, and (iv) results of measurements are perceived to be dubious and unreliable. This paper theoretically contributes to provide recommendations to application developers and usability designers on the importance of meeting the usability elements desired by the users, especially mobile applications for chronic diseases.

Keywords: Cardiac monitoring · Chronic diseases · mHealth · PSSUQ · Human computer interaction

1 Introduction

Heart disease is one of the chronic diseases that has become one of the most prominent killers in the world with 11.8% of deaths reported. Other chronic diseases such as tuberculosis contributed 3.3%, cancer 2.0%, and diabetes 1.8% to global death percentages [1–3]. This situation is similar in Indonesia based on survey conducted by the Bureau of Communication and Community Services, Ministry of Health, Indonesian

© Springer Nature Switzerland AG 2019
H. Badioze Zaman et al. (Eds.): IVIC 2019, LNCS 11870, pp. 653–662, 2019.
https://doi.org/10.1007/978-3-030-34032-2_58

Government [4]. In the survey, heart disease was reported to be the highest cause of death in all ages of 151,000 people and this number was higher than other diseases such as stroke (90,000 people), tuberculosis (32,000 people), and diabetes (29,000 people). Contributing factors for heart disease include high cholesterol levels, diabetes, hypertension, obesity, smoking, lack of exercise, and aging process [5]. In addition, the high cost of medicine that reaches tens of millions of Indonesian Rupiah [4] can make heart disease untreatable to the less privileged or poor patients. However, this is not exclusive to Indonesia only. Even in the United States of America, the cost of treatment for 30 days of protection may reached RM 93,026 (USD $ 22,416) [6]. In the era of the Fourth Industrial Revolution (4IR), heart patients are able to monitor the health condition of their hearts using heart disease monitoring mobile applications anywhere and everywhere [7, 8]. Most heart disease monitoring mobile applications are available and offered on major platforms such as Google Play for Android devices and the Apple App Store for iOS-based devices. These applications are available for purchase by heart patients. For example, the price of the Cardio Visual application is around USD 2.84 - USD 9.62 (MYR 11.64 – MYR 39.44), the Heart Disease application requires payment after the user uses it, while some other applications can be downloaded for free. These application make it easy for the heart patients and cardiologist to stay constantly in communication as well as enabling the patients to carry out self-monitoring of the heart conditions [7].

However, according to the results of some researches [9–12] software designers of heart disease monitoring applications often do not think deeply about the needs of users. This current study argues that, patients and cardiologists should be involved in the design and development of the heart disease applications. Designing an effective user interface is a big challenge as it will impact, the usability of applications [13].

Therefore, the objective of this study is to conduct usability evaluation of three heart disease monitoring mobile applications from the perspective of the heart patients. The next section reviews, extant literature related to this study. The third section presents the methods used for this study. The results and discussion are presented in the fifth section. The last section sums up the paper by concluding the research and offers pointers for future works.

2   Literature Review

There are three areas relevant to this current study. A literature review of the extant research have been conducted and discussions are divided into three topics: (a) the concept of usability, (b) usability evaluations questionnaires, (c) heart disease monitoring mobile applications, and (d) the heart disease monitoring mobile applications.

2.1   The Concept of Usability

According to usability experts [14], usability is a measure of how simple an application interface to use. Whereas according to ISO DIS 9241-11 [15], usability is the stage where products can be used by certain users to achieve their goals effectiveness, efficiency and satisfaction in their scope. As for some of the existing researches on usability and its elements, such as [14] among its usability elements: (i) learnability, efficiency, memorability, errors, and satisfaction. ISO DIS 9241-11 [15] states three usability elements: (i) effectiveness, (iii) efficiency and (iii) satisfaction.

Meanwhile [16] who conducted usability research for mobile applications called PACMAD (People At the Center of Mobile Application Development) proposed seven elements of usability, namely: (i) effectiveness, (ii) efficiency, (iii) satisfaction, (iv) learnability, (v) memorability, (vii) errors and (vii) cognitive loads. [17] Suggested the usability model for chronic mobile applications to include six elements of usability: (i) efficiency, (ii) satisfaction, (iii) effectiveness, (iv) learnability, (v) information security, and (vii) functionality. Table 1 shows the comparison of usability elements by previous researchers.

Table 1. Comparison of usability elements by previous researchers

Usability elements	Previous researchers			
	[14]	[15]	[16]	[17]
Learnability	✓		✓	✓
Efficiency	✓	✓	✓	✓
Memorability	✓		✓	
Errors	✓		✓	
Satisfaction	✓	✓	✓	✓
Effectiveness		✓	✓	✓
Cognitive loads			✓	
Information security				✓
Functionality				✓

Based on Table 1, this study adapted Nielsen's model because (i) the Nielsen's model is applicable in various research scopes, (ii) already been adopted by many usability researchers, and (iii) it has a standard questionnaire that can be used to interpret the application of usability evaluation [18]. Usability evaluation is an important aspect of identifying the usability of heart disease monitoring mobile applications for existing patients on Google Play and the Apple App Store. The next discussion explains in greater detail the different usability evaluation questionnaires and the different usability elements relevant to this study.

2.2 Usability Evaluations Questionnaires

The evaluation of health mobile application from the health professionals and patients is critical for its success [19]. For measuring and assessing usability, there are 4 (four) usability questionnaires commonly referred to ANSI report [20], and ISO 9241-11 [21] and they are:

- The Questionnaire for User Interaction Satisfaction (QUIS) [22] to assess users' subjective satisfaction with specific aspects (screen factors, terminology and system feedback, learning factors, system capabilities, technical manuals, online tutorials, multimedia, teleconferencing, and software installation) of the human–computer interface. The current version of the QUIS (7.0) contains a demographic questionnaire, a measure of overall system satisfaction along six scales, and hierarchically organised measures,

- The Software Usability Measurement Inventory (SUMI) [23, 24]. The SUMI is a 50-item questionnaire with a Global scale based on 25 items and five subscales for Efficiency, Affect, Helpfulness, Control, and Learnability (10 items each), the items have three scales (Agree, Undecided, Disagree). The SUMI contains a mixture of positive and negative statements (e.g., "The instructions and prompts are help-ful"). To view and the use of the SUMI requires a license from the Human Factors Research Group (HFRG),
- The System Usability Scale (SUS) [25]. The SUS is a questionnaire with ten items, each with five scale steps range from 0 to 4. The odd-numbered items have a positive tone; the tone of the even-numbered items is negative. The SUS scoring method requires participants to provide a response to all ten items. The SUS does not require any license fee, and
- The Post-Study System Usability Questionnaire (PSSUQ) is used due to assess users' perceived satisfaction after using computer systems or applications [26, 27]. In the third version of PSSUQ, it authors categorised the questionnaires into each the usability factors namely: 2 items on learnability, 3 items on efficiency, 2 items on memorability, 2 items on error, and 3 items on satisfaction. For the purpose of this study, PSSUQ will be used as the paper is using the five usability elements (as listed below) emphasised by the PSSUQ evaluation technique.

2.3   Usability Elements Relevant to This Study

There are many usability elements, but this research adapted Nielsen's [14] because its proposed usability elements which can be used in a wide range of research fields, already adopted by many usability researchers [18]. These, usability elements are:

- Learnability: are the features of the heart disease monitoring mobile application easy to understand, easy to search for specific information, and easy to identify their navigational mechanism?
- Efficiency: are the features of the heart disease monitoring mobile application easy to measure health conditions (e.g. measuring heart rate), and easy to get the results displayed (e.g. the results of heart rate reading)?
- Memorability: are the menus of the heart disease monitoring mobile application easy to remember?
- Errors: when using the application, does the application provides information on how to correct the mistakes made?
- Satisfaction: overall, are the heart disease monitoring mobile application is pleasant and comfortable to use?

2.4 The Heart Disease Monitoring Mobile Applications

Based on study of Institute for Healthcare Informatics there are 97,000 heart disease monitoring mobile application offered on platforms such as Google Play for Android devices and the Apple App Store for iOS devices [28]. The aim of this study is to conduct usability evaluation of the selected of heart disease monitoring mobile applications available at Apple App Store and Google Play Store. Using keyword phrases "heart disease", "heart health monitoring", "mobile health applications" and "health and fitness". The search results yielded 127 applications. The applications were read mainly for the criteria used in selecting the relevant applications for this study which are (i) have rating > 4.0, (ii) reviewed > 5,000, (iii) it has been downloaded by > 100,000 times, (iv) applications have last update > 2018, (v) available for free, and (vi) features a variety of menus such as heart rate, blood pressure, and report. The three selected heart disease monitoring mobile applications are shown in Fig. 1.

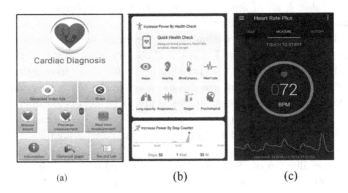

Fig. 1. The selected the heart disease monitoring mobile applications, (a) Cardiag Diagnosis, (b) iCare Health Monitoring Full, and Heart Rate Plus.

Cardiag Diagnosis was developed in 2015 by Sun Do Kim, iCare Health monitoring was developed in 2018 by Health Data Chain while Heart Rate Plus was developed in 2017 by XDA Developer. All of these applications are available for free, have features such as heart rate, blood pressure, and reporting capability.

3 Methods

The aim of this study is to conduct a comparative usability evaluation of the three selected heart disease monitoring mobile applications identified and retrieved from Apple App Store and Google Play Store. Table 2 provides comparisons of the selected applications.

Table 2. Comparison of the selected of heart disease monitoring mobile applications

The application criteria used for this study	The selected of heart disease monitoring mobile applications		
	Cardiag diagnosis	iCare health monitoring full	Heart rate plus
Rating	4.2	4.5	4.3
Reviewed	7,325	26,762	16,673
Downloaded	500,000	1,000,000	1,000,000
Latest update	Jul 2, 2019	May 2, 2019	Apr 8, 2019
Free	✓	✓	✓
Features (e.g. measuring heart rate)	✓	✓	✓

Based on Table 2, all of the selected of heart disease monitoring mobile applications met all criteria used for this study.

The study to the usability evaluation of the heart disease monitoring mobile applications was performed for 3 months (February until April 2019) at Myria Hospital, Palembang, Indonesia. The participants of this study have agreed to participate in the research by signing informed consent letter. The Myria Hospital authorities have also provided a special room for this study to be conducted after formal permission was granted by the hospital's Director. Twenty (20) heart patients were involved in this study. With the demographics for heart patients are 65% male and 35% female, mean age range of 40–49 years (15%), 50–59 years (25%) and 60 years over (60%). For the evaluation of the usability of the selected the heart disease monitoring mobile applications, this study used the PSSUQ usability questionnaires for 2 (two) phases measure: (i) pre-test before using heart disease monitoring mobile applications, and (ii) post-test after using heart disease monitoring mobile applications.

Before the participants (i.e. heart patients) fill in the questionnaire, the main researcher gave training on how to use of the different heart disease monitoring mobile applications to the participants (i.e., pre-test). They were expected to use heart disease monitoring mobile applications for 2 weeks. After that, the participants will complete the questionnaires for the post-test study.

4   Results and Discussion

The result of data analysis to the usability evaluation of heart disease monitoring mobile applications was done by measuring its Cronbach alpha using SPSS software. For this study, that all questionnaires (PSSUQ usability questionnaires for 2 (two) phases measure: (i) pre-test and (ii) post-test)) for heart patients before interacting with of heart disease monitoring mobile applications are acceptable.

For the value of Cronbach alpha for questionnaire before interacting (pre-test), application (a) (Cardiac Diagnosis) of 0.704, for application (b) (iCare Health Monitor

Full) of 0.756 and for (c) (Heart Rate Monitor) of 0.720. While the results of data processing for questionnaires the heart patients after interacting (post-test), application (a) (Cardiac Diagnosis) increased to 0.742, application (b) (iCare Health Monitor Full) increased to 0.802 and application (c) (Heart Rate Plus) increased to 0.722. If the Cronbach alpha score > 0.7 showing that the questionnaire is accepted [29]. This means that all of the instrument of questionnaire for the heart disease after interacting with of heart disease monitoring mobile applications are acceptable.

The following are the results of statistical calculations based on indicators in the usability elements as advocated in Nielsen's Model. Table 3 shows the statistic testing of pre-test and post-test of heart disease monitoring mobile applications while Table 4 summarises the evaluation result based on indicators of usability elements.

Table 3 Statistic testing pre-test and post-test of heart disease monitoring mobile applications

Usability elements	Statistic testing					
	Pre-test			Post-test		
	(a)	(b)	(c)	(a)	(b)	(c)
Learnability	5.32	5.27	5.23	4.28	4.13	3.33
Efficiency	4.33	5.25	5.33	3.33	4.2	4.33
Memorability	5.4	6.3	4.3	4.4	5.3	3.3
Errors	5.38	5.3	5.3	4.38	4.3	4.3
Satisfaction	5.4	5.28	5.23	4.4	4.2	4.45

Table 4 The evaluation result based on indicators of usability elements

Usability elements	Indicator	The selected of heart disease monitoring mobile applications		
		(a)	(b)	(c)
Learnability	The number of clicks to measure heart rate	2 clicks	2 clicks	1 click
	The number of clicks to view record	1 click	2 clicks	1 click
Efficiency	Time taken to measure heart rate	20 s	35 s	50 s
Memorability	The number of features the application has	8 features	35 features	3 features
Errors	There is information to how use it and if there is misuse	✓	✓	✓
Satisfaction	Does the app provide benefits to the user after using it	Not yet satisfied because the results change and dubious	Not yet satisfied because the results change and dubious	Not yet satisfied because the results change and dubious

Based on Tables 3 and 4, the findings of this paper of usability evaluation of the selected of heart disease monitoring mobile applications from the perspective of heart patients are:

In terms of learnability, application (c) without having a lot of interfaces just 1 click to measure the heart rate, blood pressure and reading their health records is found to be better than application (a) and (b) which require 2 clicks. However, application (b) is not far behind application (c). Furthermore, for efficiency, application (a) is better than application (b) and application (c) because the rapidness of measurements such as heart rate and display the result in 20 s.

Meanwhile, for memorability, application (c) is better than application (a) and application (b) because it has the fewest number of main (necessary) features for measuring heart rate, measuring blood pressure and keeping records while the other two applications: application (a) and application (b) are having more unmemorable features in addition to the main features. For errors, overall, participants felt that all three applications are pleasant and comfortable to use. Despite the above, the participants thought that they are not yet satisfied because according to them, the results or readings from their heart rate and blood pressure measurements are perceived to be dubious and unreliable. Meanwhile, the limitation of this study is not yet involving the cardiologist and only recruited heart patients. The findings of this study can help fill the gap with existing mobile applications for heart disease monitoring purposes in the way applications to be built (1) without having a lot of interfaces, (2) the rapidness of measurements reading and display, (3) has the fewest number of main (necessary) features, and (4) the results or readings measurements are easy to understand and reliable.

5 Conclusion and Future Work

The usability evaluations conducted on three different heart disease monitoring mobile applications discovered that usability elements are crucial to ensure users' satisfaction as well as in ensuring overall usability of the applications. This paper theoretically contributes to provide recommendations to application developers and usability designers on the importance of meeting the usability elements desired by the users, especially for applications to be used by chronic disease patients. The limitation of this study is that the study only recruited heart patients and not yet involving the cardiologists. Future work shall include the health professionals' viewpoints pertaining to usability from their perspectives, as well as offering conceptual model and prototype on how usability can be achieved across all usability elements for chronic diseases in general and for heart disease monitoring mobile applications in particular.

Acknowledgements. The main researcher thanked Universitas Bina Darma for providing grant funding to conduct this research.

References

1. Mathers, C.D., Lopez, A.D., Murray, C.J.L.: Chapter 3: The burden of disease and mortality by condition: data, methods, and results for 2001. In: Global Burden of Disease and Risk Factors, vol. 2003, pp. 45–93 (2006)
2. Dariush, M., et al.: Heart Disease and Stroke Statistics—2016 Update, vol. 133, no. 4. American Heart Association (2016)
3. Sobri, M., Ijab, M.T., Mat Nayan, N.: Systematic literature review untuk membuat model aplikasi pemantauan kesehatan cardiovascular. J. RESTI (Rekayasa Sist. dan Teknol. Informasi) 2(2), 458–464 (2018)
4. Yusro, A.H.: Penyakit Jantung Koroner di indonesia Penyebab Kematian Nomor 1 Manusia, 2 (2017). http://www.sehatalamiyah.com/2017/05/mengenal-pembunuh-nomor-1-manusia.html. Accessed 13 Dec 2017
5. Frank, J.W., et al.: Coronary heart disease, heart failure, and the risk of dementia: a systematic review and meta-analysis. Alzheimer's Dement. 14(11), 1–12 (2018)
6. Ileana, L.P., Desai, N.R., Allen, L.A., Heidenreich, P.: Managing the economic challenges in the treatment of heart failure. Prog. Cardiovasc. Dis. 61(5–6), 476–483 (2018)
7. Anshari, M., Nabil, M.: Mobile health (mHealth) services and online health educators. Biomed. Inform. Insights 8, 19–28 (2016)
8. Zahra, F., Hussain, A., Mohd, H.: Factors affecting mobile health application for chronic diseases. J. Telecommun. Electron. Comput. Eng. 10(1), 77–81 (2018)
9. Khajouei, R., De Jongh, D., Jaspers, M.W.M.: Usability evaluation of a computerized physician order entry for medication ordering. Stud. Health Technol. Inform. 150, 532–536 (2009)
10. Menachemi, N., Collum, T.H.: Benefits and drawbacks of electronic health record systems. Risk Manag. Healthc. Policy 4, 47–55 (2011)
11. Yucel, G., Cebi, S., Hoege, B., Ozok, A.F.: A fuzzy risk assessment model for hospital information system implementation. Expert Syst. Appl. 39(1), 1211–1218 (2012)
12. Collen, M.F., Ball, M.J. (eds.): The History of Medical Informatics in the United States. HI. Springer, London (2015). https://doi.org/10.1007/978-1-4471-6732-7
13. Bennett, K.B., Nagy, A.L., Flach, J.M.: Visual Display. Wiley, Hoboken (2012)
14. Nielsen, J.: Usability Engineering. Morgan Kaufman, San Francisco (1993)
15. ISO: Ergonomic requirements for office work with visual display terminals. Part 11: Guidance on usability (ISO DIS 9241–11), ISO DIS 92. International Standards Organization, London (1994)
16. Rachel, H., Derek, F., David, D.: Usability of mobile applications: literature review and rationale for a new usability model. J. Interact. Sci. 1(1), 1 (2013)
17. Fatima, Z., Haslina, M., Azham, H., Mazni, O.: Usability dimensions for chronic disease mobile applications: a systematics literature review. In: Knowledge Management International Conference (KMICe), pp. 363–368 (2018)
18. Muqtadiroh, F.A., Astuti, H.M., Tyas Darmaningrat, E.W., Aprilian, F.R.: Usability evaluation to enhance software quality of cultural conservation system based on Nielsen model (WikiBudaya). Procedia Comput. Sci. 124, 513–521 (2017)
19. Crepaldi, N.Y., et al.: Satisfaction evaluation of health professionals in the usability of software for monitoring the tuberculosis treatment. Procedia Comput. Sci. 121, 889–896 (2017)
20. ANSI: Common Industry Format for Usability Test Reports (ANSI-NCITS 354–2001), Washington DC (2001)

21. ISO: Ergonomic requirements for office work with visual display terminals (VDTs) e Part 11: guidance on usability (ISO 9241-11:1998E), Geneva (1998)
22. Chin, J.P., Diehl, V.A., Norman, K.L.: Development of an instrument measuring user satisfaction of the human-computer interface. In: CHI 1998, pp. 213–218 (1988)
23. Kirakowski, J., Corbett, M.: SUMI: the software usability measurement inventory. Br. J. Educ. Technol. **24**(3), 210–212 (1993)
24. McSweeney, R.: SUMI: a psychometric approach to software evaluation. University College of Cork (1992)
25. Brooke, J.: SUS: a 'quick and dirty' usability scale. In: Usability Evaluation in Industry, pp. 189–194 (1996)
26. Lewis, J.R.: Psychometric evaluation of the PSSUQ using data from five years of usability studies. Int. J. Hum. Comput. Interact. **14**, 463–488 (2002)
27. Sauro, J., Lewis, J.R.: Chapter 8 - Standardized usability questionnaires in quantifying the user experience, 2nd edn., pp. 185–248. Elsevier Inc. (2016)
28. Aitken, M., et al.: Patient apps for improved healthcare from novelty to mainstream. IMS Inst. Healthc. Inform., 1–65 (2013)
29. Cronbach, L.J.: Coefficient alpha and the internal structure of tests. Psychometrika **16**(3), 297–334 (1951)

User Profiling to Overcome the Social Effects of Student Dropout

Justin Gilbert and Suraya Hamid$^{(\boxtimes)}$

Department of Information Systems, Faculty of Computer Science and
Information Technology, University of Malaya, Kuala Lumpur, Malaysia
suraya_hamid@um.edu.my

Abstract. Higher education institutions or specifically tertiary education are
aimed at producing quality fresh graduates for the global market of today's
world. However, dropout rates and retention levels of university students continue to be a key matter of concern at the administration level. Thus, this paper
seeks to build a theoretical understanding of student dropout in universities from
a social perspective and the application of User Profiling as a possible solution.
This was done based on findings by evaluating a thorough review of literature
from the global context to obtain an in-depth idea of how student dropout rates
are affected by social related issues. Previous studies show that the use of
student profiling has been able to address academic related problems such as
effective learning methods. The findings from literature reveal that among the
social interventions of student dropouts include poor academic performance,
inability to adapt to a new environment as well as personal and family-related
issues. These problems may involve the influence of several external and
internal factors. Finally, the conclusion from the literature could be used to cope
with the social issues related to student dropout in universities through the
profiling, which involves means of gathering student data and performing a
behavioral analysis of each individual student.

Keywords: User profiling · Student dropout · Social perspective · Higher
education

1 Introduction

Higher education modernization is not a new venture instead something targeted by
most tertiary education institutions in the world today. One of the key issues faced by
this evolution is the balance between relevant inputs and corresponding outputs, in
other words, striking an optimal balance of enrolled and graduating students [1]. The
number of student's intake and the number of graduates produced annually have
always been a fair point of assessment of a university. However, a comparison of both
these factors together does lead us to a major loophole in the system, which is the
dropout rate. Dropout by definition refers to the abandonment of a particular course or
program, regardless of the reason for doing so [2]. This phenomenon is considered to
be a crisis because it does not only impact the individuals in question and their
education, but it also does, to a certain extent, affects local communities socially and

© Springer Nature Switzerland AG 2019
H. Badioze Zaman et al. (Eds.): IVIC 2019, LNCS 11870, pp. 663–671, 2019.
https://doi.org/10.1007/978-3-030-34032-2_59

economically [3]. Communities suffer from a lack of productive workers and higher costs associated with incarceration, health care and other social services [3]. University student dropout is a national issue in many countries throughout the world, namely Brazil [2], Colombia [4], South Korea [5], Turkey [6], Japan [7] as well as in major parts of Europe and USA [14]. Many factors contribute to the dropout rate in universities and these variables may either be social, economic, emotional or spiritual factors. In this paper, the social attributes constraining to student dropout have been studied to highlight key factors that need to be considered to develop a possible solution.

There may exist several approaches to cope with this issue. This research, however, is confined to the possible application of a Student's Profiling method as a solution. User profiling is defined as the process of gathering information regarding a certain user with the objective of creating their profile. Several information may be used to develop a user profile including geographical location, academic and professional background, membership in groups, interests, preferences, opinions and other attributes of a user. Big data techniques enable collecting accurate and rich information for user profiles, in particular due to their ability to process unstructured as well as structured information in high volumes from multiple sources [9]. The main idea behind the suggestion of user profiling is because studies have shown that profiling has been successfully applied to past academic-related issues such as recommender systems [10], self-regulated learning [11] and fuzzy models [12]. The paper is structured as follows; The next section expounds on the student enrolment and dropout as well as user profiling. This is followed by the methods deployed in conducting the research. The last section will discuss the relevant results and findings of the research, future prospective and conclusion.

2   Related Works

2.1   Student Enrollment and Dropout

Every country has its own government or private sector that is responsible for the operation and administration of its higher education institutions. Through this governance, the structure of the country's higher education system can be apprehend in terms of student's intake and graduation. In Malaysia, the Ministry of Higher Education (MOHE) reported that Malaysian universities house more than a million students as of 2017, of which 95000 were international students from more than 100 countries worldwide [13]. It is an undeniable fact that education is a highly dependent measure of a nation's progress, so important that it can be said that education plays a central role and has a cross-cutting impact on all aspects of human life [14]. However, one of the main problems facing the higher education system these days concerns the high dropout level [4]. This severity of this problem can be seen affecting several countries across the globe. Malaysian statistics show that in 2017 alone, 21% of undergraduates and 82% of postgraduate students have opted out the course before completion [32]. Elsewhere, in Japan as a whole, 8% of students dropout of college, while the dropout rate of national university and public university is lower than 8%, and private university is higher than 8% [7]. According to the Ministry of National Education of Colombia, from every one hundred students who are enrolled at a university, about half of them (50%) actually fail to complete their academic year and obtain graduation [4]. The dropout is estimated to be at 51% now from 49% in 2004 [4]. In 2015, a research across 40 universities in Brazil have revealed a dropout percentage of 39.2% with certain universities posting figures up to 53% [2]. Studies in South Korea has shown that the dropout level is increasing by 0.3% annually since 2005 [5]. Meanwhile in Turkey about 40% to 50% of engineering students dropout after their first year of studies [6]. From these examples, it can be dictated that student dropout is not just a regional or continental issue but one that is affecting the whole globe. Basically, the phenomenon of student dropout can be influenced by several impact factors as shown in Fig. 1 below:

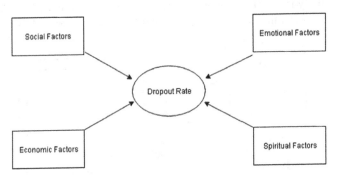

Fig. 1. Factors that impact dropout rates

Based on the figure above, emotional factors include problems related to stress, anxiety, depression and anger. Spiritual factors may include religious beliefs or patriotism. Economic factors constitute mainly on financial problems. Since the scope of the paper is to only focus on social factors that affect dropout, the other factors are not expounded on.

2.2   User Profiling

Data-driven society is a lot about the ability to capture, understand, and act on a certain data possessed, which then has the potential to create a healthier, safer, and fairer society for us all to enjoy. Data-driven analytics as a new practice of knowledge creation are on the rise [15] and a substantial component of this analytics is – profiling. A user profile is a collection of information that describes the various attributes of a user. These attributes may include geographical location, academic and professional background, membership in groups, interests, preferences, opinions, etc. [9]. User profiling is the process of collecting information about a user in order to construct their user profile. User profiles are utilized by a variety of web-based services for different purposes. One of the primary uses of user profiles is for recommendation of items, elements or general information that a user has not yet considered but may find useful

[10, 16]. Profiling is a powerful technique that is currently experiencing major changes related to the way in which knowledge about populations and futures is created [15]. This technique is further enhanced with the involvement of social network. In order to perform user profiling in online social network, one requires data pertaining to online activities of such user who performs different kinds of activities, which may either depend on one's interest or some effect of some influence on them [17]. To be able to profile the users based on their activities on different social networks requires the whole aggregated data of all social networking sites which are practically difficult for the researchers to collect. But based on the activities performed in one particular site for some period of time, the user can be profiled using various approaches separately [17]. If profiled correctly, this technique will enable a better management of students through their profiles. This will track their progress from the moment of their intake up until the moment of graduation. Hence a full-scaled profiling will better monitor students which could substantially reduce the dropout rates in the university. Figure 2 displays a case-based profiling model that could possibly be put to work to cope with dropout issues.

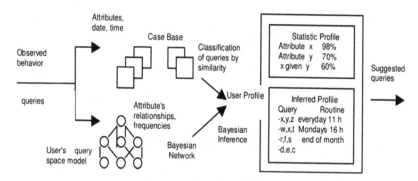

Fig. 2. Case-based profiling [22]

As depicted in the model above, the data will constitute of observed user behaviour and queries from sources. The gathered attributes will then go through two separate processes. Firstly, a case-based reasoning (CBR) that classifies queries according to their similar aspects. Secondly, the development of a bayesian network based on the attributes' relationships and frequencies. These two processes are then integrated to obtain a single user profile which will then be able to produce suggested queries.

3   Methodology

This section explains the methods deployed for this research that involves three main phases. The first phase involves the synthesis of literature review to obtain an under-standing of the global phenomenon of student dropout and the existing applications that have been used. The second phase is the identification of social factors that contribute to student dropout. The third part is to analyze the application of user profiling for the mentioned social factors. These tasks were performed to obtain a clear idea of the social constraints of student dropout and the possibility of applying user profiling as a solution (Fig. 3).

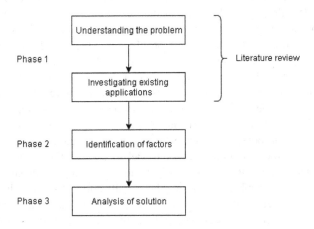

Fig. 3. Research methods flow

During the initial search, a total of 150 articles were obtained from several online databases namely Elsevier, IEEE, Web of Science, Scopus and ScienceDirect. The year of the articles selected was limited to 10 years frame from 2009 to 2018, because it is assumed as the optimal timeframe for the analysis purpose. Keywords used include student dropout, university, user profiling and social factors. In the first phase, a comprehensive literature review was conducted to find evidence based on previous studies by relevant authors. This was done to fulfill two particular purposes. Firstly, to develop an understanding about student dropout, their causes and effects. Secondly, to carry out an investigation on some of the existing models of that are in use in the academic field today, with particular emphasis on coping student dropout.

Next, the second phase involves an attempt to get a thorough insight of student dropout from a social perspective. Common traits of social causes were analyzed and grouped together (Table 1). For this part, information is extracted from a select 15 papers to obtain a more specific result. A brief description of each attribute is also provided for the reader to have a clearer picture of the particular factor.

The third phase is to analyze and detect the specific deployment of user profiling for each of the social factors identified earlier. For this part, the solution is considered from a select 10 articles only. These are also grouped in Table 1.

4 Results and Discussion

From this research, it is evident that student dropout is an issue experienced by many countries across the globe. It may be the result of several social, emotional, economic and spiritual reasons, but as discussed earlier the paper only accounts for the social impacts of student dropout (Table 1). Through literature, several existing applications for student dropout have been identified. Amongst them is the application of decision trees for the detection of student dropout profiles [4]. This model aims at identifying patterns of student dropout from socioeconomic, academic, disciplinary and institutional data of students. Policy writers and specialists in education have been encouraged to work together to implement a successful education system that better suits the new generation of students to compete better in the job markets and meet the challenges of globalization [18]. Another viable approach is the application of Bayesian networks to model dropout behaviour patterns [7]. This method combines the whole student model and the individual student model to express three kinds of dropping behaviour - heterogeneity of the dropping behaviour and temporal heterogeneity. Next is the use of cluster ensemble to improve the classification of student dropout, which involves the novel reuse of link-based cluster ensemble as a data transformation framework for more accurate prediction [21]. Lastly the application of user profiling to subdue to effects of student dropout through close surveillance of students in relation to their user profiles [9–11]. In this paper, user profiling has been selected as the optimal solution after due consideration. Whilst most applications are able to identify and classify students who have dropped out, the models are however unable to address and provide a viable solution for the problem. User profiling, on the other hand, provides a platform to track students' progress from the moment of their registration and throughout their time in university. This provides a better alternative to provide assistance to these individuals at the earliest stage possible, which can then in turn reduce the tendency to dropout. Though many external factors affect the rate of dropout, this research only focuses on the social factors involved. The target of this research is to provide an overview of the social impacts behind student dropout and how profiling will be able to provide an optimal solution.

The table below displays the results of the research. The first column categorizes the major social factors of dropout while the second column shows the list of papers that have covered them. The third column provides a brief elaboration of each factor. Finally, the fourth and last column discusses the possible application of user profiling techniques or knowledge for the corresponding factor.

Table 1. Social factors of student dropout and user profiling as a possible solution.

Factors	List of papers	Explanation	User profiling application
Poor academic performance	[1, 2, 4, 5, 7, 18, 21]	Below standards examination results, repetitive failing of a particular or different course, academically weak	Machine learning to track students academic progress from the beginning to be able to identify weak students from the start and not at the point of dropout. Using data-driven information of students results prior to intake and subsequent achievements [9, 10, 15]

(continued)

Table 1. (*continued*)

Factors	List of papers	Explanation	User profiling application
Vocational and professional disorientation	[4, 7, 19]	Confusion arising due to one's conflicting professional interest and course pursued. May also difference in expectation of course structure vs reality	Use of classification or clustering techniques to deviate content/semantic analysis to map accurate vocational pathway based on interest [17]
Difficulty adjusting to new environment	[1, 4–6, 20]	Inability to cope with moving on from schooling life to college/university. Also includes moving from rural to city or local to foreign states	Using knowledge from adaptation process in web-based for adequate learning environment [16]
Unfavorable/too difficult course	[1, 6]	Forced into accepting a course, lack of interest, too complex for one's ability/skills, low understanding level	Profiling algorithm to enable identification of students struggles with regards to syllabus or content matter. Analysis of individuals understanding levels [10, 25]
Family/personal issues	[7, 8, 18, 20, 21]	Poor upbringing, problem within family or pressure. Personal issues may include health, disability or other mental related issues	Use privacy-related attributes and adaptation process to cope with the relevant issues [16, 23]
Poor attendance	[14, 18]	Skipping classes without any valid reasoning, lack of participation in course activities	Classification technique to perform behavioral analysis, obtain causes and impacts to improve attendance records [17, 24]
Poor facilitation	[5, 8, 14]	Institutions with lack of facilities for learning and teaching procedures or fulfill student's needs	Analyzing fuzzy models logic for adequate learning strategies and improve facilitation [12]
Incompatible teachers/teaching	[6, 8]	Unfavorable teaching techniques or style	Adaptive learning methods and also improve user engagement techniques [11, 12, 23]

Based on the table above, there are eight (8) social factors that have been identified as common causes of student dropout, which can be perceived in the first column. Of these, it is evident that there are three (3) major social causes - poor academic achievement, difficulty adjusting to new environment and family or personal issues - since it appears more frequently as seen in the second column. A brief explanation is provided for each social factor. Based on the fourth column, it can be observed how different user profiling techniques can be applied to different problems as a solution.

5   Conclusion

A decrease in the rate of students dropout in higher education will certainly bring upon a positive impact to society and a nation's development. In conclusion, identifying the social factors that contribute to these rates is the stepping stone towards achieving an optimal solution. Different causes will certainly require different approaches to solve. However, this paper proposes the application of user profiling as a conducive medium to address each factor using several techniques such as machine learning, clustering and algorithms among others. Hence, it is expected that through a planned and constructive approach of user profiling, each impacting factor will be contained and consequently cope with the issue of student dropout. This would in turn increase the standards of universities and lead to the betterment of society. Dropout will continue to occur nevertheless, hence future work may be able to divert attention to eliminating the issue.

Acknowledgement. The authors sincerely appreciate and acknowledge the support provided by the FRGS Program 2018 at University Malaya and the Ministry of Higher Education under the research grant FP 112-2018A.

References

1. Paura, L., Arhipova, I.: Cause of analysis of students' dropout rate in higher education study program. Procedia – Soc. Behav. Sci. **109**, 1282–1286 (2014)
2. Costa, F., Bispo, M., Pereira, R.: Dropout and retention of undergraduate students in management: a study at a Brazilian Federal University. RAUSP Manag. J. **53**, 74–85 (2018)
3. TRENDS homepage. http://trendsinstitution.org/dropping-out-challenges-and-solutions. Accessed 6 July 2019
4. Pereira, R., Zambrano, J.: Application of decision trees for detection of student dropout profiles. In: 16th IEEE International Conference on Machine Learning and Applications, pp. 528–531 (2017)
5. Jung, J., Kim, Y.: Exploring regional and institutional factors of international students' dropout: the South Korea case. Wiley High. Educ. Q. **72**, 141–159 (2017)
6. Ktoridou, D., Epaminonda, E.: Measuring the compatibility between engineering students' personality types and major of study: a first step towards preventing engineering education dropouts. In: IEEE Global Engineering Education Conference (EDUCON), pp. 192–195 (2014)
7. Shiratori, N.: Modeling dropout behavior patterns using Bayesian networks in small-scale private university. In: 6th IIAI International Congress on Advanced Applied Informatics, pp. 170–173 (2017)
8. Rasmy, M.I., Selvadurai, S., Sulehan, J.: Social environmental determinants of student dropout in the plantation settlement. Malays. J. Soc. Space **13**(2), 54–64 (2017)
9. Hasan, O., Habegger, B., Brunie, L., Bennani, N., Damiani, E.: A Discussion of Privacy Challenges in User Profiling with Big Data Techniques: The EEXCESS Use Case, p. 1
10. Middleton, S., De Roure, D., Shadbolt, N.: Capturing knowledge of user preferences: ontologies in recommender systems, Southampton, pp. 1–8
11. Bouchet, F., Harley, J., Trevors, G., Azevedo, R.: Clustering and Profiling students according to their interactions with an intelligent tutoring system fostering self-regulated learning. J. Educ. Data Min. **5**, 104–146 (2013)
12. Xu, D., Wang, H., Su, K.: Intelligent student profiling with fuzzy models. In: Proceedings of the 35th Hawaii International Conference on System Sciences, Kowloon, pp. 1–8 (2002)
13. MOHE webpage. https://www.studymalaysia.com/education/higher-education-in-malaysia/the-malaysian-higher-education-system-an-overview. Accessed 1 July 2019
14. Latif, A., Choudhary, A.I., Hammayun, A.A.: Economic effects of student dropouts: a comparative study. J. Glob. Econ. **3**, 2–4 (2015)
15. Leese, M.: The new profiling: algorithms, black boxes, and the failure of anti-discriminatory safeguards in the European Union. Int. Centre Ethics Sci. Humanit. (IZEW) **45**(5), 494–511 (2014)

16. Lee, M.G.: Profiling students' adaptation styles in web-based learning. Comput. Edu. **36**, 121–132 (2001)
17. Vasanthakumar, G., Sunithamma, K., Deepa Shenoy, P., Venugopal, K.: An overview on user profiling in online social networks. Int. J. Appl. Inf. Syst. (IJAIS) **11**(8), 25–42 (2017)
18. Usman, S.: Dropping out, challenges and solutions, pp. 1–3. Trends Research & Advisory (2015)
19. Othman, R., Othman, R.: Higher educations institutions and social performance: evidence from public and private universities. Int. J. Bus. Soc. **15**(1), 1–18 (2014)
20. Rumberger, R., Larson, K.: Student mobility and the increased risk of high school dropout. Am. J. Edu. **107**(1), 1–35 (1998). The University of Chicago Press
21. Iam-On, N., Boongoen, T.: Using cluster ensemble to improve classification of student dropout in Thai University, pp. 452–457 (2014)
22. Schiaffino, S.N., Amandi, A.: User profiling with case-based reasoning and Bayesian networks. In: International Joint Conference IBERAMIA-SBIA, pp. 12–21 (2000)
23. Helberger, N.: Policy implications from algorithmic profiling and the changing relationship between newsreaders and the media. J. Eur. Inst. Commun. Cult. **23**, 188–203 (2016)
24. Utami, E., Luthfi, E.T.: Profiling analysis based on social media for prospective employees recruitment using SVM and Chi-Square. In: Journal of Physics: Conference Series (2018)
25. Profiling of Algorithms, pp. 1–19, 10 September 1999
26. Das, K., Kumar Sinha, S.: A survey on user behaviour analysis in social networks. Int. J. Comput. Sci. Inf. Secur. (IJCSIS) **14**(11), 895–908 (2016)
27. Borjas, G.: An evaluation of the foreign student program. John F. Kennedy School of Government Harvard University Faculty Research Working Papers Series, pp. 2–14, July 2002
28. Umar, A., Noon, N.A., Abdullahi, M.: Challenges confronting African students in Malaysia: a case of postgraduate Nigerian students at International Islamic University Malaysia (IIUM) Kuala Lumpur. J. Afr. Stud. Dev. **6**(9), 161–168 (2014)
29. Lewis, V.: Embedding marketing in international campus development: lessons from UK universities. Perspect. Policy Pract. High. Educ. **20**, 1–18 (2015)
30. Ministry of Education Malaysia: Malaysia Education Blueprint 2015–2025 (Higher Education), pp. 1–40 (2015)
31. QS Enrolment Solutions: Harnessing Opportunities in Global Higher Education. Global International Student Survey, pp. 2–25 (2018)
32. Educational Planning and Research Division, Ministry of Education Malaysia, Quick Facts 2018, Malaysia Educational Statistics, p. 34 (2018)
33. Verbik, L.: The International Branch Campus: Models and Trends. Observatory on Borderless Higher Education, London, pp. 14–15
34. Ministry of Higher of Education Malaysia: Enhancing Academic Productivity and Cost Efficiency. University Transformation Programme Silver Book, pp. 2–107. Ministry of Higher Education Malaysia (2016)

Usability Evaluation of Smartphone Gestures in Supporting Elderly Users

Hasanin Mohammed Salman[✉], Wan Fatimah Wan Ahmad,
and Suziah Sulaiman

Computer and Information Sciences Department, Universiti Teknologi
PETRONAS, 32610 Seri Iskandar, Perak, Malaysia
{hasanin_g03421, fatimhd, suziah}@utp.edu.my

Abstract. The elderly often experience usability problems in using touchscreen gestures to operate smartphones. Compared to adults and children, elderly users are outperformed in executing gestures on smartphone devices. Previous studies have recommended the tap and swipe gesture when designing apps for the elderly while criticising "tap and hold", drag, and pinch as overly complex gestures for the elderly. The objective of this study is to evaluate the usability of smartphone gestures in supporting elderly users. Ten elderly participants were recruited in conducting a two-stage experiment. The first stage of this study reassessed the usability of the current tap and swipe. While the second stage investigated the usability of the three criticised gestures against the usability of three alternative gestures proposed in this study. The results of the study affirmed the high usability of the tap and swipe gestures and the three proposed gestures. The study has contributed to providing a better understanding of the usability of gestures in supporting the elderly.

Keywords: Elderly · Gestures · Smartphone · Gestural interface ·
Touchscreens · Usability

1 Introduction

Modern smartphones offer advanced features and functionalities that require gestural interfaces in order to operate them efficiently. Gestural interfaces can be categorised as either free-form or touchscreen [1]. Free-form gestural interfaces do not require the user to touch the device directly, but instead to move the device to initiate functions, for example, rotate the device to orientate the screen [2]. While, touchscreen gestural interfaces require the user to be touching the device directly through employing various gestures [1], that include; tap, drag, pinch/spread gestures [3]. Using touchscreen gestural interfaces has been suggested compared to conventional input, like using a physical keyboard [4, 5]. Despite the benefits of using gestures as input, elderly users, aged 60 years and above [6], often experience problems in using touchscreen gestures in operating smartphones [7, 8]. The challenges faced by elderly users in operating touchscreen devices, including smartphones, can be attributed to age-related deteriorations in their physical and cognitive abilities. Smartphones are accompanied with a

© Springer Nature Switzerland AG 2019
H. Badioze Zaman et al. (Eds.): IVIC 2019, LNCS 11870, pp. 672–683, 2019.
https://doi.org/10.1007/978-3-030-34032-2_60

range of gestures ranging from a single tap to swipe, "tap and hold", "pinch/spread", and drag [2, 3]. Tap and swipe gestures are recommended for elderly users as being easier to use and comprehend [8]. Other gestures, such as "tap and hold", drag, and pinch/spread have been identified as overly complex gestures for elderly users [8]. The usability evaluation of smartphone gestures could help to enhance the understanding of smartphone designers regarding implementing proper gestures for the elderly.

The study is structured into sections. Section 2 introduces the main concepts of the study regarding usability, elaborating on the usability of smartphone gestures for the elderly. Section 3 explains the concept of the proposed gestures. Section 4 discusses the method employed in this study. Section 5 presents the evaluation results which is followed by Sect. 6 which presents the discussion. The conclusions of the overall study are presented in Sect. 7.

2 Background of the Study

Usability is a vital necessity to design new products and is a highly sought feature for individuals when selecting a product [9–11]. A product is usable if people can use it effectively, efficiently and feel satisfied [12]. [4, 5] suggested using touchscreen gestural interfaces compared to conventional input such as using a physical keyboard. But, elderly users often experience usability problems in using touchscreen gestures in operating smartphones [7, 8]. [8] tested the usability of smartphone surface gestures on different sized smartphones used by children and adults, including the elderly. The study has shown that children and adults outperformed the elderly in both the operation and execution of using gestures. Elderly participants were the slowest concerning overall time and success. The elderly also exhibited the lowest accuracy of executing the gestures. Regarding gestures, key findings were obtained from four (4) relevant studies [13–17], summarising the following issues; (1) the elderly have difficulty in recognising when a button or target is tapped, which frequently leads to long taps and pressing of wrong buttons; (2) due to slow elderly operation when tapping and executing tasks, the elderly also encounter problems with text entry using virtual keyboards; (3) additional time is needed to comprehend the movements needed for touchscreen gestures; and (4) difficulties in recognising tappable spots on touchscreens.

3 Proposed Gestures

In light of the findings by [3, 8] recommending the tap gesture to operate smartphones for the elderly, we proposed tap-activated and tap-based gestures as an alternative to the three complex gestures. The concept of a tap-activated gesture is to simplify the activation of functions that currently require performing the criticized gestures. The simplification is by means of providing a single tap gesture that could directly activate the corresponding function. While, the proposed tap-based gestures were designed to close the gap as identified by the key findings presented by [7]. Accordingly, the design of tap-based gestures considers: (1) providing proper feedback when the target is tapped; (2) supporting gesture comprehension with guidance, (i.e., visual cues and textual instruction); and (3) keeping tappable targets recognisable.

4 Method

4.1 Participants

Ten elderly participants aged 60 years and above were recruited, with diverse backgrounds, gender and education levels. Six of the participants were male, while the remainder were female. Four participants were college graduates or had a postgraduate degree, four had some college/high school credits, and two had not completed their schooling. All participants were capable of using smartphones with English language settings and had been using smartphones for six months or more.

4.2 Procedure

The design of this study employed a two-stage approach. The first stage reassessed the usability of tap and swipe gestures. While in the second stage, the usability of the complex gestures ("tap and hold", drag, and pinch/spread) was examined versus the usability of the proposed tap-activated and tap-based gestures. To test the usability of the gestures, five representative tasks were identified in which each task required a specific gesture. Table 1 illustrates the tasks (in both stages) and their associated existing and proposed gestures. Prior to the first stage, the experimenter briefed all participants, informing them that there were no time restrictions in performing a task and the decision to give up from completing the task was solely at their own discretion. Representative tasks were printed and placed in front of each participant. The procedure related to each stage is demonstrated in the following two sections.

Table 1. Representative tasks and their related gestures.

	Task	Task definition	Gesture	
			Existing	Proposed
Stage 1	1	Open camera application	Tap	Not available
	2	In the gallery application, find the black picture	Swipe	Not available
Stage 2	3	Remove the "YouTube" application	"Tap and hold", then drag	Tap-activated
	4	Highlight the text starts with "Please" and ends with "Number:" in the email in front of you	"Tap and hold", then drag	Highlight tap-based
	5	Zoom in the "triangle" appeared in the picture to the maximum size	Pinch (or spread to zoom out)	Zoom tap-based

First Stage. The first stage reassessed the usability of tap and swipe gestures. To reassess their usability, tasks 1 and 2 were identified that required performing tap and swipe respectively. Since tap and swipe, specifically tap, are the essential gestures to interact with any smartphone, reassessing their usability is crucial as it could affirm the high usability of these two gestures in supporting the elderly. Hence, no improvements in these two gestures were proposed in this study, i.e., no alternative gestures were proposed to do tasks 1 and 2. Once the first task completed, each participant was asked to respond to a questionnaire in rating his/her satisfaction level for the tap gesture. Completing the questionnaire, the participants rested for about 10 s before being subjected to the second task. Once the second task was completed, each participant was asked to respond to another questionnaire in rating his/her satisfaction level for the swipe gesture.

Second Stage. In the second stage, each participant attempted tasks 3 to 5 using the existing gestures and proposed gestures. In the first instance, five participants performed the tasks using the existing gestures while the second five participants performed the tasks using the proposed gestures first. Tasks 3 to 5 were randomly presented to each participant. Before performing each of the three tasks using the existing gestures, the experimenter showed the participants a video which demonstrated the appropriate gesture corresponding to the current task. Next, the participant attempted to perform the task, with his/her performance simultaneously recorded. Upon the completion of each task using the existing gestures, each participant was asked to respond to the questionnaire, (identical to the questionnaire administrated in first stage), to rate his/her satisfaction level for the tested gesture.

Once the second stage was completed by performing the three tasks using the existing and proposed gestures, the participants rested for around 2 min before beginning a second iteration of the stage. In the second iteration, the same ten participants reattempted only the proposed gestures, and their performance was recorded. Given that in the first iteration of the second stage the participants lacked prior experience in applying the proposed gestures, by reattempting gestures it was anticipated to reveal a more stable level of participants' performance as well as revealing the proposed gestures' learnability. At the completion of the second iteration of each proposed gesture, the participants answered an identical questionnaire in rating his/her satisfaction level overall for the proposed gesture.

4.3 Materials and Design

Android smartphone devices are relatively popular among elderly users [18], the device used in this stage was an Android-based Samsung Galaxy J7 smartphone having a 5.5-inch Super AMOLED capacitive touchscreen with a resolution of 720×1280 pixels. The proposed gestures were implemented using the Just in mind prototype tool (https://www.justinmind.com). The gestures were installed on the Galaxy J7 device using the Just in mind application, which is a prototype viewer through which prototypes can be viewed directly using the entire [full] screen on a smartphone. The user interface (UI) design related to performing tasks 3 to 5 had the identical J7 UI (e.g., icons, and colors). The main reason for choosing the identical J7 device to host the gestures during the second stage was to avoid any prospected differences in the participant's performance due to the UI design of the smartphone and its physical characteristics, (e.g., screen size and resolution, device weight, etc.). For task 3, to remove the application using existing gestures, the user is required to "tap and hold" on the target application icon and proceed by dragging the icon across the home screen to the "remove option" appearing on top of the screen (refer to Fig. 1(a)). As an alternative, we proposed a tap-activated remove function (refer to Fig. 1(b)). To remove any application (i.e. You-Tube in task three) a single tap on the remove button activates the function.

(a)

(b)

Fig. 1. Screen images of the existing "tap and hold" then drag gesture (a), versus the proposed tap-activated gesture (b).

Tasks 4 and 5, tap-based gestures were proposed as an alternative to their counterpart gestures. To differentiate between the two tap-based gestures employed in task 4 and task 5, a gesture used in task 4 is referred to as highlight tap-based, and the proposed gesture used in task 5 is referred to as zoom tap-based.

In task 4, to highlight text with the existing gestures, the user is required to "tap and hold" starting from the first word of the corresponding sentence and then drag the set of the appeared bounding handles to highlight the required text (refer to Fig. 2(a)). The alternative highlight tap-based gesture provided successive taps with guidance to perform task 4. Here, textual instruction was supported by step indicator (as a visual cue), directing the user to tap on the first word in the text required to be highlighted (Fig. 2(b)). Once the word was tapped, it will be highlighted in yellow (Fig. 2(c), indicated by the upper arrow), with a step two instruction appearing directing the participant to tap on the last word in the required text (Fig. 2(c), indicated by the lower arrow). In response to these two taps, the text between the first and last word will be highlighted in yellow (Fig. 2(d)).

Concerning task 5, in order to zoom the object to the optimal size, successive taps with guidance was the gesture proposed as an alternative to the current pinch gesture. The zoom tap-based gesture design comprises of a single tap on the target followed by immediate feedback using focus, that will be positioned on the target with a question statement: "is this the correct target that you want to zoom in?"; accompanied by 'yes' and 'no' recognisable buttons (Fig. 3(a)). If the user taps on the no button, the attempt will be repeated allowing the user to reselect the proper target again. If the user taps on the yes button, the target will be enlarged, and plus and minus signs will appear beside the target (Fig. 3(b)). As shown in Fig. 3(b) each sign will be accompanied with a label explaining its function; "plus sign" to zoom in, and the "minus sign" to zoom out.

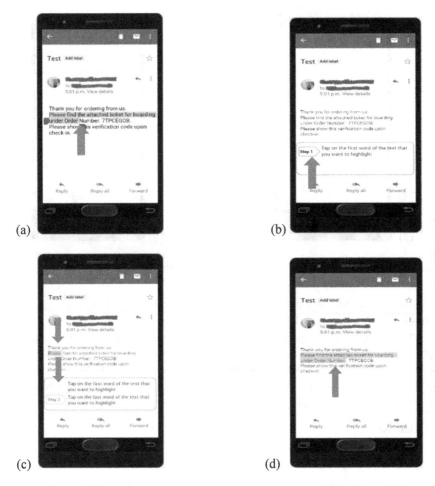

Fig. 2. Screen images of the existing "tap and hold" then drag gesture (a), versus the proposed highlight tap-based gesture (b) to (d)

4.4 Evaluation

The evaluation regarding the usability of gestures was performed by measuring the participants' performance and satisfaction while performing the representative tasks. A higher level of performance and satisfaction of the participants' is an indication of more usable gestures. As suggested by [12], the product is usable when people can use it for the product's intended purpose, both effectively, efficiently, feeling satisfied. The task completion rate referred to the number of participants who completed the task divided by the number who attempted the task, then multiplied by 100 [19]. The task completion time, measured in seconds, referred to the time required to successfully complete the task [20]. Regarding the subjective measurements, the participants were

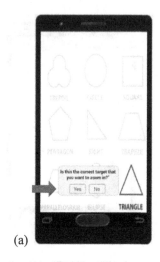

(a)   (b)

Fig. 3. Screen images of the proposed zoom tap-based gesture

asked to respond to a questionnaire to rate their level of satisfaction for the tested gestures using a 7-point Likert scale ranging from 1 = "strongly disagree" to 7 = "strongly agree". The questionnaire consisted of two questions. The first question investigated participants' satisfaction level with the ease of completing the task using the tested gesture, and the second question investigated the participants' satisfaction level regarding the amount of time taken to complete the task using the tested gesture.

5   Results

5.1   First Stage

A task completion rate of 100% was recorded for both tasks. All participants could apply the gestures correctly. 1.91 s was recorded as the mean task completion time for task 1, and 4.63 s as the mean task completion time for task 2. Concerning satisfaction, an optimum result for participants' satisfaction, (mean equals to 7), with the ease of completing the task was recorded for the tap and swipe related tasks. Optimum satisfaction with the completion time was recorded for the tap related task (task 1), along with high satisfaction recorded for the swipe related task (task 2), (mean rating of 6.9) (Table 2).

Table 2. First stage record

Task	Task completion rate (%)	Task completion time (s)	Satisfaction with the ease of completion rating	Satisfaction with the completion time rating
1	100	1.91	7	7
2	100	4.63	7	6.9

To further affirm the high usability of tap and swipe, tasks 1 and 2 were performed by a group of 10 young participants (aged 26–34 years). 1.73 s was recorded as the mean task completion time for task 1, and 4.52 s as the mean task completion time for task 2. Even though young participants required less time to apply tap and swipe gestures, independent samples t-test revealed that difference in performance between the two groups was not statistically significant ($p > .05$).

5.2   Second Stage

The task completion rate for the second stage (first iteration) for the representative tasks is depicted in Table 3. For task 3, an identical task completion rate of (80%) was recorded when the participants performed the task using an existing gesture and the proposed tap-activated gesture. For task 4, a higher task completion rate was recorded using a proposed highlight tap-based gesture, Contrary to findings observed in task 5, where a higher task completion rate was recorded using the existing gesture. As shown in Table 3, the proposed gestures mean task completion rate recorded in the first iteration was 80% which was higher compared to the mean of 63.33% recorded for the existing gesture. For the second iteration, Table 3 shows an optimum task completion rate recorded for tasks 3 and 4 (100%). Overall, as illustrated in Table 3, the proposed gestures mean task completion rate is 93.33% which was higher than the mean of 80% recorded in the first iteration.

Table 3. Task completion rate

	Task completion rate (%)		
	Existing	Proposed	
Task	1st iteration (one iteration)	1st iteration	2nd iteration
3	80	80	100
4	20	90	100
5	90	70	80
	Mean = 63.33	Mean = 80	Mean = 93.33

The mean task completion time for the first iteration of the second stage of representative tasks is illustrated in Fig. 4. For task 3, a slight improvement in the mean task completion time was recorded using the proposed tap-activated gesture (7.5 s for the proposed gestures versus 7.86 s for the existing gesture). For task 4, an observable improvement in the mean task completion time was recorded using a highlight tap-based proposed gesture (18.46 s for the proposed gestures versus 50.65 s for the existing gesture). An opposite finding was documented for task 5 where a higher mean task completion time was recorded using a zoom tap-based proposed gesture (35.47 s for the proposed gesture versus 5.69 s for the existing gesture). In the second iteration in performing the proposed gestures, an improved mean task completion time was recorded for all tasks as illustrated in Fig. 4.

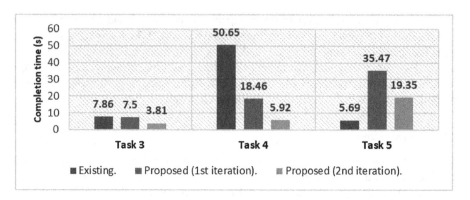

Fig. 4. Mean task completion time

The participants' ratings corresponding to tasks 3 to 5 are illustrated in Figs. 5 and 6. Regarding tasks 3 and 4, satisfaction with ease of completion and completion time were higher using the proposed gestures in comparison to their counterpart existing gestures. In task 5 using the proposed gesture recorded a higher satisfaction level with respect to ease of completion and lower satisfaction regarding the completion time.

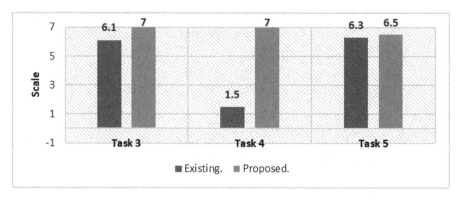

Fig. 5. Satisfaction with the ease of completion

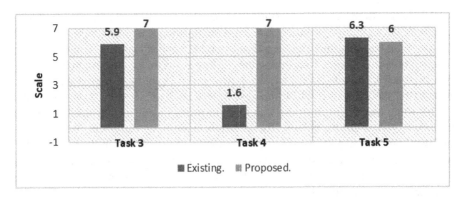

Fig. 6. Satisfaction with the completion time

6 Discussions

The results obtained affirms the tap and swipe gestures as having high usability. Thereby, the difficulty does not originate from execution or operation of the gesture or understanding but rather, originates from insufficient system feedback to the user. In tasks 3 and 4, the participants' performance was found to be usable gestures that support the elderly even without any prior experience. The improvements in the participants' performance following the second iteration also suggest the proposed gestures learnability.

In contrast to pinch gesture as a complex gesture for the elderly, high usability of the existing pinch gesture was witnessed in task 5. A higher usability pinch gesture was observed versus the proposed zoom tap-based gesture. Regardless of this superiority, the participants' performance employing zoom tap-based gesture depicts a usable gesture supporting the elderly even without experience. Following the second iteration, the recorded improvement affirmed the zoom tap-based usability. Therefore, the zoom tap-based gesture can be utilized in scenarios that require accurate zoom on a small target, like in map applications. Further, the concept of gesture can be enhanced by adding a direct-to-full-size zoom option which will invariably reduce the number of taps required to fully enlarge an object using one tap, in which the gesture's usage efficiency and completion time, will be improved.

7 Conclusions

This study extends the understanding surrounding the usability of gestures in supporting elderly users. First stage results affirmed the high usability of the tap and swipe gestures backed through the comparison with the young participants that showed a close performance between young and elderly. While the second stage affirmed superior usability of the tap-activated and highlighted tap-based gestures compared to their counterpart existing gesture. The zoom tap-based gesture recorded a high level of usability, especially following the second iteration, which was near to the existing pinch gesture. Both the zoom gesture for both the existing and proposed gestures, achieved high usability, for instance, the task completion rate. Indeed, the concept of the zoom tap-based gesture can be utilized in other applications that require accurate zooming on a small target. Concerning the existing gestures, the conclusion in terms of their usability is presented in the following two points: Usability of the existing gesture depends on the context in which the gesture was applied. The high usability of the pinch gesture which is inconsistent with a previous study identified the pinch gesture as a complex gesture for the elderly. The implementation of an early beta version of the launcher application is continuing and is planned to be published in the Google play store once accomplished. After publishing the launcher application, further improvements on the gestures will be reflected in the upcoming release of the launcher based on user feedback and comments.

Acknowledgments. This work was supported by the Fundamental Research Grant Scheme (FRGS) from the Ministry of Higher Education of Malaysia under Grant FRGS/1/2017/ICT04/UTP/02/2. The authors would like to thank Universiti Teknologi PETRONAS and all the participants who took part in the experiment of this study.

References

1. Saffer, D.: Designing Gestural Interfaces: Touchscreens and Interactive Devices. O'Reilly Media, Inc. (2008)
2. Wörndl, W., Weicker, J., Lamche, B.: Selecting gestural user interaction patterns for recommender applications on smartphones. In: Decisions@ RecSys, pp. 17–20. Citeseer (2013)
3. Leitão, R.A.: Creating mobile gesture-based interaction design patterns for older adults: a study of tap and swipe gestures with Portuguese seniors. Faculdade Eng., M.S. thesis. Univ. Porto, Porto, Portugal (2012)
4. Piper, A.M., Campbell, R., Hollan, J.D.: Exploring the accessibility and appeal of surface computing for older adult health care support. In: Proceedings of the SIGCHI Conference on Human Factors in Computing Systems, pp. 907–916. ACM, Atlanta (2010)
5. Guenther, J., Volk, F., Shaneck, M.: Proposing a multi-touch interface for intrusion detection environments. In: Proceedings of the Seventh International Symposium on Visualization for Cyber Security, pp. 13–21. ACM, Ottawa (2010)
6. Desa, U.: World Population Prospects: The 2017 Revision. Population Division of the Department of Economic and Social Affairs of the United Nations Secretariat, New York (2017)
7. Petrovčič, A., Taipale, S., Rogelj, A., Dolničar, V.: Design of mobile phones for older adults: an empirical analysis of design guidelines and checklists for feature phones and smartphones. Int. J. Hum.-Comput. Interact. **34**, 251–264 (2018)
8. Tsai, T.-H., Tseng, K.C., Chang, Y.-S.: Testing the usability of smartphone surface gestures on different sizes of smartphones by different age groups of users. Comput. Hum. Behav. **75**, 103–116 (2017)
9. Choe, P., Liao, C., Sun, W.: Providing customisation guidelines of mobile phones for manufacturers. Behav. Inf. Technol. **31**, 983–994 (2012)
10. Mack, Z., Sharples, S.: The importance of usability in product choice: a mobile phone case study. Ergonomics **52**, 1514–1528 (2009)

11. Inostroza, R., Rusu, C., Roncagliolo, S., Rusu, V., Collazos, C.A.: Developing SMASH: a set of smartphone's usability heuristics. Comput. Stan. Interfaces **43**, 40–52 (2016)   ,
12. Lewis, J.R.: Usability: lessons learned … and yet to be learned. Int. J. Hum.-Comput. Interact. **30**, 663–684 (2014)
13. Motti, L.G., Vigouroux, N., Gorce, P.: Interaction techniques for older adults using touchscreen devices: a literature review. In: Proceedings of the 25th Conference on l'Interaction Homme-Machine, pp. 125–134. ACM, Talence (2013)
14. Zhou, J., Rau, P.-L.P., Salvendy, G.: Age-related difference in the use of mobile phones. Univ. Access Inf. Soc. **13**, 401–413 (2014)
15. Harada, S., Sato, D., Takagi, H., Asakawa, C.: Characteristics of elderly user behavior on mobile multi-touch devices. In: Kotzé, P., Marsden, G., Lindgaard, G., Wesson, J., Winckler, M. (eds.) INTERACT 2013. LNCS, vol. 8120, pp. 323–341. Springer, Heidelberg (2013). https://doi.org/10.1007/978-3-642-40498-6_25
16. Zhou, J., Rau, P.-L.P., Salvendy, G.: Use and design of handheld computers for older adults: a review and appraisal. Int. J. Hum.-Comput. Interact. **28**, 799–826 (2012)
17. Furuki, K., Kikuchi, Y.: Approach to commercialization of Raku-Raku smartphone. Fujitsu Sci. Tech. J. **49**, 196–201 (2013)
18. Wong, C.Y., Ibrahim, R., Hamid, T.A., Mansor, E.I.: Mismatch between older adults' expectation and smartphone user interface. Malays. J. Comput. **3**, 138–153 (2018)
19. Mifsud, J.: Usability metrics – a guide to quantify the usability of any system (2015). https://usabilitygeek.com/usability-metrics-a-guide-to-quantify-system-usability/
20. Sauro, J.: 10 things to know about task times (2011). https://measuringu.com/task-times/

The Design Criteria of Product Label Assisting Purchase Decision

Mohd Hafiz Faizal Mohamad Kamil[(✉)] and Dahlan Abdul Ghani

Malaysian Institute of Information Technology, Universiti Kuala Lumpur,
1016 Jalan Sultan Ismail, 50250 Kuala Lumpur, Malaysia
hafizfaizal@unikl.edu.my

Abstract. Purchase decision making needs to be done wisely. Product labels are one of the delivery mediums of product information for product purchases in store by consumers. However, product label design criteria need to be identified so that the roles of product purchases will be achieved. Therefore, this study proposes a conceptual framework for food and beverage product label design criteria for university students. Observation and questionnaire were conducted on consumers and experts in 2 phases of study. The study found that, front section of product label was used for 9 types of purchase products by students, 4 product information on product labels viewed by students, 5 text design criteria and 2 images design criteria for information on product labels and impact on students as consumers during purchasing. The findings obtained are the most appropriate combination of text and image design criteria on product label in assisting student for purchase decision.

Keywords: Usability · Product label design criteria · Purchase decision · Human computer interaction

1 Introduction

The main role of product label design is to make the product packaging more attractive through combination of multimedia elements such as text and images. The function of design criteria is to deliver important product information to consumer. Good combination of design criteria can stand out the product to be selected by consumer over than competing product available. The usability evaluation on label product design criteria will be adapted to suit the environment of product marketing.

The study purpose is to identify the label product design criteria base on consumer behaviour during product purchase decision. Consumers consider labels on product packaging are effective product information medium if it able to attract and assist in purchasing decisions [19]. At the same time, the information presented can reduce consumer uncertainty about the product [9]. In addition, product labels also serve as one of the attractions for the product sales [16]. Product labels are the easiest element to detect and view because every product in the market will be display and organized according to the of product labels to consumers [24]. Studies have found that consumers spend less time when searching for products for purchase purposes when they refer to product labels [18].

© Springer Nature Switzerland AG 2019
H. Badioze Zaman et al. (Eds.): IVIC 2019, LNCS 11870, pp. 684–693, 2019.
https://doi.org/10.1007/978-3-030-34032-2_61

The study will evaluate design criteria consist of text and image criteria on label design section that visual by consumer during purchase decision in store. The evaluation criteria are based on human interaction behaviour, product label design criteria and usability. The findings to be obtained are the most appropriate combination of text and image design criteria on product label assisting purchase decision.

2 Human Interaction Behaviour During Purchase Decision Making

Human computer interactions related to interface that are used as interaction mediums between computer and human. Success in human and computer interaction can be illustrated by the success of computer system that works and utilized by user through the interfaces provided.

Interaction between human and computer is based on usability aspects. Usability is an ability of design created to assist users to complete task easily and thereby improve the human ability in completing task [7]. Design is created through computer systems using technologies and software. Meanwhile, users are consumers of design from technologies in supermarket, office, home and learning environment [21].

Interaction assessments between human and computer are a method that can be used to identify usability problem involving real users and expert users [10, 11, 13, 14, 18, 31]. The appropriate time for usability assessment process to be done are during the development process called formative evaluation process and after fully completed development called summative assessment [10, 11, 13, 18, 22, 23, 27]. The category of appraisers required to carry out usability assessments are real or potential users and experts [10, 11, 13, 14, 18, 31].

There are three aspects of usability assessment consist of assessment criteria, appraisers and assessment process [10, 13, 15]. First, assessment criteria are an aspect that needs to be assessed on design. The importance of that aspect should be known so that it contributes a meaning to product manufacturers, user interface designers and consumers.

Second, the appraiser's aspect are needs to be determined accurately, so feedback will in line with the assessment. Third, the assessment process is the last aspect to consider. Which technique or method used should be appropriate and meet the purpose of the assessment such as creating a design through user perceptions, designs improvement through effectiveness feedback or both.

3 Product Label Design Criteria for Purchase Decision

The function of product label is to deliver product information to consumers for purchase decision making that meet the needs and requirement [12, 30]. The product information to be delivered needs to use the appropriate techniques and methods so that it can be understood by the consumer and able to attract attention in purchasing [4–6, 29].

In addition, product label function as product identity that help consumers easily distinguish products between each other's when making purchases [2, 8, 17]. Consequently, consumers spend a little time when searching a product for purchase [25].

The use of multimedia elements on label products are limited. Product label design developed through computer technology and used by consumers after printing and displaying on packaging products. The multimedia elements found in products label design are text and images. While the elements of colour, shape, size and composition are complementary to perfecting a label design product. Therefore, the delivery of product information to consumers are highly dependent on the success of multimedia and complementary elements that always meet the labels design for the product.

4   Usability of Product Label for Purchase Decision

The growth of technology and lifestyle to meet the requirement and desire will often change as time goes by. It makes the design principle such as a product label also requires development and progress [28].

The product label assessment process is implemented based on usability aspects that rely on the information delivery through design elements such as text and images. The selection and use of each element are determined to be in line with the usability aspects for delivering products information [3]. Therefore, the determination of a good product label is a design criteria that can influence the consumers in product purchase selecting based on the suitability, importance and priorities required. So that the label product to be used more effectively.

Therefore, product purchase selection is one of the product label criteria assessment in physically [3]. The assessment is based on usability aspect that can be used to ensure a good and effective label can be produced.

Research Method. The purpose of this study is to examine the product label design criteria base on consumer behaviour during product purchase decision. The design criteria consist of text and image on product label. The assessment conducted to identify the product label section, product information and type of design that are used by consumer during purchase decision. Then, text and image design criteria for product label determine by an expert. As a result, a conceptual framework is designed. This framework will be used for development of research method called Criteria-Label Design Relationship (C-LaDeR) as illustrated in Fig. 1.

According to C-LaDeR, there are 2 phases of study. Phase 1 is to identify the use of product label during purchase decision by consumers through observation. The output are product label section and product information that has seen and examined by consumers during the product purchases selection. Phase 2 is to determine the text and image design criteria on product label for purchase decision based on expert survey. The research output are design criteria of text and image for product information on label section that most viewed by consumers and impact on purchase decision.

Phase 1 data collection process is observation method through video recording have been implemented during product purchase by consumers. The data collection process was conducted on 18 students at university store in residential college. The sampling

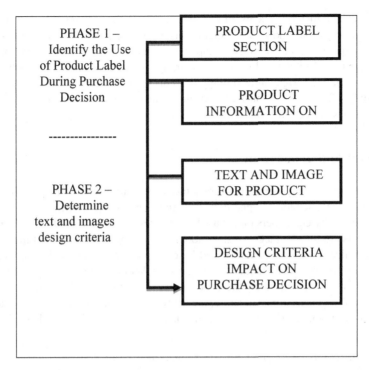

Fig. 1. Criteria – Label Design Relationship (C-LaDeR) research method

technique was randomly grouped into subject. Therefore, the study involved three categories of students selected to represent the population of university students. They are students of the Universiti Kebangsaan Malaysia in multimedia, marketing management and other courses.

The study identifies three consumer behaviour during selecting product for purchases; (i) viewing product labels on product arrangement on a shelf - means the user only sees the front section of product label only when making a purchase selection; (ii) viewing, holding products and viewing product labels - further detail viewing the front section of product label when making a purchase selection and (iii) viewing, holding the product and turn around the label section to see - indicates that consumers are looking at each product label section in detail when making a product purchase selection [26]. The percentage analysis of consumer behaviour will determine the product label section that most commonly used by consumer during purchasing and the product information according to label section.

Phase 2 data collection process is implemented to determine the criteria for text and image design on product label based on expert survey. The data collection through 7 experts; 4 lecturers from Faculty of Creative Technology and Heritage (FTKW), Universiti Malaysia Kelantan (UMK); 3 designers from Toolbox Media and Orze Media companies.

The criteria specified through two stages of the study. In the first stage, the design criteria of text and image for assisting in product purchase decision are identified using the questionnaire method. The list of text design criteria consists of (i) Roman and italic - slope texts, (ii) bold and light - weight texts, (iii) expended and condensed - width texts, (iv) uppercase and lowercase - shape text, and (v) sanserif, serif and script - type family text [1]. While, the list of image design criteria consists of (i) photo and illustration – nature image, and (ii) living and non-living – motive image [1]. In second stage, study identify the impact of text and image design criteria on product label during purchase selection [20].

5   Result and Discussion

Table 1 shows the analysis results of consumer behaviour observation on product label during purchase selection for phase 1. The study analysis results found that 89% of product viewed by consumers on front label and they choose the product for purchase. The products are bread, cracker, instant noodle, chocolate, milk, energy drink, mineral water and juice. 11% of product viewed by consumers on front label by holding the product and selecting the product for purchasing. While, none consumers behaviour looking at front label, holding the product and looking every label section during product purchases selection. Therefore, the analysis finds that consumers prefer to look at front product label compare to back and side label section during purchase selection.

Table 1. The results of consumer behaviour observation on product labels during purchase selection

No.	Front section viewing and selection	Front section viewing, holding and selection	Front, side and back section viewing, holding, turn around and selection
1	Bread	Biscuit	–
2	Cracker	–	–
3	Instant noodle	–	–
4	Chocolate	–	–
5	Milk	–	–
6	Energy drink	–	–
7	Mineral water	–	–
8	Juice	–	–
Total	89%	11%	0%

Table 2 shows descriptive analysis of product information percentage on product labels for phase 1. Study have found that 100% product information placed on front section of product label are brand, product type, flavour and slogan.

Table 3 shows the percentage of text and image design according to product information on the front section product label for phase 1. 100% brand information, product types, flavour and slogan are using text design. Meanwhile, 71% brand information, product types and flavour are using image design. 71% image design used for product type information, 71% image design used for flavour information. Slogan information does not use image design.

Table 2. The percentage of information on product labels

No.	Informations	Front	Side	Back
1	Brand	100%	0	0
2	Product type	100%	0	0
3	Flavour	100%	0	0
4	Slogan	100%	0	0
5	Nutrition	0	71%	29%
6	Manufacturer	0	71%	29%
7	Ingredient	0	57%	43%
8	Instruction	0	57%	43%
9	Weight	29%	29%	43%
10	Expired date	14%	43%	43%

Table 3. The percentage of text and image design according to product information

No.	Informations	Text		Image	
		Yes	No	Yes	No
1	Brand	100%	0	71%	29%
2	Product type	100%	0	71%	29%
3	Flavour	100%	0	71%	29%
4	Slogan	100%	0	0	100%

Figure 2 shows the text design criteria for front label of food and beverage products for phase 2. The study has found that 75% roman text are more appropriate than italic text on brand, product category and flavour information. 75% light text is better than bold text on product type, flavour, and slogan information. 75% expended text is better than condensed text on brand, product type and flavour information. 75% lowercase text is more suitable than uppercase text on product type, flavour and slogan information. While, 60% sanserif text is more appropriate than serif text and script on brand, product type and flavour information.

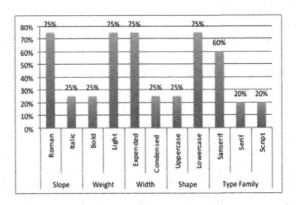

Fig. 2. Text design criteria for front label of food and beverage products

Figure 3 shows the images design criteria for front label of food and beverage product for phase 2. The analysis results showed that 67% illustration images are more appropriate than photo images on flavour and brand information. Whereas, 67% live images are more suitable than non-living images on product type and flavour.

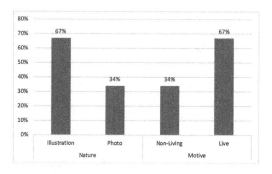

Fig. 3. Image design criteria for front label of food and beverage product

Table 4 shows the impact of using text design criteria on food and beverage product labels in purchases selection for phase 2. The study analysis shows 30% of text design criteria impact can give a theme or identity to the product. 20% of impact in terms of the capability in attracting the consumers attention. Whereas, 15% of design criteria impact may facilitating the delivery and acceptance of product information to consumers, having the ability to outline key information for consumer attention and assist consumers in reading product information on labels. 5% impact on the suitability to be used by different groups of consumers.

Table 4. Impact of using text design criteria on food and beverage product labels in purchases selection

No.	Impact of text design in purchase selection	Percentage (%)
1	Facilitate the delivery and acceptance of product information by consumer	15
2	Outline important information	15
3	Helps users in reading	15
4	Attract users' attention	20
5	Giving themes or identities to the product	30
6	Suitable for different classes of consumers	5

Table 5 shows the impact of using image design criteria on food and beverage product label for purchase selection for phase 2. Study found that 27% of image design criteria impact are to attract consumers attention. 23% impact on ability to assist in communicate and understand the information delivered to consumers. 14% impact on clear and more accurate information presented and becomes the identity in purchase selection. 9% impact on providing an overview of messages delivered and assisting consumers in search facilitating of product information. 5% impact on meeting the consumer needs.

Table 5. Impact of using image design criteria on food and beverage product label for purchase selection

No.	Impact of images design in purchase selection	Percentage (%)
1	Ability to assist in communicate and understand the information delivered to consumers	23
2	Clear and more accurate information presented becomes the identity in purchase selection	14
3	Providing an overview of messages delivered	9
4	Attract consumers attention	27
5	Assisting consumers in search facilitating of product information	9
6	Becomes an identity in purchase selection	14
7	Meeting the consumer needs	5

6   Conclusion and Future Work

Therefore, the analysis found that consumers prefer to look at front product label compare to back and side section of label during purchasing 9 types of product. There are 4 product information stated on front section of product label; (i) brand, (ii) type of product, (iii) flavour and (iv) slogan. Text are appropriate for all of front product information design. Meanwhile, images are suitable for (i) brand, (ii) type of product and (iii) flavour.

Text design criteria for front information on product label are roman – slope text; light – weight text; expended – width text; lowercase – shape text and sanserif – type family text. Text are able to be a theme or identity to the product. Meanwhile, images design criteria for front information on product label are illustration – nature image and live – motive images. Images are able to attract consumers attention.

The findings will assist to design effective product labels for consumers in making the right product purchase decision. For validation of text and images design criteria that has found, study will be extended to the development stage of product label design prototype and usability assessment based on the consumer`s eye movement.

References

1. Ampuero, O., dan Vila, N.: Consumer perceptions of product packaging. J. Consumer marketing, **23**(2), 100–112 (2006)
2. Arrúa, A., et al.: Impact of front-of-pack nutrition information and label design on children's choice of two snack foods: comparison of warnings and the traffic-light system. Appetite **116**, 139–146 (2017)

3. Bahrainizad, M., Rajabi, A.: Consumers' perception of usability of product packaging and impulse buying: considering consumers' mood and time pressure as moderating variables. J. Islamic Mark. **9**(2), 262–282 (2018)
4. Bandara, B.E.S., De Silva, D.A.M., Maduwanthi, B.C.H., Warunasinghe, W.A.A.I.: Impact of food labeling information on consumer purchasing decision: with special reference to faculty of agricultural sciences. Proc. Food Sci. **6**, 309–313 (2016)
5. Besler, H.T., Buyuktuncer, Z., dan Uyar, M.F.: Consumer understanding and use of food and nutrition labeling in Turkey. J. Nutr. Educ. Behav. **44**(6), 584–591 (2012)
6. Chen, A., Lu, Y., Wang, B.: Customers' purchase decision-making process in social commerce: a social learning perspective. Int. J. Inf. Manag. **37**(6), 627–638 (2017)
7. Dix, A.: Human-computer interaction and web design (2004)
8. Findling, M.T.G., et al.: Comparing five front-of-pack nutrition labels' influence on consumers' perceptions and purchase intentions. Prev. Med. **106**, 114–121 (2018)
9. Sogn-Grundvåg, G., Østli, J.: Consumer evaluation of unbranded and unlabelled food products: the case of bacalhau. Eur. J. Mark. **43**(1/2), 213–228 (2009)
10. Hannu, K., Elina, M.I.K.: Playability heuristics for mobile games. In: Proceedings of the 8th Conference on Human-Computer Interaction with Mobile Devices and Services. ACM Press, Helsinki (2006)
11. Hartson, H.R., Andre, T.S., Williges, R.C.: Criteria for evaluating usability evaluation methods. Int. J. Hum.-Comput. Inter. **13**(4), 373–410 (2001)
12. Hussain, S., Ali, S., Ibrahim, M., Noreen, A., Ahmad, S.F.: Impact of product packaging on consumer perception and purchase intention. J. Mark. Consum. Res. **10**(2011), 1–10 (2015)
13. Hornbaek, K.: Current practice in measuring usability: challenges to usability studies and research. Int. J. Hum.-Comput. Stud. **64**(2), 79–102 (2006)
14. Keylor, E., Burleson, W.: Experience-scapes. In: CHI 2008 Extended Abstracts on Human Factors in Computing Systems, pp. 2961–2966. ACM, April 2008
15. Koca, A., Brombacher, A.C.: User-centered analysis of feedback operations for quality improvement in new product development (2008)
16. Kuvykaite, R., Dovaliene, A., Navickiene, L.: Impact of consumer package communication on consumer decision making process'. Econ. Manag. **14**, 441–447 (2009)
17. Morris, J.: Green goods?: consumers, product labels and the environment. IEA Environment Unit (1997)
18. Nielsen, J.: Usability inspection methods. In: Conference Companion on Human Factors in Computing Systems, pp. 413–414. ACM, April 1994
19. Olsmats, C.: The Business Mission of Packaging: Packaging as a Strategic Tool for Business Development Towards the Future. University Press House, Åbo Akad (2002)
20. Ormrod, J.E., Davis, K.M.: Human learning, Merrill (2004)
21. Preece, J.: Sociability and usability in online communities: determining and measuring success. Behav. Inf. Technol. **20**(5), 347–356 (2001)
22. Ramey, J., Cuddihy, E., Guan, Z., Rosenbaum, S., Rose, E.: Beyond current user research: designing methods for new users, technologies, and design processes. In: CHI 2007 Extended Abstracts on Human Factors in Computing Systems, pp. 2865–2868. ACM (2007)
23. Rosinski, P., Squire, M.: Strange bedfellows: human-computer interaction, interface design, and composition pedagogy. Comput. Compos. **26**(3), 149–163 (2009)
24. Shah, S., Ahmed, A., Ahmad, N.: Role of packaging in consumer buying behavior. Int. Rev. Basic Appl. Sci. **1**(2), 35–41 (2013)
25. Silayoi, P., Speece, M.: Packaging and purchase decisions: an exploratory study on the impact of involvement level and time pressure. Br. Food J. **106**(8), 607–628 (2004)

26. Solomon, M., Russell-Bennett, R., Previte, J.: Consumer behaviour. Pearson Higher Education AU (2012)
27. Squires, D., Preece, J.: Usability and learning: evaluating the potential of educational software. Comput. Educ. **27**(1), 15–22 (1996)
28. Schadewitz, N.: Design pattern for cross-cultural collaboration. Int. J. Des. **3**(3), 37–53 (2009)
29. Tait, P., Saunders, C., Guenther, M., Rutherford, P., Miller, S.: Exploring the impacts of food label format on consumer willingness to pay for environmental sustainability: a choice experiment approach in the United Kingdom and Japan. Int. Food Res. J. **23**(4), 1787–1796 (2016)
30. Van Herpen, E., dan Van Trijp, H.C.: Front-of-pack nutrition labels: their effect on attention and choices when consumers have varying goals and time constraints. Appetite **57**(1), 148–160 (2011)
31. Verenikina, I., Harris, P., Lysaght, P.: Child's play: computer games, theories of play and children's development. In: Proceedings of the International Federation for Information Processing Working Group 3.5 Open Conference on Young Children and Learning Technologies, vol. 34, pp. 99–106. Australian Computer Society, Inc. (2003)

Academic Writing for Higher Learning Institution Students: Implications from User Needs Analysis for a Specific Plagiarism Module in e-Learning Platform

Hafizhah Suzana Hussien[1(✉)], Fariza Khalid[1], Supyan Hussin[1],
and Dini Farhana Baharuddin[2]

[1] Universiti Kebangsaan Malaysia, Bangi, Malaysia
suzana@ukm.edu.my
[2] Universiti Sains Islam Malaysia, Nilai, Malaysia

Abstract. Academic writing is a benchmark in most academic institution towards maintaining academic excellence among graduate students. However, to avoid plagiarism was found to be one of the most challenging tasks in academic writing among graduates in the digital era. A deeper understanding of plagiarism would be an important addition to students' competencies in academic writing. This study aimed to develop a one-stop e-learning platform that is able to assist graduate students in addressing their knowledge and understanding towards plagiarism. ICCEE instructional design method was used in developing the proposed platform. Need analysis was the first step approached in the development process. A survey was conducted among 440 post-graduate students using self-designed questionnaire. The outcome of the survey was quantitatively analyzed using descriptive technique. Results show that majority of the respondents have general knowledge about plagiarism. Even though most respondents agreed plagiarism is a serious matter, their attitude shows the opposite. This may be because they have never taken any specific course related to plagiarism nor used any plagiarism detection tool. The respondents also stated the need for a specific online course on plagiarism in the form of Massive Open Online Course (MOOC). This information about students' need can be a guide in developing the one-stop e-learning platform to understand about plagiarism.

Keywords: Needs analysis · Knowledge and attitude · Plagiarism · Academic writing · Students

1 Introduction

Academic writing is a benchmark in most academic institution towards maintaining academic excellence among graduate students. However, even though technology brought substantial improvements on educational practices in teaching and learning, unethical and irresponsible use of the tool especially in the area of academic writing can affect the educational system. One example of this unethical and irresponsible practice that caused increasing concern among the academic community is plagiarism.

© Springer Nature Switzerland AG 2019
H. Badioze Zaman et al. (Eds.): IVIC 2019, LNCS 11870, pp. 694–703, 2019.
https://doi.org/10.1007/978-3-030-34032-2_62

Plagiarism can be defined as the practice of using someone else's words, ideas, or even whole work and presenting them as your own without credit to the original author or source [1]. Plagiarism has been one of the major issues that is yet to be resolved as its prevalence, causes, detection, and punishment are still widely discussed [2, 3].

Previous studies show that plagiarism has been observed to occur in institutions of higher learning in Malaysia [4] which may be due to limited time to cover many topics in the curriculum or lack of awareness on the importance of the issue [4]. Graduate students are expected to come up with quality writing for assignments and thesis/dissertation and therefore, they need to be equipped with the knowledge and skills related to plagiarism, which is an important element in academic writing to ensure that they are being ethical and respectful of other's work. Despite the previous studies on the importance of academic integrity, research into students' attitude and skills about plagiarism in academic writing is still lacking. There is also lack of research that examine students' needs for a specific module on plagiarism.

Evidence of this may be utilized to introduce a one-stop e-learning platform to help bridge this gap. Therefore, the aim of this paper is to examine post-graduate students' knowledge and attitudes towards plagiarism as well as their needs for a specific e-learning platform. The analyzed data is then used to design and develop e-learning materials. This paper thus highlights the need for an e-learning platform from the students' responses. Therefore, the aim of this paper is to assess the knowledge and attitudes towards plagiarism among graduate students at one higher institution of learning in Malaysia. The paper also highlights the need for an e-learning platform from the students' responses.

The main objectives of this study are to examine students' level of knowledge about plagiarism in academic writing, to identify students' attitudes towards plagiarism in academic writing and to analyze students' needs for a specific e-learning platform on plagiarism to increase their writing abilities.

2   Literature Review

This section synthesizes the previous literature that has been presented in the field of academic writing (particularly plagiarism) and e-learning.

2.1   Plagiarism

Plagiarism is part of academic integrity. The word plagiarism originated from the word 'plagiarium', a Latin word that means 'kidnapper'. It was later adapted into English; referring to a person who engages in literary theft [5]. Plagiarism can be defined as the practice of using someone else's words, ideas, or even whole work and presenting them as your own without credit to the original author or source [1]. In other words, plagiarism is considered as taking the intellectual property of another.

2.2   Academic Writing and Plagiarism in Higher Education Institution

As mentioned earlier, plagiarism is part of academic misconduct. Previous studies have shown that plagiarism in the higher education institution are concerning in many countries all over the world [6]. Plagiarism is one of the major issues in higher education institutions including in Malaysia [4]. The research in higher education institution on this issue started in the 1960s [7]. Studies were conducted from a variety of disciplines comprising of both the sciences (e.g. engineering, nursing, information technology, architecture, mathematics) and non-sciences (e.g. education, humanities, law, social work, business) [8, 9]. The focus of previous research includes plagiarism prevalence rate, factors that lead to plagiarism, and strategies to prevent and detect plagiarism [10]. Previous studies show that even though plagiarism has been studied for the past fifty years, the number of those engaged in plagiarism is still on the rise.

2.3   Graduate Student Writing Culture and Knowledge in Plagiarism

Previous studies have found that students lack awareness that they are involved in plagiarism. Additionally, they also have limited understanding of how to avoid plagiarism. Base on research [11] believes that plagiarism education that explains about plagiarism and academic writing skills may benefit students. Unfortunately, there is limited discussion about plagiarism in academic writing courses, which may be due to limited time to cover many topics in the curriculum [4, 12]. Graduate students who are expected to come up with quality writing for assignments and thesis/dissertation would need to be equipped with the knowledge and skills related to plagiarism, which is an important element in academic writing to ensure that they are being ethical and respectful of other's work.

Despite the previous studies on the importance of academic integrity, research into students' attitude and skills about plagiarism in academic writing is lacking. There is also lack of research that examine students' needs for a specific module on plagiarism. Evidence of this may be utilized to introduce a one-stop e-learning platform to help bridge this gap. According to [13] the use of technology is necessary to avoid plagiarism. Hence, the use of plagiarism application is also suitable for preventing plagiarism. This awareness and knowledge are very important for students in learning and using the application of detection tool software.

3   Methodology

The main purpose of this paper is to examine post-graduate students' knowledge and attitudes towards plagiarism as well as their needs for a specific e-learning platform on plagiarism. The ICCEE online instructional design model was used in developing the proposed platform. ICCEE is an online instructional design model developed by [14]. There are five main steps in the model comprising (1) Identify, (2) Choose, (3) Create, (4) Engage, and (5) Evaluate. The unique characteristic in this model is that all main steps and their associated sub-steps follow a sequential order and at the same time can be in circular order as well. [14] proposed this model as it can help an online instructor to maximize the efficiency of designing an online course. Figure 1 shows steps in the ICCEE instructional design model.

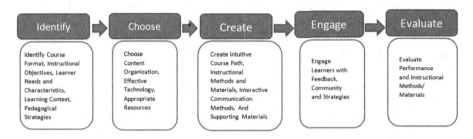

Fig. 1. ICCEE instructional design model. Source: [14]

The first step in ICCEE instructional design model is Identify. As traditional course differs from online course, identifying course format is important in the initial process when designing an online course. First, an online instructor needs to identify which course format that he or she would like to adopt for instruction. This will help the instructor to better identify instructional objectives. After setting the course format, the next step is to identify instructional objectives. When this is set, learners' needs and characteristics is next to be identified. Online instructor can better identify technologies that can maximize students' learning when they understand the needs and characteristics of the learners. Additionally, the learning context should also be identified by the instructor. Online learning context focuses on web-based learning environment thus making it crucial to provide safe and comfortable learning environment to the learners. Finally, the instructor must identify appropriate pedagogical strategies that they want to use in their course.

In the ICCEE instructional design model, need analysis was part of the first step in Identify as approached in the development process. Thus, a cross-sectional survey method was utilized for the need analysis. A questionnaire was self-designed to establish students' knowledge and attitudes toward plagiarism in academic writing and identify the need for a one-stop e-learning platform. Figure 2 show the flow of the need analysis.

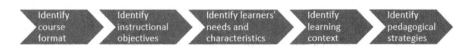

Fig. 2. Flow of the need analysis Source: [14]

3.1   Research Instruments

The questionnaire in this study was developed by the researcher based on a review of previous literature comprised of the knowledge, attitude, and needs of students and interviews with academics in the field. The questionnaire was structured into four sections including demographic items. The total number of items is 30. Section 1 focuses on demographic and personal information which aims to describe the participants' gender, age, educational background, level and field of study, and nationality. Section 2 comprises of Knowledge items that measures students' knowledge in plagiarism. Section 3 includes Attitude items that measure students' attitudes towards plagiarism. Finally, the last section investigates the participants' needs regarding information and learning processes in the e-learning platform. The questionnaire constructs a 5-point Likert scale using the following labels for each scale: (1) = Strongly Disagree, (2) = Disagree, (3) = Neither Agree or Disagree, (4) Agree, and (5) Strongly Agree. Since the questionnaire was self-designed, the researcher went through necessary procedures to ensure its validity and reliability. Following the review process, the instrument was tested on ten students to ensure face validity. Finally, a pilot study is conducting to test instruments for postgraduate students from various fields from several faculties. Corrections were made to the questionnaire. The final version of the questionnaire was then administered online using Google form. The reliability test to each construct and refer to Literature Review on the interpretation of the alpha Cronbach value and the decision made based on the test.

3.2 Sample and Population

The population of this study were 9546 (2018) post-graduate students from one public university. For a sampling purpose, we employed a simple random sampling, while the sample size was determined by [15]. Based on the calculation, the suggested minimum number of sample was n = 368. For the purpose of the study and to ensure a sufficient return rate of the questionnaire, we sent the questionnaire 4000 respondents. As a result, 440 filled up the form.

Simple random sampling was chosen because it ensures all possible samples of fixed size n have the same probability of being selected and that there is no need to number the entries in the population before drawing a sample [15]. The number of sample was determined after considering the recommendation by [16]. Out of the population of 9546 post-graduate students, the sample size recommended was calculated to be a minimum of 368.

3.3 Data Collection Procedures

The questionnaire was distributed via e-mail to all potential participants. The list of names and email addresses was derived from the university's database. The participants were given explanation about the research objectives and was assured of their privacy and confidentiality, and that the participation is voluntary. All information is included in the online form distributed by e-mail.

3.4 Data Analysis

Data from the completed questionnaire was analyzed using the Statistical Package for Social Sciences (SPSS version 25). Descriptive statistic was used to examine the results in this study.

4   Findings and Discussion

4.1   Demographic Report

Out of 4000 students, 440 completed the questionnaire resulting in a response rate of 11%. In this study, all 440 participants completed the questionnaire. The students provided answers to all questions in the demographics, knowledge, attitude, and need sections.

From the total number of participants, 46.6% are from the Faculty of Education and 53.4% are from other faculties from different fields and specializations. In terms of gender, the distribution is 32% male and 68% female. Their age ranges between 24 to 50 years old. 75% of the total sample are Master students while 25% are PhD students. 393 students are local and 47 students are international. Table 1 shows demographics information of the participants.

Table 1. Demographics information

Variables		Frequency	Percentage
Field of study	Faculty of education	205	46.6%
	Others	235	53.4%
Gender	Male	141	32%
	Female	299	68%
Age	30 years and below	120	27%
	31–40 years	268	61%
	41–50 years	52	12%
Level of study	Master	330	75%
	PhD	110	25%
Nationality	Local	393	89%
	International	47	11%

4.2   Students' Knowledge on Plagiarism

Results show that majority of the respondents have general knowledge about plagiarism. This refers to content relating to definition of plagiarism, policies and reasons for plagiarizing. It can be concluded that plagiarism from the respondents' perspectives can be divided into two – what is being plagiarized and how plagiarism occurs. The action of plagiarizing includes 'copying', 'reproducing' and 'duplicating' of a certain idea, information, assignment, and article among others. Only a small number of the respondents agreed that they have references on plagiarism such as the University's Act and Regulations, as well as plagiarism detection tool. According to the respondents, the main reason for plagiarizing is lack of skills in academic writing (92.5%).

Table 2. Knowledge in plagiarism

Item	Knowledge in plagiarism	Mean	Std. deviation	Level
S1	Lack of knowledge about plagiarism	3.70	1.078	High
S2	Less awareness about plagiarism	3.81	1.038	High
S3	Less skill on academic writing techniques	4.33	0.788	Very high
S4	Not using software to check plagiarism	4.21	0.913	Very high
S5	Copy and paste	4.36	0.877	Very high
S6	Someone else gives others permission to imitate their work	3.35	1.164	Fair
S7	Attitudes do not care about plagiarism	3.93	1.018	High
S8	There is no specific law on plagiarism	3.56	1.103	High
S9	Do not know the platform to learn to check plagiarism	4.06	0.960	High
S10	No plagiary-related courses	4.00	1.047	High
S11	Information is easily accessible via the internet	4.36	0.855	Very high
S12	Poor paraphrase technique	4.27	0.773	Very high
S13	Incorrect "quote" technique	4.20	0.782	Very high
S14	There is no exposure and knowledge from the lecturer	3.26	1.120	Fair
S15	Do not know the act is plagiarism	3.30	1.236	Fair
	Overall mean	3.91	0.532	High

Table 2, the participants' knowledge in plagiarism overall mean is (M = 3.91; S.D = 0.532). This mean can be considered as high level. Item S5 Copy and Paste (M = 4.36; S.D = 0.877) and item S11 information is easily accessible via the internet (M = 4.36; S.D = 0.855). It shows that learners firmly agree that "Internet use" and "copy and paste" makes it easier for learners to plagiarize. Item S3 "Less skill on academic writing techniques" (M = 4.33; S.D = 0.788), item S12 "Poor paraphrase technique" (M = 4.27; S.D = 0.77), item S13 "Incorrect quote technique" (M = 4.20, S.D = 0.78) showing less knowledgeable students in writing techniques. Student agree that they "Do not know the platform to learn to check plagiarism" (M = 4.06; S. D = 0.96). This shows that the development of a one-stop platform is ideally developed to meet the needs of students.

4.3   Students' Attitude Towards Plagiarism

The study shows high scores on statements showing negative attitude towards plagiarism (95%) and low scores on positive attitude (5%) as responded by the postgraduate students. Most respondent 97.2% with (M = 4.25; S.D = 0.82) agree that plagiarism is a serious matter. Only 2.7% of the respondents stated that it as not serious. Based on the data analysis, 85.1% (M = 3.49; S.D = 1.06) agreed that fines and penalties need to be implemented for the plagiarism behavior. A total of 94.8%

(M = 3.88; S.D = 0.86) students agree on any plagiarism activity to be reported. The findings of Table 3 show plagiarism is an issue that needs to be taken to prevent from extinction [2, 3].

Table 3. Students' attitude towards plagiarism

Item	Question	%	Mean	Std. deviation	Level
S16	Strikes and warnings	87.3	4.23	0.708	Very high
S17	Submit a complaint	94.8	3.88	0.862	High
S18	Fines and penalties	85.1	3.49	1.056	High
S19	Plagiarism is a serious mistake	97.2	4.25	0.818	Very high
	Total mean		3.96	0.643	High

4.4 Students' Need for Specific e-Learning Platform

Results show that majority of the respondents (81.4%) never attended any specific course on plagiarism nor used any plagiarism detection tool. The respondents stated the need for a specific course online on plagiarism. According to the respondents, the most suitable learning method for the understanding of plagiarism is in the form of step-by-step training, problem-solving, and self-driven learning. It was suggested that the content of the course include information about plagiarism (types, causes, and techniques to avoid), policies and regulations related to plagiarism, academic writing techniques (paraphrasing, citation, and summarizing) and problem-based exercises.

Table 4 Q1 shows that a total of 358 (81%) students have never followed any course on plagiarism. Even though most respondents have general knowledge about plagiarism and agreed that plagiarism is a serious matter, there is a need for improvement. This may be because they have never taken any specific course related to plagiarism nor used any plagiarism detection tool. The respondents also stated the need for a specific online course on plagiarism in the form of MOOC.

This information about students' need can be a guide in developing a module in the form of a one-stop online platform to understand about plagiarism.

Table 4 Q2 shows the findings of online module development requirements. The data showed that 413 (94%) respondents agreed on the development of plagiarism module online. Data analysis shows that the development of online plagiarism module will benefit the students and educate students to learn the techniques of plagiarism in accordance with research [9] that plagiarism learning to students will benefit them.

Table 4. Students' experience in attending courses on plagiarism and need for Online Module

Question	Yes	No
Q1. Have you ever attended a plagiarism course?	19% (82)	81% (358)
Q2. Is there a need for a plagiarism online module developed?	413 (94%)	27 6%

Students are found to be weak in paraphrasing techniques, knowledge in plagiarism checking applications, plagiarism acts, dumping information on the internet that is not prudent. Students are also less aware that they are still practicing "copy and paste" cultures, assigning friends to copy easily and also among students who are unaware of plagiarism. This necessitates the need for a platform for students to learn and take action on plagiarism to further enhance the level of knowledge and awareness in academic writing.

5   Conclusion

Plagiarism is one of the major issues in higher education institution. The findings in this study supports the need to introduce a one-stop e-learning platform that can help bridge the gap between the ideal and the reality. Lecturers and universities are encouraged to assist and monitor students in improving their understanding and knowledge they were involved in plagiarism throughout the university's student life. Action must be taken on the integrity issue to avoid plagiarism. Use of modules is mandatory for all students who are newly enrolled at university to avoid plagiarism. The university may then require students to conduct a plagiarism degree test online at a student enrollment session or after receiving a university admission offer.

References

1. Yamano, P.H.: Cyberethics in the elementary classroom: teaching the responsible use of technology. Dissertation (2004)
2. Bouman, K.: A phenomenological investigation of college students' construction and representation of plagiarism. Indiana Univ. Pennsylvania Knowl Repos @ IUP, vol. 397, pp. 12–21 (2009)
3. Kymberley, K., Bennett, L.S., Behrendt, J.L.B.: Instructor perceptions of plagiarism: are we finding common ground? Teach. Psychol. **1/2** (2011). https://doi.org/10.1207/s15328023top3301
4. Karim, N.S.A., Zamzuri, N.H.A., Nor, Y.M.: Exploring the relationship between internet ethics in university students and the big five model of personality. **1–2** (2009). https://doi.org/10.1016/j.compedu.2009.01.001
5. Katavić, V.: Five-year report of Croatian Medical Journal's Research Integrity Editor - policy, policing, or policing policy. Croat. Med. J. **47**, 220–227 (2006)
6. Guy, J., Curtis, L.V.: Is plagiarism changing over time? A 10-year time-lag study with three points of measurement. Br. J. Psychiatry **112**, 211–212 (1966). https://doi.org/10.1192/bjp.112.483.211-a
7. Cummings, R., Maddux, C.D., Harlow, S., Dyas, L.: Academic misconduct in undergraduate teacher education students and its relationship to their principled moral reasoning. J. Instr. Psychol. **29**, 286–296 (2002)
8. Selwyn, N.: "Not necessarily a bad thing…": a study of online plagiarism amongst undergraduate students. Assess Eval. High. Educ. **33**, 465–479 (2008). https://doi.org/10.1080/02602930701563104

9. Aasheim, C.L., Rutner, P.S., Lixin Li, S.R.W.: Plagiarism and programming: a survey of student attitudes. Br. J. Psychiatry **3**, 297–313 (2012). https://doi.org/10.1192/bjp.112.483. 211-a

10. Evans, R.: Evaluating an electronic plagiarism detection service: the importance of trust and the difficulty of proving students don't cheat. Act. Learn. High Educ. **7**, 87–99 (2006). https://doi.org/10.1177/1469787406061150

11. Chuda, D., Navrat, P., Kovacova, B., Humay, P.: The issue of (software) plagiarism: a student view. IEEE Trans. Educ. **55**, 22–28 (2012). https://doi.org/10.1109/TE.2011. 2112768

12. Mohd Isa, P., Jusoff, K., Abu Samah, S.A.: Sustenance of values and ethics in the Malaysian higher education e-learning drive. Asian Soc. Sci. **4**, 115–121 (2009). https://doi.org/10. 5539/ass.v4n6p115

13. Hart, M., Friesner, T.: Plagiarism and poor academic practice – a threat to the extension of e-learning in higher education? (2000)

14. Chen, L.L.: Pedagogically effective online instructional design model, vol. 6, pp. 1551–1554 (2016)

15. Cooper, D.R., Schindler, P.: Business Research Methods (1998)

16. Krejcie, R.V., Morgan, D.W.: Determining sample size for research activities. Educ. Psychol. Meas. **30**, 607–610 (1970)

A Framework for Sustainable Eco-Friendly Product Development Based on TRIZ

Nur Syaza Zainali[1], Mei Choo Ang[1(✉)], Kok Weng Ng[2], and Mohamad Taha Ijab[1]

[1] Institute of Visual Informatics, Universiti Kebangsaan Malaysia, Bangi, Malaysia
amc@ukm.edu.my
[2] Department of Mechanical, Materials and Manufacturing, Faculty of Science and Engineering, University of Nottingham Malaysia, Semenyih, Malaysia

Abstract. Nowadays designers are facing challenges in designing sustainable eco-friendly products. Sustainable eco-friendly product design requires designers to conduct rigorous product research and have a development process that incorporates existing eco-efficiency elements. Sustainable eco-friendly product requirements are becoming more critical and are compulsory for all new product development in order to comply with the newly enacted environmental protection legislation. TRIZ consists of well-established tools utilized by many enterprises and has been successful in assisting designers in solving problems during new product development. However, TRIZ tools did not directly consider sustainable and environmentally friendly features in their recommended solutions for new product development. Hence, it is necessary to explore and investigate whether TRIZ can be adapted to assist designers to derive innovative and sustainable eco-friendly products. In this research work, we proposed an initial framework that links TRIZ Contradiction Matrix and eco-efficiency elements to assist designers in the development of sustainable eco-friendly products such as a lid fastener for food containers.

Keywords: Eco-friendly product · Sustainable development · TRIZ

1 Introduction

For the past several decades, the global threats of climate change have driven environmental concern in many countries around the world [1]. Many countries have established policies to deal with the effect of climate change, leading to increasing demand for companies to develop sustainable eco-friendly products and services [2]. With the growing demand on developing sustainable eco-friendly products, companies have to come out with products that are innovative, improve profits and enhance competitiveness whilst reducing environmental impacts.

A lot of research work on sustainable design have been carried out and they can be categorized into two groups, namely eco-assessment based on statistical elaboration of past data such as life cycle assessment (LCA) [3] and experience-driven guidelines

© Springer Nature Switzerland AG 2019
H. Badioze Zaman et al. (Eds.): IVIC 2019, LNCS 11870, pp. 704–712, 2019.
https://doi.org/10.1007/978-3-030-34032-2_63

such as "Ten Golden Rules" [4, 5]. However, these research works, particularly LCA, mostly focused on assessment at the later stage of design, i.e. in detail design stage where the design is near completion and is very dependent on the accuracy of past data [6]. Thus, there is a lack of support for designers during conceptual design phase to derive innovative sustainable eco-friendly products [5, 7]. Furthermore, studies have shown that most LCA-type of assessment is complex and time-consuming to be applied by designers during design [8, 9]. Hence, the application of TRIZ which is already well-established in product innovation was studied by researchers to help designers in sustainable eco-friendly product development [8]. This study is an initial attempt to propose a framework to apply TRIZ inventive principles to support designers in developing new sustainable products. This paper consists of eight sections. Section 1 introduces the background and the purpose of this research. Sections 2 and 3 reviews past studies on sustainable products and the integration of TRIZ tools for sustainable design. Section 4 presents an initial TRIZ framework for problem solving. Section 5 integrates the eco-efficiency elements to the initial TRIZ framework presented in Sect. 4. Section 6 validates the proposed framework in Sect. 5 to derive sustainable innovative product using a case study on a lid fastener for food containers. Section 7 discusses the outcomes of the case study in Sect. 6. Section 8 concludes the research work with recommendations on further improvement for future work.

2 Sustainable Eco-Friendly Product

A sustainable eco-friendly design process can create a system or product with the lowest impact to the environment throughout its life cycle. For instance, a sustainable eco-friendly designed electric car will consider the reduction of pollution due to carbon emission. In a product development process, it is critical for companies to make environmentally friendly decisions, apply proper sustainability tools and techniques to implement sustainable development [3]. It is important to consider from life cycle perspectives how to improve product sustainability in early design stages.

In order to survive in this competitive world, companies need to adopt sustainability principles and include innovation in product development [10]. Analytical Hierarchy Process (AHP) was integrated with Environmental Conscious Quality Function Development (ECQFD) and TRIZ in a case study for innovative and sustainable product development of automotive components [10]. However, there is a limitation in AHP when there is scale-point that might be hard for decision-maker to distinguish the outcomes.

Product Life Cycle Planning (LCP) has become an important methodology to be considered in product design [9]. It is important to understand and analyze the existing products in order to design a product in development process. Life Cycle Assessment (LCA) includes problems associated with environmental impact, formulation and concept generation and it considers the whole life cycle of the product. LCA will evaluate the product's impact to the environment during its entire life cycle [11]. Other than considerations on the environmental impact, maintaining product quality at the initial stage of design is also one of the key elements in developing a successful new product development and this is also being considered in LCA in some research works [3].

LCA tools that are used for product enhancement are also used to provide a basic model for assessing environmental loads and their effects. LCA is used frequently to investigate green products, generating fundamental research information on environment impact and product reliability [12]. Despite the variety of tools and effective smart system nowadays such as artificial intelligence (AI), multi-criteria decision support (MCDS), there are still limitations in the early design stage of products.

In summary, the application of sustainable strategies is crucial to support sustainable eco-friendly product design. LCA is not a product design tool and is applied to assess environmental impact of a product. Therefore, there is a need to derive a framework for sustainable product design where a sustainable product design tool that can support designers during design process particularly in the conceptual design phase. This research work explores the adaptation of TRIZ to become a sustainable product design tool.

3   Sustainable Design and TRIZ

There have been some recent research works on deriving a systematic design method to help designers to come up sustainable eco-friendly products in conceptual design phase. Some of these research works involved applying TRIZ tools i.e. Trends of Engineering Evolution) [5] and combining TRIZ (Engineering Contradiction) with other tools such as QFD [7].

The research work based on Trends of Engineering Evolution [5] lead to a design method (in the form of guidelines) that is able to help designers to derive a sustainable product. For the research work that combined QFD and Engineering Contradiction of TRIZ [7], the research work mapped customer requirements from QFD with 7 characteristics of reducing environmental impact and replaced them with standard features of the TRIZ engineering contradiction matrix and identified recommended inventive principles (solution). This was done so that the solutions from the contradiction matrix considered the 7 characteristics of reducing environmental impact in accordance with the customer's preference. Weightage or preference from customers affects the result significantly and the results may not be a good sustainable product as it is dependent on the preference of the customer.

Therefore, this research explore the prospect a framework based on applying and adapting TRIZ [13] in the ideas generation or conceptual design phase of a new product development process in sustainable product innovation. The framework will be validated using a case study on a lid fastener for food containers will be considered. Food containers have a variety of designs and sizes as well as materials. Users usually will choose food containers with a lid (cover) to store food. The problem arises when food containers lose their cover but the food containers are still in good condition. If a new product can be designed such that it allows continuous usage of the food container even though it has lost its cover, then it can save people from buying an additional food container. Hence, this case study will explore and discover potential sustainable designs for a lid fastener for food containers through the proposed framework.

4 Initial Framework Based on TRIZ

Theory of Invention Problem Solving (TRIZ) is one of the preferred methods in product design [13–18]. The 40 Inventive Principles constructed by Altshuller have provided basic concepts and guidelines. TRIZ is a systematic method to develop innovative products. The standard procedure of problem solving method through the 40 Inventive Principles is illustrated in Fig. 1. There are five processes in the problem definition stage. The five processes are

- Product analysis to identify components of the product
- Function analysis to define the interactions between components
- Cause and effect chain analysis (CECA) is used to identify root causes
- Contradictions are formed based on the findings in CECA
- Improving parameters and worsening parameters are identified in the contradiction.

Based on the improving and worsening parameters, specific TRIZ principles will be selected from the TRIZ contradiction matrix [19]. The related potential solutions are then derived from these inventive principles.

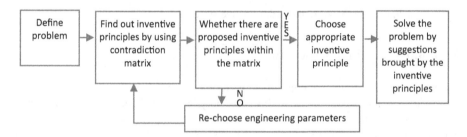

Fig. 1. Flowchart of TRIZ contradiction matrix [19].

5 Sustainable Product Design Approach

The development of innovative products is a necessity for economic growth; however, environmental impact cannot be ignored. In order to create an innovative product, designers/engineers need to consider the balance between technical innovation and environmental protection issues during the design process. Thus, the eco-efficiency elements are identified from literature study and its element is considered as a parameter in this paper. The eco-efficiency elements will be based on the official report of the World Business Council of Sustainable Development (WBCSD) [20]. The WBCSD has identified seven major eco-efficiency elements in producing eco-friendly products [20].

- Reduce material intensity
- Reduce energy intensity
- Reduce dispersion of toxic substances materials
- Enhance recyclability

- Maximize use of renewable
- Extend product durability
- Increase service intensity

Each element above needs to be considered simultaneously in order to produce eco-efficient products. Eco-efficiency elements and the TRIZ method will be adapted in this research in the development of new products at the early stage of design. Figure 2 shows a proposed initial framework to derive a sustainable eco-friendly product.

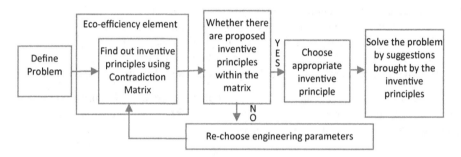

Fig. 2. Proposed framework to derive sustainable innovative product.

6   Food Container Case Study

Losing the lid for a food container when the food container is still in good condition is a common problem among users. In this case study, we carried out component analysis, function analysis in order to identify the components (Fig. 3) and function characteristics of lid fasteners for food containers (Fig. 4), which is followed by cause and effect chain analysis (CECA) to identify the root cause of the problem (Fig. 5).

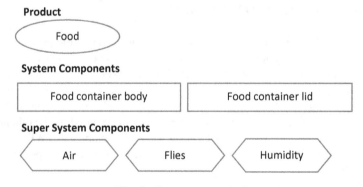

Fig. 3. Component analysis

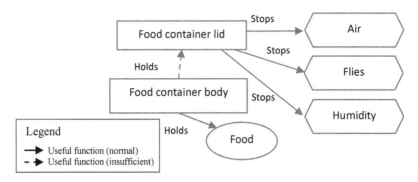

Fig. 4. Function analysis

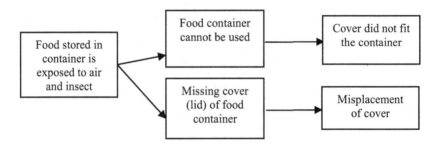

Fig. 5. Cause and effect chain analysis

In this initial study, we have considered issues related to this food container with a lid fastener case study based on common consumer comments from the internet. A mapping of the WBCSD eco-efficiency elements with TRIZ parameters is shown in Table 1. Two contradictions were formed, and the respective improving and worsening parameters were identified as shown in Table 2. Two potential solutions were then obtained as shown in Table 3.

Table 1. Mapping of WBCSD eco-efficiency elements and the TRIZ parameters

WBCSD eco-efficiency elements	TRIZ Parameters
Reduce material intensity	#23 Loss of substance
Reduce energy intensity	#20 Use of energy by stationary object
Reduce dispersion of toxic substances materials	#31 Object generated harmful factors
Enhance recyclability	#34 Ease of repair
Maximize use of renewable	#35 Adaptability or versatility
Extend product durability	#27 Reliability (Robustness)
Increase service intensity	#33 Ease of operation

Table 2. Determination of TRIZ inventive principles for sustainable eco-efficient products

Problem statement	Possible cause level 1	Possible cause level 2	Contradiction	Improving feature	Worsening feature	Related WBCSD eco-efficiency elements	Inventive principles
Food stored in container is exposed to air and insects	Food container cannot be used	Cover did not fit the container	If we use another cover to contain the food, then the food will be stored safely avoiding air and insects, but this will cause plastic waste	#26 Quantity of substance	#23 Loss of substance	Reduce material intensity	6, 3, 10, 24
	Missing cover of food container	Misplaced cover	If we tag each cover with special identification, then we can locate the cover but this incurs extra energy usage and complexity	#37 Difficulty of detecting and measuring	#20 Use of energy by stationary object	Reduce energy intensity	19, 35, 16

Table 3. Potential solutions

Recommended invention principles	Selected principle solution	Potential solutions
6, 3, 10, 24, 19, 35, 16	Principle 3: Local quality	Design a container where lid attached
	Principle 24: Intermediary	Use a flexible medium that can fit the size of the container and to cover the container, for e.g. a thin plastic film

7 Discussion

Based on past literature, TRIZ is shown to enrich the theory of creativity in multiple ways. The TRIZ Inventive Principles were proposed in the initial framework in this paper with the aim to support the research and development process and help designers in generating ideas to design the product. However, in this initial study, the improving parameters are manually selected from the TRIZ Contradiction Matrix based on common consumer comments from the internet. This selection may be subject to bias and lack of justification. There may also be other important qualities or issues that were not considered in this case study. Thus, there is a need to enhance this initial proposed framework. To replace ways of selecting parameters, a data mining approach is proposed in future work to adopt a computational process of discovering exact elements to consider.

8   Conclusion and Future Research Work

It is necessary to consider better ways to obtain the relevant data needed to support the decision on the consumer preferred qualities and issues related to the product being investigated. In our future work, we are considering the use of a data mining approach to be added into our proposed framework to provide information (in particular issues) related to the existing product during problem definition stage and also solution stage (in particular ideas for potential solutions). The improved proposed framework is shown in Fig. 6.

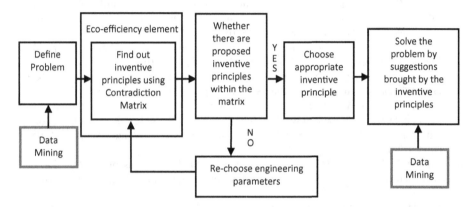

Fig. 6. Improving the proposed framework to derive sustainable innovative product

Acknowledgments. The authors would like to thank the Universiti Kebangsaan Malaysia and the Ministry of Education Malaysia (Kementerian Pendidikan Malaysia) for supporting the work through research grants GUP-2018-124 and FRGS/1/2018/TK03/UKM/02/6.

References

1. Crul, M., Diehl, J.C.: Design for Sustainability: A Practical Approach for Developing Economies. United Nations Environment Programme, Paris (2006)
2. Diehl, J.C., Crul, M., Ryan, C.: Design for Sustainability: A Step-by-Step Approach. United Nations Environment Programme, Paris (2009)
3. Chiu, M.-C., Chu, C.-H.: Review of sustainable product design from life cycle perspectives. Int. J. Precis. Eng. Manuf. **13**, 1259–1272 (2012)
4. Luttropp, C., Lagerstedt, J.: EcoDesign and The Ten Golden Rules: generic advice for merging environmental aspects into product development. J. Clean. Prod. **14**, 1396–1408 (2006)
5. Russo, D., Regazzoni, D., Montecchi, T.: Eco-design with TRIZ laws of evolution. Procedia Eng. **9**, 311–322 (2011)
6. Rebitzer, G., et al.: Life cycle assessment: part 1: framework, goal and scope definition, inventory analysis, and applications. Environ. Int. **30**, 701–720 (2004)

7. Ko, Y.-T., Chen, M.-S., Lu, C.-C.: A systematic-innovation design approach for green product. Int. J. Constr. Eng. Manag. **5**, 102–107 (2016)
8. Feniser, C., Burz, G., Mocan, M., Ivascu, L., Gherhes, V., Otel, C.C.: The evaluation and application of the TRIZ method for increasing eco-innovative levels in SMEs. Sustainability **9**, 1125 (2017)
9. Kobayashi, H.: Strategic evolution of eco-products: a product life cycle planning methodology. Res. Eng. Des. **16**, 1–16 (2005)
10. Vinodh, S., Kamala, V., Jayakrishna, K.: Integration of ECQFD, TRIZ, and AHP for innovative and sustainable product development. Appl. Math. Model. **38**, 2758–2770 (2014)
11. Yu, H.L., Guo, J., Fan, D.L.: Integrated TRIZ and MEMS in eco-innovative design. Appl. Mech. Mater. **441**, 1064–1067 (2014)
12. Chan, C.C., Yu, K., Yung, K.: Green product development by using life cycle assessment (LCA), theory of inventive of problems solving (TRIZ). In: 2010 International Conference on Manufacturing Automation, pp. 24–29 (2010)
13. Lim, S.S., Teoh, K.S.: Eco-efficient product design using theory of inventive problem solving (TRIZ) principles. Am. J. Appl. Sci. **7**, 852–858 (2010)
14. Ahmad, S.A., Ang, M.C., Ng, K.W., Wahab, A.N.A.: Reducing home energy usage based on TRIZ concept. Adv. Environ. Biol. **9**, 6–11 (2015)
15. Ang, M.C., Ng, K.W., Ahmad, S.A., Wahab, A.N.A.: An engineering design support tool based on TRIZ. In: Zaman, H.B., Robinson, P., Olivier, P., Shih, T.K., Velastin, S. (eds.) IVIC 2013. LNCS, vol. 8237, pp. 115–127. Springer, Cham (2013). https://doi.org/10.1007/978-3-319-02958-0_11
16. Ang, M.C., Ng, K.W., Cher, D.T.: Verifying innovative solutions of TRIZ engineering contradiction matrix using substance-field analysis. Appl. Mech. Mater. **761**, 196–201 (2015)
17. Ang, M.C., Ng, K.W., Ghazali, F.H.M.: Pencetusan Idea Reka Bentuk Produk Menggunakan TRIZ. J. Inf. Technol. Multimedia **11**, 1–9 (2011)
18. Ng, K.W., Ang, M.C., Pham, D.T.: Applying TRIZ to support designers in a descriptive design framework. In: The ASME 2009 International Design Engineering Technical Conferences & Computers and Information in Engineering Conference (IDETC/CIE 2009), San Diego, US (2009)
19. Altshuller, G.: Innovation algorithm: TRIZ, systematic innovation and technical creativity. Technical Innovation Center, Worcester (1999)
20. Lehni, M.: Eco-efficiency: creating more value with less impact. World Business Council for Sustainable, Development (WBCSD), Conches-Geneva, Switzerland (2000)

Computational Thinking (CT) Problem Solving Orientation Based on Logic-Decomposition-Abstraction (LDA) by Rural Elementary School Children Using Visual-Based Presentations

Halimah Badioze Zaman[1]([⊠]), Azlina Ahmad[1], Aliimran Nordin[1],
Hamidah Yamat@Ahmad[2], A. Aliza[3], M. C. Ang[1],
N. Azwan Shaiza[3], S. Riza[1], C. M. Normazidah[3], J. Azizah[1],
W. Wahiza[3], M. A. Nazlena[1], K. Fauzanita[1], N. Puteri Nor Ellyza[1],
H. Baharin[1], I. Mohamad Taha, A. K. Rabiah[1], M. N. Norshita[1],
M. Ummul Hanan[1], and M. S. Ely Salwana[1]

[1] Institute of Visual Informatics (IVI), Universiti Kebangsaan Malaysia,
43600 Bangi, Selangor, Malaysia
halimahivi@ukm.edu.com
[2] Faculty of Education, Universiti Kebangsaan Malaysia,
43600 Bangi, Selangor, Malaysia
[3] CITRA [Liberal Arts] Centre, Universiti Kebangsaan Malaysia,
43600 Bangi, Selangor, Malaysia

Abstract. This qualitative and ethnographic study examines how interactions embedded in the Collaborative Computational Thinking Design Practices (CCTDP) framework, has helped rural children think to solve STEM related open ended problems in English lessons. Our multimodal interactive approach revealed that students naturally has an orientation to problem solving that can be nurtured and trained towards a certain preferred computational thinking concept practices. The CCTDP has specifically three problem solving orientations, but this paper highlights only one of these orientation; *'logic-decomposition-abstraction'* (LDA) orientation which is identified as the second level of problem solving orientation in the CCTDP framework. This study also highlights the importance of group interactions in computational design thinking practices integrated in learning of English across science, technology, engineering and mathematics (STEM).

Keywords: Rural elementary school children · Learning english across STEM · Computational Thinking (CT) · Collaborative Computational Thinking Design Practices (CCTDP) · Visual-based presentations

1 Introduction

As we enter the digital economy, digital transformation towards a more smart society 5.0 has become inevitable. Rural society generally, and rural school children specifically, need to be prepared for this transformation and the importance of Computational

© Springer Nature Switzerland AG 2019
H. Badioze Zaman et al. (Eds.): IVIC 2019, LNCS 11870, pp. 713–728, 2019.
https://doi.org/10.1007/978-3-030-34032-2_64

Thinking (CT) and Science, Technology, Engineering and Mathematics (STEM) is crucial, in order that they can be meaningfully involved in the transformation of the country. Thus, the current study that integrates CT with the learning of English across STEM in rural schools is not only an interesting way to get children be engaged in learning a language that is not their native language, but at the same time help them acquire critical and scientific thinking skills that would match the needs of the an advanced smart society 5.0. Thus, this study was conducted amongst 10 year-olds elementary school children in the rural State of Kedah, in Malaysia, through problem solving activities conducted based on the Collaborative Computational Thinking (CT) design practices (CCTDP) framework [1, 2]. The CCTDP framework was developed based on the concepts of Computational Thinking, Optimization, Meta Cognition, Engagement Strategy and Learning Outcomes (COMEL). COMEL was created through a research program integrating CT with the teaching of English across STEM [1, 2]. The main objective of the program was to help rural children acquire CT skills through a technique called TRIZ [3–5], by integrating learning of English across STEM to help these children solve problems in a fun and engaging way through an interactive collaborative CT design practices.

This paper attends to the above issue by observing patterns of cognitive interaction flows of discussions between peers inter and intra groups, based on the CCTDP framework. A more close observational analytical scrutiny is given on how interactions occur and their orientations based on the preferred computational thinking concepts.

2 Literature Review

The process of developing the Collaborative Computational Thinking Design Practices (CCTDP) Framework involved an earlier study conducted by the authors, and related works of other authors. Earlier works by the authors based on the COMEL model design, development and verification of the model has been discussed in other published works and will not be discussed in this paper. Highlighted in previous literature is that many students lack the ability to solve open-ended problems due to the fact that they do not have the skills to think creatively and innovatively. Many researchers explained these inability to think creatively, critically, logically, reflectively, scientifically or innovatively by students [6–9]. Generally, it has been accepted that learners who have difficulty in thinking creatively, logically and scientifically during a problem solving process, are considered as learners who are not bright or possess low ability in their overall academic achievement [6–10]. This has proven not to be really true, because there are students who are high achievers, but also have problems in solving open-ended problems [11], and that incorporating a technique of CT approach can help learners acquire the type of thinking skills mentioned earlier.

2.1 Collaborative Computational Thinking Design Practices (CCTDP)

Existing literature on CT highlights that to ensure students benefit from this approach, a structured method of integration practices need to be introduced. Some of the main principles that need to be instilled in the process is students' self-efficacy and sense of confidence in order to think critically; and the lessons have been fun and engaging. Thus, activities conducted based on the Collaborative Computational Thinking Design Practices (CCTDP) framework (which have been verified in another publication), was fun, engaging and empower students to be self-reliant and confident. This was able to assist students struggling with English and subjects related to STEM [12, 13]. Education experts and scholars globally agreed that it is imperative that an interesting, fun, learner-centric thinking approach to learning be integrated into the education curriculum, so that there is democratisation and inclusivity of education for all learners, especially as we move towards society 5.0. There must be an approach that can integrate CT across curriculum including STEM amongst peers collaboratively [14–16].

An effective CT design framework that incorporates CT based on a sound learning model that integrates English across STEM thematic topics is crucial. Many learning models available have not been able to do this effectively. Many instructional design models that have been developed either locally or globally have tried to incorporate higher order thinking skills in the learning process, but all have not been able to do this effectively [17–19].

Other findings from previous literature also emphasised that incorporating suitable learning approaches such as CT across STEM through the use of interesting virtual environment applications and new media [9, 19, 20]; gamification or fun and meaningful 'hands-on' activities are also effective [17]. New media-based dynamic assessment [21, 22], and the use of TRIZ techniques [4, 8] had positive results meeting both behavioural and cognitive theory assumptions [23]. These studies also found that considerably less studies were conducted on CT across non-science subjects. Therefore, there is a need to study the incorporation of CT in non-science subjects such as English across STEM, using 'hands-on' visual based gaming approach that is fun and engaging, can help learners apply thinking skills to solve problems more effectively. Therefore, based on previous literature, there are a variety of learning approaches that can assist learners enhance their creative, logical and innovative thinking skills. These strategies were designed based on conventional approaches which can be embedded in a specific programme to assist students think and eventually help them gain self-efficacy and confidence in their learning process [24, 25]

According to Bower et al. [26] and the authors [1, 2], CT had constantly been mistaken for learning coding and robotics skills. Learning coding and robotics alone without learning thinking is not enough. This is because both these skills are the lower level of the CT order. The higher level is the instillation of higher order thinking skills, particularly the ability to solve complex open-ended problems through a series of ordered algorithms confidently [1, 2]. Related work by Tak et al. [27], on CT through social game play also discovered that computational thinking, using TRIZ through engaging and fun activities can help learners acquire more effective logical and creative thinking skills amongst school age children generally, and 4th grade elementary school learners (10 year-olds), specifically. CCTDP was designed and used in this experiment that was conducted in the four (4) schools in the rural state of Kedah. Details of the validation of the model was already published and will not be discussed in this paper [1, 2].

2.2 CCTDP and TRIZ

Today CT is considered as a 21st century skill that needs to be mastered if possible by every citizen to solve not just the science, engineering and mathematics but also the arts and other domains related to everyday life problems. CT has become so important because we need to find the most efficient way to solve problems [15, 28]. Basically, we want to find the best solution that solves the problem correctly, in the fastest way, and using the least amount of resources (time and/or space). Although CT involves thinking engaged by computer scientists and software developers, there are many others in the other domains that use this thinking process and approach too. It is imperative to take into consideration the concepts and approaches involved in CT.

The fundamental concepts such as logic (analysing and predicting), algorithms (making steps and rules), decomposition (breaking down into parts), patterns (spotting and using similarities), abstraction (removing unnecessary detail), displaying (visualising through visualisation) and evaluation (making judgment); and its related approaches such as tinkering (experimenting and playing), creating (designing and making), debugging (finding and fixing errors), persevering (keeping going) and collaborating (working together, teamwork); all complete the CT process in a holistic and systematic manner. Due to the fact that it is crucial to introduce CT to children at elementary school, it is imperative that it should be introduced beyond the computing curriculum.

TRIZ is the Russian acronym *"Teoriya Resheniya Izobretatelskikh Zadatch"* meaning the *Theory of Inventive Problem Solving* developed in 1946, by a soviet inventor named Genrich Altshuller and his colleagues. Basically, it is a problem-solving analysis and forecasting tool based on 40 principles, derived from the study of patterns of invention in the global patent literature [26, 29–31]. Both CT and TRIZ through CCTDP, has shown to possess a significant future educational learning potential in this digital economy society 5.0 environment.

2.3 Advantages of CCTDP Across STEM

Developing CT skill set among STEM educators and students to sustain scientific revolution in the digital economy society 5.0 era is imperative. It is also important that they are able to apply CT skill set in solving problems in a collaborative manner. Team work in the digital economy society 5.0 era, in preparing future generations to be digital-based data-driven knowledge worker is crucial. Although CT has been applied widely in STEM research, limited studies have been conducted, especially in elementary schools to introduce students to collaborative CT across STEM [32, 33, 36, 37]. Various studies such as the Northwest Distributed Computer Science Department (NW-DCSD) project that brings together multi-disciplinary faculty from diverse colleges and universities to foster inter-institutional collaboration in a multi-disciplinary computing approach [34, 35, 38–40]. Thus, this study conducted amongst rural elementary school children in Kedah, Malaysia, integrating CT with a humanities subject across STEM is novel.

There are various advantages to introduce a humanities subject across STEM in classrooms based on the CCTDP framework that have traditionally not involved computation. CT includes skill sets that are applicable to a broad range of problems and settings, and not tied to a specific domain. By integrating CCTDP framework in a humanities subject across STEM, students in elementary schools can explore and apply CT skills within a more established STEM contexts through 'hands-on' fun and play learning activities. Another benefit of integrating CCTDP framework in a humanities subject across STEM in classrooms is that it allows it to be reached to a wider audience than it would be possible if it was thought independently. Moreover, direct issues such as lack of resources, for example, qualified teachers who understand CT and dedicated computational based classrooms on problem solving can be addressed.

3   Methodology

The methodology adopted was a qualitative ethnographic approach to provide a naturalistic account of literacy and cognitive flow of elementary teachers' and students' multimodal during an interactive CT activity that is integrated into English lessons across STEM based on the CCTDP framework. The process was videotaped and the social interactions that took place through informal discussions among peers in the groups both inter and intra were observed. Our exploratory research design was reflective of our analytical goal of better understanding of students' plausible inclination problem solving orientations based on CT concepts. In this paper, only one plausible orientation that emerged will be discussed, that is: 'logic-abstraction-evaluation'. This was done through observational assessment. The Observational Assessment (OA) is crucial to ensure that the program conducted in the schools for the purpose to improve the thinking process of learners are effective.

Thus, this paper highlights the observational assessment conducted, based on a sample of students' group discussion session, through an extract from video recordings of the interactional CT strategy to solve a problem presented in written form. The actual observational experiments conducted in the school was run continuously for two (2) years. The observational checklist used during observation included the five (5) components of COMEL learning model mentioned earlier. The analyses focused on the interactional strategies used by the students to acquire, construct, sustain and develop knowledge within the peer group; how they make necessary adjustments to changing what they know by drawing upon prior experience and knowledge in visual presentation and the socialisation that happens naturally which then emerged the organisation of thoughts and actions pertaining to the plausible problem solving LDA orientation.

3.1   Participants

Participants of the whole research involved eight (8) teachers and 120 students from four (4) schools in the rural state of Kedah, Malaysia. However, this paper reports on the participation of three (3) teachers and thirty (30) students in a classroom of the one (1) school selected by the State Department of Education, based on a case of one (1) group. Participation selection was purposeful and based on selection of schools by the State Department of Education, which took into consideration experienced teachers and schools with similar instructional settings and location to ensure a reasonable degree of contextual comparisons that can be made when necessary.

3.2   Data Collection

Data for this study comprised of digitally captured video-recordings of students undergoing actual English lessons across STEM using the COMEL model, based on the CCTDP framework. The videos were captured using the digital camcorder focused primarily on group discussion sessions concentrating on the part when problem has been assigned to the groups in the class by the teacher. Detailed observation of the interactions was conducted using observational checklist instrument. This data collection approach provided very useful results in recent works conducted on collaborative CT learning approaches as well as collaborative community approaches [41, 42].

The videos were transcribed in full. The resulting corpus of video recordings collected were used as our primary data source. Specifically, we also collected artifacts such as lesson plans, drawings, 'hand-outs' as well as text and visual diagrams on 'rough papers', 'mahjong papers' and small portable whiteboards. These multiple data sources revealed the plausible LDA orientation of problem solving practices employed by the students in this study.

3.3   Data Analyses

The visual and verbal discourses that took place during the group work tasks were analysed to determine the interactions that happened between the students and their peers in the particular plausible LDA orientation of approaching the process of solving an open ended problem using the CCTDP framework. Our analysis of the CT modality focused on how the discussions are geared from unstructured towards more structured discussions that took into consideration the concepts of CT, in a naturalistic form. In between the discussions we also take note of the social interactions (which include social norms) that surfaced during the discussions. As they conduct their discussions, we also observe very closely how they reach their conclusions in closing the problem that they are solving based on the plausible LDA orientation.

4   Findings

Our analysis of the rural students' plausible problem solving LDA orientation revealed interesting patterns when they were conducting discussions to solve the open ended problem posed by the teacher. It was acknowledged that there were similar strategies undertaken by the students, but we could observed a somewhat distinct LDA orientation emerged in this problem solving session when the open ended question was posed based on the written task.

4.1   Problem Solving Based on the CCTDP Framework: LDA Orientation

The objective of this observational assessment was to focus on the plausible problem solving LDA orientation by peers when discussing a solution to an open ended problem on a written task. The interactions that took place were carefully observed to study the distinct patterns of plausible problem solving LDA orientation that occurred. The detailed observational study conducted, involved analysis that followed a sequential flow of activities during the peer group discussion, leading to the final solution reached by the group in written form. Focus was on how students interact with their peers in the groups through the *'logic-decomposition-abstraction' (LDA) orientation,* that emerged naturally, to solve the open ended problem posed by the teacher. The flow is explained through a 'used case' indicated in extract 2.

> Extract 2: Level 2 CCTDP: OAWF: *'logic-decomposition-abstraction' (LDA) orientation* [2017-21-12 11:01:23]
> *SK Jalan Pegawai [National Primary School, Pegawai Road]*
>
> *Students are in special COMEL Classroom environment [they sit on the floor with low tables; each group have a small white board on their tables to write down their groups' solutions; there is LCD and a computer in the classroom]*
> *<Students have just watched a video on a group of children doing voluntary work cleaning homes of the elderly. Now they are asked to work in their respective groups to solve a problem given by the teacher> .*

The problem is as Follows:
["*In the village, there live an old man called Hitam who has no family. He lives by himself in a small hut with one room to sleep, a small kitchen and a toilet. He needs help in cleaning the house and the compound. He also need help to have a space to relax and have peace of mind at his old age. How can you solve this problem for the old man. Solve the problem by writing a plan*".]

> *<Can hear sounds of students chattering away and discussing in their respective groups, discussions are intermitted with laughter..... T and TA walks from one group to another, they try to allow the discussions without any help from them, unless they are really needed.>*
>
> *<Group 4 (Winx Club) are having their discussion>*

<Adriana (S2G4) quickly takes the lead>

1. **Adriana (S2G4) :** lets divide the work...Syasya you good english, you write
   our group answer on   whiteboard.
2. *<Syasya (S4G4) nods in agreement>*
3. **Shafi (S3G4):** we must *tulis* on the paper first (malay word for write)
4. **Addin (S1G4):** yes...., paper first...better...
   <others agree by nodding and saying yes!>
5. **Adriana (S2G4):** who will *raite* on paper? (she meant write)
   <Darwisya (S5G4) and Sufi (S6G4)put their hands up>
6. **Sufi (S6G4):** Me....me...me....
7. **Adriana (S2G4):** ok Sufi, you *writ* on paper first (meant write),
8.   then we decide who do job.

<Sufi nods in agreement, whilst Darwisya puts her hand

down with slight disappointment but still smiling >

9. **Addin (S1G4):** er...er..I think we have to write
   what jobs to do at *Pak cik Tam's* house. Then
   bahagi kerja (malay term for 'Uncle' based on
   cultural respect directed to any old man and
   in the village, their names are fondly shortened
   (Hitam to Tam) and *distribute the chores,*
   respectively) *<everyone in the group agree>*
10. **Adriana (S2G4):** Oh yes!, you right Addin.
    Ok what jobs to do?

    <everyone in the group start to give their

    opinion eagerly>
11. **Sufi (S6G4):** clean all rubbish out....garden
12. **Adriana (S2G4):** first clean kitchen, mob

    kitchen, wipe *peti ais*
    (malay word for *refrigerator*)

13. **Sufi (S6G4) :** Adriana, pak cik tua is poor....no *peti ais*
    (malay word for *refrigerator*)

    <can hear laughter and utterances)
14. *<Teacher (T) walk to group, listen to their discussion,
    smile as sign of approval and walk away>*
15. **Syasya (S4G4):** Sufi write down the jobs that is mentioned
    first. List them first and we sort them later.

    <all the students in the group nod in agreement>
16. **Darwisya (S5G4):** use rake to clean all fallen leaves,
    use wheelbarrow to throw fallen leaves.
17. **Shafi (S3G4):** Clean bedroom
18. **Sufi (S6G4):** Clean toilet...need to bring soap,
    ubat cuci lantai (malay word
    for floor detergent).
19. **Adriana (S2G4):** we must also write rules...
    like cannot play when cleaning the rubbish
<everyone in the group agrees...and laugh>
20. **Syasya (S4G4):** need good teamwork
21. **Adriana (S2G4):** that is a good rule, Syasya!
22. **Shafi (S3G4):** we need vacuum to clean
    bedroom, broom, mob and some *kain buruk*...
    to clean kitchen and toilet (malay word for *rags*)

At this point we observe the *logic* orientation of 'predicting and analysing the groups' strengths and a logical approach on writing on a rough paper first

We observe yet again *logical* and *decomposition* orientation to making decision on how to go about solving the problem (with socio-cultural norms taking place)- predicting chores in relation to logical thinking of what exists and sorting out chores to be done in the old man's hut.

At this point we observe the students yet using *logic* and *decomposition* orientation divide work amongst them

23. *<Assistant teacher (TA) walk towards the group and stop to listen>*

24. *<students are happy that TA stop by their group... they continue to discuss ... with intermittent laughter and chuckles>*

25. *<TA stays a little while more, gave the group two(2) stars and then leaves the group to go to another group. >*
     <Winx Club members were happy >

26. **Sufi (S3G4)** : we need to work in pairs....two persons sweep, two persons collect rubbish, two clean kitchen... like that...

27. **Adriana (S2G4):** Sufi good idea...that can be another rule...

28. **Shafi (S3G4):** Ok...but some only one person can do...got *satu saja* vacuum, *satu je* wheelbarrow (malay word/expression for *only one*)...

29. **Adriana (S2G4):** you are right....but still can work in pairs...like two person clean garden....one person use wheelbarrow, one person use rake...*<everyone nods in agreement.>*

30. **Syasya (S4G4):** I think I can start to write our answers on the white board now... *<Syasya takes the white board and check the list of things written on the paper by Sufi>*

31. *<everyone in Winx Club group, begin to help Syasya as she writes their solution on the white board>*

32. **Syasya (S4G4):** Right..here we go..how do I start...? *<everyone starts to give their opinion and Syasya began to write something on the whiteboard and then erases it>*

33. **Sayasya (S4G4):** wait...let me draw the whole picture of our answer first....

34. *<Syasya began to draw a diagram at on another piece of paper based on the list done by Sufi>*

35. **Adriana (S2G4):** That's a good idea Syasya..

36. **Sufi (S6G4):** Oh Yes!...then only write the plan on board..but you missed the toilet...

37. **Syasya (S4G4)**: You are right Sufi...ohh ok ... Adriana and Darwisya can clean the toilet and the kitchen then..

38. *<Adriana and Darwisya both agreed by nodding their heads>*

39. *<everyone agreed....then they were chatting away... intermittent laughter could be heard*

40. *<Syasya then began to write the plan on the white board>*

     < Everyone tries to be helpful, by giving their suggestions....some of the suggestions are accepted by Syasya and she writes it on the whiteboard

The logic-decomposition Orientation continues at this point we see they start to do abstraction – and creating a check list on a rough paper (Figure 1)

<Figure 3 shows their solution written on the white board ready to be discussed with the rest of the other groups in the class together with their teacher (T) and assistant teacher (TA)>

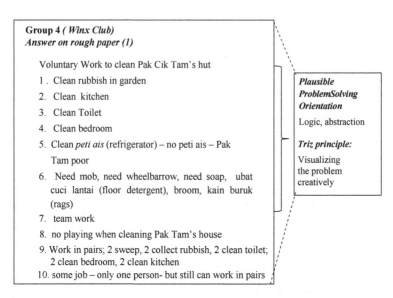

Group 4 (*Winx Club*)
Answer on rough paper (1)

Voluntary Work to clean Pak Cik Tam's hut

1. Clean rubbish in garden
2. Clean kitchen
3. Clean Toilet
4. Clean bedroom
5. Clean *peti ais* (refrigerator) – no peti ais – Pak
   Tam poor
6. Need mob, need wheelbarrow, need soap, ubat
   cuci lantai (floor detergent), broom, kain buruk
   (rags)
7. team work
8. no playing when cleaning Pak Tam's house
9. Work in pairs; 2 sweep, 2 collect rubbish, 2 clean toilet;
   2 clean bedroom, 2 clean kitchen
10. some job – only one person- but still can work in pairs

Plausible
ProblemSolving
Orientation

Logic, abstraction

Triz principle:

Visualizing
the problem
creatively

Fig. 1. Group 4 answer on rough paper (1)

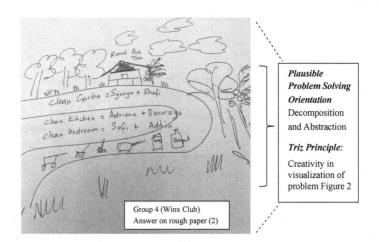

Plausible
Problem Solving
Orientation
Decomposition
and Abstraction

Triz Principle:

Creativity in
visualization of
problem Figure 2

Group 4 (Winx Club)
Answer on rough paper (2)

Fig. 2. Group 4 answer on rough paper (2)

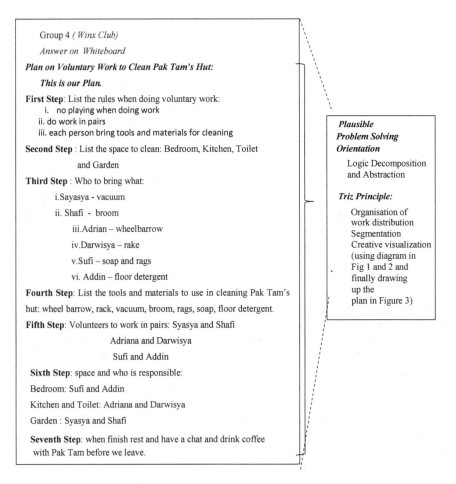

Fig. 3. Group 4 answer on whiteboard

5 Discussions

In this study, the teacher (T) and assistant teacher (TA) were in the classroom only to facilitate the groups. Clearly, this was to ensure students work together as a team, organise themselves, discuss, argue and come to a consensus for the final decision on the solution. Students used the skills (Triz and CT skills) they have learnt. From the extract, students from the 'Winx Club' group began the discussion with their peers on the English unit of 'Planning a Voluntary Work' to clean a home of an elderly man called Hitam or *<Pak Cik Tam>* who lives in the village. This English unit was integrated with STEM on the theme of cleanliness and environment.

The group was quick to organise themselves when Adriana (S2G4), took up a leadership role and began with *<lets divide the work...Syasya you good English you write our group answer on whiteboard>* . The group members were agreeable and were quick to think and response. For example Shafi (S3G4) suggested <*we must tulis* (malay word for write) *on paper first .....better*> . It was a positive suggestion and whilst they discuss who should be the one to write their discussion on a rough paper first, Adriana again played her leadership role and said <ok Sufi, *you raite on paper* (she meant write), *then we decide who do job*> . We observe that the discussion went quite smooth although there was constant <*chatting, intermittent with laughter*> Almost every member of the group contributed to the final solution of the problem. There were moments when a disagreement was made to a suggestion given <*we need to work in pairs...two persons to sweep, two persons to collect rubbish, two clean kitchen...like that*> [S3G4]....Shafi (S6G4) rebutted <*ok. but some only one person can do...got satu saja vacuum, satu je wheelbarrow (malay word/expression for only one*> . An interesting step taken during the session was when Syasya (S4G4), despite everyone `trying to give ideas in an unstructured manner at the same time, she took a unique approach <*wait...let me draw the whole picture of our answer first....*> she began to draw part of the 'whole solution' in an interesting visual diagram [Fig. 2] before writing the final solution in text form on the whiteboard [Fig. 3]. Throughout the 'brainstorming session' conducted amongst the peers in the Winx Club group, we observe a very 'skillful' discussion being conducted in the group to achieve the outcome using the plausible problem solving *logic-decomposition-abstraction* orientation.

From the extract, we also saw the interactions between the peers in the group portrayed very positive display of CT strategy behaviour and the CT skills logic-decomposition-abstraction (LDA) orientation to problem solving, TRIZ principles (segmentation, organization and universality), the optimisation of approach to presentation of ideas <writing on rough paper 1 [Fig. 1], drawing using rough paper 2 [Fig. 2]> , the obvious manifestation of meta cognition through self-efficacy, seen in confidence shown by the members especially Adriana (S2G4); the commitment of total engagement to conduct the discussion (of course with lots of intermittent laughter) and showing the way to acquire the solution to meet the learning outcome in a very positive practice using the CCTDP framework by adopting the plausible problem solving *logic-decomposition-abstraction* (LDA) orientation.

5.1   Theoretical and Practical Implications

The reported findings of this study has significant implications both theoretical and practical. Our findings underscore the critical need for further theorising interaction orientations in collaborative CT multimodal design practices, for teaching and learning strategies of both science and non-science domains (in this case, learning English across STEM). Compared to other scholars and practitioners in other academic fields, science educators are yet to interrogate interaction orientations based on CT concepts through non-science fields across STEM (Science based materials). This is also important, because attention to learning has constantly been focused on cognitive challenges broadly, overlooking the interaction orientations that affects cognitive thinking process and decision making. Thinking orientations through CT based on the CCTDP framework, clearly shows that students in collaborative situations may interact and solve problems based on the plausible *Logic-Decomposition-Abstraction(LDA)* orientation. The findings seemed to indicate that the interaction orientation on solving problems occurred when certain interaction entities took place at different levels of discussions.

For instance, when the interaction happens in a situation where students dominate in the collaborative environment the orientation was naturally geared to one that was based on the presentation requirements of the solution as instructed by the teacher. In situation, where students dominate almost fully in the lessons conducted, the interaction orientation that emerged was clearly based on the requirement for the students to present their solutions in either written or visual form. Thus, emerged the plausible LDA orientation. As our findings has shown, such expansive ways of problem solving can provide elementary educators with valuable insights into specific problem solving orientation that can be fostered by their pedagogical practices during both science and non-science lessons involved.

The findings also has practical implications. Our findings suggest a critical need for elementary school teachers generally, and rural elementary school teachers specifically, children from the B40 economic status section of the society, are afforded the opportunity to experience collaborative interactions in solving problems that are open, encourages self-efficacy and self-confidence to conduct thinking in a second language such as English (which is the lingua-franca of the digital environment), yet have the exposure to STEM materials at an early age. This CCTDP framework was initially able to convince us that it can help students to acquire a more logical, scientific, creative and innovative approach to thinking and solving open ended problems. A significant practical finding too, is that the CCTDP framework has allowed the pedagogical strategy conducted by teachers to be more 'open' in the use of students' natural collaborative interactions (that sometimes seemed casual) during dialogues and negotiations with the use of gestural and cultural interpretations. This early findings have the potential to shape young students' emergent identities as empowered English proficient science learners who interacts in collaborative discussions not simply to extract and state a fact but to actively contribute to formulate deeper understanding of the problem posed that need to be solved. This is really the objective of the CCTDP framework. It would eventually allow learners to be able to migrate from rote thinking, where ideas are fed by teachers in the conventional strategy; to open CT where learners use certain orientations to generate own ideas and construct new novel approach to problem solving. We believe that only after students have acquired the 'open' thinking through CT and Triz strategies embedded in the CCTDP framework, can they be more embracing of learning programing codes. This would be the final level of the CCTDP framework, which is not discussed in this paper.

6 Conclusion

As it turned out, an important part of elementary students' collaborative interaction to solve open ended problem, based on the Collaborative Computational Thinking Design Practices (CCTDP) Framework showed an almost natural tendency for them to interact in certain plausible problem solving orientation, in this case, the *logic-decomposition-abstraction* (LDA). This plausible orientation as we observed, was further enriched, with the students' natural socialisation experiences, through gestural (both verbal and non-verbal) and cultural norms that enhance the interactions resulting in innovative and creative solutions. When the collaborative interactions in solving problems were first guided by the teachers based on the CCTDP framework, students tended to wait for cues and expected scaffolds from teachers each step of the problem solving process. However, as the students were slowly 'weaned off' from the teachers' help, they gained confidence and began to conduct the discussions and arrived at innovative solutions themselves. Judging by their gestural voices, facial expressions, intermittent laughters and giggles, the students were having fun in constructing and formulating their own solutions based on the visual based presentation using the plausible problem solving LDA orientation of the CCTDP framework.

Acknowledgement. This work was supported by the Kedah State Government (Grant no. ZG-2015-001) and the Universiti Kebangsaan Malaysia (UKM) Grand Challenge Grant (Grant no. AP-2017-0051).

References

1. Zaman, H.B., et al.: Integrating Computational Thinking (CT) with English across STEM.: proposal. Bangi: Universiti Kebangsaan Malaysia, Bangi (2016)
2. Zaman, H.B., et al.: Computational Thinking (CT) across STEM model in teaching English amongst elementary school children in Kedah, Malaysia. Digital Transformation Landscape in the Fourth Industrial Revolution (4IR) era. In VIIS 2018, Bangi: IVI, UKM (2018)
3. Cavalluci, D., Lutz, P.: Beyond TRIZ limits. Triz J. (1998). https://triz.journal.com
4. Chechurin, L., Collan, M.: Advances in Systematic Creativity: Creating and Managing Innovation, 1st edn. Prime Student, New York (2016)
5. Chechurin, L.: TRIZ in science. In: Reviewing indexed publications School of Business 538 Procedia CIRP ScienceDirect TFC 2015 – TRIZ 2018. FUTURE 2015 and Management Lappeenranta University of Technology Lappeenranta, Finland, vol. 39, pp. 156–165 (2017)
6. Hadi, S.A., Susantini, E., Agustini, R.: Training of students' critical thinking skills through the implementation of a modified free inquiry model. In: Journal of Physics: Conference Series, vol. 947, p. 012063 (2018)
7. Hurd, P.: The state of critical thinking today. In: Developing Blu prints for Institutional Change Foundation for Critical Change, New York (2018)
8. Foster, J., Yaoyuneyong, G.: Teaching innovation: equipping students to overcome real-world challenge. J. Higher Educ. Pedagogies 1(1), 42–56 (2016)
9. Norzari, A.Y., Saimian, H.: The effects of problem-solving teaching on creative thinking among district 2 high school students in Sari city. J. Acad. Med. Sci. Bosnia Herzegovina 26(6), 360–363 (2014)
10. Sullenger, K.: Fostering higher level of scientific literacy: confronting potential barriers to science understanding. University of New Brunswick, New Brunswick (2005)
11. Anwar, M.N., Shamim-ur-Parsool, S., Haq, R.: A comparison of creative thinking abilities of high and low achievers secondary computer interaction school students. Int. Interdiscip. J.0 Educ. 1(1), 1–10 (2012)
12. Yasar, O.: A new perspective on Computational Thinking. Commun. ACM 61(7), 33–38 (2018)

13. Snalune, P.: The benefits of Computational Thinking. Chartered Institute for IT, British Computer Society, London (2015)
14. Sheldon, E.: Computational thinking across the curriculum (2017). https://www.edutopia.org/blog/computational-thinking-across-the-curriculum-eli-sheldon
15. Wolfram, S.: How to teach Computational Thinking (2017). https://www.wired.com/2016/09/how-to-teach-computational-thinking
16. Bowden Melander, H.: Problem Solving in collaborative game design practices: epistemic stance, affect and engagement. Learn. Media Technol. **44**(2), 124–143 (2019). https://doi.org/10.1080/17439884.2018.1563106
17. Barr, V., Stephenson, C.: Bringing Computational Thinking to K-12: what is involved and what is the role of the computer science education community? Inroads **2**, 48–54 (2018). New York
18. Mardiyana, N.M., Pramudya, I.: Science, technology, engineering, mathematics (STEM) as mathematics learning approach in 21st century. In: AIP Conference Proceedings, vol. 1868, p. 050024. American Institute of Physics (2017). https://doi.org/10.1063/1.4995151. http://aip.scitation.org/toc/apc/1868/1
19. Sullivan, A., Bers, M.U.: Robotics in the early childhood classroom: Learning outcomes from an 8-week robotics curriculum in pre-kindergarten through second grade. Int. J. Technol. Des. Educ. **26**(1), 3–20 (2016). https://doi.org/10.1007/s10798-015-9304-5
20. United States of America. Department of Education.: Science, Technology, Engineering and Maths: Education for Global Leadership. Washington: US Department of Education (2015)
21. Kopp, K.H., Stowitschek, J.J.: Effects of Teachers' Planning on Mathematics Computation skills. Wiley, New York (1980)
22. Cannon, M., Potter, J., Andrew, B.: Dynamic, playful, and predictive literacies. Changing English **25**(2), 180–192 (2018). https://doi.org/10.1080/1358684x2018.1452146
23. Jiang, J., Jeffery, B., Katherine, H., Tobias, E.: An insula-Frontostrial network mediates flexible Cognitive control by adaptively predicting changing control demands. Nat. Commun. [Nat. Res. J.] **6**, 8165 (2015)
24. Kazomoglu, C., Kiernan, M., Bacon, L., Mackinnon, L.: A serious game for developing Computational Thinking and learning introductory computer programming. Procedia Soc. Behav. Sci. **47**, 1991–1999 (2012)
25. Brennan, K., Mitchel, B.: New framework for studying and assessing the development of computational thinking. In: AERA, MIT Lab, pp. 1–5 (2012)
26. Bower, M., Wood, L.N., Lai, J.W.M., Hore, C.: Improving the Computational Thinking pedagogical capabilities of school teachers. Aust. J. Sch. Teachers **42**(3), 53–71 (2017)
27. Tak, Y.L., Mauriello, L., Ahn, J., Bederson, B.: CTArcade: Computational thinking with games in school age children. Int. J. Child-Comput. Interact. **2**(1), 26–33 (2014)
28. Ventura, M., Lai, E., DiCerbo, K.: Skills for today: What we know about teaching and assessing critical thinking [White paper] (2017). Accessed 29 Mar 2018. http://www.p21.org/storage/documents/Skills_For_Today_Series-Pearson/White_Paper
29. Sun, Y.T., Tin, Y.J., Li, S.C.: Triz level 1: Theory of Inventive Problem Solving. Firstfruits Sdn Bhd, Kuala Lumpur (2010)
30. Sun, Y.T., Tin, Y.J., Li, S.C.: Triz level 2: Theory of Inventive Problem Solving. Firstfruits Sdn Bhd, Kuala Lumpur (2012)
31. Sun, Y.T., Tin, Y.J., Li, S.C.: Systematic Innovation in Business and Management. Firstfruits Sdn Bhd, Kuala Lumpur (2014)
32. Yadav, A., Hong, H., Stephenson, C.: Computational thinking for all: Pedagogical approaches to embedding 21st century problem solving in K-12 classrooms. TechTrends **60**(6), 565–568 (2016). https://doi.org/10.1007/s11528-016-0087-7

33. Yadav, A., Stephenson, C., Hong, H.: Computational thinking for teacher education. Communications of the ACM **60**(4), 55–62 (2017). https://doi.org/10.1145/2994591
34. Wing, J.M.: Computational thinking. Communications of the ACM **49**(3), 33–35 (2006). https://doi.org/10.1145/1118178.1118215
35. Wing, J.M.: Computational thinking's influence on research and education for all. Ital. J. Educ. Technol. **25**(5), 7–14 (2017). https://doi.org/10.17471/2499-4324/927
36. Dorling, M., Stephens, S.: Problem solving in computational thinking rubric (2016). http://community.computingatschool.org.uk/resources/4793
37. Dorling, M., Walker, M.: Computing at school progressive pathways (2014). https://community.computingatschool.org.uk/resources/1692
38. Kranov, A., Bryant, R., Orr, G., Wallace, S., Zhang, M.: Developing a community definition and teaching modules for Computational thinking: Accomplishment and challenges. In: SIGITE, Midland, Michigan, USA, 10 October 2010 (2010)
39. Jui, C.J., Sun, P., An, J.S.: Six cognitive gaps by using Triz and tools for service system design. Expert Syst. Appl. **38**(12), 14751–14755 (2011)
40. Swaid, S.I.: Bringing Computational thinking to STEM. Sci. Dir. **3**, 3657–3662 (2015)
41. Binet, A., Gavin, V., Leigh, C., Arcaya, M.: Designing and facilitating collaborative research design and data analysis workshops: lessons learned in the healthy neighborhoods study. Int. J. Environ. Res. Publ. Health **16** (2019). https://www.mdpi.com/about/openaccess
42. West, B., Conrad, F.: Collaborative research: video communication technologies in survey data collection. University of Michigan, Ann Arbor (2019). SCR

E-Community Program: A Study on ICT Knowledge Transfer to Labuan Community

Wan Nooraishya Wan Ahmad[(✉)], Ahmad Rizal Ahmad Rodzuan,
Khan Vun Teong, Nuraini Jamil, and Nooralisa Mohd Tuah

Faculty of Computing and Informatics, Universiti Malaysia Sabah,
Federal Territory Labuan, Malaysia
{aishya, arizal, nichtkv, ainjamil, aelise}@ums.edu.my

Abstract. The transfer of knowledge enables local communities to keep up with the current revolution of ICT and later to create a knowledge society. This study reviews knowledge transfer activities to local communities in Labuan through the E-Community Program conducted by the Faculty of Computing and Informatics (FCI), Universiti Malaysia Sabah Labuan International Campus (UMSLIC). The objective of this study is to investigate the trend of selecting and implementing e-community projects. The study was conducted quantitatively and qualitatively towards the e-community project reports as well as discussions between lecturers. The finding shows that graphic design projects are popular e-community projects and school students are the most benefited communities. Impacts, challenges and suggestions for improvements to the program are also discussed.

Keywords: Knowledge transfer · Community activities · E-community · Labuan

1 Introduction

With a population density of 100,000 on 2018 [1], Labuan Island is located in offshore Sabah and is one of the federal territories of Malaysia. However, Labuan is somewhat lagging behind compared to other federal territories in terms of information technology literacy, due to its relatively isolated location [2]. Hence, the transfer of information and communication technology (ICT) knowledge to the Labuan community is particularly important to improve the quality of life and boost the economy of this island through the E-Community Program. Community is defined as a group of people who live together in a local geographic area, or who are not in the same area but have an element of similarity such as social identity, trade relations, and interests [3]. E-community enables the exchange of data and knowledge via digital networks between people and/or institutions [4].

The E-Community Program in Faculty of Computers and Informatics (FCI) was first introduced in August 2009 for E-Marketing course. Initially, only E-Commerce students were involved in the program specifically targeting rural areas with the aim of promoting internet use in connecting communities with similar interests [2]. Mindful of the importance of ICT development and the role played by the University within local

© Springer Nature Switzerland AG 2019
H. Badioze Zaman et al. (Eds.): IVIC 2019, LNCS 11870, pp. 729–740, 2019.
https://doi.org/10.1007/978-3-030-34032-2_65

communities, the Faculty at first has initiated an Industrial Training course by making the e-community project the main assignment. This e-community project assignment is seen as a preparation for the students before being placed for industry training under arrangements made by the university. Starting 2014, the e-community project becomes a major task for IT31103 Topics and Current Issues with the ultimate goal of sharing ICT knowledge and skills to nurture and increase interest in ICT among Labuan communities.

Therefore, this study aims to focus on the involvement of the local community, academicians and FCI students to transfer the ICT knowledge to the local community of Labuan. The objective of this study is to identify the trend of selecting and implementing e-community program. An E-Community program framework constructed consists of factors influencing the implementation of the e-community program, the challenges faced and recommendations for improvement. In practice, the findings can be used to propose relevant and appropriate topics for e-community projects which not only demonstrate students' knowledge and skill but benefit the local or target communities the most.

2 Background Work

2.1 Knowledge Transfer

Knowledge transfer is a term used to summarize various activities aimed in facilitating cooperation between universities and the public sectors [5], such as schools, government agencies and local communities. Among the activities conducted include the transfer of intellectual properties, expertises, learning and skills between the academic and non-academic community. These are also identified by the government and the private sector as a good 'return on investment' which is important in academic studies, because of its ability to stimulate economic development and community well-being. For academicians and students, the transfer of knowledge is one of the means to gain experience on what has been learned, taught and studied in the institution, as well as giving back to society [6].

Training through teaching and learning activities is one of the approaches that can be practiced in transferring knowledge apart from consultation, contract research, joint research and staff mobility [7]. Universities should play an active role in giving back to the community, through programs or activities that contribute to sharing of knowledge and expertise, so that they can be learned and mastered by the general public without restrictions and boundaries, to produce knowledgeable and skilled societies.

2.2 E-Community Program

The E-Community Program not only expose the students to community services, but also benefits them in terms of (1) sharing and transferring knowledge to other people in real-world situations, (2) polishing soft skills in terms of communication, management, teamwork and leadership by interacting with local communities, and (3) practicing and adapting the use of technology to solve real-world problems in ICT. Through this program, Labuan communities such as schoolchildren, government agency officials, small industry entrepreneurs and locals can learn and draw on the ever-expanding ICT knowledge. At the same time, it also helps to build close relationships between the University and the local community. Subsequently, this project has become an annual activity for the Faculty in serving the local community.

The program involves all FCI 4th year students from the Multimedia and Business Computing course, divided into 20 to 23 groups (depending on the number of enrolled students in Semester (1) and work together with their preferred lecturers to start projects with any target community groups. First, each group of students is required to discuss with their respective lecturers who are their academic supervisor, on the type of project that they wish to conduct, and later prepare a proposal based on that discussions. The proposal paper is then forwarded to the target community for discussions, amendment if there is any, and the final approval. After obtaining the consent of all related parties, preparations including the venue, facilities (e.g. computer and software) and learning materials are managed by the group of students involved with the assistance of their academic supervisors. Nevertheless, there are groups of target communities such as schools which offer their facilities for the use of the project. Each student group is given financial assistance in carrying out their project with a spending limit of up to RM 200 which can be claimed from the Faculty, for the purpose of providing teaching and learning materials as well as food for the participants.

3 Methodology

The method used in conducting this study is based on the analysis of primary data, obtained from current and previous coordinators of the e-community program, through project reports sent by students as well as discussion sessions among Multimedia and Business Computing lecturers.

The sample data analyzed contains 148 e-community projects from 2011 to 2018, excluding 2014 due to the lack of the number of students attending this course as a result of the transition year from three years to four years. There are 24 e-community projects in 2011, 23 projects each in both 2012 and 2013, 17 projects in 2015, 19 projects in 2016, 21 projects in 2017 and 22 projects in 2018. The total number of projects each year depends on the number of students enrolled for the IT31103 Topics and Current Issues course.

A total of 6 lecturers who have at least 5 years of experience in supervising the e-community project, were selected to discuss the problems and challenges faced during the project implementations, as well as suggestions for improvements. Through the discussion, project categories are determined using critical thinking methods, where the titles of e-community projects are listed and similar features of each project are identified and classified according to categories based on the literature review. Table 1 shows the categories of e-community projects along with the description and criteria.

The data collected were analyzed using quantitative and qualitative methods. For quantitative data, a total of 148 e-community project reports from 2011 to 2018 were analyzed to determine the frequency of project categories, the types of target community groups involved and the implementation of project types according to target

Table 1. Categories of e-community project

Category	Description	Project criteria
Animation	Animation is "a simulated motion picture depicting movement of drawn (or simulated) objects" [8]	– Teach animation techniques – Used certain animation software – Animated product as project output
Game development	Game development is a process of designing and creating a computer game. Game design is a subset of game development that involves designing game content and rules to play [9]	– Design a computer or mobile game – Used certain software to develop a game – Game products as project output
Video production	Video production is a process of creating video content using digitally recorded images [10]	– Teach video editing techniques – Used certain video editing software – Video products as project output
Graphic design	Graphic design is a form of visual communication on a two-dimensional or three-dimensional surface, used to convey message or information to audience [11]	– Teach graphic editing techniques – Used certain graphic editor software – Graphic products as project output
E-entrepreneurship	E-entrepreneurship is an exchange of purchase, sales and trades of products or services via digital networks [4]	– Teach online marketing techniques – Used online applications as a marketing/business platform
Awareness talk	A talk on certain issues or topic to create awareness	– Delivering issues, technologies or information related to ICT – A demonstration of ICT technology or application
Information system	Information system is a set of interrelated components that helps people or organization to achieve goals by collecting, processing, storing, and disseminate data and information [12]	– Introduce the basic of computing to participants (i.e. collect, store, distribute and disseminate) – Used certain application in learning basic computing
Website/Blog Design	Development of website including writing markup and interface design for client-side use [13]	– Design a website/blog – Used certain application or software to develop a website/blog – A website/blog as project output
Fun learning	Learning is defined as fun when it allows for interaction that involved collaboration and guidance, infuses curiosity and interest [14]	– Apply game-like activities in learning – Used exhibit or computer application in the learning process
Programming	Programming involves computational thinking through the construction of executable computer program [15, 16]	– Teach programming concept – Used programming software – A small part of a system or an application as project output

community groups. Data on the discussion session between lecturers is qualitatively analyzed. Their feedback in terms of problems, challenges and suggestions are gathered to support the quantitative analysis results.

4   Results

4.1   Quantitative Analysis

Figure 1 shows the percentages of the type of e-community project that has been conducted from 2011 until 2018. The findings show that graphic design projects (26%) dominate the type of e-community project implemented by FKI students compared to information systems (20%), awareness talk (17%), animation (13%), video production (10%), and website/blog design (7%). The least-developed projects for e-community are fun learning (3%), e-entrepreneurship (2%), and 1% each for both game development and programming.

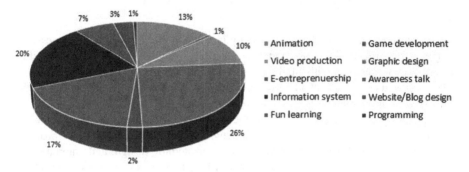

Fig. 1.   Categories of e-community project.

Analysis on the tendency of implementing e-community projects carried out by year is illustrated in Fig. 2. The year 2011 and 2012 show consistent selection of graphic design projects (25% and 26% respectively), while the lesser picked projects in 2011 are video production (4%) and programming (4%). However, in 2012, video production, e-entrepreneurship, entertainment and programming programs were not chosen to be implemented by the students. Significant differences can be seen in the increase in the percentage from 2011 to 2012, for animated category projects from 8% to 22% as well as information systems from 17% to 26%. Awareness talk and web site/blog designs remain at 13% for the two consecutive years.

In 2013, the trend of choosing the graphic design category in the e-community project rose to 36%, leaving behind the lesser picked video production project and awareness talk with 5% each. In addition, there was a significant decrease in the animated category projects and information systems projects by 18% respectively, while website/blog designs and fun learning were 9% each.

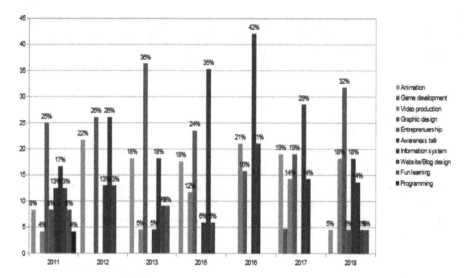

Fig. 2. Trend of e-community projects by year.

The years of 2015 and 2016 saw an sharp increase in the category of awareness talk category (from 6% to 42%) and video production (from 12% to 21%), while information systems were met with a fall from 35% to 21%, and graphic design from 24% to 16%. Animated projects (18%) and web/blog design projects (6%) were chosen by the students to be implemented in 2015, but not in 2016.

The years of 2017 and 2018 also saw the change in the domination of e-community project chosen by the students, and a few new additions in the category of projects, amounting to 5% each for e-entrepreneurship, website/blog design, and entertainment respectively. Animation category projects (from 19% to 5%) as well as awareness talks (from 29% to 18%) experienced significant declines while graphic designs (from 19% to 32%) returns to dominate the e-community project category.

Overall, graphic design, information systems and awareness talk projects are the three most preferred projects that are likely to be implemented every year. The number of e-community project categories also showed inconsistent changes, for example, 2011 and 2018 saw 9 and 8 categories respectively out of 10 projected categories compared to other years, while in the year 2016, only 4 categories of projects chosen to be implemented, and 5 categories in 2012.

Of all the e-community projects that have been implemented, 81% of them are practically conducted where project participants perform hands-on activities using specific software related to the project involved. Some of the types of e-community projects that carry out practical activities are animation, video production, information technology, games development, graphic design, e-entrepreneurship, web/blog development, and programming. About 17% of the projects were briefings such as the awareness talks, while the other 2% were in the form of fun learning and other related activities. Table 2 shows the types of software that the project participants learned.

Table 2. Types of software used for hands-on e-community project

Category	Software/Application/Language
Animation	Adobe Flash, Toon Boom Animate Pro, Scratch
Game development	Scratch
Video production	Audacity, Adobe Premiere, Adobe After Effects
Graphic design	Adobe InDesign, Adobe Photoshop, Adobe Illustrator, Adobe After Effects, Windows Paint
E-entrepreneurship	Facebook, Instagram
Information technology	Google Drive, Microsoft Word, Microsoft Powerpoint, Prezi
Website/Blog Design	Adobe Dreamweaver, Blogspot, Wordpress, WIX
Programming	C++

During its seven years of operation, the E-Community program has served 8 community groups with a total of 4226 participants. Figure 3 shows the distribution of categories of target communities that have been involved in e-community programs throughout the years. A total of 70% from 148 projects implemented from 2011 to 2018 involves schools as the participants, leaving behind other target communities such as villages (8%), associations/clubs/care centers (5%), kindergartens and colleges/institute (4% each), government departments and universities (2% each), and 5% for the groups (combinations of more than one target groups).

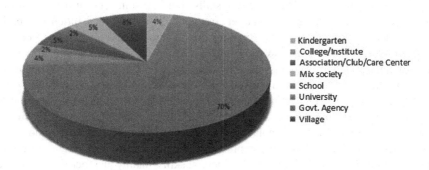

Fig. 3. Categories of target community.

Figure 4 illustrates the distribution of engagement of target community groups by the years. During its 7 years of operation, schools have been by far the largest target community every year between 12 to 20 projects. The year 2017 saw the school's highest targeted community involvement with 20 projects, while the second highest targeted community was the village with 5 projects for 2011 followed by the association/club/care center with 4 projects in 2018.

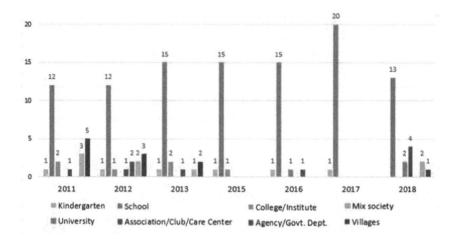

Fig. 4. Involvement of community group by year.

4.2 Qualitative Analysis

Two factors have been identified that are believed to influence the implementation of the E-Community Program, namely the selection of project categories and target communities. The factors that influence the selection of e-community project categories are classified according to the students and subjects offered as follows:

Students. Based on the discussion findings, students are seen to be more likely to choose projects involving graphic design, information systems and awareness talk as they are easy to implement. The basic ICT skills alone are sufficient for the students to carry out the project to the selected target community, who often has little to no basic ICT knowledge. For example, the training on how to use basic software such as Microsoft Word, PowerPoint, and Google Drive which are not only useful in day-to-day activities for school students but for business owners in their business management. The majority of students involved in e-community projects are in Multimedia Technology compared to those in Business Computing, and this has made the projects such as graphic design a top choice. Furthermore, there are more demands for multimedia related projects such as graphic design, video production, animations and game development, compared to the e-entrepreneurship category projects which are rarely implemented due to lack of shared entrepreneurial skills, mainly just focusing on online marketing using Facebook and Instagram. In addition, students usually avoid implementing computer programming projects even though students from both majors have studied programming subjects such as C++ and Java. Programming category projects are deemed to be difficult to master and require a long training period to be taught to the target community. Besides, target community groups such as schools have also learned programming languages such as Python and C++, while other target communities have little to no need of the programming skills.

Subject Offers. Subject offerings are also seen to influence the selection of e-community project categories. Game development and design related subjects have not been taught to the FCI students, which has made this category project not a popular choice among the students. As such, the students who picked this category took their own initiative to learn the related software before making this category their preferred project. However, a subject related to the game design and development has been listed as one of the Elective subjects for the subject offering beginning of the 2019/2020 intake. Gamification concept studied through the subject of IM31203 Human-Computer Interaction and IP0503 Creative Thinking is also less likely to be applied by the FCI students as the target communities such as schools still mainly use conventional learning methods. Kahoot! is some of the examples of electronic learning methods that utilize the concept of gamification that FCI students can use in implementing the fun learning category project. The learning of graphic design, animation and video production software from the series of Adobe's software since the 1st year, through tutorials for the IM12103 Fundamentals of Multimedia, IM22203 Animation and IM22103 Video Production subjects, have helped the FCI students to hone their skills and deliver the knowledge learned to the target community. Subjects such as IE12103 E-Commerce and the IE41103 Security and E-Commerce Payment System have also allowed students to share information in projects such as awareness talk and e-entrepreneurship categories.

Factors influencing the selection of the target community are classified by accessibility and lecturer networking categories:

Accessibility. The location which is next to UMSKAL has made Sek. Men. Sains Labuan (SMSL) a popular option for FCI students to carry out their e-community projects there, especially for the new school students in grades one and two. This is because the close proximity facilitates the movement of SMSL students to the Faculty's computer labs that offer a variety of computer software for the use in the project involved. Similarly, SMK Mutiara and SK Bebuloh are less than 8 km to UMSKAL. FCI students are very careful in spending the RM200 budget provided by the Faculty for transportation expenses. However, this is resolved by them by implementing projects in the location of the selected target community itself such in the respective school labs, by first ensuring that the specific software/application are provided by the target community, or else employ other similar software/applications.

Lecturer Networking. Each lecturer, who is also the academic supervisor for the respective e-community project, usually has an extensive and diverse network of relationships within the community. This may influence the selection of the target community by the students under them. The early period of the E-community program shows the lecturers proposed e-community projects using their current connections in the social community (i.e. having a high post in the community), work relationships through consulting projects and contacts through contacts (i.e. friends, neighbors, former students). This makes it easier for their students to get in touch with the target community directly. Given that the E-community program has been around for 7 years, the co-operation of past e-community projects has helped to bolster opportunities for future e-community projects.

5 Discussion

5.1 Findings

Overall findings have shown that students tend to choose graphic design and information system project as it is perceived to be easy by just relying on the basic knowledge of the software related to both categories. In addition, students have used the software regularly used from year 1 through subjects such as Fundamentals of Multimedia, Multimedia Design, Management Information System, and Operating Systems, also in their daily activities (i.e. making posters, editing pictures, storing important files) or learning (i.e. preparing assignments, presentations).

Schools have the highest involvement in the E-Community program than any other target community. This is because the E-Community program has received many requests from the school itself to be held in schools as an additional activity for students after the final exams. This is due to the fact that the E-Community program is held from October to November each year. This can be seen from the involvement of 22 government schools and one private school participating in the E-Community program. From the 22 government schools involved, 14 were primary schools and 8 were secondary schools. This indicates that there are only left 3 primary schools (namely SK Tanjung Aru, SK Dedication and SRJK (C) Chung Hwa) and 2 secondary schools (i.e. SM St. Anthony and SM Lajau) that have never been involved and enjoy the benefits of e-community program.

5.2 Impact and Challenges

The benefits of implementing the E-Community Program in learning ICT are evident over time through feedback given by the target community. For example, the program has helped the school students prepared themselves for competitions such as short video production, and game design in State and National level. The E-Community Program also educate school students to properly apply the latest ICT skills and knowledge in the right ways such as in daily life, learning as well as giving them awareness on the issues regarding ICT abuse. Furthermore, online business activities are also growing and expanding in Labuan Island through exposure to digital business conducted through the E-Community program. In general, the E-community Program has successfully raised awareness and knowledge of ICT among Labuan youth and communities.

While efforts to implement the transfer of ICT knowledge to the communities in Labuan is ongoing, the problems encountered in the implementation of these activities need to be identified and addressed effectively. Mandatory ICT infrastructure and facilities in most schools and colleges are incomplete and inadequate. Inadequate ICT facilities and equipment or lack of technical support are due to lack of financial support. This has hindered the implementation of this E-Community program. The benefits obtained from this program cannot be fully guaranteed if there are only educators with ICT knowledge, skills and competencies. The effectiveness and efficiency of this E-Community program also depend on adequate and timely technical support (problem solving, maintenance and repair of equipment). Without a complete infrastructure and good technical support in a classroom or computer lab, this program will be at risk of exposure to external interference or interruption due to any technical deficiencies. These technical barriers including sluggish computer processing problems, internet connection failures, internet signal disruption, virus threats, poor computer conditions, and malfunctioning computers have hindered the delivery of seamless ICT learning and disrupted the flow of e-community activities.

Another obstacle to this e-community project is time constraints. Most students perceived that time is a constraint in project management. This is because it takes a lot of time for them to prepare the teaching materials for their target community. The students need to find information related to their projects from internet sources and reference books, besides completing course work provided by lecturers and participate in university co-curriculum activities at the same time. Clearly, time constraints have been a major challenge that will affect the quality, objectives and performance of E-Community programs.

5.3   Recommendation for Improvement

Several suggestions have been identified to address the issues that make E-Community more successful. It is dedicated to the emphasis on ICT infrastructure and facilities for every school, college, village and association and club located in Labuan. These proposals are in the process of enhancing infrastructure facilities especially for computer equipment and hardware and internet access to meet ICT requirements. This improvement can be achieved with the help from the government, or private sector, or non-government organizations (NGOs) to work together to upgrade the infrastructure. The improvement in ICT infrastructure will enhance the local economy as well as education.

The E-Community program is often implemented in semester 7th in which at that point, they were facing a Final Year Project (FYP). Therefore, it is recommended that the implementation of the E-Community program through the subject of IT31103 be changed to another semester so that they can devote their full attention and commitment to the success of E-Community and serve local people successfully. In addition, it is also recommended that this E-Community program be implemented in stages so that they can prepare from the first semester for careful planning and that the E-Community program can be successfully implemented.

6   Conclusion

The E-Community Program has long been in operation and will continue from year to year. The importance of this project is to mediate and prepare the FCI students to engage with the community and to reinforce and apply the soft skills that are practiced at the university level. Furthermore, it can be viewed as a training for students to communicate with the community and as an appreciation for accepting FCI students as Labuan citizens. Sharing ICT with the people of Labuan can be a platform for FCI students to be more independent, responsible and share all knowledge learned. On the other hand, for the people of Labuan, it is an opportunity for them to be more open to the latest technology that has become daily needs not only to reduce the digital divide gap, but also as the preparation for the industrial revolution 4.0. ICT is the medium of communication for every local citizen to disseminate information and is also the best platform for small traders in Labuan to promote their local goods. It is hoped that this project continues every year and is not only focused on Labuan, but it can also be expanded at the Borneo level. It is expected that many parties not only from government agencies but from the private sector support FCI's efforts to serve the locals.

References

1. Department of Statistics Malaysia. https://www.dosm.gov.my
2. Ag. Ibrahim, A.A., Bolongkikit, J., Yusak, M.Y., Yussof, S.: SSIL e-community project: bridging the digital divide of Labuan community. Labuan e-J. Muamalat Soc. **4**, 45–53 (2010)
3. George, A.S., Mehra, V., Scott, K., Sriram, V.: Community participation in health systems research: a systematic review assessing the state of research, the nature of interventions involved and the features of engagement with communities. PLoS ONE **10**(1), 1–25 (2015). https://doi.org/10.1371/journal.pone.0141091
4. Kollmann, T.: What is e-entrepreneurship?- Fundamentals of company founding in the net economy. Int. J. Technol. Manag. **33**(4), 322–340 (2006). https://doi.org/10.1504/ijtm.2006.009247
5. Dos Santos, M.E.R.: Mechanism for knowledge transfer in the health sector. In: Seminar Knowledge Transfer Best Practices Between APEC Economies. Lima, Peru, pp. 1–24 (2018). https://knowledgetransferproject.com/
6. Ritzen, J.: Making ideas work for society: university cooperation in knowledge transfer. In: MERIT Working Paper 042: United Nations University - Maastricht Economic and Social Research Institute on Innovation and Technology (UNU-MERIT), Netherlands, pp. 1–48 (2018). https://ideas.repec.org/p/unm/unumer/2018042.html
7. Ducourneau, A.: Knowledge transfer: making the most of research. In: Workshop Administrative and Financial Management of Research, Innovation and Educational Projects, pp. 1–12 (2018). https://www.geresh-cam.eu/IMG/pdf/13._prc_sentation_-_geresh cam_valo.pdf
8. Mayer, R.E., Moreno, R.: Animation as an aid to multimedia learning. Educ. Psychol. Rev. **4**(1), 87–99 (2002). https://doi.org/10.1023/a:1013184611077
9. Schell, J.: The Art of Game Design: A Book of Lenses. Morgan Kaufmann, USA (2008)
10. Owens, J.: Video Production Handbook. Routledge, New York (2017)
11. Landa, R.: Graphic Design Solutions. Cengage Learning, Boston (2010)
12. Stair, R., Reynolds, G.: Principles of Information Systems. Cengage Learning, Boston (2014)
13. Sfetcu, N.: Web Design & Development (2014)
14. Perry, D.L.: What Makes Learning Fun? Principles for the Design of Intrinsically Motivating Museum Exhibit. Altamira Press, Plymouth (2012)
15. Lye, S.Y., Koh, J.H.L.: Review on teaching and learning of computational thinking through programming: what is next for K-12? Comput. Hum. Behav. **41**, 51–61 (2014). https://doi.org/10.1016/j.chb.2014.09.012
16. Kafai, Y., Burke, Q.: Computer programming goes back to school. Phi Delta Kappan **95**(1), 61–65 (2013)

Author Index

Printed in the United States
By Bookmasters